Terrence Malick and
the Examined Life

TERRENCE MALICK AND THE EXAMINED LIFE

Martin Woessner

PENN

UNIVERSITY OF PENNSYLVANIA PRESS

PHILADELPHIA

INTELLECTUAL HISTORY
OF THE MODERN AGE

Series Editors
Angus Burgin
Peter E. Gordon
Joel Isaac
Karuna Mantena
Samuel Moyn
Jennifer Ratner-Rosenhagen
Camille Robcis
Sophia Rosenfeld

Published by
University of Pennsylvania Press
Philadelphia, Pennsylvania 19104-4112
www.upenn.edu/pennpress

Printed in the United States of America on acid-free paper
10 9 8 7 6 5 4 3 2 1

Hardcover ISBN: 978-1-5128-2560-2
eBook ISBN: 978-1-5128-2561-9

A Cataloging-in-Publication record is available from the
Library of Congress

Frontispiece. Terrence Malick on the set of *Lanton Mills* ©1970. Courtesy of
American Film Institute.

For Mom and Dad

We watch a film to know the filmmaker. It's his company we're after, not his skill.

—Jean Renoir

If this is a good film, it ought to, if I let it, help teach me how to think about my relation to it.

—Stanley Cavell

CONTENTS

The Important Things in Life

I made my first foray into the world of film criticism in 1985, when I was eight. Richard Donner's *The Goonies* had just been released. I have no memory of actually seeing it, but certain scenes are lodged deep in the recesses of my mind, especially the one with the resplendent, jewel-and-skeleton-strewn pirate ship at the end. When I first saw the movie, or where, or with whom, I have no idea. My dad, an avid moviegoer then as now, could have taken me to see *Goonies* (nobody ever made use of the definite article), or maybe it was one of my older brothers. Maybe all four of us went together. I doubt Mom would have come along; she often worked the night shift back then.

I do remember sitting at the kitchen table, watching our tiny, black-and-white tabletop television as the local film critic Gary Franklin, the inventor of the famous "Franklin Scale"—"1 to 10, 10 being best"—panned *Goonies* on the afternoon news. It was an outrage. A scandal. An affront to everything I held dear. This old guy had no idea what he was talking about and somebody had to tell him as much.

My parents probably convinced me to write Mr. Franklin a letter, maybe as a tactic to keep me occupied for a while. Putting pencil to paper, I turned my outrage into prose. The evidence of my juvenile attempt to convince Mr. Franklin of his error now sits on my desk, yellowed a little with age. It is not a childish letter of complaint scrawled on college-ruled paper, but rather a meticulously typed reply on television-studio letterhead. Amazingly, Mr. Franklin wrote me back.

"Dear Martin," his missive begins, "Many thanks for your interesting note." It was a gracious opening, but true to his on-air persona, which was authoritative—maybe even a little professorial, now that I think of it—Gary Franklin did not waste any time putting me in my place:

The French have an expression—"Chacun a sont gout"—which means "to each his own taste." When my kids were your age I discouraged them from going to little-kid movies.

Yours is the age, when you become aware of the world, outside your home and your street, and you deserve to be exposed to things that are truly exciting, interesting and fresh . . . rather than the same old kiddie-garbage.

There's more to life than watching a group of little nincompoops chasing after a make-believe pirate ship.

Time to get excited, Martin, about the important things in life![1]

Never mind the French, *nincompoop* immediately became part of my vocabulary. But it took me many years to appreciate Mr. Franklin's larger point, which is that movies can help us to see and understand the world, not just escape from it.

Only while finalizing this manuscript did the memory of Gary Franklin's letter flash into my mind. It took some searching at my parents' suburban Los Angeles home, but buried in a box of memorabilia from that long-lost, analog age, Mom found the envelope with the KCBS-TV return address. It was like a message in a bottle, a magical piece of flotsam from my past washing up on the shores of the present.

Re-receiving Mr. Franklin's letter was the kind of serendipitous discovery that makes people talk about fate or destiny or luck—the very tropes out of which so many movies are made. Take *Badlands*, for instance. The first draft of Terrence Malick's screenplay, from November 1971, opens with a scene that never made it into the final film. In it, Kit, the protagonist, finds a bottle with a message inside: "You are many times blessed," it reads, "for you will journey far, look upon many secrets, find someone who is dear to you, and you will never see your like upon this earth."[2] And with that, the story begins.

Most of us would like to think we are unique and special, that we are "many times blessed." We want to believe we were meant to be *here*, doing precisely *this*, right *now*. But how often is it that such knowledge comes to us in the form of an actual letter, whether in a bottle or, in my case, a dusty old envelope?

Gary Franklin was a colorful character. I never realized just how remarkable his life had been until I searched for information about him. Born in

1928 into a German Jewish family in Leipzig—a city where, over seventy
years later, I would try to improve my textbook German, with only minimal
success—Mr. Franklin did not enjoy the sort of comfortable existence I took
for granted growing up in 1980s Southern California. By the time he was ten,
his family had fled Nazi persecution, ending up in the Bronx. Mr. Franklin
studied film nearby at the City College of New York (where I am now fortunate
enough to teach), then went on to serve in the army, becoming a cameraman
in Korea. That experience led to work in documentary production. A career
as a radio reporter followed, which took Mr. Franklin from Virginia to Los
Angeles. It was only a matter of time before he began reviewing movies,
switching from radio to television in 1981, just four short years before the
release of *Goonies*.[3]

After an eventful life, Gary Franklin passed away in 2007. I missed the
news of his death, no longer living in Los Angeles at the time and doing things
far removed from the movies, it felt like. I had not thought about him, or
about *Goonies*, for ages. But as I write this, the memories come rushing back.
I see his bald head gleaming under the harsh lighting of the television news
studio. I hear his distinctive voice. And I feel the weight of his aesthetic judgment. Gary Franklin's dismissal of *Goonies* still stings.

My inner eight-year-old may never be able to bring himself to agree
with Mr. Franklin about the merits of make-believe pirate ships, but
whatever part of me can claim to be an adult has learned the value of remaining curious about the wider world. My early enthusiasm for "kiddie-
garbage" has matured into an appreciation of *The Tree of Life*, a story about
childhood—and memory and growing up—Gary Franklin probably would
have liked, if only because it addresses, as I hope to show, "the important
things in life."

*   *   *

The films of Terrence Malick are some of the most well-known cinematic
works of recent (and, in some cases, not so recent) memory; they have received widespread praise and recognition not simply in Hollywood or the
United States but all around the world. They headline festivals, pack audito-
riums, and win awards. They also generate an astounding amount of critical
commentary, which shines some light on the artistry of a famously reclusive
director who—apart from a few exceptions that simply prove the rule—has
not spoken publicly about his films since the 1970s.

In this growing body of literature, one fact about Malick's unique career in cinema tends to stand out, which is that he almost became an academic. Malick studied philosophy as an undergraduate at Harvard in the 1960s, doing well enough there to impress his teachers and win a Rhodes scholarship to undertake graduate work at Oxford. He befriended philosophers who were on their way to becoming famous—including Stanley Cavell, his undergraduate mentor—and translated the writings of others, like Martin Heidegger, who already were. Few other filmmakers can boast such an illustrious intellectual pedigree.

Still, nobody would be talking about Malick's background in philosophy were it not for the stellar success of his films. The desire to know more about his ideas stems from the power of the pictures themselves. While writing this book I have assumed that most readers who might pick up a book titled *Terrence Malick and the Examined Life* have experienced these movies already, and probably many times over at that. Nevertheless, I encourage readers to revisit the films either before or soon after reading the chapters I have devoted to them, for if there is one thing that researching and writing this book has taught me, it is that Malick's movies repay rewatching.

Malick's films are finely crafted works of art: analyzing their constitutive elements—their scripts, their cinematography, their acting and editing—proves as much. But in the following pages I eschew a narrow film-studies approach, focusing instead on the ways in which these pictures participate in conversations we can trace all the way back to Socrates, who famously suggested that the unexamined life is not worth living.[4] Viewing Malick's movies as a record of the examined life invites us to rethink the boundaries of philosophy, to see it less as a cloistered academic discipline and more as a way of life.

It is time for Malick's movies to be incorporated into the history of ideas—and not merely as some kind of curiosity or afterthought, either.[5] Inspired by philosophers, but also by novelists, poets, painters, and, of course, other filmmakers, they are further proof of American philosophical culture's extra-academic vitality, its ecumenical, wide-ranging inquisitiveness. *Terrence Malick and the Examined Life* shows how the so-called high ideas we typically associate with intellectual history permeate just about every aspect of our social and cultural life.[6] Philosophy is both in and of the world, and we can find it there, provided we take the time to look for it. We might even find it at the movies.

From Philosophy to Film

It was over fifty years ago that the American director Terrence Malick abandoned his graduate studies in philosophy and embarked upon a radically different career path. Welcomed into the inaugural class of the newly founded Center for Advanced Film Studies at the American Film Institute, he embraced a vocation little discussed, at that time, in the lecture halls and seminar rooms of the philosophical profession he had left behind. Malick traded philosophy for film, Heidegger for Hollywood, and he did not look back: he was nearing "the end of my rope as an academic," he later said, and needed a new start.[1]

Five decades on, Terrence Malick is now widely regarded as one of cinema's most celebrated filmmakers. His films—from *Badlands* (1973) through *Days of Heaven* (1978) and *The Thin Red Line* (1998), up to *The New World* (2005), *The Tree of Life* (2011), *To the Wonder* (2013), *Knight of Cups* (2016), *Voyage of Time* (2016), *Song to Song* (2017), and, most recently, *A Hidden Life* (2019)—have engendered intense admiration and extensive critical examination, tendencies compounded by their director's reclusiveness. As is perhaps to be expected, Malick's general refusal to publicly discuss his work has only intensified efforts to dissect every last detail of his films, ensuring that critics and fans, bloggers and scholars, will be kept busy for decades to come.[2]

Malick's films are stunning works of art. They have beautiful natural settings, poetic voice-overs, and sweeping story lines. Interpreting them from what we might call a film-studies perspective, numerous scholars have sung their praises.[3] Yet what really seems to set Malick's works apart is not just their stylistic singularity but also their intellectual daring, their willingness to go beyond the received wisdom of genre expectations to survey territory not often explored in suburban multiplexes. In the words of film critic A. O. Scott, few directors "venture so boldly or grandly onto the primordial terrain of philosophical and religious inquiry where the answers to basic and perennial questions seem to lie. Why are we here? How do we know? What does it mean?"[4]

It is my contention that Terrence Malick has remained a philosopher as much as a movie director. But he is a unique kind of philosopher, one who could not have survived in the contemporary academy, where perennial questions are often avoided. Malick's philosophical pursuits do not correspond with disciplinary dictates. His thinking begins with personal, lived experience, not a preset research agenda. His films wander far and wide, exploring all manner of things. They are simultaneously confessional and universal, searching for meaning just about everywhere. Animated by a profound sense of wonder, they examine everything from distant stars to daily routines. They are a record of the examined life.

Even as a boarding student at St. Stephen's Episcopal School in Austin, Texas, the teenage Malick struck his teachers as "deeply thoughtful, philosophically very inquiring," never one to "take things superficially."[5] He wanted to know what it all meant, where he belonged, and why anything mattered. Unfortunately, Malick started studying philosophy at a time when the profession, at least as it was practiced in the Anglo-American world, no longer offered answers to such questions—in fact, it did not even bother asking them. In an attempt to make philosophy as rigorous and as results-oriented as the natural sciences, academic philosophers in the United States traded metaphysics for physics, ethics for logic, and ontology for linguistics. They did away with speculative philosophy and embraced what philosopher Hans Reichenbach called, in an influential 1951 monograph, "scientific philosophy."[6]

In this climate, philosophy was no longer, as it was for Socrates, "a way of life." It became, as historian James Miller has put it, just another "mainstream discipline" housed in one of the many modern "academic institutions around the world." Emphasizing "rigorous inquiry" over and above "exemplary conduct," academic philosophy shunted aside important questions about how to live.[7] In the race to become scientific—"Philosophy of science is philosophy enough," as the Harvard philosopher W. V. Quine memorably put it in 1953—philosophers relinquished much of their former purview.[8] Questions about the meaning of life were best left to religion.[9]

But what happened to those philosophy students who wanted to learn about such things? Where did they go? As intellectual historian Jennifer Ratner-Rosenhagen has suggested, "we might discover more about the dynamism of philosophy in America by following the intellectual paths of those who felt the need to break free from it."[10] Taking leave of moribund academic philosophy, in other words, we might find another tradition of thought, one that is very much alive.

As a student, Malick was drawn to philosophy precisely because he took questions about ethics, aesthetics, and "the meaning of life" all too seriously. Professional philosophy's avoidance of these questions may have been the very thing that led him to abandon a career in academia. During the summer of 1980, more than a decade after ditching his dissertation to pursue a career in film, Malick appeared—as "a surprise participant"—at a National Endowment for the Humanities–sponsored institute at the University of California, Berkeley, organized by one of his philosophy mentors from his Harvard days, Hubert Dreyfus.[11] The event was devoted to the teaching of philosophy in the American academy and, more specifically, to how it could be improved. Malick's invited talk addressed the question "Why do philosophy?" He told an audience including such noted American philosophers as Richard Rorty, John Haugeland, and Robert Brandom that he felt disappointed at Harvard because none of the philosophy classes he took "helped him understand himself and his place in the order of the cosmos."[12] In other words, his teachers had let him down. But disappointment can be a powerful motivator: what Malick could not get out of academic philosophy he has been seeking in motion pictures ever since. The films he has made are both a result of and a testament to his search.

*   *   *

Malick's penchant for cinematic philosophizing has become more pronounced over the course of his career. The films he has made since *The Tree of Life*, especially, seem to push the limits of what the movies, as a popular artistic medium, can do. These films are elliptical rather than linear. They display little concern for the conventions of dialogue, narrative, or plot. At almost every level, they resist the pull of the theatrical. Nevertheless, they are of a piece with Malick's earliest forays into filmmaking, which also sidestepped the established expectations of the movie business, though in a less obvious fashion.

Malick's films have never really told stories; instead, they have attempted to capture what the famed French director Robert Bresson once called the "states of the soul."[13] In this regard, Malick's works might best be described as aesthetic, philosophical experiments. They explore the possibilities of cinema, but they also extend the boundaries of philosophical inquiry. These are reciprocal, perhaps even symbiotic, impulses that have shaped a roster of films that, despite their formal differences, share a remarkably coherent tone and sensibility. Tracing the development of that tone and sensibility is one of the principle aims of this book. To understand the uniqueness of Malick's filmmaking, I argue, we must first consider the very specific arc of his career, taking stock of the cultural, intellectual, and historical contexts that made it possible. As I view them, Malick's films should not be viewed as stand-alone works of art, but as contributions to an ongoing conversation with other filmmakers, writers, artists, scientists, and philosophers who have set themselves the task of searching not just for answers but also, and more importantly, for meaning.

That conversation began with a popular novel that won the National Book Award while Malick was at Harvard: Walker Percy's *The Moviegoer*.[14] A classic example of American existentialism, it tells the story of Binx Bolling, an alienated, disaffected New Orleans bachelor who obsesses over what he calls "the search." He looks everywhere for meaning and purpose in life but is constantly disappointed with what he finds. Even cinema—hence the title—is of no help: "The movies are onto the search," he says, "but they screw it up."[15] Still, like some Kierkegaardian knight of faith, Bolling never gives up. Worldly concerns will not knock him off his path: "not for five minutes," he proclaims, "will I be distracted from the wonder."[16]

Malick was rumored to be working on an adaptation of *The Moviegoer* for decades and eventually made a film titled *To the Wonder*. It has a protagonist who, like Bolling, is trying to find his place in the world. This is the most consistent theme in Malick's cinema. The search for meaning is what gives his complex body of work its coherence. Whether his films depict historical worlds or contemporary ones, whether they are driven by dialogue or unfurl without much more than a few poetic lines of voice-over narration, whether they derive from literary works or from original screenplays, Malick's films all have one thing in common: a fascination with the intellectual and emotional drama that accompanies the examined life. His pictures are suffused with wonder: they marvel at human existence and explore its every nuance, from the most extraordinary events to the entirely mundane moments that imperceptibly shape our daily lives. So unique is his filmmaking that some critics call it not cinema but philosophy.[17]

One of the central claims of this book is that Malick's entire oeuvre constitutes a philosophy by other means and is worth taking seriously as such.[18]

This is not to say, simply, that the films of Terrence Malick have philosophical moments, or that each of them can be made to speak to philosophical concerns. Rather, it is my contention that Malick's films represent a continuous philosophical project in their own right, one that draws upon preexisting philosophical discourses and traditions yet also calls them into question and even, in some instances, transcends them. They remind us that philosophy can be not just an academic subject but also a way of life.[19]

To appreciate this aspect of Malick's filmmaking requires a new approach to analyzing his films. It requires contextualization. Context cannot explain everything, of course, but it can add layers of depth and nuance to our understanding of Malick's place in cinematic history, as well as in American intellectual and cultural history more broadly.[20] "The fact that film has been the most potent vehicle of the American imagination," Arthur M. Schlesinger Jr. once wrote, suggests "that the movies have something to tell us not just about the surfaces but about the mysteries of American life."[21] It is a point proven by Malick's movies, which have explored everything from the founding of Jamestown to the contemporary indie music scene in Austin, Texas.

Explicating films made in conversation not just with Hollywood and world cinema but also with many of the intellectual and cultural endeavors that seek to understand the mysteries of human existence—history, literature, science, drama, memoir, music, painting, popular culture, and religion, to name just a few—requires an interdisciplinary approach. That said, there will be a good deal of philosophy in the pages that follow. Malick is by no means the only person with a background in philosophy to have succeeded in the movie business: Pauline Kael studied philosophy at Berkeley, and Bob Rafelson did the same at Dartmouth. There are plenty of filmmakers who know their Kierkegaard from their Kant, but it is nonetheless true that few of them have so consistently circled back to topics and texts in the history of philosophy as has Malick. How he has done so and why are some of the very questions this book sets out to answer.

Only when they are viewed in relation to the specific intellectual and cultural contexts out of which they emerged do the mysteries of Malick's films begin to come into full view. Against such backdrops, their rich and complex "film worlds"—to borrow a term from the film theorist Daniel Yacavone—stand out in high relief.[22] But this means interpreting films such as *Badlands*, *The Thin Red Line*, or *The Tree of Life* as something other than mere movies. It means viewing them as pursuits of meaning, shaped by very specific conditions. It means viewing them as forms of experience worthy of serious study.[23] This book argues that viewing Malick's films in relation to recent intellectual and cultural history—the context of Harvard philosophy in the mid-1960s, say, or that of Hollywood filmmaking after the decline of the studio system in the early 1970s, or even the post-secular turn in American thought more recently—offers a whole new perspective not just on each particular film, nor even on Malick's unique career as a whole, but also on what sometimes gets called, maybe a little too ponderously, the life of the mind.

A Portrait of the Artist as a Young Philosopher

Terrence Malick arrived at Harvard at a propitious time. The university was undergoing profound changes, the most significant of these being the slow integration of Radcliffe College for women during the 1962–63 academic year, when Malick was a sophomore.[24] While the philosophy department at Harvard remained an almost exclusively masculine domain, the winds of change were blowing through it as well. New faculty members hired during this time went on to enjoy long and storied careers in Cambridge. The first notable appointment was that of political and moral philosopher John Rawls, who joined the faculty in 1962. He began offering courses in ethics and political philosophy on a regular basis and, within a decade, published his influential work *A Theory of Justice* (1971).

The other significant appointment to the Harvard philosophy department was that of Stanley Cavell. Cavell was hired to teach aesthetics, but he also took the helm of "The Self-Interpretation of Man in Western Thought," a catchall general education course previously taught by the existentialist theologian Paul Tillich (with whom Malick had taken it).[25] In some respects, the course was a perfect fit for Cavell, combining as it did the study of philosophical texts with works of prose, poetry, and drama. Its reading list included Descartes, Locke, and Nietzsche, but also Shakespeare and Beckett.

"The Self-Interpretation of Man in Western Thought" allowed Cavell to explore his own "restiveness with philosophical professionalism" and to develop—as he has described it in his 2010 memoir, *Little Did I Know*—his interest in the "intersecting worlds of art and of thought," or what he also called, putting it a little more provocatively, "the erotic and intellectual registers of human encounter."[26] Cavell's enthusiasm for film eventually found its way into the course, as he drafted a book published the very same year as Rawls's *A Theory of Justice*—namely, *The World Viewed: Reflections on the*

Ontology of Film. Cavell's book also came to dominate its field, but it probably would be more accurate to say it established it. *The World Viewed* was a watershed work in film studies. In it, Cavell attempted to make cinema a worthy subject of philosophical discussion. In later editions, he used the work of one of his former Harvard pupils—a gifted student who had roomed, like him, in Adams House—to help him do so.

The World Viewed was idiosyncratic but not unprecedented.[27] Cavell was not the first philosopher in America to write a book about the movies—in fact, he was not even the first Harvard philosopher to do so. That honor goes to the German psychologist Hugo Münsterberg, a member of the Harvard philosophy department long before Cavell, who in 1916 published *The Photoplay: A Psychological Study*.[28] Münsterberg was among the earliest intellectuals in the world to recognize the unique alliance of art and science the cinema represented, yet getting to that point took effort: "Although I was always a passionate lover of the theater," he admitted in a piece for *The Cosmopolitan*, "I should have felt it as undignified for a Harvard Professor to attend a moving-picture show."[29] As soon as he deigned to attend one, though, Münsterberg became convinced that the photoplay was "the only visual art in which the whole richness of our inner life, our perceptions, our memory, and our imagination, our expectation and our attention can be made living in the outer impressions themselves."[30] In other words, film had the unique ability to reveal secrets about a topic in which psychologists and philosophers both had a keen interest—namely, "the working of the mind."[31]

Needless to say, the Harvard philosophy department changed quite a bit between Münsterberg's day and Cavell's. But studying film in a serious way, treating it as a topic worthy of academic investigation, was still all but unheard of when Malick arrived in Cambridge, Massachusetts, in 1961. A half century after the publication of *The Photoplay*, film remained at best a marginal subject. Yet that was part of its appeal, especially for Cavell. He admitted to feeling "a certain pleasurable indecorousness in the idea of taking film into a philosophy classroom."[32] Instead of bringing philosophy or psychology to bear upon the lowly subject of the movies, as Münsterberg had, Cavell pushed the movies themselves up to the heights of philosophical thought. It was not the professor who made cinema worthy of discussion; it was cinema itself that demanded recognition from the professors—a recognition that eventually resulted in the establishment of the prestigious Harvard Film Archive in 1979.

During Malick's undergraduate career, moviegoing remained an extracurricular pursuit. But it was pursued passionately, by a wide variety of people.

As film scholar Robert B. Ray has remembered it, Harvard in the 1960s was a hotbed of cinephilia. Tiny Cambridge hosted not one, not two, but three separate film societies.[33] Especially in those pre-VHS, pre-DVD, pre-streaming days, such a concentration of high-quality film programming, much of it devoted to the European art-house cinema then in vogue, proved to be a decisive influence on a great many people, including not just Ray, but also William Rothman (another film scholar), and Malick's good friend and roommate, the future critic, lyricist, screenwriter, and Hollywood producer Jacob Brackman.[34]

Brackman was a good friend to have. After graduating from Harvard, he moved to New York and began writing about film and popular culture for *Newsweek*, the *New Yorker*, and, eventually, *Esquire*. Among a colorful circle of friends and lovers, Brackman quickly developed a Svengali-like reputation for orchestrating things behind the scenes, bringing the aspiring actors, musicians, and writers he knew to the attention of interested parties. He was, in other words, a matchmaker. According to the singer Carly Simon, with whom both he and Malick were involved for a time, Brackman specialized in creating "situations," meaningful encounters between creative people that led to lasting relationships, some of them more—and some of the less—platonic than others.[35] No doubt a Brackman-Malick-Simon love triangle could have been a "situation," perhaps even one resembling the story line of Malick's late-career film *Song to Song*, but it seems that romantic rivalry never got in the way of a friendship that had solidified years earlier at Harvard. As Simon has recalled, "neither Jake nor Terry was as interested in me as they were in each other's company."[36]

It was Brackman who convinced Malick to apply to the American Film Institute. And it may have been Brackman who got him in. Unexpectedly landing a spot on the admissions committee for the first year of fellows, Brackman did not hesitate to sing his former classmate's praises: "Terrence Malick is the most likely to succeed of anybody I have ever met," he insisted.[37]

The founding director of AFI, George Stevens Jr., son of the famed Hollywood filmmaker, took this recommendation to heart and invited Malick to Southern California. With his foot in the door, Malick began making good impressions wherever he went. It may have helped that he was "the only applicant who showed up for his interview in a jacket and tie."[38] What struck Stevens about Malick was not just his sartorial style, though, but also how "well-rounded" he was. He knew his European cinema, his "Truffaut, Antonioni, Fellini, Bergman," but Malick knew a lot of other things besides.[39] He also had profound interests in literature and the arts, not to mention theology and politics. Philosophy was just one of the many areas in which Malick's expertise exceeded that of his peers. Carly Simon was by no means alone, it seems, in thinking him "intimidatingly smart."[40]

But if Malick emerged from the Harvard philosophy program "a well-rounded individual," it was more likely despite his course of instruction than because of it. The curriculum at the time leaned more toward specialization than it ever had in previous decades. The rise of Harvard's philosophy department is synonymous with the rise of American philosophy itself.[41] It was at Harvard where professional philosophy took shape in the United States, thanks to the efforts of William James and Josiah Royce, whose interests were vast and varied. But by the middle decades of the twentieth century, their legacy and influence, along with Münsterberg's, had waned considerably. One could still find a course or two on pragmatism (offered by Henry D. Aiken or Morton White), or perhaps even a course on metaphysics (usually taught by the aging Donald Cary Williams), but logic and semantics reigned supreme.

This was thanks to W. V. Quine, one of the first promoters of logical positivism in the United States. As Joel Isaac has shown, Quine made the transatlantic transplantation of this scientizing trend in philosophy possible.[42] Although he later questioned the positivism he had once done so much to champion, Quine made sure that the analytic philosophy stemming from it held sway at Harvard.[43] While the department's undergraduate offerings reflected a long-standing commitment to teaching the history of philosophy from the Greeks up through the modern period, the graduate curriculum was weighted far more toward logic. The appointments of Rawls and Cavell began to change this dynamic somewhat, but as is always the case with institutional change (especially when it takes place within the academy), the transformation was gradual enough to seem almost glacial.

The pace of its midcentury evolution may not have impressed many at the time, but the metamorphosis Harvard's philosophy department was undergoing when Malick arrived there as a student is noteworthy nonetheless, especially since it ended up informing so much of his work as a filmmaker. Because American philosophy was in the midst of a pretty serious identity crisis in the early 1960s, professors were torn between various, often competing, allegiances. Many emulated the scientific rigor of analytic philosophy, but some were pulled to the latest trends in what came to be called continental philosophy. A few even tried to keep alive the democratic drive of pragmatism, which seemed, even to them, well past its prime.

Marrying or somehow synthesizing these various trends was difficult, but by no means impossible. In the 1950s, the influential philosopher John Wild, who began his career as a Platonic realist, started offering courses on existentialism. A year before Malick arrived in Cambridge, Wild even offered a course on European existentialism and pragmatism, one of the first of its kind anywhere in the country. But Wild's subsequent departure for Northwestern left the Harvard philosophy department with "a gap"—as an internal memo put it—in "the History and Philosophy of Religion."[44] It was a gap into which Stanley Cavell would venture just a couple years later. He ended up exploring this terrain alongside a talented young student who was drawn to the religiously inflected work of a German existentialist named Martin Heidegger.

It is well known today that Malick not only read many of Heidegger's works at Harvard, but also that he attended some of Heidegger's lectures while studying abroad in Germany. (It appears he even got the chance to speak to Heidegger personally, in a meeting facilitated by Hannah Arendt.)[45] Heidegger may be common currency in seminar rooms these days, but back then his work was just starting to appear in English. Compared to their European counterparts, American students and their professors were playing catch-up.[46] It was not until 1962, in fact, that Heidegger's most famous work, *Sein und Zeit*, first published in 1927, became, in English, *Being and Time*.[47] Many of Heidegger's other works remained untranslated, forcing students, such as Malick, to work through them in the original German.

Malick went on to write an "expert honors thesis" under Cavell's direction.[48] "The Concept of Horizon in Husserl and Heidegger" explored the difference between Edmund Husserl's concept of *Lebenswelt* and Heidegger's talk of the "worldhood of the world."[49] It remains an insightful piece of scholarship. Cavell was the first to admit it represented an instance of the student teaching his teacher, for nobody in the department at that time knew as much about Heidegger as Malick did. The only person who came close was Hubert Dreyfus. He later became one of the most important authorities on Heidegger in the United States, but back then Dreyfus was just completing a doctoral thesis of his own while teaching at the nearby Massachusetts Institute of Technology.[50] Malick would make the short, crosstown commute to audit his course on Heidegger, a course Malick would one day teach, subbing in for Dreyfus while he was away in Europe on research leave.[51]

Malick won a Rhodes scholarship to continue his studies in philosophy at Oxford. It was there, while working on a dissertation that would remain unfinished, perhaps even unstarted—rumor has it that philosopher Gilbert Ryle dismissed his proposed dissertation on "the concept of world in the works of Heidegger, Kierkegaard, and Wittgenstein" as not quite "philosophical" enough—Malick undertook a translation of Heidegger's 1929 text "Vom Wesen des Grundes."[52] In his hands, it became *The Essence of Reasons*.[53] Although few commentators have taken the time to examine Malick's undergraduate thesis, almost anybody who writes about him today mentions this translation, if only in passing. Even heavily worn and annotated, the book fetches a handsome price online as something of a collector's item.

For critics and fans alike, Heidegger serves as both talisman and key, simultaneously reinforcing and unlocking the magic of Malick's films. But the assumption that Heidegger's influence is somehow behind everything he has written and directed is both too neat and too easy.[54] For starters, we must ask, just which Heidegger did Malick encounter at Harvard, and how did he encounter him? After all, Malick's translation of Heidegger appeared in a book series edited by John Wild, the Platonic realist turned existential pragmatist, but the course on Heidegger and Sartre that was offered during Malick's junior year was taught by Dagfinn Føllesdall, a student of Quine's who attempted to graft continental philosophical discourses—such as that of phenomenology—onto analytic roots.[55] To complicate matters further, Føllesdall was one of Hubert Dreyfus's teachers at Harvard, and it was Dreyfus's classes at MIT that Malick taught during his all too brief attempt at an academic career once he returned to the States from his aborted studies at Oxford. And let us not forget Cavell, Malick's undergraduate mentor. Cavell advised Malick's thesis, but was busy teaching classes on subjects seemingly far removed from Heidegger at the time, including Harvard's general education lectures, a course on the later philosophy of Wittgenstein, and, in the fall of 1963, a course on the philosophy of religion.

As I have tried to show elsewhere, the American reception of Heidegger was a complex phenomenon, and the fact that Malick was exposed to so many different readers of Heidegger while still an undergraduate underscores the point.[56] Somewhere between the pragmatist-existentialism of Wild, the analytic phenomenology of Føllesdall, and the eclectic, if not to say eccentric, work of Dreyfus and Cavell, Malick found his way not only toward but also through and perhaps even away from Heidegger. Malick's philosophical interests were—as they remain today—more ecumenical than many commentators have realized, which makes sense, because if anything defines his cinema it is a restless searching for new perspectives, new insights, new meanings.

Even as analytic philosophy gained and retained institutional supremacy at Harvard, there were still a number of other philosophical currents swirling around Cambridge, Massachusetts, in those days to encourage philosophical diversity; enough, anyway, to influence Malick's unique choice of dissertation topic at Oxford—a study not just of Heidegger and Husserl but also of Kierkegaard and Wittgenstein. Malick's exposure to Husserl could have come from Følesdall's regularly offered course on phenomenology, which was in the Harvard rotation from the spring of 1962 onward.[57] Having been mentored by Cavell, Malick also would have worked his way through Wittgenstein. But which Wittgenstein? As was the case with Heidegger's influence, Wittgenstein's legacy represented different things to different interpreters: there was no consensus on how best to understand his sparse, gnomic pronouncements about logic, language, and the limits of philosophy. Over a decade after his death, more and more of those pronouncements were finding their way into print, including the text of a 1929 lecture on ethics he gave to a student group, in which he described his thoughts on "the ultimate meaning of life" and his "wonder at the existence of the world."[58] Wittgenstein's rediscovered "Lecture on Ethics" appeared in 1965, when Malick was deep into his philosophical studies, searching for his place in the cosmos.

Malick's interest in Kierkegaard, whose influence emerges in late-career films such as *The Tree of Life*, *Knight of Cups*, and *A Hidden Life*, is a little more difficult to pinpoint. It may have stemmed from the course on Hegel, Nietzsche, and Kierkegaard offered by the Harvard doctoral student Ian Mueller when Malick was a junior. But it also could have come from Tillich, a theologian who not only taught alongside Heidegger in Marburg back in the 1920s but who also incorporated Heideggerian and Kierkegaardian elements into his own best-selling 1952 work, *The Courage to Be*.[59] Or maybe it was thanks to Dreyfus, who was still writing about Kierkegaard in the last decades of his long, prolific career, when Malick was working on *The Tree of Life*.[60] There is also a chance Malick read works like *The Sickness unto Death* on his own, of course, learning from it "to look at actual life," not merely "logic" or "pure thought."[61]

All this should make it clear that Malick did far more than just sit around and read Heidegger at Harvard, or Oxford, or anywhere else. His academic studies led him beyond existentialism, beyond phenomenology, beyond pragmatism, beyond even philosophy itself, maybe. His films demonstrate that he has dabbled in transcendentalism and theology, that he has devoured novels, poems, and plays. All of it has shaped his filmmaking. In the chapters that follow, I hope to show how these various influences are woven into every aspect of his pictures. In addition to tracing the influence of Heidegger and Husserl, Kierkegaard and Wittgenstein, I explain why the script for *Days of Heaven* opens with an epigraph from the midwestern novelist Hamlin Garland; why the voice-over narrations of *The Thin Red Line* quote not just Emerson and Thoreau, but also John Steinbeck; and why *A Hidden Life* ends with a quotation from George Eliot's *Middlemarch*.

No single thinker, book, or source explains Malick's cinema. Rather than search for a single idea that might explain each and every one of his films, the following chapters suggest that it is more profitable to dwell on the surprisingly fortuitous ways in which various influences have come together over the course of his career. Malick was often in the right place at the right time. He studied philosophy at Harvard at just the right time; studied filmmaking at the American Film Institute at just the right time; started writing scripts and making movies in Hollywood at just the right time. He even dropped out of filmmaking at just the right time, precisely when big-budget blockbusters began displacing director-driven storytelling. Malick returned twenty years later, when a window of opportunity reopened for his brand of filmmaking to once again find financial backers.

It may not always have seemed that way, especially when Malick was a student. Academic philosophy drew him in, but it also pushed him away as it transformed itself into a resolutely "technical discipline."[62] This may have been why Malick abandoned a planned career as a philosopher, later telling a roomful of prominent academics that he was "disappointed as a philosophy major" because his teachers denied him "the metaphysical comfort" of better knowing himself and his place in the cosmos.[63] Malick once told an interviewer that he "was not a good teacher," because he "didn't have the sort of edge one should have on students."[64] He had been indoctrinated into thinking that being sharp was the only thing that mattered in philosophy, that fuzzy, comforting thinking was something to be avoided at all costs.[65]

Midcentury American philosophers who believed that self-examination and the investigation of the wider world went hand in hand—that the highest aim of philosophy was, as the philosopher Henry Bugbee (paraphrasing Spinoza) once put it, the "discovery of the union between oneself and all beings"— were ignored or marginalized.[66] Indeed, the Harvard philosophy department denied Bugbee tenure in 1957, spurring him to publish his experimental work of personal philosophy, *The Inward Morning: A Philosophical Exploration in Journal Form*, a year later. It quietly became a cult classic, a lesser-known forerunner of more popular works like Robert M. Pirsig's *Zen and the Art of Motorcycle Maintenance*, but it did not rescue its author's reputation in and around the Harvard philosophy department.[67] No wonder a soulful student like Malick could graduate summa cum laude from it less than a decade later and still not know where he belonged in the world, let alone the cosmos.

From Harvard to Hollywood and Back Again

Unable to find answers to his cosmic queries in professional philosophy, Malick traded Cambridge for California, academic scholarship for cinematic apprenticeship. But abandoning a career in professional philosophy did not mean abandoning the examined life.[68] As some of our nation's greatest philosophers have demonstrated, just the opposite might have been the case. "There are nowadays professors of philosophy," Thoreau famously declared in *Walden*, "but not philosophers."[69]

When viewed from the perspective of this venerable anti-academic tradition, Malick's turn away from professionalized philosophical work may have been the very thing that allowed him to become a true philosopher, not just some "professor of philosophy." It may have been the very thing that gave him the time and the freedom to pursue the task of thinking in a more personal, more meaningful way than any professorship would have allowed. This is philosophy unencumbered by reading lists and recitations, philosophy free of departmental meetings, midterm examinations, and annual reports. This is philosophy as a way of life, as "an economy of living," to once again borrow—as Cavell often did—from Thoreau.[70]

Hollywood would seem like an unlikely destination for somebody pursuing philosophical wisdom, though. After all, it is a place where being "too intellectual" can be a liability, as John Gregory Dunne pointed out long ago in *The Studio*, his exposé of movie industry wheeling and dealing.[71] Nevertheless, as was the case with his matriculation at Harvard, Malick's arrival in Hollywood was well timed. By 1967, the year Dunne talked Richard Zanuck into granting him full access into the inner workings of Twentieth Century Fox, Hollywood was showing the early signs of what quickly became a very public personality crisis, one that would grant up-and-coming filmmakers like Malick more artistic freedom than was previously imaginable. It was around this time that the "Old Hollywood" gave way, suddenly and somewhat dramatically, to the "New Hollywood."[72]

The year 1968 was a turning point. Gone were the big-studio musicals, the madcap farces, and the patriotic family fare of previous decades—the stuff that defined Golden Age Hollywood cinema from around the late 1930s on. "Hollywood was still a place (and the studios were far from dead)," as Michael Wood has argued, "but it was no longer a style and a world and a national monument." The "ugly, unavoidable realities" of the day—"racism, torture, and assassination; Paris, Prague, Chicago, and the war in Vietnam; drugs, muggings, and turbulent, unmanageable cities"—killed off all of the myths and mystique of movie-magic make-believe.[73] In stepped an avant-garde composed of misfits and outcasts, making films that challenged and offended audiences more than they comforted, consoled, or even, at times, entertained them—films such as Haskell Wexler's *Medium Cool*, for example, which was set, and in fact filmed, cinema verité–style, amid the protests surrounding the 1968 Democratic National Convention in Chicago.

Surprisingly, this avant-garde got a little help from the government.[74] But it was not out of sympathy for any of their various causes and crusades: politicians in Washington, D.C., had their own reasons for getting involved in the movie business. Officially established by Lyndon B. Johnson in 1965 under the auspices of the National Endowment for the Arts, the American Film Institute, which took as its mission both the preservation of American cinematic history—"nitrate won't wait" was one of its unofficial slogans—and the education of future filmmakers, benefited from a midcentury concern that scientific learning had outpaced humanistic understanding.[75] The consequences of this knowledge gap—a result, in part, of increased funding for the sciences after the 1957 launch of the Soviet Sputnik satellite—were thought to be detrimental to democracy. The humanities, and especially the arts, were suddenly matters of national interest. As a 1967 study by the Stanford Research Institute put it, AFI should "foster and promote national policy to develop leadership of the United States in artistic and cultural film endeavors and the use of film, both nationally and internationally, in the best interests of the country."[76]

As a site where innovation in both the arts and the sciences intersected, cinema could be a powerful weapon in the Cold War. As a propaganda tool, it could demonstrate both technical achievement and cultural freedom simultaneously. A draft memo drawn up by George Stevens Jr. in the earliest days of the American Film Institute's planning for a film school put it plainly: the Center for Advanced Film Studies emphatically would not be "the all-union institute for Soviet cinematography."[77] AFI would strike the right balance between scientific rigor and artistic freedom, technological innovation and humanistic imagination. On this point, Hollywood and Washington were in agreement. A year prior to the establishment of AFI, a National Commission on the Humanities–issued report declared that "if the interdependence of science and the humanities were more generally understood, men would be more likely to become masters of their technology and not its unthinking servants."[78]

By 1969, the year the Center for Advanced Film Studies welcomed its first cohort of students—including not just Malick but also Paul Schrader, who would, after dropping out of AFI, go on to write *Taxi Driver* (dir. Martin Scorsese, 1976), and the cinematographer Caleb Deschanel, who, after working on Malick's student film *Lanton Mills* (1970), shot the loosely Heideggerian Peter Sellers film *Being There* (dir. Hal Ashby, 1979)—the sense of geopolitical and cultural crisis stretched far beyond the Cold War concerns of East Coast politicians and West Coast think tanks.[79] A generational shift was underway, one that would have tremendous consequences for how Hollywood would operate for at least the next decade, until the rise of the summer blockbuster in the late 1970s.

Change was in the air. In the words of philosopher Noël Carroll, "Hollywood's insecurity made it open up to new ideas and new blood."[80] But the transfusion was messy. An awkward comingling of the old and new left everybody woozy and confused, as the roster of films nominated for best picture at the 1968 Academy Awards demonstrated all too well: they ranged from countercultural hits such as *Bonnie and Clyde* and *The Graduate* (dir. Arthur Penn and Mike Nichols, respectively) to the musical *Doctor Doolittle* (dir. Richard Fleischer).

It is tempting to interpret Malick's early success as a consequence of the rise of the New Hollywood paradigm, but the truth is that his work has never been entirely in line with films such as *Bonnie and Clyde*, *The Graduate*, or *Easy Rider* (dir. Dennis Hopper, 1969). *Badlands* may have been made in a truly independent fashion (with a limited, nonunion crew and fresh-faced actors) and *Days of Heaven* may have been produced not just by Jacob Brackman but also Bert Schneider, who as one-third of BBS Productions (along with Bob Rafelson and Stephen Blauner) did so much to usher in the era of culturally revolutionary filmmaking in the early 1970s, but neither was anything like *Head* (1968), that kaleidoscopic send-up of all things sixties written by Rafelson and Jack Nicholson, directed by Rafelson, and produced by Schneider.

Malick was headed in another direction. But to get anywhere, he needed money. Some of the earliest assignments he landed out west had him working on New Hollywood scripts. The upstart agent Mike Medavoy started representing Malick after coming across a treatment he had written for Monte Hellman's existential road movie, *Two-Lane Blacktop* (1971).[81] Hellman ended up picking somebody else to finalize his script, but Malick, now with representation, did not go hungry. In addition to penning Stuart Rosenberg's *Pocket Money* (1972) and Vernon Zimmerman's *Deadhead Miles* (1972), he also contributed to Jack Nicholson's *Drive, He Said* (1971) as well as Jack Starrett's *The Dion Brothers* (1974). He even worked on an early *Dirty Harry* script that was making the rounds in Hollywood at the time.

Malick took from these projects what he needed for his own artistic journey. The New Hollywood model gave him a template to tweak. Consequently, similarities between a film like Rafelson's *Five Easy Pieces* (1970), say, and *Badlands* (not to mention, more recently, *Song to Song*) are easy to spot: both revolve around disaffected protagonists; both juxtapose aloof irony and earnest introspection; and both, having been filmed exclusively on location, find the time to linger on picturesque sunrises or sunsets. Both are also prime examples of what Jeff Menne has dubbed "the cinema of defection."[82] But Malick's early films, despite addressing many of the same themes explored in New Hollywood cinema—alienation, isolation, dissatisfaction, frustration— have a religious aura that sets them apart. They may have had crime and murder in their plotlines, but Malick's first films exuded a quiet, almost meditative calm that was unlike anything to be found in Hollywood at the time. They showed the influence of European auteurs Malick had studied in film school and authors he had read as a philosophy student. These films had more in common with Kierkegaard than Electric Kool-Aid.

Nothing makes scholars squirm more than the mention of transcendence. Within the academy, especially, the fine arts have been thoroughly secularized. "We have been trained," writes film scholar George Toles, "to regard with suspicion and condescension any transcendent or quasi-theological discourse about the impact of art."[83] Even theologians concede the point: "Transcendence is a concept," writes M. Gail Hamner, "that rightly attracts healthy skepticism these days."[84] But transcendence is what Malick's cinema seeks. His most recent films, suffused with Kierkegaardian introspection and Christian contemplation, portray a decidedly post-secular sublime. They do not represent a radical departure from his earlier work. What Paul Schrader memorably described as the "transcendental style" in cinema is in fact a hallmark of each and every one of Malick's films, from the first right down to the most recent (the forthcoming *The Way of the Wind* depicts the life of Jesus). Like Yasujiro Ozu, Robert Bresson, and Carl Theodor Dreyer—the subjects of Schrader's still influential book—Malick also "seeks to maximize the mystery of existence." His work also "eschews all conventional interpretations of reality: realism, naturalism, psychologism, romanticism, expressionism, impressionism, and, finally, rationalism."[85] Reassessing *Transcendental Style in Film* some forty-five years after its release, Shrader had no problem placing Malick's work near the center of the bull's-eye-like diagram he concocted to illustrate the various factions within the transcendental filmmaking tradition.[86] Like every other filmmaker within what Schrader dubs the "Tarkovsky Ring," Malick is more a "spirit guide" than a director.[87]

Thanks, in part, to their transcendental style, Malick's first films have more in common with European art-house films than New Hollywood ones. They feel closer to the works of Antonioni, Bresson, and Wajda than those of Coppola, De Palma, or Hopper. Malick's time at AFI had something to do with this.[88] It was there, as I hope to show in the following chapters, that he developed an abiding admiration for directors, such as Jean Renoir, who showed him how to detect "a world of proliferating mystery" in the smallest, most mundane moments of everyday life—the way the light changes on a river's surface, say, or how a tree sways in the breeze.[89] It was at AFI that Malick's sense of wonder, frustrated in academic philosophy, found an outlet in moviemaking.

It was at AFI that Malick also learned how to make a truly personal film. From the beginning, the Center for Advanced Film Studies sought to emulate the national film schools responsible for fostering and sustaining European art-house cinema—the cinema of the auteur rather than the assembly line.[90] In countries such as France, Italy, Poland, Sweden, and Czechoslovakia, cinema had been treated as a legitimate cultural endeavor, one worthy of substantial government support. But in the United States, as the Stanford Research Institute report put it, "film as an art is considered to lack the stature and emphasis afforded other art forms."[91] Making something other than mass-market movies thus meant playing catch-up—and there was a lot of catching up to do. The hope was that a new generation of properly trained filmmakers might change things by making art instead of commodities.

Malick's artistic style took shape at AFI, which meant that it evolved adjacent to, rather than in line with, the New Hollywood ethos. Like the "cinema of loneliness" that came to prominence in the late 1960s and early 1970s,

Malick's films have explored the costs, both social and psychological, of standing apart from the status quo.[92] But this is where they begin, not necessarily where they end. The protagonists of Malick's films are searchers, pilgrims, the descendants of Binx Bolling. They include a fame-seeking outlaw (*Badlands*), spurned lovers (*Days of Heaven*), forsaken soldiers (*The Thin Red Line*), uprooted Native Americans (*The New World*), an alienated architect (*The Tree of Life*), a brooding husband (*To the Wonder*), a dissatisfied scriptwriter (*Knight of Cups*), a malevolent music producer and the artists he tortures (*Song to Song*), and, last but not least, a devout conscientious objector, ostracized by his friends and neighbors (*A Hidden Life*). Each character is on a quest, a journey of some kind. Each one of them searches for meaning, the same kind of meaning Malick sought out as a budding filmmaker in Hollywood, as a philosophy student at Harvard, and as a curious kid back in Oklahoma and Texas.

The continuity between Malick's academic pursuits and his cinematic endeavors might explain why so many of the former have found such a central place in the latter. His films allude to a wide variety of literary, religious, and philosophical sources—everything from Heidegger and the Bible to F. Scott Fitzgerald, George Eliot, and Peter Matthiessen. Taken together, Malick's films offer something like the cinematic equivalent of Harvard's general education course "The Self-Interpretation of Man in Western Thought": *The Pilgrim's Progress* this week (from which the epigraph for *Knight of Cups* is drawn), followed by some Virginia Woolf the next (*The Waves* provided inspiration for *Song to Song*). In other weeks: F. Scott Fitzgerald (*Badlands*), Heidegger (*Days of Heaven*), Emerson (*The Thin Red Line*), and, maybe even some Hume (*The New World*). To a Scots fan who had inquired about that last connection, Malick admitted that he still "liked talking about philosophy."[93] Or how about something from the Book of Job (*The Tree of Life*) with a dash of Walker Percy (*To the Wonder* and *Knight of Cups*) thrown in for good measure?

There is a delicious irony in all this, for just as Malick was injecting some vaunted reading material into Hollywood filmmaking, the academy he had left behind finally began absorbing Hollywood cinema into its curricula.[94] The culmination of this tendency might very well be the course on "moral perfectionism" Stanley Cavell developed, late in his teaching career, at Harvard. Inspired by Emerson, it paired lectures on classic works in moral philosophy (Plato, Aristotle, Locke, Kant, Mill, Nietzsche, and Rawls) with companion lectures on classic cinema from the Golden Age of Hollywood,

films such as George Cukor's *The Philadelphia Story* (1940) and Howard
Hawks's *His Girl Friday* (also 1940).[95] Far from being a seesaw adventure—
highbrow philosophy one moment and lowbrow mass entertainment the
next—the course posited a fundamental unity of purpose: moral inquiry and
cinematic art often sought, Cavell claimed, the same kinds of insights into
the meaning of human affairs. Movies kept the Emersonian dream of philosophy as a way of life alive, they kept philosophy from becoming just another "discipline among others in the modern university."[96]

Just as Malick was beginning to bring his philosophical education to bear
on scriptwriting and directing, academia became ever more interested in in-
vestigating Hugo Münsterberg's claim, from way back in 1916, that cinema
was an art form worth taking seriously. Industry magazines such as *Variety*
and the *Hollywood Reporter* had covered the business side of things for
decades, of course, and racy celebrity gossip—the staple of periodicals like
Movie Mirror, Photoplay, Picture-Play, Silver Screen, and *Screen Stars*, among
many other titles—was always popular. (Already in 1935, Walker Percy, then
a precocious undergraduate at the University of North Carolina, took note
of the "regular vomiting of prodigious quantities and varieties of magazines"
by what he called "the motion-picture magazine industry.")[97] Furthermore,
filmmaking, as a technical, teachable skill, had been around since at least
1932, when the University of Southern California began offering courses in
the subject. But film criticism and appreciation lagged behind for decades.[98]

It was not until the 1960s that professors in humanities departments,
trailing on the heels of the cinematic avant-garde, made the strongest case
for seeing film as a true art form, on par with poetry, drama, and the great
works of literature. Like Shakespeare or Proust, Dickinson or Melville, they
argued, Hollywood films were worthy of studied contemplation, discussion,
and explication. It was not an original argument: the *Cahiers du Cinéma*
crowd in Paris had been making this case—in both their criticism and their
films—for some time. When, in 1959, François Truffaut won the best director prize at Cannes for *The 400 Blows*, Jean-Luc Godard went on to proclaim
the French New Wave victorious: they had succeeded "in having it acknowledged in principle," he wrote, "that a film by Hitchcock, for example, is as
important as a book by [the poet Louis] Aragon."[99] Within a decade, college
professors stateside were singing the same chorus. Astonishingly, university
administrators listened to them. They found money for film pedagogy and
transformed curricula across the country in the process. At long last—as
David Thomson remembers it—"universities and colleges began to present

film courses in their catalogues."[100] Dartmouth College, where Thomson taught, even hosted a major conference devoted to the emerging discipline of film studies in 1965.[101] By 1976, Brown University was welcoming famed Hollywood producer Robert Evans into its English department to teach a new course, "The Anatomy of Film," even though he had never finished high school.[102]

Malick benefited tremendously from the newfound respect the cinema was receiving in the late 1960s and early 1970s. AFI had been established on the principle that film was a high art and should be taught as such. The Center for Advanced Film Studies was to be a beacon of interdisciplinary study, a place where filmmakers with "promise" were expected to have and to hone "a humanistic background" as well as "an artistic sensibility."[103] It was the perfect place for somebody with wide-ranging interests. Still, it is difficult to overlook the paradoxical nature of Malick's career change: fleeing the academy for a profession that, during the course of his lifetime, would be annexed by it, he traded philosophy for filmmaking precisely when American professors started going to the movies in a serious way.

Distinguished film critics, such as Siegfried Kracauer, James Agee, and Robert Warshow had of course been commenting insightfully on film for decades, and younger critics, such as Andrew Sarris, had helped to disseminate the auteurist approach of Truffaut and friends on this side of the Atlantic.[104] But even as movie criticism and cinema appreciation gained recognition in the culture at large, the idea of film-philosophy was seen as a contradiction in terms. After all, for much of the twentieth century, going to the movies represented a reprieve from the task of thinking, not an invitation to it. Stories abound of Wittgenstein running straight from his seminars to the front row of the nearest cinema, so he could cleanse his brain: "This is like a shower bath!" he once confessed.[105]

These days the tables have turned decisively. Film is a legitimate object of academic study in both the fine arts and the humanities. Indeed, it is no longer a question of establishing an appreciation of cinema anymore; it is, as Stanley Cavell once put it, "a matter of curriculum."[106] Movies now represent occasions for philosophical reflection rather than its avoidance: they are the stuff of symposia, not shower baths. In fact, it is now quite possible that more people are introduced to philosophy by cinema than by being forced to read Descartes's *Meditations*. A recent work by political philosopher Paul W. Kahn goes so far as to suggest that the movies have the potential to offer "philosophy for a new generation."[107]

Nobody did more to make cinema philosophically respectable than Stanley Cavell. But it is worth remembering that his early efforts with, and on behalf of, the Carpenter Center for Visual Studies at Harvard to promote the humanistic study of the movies coincided with Malick's first forays into filmmaking.[108] In other words, the lines of influence went both ways: Malick learned a great deal from Cavell about the importance and the seriousness of film, but in his pictures Cavell saw that philosophy still had much to learn from Hollywood.

Early in his career, Cavell had found that philosophers, "almost without exception," avoided anything to do with the movies.[109] He wanted to replace the usual condescension and derision with recognition and appreciation. Malick gave him the chance to do so. In the foreword to the enlarged edition of *The World Viewed* that appeared in 1979, Cavell said it was time to "grant film the status of a subject that invites and rewards philosophical speculation."[110] He made his case by juxtaposing his former student's latest film, *Days of Heaven*, not with other films but with passages pulled directly from Heidegger. This was film as philosophy and philosophy as film. The boundary lines between them had been blurred. They have stayed that way ever since.

The Fresh Prince of Beverly Hills

It is a late February afternoon and I am walking the grounds of Greystone Mansion Park in Beverly Hills. The sun is warm, the skies are blue, the flowers are blooming, and the birds are chirping. It is one of those clichéd winter days in Los Angeles that my Minnesota-born paternal grandfather hated; the kind of day on which the Pasadena Rose Parade always seems to fall; the kind of day that, when it is broadcast on television to midwesterners buried beneath mounds of snow, inevitably leads to yet another West Coast migration, yet another influx of hopefuls seeking a better—or at least warmer, sunnier—life. My grandfather had made the western trek himself, in a Model T, but once he and my grandmother had settled into their Los Angeles life in the early 1930s, once he saw the Pacific Ocean with his own eyes, saw the avocado and citrus trees in almost every yard, he did not want the secret to get out: it would only mean more crowds, more cars, more traffic.

Greystone's construction was made possible by the oil wealth that would engender Southern California's century-long love affair with the automobile. It was built by E. L. Doheny Sr., the "first discoverer of oil in the Los Angeles area," as an early AFI Conservatory Fellows Handbook put it.[111] But Greystone is far removed from the traffic-choked streets of greater Los Angeles down below it. Still today, it is the kind of place where money retreats and barricades itself behind walls and hedges and wrought-iron gates, away from the masses. You forget all this, though, when you walk the grounds of Greystone. There are trees to distract you, lots of them: eucalyptus, Italian cypress, magnolia, pine, oak, olive, even a few redwoods scattered here and there. There are palm trees, too. The arboreal abundance mirrors the subtle ostentation of the mansion itself.

Up close, Greystone has the feel of a movie set, which might explain why it so often appears in films and television. The interior of the mansion is closed off to the public most days, but anybody who has seen Paul Thomas Anderson's *There Will Be Blood* (2007) or Tony Richardson's black comedy *The Loved One* (1965) will know what the rooms inside look like: abundant stone, tile, and marble; parquet flooring offset by luxurious wood wall paneling; carved banisters; intricate chandeliers. The handbook prepared for incoming AFI fellows in 1969 made a big deal of all this grandeur. The stairway to Greystone's entrance hall, it pointed out, was a copy of the renowned "Grinling Gibbons Stairway at Cassiobury Park, English Seat of the Earl of Essex," and the murals in the card room were the work of John Frost, an early twentieth-century landscape painter known for his depictions of the American West.[112] These were not the surroundings of your typical film school. George Stevens Jr. took to calling the first home of the Center for Advanced Film Studies "Xanadu."[113]

Greystone was originally a wedding present for E. L. Doheny Jr., known as Ned. It was erected in the wake of the Teapot Dome scandal, which (until recently) was the most blatant example of political bribery in United States history. But Doheny Sr.'s suspect dealings with officials from the Harding administration were eventually overshadowed by events at Greystone itself, most especially the murder-suicide on February 16, 1929, of Ned and Hugh Plunkett, who may or may not have been his lover. Decades later, in the mid-1950s, the property was sold to Chicago businessman Henry Crown, who rented the mansion out for film shoots—still its primary function to this day—more often than he actually resided there. (Mrs. Crown's response to her husband's relocation plans was a blunt one, apparently: "over my dead body.")[114] The city of Beverly Hills eventually got Greystone on the cheap, as part of a deal that erased a sizable amount of municipal back taxes. Astonishingly, George Stevens Jr. managed to convince city administrators to rent the mansion to the American Film Institute for only one dollar a year.

With the lease finalized, Greystone was quickly converted into something resembling a film school, complete with administrative offices and seminar rooms, not to mention the requisite screening rooms, one of which replaced Doheny's private bowling alley.[115] Prints of various gauges were shown on-site daily, allowing students to see films as they were intended to be seen, and with the kind of instant access that would only become possible decades later with the advent of home video, DVDs, and digital streaming.[116] "We would order up all the films from Alfred Hitchcock or John Ford or any of the directors who we were interested in," recalled Caleb Deschanel at an event celebrating the fiftieth anniversary of the Center for Advanced Film Studies. "Our real education was all gathering together after watching lots of movies, and talking about them, and figuring out how they were made."[117] These days, Greystone may be a hushed, manicured, well-policed park—No pictures! No filming without a permit!—but in the late summer of 1969 it was a buzzing hive of conversation and creative activity. In time, every inch of the property was repurposed, including even its dilapidated horse stables: David Lynch later set up shop in them and, for half a decade, worked on *Eraserhead* (1977).

Fifty years on, the idea of these imposing Beverly Hills environs housing such a ragtag collection of aspiring filmmakers and teachers evokes all the tropes of a fairytale, Hollywood's preferred mode of self-narration. That story goes something like this: The American Film Institute's appropriation of Greystone in 1969 represented, in miniature, the brief and delirious moment when outsiders seemed poised to overthrow the old studio system—the moment when, in conjunction with the countercultural ferment of the time, the *ancien régime* of American cinema would give way to young and adventurous upstarts. It was a break, a rupture, a new beginning. It was a time of artistic freedom. It was a time of New Hollywood ascendancy.

It is a nice story, but it is not true. Although the neighbors surely must have had their suspicions about the longhairs and bell-bottoms arriving in gigantic cars for their seminars at Greystone—under the heading of "Community Relations," the Conservatory Fellows Handbook urged aspiring filmmakers to avoid giving the impression "that anything 'illegal' or 'immoral' is happening on the premises"—the early years of the American Film Institute did not constitute a storming of the palace.[118] It was quite the opposite, actually. The whole point of housing AFI at Greystone was to establish a suitably lavish setting where the Old Hollywood and the New Hollywood could meet and mingle, often over drinks.[119] As Billy Wilder quipped, the

Center for Advanced Film Studies was in the business of "teaching new dogs old tricks."[120]

Without a set curriculum, instruction at AFI revolved around seminars and tutorials, in which some of "the great figures in Hollywood film"—as an early *Hollywood Reporter* article described it—would stop by and impart their wisdom upon a select group of individuals intent on creating great and lasting art.[121] "Learn by doing; study with the Masters" was the unofficial motto of the program.[122] It "was the sort of place," Malick later explained, "where you could really get your chops together."[123] Nevertheless, despite the practical focus of the Center for Advanced Film Studies, Greystone often seemed more like a social club than an MFA program, which is why Paul Schrader, who eventually dropped out, described the decision to set up shop at Greystone as a "definitive mistake."[124] Artists should be taught to suffer for their art, he thought, not sell out to studio bosses or wealthy Westsiders for it.

But for anybody who was passionate about movies, AFI was the place to be. Hitchcock stopped by for seminars on directing. William Wyler and Billy Wilder participated in conversations with fellows. Fellini, one of Malick's favorite directors, even showed up to screen and discuss his latest film, *Satyricon* (1969), alongside Anthony Quinn, who had starred in *La Strada* (1956).[125] And that just scratches the surface. In its first year as a fully functioning program, the Center for Advanced Film Studies also welcomed Roger Corman, Sam Fuller, Costa-Gavras, Howard Hawks, John Huston, Elia Kazan, Sam Peckinpah, Arthur Penn, Jean Renoir, and Haskell Wexler.[126] Fittingly, these discussions were held in Greystone's "great hall." It was there that Malick listened to the first of the center's illustrious guests: Harold Lloyd, after whom the AFI seminar series would be named. Joining the bespectacled star of the silent era on the seminar stage was another living legend, the director King Vidor.

In such surroundings, Malick may have felt rather like a king himself. Etymologically, his name, Malick, part of an Assyrian inheritance, suggests royalty. It is a theme explored in *Knight of Cups*, an autobiographical film about a "prince from the east" who heads west on a quest, only to fall under a spell and forget who he is. A journey undertaken to prove himself becomes, in time, a journey to find himself. It is this journey of self-exploration that defines not just Malick's career in Hollywood but also his pursuit of the examined life more generally. For Malick, the search is everything, and sticking to it entails a willingness to start over again, again and again and again.

Perhaps it is fitting, then, that one of the films Harold Lloyd screened for students and guests when he visited AFI was his 1925 picture *The Freshman*. Malick had tried his hand at academic philosophy, had worked for a while as a journalist, but here was making a new start, a freshman.

*   *   *

Terrence Malick's first proper film, the short *Lanton Mills*, was made at the American Film Institute. It owes far more to Harold Lloyd—to *The Freshman*, but also to *The Kid Brother* (1927), which also played at AFI's opening-day festivities on September 23, 1969—than to anything that can be found in the pages of Heidegger. It is funny: a spoof Western starring Harry Dean Stanton and Warren Oates, it has a character known as "the slowest gun in the West" who dies, as one might expect, in a shootout. But Malick would never make anything as silly or as free-spirited as *Lanton Mills* ever again.[127] His first feature film, *Badlands*, was a wholly different work. It premiered at the New York Film Festival in 1973.[128] In just a few short years, everything had changed. And Malick went from being just another freshman to a celebrated filmmaker in the process.

CHAPTER 1

Crime Wave

The Pursuit of Personhood in *Badlands*

> Motion pictures were in some sense a response to the
> urgent social question much debated in the period in
> which the movies were born: how can an individual
> survive in the world of the crowd?
> —Warren I. Susman

The year 1969 was a good time to be in Los Angeles, especially if you were young, available, and ready to have some fun. And white, of course: the Watts Rebellion of 1965 and the East Los Angeles Walkouts of 1968 alerted everyone to the racial disparities hidden behind the city's glamorous, Hollywood-constructed facade.[1] But the myths of Southern California exerted greater gravitational pull than the news reports. In those days before the Manson murders changed everything, Los Angeles continued to be thought of as a creative's paradise, an open landscape of possibility for the artistically ambitious. It was a place of reinvention and escape—a place, most of all, of freedom. All one needed was an automobile to get to the party.

Conveniently, cars were easy enough to come by, gas was cheap, and the roads were open, traffic having not yet descended into the perpetual state of gridlock we now associate with Southland commuting. Cruising in the 1960s was a choice, not a necessity, and a new genre of pop music—the car song— offered the perfect soundtrack for it.[2] As artist Ed Ruscha's groundbreaking book *Every Building on the Sunset Strip* demonstrated, there was a lot to see as one trekked across town toward the beach, listening to "Little Deuce Coupe."[3] Ruscha celebrated the vernacular architecture of Los Angeles that stood out—like the songs of the Beach Boys—in the popular imagination. He did not distinguish between the mundane and the outlandish: gas stations on this block were just as significant as the Whisky a Go Go, where the Doors were finding fame, over on that one. For Ruscha, Southern California was a cornucopia of pop culture creativity, provided you looked at it the right way, which was from the window of a passing car.

In much the same spirit as Rushca's work, the architectural critic and urban theorist Reyner Banham, visiting from Britain, would make the most famous case for celebrating the region's unique sense of place in *Los Angeles: The Architecture of the Four Ecologies*, published just a few years after Ruscha's ode to the Sunset Strip.[4] In it, Banham hailed Southern California as an "Autopia," a vision of the global city to come, built entirely around cars. He sang of Angelenos as "freeway-pilots" gliding over street surfaces, "the selector levers of their automatic gearboxes" set "firmly in *Drive*." Banham viewed these Autopians as symbols of independence, "acting out one of the most spectacular paradoxes in the great debate between private freedom and public discipline that pervades every affluent, mechanized urban society."[5] No wonder these young "freeway-pilots," eager to throw off the chains of cultural conformity, would flock to movies about cars and motorcycles, criminals and rebels.

Young Hollywood directors of the late sixties and early seventies were drawn to the road movie as a genre because they were the children of the open road, more familiar with the tensions between private freedom and public discipline than any generation before them ever had been—or so they liked to think. From 1969's *Easy Rider*—directed by Ruscha's art-world pal Dennis Hopper—to *American Graffiti* (dir. George Lucas, 1973), the drama Banham saw playing out on Southern California roads informed a slew of New Hollywood films about personal freedom and societal constraint.[6] Car culture, it turns out, was about much more than automobiles.

For moviemakers, road movies were an occupational—not just generational—preoccupation.[7] Stories about cars and cruising, outlaws and open roads, became the subject matter of choice for a cohort of filmmakers who fancied themselves rebels for daring to make personal films that eluded the grip of studio control. The road movie was the perfect allegory for their artistic struggles: it prioritized conflict and liberation. No wonder so many New Hollywood car-culture stories—like that of Malick's first feature film, *Badlands* (1973)—turned out to be about crime, passion, and, most of all, running away.

But from what, exactly, were the protagonists of these pictures really running? Was it just the reach of the authorities and the constraints of society, or was it also, in a way, themselves? And just what did all this say about the filmmakers who brought these characters to life? From what did *they* think they were running? From studio bosses? From bean-counting producers? Or was it also, perhaps, from the crushing burden of expectations?

*   *   *

Badlands has been described as "one of the great debuts in American film."[8] The Library of Congress added it to its National Film Registry in 1993. But the recognition came twenty years after its initial release, the result of a significant shift in critical opinion.[9] Although it garnered its fair share praise when it premiered at the New York Film Festival in 1973 and went on to influence a good many artists—everyone from Bruce Springsteen to Raymond Pettibon—*Badlands* took a long time to become a classic.[10]

Badlands flummoxed early viewers. Some admired its artistry, but many others struggled to understand how its seemingly naive, teenage protagonists, young lovers on the run Kit Carruthers (Martin Sheen) and Holly Sargis (Sissy Spacek), could be so blasé about the trail of violence they leave in their wake. At its most basic level, *Badlands* is a movie about a murder spree. Although later filmmakers, such as Quentin Tarantino and Oliver Stone, would glorify this aspect of the film, creating works that borrowed heavily from its precedent, many of *Badlands'* first critics failed to see the point of putting a couple of affectless murderers up on the screen to be imitated or admired.[11] Pauline Kael dismissed it as an overly "intellectualized movie." It was "shrewd and artful," she conceded, but otherwise empty.[12]

To be sure, other critics were less demanding. They praised *Badlands* as a well-executed genre film—a backhanded compliment, but nevertheless true.[13] Malick's first feature film has everything an outlaw road movie should: car chases, shoot-outs, sex, and violence—well, no sex really, but quite a bit of violence. In cold blood, Kit murders not only Holly's father (Warren Oates), but also a trio of bounty hunters; his best friend, Cato (Ramon Bieri); and a young couple who happen to show up at Cato's place at just the wrong moment. Plenty more blood is shed before the final credits roll. None of it seems to mean anything. Largely frustrating viewer expectations when it comes to the magical cause-and-effect calculus of movie violence, *Badlands* offers no motives for all the killing. There is no dramatic resolution to the film, either, no cathartic narrative closure.

Critics kinder than Kael interpreted Malick's reticence to wrap up his story neatly as a subtle subversion of the road movie genre, which was already sputtering to a stop.[14] In this light, Malick's debut could be viewed as something of a statement. Malick's "vision of violence and death," Vincent Canby wrote in the *New York Times*, was a comment on mass cultural "boredom." "Kit and Holly are," he famously suggested, "members of the television generation run amok."[15]

As Canby noted, *Badlands* mines the 1950s true-crime story of teenage killer Charles Starkweather and his underage girlfriend, Caril Ann Fugate, who together terrorized midwestern communities in their home state of Nebraska and neighboring Wyoming, where they were eventually captured. Between December 1957 and late January 1958, Starkweather murdered eleven people. For some of these killings, Fugate was by his side, though whether as a willing or captive accomplice was open to interpretation. It was a senseless string of violence, one that mobilized not just local law enforcement but also the National Guard. The young outlaws did not escape the elaborate dragnet that was put into place to capture them: Fugate eventually surrendered and Starkweather, after being wounded in a wild car chase and shoot-out with police, was taken into custody. Extradited to Nebraska, he was found guilty of murder and sentenced to death, executed by electric chair a little over a year later. Fugate was given life in prison. She was later paroled, after serving seventeen years of her sentence.[16]

The Starkweather-Fugate story had all the elements of tabloid gold: a gun, a car, a girl, even a leather-jacket-wearing antihero who styled his hair like James Dean. News coverage of the interstate pursuit of Starkweather and Fugate captivated the Midwest and, in time, the nation at large. The fact that the murders seemed to resemble the plot of a Hollywood movie—Joseph H. Lewis's *Gun Crazy* (1950), for example—only heightened popular interest, fueling a moral panic: if this is what the kids were up to, they were not alright. Many thought Hollywood was to blame. Teenagers raised on Saturday afternoon double features had finally gone movie-mad. Could they no longer separate out fantasy from reality?

Although it is loosely based on actual events, *Badlands* is not a true-crime story. It is a movie about the movies—and about our relation to them. It is a picture preoccupied with playacting. Malick seems rather uninterested in the murders that propel his plot forward, focusing instead on the midcentury

American anxieties that the Starkweather story, as a story, came to represent in the popular imagination—anxieties about authenticity and individuality, freedom and constraint, rebellion and conformism, performance and personhood. In the modern world that mass entertainment had made, just what did it mean to be an individual, somebody who stood out from the crowd? In what ways do the movies help us to find ourselves? In what ways do they lead us astray?

Badlands explores these themes in a highly mediated, self-referential way. In repurposing the story of Charles Starkweather and Caril Ann Fugate for his own ends, Malick was making a statement not just about the conformism of the 1950s Midwest but also about 1970s Hollywood and about the place that he, a cinematic upstart, hoped to claim in it. Instead of focusing on moralizing questions of good or evil, right or wrong, he emphasizes chance, ambiguity, and incomprehension. One of the most unsettling aspects of *Badlands* is that Kit and Holly never really seem to know who they are, even and especially as they embark, almost by accident, on their life of crime. They fall in and out of things by happenstance, without so much as a moment's reflection. "How'd that be?" Kit often asks, as if he were trying out an idea, not knowing what to do next. He is constantly looking for approval, always trying to convince himself he is the person he pretends to be.

Malick knew something about falling into things and looking for approval. After having tried his hand at academic philosophy and long-form journalism, he was, in the early 1970s, trying to make a name for himself in that most fanciful of professions, the movie business. Like everyone else in Hollywood, he was putting on a show. *Badlands* is a film about posturing made by a filmmaker playing the role of the big-shot director.

Only at the American Film Institute could a film like *Badlands* have been imagined, developed, and brought to fruition. From the start, the Center for Advanced Film Studies styled itself as an independent alternative to the corporate conformism of the studio system. It tried hard to stand out. But it also hoped to bathe itself in the allure of old-time Hollywood glamour. AFI wanted its fellows—many of whom, like Malick, had only limited exposure to actual instruction in filmmaking before entering the program—to create rebellious, avant-garde cinema; but not too rebellious and not too avant-garde. The mixed messaging was, for some, rather anxiety inducing. The roles these filmmakers in training were expected to play were hazy and indeterminate. Just what did it mean to be a film worker in the era of the New Hollywood?[17] Did it mean adapting to genre conventions or subverting them?

Was directing just another technical skill to be learned through imitation and repetition, or was it an exercise in authentic self-expression? Everything, it seemed, was up for grabs. No wonder Malick felt like a "total imposter" when he was shooting his first feature. "I had read about directors who just go out there and express themselves on the set, who have total authority," he told an AFI audience in 1974, not long after making *Badlands*. "Here I was, shaking like a leaf. I literally felt embarrassed just saying 'Action!' I tried to find some other way to say it."[18]

Crime and Punishment

Surveying Malick's apprentice work—as both a film student and a scriptwriter for hire—reveals a great deal about his evolution as a director, long before he dreamed up the story of Kit and Holly. At AFI, he studied not just the finer points of prestige pictures or the ins and outs of European art-house cinema, but also the tropes and truisms of well-established Hollywood genres: Westerns, crime films, even trucker movies. An understanding of these influences goes a long way toward explaining the odd mixture of conventionality and originality to be found in his feature-length debut.

In the early 1970s, the genre of the outlaw road movie was a Hollywood staple undergoing something of a renaissance. Films such as *Easy Rider* and, before it, Arthur Penn's *Bonnie and Clyde* (1967) had injected new life into a cinematic narrative that had its previous heyday in the 1940s, when films like Raoul Walsh's *They Drive by Night* (1940), Edgar G. Ulmer's *Detour* (1945), and Nicholas Ray's *They Live by Night* (1949) graced the silver screen. In a few short years, Monte Hellman, Terrence Malick, Steven Spielberg, and Robert Altman would make road movies of their own.

The Hollywood into which Malick was thrown was the Hollywood of Hellman's *Two-Lane Blacktop* (1971). The film was more than just a possible influence on him: it was also a potential job. The upstart Hollywood agent Mike Medavoy came across Malick's name during a business meeting with Hellman: "I was sitting on the opposite side of Monte Hellman's desk," he recalls in his 2002 memoir, "and there was a treatment for *Two-Lane Blacktop* on his desk, written by an AFI student named Terrence Malick. I thought it was pretty good—even upside down and even though Monte wasn't going to use it—so I called Terry and offered to be his agent."[19]

The rest, as they say, is history. Medavoy got Malick more scriptwriting work, including the first features to which his name would be attached: Stuart Rosenberg's cowboy comedy *Pocket Money* (1972) and Vernon Zimmerman's madcap trucker film *Deadhead Miles* (1972). Alongside John Milius, Malick also worked on the initial version of *Dirty Harry* (1971), which might explain why one of the cops in the story is named Medavoy.[20] Though that script did not get used, Malick's contributions to other projects, such as Jack Nicholson's *Drive, He Said* (1971) and Jack Starrett's *The Dion Brothers* (1974), helped pay the bills while he was plotting a course toward his directorial debut.[21]

It was not a long wait. When it came to scriptwriting and filmmaking, Malick was a fast learner. But his prior studies in philosophy also proved beneficial, since they touched upon topics dominating New Hollywood filmmaking at the time. Malick's early scripts were almost always explorations of alienation, dislocation, and isolation—the general sense that the world was out of joint, maybe even absurd, but one had to carry on anyhow, like Sisyphus.

Two-Lane Blacktop was the embodiment of existentialist cinema. Its script was written by the avant-garde novelist—and musical organ heir—Rudolph Wurlitzer. He and Hellman agreed that their road movie should follow the example of Samuel Beckett's *Waiting for Godot*—a play Hellman once staged for the Theatergoers Company in Los Angeles as a Western.[22] Turning *Godot* into a road movie would be no big deal. What Beckett did for bums in bowler hats Wurlitzer and Hellman would do for long-haired drag racers in blue jeans. The result was existentialist filmmaking distilled down to its most basic components: a couple characters; a few lines of fragmented, occasionally comic dialogue; a perhaps-futile search for meaning.[23]

Like Beckett's Vladimir and Estragon, the protagonists of *Two-Lane Blacktop*—the anonymously named Driver (James Taylor) and Mechanic (Dennis Wilson)—are unmoored. As film historian Sylvia Townsend puts it, "the Driver and the Mechanic have no plans, no goals, no attachments, no anchor."[24] The same goes for the other characters in the film, the frugally named Girl (Laurie Bird) and GTO (Warren Oates). They are empty characters trying to become people but to no avail. Everybody in *Two-Lane Blacktop* is aimlessly wandering; not a single one of them "finds a fulfilling identity or a purpose to life."[25] Wurlitzer's script revolves around what Townsend calls a "search for identity," and the film Hellman made of it gives us characters "seeking to find themselves and their purpose" but coming up short.[26]

As in *Godot*, there is no dramatic resolution in *Two-Lane Blacktop*. In a metacinematic twist, Hellman's movie ends with a simulated ignition of its film stock: unfinished and unresolved, the picture dissolves before viewers' eyes, frustrating any hopes they might have for a happy ending—or, indeed, for any kind of proper ending at all. Despite lavish advertising, the film flopped, only to be rediscovered years later and hailed as a cult classic.

For Malick's budding career, *Two-Lane Blacktop* was a near miss. But it gave him an agent and a cinematic theme he could make his own: the existential search for meaning. This quest—and the many ways it can go (comically) wrong—animates an early script Malick wrote that *did* get produced in the early seventies, *Pocket Money*. The film made from it was not a success. Despite starring Paul Newman (as Jim) and Lee Marvin (as Leonard), Stuart Rosenberg's contemporary cowboy comedy fell a little flat. It was, as Vincent Canby described it, "a fragmented, far-from-great movie."[27] But *Pocket Money* was another exercise in existentialist cinema, and the fees Malick collected for penning it funded the making of *Badlands*, so one should not dismiss it too quickly.[28]

Like *Two-Lane Blacktop*, *Pocket Money* frustrates viewer expectations. Its protagonists are neither successful nor particularly likable. But they are, in their own peculiar way, sort of lovable. Jim is a little dim, or at the very least naive; he takes everything too literally. Leonard catches on quicker, but only because he is a bit of a schemer—as is suggested by his wardrobe, which consists of rumpled suits and fedoras rather than dungarees and cowboy hats. The plot of the film—Malick was working from an adaptation by John Gay of the 1970 novel *Jim Kane*, written by real-life Arizona cowboy J. P. S. Brown—involves purchasing, then driving, Mexican cattle to the United States for a dubious American businessman who is trying to make a quick buck supplying steer for the rodeo circuit.

Taking a cue from Sam Peckinpah's *The Wild Bunch* (1969)—a film Malick's cohort of AFI fellows had discussed in some detail—*Pocket Money* scrambles the codes of the Hollywood Western.[29] In Mexico, everything comes undone as Jim and Leonard go off the rails. Their conversation descends into a kind of vaudevillian cross talk that sounds, at times, rather *Godot*-like, veering wildly from the roundabout and the verbose (usually Leonard, as he works up a scheme) to the so-literal-it-is-in-fact-obtuse (usually Jim, for whom radical honesty is a kind of masochistic virtue). The cliché-riddled dialogue—"incomprehensible cowboy jargon," according to Canby, or "shit-kicker dialogue" as Jacob Brackman has called it—is like an Abbott

and Costello routine run into the ground.[30] Conversations never seem to accomplish anything; debates rarely lead to decisions or resolutions. Words
constantly seem to fail Jim, especially. In an almost permanent state of frustration, he often ends up kicking car bumpers, trash cans, or, when neither
of these is available, the dirt, Billy Martin-style.

In *The Wild Bunch* Peckinpah veered toward unredemptive ultraviolence,
but in his screenplay for *Pocket Money*, Malick went the other way, opting
for comedy and absurdist wordplay. But the messages are similar: everything
is now pointless, meaningless, absurd—a dead end. One can adopt a posture
of heroic resolve—a determination to *act*—but nothing will ever change. It
is an idea Beckett placed at the center of *Godot*: "Let us not waste our time in
idle discourse!" Vladimir urges Estragon. "Let us do something, while we
have the chance!"[31] Yet the two tramps go on to accomplish nothing: at the
conclusion of the play, they are right back where they started, still waiting
for Godot to arrive.

The same sense of existential exhaustion permeates *Pocket Money*. Like
Beckett's play, the film pokes fun at its protagonists. Most of the comedy
comes from the fact that Jim and Leonard are cowboy types living in a cow-
boyless world, more Don Quixote and Sancho Panza than Lone Ranger and
Tonto. No longer the heroic figures of the popular imagination they once
were, the cattlemen of 1972 are merely underemployed proletarians, driving
around in beat-up automobiles, staying in cheap, rundown motels. There is
nothing exciting about modern-day cowboy life, but there is no way for
modern-day cowboys to escape from it, either.

Pocket Money suggests that Jim and Leonard are caught in a kind of permanent loop, just like the protagonists of *Two-Lane Blacktop* and, before that,
Waiting for Godot. The final shots of the picture show them waiting, hobo-
like, at a remote station for a train to arrive. One gets the sense that they, like
Vladimir and Estragon, will be waiting there endlessly. No train appears as
the skies darken. "Black clouds in the distance gettin' closer all the time,"
sings Carole King on the film's title track, which plays over a still freezing
Jim and Leonard forever in their place. It is yet another conclusion—like *Godot*, like *Two-Lane*—lacking catharsis.

That these existentialist tropes found their way into *Badlands* should not
have come as a surprise to anyone in and around Hollywood at the time.
After all, Malick had arrived at the American Film Institute's Center for Advanced Film Studies not just as a Harvard-educated intellectual but also, and
more importantly, as—to use the words of one his AFI instructors—"an

expert on existential philosophy."[32] If anyone could do *Godot* properly, it was Malick. "Hollywood is still a hick town," one veteran movie producer was quoted as saying in *Esquire* in 1975, "and Terry dazzled 'em with his Harvard-Oxford style."[33]

Being able to count a philosopher among the inaugural cohort of students was a point of pride for George Stevens Jr., AFI's founding director. In fact, it was an essential component of his vision for the place. In remarks delivered during the Center for Advanced Film Studies' formal inauguration, he said he hoped Greystone would be much more than a film school: he wanted it to be a center "for inquiry and discourse about the world we live in." In addition to hosting famous actors, directors, cinematographers, and screenwriters for seminars and public events, AFI would be inviting "philosophers and scientists" to its outpost in Beverly Hills.[34] It was to be a place for intellectuals with big ideas. How fortunate for Stevens, then, that one of his first fellows was a philosopher *and* a filmmaker—or a filmmaker in training, at least.

The film Malick submitted as part of his application to the Center for Advanced Film Studies was a forty-minute short titled *An Unlikely Story*. It was screened alongside other student works during the first week of activities at Greystone, in late September 1969.[35] Very little about the film has surfaced in the decades since Malick made it, but a telling clue about its subject matter can be found in a document buried in the American Film Institute's institutional files. It is nothing grand, just a compilation of biographical blurbs describing the first cohort of fellows. Composed after Malick had left AFI—sometime in 1972, most likely, while he was working on the film that would become *Badlands*—Malick's bio bears all the marks of his wry sense of humor, which he was busy pouring into scripts such as *Pocket Money*.[36] He describes himself, first and foremost, as a Harvard graduate, "Phi Beta Kappa," who also "studied as a Rhodes Scholar at Oxford University." Immediately after this comes a list of odd jobs that mixes blue-collar bona fides with white-collar pedigrees: "He has been employed as an oil field roustabout, air-hammer operator, short order cook, truck driver, wheat harvester and as a journalist for LIFE, NEWSWEEK, and THE NEW YORKER." But Malick then returns to his academic credentials, noting how he was "a guest lecturer in philosophy at the Massachusetts Institute of Technology." And then, at last, comes this clue about *An Unlikely Story*: "Before coming to the Center," Malick writes, he "had made one short film about a respected young man who decided to commit a crime to prove his existence to himself."[37]

It sounds like it could have been an adaptation of something out of Dostoevsky, a version of *Crime and Punishment* set in Cambridge, Massachusetts (where the film was made), maybe.[38] But Malick's initial foray into filmmaking was not so weighty. Friends and colleagues from his Harvard and MIT days recall a largely improvised sixteen-millimeter film, done on the cheap with borrowed equipment, about an office worker who climbed dangerously tall buildings on his lunch breaks. It was a film about surviving the drudgery of office work, about finding meaning in something other than the daily grind.[39]

Whether or not it had an adequately Raskolnikovian protagonist, *An Unlikely Story* certainly demonstrates that Malick's turn to filmmaking was not a diversion from his studies in existential philosophy but rather an extension of them. What drew him to philosophy in the first place—namely, a fascination with the meaning and purpose of existence—would animate the stories he would seek to tell as a director. From *An Unlikely Story* on, his motion pictures have been about characters seeking out some kind of reminder that they were, indeed, alive—that they were individuals who stood out from the crowd.

The Brave Cowboy

When he arrived at AFI in late September 1969, Malick may have had all the philosophy he needed for the purposes of scriptwriting, but it was clear that when it came to actual filmmaking there was room for improvement. As he told his instructors when he finally got to Greystone, he had "a lot to learn about the technical side of stuff," especially since he "never had any experience with film school."[40]

One of the appeals of AFI in its early years was the tailored course of training each fellow received. A draft outline for Malick's coursework provides insight into his cinematic interests as an apprentice filmmaker. It recommends both practical exercises and interpretive assignments:

WORK

Preparation of a feature film script. TV rehearsals with actors from written script and improvisations. Lighting exercises. Unit managing a Fellows film. Ten minute 16mm film telling a story without dialogue. Editing of a Feature film sequence. 35MM ten to 15 minute film based on a sequence from his feature script.

STUDY

Write a short breakdown from two sequences of a feature film. Analysis of selected pictures for dramatic structure, acting performance, lighting, music and storytelling through the image. Study of production and distribution problems. Study of use of music, lighting and camera work. Technical aspects of 35MM productions. Presentation to Fellows of films dealing with historical figures. Study of films set in the Southwest.[41]

Though the outline describes a detailed curriculum, it does not cover everything. It does not even address everything Malick wanted to learn. He was also keen to learn how "to score my own films," he told his classmates.[42] Given the many memorable ways in which Malick has used both popular and classical music to shape the mood and meaning of his films—from Nat King Cole's "A Blossom Fell" in *Badlands* and Camille Saint-Saëns's *The Carnival of the Animals* in *Days of Heaven* to Zbigniew Preisner's *Requiem for My Friend* in *The Tree of Life* and Henryk Górecki's *Symphony of Sorrowful Songs* in *A Hidden Life*—this hardly surprising admission demonstrates that, from the start, Malick was interested in mastering as many aspects of the filmmaking process as he possibly could, from generating story ideas and production budgets to finessing the finer details of editing and sound design. Even as a student Malick knew that being competent in cinematic trades both above and below the line would ensure his artistic independence. Such freedom was a central preoccupation of the day, one Malick shared with many of the emerging filmmakers of the New Hollywood era.

Malick may have had a lot to learn about *how* to make a movie, but he knew *what kind* of movie he wanted to make: a Western. Hence the suggested study of "films set in the Southwest." In a memo sent to the staff of AFI, September 8, 1969, from Amarillo, Texas, where Malick was still based at the time (friends and acquaintances have recalled his fondness for an Amarillo Dragway T-shirt, which he used to wear beneath his button-downs, apparently), he outlined some of his cinematic interests. These included a good many prestige pictures, but also a fair share of cowboy movies.[43] Alongside the early films of Federico Fellini, Elia Kazan, and François Truffaut, as well as masterworks by Orson Welles (*Mr. Arkadin* [1955] and *The Magnificent Ambersons* [1942]) and Max Ophuls (*Lola Montès* [1955]), Malick's wish list of films he hoped to view at AFI included Arthur Penn's *The Left Handed Gun* (1958),

David Miller's *Lonely Are the Brave* (1962), Sam Peckinpah's *Ride the High Country* (1962), and George Stevens's *Giant* (1956). The last was a particular favorite of his, apparently, but it was also a film made by the father of AFI's founding director.[44]

In the same memo, Malick suggested AFI invite his former philosophy mentor Stanley Cavell to speak at the center, a recommendation we might interpret as proof that his interest in Westerns was not a typical one.[45] This is not to say that the genre was unworthy of philosophical analysis, that cowboy movies and philosophy should not mix. For almost as long as it has been around, the Western has been a site of profound reflection—even if only in a stylized or mythological sense—on ideas of freedom and constraint, moral duty and obligation. For better or worse, the Western is our political philosophy.[46] Some of the most astute American film critics, such as Robert Warshow, noticed early on how the Western reflected some of our most troubling preconceptions about the tensions between self and society.[47] When Stanley Cavell first began teaching courses on philosophy and film at Harvard in 1963, he made sure to include Warshow's essays—on the Western, especially—in his syllabus.[48]

Mediated as it was by his Harvard studies, Malick's interest in Westerns was not that of a fanboy raised on a steady diet of John Ford films.[49] But neither was it what we might call overdetermined. A too-tidy genealogy, stretching from Warshow to Cavell to Malick, might suggest an excessively theoretical approach to the Western, originating solely in seminar-room discussions of little magazines and culminating in a film like *Badlands* or *Days of Heaven*. But this narrative would be external to Hollywood, a view from the outside, as it were. An internal explanation works just as well.

The Westerns Malick studied at AFI were existentialist in their own right. They featured alienated protagonists struggling to survive in increasingly modern, ever more regimented surroundings. Two of them, released just three years apart, were helmed by George Stevens. In *Shane* (1953), Alan Ladd plays the title character, a buckskin-wearing gunslinger who is reluctantly drawn into an ongoing battle between homesteading farmers, on the one side, and a bunch of rugged, crooked cattlemen who continually threaten their claims, on the other. Though he desires to settle down, to marry and perhaps raise a family—his purchase of store-bought clothing in town is meant to symbolize this transition to polite society—Shane must remain a gunslinger. "A man has to be what he is," he says. Changing back into his buckskins, Shane defeats the black-hatted bad guys (including Jack Palance in one of his most memorable early roles), but the victory is a hollow one, for in resorting to violence Shane demonstrates that he is not, and never will be, one of the civilized. The tragedy of the story is that Shane must remain forever excluded from the very community he swoops in to rescue. He represents the repressed, sacrificial violence that founds, but must be exorcised from, civilized society.[50]

Stevens returned to these topics with *Giant* (1956), a multigenerational saga that brought the Western up to the jet-age present. The film is chiefly remembered for James Dean's supporting-cast portrayal of Jett Rink, a character whose improbable rise from lowly ranch hand to fabulously wealthy oil tycoon—an easy-to-grasp analogy for the transition of the Old West to the New—presages the death of the Western as a genre. *Giant* also foreshadows the artistic and economic transformations—if not also the generational transition—that distinguished New Hollywood cinema of the late 1960s and early 1970s from the decades of studio-based filmmaking preceding it. The Hollywood of George Stevens Jr. would not be the Hollywood of George Stevens Sr., just as the Hollywood of *Badlands* would not be the Hollywood of *Shane* and *Giant*.

The Hollywood Western went into decline right when the old studio system started showing signs of distress. Television changed everything: the longest running Western on American television, *Gunsmoke*, debuted a year before the release of *Giant*; *Bonanza*, the show with the second-longest career, hit the airwaves just three years later. The success of these shows resulted in dwindling box-office receipts in the 1950s, but a growing list of motion-picture writers, directors, and actors began to blame the bloated rigidity of the studio system. A new approach to moviemaking was needed. Up-and-coming talents turned to the Western with the hope of using it to shake up the Hollywood system. "The Hollywood western was arrogated by talent on the make," Jeff Menne has argued, who "brokered their own deals." In doing so, they subverted studio control. It was the dawn of what Menne playfully calls— invoking both the cinematic aesthetics of John Ford and the managerial economics of Henry Ford—post-Fordist filmmaking.[51]

In Menne's account of this transition, the gunslinging outsider comes to represent the renegade filmmaker challenging the entrenched authority of studio executives: the cowboy as auteur and the auteur as cowboy. But in the struggle to wrest artistic control from the clutches of those who controlled the culture industry, this new crop of filmmakers subjected the Western to something of an acid bath. Their version of the genre depicted defeat rather than victory, foolhardiness rather than heroism. Most of all, it expressed doubt rather than certainty about the things typically associated with Fordism (in both its meanings): civilization, modernity, progress. The high-water mark of the trend was Dennis Hopper's all too fittingly titled *The Last Movie* (1971), a deconstructed film about the making of a Western that never actually gets made.

There were other movies made before Dennis Hopper decamped to Peru that explored the exhaustion of both the Western and the studio system that had created it. One of them was *Lonely Are the Brave*, a 1962 film Menne interprets as a kind of *locus classicus* of the post-Fordist tradition in Hollywood, a film that was on Malick's screening wish list when he arrived at the American Film Institute seven years after its release. Its influence on *Badlands* is unmistakable.

Adapted from Edward Abbey's 1956 novel *The Brave Cowboy* by Dalton Trumbo, David Miller's *Lonely Are the Brave* opens with a striking juxtaposition. A series of shots show Jack Burns (Kirk Douglas) in perfect cowboy repose, leaning back against his bedroll, smoking a cigarette, his hat tilted forward, shadowing his face from the bright desert sun.[52] For all we know, it could be 1862. But then, breaking the spell, is a shot of a jet plane flying high above, leaving a long contrail in its wake. It is *not* 1862, and for Jack it is time to move on.

As if to reinforce the notion that Jack Burns is a man out of time, the subsequent scenes in *Lonely Are the Brave* provide a series of striking contrasts. They show him on horseback riding up to a fence. Like the contrails in the previous scene, the barbed wire stretches as far as the eye can see. The open range has been cordoned off. But Jack Burns simply cuts the wires and rides on through. A real westerner "hates fences," he will say later on. Country music plays as a series of shots capture him resuming his travels on horseback, climbing a ridge, crossing a river—all of the usual images typically associated with Westerns. But then, in another Brechtian juxtaposition, we see him approach a busy highway, with cars traveling at high speeds in both directions. Two different worlds—the old and the new—have collided again. Navigating the gap between them is trickier this time. Jack can get from one world to the other—from this side of the road to that one—only by risking great danger. He eventually manages to get his spooked horse, Whisky,

Figure 1. Worlds collide in David Miller's *Lonely Are the Brave*.

through the maze of honking cars and trucks whizzing past, but just barely. The scene foreshadows Burns's fate at the end of the film, when he and Whisky, pursued by the law, will not be so lucky.

As Kirk Douglas plays him in *Lonely Are the Brave*, Jack is a tragic figure, a relic from the past who can no longer survive in the modernized, suburbanized, border-patrolled present. He is an independent individual in a time of increasing conformity and control. Douglas was eager to portray him: "I love the theme that if you try to be an individual," he later wrote in his autobiography, "society will crush you."[53] Whereas older Westerns, like *Shane*, depicted the loneliness of a gunslinger excluded from modern society, newer Westerns, such as *Lonely Are the Brave*, bemoaned an even bleaker predicament: that of being stranded *in* a society with no possibility of escape.

Another Western that drove this point home for Malick was Arthur Penn's *The Left Handed Gun*. Released in between *Giant* and *Lonely Are the Brave*, Penn's first feature film—based on a script by Gore Vidal—was a moody retelling of the legend of Billy the Kid. Paul Newman plays him in the style of James Dean's performance as Jim Stark in Nicholas Ray's *Rebel Without a Cause* (1955): young, alienated, confused, prone to outbursts—in a word, troubled. Caught between adolescence and adulthood, he yearns to become somebody of note but struggles under the weight of self-responsibility. Penn wavers between presenting Billy as the personification of righteous justice, on the one hand, and as a misguided kid irresponsibly playing around with guns, on the other.

Over the course of the film, Billy becomes increasingly obsessed with how others view him, the press most especially. He cannot read, but he is fascinated by the figure into which news reports and dime novels have transformed him: "They say I'm a figure of glory," he gushes to his jailer. But his fame will be his undoing and he knows it. In what surely must be interpreted as Penn's commentary on the culture industry's shameless and pervasive bloodlust (a theme to which he would return in *Bonnie and Clyde* just a few years later), Billy is finally tracked down and killed in a hideout plastered with flyers calling for his arrest.

A day before Valentine's Day 1970, Malick led an AFI Fellows' Meeting at Greystone devoted to "The Western." He began by discussing the character of Billy in *The Left Handed Gun*. Malick said he was particularly interested in how Penn portrayed Billy's conflicted thoughts about his growing celebrity. As he saw it, Billy seemed both curious about his fame and disgusted by it. This suggested that he was more reflective than he first appeared. "Billy constantly seems to be embarrassed about what's deepest in him," Malick told the other fellows, his "embarrassment communicates a kind of depth." Malick thought this aspect of Billy's personality kept him within the realm of the audience's "moral sympathy" despite the fact that he was a proven killer.

What made Billy remarkable in Malick's opinion was his willingness to act out his insecurities and his emotions in ways most moviegoers would never dare. Malick thought audiences experienced Billy's on-screen death as "a kind of moral consolation for the courage we don't have." For all his flaws, Billy is courageous, righteous, determined—maybe too much so, which is why he must be killed. Billy represents a threat, a challenge, to civilized society's norms and rules. Like Shane in *Shane*, like Jett Rink in *Giant*, like Jack Burns in *Lonely Are the Brave*, Billy in *The Left Handed Gun* is a sacrificial scapegoat, an individual crushed by society.[54] He is punished for standing out from the crowd.

Screen Stories

In the early 1970s, Malick quickly went from being just another AFI fellow, arguing about movies with his classmates, to being an esteemed alumnus and guest at Greystone. It all started with his student film, which was a Western. Not so long ago, one could walk up to the American Film Institute's Louis B. Mayer Library and watch the short Malick made at AFI, *Lanton*

Mills, without much hassle. Back then, the library had a DVD copy of the film, which they allowed students and scholars to watch on a monitor that must have dated back to the dawn of home video technology. It was not the best way to watch a film, but it was a way. Today, alas, *Lanton Mills* is kept under lock and key. The Mayer Library now has better viewing technologies, a larger collection of books and film titles, and an expanded staff of librarians and archivists, but at some point *Lanton Mills* was withdrawn from the AFI collection. It is a shame, because, as anyone who has seen it will attest, the film sheds a great deal of light on Malick's subsequent work, *Badlands* and *Days of Heaven* most especially. Also, it is really funny.

Harry Dean Stanton stars as the title character. He is joined by a Sancho Panza-style sidekick, Tilman, played by Malick himself.[55] *Lanton Mills* begins as a recognizable Western. Everything is genre appropriate: the landscape, the buildings, the clothes, even the old-timey banter, which anticipates the silly wordplay of *Pocket Money*. The other characters in *Lanton Mills* are stock types, too, but tweaked just so. They include a mute (Tony Bill), who wears a sign around his neck announcing as much, and a gunslinger (Warren Oates) introduced as the "slowest gun in the West." He soon dies—as expected—in a shootout.

The opening scenes of *Lanton Mills* are episodic, maybe even a little disjointed. The have the feel of silent-film-era comedy—like Harold Lloyd's *The Kid Brother* (1927)—but retold by a stoner. A memorable jump cut in the middle of the film takes Lanton and Tilman from what seem to be nineteenth-century backwoods to the car-clogged streets of contemporary Beverly Hills. The sequence recalls the visual juxtapositions of *Lonely Are the Brave* and anticipates the comic reveal that would come at the end of Mel Brooks's spoof Western, *Blazing Saddles* (1974), in which the film's heroes trade their horses for a Cadillac and ride off into the sunset.

The anachronism is the plot point around which *Lanton Mills* pivots. On horseback, in period clothing, Lanton and Tilman are quite the sight: crowds of people stop and stare as they ride down modern-day Wilshire Boulevard.[56] When the two cowboys try to hold up a bank, customers and tellers alike react with a mixture of curiosity and befuddlement. Is this some kind of prank? An act? Is it *a movie*? Whatever it is, the cops eventually arrive, sirens blaring. In no time, they take Tilman into custody and shoot Lanton, wounding him fatally. "Don't shoot me no more," he says in Malick's script. "I'm killed."[57] Lanton expires slowly, giving the officers time to close in. They ask him why he tried to rob the bank, to which he replies—in the kind of understated, deadpan fashion that would become a trademark of Harry Dean Stanton's long and fascinating career—"Always wanted to be a criminal, I guess. Just not this big a one."[58]

The full title of Malick's AFI student film is *Lanton Mills: The Cincinnatus Hiner of Texas*.[59] It is an allusion to the nineteenth-century California poet who was as famous for the cult of personality he had fashioned for himself as for any of the poems he ever composed. Cincinnatus Hiner Miller, who went by the pen name Joaquin Miller, was a pop star *avant la lettre*. In the words of California historian Kevin Starr, he was "a lifelong poseur and figment of his own imagination: a onetime miner turned poet and compulsive fabulist (no one has ever fully been able to disentangle truth from fiction in the stories he told about himself) who decamped for London, where his *Pacific Poems* (1870) and *Songs of the Sierras* (1871) were privately published with some success, especially among the pre-Raphaelites, and where Miller attended literary soirées dressed in miner's attire and otherwise played the frontier troubadour."[60] When he finally returned to San Francisco, Miller published perhaps his most famous book, *Life Amongst the Modocs* (1873), an entirely romanticized memoir—"a typical blend of fact and fiction," says Starr—detailing his days living among the native peoples of Northern California.[61]

If Malick thought of Lanton Mills as the "Cincinnatus Hiner of Texas," then we must view him as a poseur twice over: somebody pretending to be somebody else who was most famous for pretending to be somebody he was not. Viewed from this angle, *Lanton Mills* becomes a modernist study in playacting, a movie about moviemaking. Lanton's shoddy performance as a bank robber, his half-assed attempt at being a bandit, echoes Billy's fate in *The Left Handed Gun* and foreshadows Kit's efforts to play the role of the rebel in *Badlands*.

Lanton Mills might also be interpreted as a subtle, perhaps even subconscious, expression of Malick's own anxieties about becoming a filmmaker: his worry that, in trying to play the part of the Hollywood director, he, too, was just a poseur. Impostor syndrome is common enough in professions—such as academic philosophy—requiring a certain level of performativity, but it is omnipresent in Hollywood. This might explain why *Lanton Mills* does not commit to its narrative premise any more than its title character commits to being a proper criminal (at one point, Lanton and Tilman even attempt to give back the money they have just taken from the tellers). The film never takes itself seriously. It is almost as if Malick were saying: *I wanted to be a director, I guess. Just not this big a one.*

A big-name director is precisely what Malick became, of course. After the release of *Badlands* in 1973, he was invited back to the Center for Advanced Film Studies on three different occasions—in April and December of 1974, and then again in January of 1976—to talk with students. Whether he liked it or not, he was now something of an authority and he had to play the part. In discussions that were frank and collegial, he downplayed his newfound expertise, offering practical advice to the aspiring filmmakers without pretense. Malick was keen to discuss technical issues related to filmmaking—such as fundraising, budgeting, and the handling of cast and crew—yet reluctant to dissect and interpret films the way he had when he was a fellow himself.

It is not so easy to discuss the production and distribution of a film without addressing its content, though. In the seminar on January 21, 1976, Malick expressed dismay over how Warner Brothers publicized his feature-length debut. "I was so upset about the way that they were advertising the picture," he said, "that I just tuned it all out." "The artwork was lurid, and the slogan was something like, 'In 1950 a crime of passion became a passion for crime.' It just misrepresented the picture," Malick complained. "It's important how a picture is represented."[62] The comment is a revealing one, and it suggests that, from the very start of his career, Malick exhibited a certain wariness toward the ways of the big studios, with their advertising campaigns and their unwavering focus on bottom lines. But it also raises the question of just what kind of film Malick thought *Badlands* was. If the story of Kit and Holly was not a story of crime and passion, what was it?

For better or worse, *Badlands* was received as an outlaw film. Critics viewed it as a contribution to the "lovers-on-the-lam" genre that included films such *You Only Live Once* (dir. Fritz Lang, 1937), *They Live by Night*, *Gun Crazy*, and *Bonnie and Clyde*. In interviews, Malick claimed only to have seen the last one.[63] But over and against his protests, the critics had their say. Kit and Holly's criminality dominated early discussions of the film. Critics wondered why *Badlands*' troubled protagonists, who commit murders with neither remorse nor comprehension, were not made to pay for their crimes. Kit is eventually caught and taken into custody, but his captors fawn over him. As Pauline Kael pointed out, in her perennially dyspeptic style: "The troopers who arrest him ask him why he committed the murders, and he says that he always wanted to be a criminal; they smile approvingly. No one shows any anger toward him; the townspeople are quietly eager for the souvenirs of himself he distributes. All this slanting is designed to prove that Kit and Holly are psychologically aberrant and yet that they're just like everybody else—that their moral vacuum is spreading over the flat, dead landscape."[64] *Badlands* was, she fumed, "so cold and formal that I felt as if I were watching a polished Ph.D. thesis that couldn't help making the professors exclaim 'Brilliant!'" She followed this with an even blunter attack: "I didn't admire it, I didn't enjoy it, and I don't like it."[65] It was line of criticism that was particularly distressing to Kael's editor at the *New Yorker*, William Shawn, whose son Wallace had studied with Malick at Harvard. Malick was part of the family—and in more ways than one, being both a personal acquaintance of Shawn's and a *New Yorker* alum. "I guess you didn't know that Terry is like a son to me," he told Kael after reading a draft of her piece. "Tough shit, Bill" was her considered reply.[66] The column ran as it was, unchanged.

In Kael's estimation, *Badlands* was too slick and too knowing. Unlike Spielberg's *Sugarland Express*—a film she *did* like—it reminded her only of movies she despised: "counterculture" and "art" movies directed by the likes of Monte Hellman and Michelangelo Antonioni.[67] Kael's animus toward anything associated with the art-house tradition often got the best of her critical judgment, but in this case, at least, she did have a point. *Badlands* certainly *was* closer to *Two-Lane Blacktop* and *Zabriskie Point* than to Spielberg. And the meaning and import of *Badlands* did hinge, as Kael rightly noticed, on its conclusion.

Unlike Kael, the professors loved *Badlands*. No less than Gilles Deleuze and Félix Guattari, the radical French authors of *Anti-Oedipus: Capitalism ad Schizophrenia* (1972), went on to herald it as a revolutionary depiction of what they called "schizo love."[68] They viewed Kit and Holly as mad lovers who showed just how mad society had become. Kit and Holly could also be viewed as products of what another French intellectual, Guy Debord, memorably called "the society of the spectacle," their shared preoccupation with image and appearance suggesting that role-playing was all that really mattered in modern, consumer society.[69]

Like *Lanton Mills*, *Badlands* is metacinematic. It is a movie about the mystique and the allure of motion pictures. It is about mass culture and celebrity worship. In the words of historian Andreas Killen, "No contemporary film comments more explicitly on the pathologies of the star system and the deformities it wrought on the American psyche than *Badlands*."[70] Kit and Holly are not star-crossed lovers: they are kids playing at being star-crossed lovers. Viewed from this angle, Malick's debut film is not about crime or criminality, but rather it is about the *spectacle* of crime and criminality. Just like Billy in *The Left Handed Gun*, Kit, in *Badlands*, is fascinated by his own criminal image. Holly tells us that "he wondered if he'd be able to read what the papers would say about him."

Kit commits to the role of the rebel. His look is dime-store James Dean, from his cowboy boots and jeans all the way up to his popped collar and pompadour. He wants nothing more than to be noticed. In fact, Kit repeatedly tells Holly about his desire to achieve notoriety—in life or, if need be, in death—and he curates everything around him with this singular aim in mind. What Killen rightly calls Kit's "myth-making impulses" govern everything.[71] Even at the unlikeliest of moments, he remembers to mind his image. In the middle of the film's climactic car chase, for example, he pauses to check his hair in the rearview mirror. He then proceeds to choose the spot where the chase will end, going so far as to shoot out his own car's tires to make it look like he had no other choice but to stand and fight. He checks his appearance one last time in the mirror, gathers a few stones, then piles them up making a hastily constructed monument marking the spot where he will be captured, or maybe even killed. Kit is the outlaw, the criminal, the lonely cowboy, but he is also the stagehand, setting himself up for mass-media consumption.

Kit's life is a performance in desperate search of an audience. He is one part Albert Camus and too many parts Colin Wilson (whose 1956 bestseller *The Outsider*, released only a year or so before the Starkweather murders, popularized the existentialism of works such as *The Rebel* for English-speaking audiences.)[72] He is also every role James Dean played in his brief acting career. When the deputy sheriff who has taken Kit into custody near the end of the film remarks that he looks just like Dean, the captured murderer cracks a sly but revealing smile: it is all he ever wanted to hear. Emboldened by the comment, Kit puts on a show for his captors. The lawmen—as Kael noticed—lap it up. "Why'd you do it?" one of them asks. "I don't know," Kit replies, good-naturedly, almost innocently. "I always wanted to be a criminal, I guess. Just not this big a one." His demeanor is nonchalant, as if it were all no more than a game, one he got carried away playing through no fault of his own. It is an important exchange, one Malick first tried it out in *Lanton Mills*. But whereas Lanton seems a little bewildered by what has happened to him, Kit seems eager to keep up the performance: the show must go on, because the show is all he knows.

The concluding scenes of *Badlands* portray Kit handcuffed and shackled, playing to a crowd of officers and National Guardsmen. He gives away his comb and his lighter, certain they were now valuable prizes. He seems pleased with himself, proud of the fact that people have finally taken notice of him.

His crimes proved his existence. "You're quite an individual, Kit," remarks a state trooper (played by Malick's friend, the Harvard historian of Latin America John Womack Jr.) guarding him on his flight back to South Dakota.[73] Kit knows he is on his way to his eventual execution, but he does not miss a beat: "Think they'll take that into consideration?" he asks with a smirk.

This knowing, gee-whiz naïveté is a hallmark of *Badlands*, as is Kit's pervasive obsession with how he is seen by others. In an early interview with Beverly Walker published in *Sight and Sound*, Malick tried to explain it: "Kit doesn't see himself as anything sad or pitiable," he said, "but as a subject of incredible interest, to himself and to future generations."[74] For Malick, Kit was a case study in self-regard gone wrong. The theme can be found in every stage of *Badlands*' development, from the earliest beginnings of the project up to its premiere. The first draft of Malick's screenplay, from November 1971, highlights it: Kit introduces himself to Holly as somebody with "some stuff to say." "Guess I'm lucky that way," he muses. "Most people don't have anything on their minds."[75] These lines survived Malick's many revisions of the script, as well as the improvisation that went into filming it, so as to be delivered, verbatim, by Martin Sheen.

On the page and on screen, Kit wants nothing more than to be seen as a unique individual, as somebody who stands out from the crowd. As Andreas Killen puts it: "Kit seeks constantly to leave his imprint on the world."[76] But as Stanley Cavell noticed early on, Kit has great difficulty saying much of anything beyond clichés and empty catchphrases: "It takes all kinds" is one of his hokey, endlessly recycled refrains.[77] Even the most casual viewer of *Badlands* notices pretty quickly that Kit's high opinion of himself is at odds with how others perceive him. This provides Malick with endless opportunities for comedy, but Kit's frustrated desire for fame also hints at a rather profound philosophical problem residing just beneath the surface of *Badlands*—namely, the problem of performance itself. How can we ever be sure there is something there, beneath all the layers of playacting, that defines us as uniquely ourselves? How can we ever be certain that what we have to say is not a cliché? How can we ever be sure that we are not poseurs?

Stanley Cavell was among the first to suggest that *Badlands* should be interpreted along these lines. He focused on the themes of self-knowledge and performance. As he saw it, his former student's first film explored the relationship between interiority and exteriority, the inner self and the outer world. "To whom, from where," he asked, "does one address a letter to the world?" "To what end," he went on, "does one wish to leave one's mark upon the world?"[78] *Badlands* certainly raises such questions, but it also refuses to answer them, which is why Cavell associated it with other movies illustrative of what he called "the end of romance." It was a mini-genre of Cavell's own invention, one premised on the thwarting of audience desires—the "impossible yet unappeasable human wishes" no longer satisfied by movie magic.[79] For Cavell, the "end of romance" film proved that cinema had entered what Catherine Wheatley has called "a modernist phase," in which traditional "cycles, plots and types" begin "dying out."[80]

In this regard, if not others, *Badlands* is a modernist film. Its plot offers no romantic resolution—not for Kit, not for Holly, but also not for the audience, either. No wonder *Badlands* continues to strike some viewers as cool and detached, for its main point seems to be that our messages to the world—and to each other—are always and everywhere going astray, because they are tangled up with our messy, impostor-like performances of subjectivities we no longer believe in. A certain cynicism creeps in, one echoing what Malick's pal Jacob Brackman had identified just a few years earlier in countercultural cinema and culture.[81] Everybody, everywhere, is playing a role, and what is more, we *know* this. In this context, is something like "mutual trust," Brackman asked, even possible anymore?[82]

Role-playing puts a heavy interpretive burden on our social interactions, something which the philosopher Robert B. Pippin has labeled—with reference to the convoluted plot of Alfred Hitchcock's *Vertigo*, yet another film Cavell linked to "the end of romance"—a "common struggle for *mutual interpretability.*"[83] Because we so often remain opaque not just to others but also, and more fundamentally, to ourselves, we have trouble both knowing *and* being known. Too often we are taken in by the performance of self; we fail to discern the performer only half-hidden behind it—especially if we are that performer.

Hollywood is not usually associated with existential authenticity. It is the land of make-believe, all artifice and fantasy. And yet, when it went in search of an inaugural cohort of fellows in 1969, the American Film Institute advertised itself as a program built around self-examination. Promising much more than technical training, it emphasized earnest humanistic inquiry and serious artistic practice. George Stevens Jr. saw the Center for Advanced Film Studies as a place where people who had something unique, personal, and, most of all, authentic to say could find their footing and go about exploring the important things in life. An early program brochure asked prospective fellows—whom it tacitly assumed to be male, judging by the exclusive use of masculine pronouns—to introduce themselves by way of their personalities rather than their résumés. "We want to get an idea of what kind of person you are, what kind of head you have," it reads. "What do you think about often?" And then, finally, the most important question: "What, if any, is your message to the world?"[84]

Badlands is a movie full of messages—messages sent, but never really received. In a number of scenes, Kit and Holly compose missives to the world that repeatedly go unread, rejected, returned. The only one that escapes this fate is Holly's narration, which reaches us somewhat miraculously, via voice-over. We never see her recording her thoughts, which means that we enter into her consciousness without ever realizing how or why or from whence she is speaking. At one point she tells us that she spells out words on the roof her mouth with her tongue, like a child speaking her own private language, but this does not explain why we, the audience, have been granted access to such secret codes.

Kit takes a far more public approach to message-writing. He constructs testaments to his worldly presence everywhere he goes. *Badlands* is chock full of his letters and signposts, his existential trail markers. He improvises monuments and buries time capsules.[85] At one point he releases a balloon tied to a basket of scrawled notes. On another occasion, he takes rocks from the spot where he and Holly have consummated, somewhat comically, their love ("Is that all there is to it?" she asks). Later, in an attempt to throw off the police, Kit even records a phony suicide message in a phonograph booth, running out of things to say before his time is up. Maybe Kit does not have so much "stuff to say" after all.

Still, Kit pontificates whenever he gets the chance. He pretends to be an authority on all things, but his opinions are no more than regurgitations of received wisdom, what Heidegger, in *Being and Time*, called "idle talk."[86] In another memorable scene, which takes place at the rich man's house (where he and Holly have holed up after committing a home invasion), he offers the world his hollow musings about how best to live. Surrounded by the trappings of adult life, he plays at being older and wiser than he is. "Consider the minority opinion," he says, speaking into a dictation machine as if it were a news reporter's microphone, "but try to get along with the majority opinion once it's accepted." In other words, conform. It is the least rebellious thing a rebel could say.

In a revealing twist on this theme of message-leaving, Malick himself appears on screen not long after the sequence, playing an architect who arrives at the house for a previously scheduled meeting. Kit tries to brush him off, but Malick's character persists. If he cannot come inside, can he "leave a message," he asks. Kit indulges him, only to drop the piece of paper on which the architect has scribbled something into an elaborate Chinese vase once the door is closed. It is yet another message—the auteur's message, perhaps?—sent but not received. Was Malick worrying about how his film would be received? Would he be able to get his message across?

Malick learned a thing or two about auteurist cinema from Arthur Penn. His 1967 film *Bonnie and Clyde*—the movie that "changed American movie culture"—was the only lovers-on-the-lam picture Malick claimed to have seen before embarking on *Badlands*.[87] On the surface, Malick's first feature certainly seems to have a much in common with Penn's most famous film: young protagonists fleeing the reach of the law; tabloid-worthy criminal exploits; sex and violence and mass culture celebrity. But a closer examination reveals some noteworthy differences. Instead of *Bonnie and Clyde*'s more theatrical, catchphrase dialogue, for example, *Badlands* relies upon Holly's sparse and often poetic voice-over narrations to stitch its story together. And instead of aping its predecessor's extravagant shootouts and saturated colors, Malick's film utilizes natural lighting and slow, wide-angle shots of the natural world, which serve as counterpoints to the film's gruesome plot.[88] Furthermore, *Bonnie and Clyde* had protagonists who, as one film scholar has noted, "displayed a sense of purpose or direction."[89] Almost everything in *Badlands* is directionless: Kit and Holly seem motivated by nothing more than boredom.

Instead of the Robin Hoodesque bank robberies of Bonnie Parker and Clyde Barrow, *Badlands* gives us the far more senseless Starkweather murders.[90] Malick discussed the idea of making a movie about them with Penn on several occasions, and there is no doubt his feedback was vital. The same probably applies to the input of Penn's assistant Jill Jakes, who later became Malick's wife and first producer: *Badlands* was a "Jill Jakes Production."[91]

Breaking the Rules

Though it is often celebrated as a memorable example of independent filmmaking—of young, eager, underpaid, nonunion artists battling the odds to make a film more or less on the fly—*Badlands* was also, in its own unique way, a very Hollywood product, too. A changing Hollywood, maybe,

but Hollywood nonetheless. *Badlands* was an independent film, but it was
not, for example, *Billy Jack* (1971). Tom Laughlin's low-budget, countercultural-
exploitation movie, which centered around the social justice crusading of its
title character—"a half-breed Native American and ex-Green Beret," played
by Laughlin himself, "returning to live in solitude on an Arizona reservation"—
was the talk of Hollywood for a while, mainly because it proved to be something of a box-office sensation, showing that independent films could turn a
profit. Malick referenced it repeatedly in the three AFI seminars he participated in after making *Badlands*.

But for all its economic success (two sequels would follow on its heels)
Billy Jack's preachy aesthetic was not one Malick chose to imitate. Arthur
Penn's influence was far more important. He showed Malick a path that led
away from exploitation flicks. Penn's unique career demonstrated how established Hollywood genres could be tweaked and transformed into something
new, how a director could make films that were simultaneously popular and
artistic. Independent, but not too independent. Hollywood, but not too Hollywood. It was the approach perfected by the French New Wave. Penn showed
Malick how working *within* cinematic conventions could be just as captivating as trying to escape them. One did not need to invent a new kind of cinema out of whole cloth, one just had to recut what had come before and
personalize it. Malick borrowed from *Bonnie and Clyde* the way Penn borrowed from Jean-Luc Godard's *Breathless* (1960).

Following Penn's example, Malick made just the kind of film the founders
of the American Film Institute hoped its students would make: something
old and something new at the same time, something familiar and strange simultaneously. It was a mash-up of European art-house beauty and Hollywood storytelling—a cross between René Clément's *Purple Noon* (1960), say,
and Ida Lupino's *The Hitch-Hiker* (1953)—held together by the larger vision
of the director as auteur, as a person "with a message."

Penn visited the American Film Institute on October 7, 1970. He was there
to screen and discuss *Bonnie and Clyde*, but he was also there to make a case
for precisely this kind of auteurist filmmaking. He encouraged the fellows to
put their "personal stamp" on the pictures they were creating. No matter how
much resistance they faced from studio bosses, financiers, or unionized crew
members, they should fight to protect their personal visions. Penn admitted
that New Wave directors, such as his friend François Truffaut, had it easier.
They worked in a very different context, one that afforded them far more control. Still, theirs was an example worth following if a filmmaker had the guts

Figure 2. Holly (Sissy Spacek) reading about James Dean in *Badlands*.

to give it a try: "trying to break the rules in Hollywood," Penn said, "is an important goal."[92]

Badlands wears its uneasiness about Hollywood filmmaking—and about the culture industry more generally—firmly on its sleeve. It is a personal film about characters who do not know how to be persons of their own, made by a director who is not sure if directing is for him. Everybody deflects. Kit blames his victims for making him shoot them. Holly parses the pages of a celebrity gossip magazine—with a James Dean–related headline on its cover, no less— so as to avoid all the death and destruction. And Malick pretended like his movie was not really about Starkweather and Fugate, even though he did his research on them, going so far as to gain access to the correctional facility in Lincoln, Nebraska, where Starkweather was held and eventually executed.[93]

In one sense, this is true. *Badlands* is not just, or not only, about Starkweather. It is about our fascination with the true-crime story, our perverse identification with rebels who play out our collective fantasies relating to the pursuit of personhood. This narrative focus derived from an unlikely and, so far as I can tell, hitherto unrecognized source: music journalist Michael Lydon's memoir essay "Charley Starkweather: Wheel on Fire," which appeared in the inaugural issue of *US: A Paperback Magazine* in the summer of 1969.[94] *US* was short-lived—only three issues of the countercultural publication made it into print before the magazine went belly-up—but it boasted some noteworthy bylines. Among the other contributors to its inaugural is-

sue were the iconic cartoonist Robert Crumb and a singer, poet, and former
UCLA film student by the name of Jim Morrison.

How Lydon's essay found its way into Malick's hands is a mystery, but the
fact that it did—and that it inspired *Badlands*—is not. I found a copy of it,
torn from the pages of *US*, in the administrative files of the American Film
Institute. Paper-clipped to the piece was a memo from George Stevens Jr.,
which reads: "Malick's idea for Charlie Starkweather film."[95] Annotations to
the article offer a revealing glimpse of the film project that would eventually
evolve into *Badlands*. They suggest that much of the movie's memorable imagery was taking shape long before location scouting, costuming, and set design had gotten underway. They also suggest that Lydon's interest in the
mythology of Starkweather—as opposed to the details of the actual case—was
what really captured Malick's attention.

From "Charley Starkweather: Wheel on Fire" Malick appropriated a number of telling images and motifs that became the building blocks of *Badlands*. Reminiscing about his own childhood memories, Lydon sketched a
1950s world that Malick, another child of the postwar era, brought to life on
screen. Lydon described an age that was real and stylized at the same
time: "'Tom Dooley' by the Kingston Trio," "hops in the gym," and "the
chopped, blocked, and dropped Mercs with dice hanging from the rear view
mirrors and tassels along the back windows peeling out of the school parking lot."[96] These details bring out the contours of the historical world Malick
sought to recreate, but they also evoke a *Rebel Without a Cause* romanticization of it, too.

More important than the cultural mood of the late 1950s was the image
of Starkweather as a star-obsessed impersonator: "Nature gave him a dumb
farmboy's face," Lydon had written, "but with practice and the natural ability of worshippers to resemble their idols, he came on like a cross between
James Dean and Elvis Presley."[97] An annotation next to this line marks the
origin of Kit Carruthers as a character and *Badlands* as a film. The idol worship explains why Kit and Holly adopt the aliases of James (as in Dean) and
Priscilla (as in Presley). It even explains Kit's James Dean–inspired "drug-
store swagger."[98]

Following Lydon's lead in making Kit a wannabe James Dean meant Malick was swimming in the current of what Noël Carroll famously termed—
in an influential 1982 article in *October*—"allusionism." Allusionism was the
defining feature, Carroll argued, of early 1970s U.S. cinema. It stemmed from

Figure 3. James Dean as Jett Rink in George Stevens's *Giant*.

Figure 4. Kit (Martin Sheen) as a wannabe James Dean in *Badlands*.

the "legacy of American auteurism" that had dominated the discussion of movies when Malick and his fellow allusionists—Carroll lumped together Peter Bogdanovich, Michael Cimino, Monte Hellman, John Milius, Paul Schrader, and Martin Scorsese—started honing their craft. "Armed with lists from Andrew Sarris and incompatible aesthetic theories from Eisenstein, Bazin, Godard, and McLuhan, a significant part of the generation raised in the fifties went movie mad and attacked film history," he claimed.[99]

Carroll thought allusionism defined the New Hollywood sensibility. A generation of young filmmakers raised on "quasi-academic film lore," he wrote, could play "the game of allusion" with each other, demonstrating both their fealty to movie fandom and their auteurist bona fides at the same time.[100] Though he was not particularly impressed by the approach, Carroll grudgingly recognized its merits. Allusionsism was a way for upstarts to gain access to the Hollywood system. Peter Bogdanovich's *Targets* (1968)—a film that was also on Malick's viewing wish list when he entered AFI—was a case in point. Carroll dubbed it "the most enterprising early exercise in allusionism."[101] But *Targets* is not merely an allusionist film, it is a film about the *making* of an allusionist film. "When all the good movies have been made," remarks Sammy Michaels (played by Bogdanovich himself), the young director of a picture within the picture, why not just remake them with a slight twist?

This is precisely what Bogdanovich did in *Targets*, a horror film about horror films, made in an age of horror—a truly "modern monster movie," to use the emphatic words of Quentin Tarantino.[102] But in addition to being a textbook example of cinematic allusionism, *Targets* was also prescient cultural commentary. Partially inspired by the 1963 assassination of John F. Kennedy and the 1966 shootings committed by Charles Whitman on the campus of the University of Texas at Austin, the theatrical release of *Targets* was delayed by two more murders, those of Martin Luther King Jr. and Robert Kennedy. The film's fictional story of a lone white male, Bobby Thompson (Tim O'Kelly), going on a killing spree was just too close to reality.

Malick knew about disorienting real-world violence. He had reported on it. The only piece of journalism he ended up publishing in the *New Yorker* was an unsigned "Notes and Comment" piece, April 13, 1968, coauthored with his friend Jacob Brackman and the writer Renata Adler, about the aftermath of the assassination of Martin Luther King Jr.[103] King's murder left the general public and journalists alike reeling. "Word of the assassination reached us while we were working late at our office," Malick, Brackman, and Adler wrote, "and we immediately switched on a television-network special report. Perhaps because we received each piece of news minutes after it happened, we came to feel that we were at the eye of a historical hurricane."[104] The young writers dwelled on the *mediated* nature of the event—"We sat, it seemed dumbly, in the gray haze of our television screen"—and on the miscues of news anchors and political leaders, signs of "the poverty of their response" to what had just taken place.[105]

American culture was awash in both mediated and unmediated violence. Malick did not escape any of it by going to film school. Indeed, he arrived in Los Angeles not long after the Manson murders, which perhaps explains why

senseless violence would be the subject of some of his earliest work as a screenwriter, most notably the *Dirty Harry* scripts he penned alongside John
Milius, scripts that in retrospect read like an amalgamation of his *New Yorker*
article on the assassination of King, Bogdanovich's *Targets*, and—for allusionist good measure—Hitchcock's *Rear Window* (1954).[106]

Two drafts of *Dirty Harry*, both from November 1970 (the first carrying
the title "Dead Right"), investigate how *visual* a phenomenon violence had
become. They explore the spectacle of violence and, more specifically, the
complicity of the spectator in its perpetuation. The scripts imply that mass
consumption of mediated violence makes everyone, to some degree, a potential criminal—a suspect. The indignant, silent majority–ism that would become a hallmark of the cruder, more politically and racially suspect
serial-killer film Don Siegel eventually made out of a later draft of *Dirty Harry*
(one to which Malick's name was not attached) is noticeably absent in the
original scripts. To be sure, the scripts Malick worked on are not innocent.
They are by no means free of the racial, class, and gender anxieties of the late
sixties, but they are not so fixated on them as the *Dirty Harry* franchise eventually became. Rather than depict all too easily demonized outsiders—poor,
inner-city minorities, by and large—as criminals, Malick and Milius suggested that the real criminal, the real killer, was everywhere, inside each and
every moviegoer. Maybe even in every filmmaker, too: Harry and Travis bear
a striking resemblance to their creators—or to one of them, at least. Harry is
a "professor," and Travis speaks in "the mildest southwestern accent," one that
sounds (or reads) suspiciously like Malick's own.[107]

When making *Badlands*, Malick chose to depict violence in a far more
distanced, abstract fashion than *Dirty Harry*. The killings Kit commits are
instances of allusionistic violence rather than real-world violence. Perhaps it
was because Malick thought of *Badlands* as a film not about violence per se
but about *Hollywood violence*. Kit's fascination with the image of the James
Dean rebel is important to note here, for it complicates any attempt to interpret his behavior in the film.

Kit may lack direction, but he has motives galore. And those motives have
everything to do with the movies. It is not so much that Kit *is* James Dean,
but that he *wants to be* James Dean. It is this longing—this mimetic desire—
to be *seen as* Jim Stark/Jett Rink/James Dean that propels Kit forward and
leads him to commit acts of violence.[108] It is all part of the act, as it was for
Starkweather. But in sticking so closely to his imagined script, Kit steers himself away from true autonomy. He plays the ready-made role of the screen

idol so as to avoid taking responsibility for his actions. In *Badlands*, Kit is the doomed hero, the misunderstood outsider, the charismatic rebel—he is anybody and everybody but himself.

For all his bluff and bluster, Kit is really just another example of what the sociologist David Riesman famously called—in *The Lonely Crowd*, the 1950 sociological study he coauthored with Nathan Glazer and Reuel Denny—the "other-directed" individual, somebody whose self-worth was entirely contingent upon the attention and validation of others.[109] The "other-directed" individual is a conformist. Viewed from this angle, Kit represents less the irredeemable sociopath and more the respectable rebel, the wild child who is secretly a rule follower. He is the cold-blooded killer who bemoans people littering on public streets. In that 1975 *Sight and Sound* interview with Beverly Walker, Malick explained the paradox perfectly: "He thinks of himself as a successor to James Dean—a rebel without a cause—when in reality he's more like an Eisenhower conservative."[110]

Persona

In the very same interview, Malick also said he wanted *Badlands* to have the feel of a "fairy tale, outside time, like *Treasure Island*." He claimed to have been influenced not so much by other films as by children's books: "*The Hardy Boys*, *Swiss Family Robinson*, *Tom Sawyer*, *Huck Finn*," stories "involving an innocent in a drama over his or her head."[111] The theme was underscored by his decision to make Carl Orff's whimsical and childlike, xylophone-based *Gassenhauer* arrangement a centerpiece of his film's soundtrack.[112] Its twinkling sounds transform Kit and Holly into curious kids, setting out on an adventure. The film's true-crime bloodbath becomes an idiosyncratic coming-of-age story, one chock full of what musicologist Daniel Bishop has called "ambiguous melancholy."[113]

Malick borrowed this idea from Lydon's "Wheel on Fire" essay, which showed how Starkweather's self-mythologizing was appropriated by a generation of kids that had grown up in its shadow. Starkweather embodied the conflicting, contradictory yearnings of adolescence: the urge to be autonomous, but also the refusal to relinquish childhood fantasies. Lydon's essay portrayed Starkweather not as a killer but as a dreamer. He was a lonely kid who viewed the world around him as "an enchanted forest," complete with "beautiful colors in the western sky" and "birds singing in the melodies that came softly from the trees."[114] These lines are marked with an "NB" for *nota bene*. And for good reason, since they seem to describe Starkweather in what we might call, anachronistically, Malickian terms: as a lover of trees who would sit in their branches all afternoon gazing up at the sky until an "irresistible feeling would sweep over my soul," bringing "intimate knowledge of myself."[115] Malick gave Kit very similar lines: "I'm the type that loves to climb trees," he declares in an early script. "Sometimes I feel like they're listening to me."[116]

As Lydon saw it, Starkweather, in refusing to grow up, personified the rejection of adult society. "I knew that he as my hero was fighting, on a scale grander than one to which I could aspire," he wrote, "to preserve our right to childish fantasy."[117] Malick was struck by the passage, for it is underlined on the page. But however inviting it may have been to imagine Starkweather as some kind of existential Peter Pan, the gruesomeness of his crimes remained. As Lydon put it: "I can't get back to where I was at 15. I can dig the painful cry of 'I am!,' but the slaughter stops and baffles me."[118] Beneath the serial killer exterior was an existential *cri de coeur*—but it was not enough, in the end, to justify all the violence.

Badlands is similarly conflicted about Kit. Malick could not decide if he should be a tragic antihero or an insufferable blowhard. A revealing scene in his first screenplay draft, which did not end up making it into the final film, suggests as much. The scene would have constituted but a fleeting moment in the film, but it tells us a great deal about Kit's character, merely by cataloging the few possessions he owns in the world, including a few fossils and "an underlined library copy of Fitzgerald's *This Side of Paradise*."[119] F. Scott Fitzgerald's first novel is a tale of adolescent self-formation, romantic longing, and literary aspiration. It tells the story of a protagonist, Amory Blaine, who is not all that different from Kit, if only Kit had been born earlier, wealthier, handsomer, and much better read. In *Badlands*, Kit is no Princeton prince, but he shares Amory's burning desire to be somebody, to leave his mark, and most of all, to have sex.

Like adolescence itself, *This Side of Paradise* is painfully awkward, seemingly profound at times but more often than not rather cringeworthy. It is full of pretense. Discussions of Tolstoy, Nietzsche, and William James segue into scenes of attempted heavy petting with some high society "popular daughter" or other.[120] For Amory, intellectual and sexual frustration go hand in hand. His thoughts on both subjects often sound rather silly. Amory is immature, nothing but a naïf playing at being a grown-up. Some early reviewers even went so far as to suggest that he was Fitzgerald's avatar, which meant the scorn they piled upon the character was a less-than-subtle dig at the author who had created him.[121]

The fact that Fitzgerald titled his first book of short stories *Flappers and Philosophers* and at one point considered calling his first novel *The Romantic Egotist* suggests the critics were on to something.[122] *This Side of Paradise* is a novel of shameless ambition and Amory is, indeed, very much like his creator, especially in the way he yearns to be somebody big, somebody important. His quest to become a unique individual animates *This Side of Paradise* from the first page to the last. The second half of the book is titled, with a nod to Henry Adams, "The education of a personage." But Amory never really becomes a person of his own. One of the lessons of the book is that his preoccupation with his persona hinders his ability to encounter, truly and meaningfully, anything or anyone else around him. He remains a romantic egotist to the very end. *This Side of Paradise*'s oft-quoted final sentence is Amory's famous lament: "'I know myself,' he cried, 'but that is all.'"[123]

Much of Amory's navel-gazing egotism can be detected in Kit's interactions with Holly. In Malick's screenplay, he repeatedly suggests to her that he might be a genius, hence his remark, when they first meet, about having "some stuff to say." But everything he ends up saying is borrowed from somebody else. Having no words he can call his own, he speaks in nothing but stock phrases and borrowed lines. A noteworthy passage in the first draft of Malick's screenplay sends up his relentless impersonating. It describes a meta-cinematic sequence set, somewhat comically, in a junkyard. Kit enlists Holly in a reenactment of "the scene from *Giant* in which James Dean turns down Rock Hudson's offer on his land, the Little Reata." "Kit speaks Dean's lines from memory," the screenplay says, "while Holly recites those of Hudson and his advisors from a notebook." Tellingly, she "is much less enthusiastic about it all than Kit."[124]

Just about every idea Kit has about becoming an individual derives from this one scene in *Giant*. Jett Rink/James Dean is everything he hopes to be. Malick emphasizes this point repeatedly. Kit's playacting is obvious in *Badlands*—he is, as one commentator has put it, a "peon to 'personality'"—but it is even more pronounced in Malick's scripts, which make continuous reference to Kit's Dean-like mannerisms, from the way he throws his head back or waves his hand to the deliberately "Deanish" way he slips a cigarette between his teeth.[125] In an era obsessed with the concept of personality, Kit is determined to exude as much of it as he possibly can, even if that means impersonating somebody else.

At first, Holly is taken in by the performance: one of the first things she says about Kit in *Badlands* was that he was "handsomer than anybody I'd ever met" and "looked just like James Dean." But over the course of the film, she begins to see through the act. The junkyard scene in Malick's screenplay is the first suggestion of this, hinting at how bored of the playacting she eventually becomes. (It may very well be an allusion to Godard's *Breathless*, in which Patricia Franchini [Jean Seberg] grows tired of the Humphrey Bogarting of Michel Poiccard [Jean-Paul Belmondo] and turns him in to the cops.) Holly begins to see through Kit's pretense. For all his talk of being somebody, of achieving fame and notoriety as a rebel and a genius, Holly realizes that Kit is going nowhere. It will not be the last time in Malick's cinema that a female protagonist punctures the hubris of her playacting male counterpart.[126]

Holly comes to see Kit as little more than a "personality," a term that Fitzgerald, tapping into a general fascination with the notion of personality in his own day, juxtaposed with the seemingly more profound concept of "personage."[127] In *This Side of Paradise*, Amory's beloved mentor, Monsignor Darcy, explains the difference: "personality is a physical matter almost entirely," he says, but personage is "a bar on which a thousand things have been hung." In other words, one is a purely external phenomenon, nothing but fleeting fashion, whereas the other denotes depth, as in the idea of—to use a clichéd phrase—"depth of character."

This Side of Paradise suggested that a "personage" was made not by pretending, but by actual experience. This is why a "personage" could be fully self-sufficient, somebody who "need never bother about anybody."[128] A personage could stand apart from the world of mere opinion, whereas a personality could not. A personality was the product of the crowd, of modern culture and mass entertainment. A personality was phony, inauthentic. Already in 1910, a serious young theology student preparing for the priesthood named Martin Heidegger decried the way "everyone talks much about 'personality'" but avoids the "truth."[129] It was a common refrain, and its commonness helps explain why Heidegger made "authenticity" such a central component of his philosophical work leading up to *Being and Time*.

Is Kit on the path from personality to personage, from inauthenticity to authenticity? Or is *This Side of Paradise* just another prop in his performance? Malick's script suggests the latter. The book gives him the excuse to pontificate. In an off-screen voice-over, Malick has him laying it on so thick as to be laughable: "I suffer a little bit, like it says where I underlined in this library book."[130] He does not stop there: desperate to appear deep, Kit waxes philosophical.

"The world is billions of years old," he says, "so who cares what happens? The guy who wrote that book is famous today," he muses, "but nobody's going to remember him in two hundred years, much less in a billion. And they're sure not going to remember me. So we're in the same boat."[131]

Had this scene made it into the film, it would have provided yet another opportunity to highlight Kit's obsession with James Dean, since the lines recall the famous sequence in Nicholas Ray's *Rebel Without a Cause*, in which, on a school trip to the planetarium at the Griffith Park Observatory, Jim Stark and his classmates learn that human existence is rather insignificant when viewed from the larger perspective of the cosmos: "Through the infinite reaches of space, the problems of man seem to be trivial and naive indeed," explains an elderly astronomer. "And man, existing alone, seems himself an episode of little consequence." It is an unsettling thought and the rowdy teenagers in the audience do not react well to it.[132] "What does he know about man alone?" asks the aggrieved Plato (Sal Mineo), whose tragic fate takes center stage in the remainder of the picture.

The second draft of Malick's screenplay for *Badlands* contains a number of minor but revealing alterations, each signaling significant shifts in Malick's evolving vision for the picture. Take, for instance, the fleeting reference to *This Side of Paradise*, on which I have placed a great deal of emphasis above. In the second draft of *Badlands*, it is not *This Side of Paradise* that Kit has in his possession, but rather *Tender Is the Night*, a later, far more tragic work of Fitzgerald's.[133] Was it just an editorial slipup? Would any old Fitzgerald title give the audience all they needed to know about Kit's penchant for pretense?

I doubt Malick would have been so casual with his references. The switch could have been a nod to Michelangelo Antonioni's *L'Avventura* (1960), an enigmatic art-house classic ostensibly about the disappearance of a wealthy young woman, Anna (Lea Massari), during a sailing trip on the Mediterranean. The books she was reading beforehand include the Bible and, you guessed it, *Tender Is the Night*. But it is also worth pointing out that *Tender Is the Night* is a more mature work than *This Side of Paradise*, especially insofar as it grants its female characters greater depth and complexity. Rosemary Hoyt and Nicole Diver, the book's principal protagonists, are more than just college coeds or Jazz Age flappers; they are fully realized characters in their own rights—and they are far more captivating than Dick Diver, the book's principal male character. Women take center stage in *Tender Is the Night*. It was something Antonioni noticed and put into *L'Avventura*. It was probably something Malick noticed, too, and put into *Badlands*. The second draft of his screenplay contains the seeds of what would eventually become Holly's unforgettable voice-over narrations in the final film, which make her, not Kit, the film's true protagonist.

One scene in the second draft is particularly noteworthy. In it, Holly plays with a Ouija board and is suddenly struck by a profound sense of wonder: "Where would I be this very moment if Kit had never met me? If Kit had never killed anybody? What would I be doing if I'd met a different boy? Been born in a different city? Or if my Mom had never met my Dad? If she'd never died?"[134] As anyone who has seen *Badlands* will recall, these lines mark a turning point. Once Holly contemplates the fundamental contingency of her existence—what we might call, using Heideggerian terminology, her "thrownness,"—she begins to take a noticeably cooler stance toward Kit and his schemes.[135] Her moment of existential anxiety changes everything.

Holly's thoughts are not accompanied by shots of a Ouija board in the finished film. Instead, they are paired with images produced by her father's stereopticon, one of the few items she rescued from the family home before Kit set it ablaze. Malick's decision to switch out the Ouija board for the stereopticon is significant, not just because it avoids associating Holly with the occult, but also because it hints at the unique ability of the cinema—a projection technology directly descended from mechanisms such as the stereopticon—to put us into a particularly reflective, if not to say philosophical, frame of mind.[136]

Figure 5. Holly's stereopticon moment, a turning point in *Badlands*.

Malick's suggestion that the stereopticon is a catalyst for Holly's existential reverie can be interpreted as an allegory for the moviegoing experience. Far from simply encouraging mere imitation—as with Kit's impersonations of James Dean—cinema also can promote contemplation. Holly's inner thoughts in the stereopticon scene might at first seem rather banal—"And what will my future husband look like? And what's he doing right this moment?"—but her questions go on to broach big topics, such as the limits of personal perspective, the nature of time, and, most importantly, the meaning of existence—*her* existence.[137] Marveling at historical images, scientific images, images of natural wonders, Holly brushes up against the limits of her world.

This is precisely what movies allow us to do, provided we stop and pay attention to them. In this regard, *Badlands* is a philosophical film that teaches us how to watch it: Holly shows us how watching and listening can lead to wonder. Her stereopticon experience echoes a scene in Walker Percy's existentialist novel *The Moviegoer* (1961). In it, Binx Bolling experiences a comparable moment of existential reverie while watching Howard Hawks's famous Western *Red River* (1948): "As Montgomery Clift was whipping John Wayne in a fist fight, an absurd scene," he says, "I made a mark on my seat arm with my thumbnail. Where, I wondered, will this particular piece of wood be twenty years from now, 543 years from now?" It was during this moviegoing experience, Bolling explains, that he "first discovered place and time, tasted it," he says, "like okra."[138]

Through her immersion in screened images, Holly begins, like Binx before her, to contemplate the mysteries of place and time, self and world. Her stereopticon moment awakens her to the vastness of the cosmos and the contingency of her world. It thrusts her into a state of anxiety—the fundamental mood, according to a long line of philosophers stretching from Kierkegaard and Heidegger all the way up to Stanley Cavell, of existentialism.[139] "For days afterward," Holly tells us in voice-over, "I lived in dread." Her stereopticon moment is a miniature version of the astronomy lecture in *Rebel Without a Cause*.

When faced with the brute fact of our finitude, we often feel small, insignificant. The natural inclination is to retreat into childish thinking, as Holly does: "Sometimes I wished I could fall asleep and be taken off to some magical land," she says, "but this never happened." Holly was no longer a child, but she was not yet an adult. And, as Michael Lydon's essay in *US* had made clear, neither was Kit, nor any of the other children who grew up in the shadow of Charles Starkweather.

Holly's laconic, deadpan narrations have rightly become a hallmark of *Badlands*, but many of her most memorable lines do not appear in the first two drafts of Malick's screenplay. Their addition, at whatever points they came during the production process—to an audience at AFI Malick admitted that "the script changed right up until shooting"—was surely a stroke of genius, for the voice-overs demonstrate Holly's willingness to think, as opposed to Kit's eagerness to perform.[140] If anyone comes close to being a grown-up in *Badlands*, it is, ironically enough, Holly, the youngest person in the film. The adults throughout are intent on playing the roles society expects of them, whether that be the part of sign painter (her father), trash collector (her boyfriend), or bounty hunter (her pursuers). As much as he pretends to rebel, Kit is one of them: he rarely takes notice of anything beyond his own nose. Holly, on the other hand, looks into things. She wonders.

Holly's voice-overs suggest that she is open to what Stanley Cavell called, in *The World Viewed*, the "world's exhibition."[141] In contrast to Kit, she is willing to experience angst and discomfort. A humorous scene in Malick's first draft screenplay anticipates this difference between the two of them. In it, Kit and Holly are squabbling. Holly is upset, but about what, she admits, is "kind of hard to say." "Well, I'm not going to waste any more time talking to lady philosophers," Kit cracks.[142] His feeble attempt at sarcasm contains a startling truth: Kit may fancy himself a brooding, existential hero, but his intellectualism is only surface deep. It is Holly who endures anxiety and dares to see the world for what it is on its own, often disorienting terms. "To satisfy the wish for the world's exhibition," Stanley Cavell had written in *The World Viewed*, "we must be willing for anxiety, to which alone the world as world, into which we are thrown, can manifest itself."[143] Kit may wield a gun, but only Holly is brave enough to stare into the stereopticon and endure a state of dread.

After the Deluge

Badlands made Malick famous. When he returned to AFI to talk about it, students were interested in hearing about how he ended up in filmmaking. With what seems like honest self-deprecation, Malick talked about possibly sneaking into the brand-new program "under the wire." He was, he said, "at the end of my rope as an academic," and going to film school "sounded like something to try, it sounded like a suicidal little adventure." What he found most appealing about the AFI program was its emphasis on technical training: "These were technicians, people who made their lives at this, who knew how to handle these machines, and who knew how to pass that knowledge on to you." The Center for Advanced Film Studies "was the sort of place where you could really get your chops together," he said. "You could learn how to edit, you could learn how to shoot, you could learn how to do anything you wanted to."[144] What Malick really wanted to do was make a Western, something that would have been "too expensive," he said, at least for a first film.[145] But now, after *Badlands*, that dream was one step closer to becoming a reality.

Badlands may not have been the first film Malick intended to make, but it allowed him to check off a number of other boxes on his cinematic wish list. He "was really interested," for example, "in making a picture about an adolescent girl."[146] This admission might explain the delight his camera took in capturing the giddy extremes of Holly's changing wardrobe, from her bobby socks and gym shorts in the opening scenes of the film to the brilliantly colored, puffy-sleeved dresses she wears at critical moments later on, including, most notably, the stereopticon scene. As Malick told a reporter from *Women's Wear Daily* in 1974, "I wanted to do a film on what it meant to be fourteen in the Midwest in 1958"—"to show," he said, "a kind of openness, a vulnerability that disappears later, when you get a little savvier."[147]

By all accounts, Malick and Sissy Spacek had a great time developing the character of Holly. "From the very beginning," Spacek recalls in her memoir, *My Extraordinary Ordinary Life*, "Terry included me in his creative process. He asked me all kinds of questions about my life, as if he was mining for gold. When he found out I'd been a majorette, he worked my twirling routine into the script. Before I knew it, we were driving down Hollywood Boulevard to a music store to buy a Starline baton like the one I'd had in high school. Terry would give me little pieces of paper with a few lines of dialogue on them, and when I read the lines out loud to him, he'd fall over laughing."[148] Spacek and Malick shared small-town Texas roots, which might be why they "fell all over each other." Malick recalled casting her "in about fifteen minutes."[149]

The filming of *Badlands* was a little less fun. As Spacek remembers it, many peanut butter and jelly sandwiches were had, especially as finances tightened, crew members quit, and lead actors ended up doing double duty as caterers. At one point, Paul Williams, one of the film's producers, had to swoop in and reassure a restless crew that they were working on a future "classic," not a "low-budget piece of shit."[150] Spacek stuck it out—maybe because her mind was on other things. It was while working on *Badlands* that she met her future husband, the art director Jack Fisk, whose charming attention to every detail of Holly's world—from the furniture in her bedroom to the intricate details of the tree house she shares with Kit down by the river—proved to be a subtle yet highly effective form of courtship.

Malick's own accounts of the process of getting *Badlands* made, detailed in the seminars he participated in at AFI after its release, paint a decidedly less romantic picture of the filmmaking process. They catalog the struggles of raising money ("you can't get a sophisticated movie investor to touch you with a ten-foot pole"); of being "a first time director" ("I was afraid to fire anybody"); of filming in southeast Colorado ("it was always hot, and the dust was up in the afternoon, and you couldn't breathe"); of dealing with on-set mishaps ("we were showing a piano and a sofa bursting into flame—the hero sets fire to the house—and the whole room just exploded, and everybody was thrown out of doors, and all the equipment just went up in flames"); of failing to get the right footage in the can ("I didn't understand the importance of over-the-shoulder shots"); of drowning in all of the details of editing and post-production ("Oh, I was involved in it all the way, far too involved"); of navigating one's way through the Hollywood system ("It's easy to get an agent; it's hard to get a *good* agent").[151] No wonder he felt that just completing the film was an important achievement, since making it was such a grueling ordeal: "my main satisfaction lies in just having finished it. I don't care what anybody thinks of it. I mean, I do care, but my main pleasure comes in just having done it."[152]

Throughout the arduous process of making *Badlands*—from writing the script to the humiliating process of asking for money from Beverly Hills dentists; from filming in Colorado to editing in Hollywood—Malick pretended he had it all under control.[153] In other words, he played the part of the Hollywood director, even when he "didn't know what he was doing."[154] Hence the feeling of being, as he put it, a "total impostor."[155] But attempting to comport himself according to the widespread "myth of the director," Malick came to realize, was pointless, and possibly even counterproductive. Being a perfectionist got in the way of things. "You know, if the picture really has a heart or if it's got the breath of life in it," he told an audience at AFI, "people aren't going to notice the mistakes and aren't going to notice the shoddiness."[156] In the end, it was not the persona of the big-time Hollywood director that mattered, only the final product itself, the film.

Reflecting on these comments, one notices a striking parallel between Malick's experiences as a young Hollywood talent on the make and Kit's desperate playacting throughout *Badlands*. Both director and character are keenly aware of the expectations of others: they know how they wish to be seen. But whereas Kit never abandons the performance, pantomiming to the very end, Malick, having tried the "myth of the director" on for size, was all too eager to slip out of the role (in a manner rather reminiscent, perhaps, of his exit from professional philosophy).[157] To AFI fellows who were hoping to follow in his footsteps, he was quick to demystify the whole process of moviemaking: "there's no mystical knowledge" required, he said.[158] It just so happens that once you make a film, other people begin to regard you as a filmmaker.

Such remarks shed light on the ease with which Malick could disappear from the director's chair for some twenty years, between the release of *Days of Heaven* (1978) and *The Thin Red Line* (1998). They also suggest that playing the role of the Hollywood director was by no means a necessary component of Malick's identity. He was suspicious of the cult of the director and had no desire to become some "colossal ego," like Otto Preminger.[159] If we look to the recent, autobiographical films Malick has made about his experiences during these decades—films such as *To the Wonder* and *Knight of Cups*—we might even say that his efforts to become a big-name Hollywood director did some damage to him as a person. These late films revolve around, as Robert Sinnerbrink has suggested, "the task of becoming a self."[160] They document Malick's attraction to, and eventual disillusionment with, the personas and personalities of Hollywood. They show him growing—like Holly—a little savvier with experience. They also document the persistence of his philosophical temperament. As his longtime art director Jack Fisk has said, "Terry's a philosopher," his films revolve around "philosophical questions."[161]

Many of those "philosophical questions" appear on the audio tracks of his films, in the voice-over narrations that have become one of the many hallmarks of his cinematic style. In the AFI seminars, Malick said working on Holly's voice-overs "was probably where I had the most fun on the picture."[162] Maybe it was because the process required interacting with the fewest number of people—there was no need to play the role of the self-confident director. Malick did not even have to leave home. Spacek recalls him stapling quilts to the walls of a room in his house so they could record the voice-overs without having to pay for a recording booth.

Spacek considers Holly's voice-overs to be "some of the most beautiful language ever written for film." They also contain some of the "funniest, most deadpan lines," too.[163] Lines such as these, which accompany images of Kit dumping the body of his friend Cato, whom he has shot and killed, into an abandoned train car: "He never seemed like a violent person before"; and "It all goes to show how you can know a person and not really know them at the same time." Not everybody got the humor, though. What had left Malick and Spacek in stitches seemed to have no effect on early audiences. When *Badlands* premiered at the New York Film Festival in 1973, the two of them were astonished by how utterly silent the crowd was: "nobody even chuckled."[164]

Some early viewers may have been slow to see the humor in Malick's send-up of 1950s mass culture, but a few were quick to notice the uniqueness of his talents as a filmmaker. Vincent Canby deemed *Badlands* "a most important and exciting film."[165] Among the many aspects of the film that diverged from the standard themes and techniques of Hollywood filmmaking at the time was Malick's decision to make Holly's commentary—which Canby adored—such a central component of the film. At the time, voice-overs were often dismissed as stylistically naive narrative crutches, used mainly to shore up films with wobbly plots or incoherent visuals. But as Malick argued in one of his AFI seminars, the pictures that made use of voice-overs were some of "the best pictures ever. I mean, CITIZEN KANE, THE MAGNIFICENT AMBERSONS, JULES AND JIM. JULES AND JIM is 90 percent voiceover," he said. "And THE WILD CHILD."[166]

He was right. Far from being a narrative quick fix for poor visual storytelling, voice-overs have the ability to enrich the cinematic experience, if only because they complicate the time frame of the story unfolding before us on screen, adding a layer of meaning that demands additional interpretive work on the part of audiences. As the philosopher of film Alexander Sesonske pointed out some time ago, voice-overs create a "complex temporal structure" in cinema, one that makes a film's narrative seem both more distant and more immediately present at the same time.[167] While they have the power to orient our perception of the images on screen, voice-overs also have the power to challenge and destabilize it, putting everything up for interpretive grabs. As the French theorist Michel Chion has put it, *Badlands* brings "new poetic power to the voiceover, breaking conventions of narration to destructure the spectator's point of view."[168]

The novelty of *Badlands* did not rest on its voice-overs alone. Its larger sound design also helped to set it apart from other films of the era. The sounds of nature, in particular, came to enjoy a privileged place in Malick's debut. For a movie about two teenage criminals on the run from the law, *Badlands* makes ample use of some surprisingly soothing sounds: birdsong, rushing river waters, rustling trees. Experimentation with sound design was a big part of the emerging radical sensibility of New Hollywood filmmaking. Before the emergence of Dolby Stereo in 1979, argues Jay Beck, "sound aestheticians explored new methods of constructing film sound tracks in an attempt to rethink regimes of seeing and hearing in narrative cinema."[169] Malick was especially adept at this. Already in *Badlands*, but certainly by the time he began work on *Days of Heaven*, he had developed an interest "in the ambient sounds of his films and their ability to allow the diegetic space to spill into the theater."[170] Malick realized early on how the sounds of nature could be used to fill out the philosophical potential of the stereopticon, putting audiences in a particularly reflective state of mind, one open to the "world's exhibition."

Malick's attention to the sights and sounds of the natural world is now considered to be another hallmark of his cinematic style. The seeds of that style were sown in *Badlands* and reaped in *Days of Heaven*, making the stylistic progression from his first film to his second easy enough to track. What commentators have had a more difficult time explaining is the seemingly abrupt shift in subject matter. Moving from what appears to be a genre film about teenage killers to a period piece that draws its title—if not also its basic plot points—from the Bible, Malick's early career trajectory left some early critics, as we shall see in the next chapter, scratching their heads.

But before we get there, it is worth pointing out that Malick's original vision for *Badlands* was anything but secular. A number of allusions to the Bible, and to churchgoing, are scattered throughout his early screenplay drafts, each of them hinting at some of the religious themes he has taken up in his most recent films.[171] None too subtly, the first draft of the screenplay for *Badlands* opens with the aftermath of a great flood—a flood of biblical proportions, even. The scene describes a devastated landscape, with symbols of American consumer culture strewn about receding floodwaters. Driving along in their garbage truck, Kit and Cato take in various other sights of the recent calamity: abandoned power plants, National Guardsmen on patrol, men leading horse-drawn carts full of worldly possessions down the side of the washed-out road.

The bleakness of the original opening might be explained by the fact that Malick had been working on an adaptation of Walter M. Miller Jr.'s tremendously popular novel *A Canticle for Leibowitz*, a work of theologically inflected apocalyptic science fiction first published in 1959, not long after Charles Starkweather was executed by the state of Nebraska.[172] Malick developed the treatment of *Canticle* for Hollywood producer Sidney Beckerman. The adaptation never made it to the screen. Miller's masterwork still attracts legions of fans, but only as a book, not a movie. (On more than one occasion, Walker Percy sang the book's praises.)[173] With a timeline spanning millennia and a diverse cast of characters, including generations of monks, wandering desert hermits, space-age scientists, and ruthless *Dungeons & Dragons*–style warlords, *Canticle* is difficult to pin down. It makes comedy out of theology, literature out of sci-fi pulp, and morality out of nuclear apocalypse and civilizational collapse. It is a lot to condense into a workable screenplay. To this day, *Canticle* is often described as unfilmable.

Adapting *A Canticle for Leibowitz* was one of the many commissions Malick took on while trying to get *Badlands* off the ground. He needed the money, surely, but the project was probably more than just a paycheck, especially since Miller's most famous work broaches the big questions the young Malick seemed interested in tackling: questions of life and death, guilt and responsibility, science and faith. The message of *Canticle* is clear: modern progress may bring us to the point of mass extinction—a nuclear apocalypse Miller's characters call the "Flame Deluge"—but faith, and a little humor, will help us survive the cataclysm.[174]

Faith takes center stage in the films that have come to define Malick's mature cinematic vision, from *The Tree of Life* and *Voyage of Time* up through *A Hidden Life* and the forthcoming *The Way of the Wind*.[175] *Badlands* bears little resemblance to these pictures, but it was the project that put him on the path toward making them.

*　*　*

"On a Tuesday in the last week of August, 1973, twenty-nine-year-old Terrence Malick, producer-writer-director of the currently acclaimed *Badlands*, flew from L.A. to New York with two cans of still-wet film cradled on his lap." So opens a profile article from the June 1974 issue of the gossipy—and gay-leaning—entertainment industry magazine *After Dark*.[176] The piece tells the story of Malick's arrival on the Hollywood scene, which began, paradoxically enough, with that trip back east, so that he could screen his first film for the organizing committee of the New York Film Festival. Having financed *Badlands* independently, rounding up some $350,000 from friends, family, and a handful of small-time investors, Malick was gambling big: inclusion in the festival's lineup could land him a distribution deal, which might help him pay off his debts and maybe even make a small profit. "On the morning I screened *Badlands* for the Festival judges," he told his interviewer, "the sweat ran down my back. I wasn't allowed into the theater; I had to stay in the projection room with the projectionist. We had a screaming battle throughout. Everything went wrong—the sound, the focus, the reel broke. I thought the committee couldn't possibly evaluate what I was offering them. Then, when the movie was over, Richard Roud, the curator of the Festival, came back and told me they agreed to show the film, not *during* the Festival but as the official closing-night show. That in itself was a powerful honor for me."[177] The New York Film Festival was still a relatively new institution when Malick arrived in Manhattan, film canisters in hand. But already it was perhaps the best place for a young director to make a splash, as Roman Polanski had, with *Knife in the Water* (1962), only a decade before.[178] By all accounts, *Badlands* did just as well: so positive was the early industry buzz that it had to be shown twice to satisfy "advance ticket demand."[179]

Badlands made Malick's reputation, but it remains a record of his youthful anxieties. It is suffused with a young person's chief preoccupations: not just a fanciful longing for adventure, but also, and perhaps more importantly, worries about identity, purpose, and the opinions of others. In his *After Dark* interview Malick said he "never *planned* on being a director." Yet *Badlands* had most definitely made him one. He was aware of the pressure that came with this new role. His next film, he knew, would be judged according to a different set of standards. "I'm no longer an underdog in this business," he said. "I miss that feeling. I love the feeling of fighting from below. *Badlands* has established my name, good or bad. From this point on I'm being watched. That could trip me up."[180]

After working more or less nonstop since arriving in Hollywood in the late summer of 1969, Malick suddenly had the time—and the resources—to consider his next move. Too much time, maybe. It took him quite a while to come up with what he considered to be "a decent screenplay" for his next project.[181] That film, *Days of Heaven*, was not released until 1978.

CHAPTER 2

Wonders of the Prairie

The Metaphysics of *Days of Heaven*

Even in such hours of toil, and through the sultry skies,
the sacred light of beauty broke; worn and grimed as we
were, we still could fall a-dream before the marvel of
golden earth and a crimson sky.

—Hamlin Garland

Among other things, the Book of Deuteronomy is about farming. Much of it revolves around divine dictates, of course, but there is the promise of land at its heart: land ready to produce crops in abundance, land rich in soil and life-nourishing water, land "flowing with milk and honey." The Lord watches over this land and those who follow the Lord's commandments are promised a leisurely existence upon it—"days of heaven upon the earth." No doubt some farmers, gazing over their estates in the rosy warmth of an early-morning sunrise, or after a day's work is done, have felt this way about their property, if they are fortunate enough to call such land their own. Their domains, no matter how meager or mean, must surely seem like heaven from time to time.

But how much effort is required to keep the water, milk, and honey flowing? Farming is difficult, labor-intensive work. It relies upon the generosity of the seasons, which can be fickle. My maternal grandfather, an immigrant from the Azores, saved enough money to buy some land of his own in the San Joaquin Valley, where, between droughts and floods, he grew walnuts and cotton. He knew full well that life on the land could be, as the Book of Deuteronomy puts it, both a "blessing and a curse."

In *Boy Life on the Prairie*, his lightly fictionalized account of growing up on an Iowa farm after the Civil War, the American writer Hamlin Garland recounted all the pleasures and pains of rural life before the turn of the twentieth century. Garland began composing his work in 1887, but it was not until two years later that *Boy Life* was first published in its entirety. By then, the adventurous life on the American plains that his book describes had all but disappeared. "The life I intended to depict was passing," Garland wrote in the preface. "The machinery of that day is already gone. The methods of haying, harvesting, threshing, are quite changed, and the boys of my generation are already middle-aged men with poor memories."[1] If there was one constant about rural life, Garland's book suggested, it was change.

Boy Life on the Prairie was a romanticized record of a bygone America—a "vanished world," as Garland later put it.[2] More than just the machinery of the day had disappeared from contemporary view. Along with the antiquated tools and equipment had gone the unique sights, sounds, and smells of a way of life. Garland evoked these sensory traces as best he could, in both prose and in poetry, interspersing pages of verse throughout the chapters of his book. He was writing against the current. His Whitmanesque paeans to the wonders of the prairie—"Who shall describe the glory of growing wheat?" "Who shall sing the song of it, its gold and its grace?"—were bookended by an awareness that "a changed world" awaited this prodigal son's return to the Middle West.[3] "The passing of the wheat-field, the growth of stock-farms, the increase in machinery, have removed," Garland lamented, "many of the old-time customs."[4] Old prairie life was no more: only ghosts and spirits populated what had become a world of yesterday. Was it any surprise, then, that Garland, after living for so long on the East Coast—in literary Boston, mostly—ended up not back on the farm but in Hollywood, where he spent his twilight years dabbling in paranormal psychology, seeking out the spectral residues of a long-lost past?[5]

The idyllic days described in Garland's nostalgic portrait of nineteenth-century rural life were always in danger of slipping away. They may have seemed to disappear slowly, but change did not always come gradually on the farm. Sometimes it was instantaneous, as sudden and violent as a thunderclap. Livelihoods could be lost in an instant: an unexpected weather pattern could ruin a harvest, and a single strike from a venomous massasauga rattlesnake was enough to bring down a prized steer, or even a farmer. There were locusts to worry about, too—both literal and metaphorical.

Biblical fears resonated in a landscape rife with potential calamities. *Boy Life on the Prairie* recounted stories involving actual locusts—"the locusts leap in clouds before our heedless feet"—and the havoc they wreak.[6] But it also cataloged threats posed by figurative locusts: all-too-human threats that signified a fall from grace, a rejection of divine munificence. Composed as it was of these various ingredients—blessings and curses; salvation and damnation—Garland's ode to the wonders of the prairie occasionally bubbled over into a morality tale. And at the heart of this morality tale, like so many other American stories stretching from *The Autobiography of Benjamin Franklin* to *The Grapes of Wrath*, was work.

Even in the nineteenth century, prairie farms were vast enterprises requiring more labor than a single family, no matter how extended, could supply. Especially as family farms were consolidated into ever vaster holdings toward the turn of the twentieth century, the need for labor increased exponentially. Then, as now, farmers turned to migrant workers, whose arrivals and departures were as regular as the changing seasons.[7] Garland described the "hired men" who descended upon the farm during harvest time as "troops of nomads from the south who swept over the country, like a visitation of locusts, in harvest, reckless young fellows, handsome, profane, licentious, given to drink, powerful but inconstant workmen, quarrelsome and difficult to manage at all times."[8] This "nomadic army," whose movements were as "mysterious as the flight of locusts," captivated young boys like Garland because, among other things, its troops "told of the city, and sinister and poisonous jungles all cities seemed, in their stories."[9]

Garland's dichotomy was a simple one: on one side, a land of "milk and honey"; on the other, locusts and poisonous jungles, those places Upton Sinclair would describe in disturbing detail just a few years later.[10] The contrast between the rural and the urban, the traditional and the modern, was a stark one, with ready-made moral presumptions baked into it. Proving as much was the fact that migrant labor camps were often called "jungles," as if the workers who inhabited them had brought all of the danger of the city along with them when they set out on the rails to work the harvest.[11] Like locusts, they were perceived, most of all, as a threat.

It says something that, out of all the prose and poetry on display in *Boy Life on the Prairie*, Terrence Malick would choose a passage devoted to a "nomadic army" of such traveling laborers to serve as the lengthy epigraph for the script of his second feature film, *Days of Heaven* (1978).[12] It suggests that Malick was interested not merely in the antique world of the prairie, which

Garland had eulogized, but also in the interaction of that world and the "sinister," far from poetic world of the modern city, the rapid and unrelenting rise of which Garland had witnessed in his own lifetime and Malick had been born into generations later.

Days of Heaven's sepia-toned prologue underscores the transition. In a manner now synonymous with the documentary filmmaking of Ken Burns, the camera pans slowly over period-appropriate photography by the likes of social reformer Lewis Hine depicting workers, immigrants, and children. These images demonstrate Malick's interest in the laboring "nomads"—the "hoboes," "tramps," or "bums," as they were called at the time—who received wary welcomes on the farm.[13] The clash of their world with that of their employers was what captured his imagination.

Days of Heaven is not just some pastoral art piece, as many of its early critics charged. ("The film actually borders on being too beautiful," one reviewer complained.)[14] Although it is famous for its Garlandesque, magic-hour shots of shining wheat fields at sunset, *Days of Heaven* is nevertheless a very human tale, too. Malick thought of it as a fine-grained drama, a story "full of desires, dreams, and appetites."[15] It is as beautiful as a landscape painting by Edward Hopper or Andrew Wyeth, but like *Christina's World* (Wyeth, 1948), *Days of Heaven*'s human characters give its landscapes a necessary sense of perspective.[16] As Dave Kehr, the regular film critic for the *Chicago Reader* put it in an appreciative review: "*Days of Heaven* is a story of human lives touched by the cosmos, and then passed over—momentary intersections between the eternal and the immediate."[17]

Days of Heaven has been celebrated as well as cursed for its almost obsessive devotion to what Garland described as the "golden earth" and "crimson sky" of the prairie. Critics marveled at its breathtaking visuals—*Rolling Stone* called it "majestic and sumptuous"—but were nonetheless suspicious of its theological rumination.[18] The fact that the film's plot borrowed freely from biblical tales of deception and adultery, such as the story of Abraham and Sarah in Genesis, did not help matters in this regard.[19] But what really drove reviewers crazy was its tone. Writing for *New York* magazine, David Denby described *Days of Heaven* as "a zombie masterpiece" devoid of real feeling.[20] Cinematic style, he exclaimed a little hysterically, had won out over narrative substance: "What an aesthete's pipe dream of a movie it is!"[21] Stanley Kauffmann said something similar in the *New Republic*. He lamented how "mopily terse," how "emptily portentous" the film was. In his opinion, *Days of Heaven* was "just a tony graduate-student gesture against old movies," an assessment with which Andrew Sarris, writing in the *Village Voice*, largely agreed.[22] Malick's second feature was a "feast for the eyes," he conceded, but he "found its drama deficient and its psychology obscure."[23]

Overlooked in such criticisms were Malick's larger aims. Stretched as it is between the quotidian and the transcendent, the anthropological and the cosmological, *Days of Heaven* is much more than an empty exercise in aesthetic style. It is a searching investigation into life, undertaken in the spirit of what Penelope Gilliatt called—in a *New Yorker* review that made up for Pauline Kael's takedown of *Badlands*—"regenerative honesty."[24] *Days of Heaven* poses more questions than it could possibly answer, but this should not prevent us from exploring just how and why those questions, many of which Malick first puzzled over as a philosophy student, make their way into the picture. They orient us not only toward the prairie's "golden earth" and "crimson sky," but also toward the "sacred light of beauty" that illuminates them.

*   *   *

Badlands used the genre of the lovers-on-the-run picture to explore the theme of subjectivity. *Days of Heaven* similarly tweaks a generic plot—that of the tragic love triangle—to its own ends. The story is simple enough: in the early years of the twentieth century, Bill (Richard Gere) and Abby (Brooke Adams), along with a young child, Linda (Linda Manz), escape the immigrant "jungle" that is Chicago and join the hordes of migrant workers laboring their way across the Western Plains (the Texas Panhandle, to be exact). Bill and Abby are lovers, but they pass themselves off as brother and sister, a ruse that becomes more complicated when, learning of the fatal illness that has doomed their current employer—a solitary farmer (Sam Shepard) with a beautiful home amid a vast holding of wheat fields—to a premature death, Bill suggests Abby win his affections for the sole purpose of inheriting his wealth. The farmer's single friend, a grizzled foreman (Robert J. Wilke), is on to their plans, but he cannot stop them. The ruse would ensure a life of leisure for the masquerading migrants, so they disregard his threats. Abby wins over the farmer. As with all marriages erected upon a foundation of lies, though, the union collapses when Bill, who had taken temporary leave from the farm, returns.

What happens next is downright operatic: a confrontation, a hellish inferno that engulfs the wheat fields, a fight, then flight, then death. But reducing *Days of Heaven* to such plot points would be like describing *Hamlet* as a coming-of-age story. Malick's second feature has much more going for it than doomed romances and unhappy endings. Gilberto Perez once described it as "a parable of the American experience."[25] That may be too grand, but the film certainly invites such lofty interpretations. It could be viewed as an account of industrial change; or as a cautionary tale about the perennial struggle between labor (migrant workers) and capital (wealthy landowners); or even, in a totally different register, as a meditation on the mysterious workings of fate and destiny. Thematically, the film anticipates Michael Cimino's unfairly maligned *Heaven's Gate* (1980), which in its retelling of the Johnson County War of 1892, pitted poor European immigrants against wealthy western cattle barons—all amid a magnificent scenery of rushing rivers and snow-capped peaks. But stylistically, *Days of Heaven* has lot more in common with Bernardo Bertolucci's epic *1900* (1976), another tale depicting the inevitable struggle between workers and landowners, this time set in early twentieth-century Italy.[26] Bertolucci's didactic Marxism does not seem to have exerted much influence on Malick's *Days of Heaven* script, but the imagery of his five-hour-long, multinational production is certainly echoed throughout the film that was made from it: symbolic scarecrows amid wheat fields, poignant portraits of the animal world juxtaposed with human dramas, portentous fire sequences.

At the very least, Malick borrowed the sound of *1900*. He got Bertolucci's composer, the famed Ennio Morricone, to create the score for *Days of Heaven* by showing him a cut of his own film that he and his editor, Billy Weber, had spliced together with a temporary soundtrack borrowed almost entirely from *1900*.[27] Upon seeing his own work recycled in such a fashion—and after beating Malick at a couple games of chess—Morricone agreed to write a new score for the film.[28] He drew upon his own work for *1900*, but he also created arrangements that echoed nineteenth-century French composer Camille Saint-Saën's "Aquarium," from the musical suite *The Carnival of the Animals*, which Malick had chosen for both the opening prelude and the closing credits of his picture.[29] The result of this unusual sonic mixture was one of Morricone's most memorable soundscapes, topped only by some of the Spaghetti Western soundtracks he had created in the previous decade for Sergio Leone.

Speaking of Westerns, *Days of Heaven* also could be viewed as a kind of anti-epic, an inversion of Howard Hawks's *Red River* (1948), say, or a minor-key interpretation of George Stevens's *Giant* (1956), which exerted a great deal of influence on *Badlands*. These loud, monumental films, which celebrate the conquering of land, cattle, and, eventually, oil, stand in stark contrast to the hushed tones and meditative stillness of *Days of Heaven*. Whereas Hawks and Stevens give us heroic, if conflicted, visions of progress—from lawlessness to law, for example, or from the rustic to the domestic—Malick gives us something quieter and more inquisitive. Stevens's epic may have inspired the set design of the farmer's grand Victorian mansion, a structure Jack Fisk built from scratch to serve as a visual centerpiece of the film, but there the comparisons end: about all that *Days of Heaven* has in common with *Giant* or *Red River* is an imaginary Texas that never really was.[30] If *Days of Heaven* is a Western, it is an idiosyncratic one.

What sets Malick's second feature apart is not its unique look or sound—its aesthete's style—but its preoccupation with perennial philosophical, perhaps even theological, questions. Following the evolution of *Days of Heaven* from script to screen, we can see how Malick explores topics such as truth, time, and transcendence. We can see how he transformed *Boy Life on the Prairie* into philosophy.

Malick appropriated much of the poetry and imagery in Garland's depiction of farm life on the plains, but he put all of it to other purposes. Take, for instance, the climactic sequence depicting the burning of the wheat fields. Malick's script calls for "a Biblical inferno of spectacular sweep" and his cinematographers—the famed Nestor Almendros, who earned an Oscar for his work on the film; and the equally important Haskell Wexler, who was all but cheated out of one, having been credited merely with an "additional photography by" credit even though he shot about as much of the film as Almendros did—gave him one.[31] The fire scenes were captured largely with roaming, handheld and Panaglide (an early competitor of the Steadicam) shots, and without any artificial lighting, either. The naturalistic approach heightened the fear and claustrophobia of the scenes.[32] The discordant notes of Morricone's accompanying score—along with the enveloping ambient sounds of the burning wheat fields, made possible by another new technology, Dolby Stereo—only heightened the anxiety of these moments when they were added later on.[33]

Boy Life on the Prairie contains a scene that may have inspired the sequence. Here is how Garland describes a fire's effect on his young protagonist, Lincoln: "The roaring flames threw a cataract of golden sparks high in the air—the wind suddenly returned, and great whisps rose like living things, with wings of flame, and sailed away into the obscure night, to fall and die in the black distance. The smoke, forming a great inky roof, shut out the light of the stars, and the gray night instantly thickened into an impenetrable wall, closing in around them, filling Lincoln's heart with a sudden awe of the world of darkness."[34] The passage describes a routine component of farm labor—the necessary burning of excess straw—but Garland uses it as an opportunity to convey both a sense of wonder and a feeling of anxiety. Malick takes the mood and runs with it. He turns the fire sequence into a cataclysm, brought about by the mutual suspicion burning—now finally erupting into an uncontrollable blaze—between romantic rivals Bill and the farmer. The scenes are an intimation of hell.[35] As locusts burn in the flames, a number of unanswered questions come crackling to life: Did Bill bring the plague with him when he returned to the farm in pursuit of Abby? Does the formerly gentle farmer cry out "Let it burn!" because he has been infected with rage or jealously? Will the inferno simply destroy, or might it also cleanse and purify? Are deception, greed, and jealousy the effects of our fallenness, or their cause?

Such questions are foreshadowed in the film's prologue, another fiery sequence, but set far away from the farm, in the steel mills of Chicago. With blast furnaces drowning out all other sounds on the audio track, the sequence recalls the wordless opening to Jean Renoir's *La Bête Humaine* (1938). In it, Bill accidentally kills his foreman, prompting his and Abby's flight away from the urban jungle. That Bill would find himself in a similar standoff with another boss later on suggests either repetition or predestination—maybe Bill's original sin was coming back to haunt him.

All this makes *Days of Heaven* sound like a biblical parable, which is surely what some critics went looking for when they first entered the screening room. They were bound to be disappointed, because Malick had other ambitions. There is much more to the film than a preoccupation with original sin. For a more nuanced account of *Days of Heaven*, one that explores not just its biblical allusions but also its philosophical foundations, we must turn to somebody with a much more intimate connection to Malick's work. Stanley Cavell's early suggestion that *Days of Heaven* offers nothing less than "a metaphysical vision of the world" remains probably the most accurate description of the film, and it goes a long way toward explaining just why it, like Malick's approach to filmmaking more generally, is so unique.[36]

In his first book devoted to the movies, *The World Viewed*, Cavell thanked only a handful of people for their comments and suggestions as he was preparing the manuscript. Malick was one of them. In 1971, he had yet to make anything other than a couple of shorts, including his thesis film at the American Film Institute, *Lanton Mills*. But by the time Cavell released an expanded edition of *The World Viewed* in 1979, both *Badlands* and *Days of*

Heaven had been released and lauded by critics—the latter even earning him a Best Director Award at Cannes. Cavell mentioned both of Malick's films in the enlarged edition of his book. His remarks about the "metaphysical vision" of *Days of Heaven* come from the lengthy foreword he penned for the new printing. In it, he suggested that no other film had quite captured "the scene of human existence" as Malick's had. So unique was *Days of Heaven*, Cavell thought, that it should be compared not to other films but rather to philosophical treatises. Some of its scenes struck him "as a realization of some sentences" from Heidegger, specifically his later series of lectures, translated into English in 1968, *What Is Called Thinking?*[37]

Coming from a Harvard professor, this was high praise. It set Malick's work apart from other films and gave it a special status—a status at least a few critics seemed willing to applaud in the waning days of what *Los Angeles Times* film critic Charles Champlin came to call "Hollywood's revolutionary decade."[38] "Terrence Malick makes his movies for intellectuals," declared Scot Haller in *Horizon* magazine in September 1978.[39] As Cavell saw it, *Days of Heaven* revealed truths about the world, and about human existence, that should be taken seriously. He wanted "to grant film the status of a subject that invites and rewards philosophical speculation," and in Malick, his former student, he had found a filmmaker who provided him with more than enough evidence to make his case.[40] *Days of Heaven* did not just dramatize philosophy, it *was* philosophy. It evoked the same sense of wonder animating the oldest of all metaphysical questions: Why is there something rather than nothing?

What Was Metaphysics?

Days of Heaven's theological glow is the product of intentional design. Malick's script makes its debt to the Bible, like its debt to Garland's *Boy Life on the Prairie*, explicit. If many of the finished film's scenes suggest religious interpretations, it is not just because they were shot in the "sacred light of beauty" Garland had celebrated, but it is also because their composition and their content were meant to evoke religious associations. When viewers first glimpse the farmer, for example, he is biting into an apple. He is also gazing upon the arrival of his hired hands, with the Eve-like Abby—as we see in the very next shot—foremost among them. If the farm is a kind of Eden, this scene suggests that expulsion from it is imminent.

Beating beneath such religious symbolism, *Days of Heaven*'s philosophical pulse can be difficult to detect, especially since the kind of philosophy that courses through its veins was, as even Cavell admitted when he invoked Heidegger, of a rather rare type. Cavell called *Days of Heaven* a "metaphysical film," but *metaphysics* had become, by 1978, something of a dirty word in American philosophy. Indeed, metaphysics had been all but banished from serious scholarship.

For most of the twentieth century, philosophers all over the world worked toward the "elimination" or the "overcoming" of metaphysics. It was the one task on which almost anybody working in philosophy could agree. The fact that thinkers as different from each other in style, tone, and outlook as Rudolf Carnap and Martin Heidegger could speak this way demonstrates just how far metaphysical inquiry had fallen from the medieval and scholastic heights it had achieved in previous centuries.[41] The rise of natural science, positivism, and experimentalism, which together had done so much to remake everyday life, had also made talk of things like "essence" and "spirit"—if not also the more religiously resonant "soul"—seem quaint at best or confused if not reactionary at worst.

Still, there was no clear consensus about how best to escape the gravitational pull of metaphysics when Malick was a philosophy student in the 1960s. Carnap's idea of "The Elimination of Metaphysics Through Logical Analysis of Language," as a 1932 paper of his was titled, differed quite dramatically, for example, from Heidegger's talk of "overcoming metaphysics."[42] Like so many of the linguistic philosophers he inspired, including W. V. Quine at Harvard, Carnap espoused a problem-solving approach: the pernicious influence of metaphysical speculation should be replaced with a specific, scientific method—namely, that of "logical analysis."[43] Seen from this perspective, getting rid of metaphysics cleared a path for more fruitful, more empirical work. As one of Quine's most oft-cited quips had put it: "philosophy of science is philosophy enough."[44]

But it was under Cavell's influence, not Quine's, that Malick ultimately fell. And whereas Quine usually taught logic at Harvard, Cavell, who arrived in the middle of Malick's undergraduate career, was hired to teach aesthetics. Not only that, but he was willing to read authors whom the proponents of logical analysis either avoided or actively disparaged, Heidegger foremost among them.[45]

Heidegger repeatedly returned to the question of metaphysics throughout the 1930s and 1940s. The work he produced during this time suggested a completely different philosophical approach than Carnap's—a working through, as opposed to a jettisoning of, old metaphysical concepts and categories. For Heidegger, metaphysics encapsulated a whole tradition of thought spanning centuries, from the ancient Greeks all the way up to modern-day natural science. It was not so easily "eliminated." Modern technology was a case in point. Heidegger described it as "completed metaphysics," but technology defined almost every aspect of the modern world: to think outside its frame required a whole new kind of philosophizing, a whole new language even, one that resembled poetry more than formal logic.[46]

With such divergent views on what constituted proper philosophical language, Heidegger and Carnap were destined to disagree. For Heidegger, logical analysis and the scientific mindset from which it stemmed were not so much the solution to metaphysics as the fullest expression of it. Carnap thought otherwise. He maintained that metaphysical speculation stemmed simply from the misuse of everyday language. If Heidegger viewed metaphysics as something like a world-historical condition, a fate that had befallen the earth and all who dwell on it, Carnap saw it as just a technical problem to be solved by the powers of logic and semantics.

Heidegger's and Carnap's differing assessments of metaphysics led to very different philosophical projects. Carnap's approach entailed running metaphysical treatises through the wringer of logical analysis. With glee he did just that to Heidegger's early work, including his essay "What Is Metaphysics?" (1929), which ended with a restating of the fundamental metaphysical question: "Why are there beings at all, and why not far rather Nothing?"[47] Heidegger envisioned a kind of struggle between things or beings and the nothingness out of which they arose. But for Carnap, to say that "the Nothing nothings," as Heidegger had, was not a statement of profound insight into the meaning of Being, but merely "a logical defect of language."[48] It was utter nonsense.

Carnap sought refuge from all things metaphysical in logic and empirical science, but Heidegger took a different approach. He attempted to work his way back through metaphysics, turning for aid not to logic but to phenomenology and, later, poetry. The fact that Carnap and Heidegger were on opposite sides of an increasingly polarized political spectrum only widened the intellectual chasm between them. In fact, thanks to the recent publication of some of Heidegger's private writings from the 1930s—especially the so-called *Black Notebooks*—we now know that the question of metaphysics was an explicitly *political* question for Heidegger, one that supposedly helped set the Germans apart from Russians, Americans, and Jews.[49]

Heidegger's approach to the question of metaphysics—especially as he returned to it in later years, offering first a postscript (in 1943) and then a lengthy introduction (in 1949) to his original 1929 essay—offered not only a more imaginative perspective than Carnap's but also a more expressly politico-theological one. Heidegger's ruminations also took on an increasingly apocalyptic tone.[50] Indeed, during what philosopher Steven Crowell has labeled his "metaphysical decade," Heidegger peered directly into the abyss of the Nothing and began to argue that metaphysics was in large part responsible for the fallenness of the modern world—for all its crass materialism and industrial soullessness. Metaphysical thinking, Heidegger insisted, had brought humanity to an intellectual and spiritual dead end. In dealing only with objects, with things that could be calculated and manipulated, metaphysics relegated everything else to the realm of the unthought.[51] It blotted everything else out.

The question of how *beings* differed from *Being*, was, for Heidegger, a far more important—and far more difficult—question to ask than how they could be counted or used. But he counseled staying with the difficulty, for it spurred us to think and ponder. "Only when the strangeness of beings oppresses us does it arouse and evoke wonder," he insisted in his inaugural lecture at Freiburg University.[52] But metaphysics sought to explain away this strangeness. As Heidegger put it (in 1949): "Metaphysics thinks beings as beings. Wherever the question is asked what beings are, beings as such are in sight. Metaphysical representation owes this sight to the light of Being. The light itself, i.e., that which such thinking experiences as light, no longer comes within the range of metaphysical thinking; for metaphysics always represents beings only as beings."[53] This visual imagery demonstrates that Heidegger's later conception of metaphysics was not merely linguistic, as it had been for Carnap. For Heidegger, thinking about metaphysics meant thinking about light and vision and appearance—all those things that preceded or escaped the confines of language, whether logically rigorous or not. It also meant thinking about disappearance, too—the "nothing" as well as the "something." Convinced that philosophy had abandoned the question of Being for the study of beings, Heidegger lamented the loss of philosophical interest in anything that could not be cataloged, defined, or itemized, as logic would have it. He described this state of affairs as the "oblivion of Being," a condition responsible for, and made worse by, metaphysics.[54] We have become so enthralled with objects that we fail to marvel at the light that illuminates them, making them visible in the first place. We no longer see that we cannot see.

Like Plato's allegory of the cave, Heidegger's critique of metaphysics hinted at a realm of truth—the "truth of Being," he occasionally called it— obscured by the images of mere beings that appeared to us in our day-to-day lives. In a 1938 essay, he went so far as to suggest that we lived in "The Age of the World Picture," in which everything was apprehended as mere representation. The world had become, as he put it, enframed. "The fundamental event of modernity," he proclaimed, was "the conquest of the world as picture," and it meant that now "man fights for the position in which he can be that being who gives every being the measure and draws up the guidelines."[55] The world had become little more than an album of snapshots awaiting systematic arrangement.

Whether or not man should be the measure of all things, as Protagoras had suggested centuries earlier, was one of the questions Heidegger had thought long and hard about over the course of his career.[56] His earlier essays on metaphysics seemed to answer in the affirmative, implying that the metaphysical heritage of the western tradition required an active, willful response from human beings. It compelled them, he argued, to "draw up the guidelines" of the world. Among Heidegger's early treatises written in this activist vein was an essay composed around the same time as "What Is Metaphysics?" titled "On the Essence of Ground," which could also be translated as "On the Essence of Reasons," since the German word *Grund* carries both connotations.[57] This is how Malick translated it.

As with "What Is Metaphysics?," Heidegger returned to "On the Essence of Reasons" in later years, obsessively inserting revisions and adding additional commentary. The two works cover some of the same terrain, but from slightly different perspectives. "What Is Metaphysics?" addresses the question of Being, but "On the Essence of Reasons" spends more time on the forgotten or overlooked reasons—the ground—upon which something like metaphysics rests. In "On the Essence of Reasons," Heidegger suggested that metaphysics was rooted in human freedom. As he saw it, the transcendence of human freedom was what created worlds, what grounded them. Such freedom meant that human existence was unique, it could not be viewed as just another component of the world picture, for it was what made that picture possible in the first place.

The fact that Malick was familiar with these ideas forces us to take a second look at *Days of Heaven*. With its sparse and often poetic narration, its patient pacing, and its deliberately distanced—if not to say "distancing"—cinematography, Malick's second feature feels like its own meditation on the essence of ground. Heidegger thought this essence derived from the uniquely human ability to unmake or remake the world, which is why he described the human being as, first and foremost, a "creature of distance."[58] Human existence, *Dasein*, is both in and of the world, dwelling within it and standing beyond or transcending it at the same time. The meaning of Being hinged on this simultaneous in-and-outness. Without *Dasein*, the world does not exist; but without the world, neither does *Dasein*. Human existence provides the necessary element of perspective for anything meaningful to appear amid the vastness of Being: it is the lonely figure standing off on the horizon that allows us to differentiate earth from sky, nearness from farness.

Such insights animate *Days of Heaven* from beginning to end. They go a long way toward explaining the film's delicate counterpoint structures, whether at the level of script, shot sequence, or sound design. *Days of Heaven* constantly juxtaposes objects in the world with the light that allows them to be seen, sounds with the silences allowing them to be heard. Everything stands apart and together all at once. All "the devices of the film seem to be meant," Penelope Gilliatt observed in her *New Yorker* review of the film, "to transmit loneliness and recovery."[59] In other words, *Days of Heaven* explores the world of human existence: it ponders nothing less than the relation of beings to Being.

The Worldhood of the World

In the introduction to his translation of "Vom Wesen des Grundes," Malick suggested that Heidegger was "largely concerned with the concept of 'world.'"[60] But he was quick to point out that Heidegger's concept of world was distinct from what we usually think of as the world of objects: it was "not the 'totality of things' but that in terms of which we understand them, that which gives them measure and purpose and validity in our schemes." Heidegger was interested most of all in asking "why we must, and no less how we *can*, share certain notions about the measure and the purpose and validity of things."[61]

This put a whole new spin on the Protagorean idea of "man" as "measure." As Malick pointed out, Heidegger did not view the notions of measure and purpose as pretty metaphors. Rather, the idea of man as measure pointed toward the limits, the very boundaries, of our experience of the world.

Measuring and drawing up guidelines of the world was, in other words, a fundamental feature of existence. It is what makes us human.

Malick likened Heidegger's concept of world, especially as it is expressed in "Vom Wesen des Grundes," to Søren Kierkegaard's notion of the "sphere of existence" and Ludwig Wittgenstein's idea of the "form of life."[62] According to each of these thinkers, the world is less like a quantifiable, external object and more like a horizon of meaning making any shared understanding possible. The world comprises all of the things underpinning communication and understanding, such as language, culture, tradition, and heritage. Malick stressed this in his introduction. Heidegger's notion of the world encompassed far more than just a viewpoint or a particular perspective. As Malick put it: "there is little sense in speaking of 'a point of view' here since precisely what Heidegger wants to indicate with the concept [of world] is that none other is possible. And there is no more sense in speaking of an interpretation when, instead of an interpretation, the 'world' is meant to be that which can keep us from seeing, or force us to see, that what we have *is* one."[63] All of this suggests that there is no external, objective distance between the world and human existence. The two are entwined in a way that escapes the strictures of logic and calculation. As Heidegger put it, in Malick's translation: "World belongs to selfhood; it is essentially related to Dasein."[64]

Malick's translation of "Vom Wesen des Grundes" draws extensively from the work he put into his undergraduate thesis at Harvard. Both the introduction and the extensive array of notes he added to Heidegger's essay demonstrate as much. Malick wrote "The Concept of Horizon in Husserl and Heidegger" under the supervision of Cavell, though Hubert Dreyfus provided guidance as well.[65] Juxtaposing Husserl's more abstract understanding of the "world of life"—which is how Malick translated Husserl's term *Lebenswelt*—and Heidegger's seemingly more practical or existential understanding of "world," Malick's Harvard thesis sided with Heidegger.[66] Something about Heidegger's desire to begin philosophizing not from the standpoint of abstract principles but instead from the experience of everyday existence seemed to resonate with the young philosophy student. Following Heidegger's lead, Malick implied that academic philosophy, including even Husserlian phenomenology, was derivative of actual being-in-the-world. It failed to recognize what was really at stake in the metaphysical understanding of worldhood. The mystery of how the world happens—of how the world "worlds," as Heidegger had put it in "Vom Wesen des Grundes"—pushes us beyond the realm of postulates and theories into the everyday mysteries of Being itself.[67]

Malick was onto something. Heidegger's concept of world really did suggest a radical reconsideration of both philosophical practice, in general, and phenomenology, in particular. Heidegger's concluding remarks in "Vom Wesen des Grundes" pointed toward the turn his own thinking would take during the 1930s and 1940s, resulting in essays such as "The Age of the World Picture" and, perhaps most famously, "The Origin of the Work of Art." His so-called *Kehre* (which was, in fact, a postwar rewriting of his intellectual history) was supposed to mark a shift from his earlier, more decisionistic conception of existence, toward a more passive or contemplative approach to the question of Being. It was a step away from individual resolve and authenticity, away from the activist response to metaphysics, and toward poetic thinking.

Heidegger's concluding remarks in "On the Essence of Reasons" emphasized the fact that *Dasein* shared a world with others. It was this sharing, Heidegger now claimed, that was truly important. But as a "creature of distance," *Dasein* was both near and far—to itself, to others, to all existing things, which meant that being with others was fraught: "Only through the primordial distances he establishes toward all being in his transcendence does a true nearness to things flourish in him. And only the knack for hearing into the distance awakens Dasein as self to the answer of its Dasein with others. For only in its Dasein with others can Dasein surrender its individuality in order to win itself as an authentic self."[68] It was something of a paradox: *Dasein* had to distance itself to appreciate nearness, but it also had to lose itself with others in order to become authentic. The characters of *Days of Heaven* learn these lessons the hard way.

Some of Heidegger's concern with nearness and distance, closeness and expanse, certainly found its way into the look and feel of Malick's second film. Like the classics of the silent screen, *Days of Heaven* relies far more on scenic suggestion than linguistic explication—and that suggestion conveys Heidegger's notion that *Dasein* is, first and foremost, a "creature of distance." In the words of Steven Rybin, "*Days of Heaven* is a film that is both about what it means to inhabit a particular space with a tactile closeness while at the same time being apart from any spiritual or metaphysical connection with others in relation to that space."[69] It is a film about community that lacks community; a film about rootedness that has nomads as it principal protagonists; a film about all-too-human hopes and dreams that spends much of its time contemplating the natural environment's indifference to such longings.

Days of Heaven depicts the necessity and the futility of human will, especially when it is viewed from the perspective of what Heidegger called the "worldhood of the world." As Malick clearly knew, the essays and lectures Heidegger prepared after the appearance of "What Is Metaphysics?" and "On the Essence of Reasons" moved away from notions of authenticity and will altogether. They seemed to imply that the urge to be the measure of all things was itself emblematic of the "oblivion of Being," just further proof of the tyranny of beings over Being. *Dasein*, the later Heidegger came to understand, was not in total control. Human transcendence—that is, human freedom— was not what made worlds. If anything, it was the other way around: it was the mysterious existence of the world that made human freedom possible.

Heidegger eventually came to think of the illusion of mastery ushered in by the age of the world picture as but a fateful sign of world-historical decline, yet another symptom of our ignorance of Being. Hence the apocalyptic tone that emerged in his later ruminations on the metaphysical legacy of the West. "Before Being can occur in its primal truth," he wrote in a piece he titled "Overcoming Metaphysics," "Being as the will must be broken, the world must be forced to collapse and the earth must be driven to desolation, and man to mere labor. Only after this decline does the abrupt dwelling of the Origin take place for a long span of time. In the decline, everything, that is, beings in the whole of the truth of metaphysics, approaches its end."[70] Without the desolation of the earth, in other words, there would be no days of heaven, no return to the Edenic origin of Being. Sadly, the darkest days of the Second World War only seemed to confirm such prophesies, leaving behind a trail of unimaginable real-world desolation that made all considerations of metaphysical desolation rather moot.

Some of the bleakness of Heidegger's later thinking about metaphysics seeps into *Days of Heaven*. Although it has sequences depicting laughter and leisure, all-too-brief respites from and rewards for the backbreaking manual labor of the harvest, *Days of Heaven* is by no means a pleasure cruise. There is a darkness that permeates it, one attributable, in part, to its imagery, but much of it comes from the voice-over narration contributed by Linda Manz, which was added long after shooting had ended, as Malick and Weber wrestled the raw footage from over a year's worth of shooting into the final shape of the film.

How much of the narration was Manz's own creation or Malick's, if only by suggestion, is hard to say; either way, the commentary certainly adds an ominous, apocalyptic element to the film, speaking as it does of "the whole earth" eventually "going up in flames," of the "devil just sittin' there laughing" because he's "glad when people does bad."[71] Sissy Spacek's voice-overs in *Badlands* had introduced an element of ironic comedy into the otherwise disturbing narrative of the film; but here, Manz's narration goes in the other direction, injecting a large dose of dread—some of it drawn from the Book of Revelation, which she had taken to reading during the postproduction process, apparently.[72] Her talk of danger and decline has an almost Heideggerian quality, but it never invokes Being or metaphysics. It sticks to the more accessible language of biblical damnation: "I think the devil was on that farm," Linda says.[73]

The Hidden Suddenness of Possible Absenting

In fact, the sentences from Heidegger that *Days of Heaven* reminded Stanley Cavell of when he first saw the film came not from the apocalyptic Heidegger, but rather from the supposedly humbled and chastened Heidegger, the postwar Heidegger. They came from a much later work of his, *What Is Called Thinking?* Composed of lecture courses Heidegger had given in 1951 and 1952—his first after having been banned from teaching by a French denazification committee in 1946—it had been translated into English by the American philosopher J. Glenn Gray, along with Fred D. Wieck, in 1968. *What Is Called Thinking?* was the book that introduced Heidegger's thought—including its disdain for the logical inquiry that reigned supreme in "Anglo-Saxon countries"—to a much wider audience.[74]

That audience included even philosophers who had been on Carnap's side of the philosophical divide in previous decades. Stanley Cavell was one of them. Making the connection between Heidegger and *Days of Heaven* in *The World Viewed*, he quoted liberally from the last two lectures of *What Is Called Thinking?* Such extensive referencing suggested that Malick's second film was more than casually connected to Heidegger's philosophy. Cavell should have been the one to know: if anyone had the right to claim that *Days of Heaven* somehow channeled Heidegger's thinking of Being directly onto the big screen, it was Malick's mentor.

Cavell's interpretation of *Days of Heaven*—and of Heidegger—is intriguing. "The first service man can render," he quotes Heidegger as arguing, "is to give thought to the Being of beings. . . . The word [being] says: presence of what is present."[75] With its long and contemplative shots, its warm appreciation for the natural world and the place of human beings within it, *Days of Heaven* certainly does seem to give thought to what is present. It exudes amazement at the fact that *presencing*—as Heidegger would have put it—occurs. After its confined prelude set in the industrial purgatory of a Chicago steel mill, the film opens up to the vastness of the world with shots of horizons so unending it is often difficult to tell where the wheat fields stop and the sky begins. Here, unlike in the big city, daily life seems rooted in timeless traditions, centered around seasons that come into being then fall away.

The landscapes of *Days of Heaven* are intimations of constancy, perhaps even eternity, but they are full of change. They give us not a world forged, like steel, but rather a world revealed, as in poetry or scripture. In this regard, especially, Cavell thought *Days of Heaven* merited a direct comparison with Heidegger's later philosophy, which contained lines such as these: "The presence we described gathers itself in the continuance which causes a mountain, a sea, a house to endure and, by that duration, to lie before us among other things that are present. . . . The Greeks experience such duration as a luminous appearance in the sense of the illumined, radiant self-manifestation."[76] What Heidegger was doing here with philosophical prose, Cavell suggested, Malick was doing with moving images. Not only did his former student manage to capture the magic of presencing, he also somehow grasped the deeper mystery of illumination and "self-manifestation," what Heidegger elsewhere would call—using an idiosyncratic translation of the ancient Greek word for truth—*Aletheia*, or "unconcealment."

If Heidegger's later thinking of Being meant thinking in terms of illumination and duration rather than so-called calculation, and if *Days of Heaven* really was inspired by Heidegger, then it is safe to say that Malick's second film was indeed shot from the perspective of Being. In this regard, the process that produced it was just as significant as the philosophy that inspired it. Famously, *Days of Heaven* used almost nothing but natural light. Many of the film's most memorable scenes were captured in the fading embers of a soft, magic-hour glow, just before the complete darkness of night set in, before presence gave way to absence, something to nothing.[77]

Malick insisted on these methods. As Jacob Brackman put it in a 1979 interview: "the concept behind the cinematography was basically Terry's," and it required "shooting later into magic hour than many people thought possible."[78] No other Hollywood production of the time looked anything like it. Although its visual style sometimes recalled the stark simplicities of silent-era cinema, *Days of Heaven* represented something entirely new, something that stood outside the familiar tropes and styles of mid-seventies American film.[79] Its depiction of the natural world, illuminated by magic-hour light-

Figure 6. Magic hour lighting in a scene from *Days of Heaven*.

ing, set it apart. "More than any other film since *The Big Trail* or *The Search-ers*," Ryan Gilbey has suggested, *Days of Heaven* "integrated landscape into American film-making, showing how it could affect, influence and comment on the action."[80] In portraying the earth as more than a mere backdrop for human drama, *Days of Heaven* spoke—or attempted to speak—a whole new cinematic language.[81]

After the *Kehre*, Heidegger, too, had attempted to write and think in an entirely new way. He refrained from even using the term *philosophy* to de-scribe what he was doing. For him, *philosophy* was a term too redolent of the metaphysical tradition he was trying to overcome, as well as the academic language he had been trying to sidestep his entire career. Whereas logic, on which contemporary philosophy had focused its attention, contented itself with analyses of grammars and objects, the kind of thinking Heidegger recommended—the kind of thinking realized by *Days of Heaven*, according to Cavell—peered behind such objects in order to contemplate that which made them visible in the first place.

Heidegger wanted to know why there was something rather than noth-ing, and Cavell was right to see the same sense of wonder at work in his for-mer student's moviemaking. Not since the Greeks, Heidegger maintained, had this kind of awe held sway. As he explained near the end of *What Is Called Thinking?* in a passage surprisingly not quoted by Cavell in *The World Viewed*, Heidegger claimed: "Wherever the thinking of the Greeks gives heed to the presence of what is present, the traits of presence which we mentioned find expression: unconcealedness, the rising from unconcealedness, the entry into unconcealedness, the coming and the going away, the duration, the gathering, the radiance, the rest, the hidden suddenness of possible absenting. These are the traits of presence in whose terms the Greeks thought of what is present."[82] To understand presence, in other words, meant contemplating *presencing*. It meant noting the ever-changing light on the prairie, or the subtle but unmistakable passing of the seasons. It meant seeing how something and nothing disappear into each other in an intimate embrace.

Had he not already chosen an epigraph from Hamlin Garland for his *Days of Heaven* script, Malick could very well have used this passage from Heidegger instead, for it captures so much of his picture's imagery and poetry, its attention to comings and goings, rest and radiance, concealments and unconcealments. *Days of Heaven* is about departures and arrivals (with countless shots of trains, planes, and automobiles; and many sequences depicting travel); about gathering and dispersing (not just as the migrant laborers arrive and depart the farm, but also as various other events mark the changing of the seasons); and, finally, about radiance and absence (with characters surrounded by magnificent beauty, but almost entirely unaware of it). If *Days of Heaven* realized any sentences from Heidegger, it was surely these. The film gives itself over to "radiance" while simultaneously contemplating the "hidden suddenness of possible absenting"—the possibility, in other words, of death, the final absence toward which the film's tragic plot pushes its protagonists.

The Fourfold on Film

Cavell could have chosen lines from any number of texts to suggest that *Days of Heaven* was Heideggerian thought realized on film, for by the late seventies, those texts were numerous and widely available. Beginning with the appearance in 1962 of *Being and Time*—a translation of Heidegger's 1927 magnum opus *Sein und Zeit*—Heidegger's works appeared in English rapidly. Under the editorial direction of J. Glenn Gray, who had been recommended for the job by his good friend Hannah Arendt, Harper & Row publishers released many translations that went a long way toward popularizing Heidegger's work in the United States. Among these were *Poetry, Language, Thought*, translated by Albert Hofstadter in 1971, and, the same year, *On the Way to Language*, translated by Peter D. Hertz. By 1977, when *The Question Concerning Technology and Other Essays* appeared in a translation by William Lovitt, Harper & Row had published over ten volumes of Heidegger's works in English. Malick's translation, *The Essence of Reasons*, was produced for a different publisher—Northwestern University Press, which specialized, as it still does today, in continental philosophy—but it, too, was part of this wave of Heideggeriana hitting American shores.

Many of these translations were unavailable when Malick was a student at Harvard just a decade or so earlier. The bibliography of his undergraduate thesis "The Concept of Horizon in Husserl and Heidegger" lists works by Heidegger only in the original German. It also lists a wealth of secondary and supplemental sources, including even Carnap's essay "The Elimination of Metaphysics Through Logical Analysis of Language," which Malick addressed in one of his endnotes.[83] But by the time *Days of Heaven* was released in 1978, Heidegger's writings were readily available in English, and many of them highlighted the more poetic, post-*Kehre* work of the Freiburg philosopher, the work to which Malick's filmmaking seemed to gravitate.

Already in his Harvard thesis, Malick had stressed that Heidegger wanted to get beyond or behind rational argument. He wanted us to enter worlds of meaning, Malick suggested, not just analyze them. He wanted us to experience the world as a whole rather than breaking it down into constituent parts. But this approach required something that more scientifically inclined philosophers generally eschewed—namely, a leave-taking from problem-solving. "To set out his thoughts as argument or theory," Malick explained in his thesis, "would do more than disarm them; it would undermine them altogether." "What Heidegger wants is not assent or disapproval," he suggested, "but something like faith." If his work had "arguments," they were closer to "dogmatic theology" than philosophy: "Heidegger wants us to believe in order that we may understand."[84] And indeed, in the United States, Heidegger was first read by theologians and religiously minded scholars.[85] They often situated his early work in the context of Christian, if not explicitly Catholic, teaching. Heidegger's later philosophy, even though it veered away from orthodoxy, was similarly faith based. As he searched for ways to ask the question of Being without slipping back into metaphysics, Heidegger resorted more and more to seemingly mystical language. He practically abandoned the philosophical practice of argumentation altogether.

As a philosopher in training, Malick had expressed some skepticism about Heidegger's poetic turn. After all, what it produced—as Heidegger was the first to confess—was not really philosophy. Working as a filmmaker, though, Malick did not have to worry about such disciplinary categorization. He could treat philosophy like poetry and poetry like philosophy. Following in the footsteps of Heidegger, he could explore a kind of thinking—a kind of seeing, a kind of listening, a kind of feeling, even—that slipped the binds of narrow academic discourse. What Heidegger called *Denken* could explore a kind of experience that was, we might say, almost cinematic. *Days of Heaven* is thoroughly indebted to it. It speaks a poetic language all its own, and its philosophical freedom is as readily apparent as its free-flowing, Panaglide camerawork.

Days of Heaven follows in Heidegger's footsteps by opting for poetic invention over argumentative coherence. It searches for meaning in the often-overlooked subtleties of everyday existence—the layered meanings of a furtive glance, say, or the afterglow of a prairie sunset. In one of his post-*Kehre* essays, "The Thing," Heidegger had managed to transform a discussion of a simple jug, a mere vessel for holding and pouring water, into a consideration of the very mystery of the world. That mystery hinged on what he called, in one of his many neologisms, "the fourfold."[86] The term he used—*das Geviert*—signified the connection between earth and sky, divinities and mortals, which he thought made all revealing and concealing possible. The four coordinates composed a unity reflecting the unity of all things: "Earth and sky dwell in the gift of the outpouring. In the gift of the outpouring earth and sky, divinities and mortals dwell *together all at once*. These four, at one because of what they themselves are, belong together. Preceding everything that is present, they are enfolded into a single fourfold."[87] The idea of the fourfold represented, for Heidegger, a new way of thinking about the phenomenon of world, a new way to understand what he called the "worldhood of the world."[88] But its appearance in his work was intimately connected to his earlier struggles with metaphysics, with the work that went into "What Is Metaphysics?" and "On the Essence of Reasons," especially.

Even if he was utilizing a new language, Heidegger was nonetheless pursuing the same philosophical questions that had puzzled him for decades, since the start of his career: What makes a world? Why is there something rather than nothing? What is the meaning of Being? In "The Thing," he declared that "the world presences by worlding," and "worlding cannot be explained by anything else nor can it be fathomed through anything else."[89] It could not be analyzed or dissected, only felt, experienced, or, through faith, perhaps, as Malick claimed, believed. "The human will to explain," Heidegger warned, "just does not reach to the simpleness of the simple onefold of worlding. The united four are already strangled in their essential nature when we think of them only as separate entities, which are to be grounded in and explained by one another."[90]

Getting to the simpleness of the fourfold was by no means simple, though. It required paying attention not just to mortals, but also divinities and—just as importantly—nature. The later Heidegger's desire to grasp the world as world—and not merely as abstraction, representation, or metaphor—animates both the look and feel of *Days of Heaven*, which in its own way depicts "the light and dusk of day, the gloom and glow of night, the clemency and inclemency of the weather, the drifting clouds and blue depth of the ether."[91] It explains why Malick's camera privileges no one element of the fourfold, but instead shows them to be entwined. In *Days of Heaven*, we find earth and sky, mortal creatures and intimations of divinity folded into each other: biblical allusions and religious imagery—including the blessing of the harvest, for instance, or the wedding of Abby and the farmer—share the screen with stunning depictions of the natural world.

Whether singing the film's praises or dismissing its pretensions, critics have tended to isolate just one of these elements, rather than consider the ways in which Malick's camera compels them to interact with each other. Nothing stands alone in *Days of Heaven*: although it mobilizes a number of specific religious, cultural, and aesthetic references, *Days of Heaven* is determined to capture the world in its fundamental interconnectedness. It shows that divinity and mortality, earth and sky, must always and everywhere be seen as standing in relation to each other. In other words, the human drama of *Days of Heaven* makes sense only in relation to divine presence and/or absence, just as seas of wheat only stand out when they are viewed against the rosy-hued backdrop of a magic-hour sunset.

Still, if *Days of Heaven* really does depict, in its own unique way, Heidegger's conception of the fourfold, it does so over and against Heidegger's wishes. Heidegger, who was born in 1889, never acclimated to the dizzying heights of twentieth-century technological innovation. His writings extol the virtues of hand tools and handicrafts; they celebrate the artisan and vilify the technician. Heidegger thought that mechanization and electrification hindered rather than helped our understanding of the fourfold. In many ways, his world was closer to that of Hamlin Garland than it was to Malick's. As a child of the technological age, Malick, born in 1943, is obviously less suspicious of technology, which might explain the subtle Heideggerian joke he inserted into *Days of Heaven*. It is a joke that not only demonstrates an admirable ability to philosophize without abdicating one's sense of humor—something sorely lacking in most professional philosophy—but also signals Malick's distance from what we might describe as knee-jerk Heideggerianism.

In his essay "The Thing," Heidegger worried that technology might one day demystify nature entirely. If that were to happen, nothing would be considered sacred or mysterious ever again. Technology would have devalued everything, allowing the "creature of distance" to think—falsely, of course—that all distances had been overcome. As a result of technology, Heidegger warned, "man puts the long distances behind him in the shortest time. He puts the greatest distances behind himself and this puts everything before him at the shortest range."[92] This allows nature to be coldly, even clinically, dissected and enframed. "The germination and growth of plants, which remained hidden throughout the seasons," he explained wearily, "is now exhibited publicly, in a single minute, on film."[93] But in a montage in the middle of *Days of Heaven*, the very sequence Heidegger describes appears. It is a National Geographic–like time-lapse, shot in close-up, of a seed germinating underground. Malick was having a little fun with his philosophy, but he was also acknowledging the fact that moviemaking combines—as V. F. Perkins once put it—both "science and style."[94] Without technology, cinema would not exist and Malick was admitting as much.

The germination sequence was no last-minute improvisation. Like so much of the finished film—except, of course, for the voice-over narration supplied by Manz—the "single minute" of footage Heidegger had warned of was already there in Malick's screenplay. The first draft of *Days of Heaven* was registered with the Writer's Guild of America on April 14, 1976. A revised draft from a few months later, dated June 2, 1976, carries the following expository synopses, which follow Bill's initial departure from the farm halfway through the film. A series of shots depicting the changing seasons and the passing of time were to be entwined with various shots of the natural world: "Views of backlit gems, stalactites, salamanders in their cold dark pools, hidden springs, and other mysteries of nature."[95] A similar sequence is described soon after: "Various wonders of the prairie: a charred tree, a huge mastodon bone, a flowering bush, a pelican, the rusted hulk of an ancient machine, etc."[96] It is amid all this that Malick situates the germination scene. His stage directions even call for stock footage to be used. Everything was scripted.

When he visited the American Film Institute on January 12, 1970, Federico Fellini told a roomful of ambitious young directors that "filmmaking isn't improvised." "Making a movie is a mathematical operation," he said. "It's like you Americans sending a missile to the moon."[97] The director of *8½*—a

Figure 7. A glimpse of animal life down below in *Days of Heaven*.

movie about the making of a movie that may or may not include a rocket ship—must have said this with a smile. After all, his films could hardly be described as mathematical, including, most of all, *Satyricon*, which he screened for the AFI audience while he was in town. Still, he had a point: it helps to have a plan. Malick's early scripts resonate with the Italian auteur's advice, for they are extremely precise. Much of the look and feel of *Days of Heaven* is already there on the page—including shots that are deliberately marked as "MAGIC HOUR," in all caps.[98] Detailed notes about capturing images of nature demonstrate that, from the start, Malick wanted his film to feature all four coordinates of the fourfold. Natural panoramas would recur throughout the picture.[99]

Malick's curiosity also extended to animals. Like Garland's *Boy Life on the Prairie*, his script highlights the rich diversity of creaturely life on the Great Plains. It calls for shots in which "bison drift over the hills like boats on the ocean"; it mentions "snakes and gophers, rabbits and foxes" darting through wheat fields, unaware that "their sanctuary is growing smaller as the reapers make their rounds"; and, after the inferno that follows the locust infestation, it describes "burnt, blind deer" and the "roasted corpses of sharptail grouse, coyotes and badgers" that "lie scattered here and there."[100]

The animals of *Days of Heaven* are victims of violence, a fate mirroring that of their human counterparts. Harvesttime means that rats and snakes and rabbits and foxes will be "killed with rakes and flails" while the hunt means that "pheasants and quail" will "tremble in their coveys, their eyes big with fear."[101] All of this coincides with cosmic portents, too, many of which did not make the final cut. An ominous shot of Mars hanging "low and red in the western sky" after the harvest, along with stock shots of "Jupiter, the Crab Nebula, the canals of Mars," might have suggested that violence was written into the fabric of the cosmos.[102]

Long before *The Thin Red Line*, *The Tree of Life*, and *Voyage of Time*, Malick had his eyes trained on the earth below and the heavens above. But whereas his later films bridge the two, finding consolation in a fundamental unity of the terrestrial and cosmic realms, his earlier films emphasize instead the distance separating them. In *Days of Heaven* the epic grandeur of the cosmos offers little more than cold comfort to those who gaze upon it. Indeed, the cosmological perspective on human affairs does not always console: it can just as easily confirm, as Heraclitus put it, the unceasing necessity of strife.

Something Like Faith

We often think of religion as a domain stretched between the earthly and the heavenly, the mortal and the divine. Perched as it is between these two poles, it should come as no surprise that the script for *Days of Heaven* hews so closely to religious tropes and themes. But as was the case with *Badlands*, the religious imagery and content that so animated Malick's scripts did not always make it into the finished film. Once again, what emerged from the production process was a fundamentally religious picture stripped of its spiritually inflected source material. To be sure, Linda Manz's voice-over narration adds some religious feeling, much of it eschatological, and there is a scene depicting the blessing of the harvest (shooting script notes mention Psalm 90, which juxtaposes the mortal frailty of humans and the omnipotence of God).[103] There is also the pageantry of Abby's marriage to the farmer. But in Malick's original screenplay, there was much more religion than all this.

Much of *Days of Heaven*'s religious rumination was cut because Malick dropped a story line associated with it before principal photography began. Originally, the farmer, played by Sam Shepard (in his first major role as a Hollywood actor), was named Chuck Artunov, the only son of a Russian immigrant who had claimed land, defended it tooth and nail, only to die of smallpox, leaving a very young Chuck to fend for himself. One scene in Malick's scripts has an eleven-year-old Chuck eating coyote meat alone on the plains as Indians look on from afar. Another scene—a dream sequence—depicts his immigrant father, "a biblical figure with a long plaited beard, in a

Figure 8. The blessing of the harvest in *Days of Heaven*.

frock coat and Astrakhan hat, sitting in a chair on the open prairie, guard-ing his land with a brace of guns."[104]

All this backstory, which puts a very different, far more symbolic, slant on the biblical reference hinted at in the film's title, was x-ed out—literally—before shooting. Also cut was religious imagery that would have made Chuck/the farmer's fateful standoff with Bill more than just a romantic rivalry. Like his homesteading father before him, Chuck/the farmer was supposed to have been portrayed not simply as a cuckolded husband but as the embodiment of divine retribution. According to Malick's original vision, there was to be a scene, after Abby's marriage to Chuck/the farmer, depicting the slaughter of a hog. The violent act would take place off screen, but just prior to it we would see Chuck/the farmer putting a "stole, a long religious scarf, around his neck." Seeing this, Bill, in his flippant, jokey way, asks, "What's the neck-tie for?" To which Chuck/the farmer responds, in all seriousness: "Keeps the stain of guilt off."[105] The exchange foreshadows their fateful showdown later on, amid the wreckage of the biblical inferno that destroys the harvest. Fi-nally aware that Bill and Abby had deceived him, that his marriage was, at root, a sham, Chuck/the farmer looks for revenge: after knocking Bill to the ground, he was supposed to have moved toward him mumbling "a prayer of absolution—in Russian."[106]

Even without these scenes—or with truncated versions of them, at least—*Days of Heaven* still exudes a religious aura. Critics picked up on it immedi-ately. Just what this aura meant or implied, however, was up for debate. In

Time magazine, Frank Rich told readers that "*Days of Heaven* climaxes with a cleansing, Old Testament plague of locusts—a nighttime apocalypse so damning that it makes the similar finale of Nathanael West's *The Day of the Locust* seem tame by comparison."[107] For Rich, the message was obvious: a day of judgment was at hand. "Like *Badlands*, director Terrence Malick's remarkable first film, his new work is a bleak and unstinting attack on America's materialistic culture."[108] Perhaps in the economic doldrums of the late seventies, during what President Jimmy Carter would label, less than a year later, a "crisis of confidence," such a reading of the film made sense. (Surely it was a notable coincidence that a film about alienated, migrant labor premiered amid the New York newspaper strike of 1978, which effectively shut down the city's three major dailies and forced the producers of *Days of Heaven* to collect and distribute all the available notices and reviews of the film on their own.) But to David Denby, writing in *New York* magazine, "this biblical calamity" was "just a lot of fancy crap, completely out of place in so modern a movie: anyone can see that God isn't present in *Days of Heaven*, that Malick's supercool style is devoid of ethical or religious fervor." It was, he ranted, "a story of exploited labor without outrage, a sexual triangle without the slightest erotic tension, a biblical parable without religious feeling."[109]

If the seemingly religious message of *Days of Heaven* divided critics it was only because that message required a fair amount of decoding and not all viewers had the patience or the willingness to undertake it. Malick's biblical allusions may be obvious, but any underlying message his film had about the fate of religion in the modern world was—and still is—open to interpretation. *Days of Heaven* depicts the birth of the modern, secular world, but it seems conflicted about what this birth signifies. Set in 1916–17, just ahead of American involvement in the First World War—the "war to end all wars," the war that was the backdrop for so much of Heidegger's early thinking— the movie is situated on the cusp of an era defined by industrial technology, mechanized mobility, and scientific exploration, some of organized religion's most powerful solvents. If Chuck/the farmer's religious rituals are a holdover from his immigrant father's days, then the many scenes of natural wonders and scientific fascination in the film are their modern, secular counterparts. Could these different worlds coexist? A telling exchange between Bill and Abby in Malick's screenplay presses the question. "Suppose we woke up tomorrow and it was a thousand years ago," Bill says. "I mean, with all we know? Electricity, the telephone, radio, that kind of stuff. They'd never figure out how we came up with it all. Maybe they'd kill us."[110]

Figure 9. Linda (Linda Manz) watching Charlie Chaplin's *The Immigrant* in *Days of Heaven*.

Days of Heaven's many images of the pursuit of knowledge and scientific exploration—conveyed in still-life-like shots of telescopes, weather vanes, and dioramas—hint that the birth of the modern world means more than just the arrival of crass materialism. Modern technology is presented as a kind of miracle, just as Bill understood it. It gives us, among other things, the magic of cinema. Malick highlights this fact by incorporating Charlie Chaplin's 1917 short *The Immigrant* into his film. The protagonists of *Days of Heaven* watch it with both glee and amazement. Like Holly's stereopticon moment in *Badlands*, this metacinematic sequence alerts us to our own vested viewership, our own capacity for wonder.

Far from displacing religious cosmology, *Day of Heaven* suggests that modern science merely echoes it in a new key. Religion and science both seek to link the earth to the heavens. They differ only in the languages they utilize to do so. Both are awesome, a mix of terror and wonder. One sequence depicted in the script, but condensed almost beyond recognition in the final cut of the film, demonstrates this quite clearly. After a day of rest spent down by the river, Chuck/the farmer, Abby, and Bill return to the house and—as the script has it—"portray the movements of the sun, earth and moon relative to each other" on the fields leading back to the house. I envision the scene—a version of which Malick later inserted into his script for *The New World*—as something like the magnificent opening sequence of Béla Tarr's *Werckmeister Harmonies*, but with Bill, Abby, and Chuck/the farmer taking

Figure 10. Rapacious technology scars the land in *Days of Heaven*.

the place of the grinning, swaying drunkards in the bar at closing time.[111] In Malick's version, it is Chuck/the farmer, the most educated of the bunch, who instructs the others on their proper positions and trajectories. The science lesson doubles as a cosmological metaphor for their tragic love triangle, with Abby, as the sun, at the center, circled by Chuck/the farmer, playing the earth, while Bill, who has "the most strenuous role of all" as the moon, circles Chuck/the farmer.[112] The scene implies that an interplanetary collision is inevitable.

If the religion of *Days of Heaven* has moments of strife and violence, so too does its science and technology. Whenever mechanization is portrayed, from the opening sequence in Chicago to the extended scenes depicting harvesting later on, both the screen image and the soundtrack are dominated by it—by its force, its deafening sound, its looming threat.[113] Laborers on the farm are but appendages to the massive tractors and reapers, rather like the impoverished proletarians depicted in Fritz Lang's *Metropolis* (1927), who are sacrificed to the industrial Moloch.

But whereas Lang settled for an all-too-easy solution to the ongoing struggle between inhuman mechanization and all-too-human labor ("the mediator between head and hands must be the heart" is the film's famous tagline), in *Days of Heaven* Malick offers only open-ended questions: Is all this part of nature, or an irremediable rupture from it? Does the machine have an agenda of its own? Do we control technology, or does it control us?

Malick's film does not romanticize the long-lost past of religious ritual, but it does not wholeheartedly celebrate the birth of the modern, either.

Modern technology gives us cinematic wonders, but it also threatens our very existence on the earth. Like the historical era in which it is set, *Days of Heaven* straddles two worlds in this regard: it laments a lost past, but it frets over a possibly precarious future, too.

In the end, *Days of Heaven* cannot decide if it will be religious tradition or scientific innovation that will save us. The truth of the matter is that neither approach, all on its own, is sufficient. And this may in fact be one of the central lessons of the film. Throughout the history of Western thought, metaphysical inquiry has shuffled between theological and scientific registers—between wisdom and knowledge, we might say. For centuries, religion and philosophy have been in constant dialogue—from Socrates through Aquinas up to Emerson, Kierkegaard, and Nietzsche. The conversation continued into the twentieth century, when metaphysics came under attack. Religion always returned. Even Wittgenstein's *Philosophical Investigations*, a work that set the stage for much of the research undertaken in the Anglo-American philosophical world in the second half of the twentieth century, including Cavell's, made a point of consistently circling back to a passage from Augustine's *Confessions*.[114]

In addition to this, many of those thinkers who, like Heidegger, called for the overcoming of metaphysics often adopted what seemed like a rather metaphysical, if not to say overtly religious, style in doing so. More often than not, they spoke the very language they advocated abandoning. *The Essence of Reasons* was a noteworthy case in point. Although Heidegger emphasized that his remarks neither confirmed nor denied the existence of God, that his inquiry was situated beyond religious categories and was thoroughly philosophical in orientation, his opaque rhetoric often had much in common with medieval Christian thinkers, such as Duns Scotus or Thomas Aquinas, who wrote at a time when philosophy and theology were allies rather than adversaries. In this regard, his work stood apart from that of his contemporaries. As Karl Löwith, one of his students, noted at the time, Heidegger looked and sounded more like a preacher than a professor.[115] His philosophizing, Löwith recalled, was a kind of "godless theology."[116] Dogmatic theology—as Malick had described it—indeed.

By the 1960s, when Malick started studying Heidegger's work at Harvard, most professional philosophers had turned their backs on theology. Scientization and secularization had driven a wedge between religious contemplation and philosophical inquiry. There were places where one could still ask questions of religious interest in a philosophical way, but they were few and far between. If one wanted to study Heidegger, who sounded so suspiciously theological, it usually meant working with Jesuit priests or Protestant theologians. By and large, analytic philosophers kept their distance.

Still, if one was inclined to seek it out, theology-tinged philosophy could be found in Cambridge, Massachusetts. At that time, Harvard was home to Paul Tillich, whose lecture course "The Self-Interpretation of Man in Western Thought" Malick attended as a freshman.[117] In addition to this, one of the philosophy department's most recent hires, John Rawls, had been shaped and influenced by years of religious study, which continued to motivate, if only implicitly, his lifelong quest to establish the philosophical foundations for a just and equitable society. And there was at least one other younger member of the department who tried to keep the dialogue between philosophy and religion alive amid all the logical analysis that dominated the curricula of the day. To those who view him only as an ordinary language philosopher, or as a philosopher of film and aesthetics, or even as an Emersonian moral theorist, it may come as a surprise to learn that Cavell taught courses such as "The Philosophy of Religion" at Harvard, which he offered in the fall of 1963. The course explored the ways in which "contemporary philosophy confronts religious discourse."[118]

Malick had already been exposed to a number of philosophical traditions that tiptoed around theology. His frame of reference included existentialism, metaphysics, and Heideggerian phenomenology. The Harvard-educated Norwegian philosopher Dagfinn Føllesdal regularly gave courses on phenomenology: he even devoted a whole course to Heidegger and Sartre. In addition to this, Cavell's good friend Kurt Fischer—a visiting professor at the time—also taught Heidegger, in courses such as "German Philosophy After Kant." There was even a course devoted to the musty old topic of metaphysics on the books, which was taught by the California-born philosopher Donald Cary Williams. Its reading list was, like Williams himself, heading rapidly toward retirement, but given Malick's expressed interest in understanding—as he later put it—"himself and his place in the order of the cosmos," the subtitle for the course is revealing: "Problems and Principles of Cosmology."[119]

All of this suggests that Malick studied philosophy at Harvard at just the right time. Any sooner and Cavell and Rawls would not have been there. Any later and metaphysics and cosmology would have been only dimly remembered relics of a distant pedagogical past. Still, for somebody searching out his place in the grand scheme of things, even these resources were not enough. Too late to resort to traditional religious belief and too soon to find solace solely in secular science, Malick would have to ask the kinds of questions he was most interested in pursuing elsewhere. He would have to study cosmology independently. Or in film school.

Garland's *Boy Life on the Prairie* closes with its protagonist leaving the farm to head off to school. *Days of Heaven* ends similarly, but with a significant twist. Linda has been enrolled in a girls' school, but in the film's final shot, captured in the last embers of a day's fading light, we see her sneak out from the schoolhouse to walk off along the train tracks; she is seeking out the wider world. It is hard not to imagine Malick channeling some of his own experience into that sequence (not to mention some of his enthusiasm for Truffaut's *The 400 Blows* [1959], which ends with similar images of escape). In search of experience, Malick, too, had left school. But while he may have ditched the lecture halls and seminar rooms of the academy for the allures of Hollywood, he by no means abandoned philosophy. Released almost a decade after his arrival in Los Angeles, *Days of Heaven* showed that he was still searching for his place in the cosmos. And the fact that some twenty years would pass before the release of his next film suggests he was not one to call off the search prematurely.

*   *   *

One of the projects on which Malick was rumored to be working during the twenty-year span between the release of *Days of Heaven* and *The Thin Red Line* was an adaptation of Walker Percy's religiously inflected existentialist novel *The Moviegoer*. Percy's book won the National Book Award in 1962. It tells the tale of a New Orleans bachelor who is, as he puts it, "on the search," looking for meaning. He has a difficult time finding it, though. "The search" takes him all around town, even to the movies, but for most of the book he remains conflicted and disappointed, the natural state of existentialist heroes stretching from Kierkegaard's knight of faith and Fyodor Dostoevsky's underground man to Richard Wright's Bigger Thomas and Albert Camus's Meursault. Still, Binx Bolling keeps going back to the movies. He keeps searching, keeps asking questions. "And there I have lived ever since," he declares at one point in the novel, "solitary and in wonder, wondering day and night, never a moment without wonder."[120]

Malick eventually made a film titled *To the Wonder*, a film that, as we shall see, channeled much of *The Moviegoer*'s contemplative introspection into a somewhat fictionalized autobiographical portrait, one that spills over into the storyline of *Knight of Cups* as well. Malick's career should be viewed as a search for meaning. In *Days of Heaven*, we can see him assembling the supplies he would take along with him on his intellectual journey. In this regard, his second feature is a far more personal work than his first, which might explain why the film "gets under your skin"—as a reviewer in *Newsweek* put it—in a way that *Badlands*, which is cooler, more detached, does not.[121]

Malick's first two films do have some important things in common, though, most notably an interest in capturing the oneness of the fourfold. Fire and water play significant roles in *Badlands* and *Days of Heaven*. Both films contain dramatic, extended sequences of conflagrations. Both films feature flowing rivers. The juxtaposition of fire and water constitutes what we might describe as a cinematic tic, one that grows more pronounced over the course of Malick's career.[122]

The river flowing through *Days of Heaven* is laden with more religious significance than the one in *Badlands*, though. More like the rivers that appear Malick's later films, such as *The Thin Red Line*, *The New World*, *The Tree of Life*, and *A Hidden Life*, the river in *Days of Heaven* is a place apart from the hustle and bustle of daily life. It provides respite from the daily routine on the farm, all of its labors and chores. The river is not only a hideout—like the one in *Badlands*—but also a refuge, a place of calm and quiet, of cooling regeneration. Hamlin Garland, in *Boy Life on the Prairie*, recalled his visits to the water's edge as a boy: "To go from the dusty field of the prairie farms to the wood shadows" near "the cool murmuring of water" was a revelation. And "to plunge into the deeps of the dappled pools," he wrote, "was like being born again."[123]

Some of the most significant turning points in *Days of Heaven* take place down by the river. It is where Bill first pitches to Abby the idea of her marrying the farmer for his money; it is where Abby and the farmer eventually marry; and it is where the farmer, Abby, and Bill, in an approximation of family life that brings to mind Jean Renoir's *A Day in the Country* (1936), enjoy their new, leisurely existence together—their short-lived days of heaven. But the river is also where everything comes undone. It is there, in a shot that seems to mirror, darkly, a baptismal dunking, Bill is shot dead near the end of the picture. The way his body splashes into the water recalls the unceremonious fashion in which Holly's father, in *Badlands*, tosses her dead dog, stuffed into an army-issue duffel bag, off a bridge. In both films, the river comes to represent a boundary separating life and death: it baptizes, but it also buries.

Ancient Greek cosmologies depicted the earth as a landmass bounded on all sides by the river Ocean. The lord of that river, also named Ocean, was one of the original Titans. He regulated the rise and fall of heavenly bodies as they emerged from, and disappeared back into, his waters. The interplay of absence and presence was his domain, which might explain why Heidegger, thinking of the Greeks, spied in the quotidian pouring of water from a pitcher the elaborate workings of the fourfold. Malick finds something similar in a river's flowing. For him, rivers are the quintessential sites of gathering and distancing. They are cosmologies in miniature.

Divinities and mortals, sky and earth: this is the stuff of which *Days of Heaven* is made. It is a film about land, but it is bounded by water, represented most noticeably by the cooling sounds of Camille Saint-Saën's "Aquarium," from *The Carnival of the Animals*, which opens and closes the film's soundtrack. As Heraclitus put it, in one of the earliest fragments of Western philosophy: "For souls to become water is to die; for water to become earth is to die; but from earth, water comes to be; from water, soul."[124] Out of water we are born, then, and into the earth we will one day be buried, perhaps someday to be born again, anew.

CHAPTER 3
_____

Heroism, Individualism, and the Over-Soul

The Transcendentalist Theodicy
of *The Thin Red Line*

> If man's attempt to live without gods appears, in the harsh
> light of present realities, a failed attempt, is a reversal of
> our course possible?
>
> —J. Glenn Gray

By his own admission, the philosopher John Rawls lost his Christian faith
sometime around June of 1945, near the end of the Second World War. Long
before becoming one of the preeminent moral and political thinkers of the
twentieth century, Rawls, after graduating from Princeton with a bachelor's
degree in philosophy, enlisted in the army. He served with the 128th Regi-
ment of the Thirty-Second Infantry in New Guinea, the Philippines, and, last,
Japan, where he was part of the occupying forces at war's end.[1] No doubt like
many other enlisted men, Rawls's time in the army substantially altered his
views of the world and his place in it.

Three separate events during this time challenged Rawls's religious beliefs, beliefs once held so dear they almost propelled him into the seminary.
After taking part in the vicious battle for Leyte in the Philippines, Rawls remembered being enraged by a Lutheran pastor's "falsehoods about divine
providence."[2] Over fifty years later, he still recalled the pastor's outrageous
claim "that God aimed our bullets at the Japanese while God protected us
from theirs."[3] Even then he knew such sentiments, however comforting to
the troops, made for shoddy theology. The random and arbitrary death of

Rawls's good friend Deacon along the Villa Verde Trail on Luzon only a few months later surely reinforced his suspicions regarding the supposed goodness of God's cosmic plans. After all, the only thing that saved Rawls from Deacon's fate was the fact that his blood type was needed in a nearby field hospital, keeping him a safe distance from the fatal Japanese mortar barrage that took his friend's life.

It was hearing about the Holocaust in Europe that finally broke Rawls's Episcopalian faith. He remembered being stunned by the news of the attempted extermination of a whole people: "How could I pray and ask God to help me, or my family, or my country, or any other cherished thing I cared about, when God could not save millions of Jews from Hitler?" In light of the Holocaust, and the bloody Pacific campaign in which he had taken part, Rawls "soon came to reject the idea of the supremacy of the divine will," finding the notion "hideous and evil." In an age of total war punctuated by genocide as well as the use of nuclear weapons, the concept of providence neither comforted nor persuaded. "To interpret history as expressing God's will," Rawls later wrote, "God's will must accord with the most basic ideas of justice as we know them."[4]

Serving in the Pacific during World War II taught Rawls to look elsewhere for such basic ideas. Instead of enrolling in divinity school upon his discharge from the army in 1946, as he had planned, he returned to Princeton on the GI Bill to pursue graduate work in philosophy.[5] Twenty-five years later, in 1971, the press of Harvard University, where Rawls taught for almost his entire career, published his seminal contribution to political and moral philosophy, *A Theory of Justice*. Nowhere in its meticulous and sprawling, eighteen-page index does the word *providence* appear.[6]

*　　*　　*

Many books and countless films have chronicled the brutality and horrors of combat in the Pacific war. Memoirs such as E. B. Sledge's *With the Old Breed* and Robert Leckie's *Helmet for My Pillow* supplied the story lines for HBO's 2010 television miniseries *The Pacific*.[7] And journalistic accounts, such as Richard Tregaskis's *Guadalcanal Diary* (the basis for the wartime-produced film of the same title starring Anthony Quinn and William Bendix), and John Hersey's *Into the Valley: A Skirmish of the Marines* remain in print some eighty years after their initial publication.[8] Amid all this nonfiction, however, it might very well be that a novel written by a veteran of the Pacific campaign best captures the faith-shattering consequences of combat as described by Rawls. It may also be the case that a former Harvard philosophy student's adaptation of the novel for the big screen comes closest to capturing its spiritual message. As a book, written by James Jones, and as a film, directed by Terrence Malick, *The Thin Red Line* represents a unique rethinking of the wartime experience.

The success of Jones's novel stems from its dismantling of the war literature genre. The same has to be said for Malick's adaptation of it for the screen, which, far from being just another war movie, is a tapestry woven from rich and sometimes surprising literary, philosophical, and theological threads. Malick's version of *The Thin Red Line* is anything but a series of choreographed battle sequences punctuated by special-effects explosions. It looks askance at traditional notions of heroism and calls into question the militaristic jingoism to be found in everything from *Sands of Iwo Jima* (dir. Allan Dwan, 1949) to *The Pacific*. How Malick came to make the picture, especially after spending some two decades away from the director's chair, is a story full of gossip and speculation, but even more important than this behind-the-scenes narrative is the intellectual journey that led to the creation of such an unprecedented war film.

This chapter teases out the various influences that made *The Thin Red Line* one of the most compelling films of Malick's career. Examining them closely, we can see how *The Thin Red Line* became something other than a genre film. We can also see how it became another path forward in Malick's quest for meaning. To understand his adaptation of *The Thin Red Line* is to understand not just the "Pacific blitzkrieg" of Guadalcanal or the literary legacy of James Jones, but also how philosophy, theodicy, and nature can help us explore nothing less than the meaning and purpose of life.[9]

Total Mobilization

The Thin Red Line represented Malick's momentous return to Hollywood after a twenty-year absence. During this time, rumors about what had happened to him after the release of *Days of Heaven* ran rampant. He was a big-name director, but he was nowhere to be found. Was he hiding out in Santa Monica? Had he gone back to Austin? Did he really fall in love, drop everything, and move to Paris? Any and all of these stories contained some small smattering of truth. What was not true was the suggestion that Malick had abandoned filmmaking. He may not have been directing, but he was still busy working on scripts and developing projects. In these so-called lost years, he wrote a screenplay about the life of Jerry Lee Lewis—"Great Balls of Fire," based on the book by Myra Lewis and Murray Silver, Jr.—and another about the origins of psychoanalysis called "The English Speaker," centered around the famous case of Anna O. chronicled by Josef Breuer and Sigmund Freud in their 1895 book *Studies in Hysteria*. He even pitched a project based on the life of Joseph Merrick, otherwise known as "The Elephant Man," until word got out that David Lynch was making a movie about the same subject, to be produced by Mel Brooks.[10]

Throughout the 1980s and 1990s, Malick also began working on an adaptation of *The Thin Red Line*. Over the years, it morphed into a massive endeavor, with producers coming and going, financiers jockeying for position with studios, and actors lining up for their chance to work on what would turn out to be one of the hottest productions in Hollywood: a Terrence Malick picture. In fact, it was Malick's 1970s reputation as a cinematic genius that helped get the project off the ground. George Stevens Jr., Malick's friend and mentor from his American Film Institute days, became a producer on the film and said as much: "One of the facts that made possible the making of the movie," he said, "was that so many good actors wanted to be part of the film." *The Thin Red Line* could be cast with "enough stars to assure 20th Century Fox that it would be a picture of some importance."[11]

The list of actors who landed a part in Malick's adaptation of *The Thin Red Line* reads like a who's who of 1990s Hollywood: Sean Penn, Woody Harrelson, Nick Nolte, John C. Reilly, John Cusack, George Clooney, Tim Blake Nelson, John Savage, Thomas Jane, Adrien Brody, Elias Koteas, John Travolta, and Jared Leto, among others. But many of them saw their roles reduced to mere cameo appearances by the end, especially Brody who, as Fife, thought he would be the protagonist of the film until he finally saw it at the premiere and realized he was anything but. He was lucky: a number of other actors—including Mickey Rourke, Bill Pullman, and Lukas Haas—filmed scenes that never even made the final cut. *The Thin Red Line* taught many of these actors that they were, to some degree at least, dispensable. In this regard, the making of the film stayed true to its source material, which suggested that modern warfare was premised on anonymity and standardization, not to mention dehumanization.

Like the military campaign it depicts, James Jones's novel is long, brutal, and dispiriting. Its fictionalized account of the battle for Guadalcanal, the site of the first major Allied victory in the fight against the Japanese in the South Pacific, takes a toll on readers. Nothing that is not war can be entirely like war, of course, but *The Thin Red Line* nevertheless comes close, especially insofar as it exposes just how unreal dramatized depictions of combat death and military violence usually are when they are compared to the real thing. Alert to this danger, Jones's novel consistently questions its own veracity. As one of Jones's primary characters, John Bell, mutters, "it was all once again like some scene from a movie, a very bad, cliché, third rate war movie. It could hardly have anything to do with death."[12]

If there is anything that permeates *The Thin Red Line*, it is, indeed, death. But in Jones's account, death is intimately associated with that other world-historical force: sex. "Could it be that *all* war was basically sexual?" Bell asks himself after surviving a battle. "Not just in psych theory, but in fact, actually and emotionally? A sort of sexual perversion? Or a complex of sexual perversions?"[13] The interplay of what Freud had labeled, after the bloodbaths of the First World War, *Eros* and *Thanatos*, is on full display in the book, which captures the physical and psychological stress of combat in unrelenting detail, while also gesturing toward the "sexual ecstasy of comradeship."[14]

In one memorable sequence not included in Malick's film, young Private First Class Bead, the assistant forward clerk of C-for-Charlie Company, heads off into the jungle to relieve himself, only to be confronted by a "very thin," "badly unshaven" Japanese soldier whose "mud-slicked, mustard-khaki uniform with its ridiculous wrap leggins hung from him in jungledamp, greasy folds."[15] A visceral fight to the death ensues, during which Bead repeatedly tries to pull his pants up from down around his ankles. His animalistic survival instincts take over:

> Bead heard a high, keening scream and thought it was the Japanese begging for mercy until finally he slowly became aware that the Japanese man was now unconscious. Then he realized it was himself making that animal scream. He could not, however, stop it. The Japanese man's face was now running blood from the clawing, and several of his teeth had broken into his throat from the punches. But Bead could not stop. Sobbing and wailing, he continued to belabor the unconscious Japanese with fingernail and fist. He wanted to tear his face off with his bare hands, but found this difficult. Then he seized his throat and tried to break his head by beating it on the soft ground but only succeeded in digging a small hole with it. Exhausted

finally, he collapsed forward on his hands and knees above the bleeding, unconscious man, only to feel the Japanese immediately twitch with life beneath him.[16]

"Outraged at such a sign of vitality," Bead grabs the Japanese soldier's rifle and runs its bayonet through his chest.[17] Jones does not leave it at this: he goes on to describe Bead's immediate bodily and emotional reaction to killing a man, being sure to include all the fear, mud, shit, and vomit that comes with it. In the end, as Bead's adrenaline subsides, the horror sinks in: "He wanted to beg the man's forgiveness in the hope of forestalling responsibility. He had not felt such oppressive guilt over anything since the last time his mother had caught him and whipped him for masturbating."[18] Sex and death, they went hand in hand.

Jones's descriptions of wounded and dying bodies is as detailed as his psychologically convincing portraits of traumatized minds. His account of Bead's mental state before, during, and after the killing of the anonymous Japanese soldier is as exacting as the sharpest surgical tool. The fact that the set piece derives from Jones's own memories of combat on Guadalcanal only redoubles its powerful effect.[19] But other passages in *The Thin Red Line*, ones *not* rooted in his personal experience, are just as convincing in their psychic anguish. Take, for instance, the following internal monologue from Fife:

> When compared to the fact that he might very well be dead by this time tomorrow, whether he was courageous or not today was pointless, empty. When compared to the fact that he might be dead tomorrow, everything was pointless. Life was pointless. Whether he looked at a tree or not was pointless. It just didn't make any difference. It was pointless to the tree, it was pointless to every man in his outfit, pointless to everybody in the whole world. Who cared? It was not pointless only to him; and when he was dead, when he ceased to exist, it would be pointless to him too. More important: Not only would it *be* pointless, it would *have been* pointless, all along.[20]

The Thin Red Line does not turn away from this pointlessness: it confronts it head-on.

Jones's novel also confronts the hollowness of justifications for going to war in the first place. Like many of his comrades, Fife "could not believe he was fighting this war for God. And he did not believe he was fighting it for freedom, or democracy, or the dignity of the human race."[21] None of these things mattered, because, whether in a slit trench or on a forced march through the jungle, they were unreal. The experience of battle demystified the abstractions of ideology and propaganda. It demystified organized religion, too.

The Thin Red Line is about the terror of combat, not the rationalizations priests and politicians proffer for its supposed necessity. Robert Gottlieb, comparing Jones's account of the battle of Guadalcanal with his previous, perhaps more famous work, makes this clear: "There's an absence of religion and not much patriotism. Instead, there's battle, there's unbearable thirst, there's terror. *From Here to Eternity* was about the army; *The Thin Red Line* is about war."[22] But what is there to say about war that has not been said already, and many times over at that? From the *Iliad* to *The Red Badge of Courage*, the brutal, unrelenting reality of battle has been portrayed plenty of times before. What makes *The Thin Red Line* unique?

At first glance, Jones's novel seems to echo previous celebrations of the grandeur of combat-forged, fraternal heroism. It seems to confirm journalist Chris Hedges's lament that "war is a force that gives us meaning."[23] The dedication Jones appended to the book suggests as much: "This book is cheerfully dedicated to those greatest and most heroic of all human endeavors, WAR and WARFARE; may they never cease to give us the pleasure, excitement and adrenal stimulation that we need, or provide us with the heroes, the presidents and leaders, the monuments and museums which we erect to them in the name of PEACE."[24] But the pages that follow these words undo them; they transform the dedication into a farce, a twisted joke. If war really is a force that gives us meaning, it does so fleetingly, and only in the most intimate, private, fundamentally alienating fashion. But even at this level, up close or down deep, war's supposedly virtuous grandeur proves entirely illusory. The only meaning to be found in war is the necessity of surviving it.

The Thin Red Line shows that the supposedly heroic nature of war is always and everywhere overshadowed by the brutal realties of modern, industrialized violence. In the era of what the German warrior-writer Ernst Jünger called—prophetically—"total mobilization," heroism cannot be viewed as anything but an empty concept.[25] Jones puts this idea into the head of James Stein, the captain of C-for-Charlie Company:

> Only this time he himself, he Jim Stein, was one of them, one of the committed ones. The committed ones going through their exagger-

ated pretenses of invoking the cool calm logic and laws of the science of tactics. And tomorrow it would be someone else. It was a horrifying vision: all of them doing the same identical thing, all of them powerless to stop it, all of them devoutly and proudly believing themselves to be free individuals. It expanded to include the scores of nations, the millions of men, doing the same on thousands of hilltops across the world. And it didn't stop there. It went on. It was the concept—concept? the fact; the reality—of the modern State in action.[26]

In the era of mass mobilization, individual soldiers are no more than tools waiting to be used—used up if necessary.

Jones spends a great deal of time pondering the illusion of individuality in modern warfare. His characters think about it constantly. In a war composed of faceless, nameless masses, a war in which soldiers were as interchangeable as jeeps and rifles and tents—and worth about as much in the ledger books of their superiors—there is no room for the unique individual. This means there is no room for the solitary hero, either. Modern soldiers, whether brave or paralyzed by fear, are no more than statistics, numbers on a balance sheet. Even death does not individualize them.

This terrifying insight about modern warfare—not only that death is omnipresent, but also that it is anonymous, empty, and meaningless—becomes the recurrent theme of *The Thin Red Line*. Fife's battlefield realization is representative: "Slowly he stopped weeping and his eyes cleared, but as the other emotions, the sorrow, the shame, the selfhatred seeped out of him under the pressure of self-preservation, the fourth component, terror, seeped in to replace them until he was only a vessel completely filled with cowardice, fear and gutlessness. And that was the way he lay. This was war? There was no superior test of strength here, no superb swordsmanship, no bellowing Viking heroism, no expert marksmanship. This was only numbers. He was being killed for numbers."[27] As if to reinforce the idea, to underscore how fundamentally fungible the modern soldier had become, Jones puts similar thoughts into the head of another solider, Bell: "*Some* men would survive, but no *one* individual man *could* survive. It was a discrepancy in methods of counting. The whole thing was too vast, too complicated, too technological for any one individual man to count in it. Only collections of men counted, only communities of men, only *numbers* of men."[28] For Bell, the "weight of such a proposition was deadening, almost too heavy to be borne," but he nevertheless concluded that individualism was "a fucking myth!" He and the rest of his company were "*numbers* of free individuals, maybe; *collectives* of free individuals," perhaps, but they were not individual souls in and of themselves.[29] They had deluded themselves into thinking otherwise: "They thought they were men. They all thought they were real people. They really did. How funny. They thought they made decisions and ran their own lives, and proudly called themselves free individual human beings."[30] The truth, of course, was otherwise.

Earlier representations of the war in the Pacific, including not just journalistic accounts but also Hollywood films, shielded the civilian public from such hard truths. If it was addressed at all, the anonymity of wartime death was something associated only with the Japanese enemy. In fact, one of the defining characteristics of American representations of Japanese soldiers and civilians during World War II was their faceless interchangeability. In contrast to American military men, who were represented as heroic individuals hailing from Brooklyn to the Bay Area, each with his own distinct accent, personality, and voice, Japanese soldiers were always portrayed as little more than brainwashed automatons at best or subhuman beasts at worst. It was *they* who were anonymous and interchangeable, not U.S. Marines.

As film scholars have shown, this trope reflected the widespread racial prejudice of the time, which situated the Asian enemy higher than the European on the enmity scale devised by the Office of War Information. Even Nazis, it seemed, could be considered human. But Japanese civilians and soldiers were never afforded such sympathy.[31] In films such as *Wake Island* (1942) and *Guadalcanal Diary* (1943) "the onscreen Japanese enemy usually appeared as anonymous phantoms who were called 'Japs' or 'Nips' (not uncommonly augmented by a racial slur such as 'little yellow')."[32] The American servicemen who confronted them, on the other hand, were anything but spectral. Not once but twice in the film version of *Guadalcanal Diary*, for example, American soldiers are praised for their unique, remarkable individuality. In one scene, a charismatic chaplain, an Irish graduate of Notre Dame (where he was a fullback on the football team, the narrator rushes to note), sermonizes over a hastily constructed battlefield graveyard. He dismisses the suggestion that "these boys," these dead American servicemen, could be described as mere "statistics." In his eyes, each whitewashed cross represented a hero. A few scenes later, two officers discuss the prospects for the next offensive. They know their men have the upper hand because, unlike their opponents—the seldom seen "apes" and "monkeys" hiding in groups behind jungle tree lines—the marines had "learned to act as individuals."[33]

War correspondent Richard Tregaskis's account of the battle for Guadalcanal was published in 1943, within a year of the events it recounted. The film
version Hollywood rushed into production only months later softened the
edges of his pointed prose, but it did not deviate from the book's fundamentally heroic celebration of American bravery under fire. Tregaskis's journalism was a paean to the U.S. Marines who had secured the first offensive
victory against the Japanese. Taking time to note the full name and hometown of each and every soldier he encountered, Tregaskis provided a group
portrait of noble everyday men, carrying out their orders in what was most
certainly an extraordinary context—on a jungle-covered island thousands of
miles away from the mainland, a place unknown to most Americans back
home. Tregaskis did all he could to humanize and personalize the battle for
Guadalcanal. Even if he "had the feeling of being at the mercy of great ac-
cumulated forces far more powerful than anything human," of being one of
the "pawns in a battle of the gods," he consistently highlighted the individual men—sometimes no more than teenage boys, really—who fought the war
raging all around him.[34] Tregaskis celebrated their "esprit de corps" and composed a "long chronicle of heroism" documenting the marines' countless
actions against the "swarming Nips."[35]

In Tregaskis's telling, the battle of Guadalcanal pitted American heroism
against Japanese treachery. To his readers he relayed the talking points of
American generals, who spoke of the battles in the Solomon Islands as "the
most wonderful work in our history," while keeping an eye out for the chance
to herald "an outstanding hero" whenever he came across one.[36] In contrast
to these American heroes, Tregaskis found the Japanese soldiers he encountered (or heard about) to be "a measly lot."[37] Time and again in *Guadalcanal
Diary* he describes them as "puny," "sallow," and "wretched."[38] Although he
distinguishes between Japanese labor troops, for whom he had "at least a trace
of sympathy," and Japanese military troops, for whom he did not, Tregaskis
nevertheless developed a kind of composite figure of the enemy as a "Jap
pigmy," a fearless soldier who would fight always and everywhere to the death,
availing himself of any means, any tactic, no matter how devious or vicious.
Tregaskis admitted to feeling "little sympathy at seeing them killed."[39]

Jones's *The Thin Red Line*, which is told largely from the perspective of
the C-for-Charlie soldiers, does not provide a much more nuanced portrait
of the Japanese enemy encountered on Guadalcanal. But unlike Tregaskis's
work, it does not assume that its American protagonists are paragons of heroic individuality. In fact, Jones was very critical of the "antiquated individual

heroism" Hollywood peddled to the masses in films such as *Sands of Iwo Jima* and *Guadalcanal Diary*. He said as much in a 1963 article for the *Saturday Evening Post*, an article tellingly titled "Phony War Films." In the era of total war, he argued, such romantic tropes "no longer pertained," but they nevertheless lived on in Hollywood, where they found expression in box-office successes like *Bataan* (1943) or, much later, *The Guns of Navarone* (1961).

In "Phony War Films," Jones suggested that modern combat made clichéd notions of individual initiative, heroism, and self-sacrifice—the hallmarks of the war-movie genre—obsolete. Total warfare rendered wartime death "totally reasonless and pointless," a result of nothing but "arbitrary chance" and "totally random selection."[40] Like frontline journalism, though, war films needed their heroes, their singular souls who fight and die in worlds with clear-cut consequences, worlds governed by an easy-to-follow calculus of cause and effect. War films needed to individualize death and make it meaningful, which is why they relied so heavily upon the idea of the hero.[41] But the real experience of war left no room for heroism. It represented nothing but "the regimentation of souls, the systematized reduction of men to animal level, the horror of pointless death, the exhaustion of living in constant fear."[42] As Jones saw it, modern war was mass annihilation all the way around, and amid its many victims the individual soldier, whether he was a "Misunderstood Leader," an "Individual Champion-Hero," or just an anonymous grunt, barely registered.[43]

The Red and the Green

Terrence Malick's adaptation of *The Thin Red Line* captures some of the haunting anonymity of total war in the Pacific. In this respect, it remains rather faithful to Jones's vision. We might even say that Malick's protagonists are even more interchangeable than Jones's, since they are not blessed with the time or the space required for full character development. Many of them contribute to the chorus of voice-over narration that accompanies the film's indelible imagery, but their contributions are indistinct and overlapping; it is often unclear which character is speaking, and from what vantage point, what place in time. So confusing was the setup that many early reviewers and critics mistakenly attributed the voice-overs of Private Train (John Dee Smith), who appears in just a handful of scenes, to Witt (Jim Caviezel), a more central character, just because they had similar accents.[44]

Figure 11. Jim Caviezel as a gentle Witt in *The Thin Red Line*.

Although we see a great deal of the gentle, inquisitive Witt on screen—and of Welsh (Sean Penn), his alter ego in both mood and demeanor—it is Train's voice that stands out on *The Thin Red Line*'s audio track.[45] In one particularly memorable soliloquy (loosely borrowed from John Steinbeck's 1939 *The Grapes of Wrath*, which John Ford made into a film a year later, starring Henry Fonda, whom Jim Caviezel resembles to an uncanny degree), he speculates that "maybe all men got one big soul who everybody's a part of. All faces of the same man. One big self."[46] Other characters, in different contexts, say similar things. Some are ruminating about their mortality, others are lamenting the fallenness of the world, lingering over past memories—of family or lovers—while doing so. But each and every voice-over represents a search for meaning, an attempt to make sense of a seemingly meaningless, death-filled, wartime experience.[47]

Although Malick's voice-overs echo the multiperspectival style of Jones's novel, they filter its narrative through precisely the kind of existential, theological sermonizing the book calls into question. Jones wanted to capture some of the dehumanizing horror of modern warfare; Malick seems intent on rescuing some of the humanizing hope that persists amid calamity and catastrophe. Jones demystifies; but Malick consoles. The process of adaptation is always one of alteration, and Malick's version of *The Thin Red Line* is a case in point, but if anything marks the transformation of the novel into the screenplay that eventually became the film, it is this shift in narrative focus: Malick trades the specifics of combat in the Pacific for a seemingly

Figure 12. Henry Fonda as Tom Joad in John Ford's *The Grapes of Wrath.*

timeless and transcendental exploration of war as kind of natural, perhaps even spiritual, force.[48]

In Malick's hands, *The Thin Red Line* becomes a more abstract, decontextualized work. Whereas Jones's novel is rooted in a gritty realism, Malick's film skews contemplative, philosophical, maybe even a little meandering. Malick's longtime agent Mike Medavoy, a producer on the film, described it as "very poetic, very religious."[49] Sloughing off the embodied psychological details of the novel, *The Thin Red Line* is reborn as a transcendental meditation for the big screen. As Stacey Peebles has argued, Malick's "dramatic excision of the book's bodily and sexual thematics" serves the purpose of highlighting the wonders and peculiarities of "the transcendental soul," especially as they are revealed in the unlikely context of combat.[50] Traces of this transformation suggest that Malick, while perhaps remaining true to Jones's overall vision, nevertheless broadened the narrative scope of *The Thin Red Line*, with a potentially distorting effect.

The changes Malick introduced into *The Thin Red Line* can be detected in his screenplay drafts, but they appear there only in embryonic form. The second draft remains close in spirit and tone to Jones's novel. The character of Witt, for example, is still the rough-around-the-edges wiseass Jones intended him to be. His redneck racism has been scrubbed away, but his standoffish nature remains. To be sure, Malick's decision to make Witt one of the central protagonists of his screenplay already marks a significant shift from

Jones's narrative, especially since Witt does not appear in the book until over a hundred pages in, but initially at least, Malick's Witt was still Jones's Witt. He was not yet the image of a selfless saint.[51]

In fact, in Malick's early screenplay drafts, each and every one of the characters remained close to Jones's descriptions of them. Captain Staros, for example, is still Captain Bugger Stein—still Jewish, that is, not Greek. And the other soldiers, from Fife to Bell to Storm to Keck to McCron and Doll and all the rest—there are some eighty-four characters listed in the "partial" company roster reproduced in the novel's prefatory pages; Malick's screenplays kept at least half of them—are identified by name and described with care. They have yet to become the eerily similar faces and almost interchangeable narrators seen and heard in the final film.

Malick's screenplays for *The Thin Red Line* show no sign of the poetic, philosophical narration that would permeate the finished film's audio track. Far from depicting a world-historical struggle between the forces of good and evil in the world—"What's this war in the heart of nature?" asks the film's famous opening voice-over from Train—Malick's second draft screenplay speaks only of the "esprit de corps," "the closeness of comradeship coming from having shared something a bit tougher than the rest."[52] On the page, Malick's adaptation remains a rather traditional war-film narrative, a story of combat-forged character and battle-tested bravery. If anything, the screenplays genuflect to the usual tropes of military heroics more often than the novel does, because they excise the psychosexual dynamics so central to Jones's narrative. Jones's frank exploration of wartime homosexuality disappears completely from Malick's scripts, even though the fraternity—and the fraternizing—remain.

In his screenplays, Malick did not change the plot of *The Thin Red Line* all that much, but he did choose to frame it in a way that readers of Jones's novel might not have expected. Signaling the shift, he added a telling epigraph to the second and third drafts of his screenplay. It came from a popular book by William Manchester, a veteran of the American campaign in the Pacific who went on to become a prominent author, journalist, and historian. *Goodbye, Darkness: A Memoir of the Pacific War* contains within its pages a moving depiction of Guadalcanal, drawn not just from contemporary description and historical research, but also, and more importantly, from personal memory. Manchester first came to know Guadalcanal as a soldier. When he arrived on the island, it was already occupied by American troops, having become a way station in the U.S. military's island-hopping campaign against the Japanese. Manchester was part of that massive assault, participating in the bloody battle for Okinawa near the end of war.

Goodbye, Darkness was published almost two decades after Jones's *The Thin Red Line*. It, too, attempts to make sense of the war, to find some kind of personal meaning in the traumas of the past. More lyrical than Jones's novel, Manchester's account of combat life nevertheless has much in common with *The Thin Red Line*, most notably its distaste for the high and mighty celebrations of martial service that continued to permeate popular culture decades later.

In Manchester's eyes, the war in the Pacific was anything but a war fought for big ideas like patriotism or democracy. Soldiers like him certainly did not see it that way. They fought mainly for their comrades. Combat was an intensely personal affair, "an act of love." "Those men on the line were my family, my home," Manchester writes. "They were closer to me than I can say, closer than my friends had been or ever would be. They had never let me down, and I could never do it to them. I had to be with them, rather than let them down and me live with the knowledge that I might have saved them. Men, I now know, do not fight for flag or country, for the Marine Corps or glory or any other abstraction. They fight for one another. Any man in combat who lacks comrades who will die for him, or for whom he is willing to do die, is not a man at all. He is truly damned."[53] This is Manchester's explanation for why, against orders, he snuck out of a field hospital and rejoined his company amid the brutal Okinawa campaign. The passage, which Malick chose as an epigraph for his screenplay, offers a clue as to how the psychosexual strain of Jones's narrative could be channeled into a seemingly less explicit account of heroic fraternity. It might also account for Witt's narrative arc in the film, culminating as it does with a heroic self-sacrifice to save the lives of his comrades. Early in the film he even says—to Hoke, while both are in the brig after going AWOL—"I love Charlie Company, they're my people."

This passage from Manchester's book was a fitting epigraph for Malick's screenplay, which focused more on fraternal bonds forged under fire and less on the physical and psychic immediacy of battle, the theme that had preoccupied Jones. The epigraph from Manchester shows that Malick was already tinkering with *The Thin Red Line*'s tone and message: he was finding room for meaning and purpose where Jones saw only the absurdity of total war.

But it was not only the subcurrent of romantic sacrifice that Malick appropriated from *Goodbye, Darkness*. He also borrowed from Manchester's descriptions of the natural environment. As any casual viewer of *The Thin*

Red Line knows, Malick's camera lingers on the natural wonders of the Melanesian landscape, with the north coast of Australia—Queensland's Daintree Rainforest—occasionally standing in for the Solomon Islands. These scenes evoke Manchester's description of his first glimpse of Guadalcanal as a young soldier:

> I thought of Baudelaire: *fleurs du mal*. It was a vision of beauty, but of evil beauty. Except for occasional patches of shoulder-high kunai grass, the blades of which could easily lay a man's hand open as quickly as a scalpel, the tropical forest swathed the island. From the APA's deck it looked solid enough to walk on. In reality the ground—if you could find it—lay a hundred feet below the cloying beauty of the treetops, the cathedrals of banyans, ipils, and eucalyptus. In between were thick, steamy, matted, almost impenetrable screens of cassia, liana vines, and twisted creepers, masked here and there by mangrove swamps and clumps of bamboo.

Guadalcanal's landscape was more sinister than even Baudelaire could have imagined. It was as if the environment itself was a threat, a mortal enemy:

> The forest seemed almost faunal: arrogant, malevolent, cruel; a great toadlike beast, squatting back, thrusting its green paws through ravines toward the shore, sulkily waiting to lunge when we were within reach, meanwhile emitting faint whiffs of foul breath, a vile stench of rotting undergrowth and stink lilies. Actually, we had been told in our briefings, there were plenty of real creatures awaiting us: serpents, crocodiles, centipedes, which could crawl across the flesh leaving a trail of swollen skin, land crabs which would scuttle in the night making noises indistinguishable from those of an infiltrating Jap, scorpions, lizards, tree leeches, cockatoos that screamed like the leader of a banzai charge, wasps as long as your finger, and spiders as large as your fist, and mosquitoes, mosquitoes, mosquitoes, all carriers of malaria.[54]

Nature could kill you just as swiftly as the Japanese.

But at the end of his chapter on Guadalcanal in *Goodbye, Darkness*, Manchester offers his readers a very different environmental portrait. The passage of time, he noticed, had transformed the place: no longer the anthropomorphically threatening entity he recalled from his time in the Marine Corps, the island is not so much threatening as indifferent. Visiting Guadalcanal as an aging tourist, Manchester finds everything changed. "The Canal is still essentially pristine," he writes. "I find the remains of a floating pier and two amphibian tractors, overgrown by vines and covered with nearly four decades of rust. Otherwise the fine-grained gray beach and the stately palms are much as they were on August 7, 1942."[55] "The war," Manchester continues, "was a major assault on the rainforests. It is scarcely remembered now. Nature holds all the cards." Seeing the battle of Guadalcanal as a struggle not merely between the Americans and the Japanese but between "man and the primeval forest," Manchester finally concludes that "the forest won; man withdrew, defeated by the masses of green and the diseases lurking there."[56]

All this is miles away from Jones's novel. But in one of the rare nonfiction texts he composed about his memories of the Second World War, Jones, too, remarked upon the spectacular natural beauty—and awesome power— of Guadalcanal. "God help me," he wrote, "it was beautiful." Decades after arriving on the island as a soldier, Jones still recalled the "delicious sparkling tropic sea" and "long beautiful beach," the palms "waving in the sea breeze" and "the dark green band of jungle" with "the mountains rising behind it." It was enough to "catch your breath with awe," to make one wonder "what it must have been like to live here before the armies came with their vehicles and numberless feet and mountains of supplies."[57]

Such imagery features prominently in Malick's version of *The Thin Red Line*. It dominates his compositions and demonstrates that he, like Manchester and Jones before him, yearned to see Guadalcanal in a pristine, pure, prelapsarian state—to catch a glimpse of it as it must have looked before the warships arrived. David Thomson has suggested that *The Thin Red Line* "is about a Pacific island where, for a moment, a war occurred. It is a botanical panorama in which the soldiers scurry and rant, like furious insects, lost in their attempt to win and survive. The island, its foliage, its fauna, and its light endure—as if the war was just a passing rainstorm."[58] Long before him, Tom Shone, reviewing *The Thin Red Line* for the *Sunday Times* of London, suggested Malick's movie was "filmed not from the point of view of the Japs who occupy the island, nor of the Americans who seek occupancy of the island, but from the point of view of the island itself."[59]

Other critics looked less kindly on the theme. *The Nation*'s Stuart Klawans deemed *The Thin Red Line* "the first New Age World War II movie," and Tom Whalen, writing in *Literature/Film Quarterly*, likened it to a "New Age promo."[60] Fans of the war-movie genre, expecting to see a detailed account of a key battle in the Pacific war, were particularly critical of the National Geographic aesthetic.[61] "*The Thin Red Line* does not tell the viewer enough about history," complained historian Kenneth T. Jackson in the American Historical Association's newsletter *Perspectives on History*. Its director "devotes too much footage to exotic animals, waving grass, happy natives, or light filtering through the trees." Jackson recommended returning to *Sands of Iwo Jima* or watching *Saving Private Ryan*—"the best American war movie of this decade"—instead.[62]

It did little to earn *The Thin Red Line* genre credibility, but the environmental focus of the film, which Malick borrowed from Manchester's memoir and squeezed out of some of Jones's occasional writings, distanced his picture from the well-worn tropes of the war film, giving it some of its philosophical patina.[63] The National Geographic aesthetic was a hallmark of Malick's vision. Recognizing this, Twentieth Century Fox made it the centerpiece of their advertising campaign. Promotional materials sent out ahead of *The Thin Red Line*'s release prepped audiences for what was in store: "The film presents a juxtaposition of a vicious mechanized battle taking place in a pristine wilderness, where the forces of destruction collide with a people living in quiet harmony with their natural surroundings; these were the Melanesians of the Solomon Islands, whose way of life centers on family and tranquility."[64] The press release read like some kind of warning label: beware, *The Thin Red Line* is not your typical war film.

Paths of Glory

The stunning natural beauty of *The Thin Red Line* sets it apart from most other war movies, especially those that spend the majority of their budgets on explosions (there are plenty of explosions in the film, though not nearly as many as in *Saving Private Ryan*). But it is not just the beauty of the Solomon Islands that interested Malick; it was also the question of how this beautiful, picturesque environment survived the cruelties inflicted upon it by the unrelenting onslaught of total warfare. Malick wanted to know just how it was that nature went about healing itself.

Examining Malick's sources and early scripts gets us only part of the way toward appreciating the nuances of this theme as it appears on screen. For it is only in later scripts, and in the braiding of cinematographer John Toll's stunning visuals with Malick's evocative voice-overs later on, that we can begin to locate the larger intentions of the picture, intentions that may have had their roots in Jones's novel and Manchester's memoir, but which stretched far beyond both, into the realms of philosophy and even, as I aim to show, theodicy.

The Thin Red Line offers a wide-angle perspective on modern combat. Its concession to war-movie action sequences is buried in the middle of the film and is framed by sights and sounds one does not typically encounter in the genre. It is these sequences, not the explosions, that should take precedence in any attempt to understand the picture. The film's patient contemplation of tropical waters, jungle canopies, and native villages has little to do with skirmishes and battles. These scenes highlight the natural beauty and harmony of Guadalcanal, but they also point to another temporality, another world, existing just outside the film's martial story line. Indeed, some of the film's most remarkable imagery seems to have been captured by accident, by looking askance at, if not away from, all the combat: a brilliantly blue butterfly floating through a firefight, for example, or shadows racing across a grassy hillside just after two soldiers are shot dead by a sniper.

Malick seems little interested in the events that propel his plot forward: capturing a hill, achieving a battlefield victory, defeating the enemy.[65] Instead, *The Thin Red Line* depicts the journey of isolated souls who, each in his own way, comes to consider the cosmic force, or forces—"the avenging power in nature" may not be "one power, but two," says Train in a voice-over at the start of the film—animating all living things. In this regard, we might say that the film aspires to ascend from the part to the whole, the particular to the universal.

This theme emerged slowly in the development of the picture. Only in the third draft of Malick's screenplay does it begin to appear. As if signaling a new, more transcendental focus, Welsh, on the very first page of the draft, describes himself as "the instrument of a laughing providence."[66] The third draft also contains the first detailed descriptions of the early scenes of the film, in which Privates Witt and Hoke hide out in an Edenic Melanesian village. As his stage directions indicate, Malick intended these scenes to stand in stark contrast to the combat sequences that would follow them. The screenplay describes Witt and Hoke, having gone AWOL, "living among the Melanesians, unconscious of the passage of days, of good and evil." "The native people," they notice, "live content with what the earth and sea provide them, in peace and harmony." Witt "marvels at a society where no one is alone or lives to himself, where all is

Figure 13. Worlds collide in a scene from *The Thin Red Line*.

based on family and clan."[67] With these lines Malick goes beyond both Jones and Manchester, steering our vision so far away from the generic themes of military valor to suggest the lineaments of something that was no war film at all. Not for nothing, then, does *The Thin Red Line* open and close with scenes depicting the Melanesian people and their world.

Taking liberties with Jones's characters and with Manchester's environmental musings (in Jones's book Witt is never AWOL, merely demoted and reassigned; in Manchester's book the Melanesians are not presented as romanticized stereotypes), Malick sets up a dramatic contrast between Indigenous and Western modes of existence, between native harmony with nature on the one hand and military-industrial demolition of it on the other. These divergent ways of being in the world produce different social arrangements—one defined by cooperation, the other alienation. Promotional materials emphasized the ways in which "the gentleness of the Melanesian people and their way of life provided a stark, often chilling contrast to the scale of wartime destruction surrounding them."[68] Malick's picture was not about American and Japanese men fighting on a faraway island; it was about the forced march of modernity, and all the ruthless violence and destruction it entailed.

Malick began exploring this theme long before his actors donned their replica uniforms. Ahead of principal photography, Jack Fisk, his trusted production designer, and John Toll, his cinematographer, put together a small "anthropological unit" so as to shoot scenes with the Melanesian people of the Solomon Islands that might later serve as a counterpoint to the military narrative anchoring the film's plot.[69] This "ethnographic" work, as Toll recalled, was "really interesting." The Solomon Islanders "had existed for centuries in this very peaceful and tropical place when they were suddenly invaded by all this large-scale violence."[70]

In addition to this, Malick began revising his screenplay: into later drafts he inserted new scenes meant to emphasize the war machine's violent incursion into the natural world. One example will suffice. As the American troops march deeper into the Guadalcanal landscape, there is this stage direction: "A stirring in the grass, a rustle of the sugar cane signals the approach of danger. At Keck's signal, the company stops. He pulls out a grenade and, stepping into the rows of cane, advances toward the source of the noise. He discovers a white cow. (A feral Indo-Chinese pig? They wandered loose, shellshocked.)"[71] The scene is a jump scare, but it is also a reminder that war brings suffering to all creatures, human and animal alike. It recalls similar images from *Days of Heaven* and foreshadows the menagerie of animals that will appear throughout the rest of *The Thin Red Line*, including tropical birds, bats, snakes, lizards, even a crocodile.[72]

These were not the only new additions to Malick's reworked screenplay. Some of the religious sentiments that would come to punctuate the film's many voice-overs began to appear as well. A scene depicting Floyd and McCron praying on the battlefield is representative of the more spiritual tone. In it, Floyd, "kneeling in the grass with his Bible" recites the well-known lines of Psalm 23 as McCron prays in his own words. "We stand here in the presence of Lucifer," he says. "I see Lucifer walking on the slopes." "I feel that if I opened my mouth, my soul might leap out of it," he frets. "This great evil—where does it come from? How did it steal into the world? What seed, what root, did it grow from?"[73] They are lines Malick would use later—almost verbatim—as voice-over narrations.

This version of *The Thin Red Line* is not interested in war or soldiers; it is interested in souls. More than this, it is interested in the way(s) in which some souls relate—or fail to relate—to others. It is interested in that power transcending all individual souls, the mysterious entity Ralph Waldo Emerson once called the "Over-Soul."[74] *The Thin Red Line* may be set in the era of total warfare, but its mood is reminiscent of nineteenth-century transcendentalism, which pondered the meaning of evil and loss, not to mention the place of the individual in society, the world, and the cosmos.

Many well-known artistic works, from the *Iliad* to *Saving Private Ryan*, have portrayed combat as a world-shaping force. Many philosophers have portrayed it this way, too. It was in confronting danger on the battlefield, Heidegger famously suggested, that a person's fundamental mortality, their "being-towards-death," was truly revealed.[75] But in *The Thin Red Line*, Malick turns away from such heroic existentialism, invoking a more pious American transcendentalism instead, which allows him to explore the feelings of loss, abandonment, and spiritual yearning obscured by romanticizations— like Heidegger's—of the "front experience." Robert Pippin is surely correct to say that Malick's film emphasizes neither the heroism nor the esprit de corps of modern combat, but rather the "isolation, alienation from others, and loneliness," that results from it.[76] But he overlooks the fact that Malick's jettisoning of the individual's perspective might leave room for an appreciation of that which stands above or beyond it.

Unlike generic war narratives, *The Thin Red Line* displays little interest in celebrating individual heroism or group camaraderie. These may have been prominent themes in Malick's earliest screenplay drafts, but they are almost entirely absent from the final film. In an attempt to manage viewer expectations, the studio sent out press materials conceding as much. "There are no heroes in THE THIN RED LINE," a season preview explained. "No one stands out under the numbing impact of war. Instead, we meet a dozen men who change, who suffer and who make essential discoveries about themselves."[77] Even if a hint of advertising hyperbole can be detected in that final clause, it is an apt description of the film. *The Thin Red Line* certainly has more to do with the search for meaning than the search for Japanese bunkers on Guadalcanal.

Malick's discomfort with the trope of military heroism owes a significant debt to Emerson, who thought heroism was something to "revere," but also something to be wary of. Representing the "extreme of individual nature," heroism "has pride" but is neither "philosophical" nor "holy."[78] Heroism's foregrounding of the individual comes at the expense of an appreciation for the larger forces of cosmic unfolding. Emerson thought focusing on heroes downplayed the importance of intersubjectivity, which makes all individualisms possible. It relegated the Over-Soul to what is, in essence, just a supporting role in world history. The heroic soul may think itself noble in its singularity, but the truth was that the Over-Soul shone through it, illuminating everything.[79] No individual, no matter how heroic, could stand wholly apart.[80] Everyone—and everything—is connected. One big soul.

In his famous essay "The Over-Soul," Emerson claims that individual souls reflect and refract wider creation. "Within one soul," he suggests, "is the soul of the whole."[81] This notion could, of course, be used to justify precisely

Figure 14. Animal life as seen up above in *The Thin Red Line*.

the kind of overweening individualism hero worship celebrates, the kind of self-satisfied solipsism that seems to mark so much of Emerson's thinking, with its emphasis on "Experience" and "Self-Reliance" (as two of his most famous essays are titled). But in "The Over-Soul" Emerson is adamant that individual uniqueness is but a small part of a much larger totality. "We see the world piece by piece, as the sun, the moon, the animal, the tree; but the whole, of which these are the shining parts, is the soul."[82] Even if individuals partake of this soul, it is clear, for Emerson, that they are but its pawns: "From within or from behind, a light shines through us upon all things, and makes us aware that we are nothing, but the light is all."[83] It is not a reverence for individual heroism that Emerson's essay "The Over-Soul" encourages, but rather "the love of the universal and eternal beauty."[84] Other individuals may propel us toward the creative activities of "conversation, competition, persuasion, cities, and war," but we must not forget "the identical nature appearing through them all." This "common nature," Emerson stressed, is "God."[85]

In many ways, "The Over-Soul" is the quintessential Emerson essay. Its romantic mood, its poetic prose, its grand philosophical gesture nestled in an intimate profession of faith—all of it conveys Emerson's unmistakable style. It makes for inspirational reading still, perhaps because it captures our continued uneasiness with the contingency and ambiguity of modern life. We have trouble accepting the idea that things do not happen for a reason. Emerson offers a way out of this abyss. His is a vision of the world, and of human life, saturated with meaning. Indeed, the profoundest error of modern thought, Emerson believed, was its vociferous denial of the cosmic interconnection of all things. Unlike the empiricists, on one side, and the rationalists, on the other, Emerson maintained that "one blood rolls uninterruptedly an endless circulation through all men, as the water of the globe is all one sea, and, truly seen, its tide is one." Emerson reminds his reader "that the Highest dwells with him; that the sources of nature are in his own mind."[86]

What Emerson thought knowledge of the Over-Soul promised was the ability to "see that the world is the perennial miracle which the soul worketh." To know this is to recognize "that there is no profane history; that all history is sacred; that the universe is represented in an atom, in a moment in time." It is to be conscious of the "divine unity" that "sees through all things."[87] This is a transcendentalist version of providence. Because it accepts as necessary the good and the bad, the joyous and the painful, it represents Emerson's attempt at articulating a theodicy.[88]

Emerson provides the inspiration for *The Thin Red Line*'s consoling conclusion: "Darkness and light. Strife and love. Are they the workings of one mind, the features of the same face?" Train asks in the film's final soliloquy. He then goes on, in true Emersonian fashion, to invite the Over-Soul into his world, to imbue it with meaning. "Oh my soul," he says, "let me be in you now. Look out through my eyes. Look out at the things you made. All things shining." The sentiment seems at odds with the images of carnage and chaos that have played out before us on screen, the sights and sounds of war that drove John Rawls and so many others away from theology—away from conceptions of God and divine providence—toward more secular understandings of truth and justice. But it is the concluding message of the film nevertheless.

In *The Thin Red Line*, it is not the worldly materialists who have the final say. They are there to tell us that there "ain't no world but this one" (Welsh), that "nature's cruel" (Tall, played with spit-and-venom-drenched rage by Nick Nolte), but it is Train who gets the last word. Playing the part of the chorus in an ancient Greek drama, he reframes all of the strife and struggle we have seen—the quarrels between Witt and Welsh, Tall and Staros, even, at one point, infighting among the Melanesians. Train reappears after all this, at the end of the film, to remind us to see the glory, to see all things shining. His voice is the last one we hear, expressing a desire to belong not merely to a family, group, unit, or nation, but to all of creation: he yearns to become one with the cosmos. Concluding with Train's words, *The Thin Red Line* fans the transcendental spark Emerson saw glowing behind all historical events.

John Rawls's later quest for justice took leave of theodicy and steered clear of such transcendentalist ideas, but one of his longtime colleagues in the philosophy department at Harvard remained intrigued by them. By the late 1960s few American philosophers bothered to read the writings of Emerson or his protégé Henry David Thoreau. Their work was deemed too rambling, too personal, too unscientific, to be taken seriously. Transcendentalism survived mostly in history, literature, or American studies departments. But things changed when Rawls's friend Stanley Cavell initiated an intellectual rescue operation of its legacy. His aim? To make Emerson and Thoreau relevant for philosophy once again.

Cavell came to Emerson and Thoreau somewhat late, turning to their work in earnest only after publishing his book on film, *The World Viewed*, in 1971. But his enthusiasm for their unique brand of moral self-reflection, which he later dubbed "perfectionism," was boundless.[89] In an essay from 1978, Cavell applauded Emerson's unswerving belief in the "evanescence of the world."[90] Glossing his essays "Experience" and "Circles," Cavell argued that "the universe is as separate from me, but as intimately part of me, as one on whose behalf I contest, and who therefore bears the color I wear. We are in a state of 'romance' with the universe," Cavell maintained. "We do not possess it, but our life is to return to it, to respond to its contesting for my attention, in ever-widening circles," until, as Emerson put it, "'the soul attains her due sphericity.'"[91]

In Cavell's eyes, Emerson's spiritualism was not something to be avoided or explained away. In search of the "sphericity" that brings all things together under the aegis of the Over-Soul, Emerson was an important voice in "the unending quarrel between philosophy and theology."[92] Echoes of his ideas could be found everywhere. Cavell thought Heidegger's idea of "poetic dwelling," for example, resonated with Emerson's desire not just to understand the world but also to receive it as a gift—to move from the tasks and chores of "philosophy" or "religion" and arrive at the true experience of "thinking," which, Heidegger suggested, was etymologically connected to "thanking."[93]

Heidegger's suggestion that "thinking" stems from "thanking" found fullest expression in some of his most well-known postwar essays, such as "Building Dwelling Thinking" and "'. . . Poetically Man Dwells. . . .'" It also appeared in the lecture course published as *What Is Called Thinking?* that Cavell had used to interpret *Days of Heaven* in *The World Viewed*.[94] In these late-career works, Heidegger suggested that true thinking, which he adamantly distinguished from academic philosophy, represented "the thanks owed for being."[95] *What Is Called Thinking?* stressed the idea. More meditative, more chastened and poetic, than Heidegger's earlier works, it was a far cry from those essays and lectures of the interwar years, in which he had embraced the existential, world-historical struggle (*Kampf*) celebrated by the many propagandists of National Socialism, Hitler foremost among them. At that time, Heidegger was a firm believer in Heraclitus's claim that "war is both father of all and king of all."[96]

After the Second World War, though, Heidegger abandoned martial rhetoric. He turned away from his earlier focus—in *Being and Time*—on "finitude" and "being-towards-death." He wrote less about strife and more about poetry and piety, attunement and gratitude. Since "we receive many gifts, of many kinds," including our "essential nature," he intoned in *What Is Called Thinking?*, we are called to thinking not by struggle, but by thankfulness. "Pure thanks" is not to "repay gift with gift," he claimed, but to "simply think—think what is really and solely given, what is there to be thought."[97]

What Is Called Thinking? was translated into English by an American veteran of the Second World War, J. Glenn Gray, who, after serving as a counterintelligence officer in Europe, taught philosophy at Colorado College.[98] Gray may have helped to disseminate Heidegger's ideas in the English-speaking world, but he did not always agree with them. Although he admired *What Is Called Thinking?* and thought it represented a good a point of entry into Heidegger's extensive philosophical corpus, he was wary of Heidegger's subterranean romanticism—the very thing to which Cavell was so attracted. In one of the last essays he wrote before his death, Gray even went so far as to caution against the easy acceptance of Heidegger's thought. He worried about Heidegger's preference for the poetic over and against the prosaic, his escape from the concrete here and now into a diffuse realm of romantic rambling. Referencing the essay "'. . . Poetically Man Dwells . . . ,'" Gray made the point that poetry remained an empty consolation if it had no real-world application: we "must first build a house in a very literal sense in order to dwell in it poetically as a home," he wrote.[99] The sentiment recalled his good friend Hannah Arendt's famous description of Heidegger as "the last (we hope) romantic" of the German intellectual tradition.[100]

Splendor in the Grass

Is Malick the last romantic of American cinema?[101] Reactions to *The Thin Red Line* were polarizing from the start, and many of them hinged on precisely this question. Responses to the film's transcendental ruminations—its

allusions to Emerson and Wordsworth, for example—stretched from the infuriated to the mesmerized.[102] Rarely, if ever, were critics indifferent. The
film's success or failure depended on how receptive viewers were to the
grand questions posed by the film's philosophical voice-overs: Why am I
here? How shall I make sense of this suffering? Or, more grandly, "What's
keeping us from reaching out, touching the glory," as Train intones in the
second half of the film, while we watch Witt return to the Melanesian village, finding the formerly peaceful locale now beset by conflict. The scene is
a vision of fallenness, of expulsion from Eden, something Malick made central to his film from the very start. "Malick's Guadalcanal," said producer
Bobby Geisler, "would be a Paradise Lost, an Eden, raped by the green poison, as Terry used to call it, of war."[103]

    But it was not just *The Thin Red Line*'s audio track that tripped up com-
mentators; for many critics, the picture's poetic visuals of this Paradise Lost
were just as confounding. Just what were all those shots of sunlight cascad-
ing through the dense jungle canopy, of exotic animals seeming to return the
gaze of the camera lens, of tall grasses bending in the breeze, doing in a war
film? Nature is afforded pride of place in Malick's *Thin Red Line* compositions, and this positioning says something important about the film's overall message, for if there is a line running from Emerson through Heidegger,
up to and including Cavell and even Gray—who in his book *The Promise of
Wisdom* held out hope for a reconciliation of "the individual and his world"—
it is the long green line of nature.[104] *The Thin Red Line* is defined as much by
this line as the red one of its title, for between the lonely, isolated subjectivity
of the soldier and the spiritual intersubjectivity of the Over-Soul, Malick spies
a creation vibrating in glorious splendor. *The Thin Red Line*'s depiction of nature's terrifying bounty points to a cosmic belonging that sustains humanity, even and especially as human beings attempt to destroy it.

    James Jones's novel suggested that "the teeming verdure" of Guadalcanal
made the men of C-for-Charlie Company "fearful."[105] It was an observation
seconded by Manchester's memoir, *Goodbye, Darkness*. Malick's film captures
some of this fear—its opening shot, set to the ominous first notes of Hans
Zimmer's score, is of a menacing crocodile slipping into algae-green
water—but it more frequently revels in the tremendous beauty of the natural
world, beauty in danger of being obliterated by the war machine.[106] The way
a warship's black, billowing smoke blots out the beautiful, rosy sunset sky of
a South Pacific seascape is but one of many such instances. Such shots, especially when accompanied by nondiegetic voice-overs, frustrate genre expec-

Figure 15. The war machine's incursion into nature in *The Thin Red Line*.

tations. They invite what Carl Plantinga has labeled "affective incongruity," which encourages "a ruminative and contemplative mode of film viewing."[107] They turn our attention to nature so as to elicit a sense of wonder, a feeling not usually associated with war movies.

Emerson thought the Over-Soul was best glimpsed in nature. The dramatic and awe-inspiring cinematography of *The Thin Red Line* seems to agree with him. It suggests that nature stands closer to the Over-Soul than humanity does. It is a telling marker of our distance from, or our nearness to, the divine. Emerson's essay "Nature" puts it plainly: "Man is fallen; nature is erect, and serves as a differential thermometer, detecting the presence or absence of the divine sentiment in man."[108] But viewed from the right perspective, nature could also be a conduit to divinity: "We are escorted on every hand through life by spiritual agents, and a beneficent purpose lies in wait for us. We cannot bandy words with nature, or deal with her as we deal with persons. If we measure our individual forces against hers, we may easily feel as if we were the sport of an insuperable destiny. But if, instead of identifying ourselves with the work, we feel that the soul of the workman streams through us, we shall find the peace of the morning dwelling first in our hearts, and the fathomless powers of gravity and chemistry, and, over them, of life, preëxisting within us in their highest form."[109]

Emerson wants us to see that we are not merely pawns in the game of providence; we are providence itself. Hence the seemingly paradoxical invitation in that final, concluding monologue from Train: "O my soul, let me be in you now. Look out through my eyes. Look out at the things you made. All things shining." Train does not ask to be a part of creation so much as for creation—the Over-Soul materialized—to be a part of him. The line recalls Emerson's stirring conclusion to "Nature": "Let the victory fall where it will, we are on that side. And the knowledge that we traverse the whole scale of being, from the centre to the poles of nature, and have some stake in every possibility, lends that sublime lustre to death, which philosophy and religion have too outwardly and literally striven to express in the popular doctrine of the immortality of the soul. The reality is more excellent than the report. Here is no ruin, no discontinuity, no spent ball. The divine circulations never rest nor linger."[110]

These words find a visual echo in the last scenes of *The Thin Red Line*. Hints of them appear in Malick's screenplays. The third draft has Fife walking along the seashore as he prepares to leave Guadalcanal. He "sees the broken shells, the wavy lines of wrack, a germinating coconut. Is life like the sea, brutal and relentless? Does it know, or care, whom it smashes on the rocks?"[111] But life goes on, the unfolding of nature, the work of the Over-Soul, continues. "Stalks of red ginger glow amid strangler figs and vines," the script says. "Outside a leaf chapel, a group of Melanesians are singing. The stream where Dale stopped to drink the bloody water flows clear again." All of it was meant to suggest that "in time the earth will cleanse itself."[112]

Malick's screenplay ends here, where Jones's novel does. It has troops walking past a newly constructed cemetery: "Big sprinklers send their long gossamer jets swirling through the air above the crosses. Already grass rises from the grave mounds."[113] But the final shot of *The Thin Red Line*, which is not in Jones's novel and is but a minor aside in Malick's screenplays, is of the germinating coconut, situated amid an expanse of sea and sky.

Such images of rebirth and regeneration—not simply the whitewashed crosses of individual gravesites, so similar to the imagery of *Guadalcanal Diary*, but also the tender grass sprouting from a graveyard's soil and a coconut sending forth new shoots—are the visual equivalent of a theodicy: they offer an explanation—a justification—for death, for loss, and for human suffering. They transform meaninglessness into meaning. The scenes channel the transcendentalist sentiments of Emerson's essays.[114] In "Circles," for example, Emerson professes that "all things renew, germinate, and spring."[115] Similar notions can be found in the writings of Thoreau, too.[116] But unlike his mentor, the future author of *Walden* knew nature was "no saint."[117] In his

Figure 16. Contemplating the end of life in *The Thin Red Line*.

Figure 17. A vision of life continuing in *The Thin Red Line*.

journals, he wondered if there was not in fact an "avenging power in nature," a contrasting power to the forces of renewal and germination. This suggested that the world might be governed by "two powers," not just one.[118]

Any theodicy worthy of the name will have to take both these forces into account, the life giving as well as the life taking. Thinkers across the centuries have accorded different weights to each. Some theodicies are meant to humble, others to console.[119] Malick's version of *The Thin Red Line* leans toward the latter. In some sequences of the film, his theodicy has an explicitly Christian cast. Witt's Christlike demeanor is illustrative of it, especially because he is seen repeatedly—almost exclusively—comforting wounded and dying soldiers. Similarly, a fleeting shot of Train early in the film, below deck on a ship taking him to Guadalcanal, invokes Christian faith in providence. In it, we see that Train has "1 John 4:4" tattooed on his upper arm. It is a reference to the First Epistle of John, which preaches faith and hope in transcendence: "You belong to God, children, and you have conquered them," the verse reads, "for the one who is in you is greater than the one who is in the world."

This visual cue sheds light on at least one of Train's voice-overs late in the film, after the major battle sequences have taken place. "One man looks at the dying bird and thinks there's nothing but unanswered pain, that death's got the final word," Train says. "Another man sees that same bird, feels the glory, feels something smiling through it." The lines bring to mind images, seen earlier in the film, of a fledgling bird struggling to survive amid the dark recesses of the jungle floor. At that point in the picture, the scene seemed to symbolize death, but Train redescribes it here as an intimation of "glory." The suffering we have seen on screen suddenly takes on a new, potentially reassuring meaning. Maybe, in retrospect, it can all be viewed differently, not as a record of pointless death and destruction, but as an intimation of transcendence.

In *The Thin Red Line*, it is not just American soldiers who come to this realization. One of the remarkable aspects of the film is the way it depicts the Japanese: they, too, are bound to each other by fraternal bonds (we see them valiantly defending their wounded); they, too, are religious (in one scene, a captured soldier meditates in a state of unbelievable serenity amid the chaos of battle); they, too, have interior monologues laced with spirituality—even after they have been killed. "Do you imagine your sufferings will be less because you loved goodness, truth?" one says to Witt, seemingly from the other side. These scenes suggest that, like Emerson, Malick views faith and belief in a more inclusive, ecumenical, and universal way than has been acknowledged by some critics and commentators. The arc of *The Thin Red Line* runs from death to life, from meaningless loss to meaningful redemption, and it gives every one of its characters the chance to participate in it—even the dead. A transcendental faith sustains the film, but it is by no means exclusively Christian.[120]

The Thin Red Line is representative of Malick's mature filmmaking style. Combining philosophical voice-overs with majestic images of the natural world, hushed tones with unexpected editing, it is inescapably his: nobody would confuse it with the work of any of his peers. Who else but Malick would

open a film with Thoreau's talk of the "avenging power in nature" and conclude it with Emerson's paean to the Over-Soul? Still, contrary to popular
opinion, Malick did not make Jones's novel into captivating cinema simply
by injecting some pretty images and a bit of philosophical dialogue into his
scripts and production notes. Contrary to what Anthony Lane humorously
suggested in his *New Yorker* review of the movie, Malick did not sit down
and slap "a copy of Emerson on top of the Jones" when he wrote his screenplays.[121] The transcendentalist glaze that makes *The Thin Red Line* shine was
applied only at a much later stage. And, as it turns out, Malick may have had
some help in fashioning it.

However Malickian it is, *The Thin Red Line* is still an adaptation. Its philosophical content stems, first and foremost, from its source material. As R.
Barton Palmer has observed, Malick's film highlights and emphasizes spiritual themes that were already very close to James Jones's own heart. While
these themes received scant attention in his Guadalcanal novel, they found
fuller expression in some of his other, even more sprawling works, including
From Here to Eternity and *Some Came Running*. The latter, in particular, contains long passages ruminating on life, death, and the possibility of reincar-
nation, passages not unlike some of the voice-overs in Malick's film.

With this in mind, we can see how Malick took up Jones's baton and ran
with it. In supplying *The Thin Red Line* "with a sense of transcendental experience," it may even be the case that, as Palmer puts it, Malick "out-Joneses
Jones."[122] His vision for the picture did not deviate from the fundamental
message of Jones's work, it merely amplified it. This might explain why Malick won the praise and admiration of Jones's widow, Gloria, as well as his
daughter Kaylie.[123] Precisely because he chose to transform *The Thin Red Line*
into a highly meditative work, Malick proved himself to be Jones's true, transcendentalist heir.

According to Steven R. Carter, James Jones was a longtime devotee of the-
osophy, Eastern mysticism (especially teachings related to the idea of
karma), and, of course, Emerson, in whose work he found not just philosophical inspiration but also an epigraph for *From Here to Eternity*: "The Sphinx
must solve her own riddle. If the whole of history is in one man, it is all to be
explained from individual experience."[124] As Carter has argued, Jones leaned
on Emerson to develop an elaborate "spiritual system" of his own over the
course of his writing career: "He believed in the unity of God or the Over-
Soul, the temporary separation of egos like drops of the ocean being left on
the shore, the expansion of these seeming fragments into selves, and their

subsequent spiritual growth through ego-reduction until they are worn
down enough (and compassionate enough) to be reabsorbed into the Over-
Soul."[125] Jones may have come to regret the "excessive didacticism" of his
early writing—especially after the critical failure of *Some Came Running*, his
follow-up to *From Here to Eternity*, which contained some of his lengthiest
digressions concerning his spiritual beliefs—but he never jettisoned the idea
that the Over-Soul was behind everything. He just tried to convey this notion
in subtler ways. We can see as much in *The Thin Red Line*, a novel that buries
its spiritual pontificating beneath many layers of gritty psychological realism.[126] But if you know where to look for them, you can see Jones's spiritual
impulses shining through many of its pages. As Carter puts it, *The Thin Red
Line*'s underlying message—that "man's separation from God is merely the
starting point for a gradual development and reabsorption into God"—is
borne out by Jones's decision to depict not the "the proud, brave, super-
masculine animals who fight wars but the sensitive humans who emerge
from the suffering of combat."[127] For Jones, divinity was to be found in weak-
ness, not strength. He believed that it truly was the meek who would inherit
the earth. It is an idea to which Malick has returned again and again throughout his career.

Perhaps the most remarkable aspect of Malick's adaptation of Jones's
novel is the way it isolates and foregrounds the vein of Emersonian belief buried deep within its pages. Not only did Malick excavate this rich, philosophical deposit, he also found a way to visualize it, to put it on the big screen.
Because so much of the film's transcendental feel was absent from Malick's
early screenplay drafts, though, we might conclude that it was only while filming and editing the picture that he found a way to do it justice. Right up until
the very last days of production, Malick was constantly exploring. John C.
Reilly, who played Sergeant Storm in the film, "quickly realized" that Malick
was "more of a philosopher than a filmmaker." He was more interested in
"looking for the truth every day" than he was in getting shots in the can.[128]
And as many of the editors who have worked with him over the years have
explained, much of Malick's artistic work occurs only after the cameras have
stopped rolling and the footage is compiled, assembled, and reassembled over
the course of many months: the editing process of *The Thin Red Line* spanned
over a year and a half.[129]

In some of his later films, Malick practically abandoned scriptwriting altogether, focusing instead on the improvisational and spontaneous possibilities that arise during the process of shooting and editing a motion

picture. Even though its script was adapted from a literary source, and underwent extensive revisions, *The Thin Red Line* points in this experimental direction. The chasm between printed word and finished film is vast. On the page, Malick's movie mirrors Jones's novel rather faithfully; on the screen, however, it is a wholly different piece of work, an audiovisual exploration—if not a celebration—of the Over-Soul that turns the genre of the war movie on its head. It is nothing less than a cinematic theodicy. Whether or not it out-Jonesed Jones, as Palmer claims, it certainly dug a little deeper into the human condition than most film audiences were willing to venture at the time. Overshadowed by Steven Spielberg's *Saving Private Ryan*, which was released just months prior to *The Thin Red Line*, Malick's film was a piece of poetry stranded in what was rapidly becoming a comic-book world.[130]

*   *   *

The Thin Red Line has generated the most critical commentary of all of Malick's films. Not all of it tends toward praise. As we have seen, early reviewers decried Malick's "pretty abstractions and ontologies," claiming they had no place in a war movie.[131] Only after other critics panned or dismissed *The Thin Red Line* as too long, too beautiful, or too philosophical—especially in comparison with *Saving Private Ryan*, for which Spielberg won the Academy Award for directing—did some commentators begin the long process of rescuing and responding to the film's more philosophical moments. Sounding an expressly theological note, a reviewer for *Commonweal*, for example, described the film as nothing less than a stirring "vision of war as Original Sin."[132] Similarly, F. X. Feeney, writing in *L.A. Weekly*—and writing against his colleague Manohla Dargis, the *Weekly*'s regular film critic at the time—defended Malick's "moral argument," praising its attempt to explore, if not to define, "what it means to be human."[133]

Malick's interest in the question of "what it means to be human" can be traced back to his student days at Harvard, and probably long before that. Over the years, he has amassed a great wealth of poetic, philosophical, and theological material to work with, some, but not all, of which made it into *The Thin Red Line*. Even aborted projects from his twenty-year absence from the director's chair found their way into the film. Chief among these were the scripted but unfilmed "The English Speaker," which used the birth of psychoanalysis in 1880s Vienna as an excuse to investigate the theme of existential suffering, and an adaptation of Kenji Mizoguchi's *Sansho the*

Bailiff (1954) for the stage. Like "The English Speaker," the *Sansho the Bailiff* project failed to find adequate financial backing, but it gave Malick yet another opportunity to address big themes, in this case nothing less than the eternal struggle between good and evil in the world. Its exploration of the theme of mercy, in particular, proved especially relevant to *The Thin Red Line*, so much so that Malick pilfered his own stage play for material to add to the dead Japanese soldier's memorable soliloquy in the film.[134]

Given the prevalence of such theodicy-redolent themes in Malick's version of *The Thin Red Line*, philosophers and philosophically minded critics have been captivated by it. Cavell thought it nothing less than "astonishing." It had "moments of transcendence" that he simply could not get out of his head.[135] But whereas he emphasized *The Thin Red Line*'s visual compositions, others tended to gravitate toward the film's lyrical and enigmatic voice-overs, replete as they are with transcendental rumination. Some commentators have fixated on the echoes of Emerson and Thoreau, others on Heidegger, John Steinbeck, even Homer.[136]

Inquiries into the philosophy of *The Thin Red Line* have ranged widely over this vast intellectual terrain, sometimes losing their bearings along the way. Marc Furstenau and Leslie MacAvoy have argued that the film constitutes a distinctly "Heideggerian cinema," a conclusion also reached, though for slightly different reasons, by Robert Sinnerbrink.[137] For their part, Leo Bersani and Ulysse Dutoit maintain, somewhat confusingly, that *The Thin Red Line* is about "the ontological impossibility of individuality."[138] Meanwhile Kaja Silverman highlights the "unbearable negativity" of *The Thin Red Line* and tries to show how it anchors a complex philosophical project of mourning.[139] Like Silverman, Simon Critchley focuses almost exclusively on the character of Witt, who runs headlong toward his sacrificial death at the film's end. Critchley interprets Witt's actions as an existentialist meditation on the meaning of mortality.[140] Against this interpretation, though, Hubert Dreyfus and Camilo Salazar Prince offer a more nuanced account of the film, emphasizing Witt's "spiritual immortality" rather than his stoicism.[141] Taking yet another approach, David Davies, drawing upon the work of phenomenologists such as Maurice Merleau-Ponty, praises the film's depiction of "embodied engagement with the world."[142] And, last but not least, Robert Pippin addresses what he calls *The Thin Red Line*'s "vernacular metaphysics."[143]

It is no doubt a testament to the richness of Malick's film that so many philosophers can come away from it with such varied responses. But isolating just one of the many philosophical and theological themes addressed in the film's many voice-overs—such as the experience of death (Critchley) or the making and unmaking of worlds (Dreyfus and Salazar Prince) or the meaning of metaphysics today (Pippin)—forces a sprawling work of art through the all-too-restricting eye of the philosophical needle. Indeed, few commentators, whether philosophically inclined or not, have widened their focus enough to examine how the intellectually suggestive voice-overs of *The Thin Red Line* are but isolated gems within the totality of film. They settle for what Emerson in his Over-Soul essay called "particular wonders," which are but small components of the larger, "perennial miracle which the soul worketh" in the world. It is this larger miracle of the soul, I would argue, that Malick attempts to capture.[144] The magic of *The Thin Red Line* derives from its weaving of so many different influences and sources into a seemingly seamless whole, one singing the praises of the Over-Soul.

It helps to view *The Thin Red Line* as a palimpsest. Its base layer comes from James Jones's novel, but even that draws upon a whole tradition of war writing going back to Tregaskis's *Guadalcanal Diary*. As we have seen, Jones's novel jettisoned the pieties of previous World War II narratives, both literary and cinematic, but that did not prevent it from being adapted, in 1964, into a generic film directed by Andrew Marton starring Keir Dullea and Jack Warden. Malick's adaptation goes beyond it, and it does so by putting *The Thin Red Line* in conversation with Jones's spiritualism. But Malick also incorporates other influences as well, such as Manchester's memoir *Goodbye, Darkness* and Stanley Kubrick's *Paths of Glory* (1957), a film he had studied at AFI.[145]

All of this preceded the bold choices yet to come, by which I mean the improvisation that marked Malick's filming and editing of *The Thin Red Line*. As actor Ben Chaplin, who played Bell, explained to an interviewer, "dialogue Terry had honed over the years, when he gets behind the camera on the hill, he doesn't care about it anymore, he just tosses it away. It's all about the moment. True film-making."[146] Malick tried everything he could to prevent *The Thin Red Line* from feeling staged. This included shooting much of the film in a documentary style, and instructing his actors to act as if they were appearing in a silent movie.[147] With a bit of humor, John C. Reilly recalled his director telling him he was "slightly disappointed when you all open your mouths to speak. I almost wish the picture could play like a silent picture." Reilly realized then and there that his character's one big speech would never make the final cut: "There's a picture of a bug on a leaf instead," he joked.[148]

Malick himself may not have known what his movie was about until he started filming it. Some hint of *The Thin Red Line*'s obsession with the natural world can be located in his screenplays, but it was only when shooting began that Malick turned his full attention to the flora, fauna, and people of the Solomon Islands. According to Leslie Jones, one of the editors who worked on the film, Malick often preferred viewing the nature footage shot by his second unit camera crew and the so-called "anthropological unit" over any of the material depicting the military sequences at the center of the film's narrative.[149] In essence, Malick "was shooting another movie at the same time."[150] Or as George Stevens Jr., one of the film's producers, put it, "Terry was making a big Hollywood war movie while ruminating cinematically on life, death, and creation."[151]

Perhaps Malick, like Witt, had seen "another world." These two worlds came together only in postproduction, with Emerson, Thoreau, and maybe a little Cavell and Heidegger serving to suture them together in voice-overs written, recorded, and added, one index card at a time.[152] Together with the film's complex and evocative sound design—as well as its score, which at one point quotes modernist composer Charles Ives's Emerson-inspired piece "The Unanswered Question"—this poetic voiceover track was but the finishing touch on a painstakingly produced picture.[153] As Sean Penn later put it: Malick "is a purist. I think he makes the movie three times, once when he writes the script, once when he's shooting it and there's another writing period in the editing room."[154]

Nowhere to be found in the previous iterations of the project, from Jones's novel to Manchester's memoir to Malick's screenplay, the thoughts and musings captured in *The Thin Red Line*'s voice-overs transform the work into something entirely unique. But they should not be interpreted as any kind of definitive final word: *The Thin Red Line* is a complex amalgamation of voice, vision, and sound; each layer of it adding something unique to its overall effect. Exploring *The Thin Red Line*'s rich and varied genealogy helps us appreciate both its philosophical daring and its openness to ongoing interpretation. It shows us that the line stretching from Tregaskis to Jones to Manchester may have been a long one, but it was no longer—and no thinner—than the one linking Heraclitus and Emerson to Heidegger, Cavell, and Malick. Whether or not these lineages reach all the way back to the Over-Soul, the gods, or God, remains an open, unanswered question.

CHAPTER 4

Ways of Worldmaking

Beginnings and Endings
in *The New World*

> For mankinde they say a woman was made first, which by
> the working of one of the goddes, conceived and brought
> foorth children: And in such sort they say they had their
> beginning.
>
> —Thomas Hariot

Jamestown holds a special, though problematic, place in the American political imaginary. As the first English settlement to survive in North America, it has come to symbolize the birth of a nation. But that birth, in 1607, was a painful one, its trauma passed down through generations. One does not have to look far for examples of Jamestown's contested legacy today. Recent national reckonings with anti-Black violence, systemic racism, and socioeconomic inequality have made it a flashpoint once again. They have reignited debates about how Jamestown should be commemorated—or, indeed, if it should be commemorated at all. Much of the current conversation has been generated by an investigative project spearheaded by the journalist Nikole Hannah-Jones at the *New York Times*. The title of the ongoing endeavor—"The 1619 Project"—is significant, for it refers not to the date of the first arrival of English colonists in what would become Virginia, but rather to that of enslaved Africans.[1]

The myth of Jamestown all too often overshadows the historical reality. For apologists and critics alike, Jamestown remains a convenient origin story for settler colonialism. It is where the Old World supposedly discovered the New; where Western civilization made contact with the so-called noble savage; where liberty and industry stamped out the evils of tyranny, idleness, and heathenism. But it also signifies devastation and exploitation, not to mention genocide.

Many stories have been told about Jamestown, almost all of them outsized and overdetermined. Their register is mythological rather than historical. The most famous one centers upon an early explorer and colonist named John Smith and a Powhatan girl he came to know as Pocahontas. Smith's accounts of their encounter—the first of them, *A True Relation*, was published in 1608, followed by the much longer, and probably more imaginative, *The Generall Historie of Virginia, New-England, and the Summer Isles* in 1624 and *The True Travels, Adventures, and Observations of Captaine John Smith* in 1630—had their fair share of fanciful flourishes, including a dramatic scene (recounted in both *The Generall Historie* and *The True Travels*) in which Pocahontas, Chief Powhatan's daughter, saved him from certain death. In one version of the story, Smith had been "taken prisoner by the Savages," "tied to a tree to be shot to death," then "fatted as he thought, for sacrifice to their Idoll," only to be rescued by Pocahontas's last-minute intercession on his behalf.[2] The other version was simpler, describing natives "ready with their clubs, to beate out his braines" until Pocahontas, "the Kings dearest daughter," arrived on the scene to stay his bludgeoning.[3] Smith would live, and, according to legend, fall in love.

However fanciful the story was, it set the tone for everything that was to come: stories, poems, songs, even, eventually, a Disney musical. What all these cultural artifacts have in common is the praise of new beginnings. Smith's writings were tall tales that described a virgin land, full of abundance and possibility, awaiting anybody daring enough to seek it out.[4] Thanks to him—and to a handful of other chroniclers and explorers, such as the polymath intellectual Thomas Hariot and the explorer-artist John White—Virginia would be remembered as something more than a minor colonial outpost in a far-flung land. It came to represent nothing less than a radical rebirth for all mankind.

It was a common trope of European Renaissance writing during the so-called Age of Discovery, but it said more about the Europeans than it did the lands and peoples they encountered. "In discovering America," historian J. H. Elliott once suggested, "Europe had discovered itself." Or the fantasy of itself, anyway: "For if America nurtured Europe's ambitions, it also kept its dreams alive. And perhaps dreams were always more important than realities in the relationship of the Old World and the New."[5]

Keeping the dream alive was a key component of the Jamestown myth. But the meaning of the dream changed over time. The writings of figures such as Hariot and Smith soon became the building blocks of not just European fantasies but also a new national mythology. Like all nationalisms, this one entailed both inclusion and exclusion: the story of Jamestown heralded the arrival of new Americans, but it also ushered everybody else into the minor roles of the nationalist pageant, if it did not usher them offstage completely. In the Jamestown myth, appearance and disappearance went hand in hand.

Seen from the perspective of the enslaved, the indentured, or the displaced (as the Indigenous populations of the mid-Atlantic soon would be), the establishment of Jamestown in 1607 was hardly something to celebrate. But in the years after 1776, people calling themselves Americans transformed it into something of a sacred origin story. Repurposing the Jamestown myth for their own ends, they came to view the colony not so much as a link back to lands and traditions across the Atlantic as a new, unprecedented venture into a utopian future. Jamestown was still the symbol of opportunity and progress Smith had prophesied, but it belonged to a new constituency.

The settlement came to embody the burgeoning national ethos of the United States of America: it represented diligence, ingenuity, and hard work; a hardened determination to turn the untamed bounty of nature into an orderly, productive plantation. All this despite the fact that Jamestown's early years were—according to the documentary record, at least—disastrous, full of privation and widespread starvation brought on not only by chance but also by the failure of English willpower. Smith himself acknowledged that some of the first colonists were at times "in such dispaire" that "they would rather starve and rot with idleness, then be perswaded to do anything for their own reliefe."[6] Things did not improve much over time: almost a hundred years later, John Locke could still view Virginia as something of a political failure, a colony run by greedy governors who displayed little to no "public spirit."[7]

But the Jamestown legend consistently won out over the facts. Throughout the history of the United States, the legend was recycled and retold so many times that it became a keystone of the nation's political self-understanding. It became the subject of ritual celebrations. Every half century throughout the nineteenth and twentieth centuries, the 1607 founding of the colony was feted with lavish commemorations. While the symbolism of these events varied according to the contemporary climate, their political import never wavered.[8] To celebrate Jamestown was to indulge in unabashed displays of jingoism. By the turn of the twentieth century—when, as Daniel

Immerwahr has noted, the nation went from being called just the United States or the Republic of the Union to the more aggrandizing America—that jingoism found a global stage on which to display itself.[9] The tercentennial Jamestown celebration of 1907 projected American imperial power abroad with a flotilla of formidably armed ships. In the words of one historian, it was "one of the greatest showings of American military force in peacetime," a showcase for Theodore Roosevelt's "big stick" foreign policy.[10]

The drumbeat resumed fifty years later, when Jamestown became a prop in Cold War–era propaganda. The 1957 celebration projected a new kind of U.S. political and military dominance. Three U.S. Air Force F-100 Super Sabre fighter jets reenacted the transatlantic voyage of the *Discovery*, the *Susan Constant*, and the *Godspeed*, the seventeenth-century ships that had brought the original colonists across the seas.[11] It was a long way from Captain Smith and Pocahontas, but the point was obvious enough: a direct line of progress connected Jamestown to NATO. The United States was—and would remain—the leader of the free world. What began as a minor colony on a far-flung coast had matured into a mighty global power, a paragon of freedom and democracy: "not the least of the achievements of the 350th anniversary celebration," a federal report concluded, was "that it drew the homage of so many who represent American democracy to this free Nation's place of birth."[12] Even the queen of England could not resist accepting an invitation to the party.

Left off the guest lists, however, were the descendants of Virginia Indians and enslaved Africans. The segregated South was not prepared to include the latter, and the former, well, they had been left behind by the forward march of progress, supposedly. An overview of archaeological research into Indigenous life published in the run-up to the celebrations concluded that "wars, imported disease, liquor, and general moral destruction did their work so well that the Virginia tribes which were numerous, strong, and dominant in 1600 had disappeared or had almost completely disintegrated by 1700." Almost nothing remained of their once-great nations, the author thought, for "when pitted against the culture of the English, the civilization of the Indians was powerless. It proved to be impossible for two cultures so fundamentally different to exist side by side."[13]

*   *   *

The New World arrived in 2005, ahead of the next major Jamestown anniversary. But the available evidence suggests Terrence Malick was little interested in making a promotional film for what organizers of that event were calling "America's 400th Anniversary."[14] Like almost every other movie he has made, *The New World* came to fruition only after a lengthy period of development, which predated all the patriotic party planning. According to Jack Fisk, Malick began working on a script about Pocahontas as early as the 1970s, when he was making *Badlands*.[15] Still, the extra attention generated by the upcoming anniversary could not have hurt the commercial prospects for the picture, so when plans fell through for another project he was working on at the time—a biopic about the revolutionary icon Che Guevara—Malick returned to his Pocahontas notes in earnest.

The timing was right in other ways as well. In a reversal of historical fortunes, Jamestown had become, somewhat surprisingly, an overlooked theatrical subject. Although Disney had a huge hit with its 1995 movie *Pocahontas*, no tidal wave of popular interest in the real history of Jamestown ever arrived in its wake. In fact, the success of the animated musical may have made Pocahontas and Captain Smith somewhat passé, their *Romeo and Juliet*–like romance having been transformed into the stuff of kids' cartoons. At the turn of the twenty-first century, Jamestown's place in the national imagination was overshadowed by tales of Pilgrims landing at Plymouth Rock over a decade after the colony had been established. As one local historian reviewing *The New World* put it in a clever double entendre: "Virginia is American memory's most illustrious backwater."[16]

Both the 2007 Jamestown Commemoration Commission and the director of *The New World* had their work cut out for them. To restore colonial Virginia to a vaunted place in the national mythology, commemoration organizers needed something subtler than a Super Sabre flyby. They opted for an ongoing program of more or less academic events, celebrating Jamestown as a symbol of American "democracy, enterprise, exploration, and diversity."[17] Similarly, in his quest to outdo Disney, which had big-name stars (Mel Gibson voicing Captain Smith) and award-wining songs ("Colors of the Wind" won both an Oscar and a Grammy) on its side, Malick opted for the less-is-more approach. In keeping with his "idiosyncratic style of moviemaking," *The New World* saw him experimenting with looser, cheaper cinematic techniques, such as extensive improvisation and documentary-style filming. Perhaps these might breathe new life into the old Jamestown myth. Whether or not Malick was successful in doing so is still up for debate, but the impact of this experimentation on his future filmmaking is not.[18] In this regard, at least, *The New World* really was something new.

Deepening and extending the probing style of his previous films, *The New World* added another component to Malick's ongoing philosophical project. Thematically, it resembles the films preceding it: *The New World* is a meditation on the fragility—temporal, environmental, existential—of human worlds. Stylistically, though, it was something of a démarche, a bold step into the fluid and flexible filmmaking that would become a hallmark of Malick's mature cinematic vision. Without *The New World*, there would have been no *The Tree of Life*, no *To the Wonder*, no *Knight of Cups*.[19] Situated at the crux of Malick's career, *The New World* is best viewed as a bridge between his earliest films and his most recent ones. Like *Days of Heaven* and *The Thin Red Line*, it marvels at the astounding beauty of nature and laments its desecration. But *The New World*'s swirling camerawork and more personal feel seem closer to the intimate aesthetic of films such as *The Tree of Life*. *The New World* radicalized Malick's unique cinematic grammar—everything made in its wake has been indebted to it.

Having much in common with his earlier films devoted to pivotal moments in American history—the coming of the modern, mechanized world in *Days of Heaven*; the global reach of total war in *The Thin Red Line*—*The New World*'s subject was ripe for Malick's layered storytelling. By the time he finally got around to filming it, he had amassed a wealth of source material with which to work, whole crateloads of drafts and notes and research materials. The long gestation period of the film shows. But *The New World* needed many midwives: it would not have been born had Malick not assembled an extraordinarily capable crew of collaborators to help bring it into being. Some of them, such as artistic director Jack Fisk and editor Billy Weber (an associate producer on the project), had worked with Malick since *Badlands*. Others, such as costume designer Jacqueline West and cinematographer Emmanuel "Chivo" Lubezki, were new recruits.[20] The mix made for a winning team—one that would realize not just *The New World* but also the increasingly daring, innovative films Malick made in rapid succession after its release.

Of Teepees and Astrodomes

There is no shortage of praise for Malick's fourth picture. As one critic put it, *The New World* is a film that does not have "fans," only "disciples and partisans and fanatics."[21] Director Chloé Zhao, whose Malick-influenced film *No-*

madland won the 2021 Academy Award for Best Motion Picture, is one of them. In an interview with the Criterion Collection, she described *The New World* as nothing less than "pure cinema."[22] Others have used similar terminology to describe it, deeming *The New World* a work of "great intelligence, ambition and radiant beauty" (Amy Taubin in *Sight & Sound*) that is both "elegiac" and "shattering" (Manohla Dargis in the *New York Times*).[23]

Despite such acclaim, though, *The New World* remains perhaps the most confounding film in Malick's cinematic oeuvre. It is long and slow; its plot wanders. For these reasons and more, the initial critical response to it was, on the whole, "generally disheartening."[24] Box-office receipts were not great, either. Audiences were turned off not just by *The New World*'s languid pace but also by its episodic construction, which relied heavily upon voice-over narration. Making things worse, those whispered voice-overs were sometimes hard to hear, resembling poetry more than easy-to-follow prose; just listening to them was not enough, one needed to decipher and interpret them.

Perhaps the most alienating aspect of *The New World*, though, is its subject: settler colonialism.[25] Despite being exhaustively researched and intricately executed, the picture props up some long-lasting myths about Jamestown—such as the misconception that Pocahontas and Captain Smith were romantically involved, a fiction exposed ages ago by Henry Adams— and about Eurocentrism and American exceptionalism more broadly.[26] When *The New World* attempts to question the received wisdom that has coalesced around these topics, it often falls back into clichés and truisms about the early colonial period, the very things that endeavors such as the 1619 Project ask us to question. Some critics have gone so far as to label *The New World* a work of "imperialist nostalgia" dedicated to the "ideological work of exculpation."[27]

The New World is not pure fantasy. It draws extensively from historical accounts—the liner notes for its Criterion Collection release reproduce quotations from primary sources used in its production, such as Robert Beverley's 1705 *The History and Present State of Virginia* and Bartolomé de Las Casas's *An Account, Much Abbreviated, of the Destruction of the Indies*, which dates back to 1542. It also invokes current anthropological research.[28] Consequently, *The New World* gets many of the details right. Some of its voice-over narrations derive directly from historical documents, such as Smith's accounts of Virginia, or the writings of other early chroniclers, such as Beverley, Hariot, and John Rolfe, the tobacco entrepreneur who married Pocahontas in 1614. Malick's script even quotes the testimony of Arthur Barlowe, one of the captains of Sir Walter Raleigh's ill-fated expedition across the

Atlantic in 1584. Barlowe famously found the people of the New World to be "gentle, loving and faithful, lacking all guile and trickery. It was as if they lived in a golden age of their own."[29]

Further contributing to its verisimilitude, *The New World* was filmed just miles from the actual Jamestown site. Malick's crew fashioned period-specific buildings, clothes, and weaponry, giving the film an impressive aura of authenticity. More remarkable still was the use of historical linguistics to re-create all but lost Algonquin languages and songs, which make fleeting, but significant, appearances at important moments in the film. Such attention to detail was extended to the natural world. *The New World* utilizes ornithologi-cally appropriate birdsong on its soundtrack, including even the songs of birds believed to be extinct. Consulting experts at Cornell University's Ornithology Lab, Malick's team recreated the sound of the lost Carolina parakeet.[30]

None of this makes *The New World* a documentary film, though. It has narrative flourishes typically found in nineteenth-century opera, or, indeed, twentieth-century Disney films: unexpected reversals of fortune, archetypi-cal struggles between good and evil, tragic love affairs. A gauze of stylized exoticism rests upon everything, resulting in a style that veers away from realism. *The New World* is much closer to romanticism—"cinematic *roman-ticism*," Robert Sinnerbrink has called it—and symbolism.[31] *The New World*'s imagery swerves from the anthropological to the art historical. It owes as much to the South Seas paintings of Paul Gaugin, for example, as to the more period and geographically appropriate watercolors of John White. Similarly, its depiction of Captain Smith owes as much to epic poetry as it does to his-tory. In Malick's vision of him, Smith is no soldier of fortune who happened to find unexpected fame across the Atlantic, but rather the "Aeneas of this New World."[32]

Anyone who has read *A True Relation*, *The Generall Historie*, or *The True Travels* will have a hard time believing that one, but the remark is revealing nonetheless, for it illuminates Malick's aims, helping us to see that he never meant for *The New World* to be viewed merely as a historical reenactment. Like his previous films, the picture is best viewed as a foray into the realm of timeless poetry and grand mythology. His script references Achilles, Calypso, and Demeter.[33] As one critic has put it, "Malick sides with myth."[34]

The New World is not a story of the historical Jamestown or of Pocahon-tas and Captain Smith. It is a story built on archetypes—a universal story of ambition, desire, and greed; a timeless parable of love lost and then found. *The New World* is myth as history, history as myth. Whether or not it rises to the level of a "countermythology," it nevertheless attempts to be both singular and universal, intimate and abstract, all at once.[35] Press materials for the film carried an epigraph from John Locke's 1690 *Second Treatise on Government*: "in the beginning all the World was America, and more so than it is now."[36] Though it is based on historical events and depicts the lives of real individuals, it treats them as symbols, as expressions of what professors of American studies once called the "American experience."[37] Pocahontas and John Smith appear in *The New World* as the essence of a national identity, the American Adam and Eve. Malick's screenplay describes them as "our hero" and "our heroine."[38]

In his research for the project, Malick was drawn to sources that spoke in sweeping terms, ones that described Smith, for example, as a personification of uniquely American "virtues"—"individualism, practicality, disdain for class rank, and esteem for those who worked hard to get ahead"—"at the heart of the new nation."[39] Somewhat understandably, essence-averse historians have been dismissive of *The New World* for precisely this reason—"the historical Smith calls out for cinematic treatment," one of them complained in the *Journal of American History*, yet "this film does not provide it."[40]

To judge *The New World* solely by the standards of history is to view the film through the wrong disciplinary lens, though. The "documentary approach" Malick urged his cast and crew to adopt during production should not obscure the fact that *The New World* is a narrative film—a mythologizing work, in other words, not an attempt at historical realism.[41] Malick has always played fast and loose with history. *Badlands* and *Days of Heaven* were set in realistic historical worlds, but their plots contained elements of melodrama (the latter even had a love triangle not unlike that of Captain Smith, Pocahontas, and John Rolfe). Similarly, *The Thin Red Line*'s stylized depiction of the very real battle of Guadalcanal was more modern-day *Iliad* than contemporary newsreel. *The New World*'s transformation of Captain Smith's writings into something resembling epic poetry pulls them out of the historical continuum and places them in the realm of ancient ballads and epics. As Manohla Dargis rightly put it in her *New York Times* review of the film, Malick is "more poet than historian."[42]

In this regard, *The New World* was an opportunity for its director to explore his own long-standing poetic and philosophical preoccupations—preoccupations having to do with the nature of time and existence, the pursuit of meaning and purpose, and the notions of dwelling and being-in-the-world. Like Witt in *The Thin Red Line*, Malick imagines Pocahontas as a character seeking transcendence, somebody who has glimpsed, and searches for, "another world." Malick's previous films had all been set in the twentieth century, amid more or less recognizable worlds similar enough to our own: the suburban Midwest of the 1950s, the Texas Panhandle of 1917, even the South Pacific of the Second World War. But now he was contemplating a far more distant epoch—and a very different world. What was this world, and, more importantly, how did it relate to *our* world? Was the New World still *our* world?

Such questions invariably lead to other questions, which are just as perplexing, because, as it turns out, we know very little about what actually makes a world. Is the world "everything that is the case" or "the totality of facts," as Wittgenstein famously declared at the outset of the *Tractatus Logico-Philosophicus*?[43] Is it, in other words, a largely linguistic phenomenon? Or was it—as the philosopher Ernst Cassirer argued way back in 1925—a matter of symbols? "Any symbolic form," he said, was "a particular way of seeing," bearing "within itself its particular and proper source of light."[44]

Perhaps it was the case that there was no one way to reveal the world, and, furthermore, no one world to reveal. Cassirer's interest in myths and symbols galvanized a great many philosophers in the United States, among them Susanne Langer, who translated his work, and Walker Percy, who got it secondhand from her. But it was the Harvard philosopher Nelson Goodman who most explicitly took up Cassirer's call to make sense of the concept of world. For him, nothing about worlds was obvious or settled. His influential 1978 book *Ways of Worldmaking* opened with a series of questions: "What are worlds made of? How are they made? What role do symbols play in the making? And how is worldmaking related to knowing?" Goodman knew this line of questioning, which stemmed from his reading of Cassirer, could lead him down the proverbial rabbit hole. But there was no other way: "These questions must be faced even if full and final answers are far off."[45]

In some ways, Goodman was reviving a debate that had taken place decades earlier, in 1929, when Cassirer squared off with Martin Heidegger in a colloquium held in the resort town of Davos, Switzerland.[46] It was there that the two German philosophers, representing two very different philosophical traditions, discussed the merits of science, reason, and metaphysics before a captivated audience. Philosophically, but also politically, Cassirer and Heidegger were from different worlds, which made sense, since they had such very different conceptions of the world. Cassirer's high-minded, abstract approach was not enough to convince Heidegger that the key to understanding the world was an exhaustive rendering of the "archetypal phenomena of human mentality."[47] For Heidegger, the world was concrete and contingent, not something we constructed in our minds. Just two years before the Davos dispute, his breakthrough book, *Being and Time*, had suggested that the world was something into which we were "thrown."[48] One had to approach it existentially. "What is this mystery, the world," he once told his students, "and above all, *how* is it?" Because the world "exists," he thought, one could not treat it as some abstract concept. To inquire into the meaning of the world was to confront anxiety, nothingness, even death.[49] To know the world entailed contemplating its absence, what Heidegger sometimes called the *Abgrund*, or abyss—at least that is what he called it in his 1929 essay "Vom Wesen des Grundes," the text Malick translated forty years later as *The Essence of Reasons*.[50]

It is to Heidegger's more enigmatic understanding of the concept of world that *The New World* is most indebted. The questions it poses are existential rather than theoretical: To what degree is the world revealed or concealed by one's mortality? If a world can be found or "discovered," can it also be lost? Does the phenomenon of world-collapse—the experience of the *Abgrund*—reveal something essential about what it means to be human?

Malick had pondered these questions for a long time. "We speak quite aptly of losing 'our hold on the world,'" he wrote in his Harvard honors thesis. "For we realize that it is only because we have such a world that things within it have claim and significance to us."[51] From Heidegger, Malick had learned that the experience of existential dread, which "marks 'the collapse of the world,'" helps us understand not just the meaning of human existence, but also Being itself.[52] In the end is the beginning: to experience the end of the world is to take the first step toward contemplating the *Seinsfrage*.[53]

Hubert Dreyfus, Malick's longtime friend and mentor (he is thanked in the honors thesis), was one of the first people to highlight this theme as being a focal point of *The New World*. Visiting the elaborately constructed recreation of Jamestown that Jack Fisk and his crew had erected not far from the site of the original 1607 settlement, the Berkeley philosopher noticed—even before Malick had finished filming his movie—how the story centered on what Heidegger called the "worldhood of the world." In this regard, *The New World* was like every other picture Malick had made. Dreyfus told students enrolled in his 2007 lecture course on Heidegger at the University of California as much: "All of his [Malick's] movies are about worlds," he claimed, "about what it is to be a world, and things that happen with worlds." "Each film" is "about some aspect of the world."[54]

The Mother of Us All

Dreyfus's remarks about *The New World* beg the question: just whose world does it seek to portray? Is it that of Smith and the English colonists, or Pocahontas and the Powhatan people? Indigenous communities did not—and rightfully still do not—think of themselves as New Worlders.[55] So just what does the idea of the "New World" mean? Could it represent something like a fusion of two worlds, a new beginning and an apocalypse, a starting point and an abyss, all at once? Answers to these questions hinge on viewer expectations, on what they *want* to see in the film.

All of the usual arguments against *The New World*—that it recycles John Smith's own self-serving exaggerations, for example, or that it silences Indigenous voices and reduces native peoples to caricatures—are justified. Many of the fetishistic myths and stereotypes associated with the first inhabitants of the Americas can be found within its cinematic frame, from the noble savage right on down to the disappearing Indian.[56] The Indigenous characters are conceptual stand-ins, their silent, harmonious existence with nature merely a point of contrast to the actions of the rapacious, duplicitous colonizers, who are themselves just stunted embodiments of the scourge of modernity. In this narrative, the Indians represent the path not taken. They stand outside of time.

Nowhere is this reliance upon preexisting tropes more apparent than in the film's portrayal of Pocahontas, who has enjoyed a long afterlife in literature, poetry, painting, opera, and cartoons.[57] In *The New World* she appears as the archetypal Indigenous mother who all too conveniently disappears from the scene once European colonialism gets a proper foothold in the Americas.[58] She personifies purity, tractability, and an untarnished connection with nature—she is always seen climbing trees in the film, sometimes even talking to them.

The New World opens with the voice of Pocahontas (Q'orianka Kilcher). Over a serene shot of gently rippling water, we hear a prayerlike soliloquy that serves as a prologue to the picture.[59] "Come Spirit," Pocahontas says. "Help us sing the story of our land. You are our mother, we, your field of corn. We rise, from out of the soul of you." A shot of Pocahontas from below follows, showing her with outstretched arms. Who is this mother? Is she the First

Mother of the Powhatan, the mother of all "mankinde," as Thomas Hariot wrote in *A Briefe and True Report of the New Found Land of Virginia*, the earliest English-language account of the beliefs of the native peoples of Virginia? Or does she represent something else, something like Mother Nature, perhaps? Malick's screenplay makes it clear that Pocahontas is communicating with the spirit of her deceased mother, who speaks to her through the "wind in the pines," but this is far from obvious in the film.[60] The prologue raises other questions. Of whose land does Pocahontas hope to sing? Will it be that of her father, Powhatan, or that of her future paramour Captain Smith (Colin Farrell) or even John Rolfe (Christian Bale), the tobacco entrepreneur she will eventually marry? Or maybe she is singing of the land of her son, Thomas (Jonathan Gonitel), the first person born of an Indigenous mother and an English father—the first so-called American.

The New World has two major story lines, which correspond to two different moments in Pocahontas's life. In the first, she is the Indigenous princess of common lore who meets, rescues, and has "a very mad affair"—as Peggy Lee once sang it—with Smith. It is the stuff of songs, poems, and Disney films.[61] But in the second, which hews closer to the historical record (and which receives far more screen time in Malick's preferred "extended cut" of the film, released in 2008), she is sent away from her people, told Smith has died at sea, sold to a conniving Samuel Argall for the price of a copper kettle, and brought to live with the English colonists as something of a security deposit.[62] After a period of despondency (in Malick's vision she contemplates suicide, only to be rescued from her despair by the whispering beauty of the forest), she eventually marries Rolfe and begins a second life as a colonial wife and mother.[63] She trades her buckskins for corsets and starched collars, learns English, and undergoes a Christian baptism.

The New World's emphasis on Pocahontas's transformation from native princess into Rebecca, the biblical name by which she would be known to the English, lends credence to the belief that some sort of cultural fusion was possible, that a new world could arise out of the confluence of two different civilizations: the son she bore Rolfe was the proof. Q'orianka Kilcher came to understand her character as a maternal bridge-builder: "I think she saw her son as an extension of a hope to bring the two worlds together; he was the bridge over the gap between the two worlds. He was the first inter-racial child, so her dream of bringing the two worlds together did come."[64] Thomas appears in only a handful of scenes in *The New World*: as a newborn in Jamestown, being swaddled lovingly by his mother (who is visibly transformed, brought back to life even, by his arrival); as a toddler roaming the tobacco plantation; and, finally, as a four-year-old back in England, running with glee through royal gardens, playing hide-and-seek.

It is of Thomas's world that *The New World* ultimately sings. But this was a world made possible by Pocahontas. At one point, Malick considered titling his fourth feature film "The Mother of Us All."[65] It was an allusion to a poem about Pocahontas by Vachel Lindsay.[66] Appearing in the magazine *Poetry* in July 1917, just a few months after the United States formally entered the First World War, the poem was a noteworthy piece of patriotic mythologizing. Its title said as much: "For America at War: Our Mother, Pocahontas."[67] To Lindsay, Pocahontas was a paragon of innocent virtue. She represented everything good and noble in the American character, everything standing in such stark contrast to the Old World. Thanks to her, Americans had no need for "gray Europe's rags": Americans could "renounce our Saxon blood," "our Teuton pride," "our Norse and Slavic boasts," as well as our "Italian dreams" and "Celtic feuds." Americans were "the newest race," born of Pocahontas's "resilient grace." Americans were her bounty, her "fields of corn."[68]

With Lindsay's poem in mind, we can now see that the prologue to *The New World* signals the start of a nationalist epic. Other source materials encouraged Malick to run with the theme. One of them was *A Book of Americans*, written by Rosemary and Stephen Vincent Benét.[69] First published in 1933—and intended primarily for children and young adults—it tells the history of the United States through a series of biographical vignettes written in verse. The book's cast of characters ranges from Christopher Columbus and Cotton Mather all the way up to Woodrow Wilson. Some of its subjects are anonymous ("Indian"), or compound ("French Pioneers"), but *A Book of Americans* focuses mostly on notable individuals with proper names: George Washington, Benjamin Franklin, Dolly Madison. The portraits display a comic touch, even and especially when the fate of the historical subject is—as with Pocahontas—rather grave.

The Benéts portray Powhatan's daughter as a fundamentally tragic figure. They liken her to "a wild thing tamed," a "poor wild bird." She represents civilizational discontent: "All through the ages: Wild things die / In the very finest cages."[70] Pocahontas is not the only Indigenous person to appear in *A Book of Americans*—Crazy Horse, for example, gets a poem—but she is unique in that she alone plays the role of the tractable native who succumbs to the march of historical progress. (Crazy Horse, by contrast, is "hard to tame," like the other "Indians of the Wild West.")[71] Pocahontas plays her role, then quietly slips off the world-historical stage: she is the live-action version of the "vanishing Indian."[72]

Captain Smith made Pocahontas famous by documenting how she had "become formall and civill after our English manner."[73] In a letter to Queen Anne, he boasted that she was "the first Christian ever of that Nation, the first Virginian ever spake English, or had a childe in marriage by an Englishman."[74] She was, in other words, a wonder. But the tragedy of her life, as later generations came to understand it, was that she was so capable of being "tamed." She became the caged bird of the Benéts.

Malick's Pocahontas is also tragic. She is the symbol of a lost world. The idea appears in both of the film's story lines—the fictional romance with Smith as well as the very real marriage to Rolfe. Smith views her mostly as a marvelous gateway to another life, a new beginning. "Start over," he says in voice-over, "exchange this false life for a new one, give up the name of Smith." Rolfe views her—initially, at least—as an extension of his duty, her domestication and conversion a project to be undertaken for the good the colony.

Malick loves a good love story. His script for *The New World* is full of passion. In it, Smith describe Pocahontas as "the very image of earthly beauty," a beauty that, later on, sends "tongues of fire" through Rolfe's veins.[75] Both men find Pocahontas captivating, beguiling. But neither comes to know her, not entirely, not completely. To Smith she remains something untamed: "you're a wild creature that belongs to a bygone era," he tells her.[76] And to Rolfe she remains a mystery until the very end: she learns to speak his language and professes his faith, but her mind, like her heart, is elsewhere. "You seem like someone who loves her freedom—who could never be caught," he says to her in Malick's screenplay.[77] This is straight out of *A Book of Americans*, which compares Pocahontas to "a wild deer"

> Or a bright, plumed bird,
> Ready then to flash away
> At one harsh word.[78]

Late in *The New World*, Rolfe takes Pocahontas back across the Atlantic. He is keen to show her off as a prize. To the English, Pocahontas is presented as a novelty, a Virginian curiosity on par with its flora and fauna, the human equivalent of a bald eagle on a tether. At one point we even see her peering, with sad solidarity, into the cages of the animals on display beside her. (In something of a winking reference to Disney's *Pocahontas*, one of them

Figure 18. Pocahontas (Q'orianka Kilcher) on display in *The New World*.

contains a raccoon, which many viewers will associate with that film's most
memorable character, Meeko.) As camera operator Joerg Widmer later put
it, Pocahontas "was there as if she was a parrot or an animal from the wild
coming into civilization. She was watched as if she was like a strange bird."[79]

But this is only part of the story Malick ends up telling. The sequences depicting Pocahontas's arrival in England show her not just being looked at, but
also looking back. On the sooty, cobble-stoned streets of London, where nearly
everybody stops to stare at her, we see Pocahontas assuredly returning the
gaze. Her own curiosity and fascination with England and the English are evident. (Malick's script has her asking Smith early on, "Are the people in London
as we are? Would they understand me?")[80] Pocahontas is not just—or at least
not only—a caged creature, an object of others' fascination. She is also an explorer, an ethnographer in her own right. As is her uncle, Opechancanough
(Wes Studi). In scenes that reverse the usual colonial perspective of films set in
this period, Opechancanough accompanies Pocahontas to England so that he
might "count Englishmen" and "see this God that they keep talking so much
about." We see him contemplating stained glass depictions of scenes from the
Bible and walking in an overly manicured, formal garden. Trimmed into geo-
metric symmetry, the topiary brings to mind Alain Resnais's *Last Year at
Marienbad* (1961), a film about alienation and loss. Opechancanough is as far
as he could be from his home, from what he would recognize as his world.

Pocahontas/Rebecca, in Western dress, joins her uncle in this rationalized space. "Life has brought me to this strange new word," she says som-

Figure 19. Pocahontas's New World in *The New World*.

berly. Suddenly, *The New World* is no longer Captain Smith's story nor John Rolfe's, nor even Jamestown's—it is Pocahontas's. In Kilcher's words, "England was the New World for Pocahontas."[81]

But in England Pocahontas could not thrive. Like the topiary in which she wanders with her uncle, she has been reshaped, restricted. Widmer described the intended symbolism: "You really see how the English cut down Nature," he said, "shaping it into a form that they created. They did not let Nature grow, which is what they did with Pocahontas," forcing her "into a shape which suited their civilization."[82] As the tractable native, Pocahontas embodied the hopes and dreams of English colonialism. But at the time of her death at Gravesend she remained a stranger in a strange land. Her son Thomas survived, but he was raised, and lived, as an Englishman—even and especially after returning to America as an adult.

The world into which Pocahontas was born would not survive. Malick portrays "the mother of us all" as somebody who knew this, deep down in her bones: "I hope that someday my people will forgive me," she tells her uncle as they walk in the garden. It is the final time in the film Pocahontas speaks in her native tongue.

Civilizing Fictions

Whereas Pocahontas was forced to contemplate the demise of her world, the English were of course invited to see the newly discovered lands across the

Atlantic as but an increase of theirs. It is worth recalling that, for them, if not for all Europeans, Virginia was first and foremost a commercial opportunity. The earliest accounts of the New World were often little more than investment brochures for joint-stock companies such as the Virginia Company of London, which funded the Jamestown expedition. In *A True Relation*, Captain Smith sang of "Acres of most excellent fertill ground, so sweete, so pleasant, so beautifull, and so strong a prospect, for an invincible strong Citty, with so many commodities, that I know as yet I have not seene."[83] The rhetoric was meant to spur investment, and such wide-eyed wonder helped loosen the purse strings of speculators.

Pamphlets about the New World, such as Smith's, proved to be tremendously popular, especially when they were repackaged with captivating images. The most famous of these works was a 1590 edition of Hariot's *A Briefe and True Report of the New Found Land of Virginia* put out by the Flemish engraver and publisher Theodor de Bry and his sons. De Bry realized that *A Briefe and True Report*, if accompanied by images, would sell. So he put an edition together combining Hariot's text with engravings based on John White's paintings of Algonquin peoples. It was a publishing sensation.[84] The frontispiece de Bry created for *A Briefe and True Report* contained statuesque portrayals of Algonquin natives. Front and center were a well-muscled warrior and a shapely maiden, situated atop a classically decorated plinth. The image was more fanciful than factual, but that was the point, since it was meant to serve as a gateway to the magical lands described in Hariot's report.

The de Bry edition of Hariot's *Briefe and True Report* was a linchpin of Malick's visual design for *The New World*. But Hariot's writings also provided him with plenty of other useful material. Hariot was a member of Sir Walter Raleigh's 1585 English expedition to Roanoke Island. *A Briefe and True Report* was his firsthand account of the journey. Seen through his eyes, America was a land of unbelievable abundance, something the cinematography of *The New World* manages to capture to amazing effect. But whereas Lubezki's camera—loaded, on occasion, with high-resolution, sixty-five-millimeter film stock—transforms nature into something poetic and beautiful, Hariot focused almost exclusively on its business potential.[85] *A Briefe and True Report* cataloged the commercial opportunities awaiting the "the adventurers, favorers, and welwillers of the enterprise for the inhabiting and planting of Virginia."[86]

The first part of the *Report* was devoted to an exhaustive recording of "merchantable commodities:" everything from silks, flax, and hemp to ce-

Figure 20. Nature's bounty as depicted in *The New World*.

dars, otter furs, and deer skins, not to mention copper, iron, and pearls.[87] The second and third parts went on to discuss Virginian victuals. Here, too, abundance was the primary theme: ripe for the taking were vegetables, roots, fruits, nuts, shellfish, fish, and fowl, as well as larger beasts that could be captured or hunted. *The New World* stresses this bounty from the start: "I've found oysters," an amazed colonist reports back to his captain at the outset of the film. "They're as thick as my hands. They're the size of stones, sir. There's fish everywhere, they're flapping against your legs. We're gonna live like kings." Just as Hariot had described it, Virginia is portrayed as a veritable paradise, a weary traveler's ultimate utopia.

Malick fixated on the idea. The first page of his screenplay for *The New World* describes a prelapsarian land without toil or strife: "Virginia is a rich, magical country, where nature has provided for every human want," it says. "Wild plums and cherries grow in profusion along the banks of the musical rivers. Grapes dangle from the boughs of tall pines and bog magnolias perfume the air." Amid this bounty, "braves tend the fishing weirs, plant corn and squash, while the women gather berries and lay meat out in strips to dry. Their work is soon finished, however, and they join the children at their life of play."[88] This description of Indigenous life comes straight from Hariot. The New World, he had written in the *Briefe and True Report*, had everything civilized life required—not just food, but also building materials. Entire cities could be built without having to bring anything across the Atlantic but a few tools and some laborers.

Only after Hariot had cataloged the natural wealth of Virginia did he finally turn his attention to "the nature and the manners of the people" who lived there.[89] His approach in this section was descriptive, even—we might say—ethnographic. He commented on the clothing of the Algonquins, the layout of their towns, the design of their homes. He examined their politics and modes of warfare. When compared to Europeans, Hariot found the natives lacking. Most galling of all was their lack of commercial sense: "In respect of us they are a people poore, and for want of skill and judgement in the knowledge and use of our things, doe esteeme our trifles before thinges of greater value."[90] But Hariot nevertheless considered the Algonquins "very ingenious." They were diamonds in the rough; with a little cultivating, a little shaping, they might one day become as polished as the colonists. The natives demonstrated such "excellencie of wit," he wrote, that "they may in short time be brought to civilitie, and the imbracing of true religion."[91]

Hariot was keenly interested in Indigenous belief and practices, especially as these pertained to their interactions with the English. In the pages of the *Briefe and True Report*, one can see traces of Indigenous curiosity, a looking-back on par with Pocahontas's in *The New World*. Hariot found the Algonquins full of questions. How come the Europeans had no women among them? Why did they not seem to get sick or die, especially when so many of their own were succumbing so soon after coming into contact with them? Were the English striking them down with "invisible bullets"?[92]

It was not "invisible bullets" that felled so many of the natives, of course, but European viruses, smallpox and measles foremost among them. Hariot thought Algonquin talk of "magical bullets" suggested they were more superstitious than the English, which made them prime targets for civilizing and evangelizing. "There is good hope they may be brought through discreet dealing and governement to the imbracing of the trueth," he wrote, "and consequently to honour, obey, feare and love us."[93]

Such comments have been interpreted as evidence of the calculating, premeditated tactics used by the English to establish and maintain colonial control in Virginia. In his essay "Invisible Bullets," Stephen Greenblatt long ago suggested that Hariot's text should be viewed as "a continuation of the colonial enterprise."[94] But the *Briefe and True Report* was subversive, too, for its proto-political anthropology also called into question the foundations of orthodox Christian belief. Who was to say that the English were not also naive and superstitious, that their faith was not also just a story concocted to explain things that could not be understood, or a noble lie used to establish and maintain political control?

As every ethnographer knows, the interpretive lens can be turned back upon the viewer very easily, making everything relative, provincial, a matter of perspective.[95] Malick portrays Captain Smith in this light, as somebody who, after seeing a vision of another kind of life that could be possible with the Powhatan, contemplates trading his old, European existence for a new one. In Malick's screenplay, he becomes "aware of a new world." After spending time with Pocahontas, "the whole scheme of his former life has been called into question," all of it now seeming nothing more than "an illusion."[96]

For the colonists of Jamestown, the idea of "going native" Smith seems to ponder in *The New World* was never really an option, though. The idea of European superiority over all things Indigenous held sway in sixteenth- and seventeenth-century European writing about the New World. It was a central component of what Greenblatt has called a "mobile technology of power."[97] Europeans arriving in the Americas believed their advantages to be not just instrumental but also moral. In the colonial imagination, the Indigenous peoples of the Americas were relegated to what intellectual historian Nicolás Wey Gómez has described as "Europe's moral periphery."[98]

Christian teaching and scholarly learning taught explorers, traders, and colonists to view the natives of the New World as, first and foremost, heathens. Whether they were heathens who could be saved via conversion or were forever damned was the subject of much debate back in Europe.[99] But medieval geographical and cosmological science did little to convince early European voyagers to the Americas that the people they would find there might be in the least bit civilized. Some doctrines, such as the ones Christopher Columbus studied, even went so far as to suggest that many regions of the newly discovered lands—the supposedly intemperate ones—were inhabited not by people at all but by monsters. So widespread was this prejudice that early mapmakers—like Martin Waldseemüller, the first person to dub the newfound lands "America"—inserted "cannibal iconography" into their cartographic renderings.[100]

But the flip side of demonization is romanticization, and that, too, found its way into colonial writing. The Algonquins were described in this more positive light occasionally. With their "goodly bodies," which were on full display in White's watercolors and de Bry's engravings, they quickly became objects of widespread fascination and wonder back in Europe—and wonder is something that, as Greenblatt has put it, "precedes, even escapes moral categories."[101] The wonder of the New World was the loophole that allowed it to be exploited and tamed, transformed from a wild space, full of wild peoples—"the naturals" is what they are called by the colonists in *The New World*—into a pastoral ideal.

The New World shows how Pocahontas's story encapsulated the hopes and aspirations of the European civilizing mission. It was precisely why she was viewed as a token, "the presumed forerunner," as one historian has put it, "of many who would eventually be won over by the colonists' culture and good intentions—opening the way for unhindered English settlement and commerce."[102] The epigraph Malick chose for his *New World* screenplay underscores the theme:

> Pocahontas easily prevailed with her father and her countrymen to allow her to indulge her passion for the captain, by often visiting the fort, and always accompanying her visits with a fresh supply of provisions: therefore it may justly be said, that the success of our first settlement in America, was chiefly owing to the love this girl had conceived for Capt Smith, and consequently in this instance, as well as in many others,
>   LOVE DOES ALL THAT'S GREAT BELOW!

The text came from a 1755 article in *London Magazine*: "A Short Account of the British Plantations in America."[103]

The epigraph refers to Pocahontas's fabled kindness to the Jamestown colonists, but it is also significant that Pocahontas's husband, John Rolfe, played such an essential role in turning the wilds of the New World into an orderly, productive tobacco plantation. Although Malick downplays it in his film, the historical Rolfe viewed his marriage to Pocahontas as an extension of this colonial mission. His nuptials afforded him the opportunity to civilize at least one of the natives, making her a Christian in the process. As Rolfe wrote to Sir Thomas Dale, the deputy governor of Virginia, it was not "unbridled desire for carnall affection" that drew him to his intended bride, but rather colonial duty: his concern was "for the good of this plantation for the honour of our countrie, for the glory of God, for my owne salvation, and for the converting to the true knowledge of God and Jesus Christ, an unbeleeving creature, namely Pokahuntas."[104] Rolfe considered himself created "not for transatory pleasures and worldly vanities, but to labor in the Lords vineyard;

there to sow and plant, to nourish and increase the fruites thereof," all with the hope of obtaining "salvation in the world to come." Not only that, but he was only doing what Pocahontas wanted. Rolfe remarked upon "her great appearance of love to me, her desire to be taught and instructed in the knowledge of God, her capablenesse of understanding, her aptnesse and willingnesse to receive anie good impression."[105]

No doubt Rolfe protested too much, but Malick takes these lines and runs with them. In *The New World*, romance wins. It is not just that Pocahontas is depicted as a "natural" with a "goodly body." (That much is obvious: in her *New York Times* review of *The New World*, Manohla Dargis remarked that "the beautiful lead actress may cause cardiac arrest among some viewers.")[106] It is that Rolfe's love for Pocahontas is made to appear purer and truer than it probably was. Malick implies that Rolfe was compelled by colonial officers to write the words cited above: in the film, it is not he who speaks them, but rather Dale. The slippage makes Rolfe's union with Pocahontas seem less like a marriage of convenience and more like a true love match, one founded on mutual attraction and affection.

This bending of the historical record is necessary for Malick's aims. It provides the necessary third point in the love triangle at the heart of his film. (His script is even more focused on the star-crossed-lovers theme, devoting pages upon pages to Smith and Pocahontas's *Romeo and Juliet*–esque rapport.) But if Smith's whirlwind romance with Pocahontas was clearly a fantasy from the very beginning, one concocted to help sales of books like *The Generall Historie of Virginia* and *The True Travels*, then surely Malick's version of Pocahontas's marriage to Rolfe is also imaginative, a way to sugarcoat the truth, to make historical reality a little more palatable to contemporary viewers.

Paradise Found and Lost

These minor but significant tweaks to the historical record serve another purpose: they prop up Malick's own pastoral ideal, to which he has returned repeatedly throughout his career. It first appeared in *Days of Heaven*, with its Hamlin Garland–inspired wheat-field majesties, matured in the romanticized primitivisms of *The Thin Red Line* and *The New World*, with their exotic Edens, taking on something of a final shape in his most recent films, such as *A Hidden Life*, which contains so many luminous images of idyllic agrarian life set against the backdrop of the resplendent Austrian Alps that

some critics have labeled it an environmental "fantasia."[107] Malick has been
drawn to these seemingly timeless locales, these places where human life
seems to unfold in harmony with nature, in keeping with the cycle of the seasons. But in American intellectual history the pastoral ideal was always, as
Leo Marx demonstrated long ago, a fantasy.[108] It represented a dream space
where both nature and the machine could be tamed and domesticated.

Since his very first days in Hollywood, Malick has been drawn to the
tragic fates of such nostalgic visions, repeatedly crafting stories that depict the
demise of idealized worlds of yesteryear. His AFI student film, *Lanton Mills*,
set the pattern: it juxtaposed the mythical Wild West and an ugly, modern-
day, car-clogged Los Angeles. The full title of his student short—*Lanton Mills:
The Cincinnatus Hiner of Texas*—was an allusion to the work of the so-called
Poet of the Sierras, Joaquin Miller (né Cincinnatus Hiner Miller), whose
works depicted an idyllic California destroyed by nineteenth-century gold
mining, not to mention the genocide of its Indigenous populations.

Miller's most famous book, the prelapsarian fable *Life Amongst the Modocs* (1873), depicted a paradise lost to the forces of progress. One part memoir and two parts mythical adventure, *Life Amongst the Modocs* was a morality
tale. It recounted Miller's arrival in Northern California as a gold miner, followed by his eventual realization that this way of life had to be rejected as
nothing less than a wrong turn for humanity. *Life Amongst the Modocs* ends
with Miller turning his back on the modern world and all that it represented:
"I have seen enough of cities and civilization—too much. I can endure storms,
floods, earthquakes, but not this rush and crush and crowding of men, this
sort of moral cannibalism, where souls eat souls, where men kill each other
to get their places. I have returned to my mountains. I have room here. No
man wants my place, there is no rivalry, no jealousy; no monster will eat me
up while I sleep, no man will stab me in the back when I stoop to drink from
the spring."[109] To Miller, the ancestral lands of the Modocs—the area in and
around what is known as Mount Shasta today—were "a little Eden," "a little
Paradise," but the miners who found their way to these magical places brought
nothing but chaos and destruction.[110] They desecrated everything they
touched. No wonder the Modocs viewed them as "evil spirits," he wrote,
because they "tear up the earth, toil like gnomes from sun-up to sun-down,
rain or sun, destroy the forests and pollute the rivers."[111]

This is exactly how Malick portrays the Jamestown colonists in *The New
World*. But it is not the only thing he may have borrowed from Miller while
toiling away at his Pocahontas scripts. His idealized depiction of the Pow-

hatan also may have derived from Miller's noble-savage romanticization of the Modocs. Resisting the forward march of progress and civilization, Miller envisioned preserving "a national park, a place, one place in all the world, where men lived in a state of nature." "When the world is done gathering gold," he proclaimed in *Life Amongst the Modocs*, "it will come to these forests to look at nature, and be thankful for the wisdom and foresight of the age that preserved this vestige of an all but extinct race."[112]

It is hard to tell how seriously Miller took his own proposal. After all, it was not as if he, a white miner who had come to California seeking gold, kept his distance from the native inhabitants of the area. Indeed, since Miller fancied himself something of a West Coast Captain Smith, he naturally found himself a Pocahontas of his own. The historical record suggests he lived for a time with a McCloud Indian named Sutatot.[113] In *Life Amongst the Modocs* (and other writings), Miller called her Paquita and waxed poetic about her beauty: "tall and lithe, and graceful as a mountain lily swayed by the breath of morning. On her face, through the tint of brown, lay the blush and flush of maidenhood, the indescribable sacred something that makes a maiden holy."[114] Sutatot/Paquita bore Miller a daughter, the poetically named Cali-Shasta, but her father would not stick around long enough to help raise her. Miller was off to explore other lands and, later on, to make his name as something of a minor celebrity in London.

Joaquin Miller was a mythologizer, and, like Captain Smith, he realized that his myth needed romance. Writing over two hundred years after his predecessor, though, Miller was able to see things Smith could not, such as the costs—human costs, environmental costs, spiritual costs—of the colonial project inaugurated by Jamestown and brought west by the forces of Manifest Destiny.[115] As he saw it, settler colonialism was a world-destroying force, leaving nothing but wastelands in its wake. Miller's account of the desecration of the Klamath River by greedy gold miners captures the idea: "A deep, swift stream it was then, beautiful and blue as the skies; but not so now," he wrote. "The miners have filled its bed with tailings from the sluice and tom; they have dumped, and dyked, and mined this beautiful river-bed till it flows sullen and turbid enough." The native name for the river meant "'giver' or 'generous,' from the wealth of salmon it gave the red men till the white man came to its banks," but as Miller lamented, the salmon would no longer "ascend the muddy water from the sea. They come no more and the red men are gone."[116]

In *The New World*, Malick overlays this somber nineteenth-century perspective upon his sixteenth- and seventeenth-century sources. The result is

a portrayal of English settlement that is stereoscopic: simultaneously won-
drous (as it may have originally been) and horrifying (as it certainly became).
Although *The New World* portrays the grandeur of an Edenic landscape
seemingly untarnished by European civilization, it also trains its attention
on the very phenomena that would eventually destroy it. Malick presents the
colonial enterprise as a brutal, dismal, demeaning endeavor for both native
peoples and colonists alike. But here, too, he cannot stop himself from swerv-
ing into the realm of myth, setting up Jamestown as the representation of an
ahistorical despoiling force, akin to a swarm of locusts that arrives to scar
and tarnish a veritable paradise. It is the same trope Miller used in *Life
Amongst the Modocs* and it is one Malick had deployed himself in *Days of
Heaven* and *The Thin Red Line*.

As in *The Thin Red Line*, the soldiers of *The New World* are carried into
the cinematic frame by warships. With their arrival, the story, and the dramatic conflict, begins. Disturbing the natural order, these embodiments of
instrumental rationality set everything in destructive motion. Their first and
most important goal—as stated by their leader, Captain Newport (Christopher Plummer)—is to clear the land so as to construct a fort, a dwelling that
will stand in stark contrast to the Powhatan village, which seems to have been
constructed in greater harmony with the natural environment—further evidence, perhaps, of the stereotypical "cosmic green thumb" Indigenous peoples
are supposed to have.[117] Even before any trees are felled, we know that the
English do not intend to inhabit the same world as the natives. These very
first scenes of *The New World* have told us as much, showing us the Powhatan
people living an Edenic life—as Malick's script has it—and the English colonists cowering behind their armored helmets and breastplates.[118]

As many commentators have noticed, the opening minutes of *The New
World* offer a concise encapsulation of the film's environmental message. Its
prologue is followed by a credit sequence built around seventeenth-century
cartographic images, which borrows liberally from the example set by Bruce
Beresford's tale of Jesuit missionaries in New France, *Black Robe* (1991).[119] But
the extended cut of *The New World* moves quickly from this to underwater
shots of three young Algonquin women swimming. Orchestral sounds stir
to life as their bodies slide through river currents. Classical music fans will
recognize the prelude to *Das Rheingold*, the opening installment of Richard
Wagner's monumental *Ring* cycle of operas. Utilizing what one musicologist
has described as "Western culture's most famous 'under-watery' music," the
cue verges on cliché, but is, as Alex Ross has noted, nevertheless appropri-

ate—"a more apt and precise application of Wagner on film is difficult to find."[120] The prelude provides suitably grand sounds for the first scenes of Malick's film, but it also foreshadows the arc of its plot.

Wagner's opera opens with three cavorting river nymphs. They are entrusted with the task of protecting gold buried beneath the Rhine. But a dwarf, Alberich, soon arrives and absconds with it, instigating the events that propel Wagner's cycle of operas into ever grander tales of cosmic conflict. *The New World*'s opening sounds invoke this mythic tale: the Powhatan girls play the part of the mythical Rhine maidens and the colonists are gold-grubbing Alberichs. With shots alternating between the perspective of Pocahontas and her people, who spy the English ships sailing toward them, and the shipbound soldiers, who gaze out in wonder upon the verdant world awaiting them at water's edge, the opening sequence of *The New World* posits a conflict of perspectives—a contrast of worlds—that will play out in the rest of the film.

Malick's use of Wagner situates his picture in a mythopoetic space, only tangentially related to actual historical events. As Ross notices, "*Rheingold* does an intriguing double duty: it sets up an allegory for white invasion of the Americas as an act of theft, casting the settlers in the role of Alberich. At the same time, the sailing ships are ennobled by the flow of the music. What follows—the story of Pocahontas and her relations with two men in the settling party—raises the fleeting possibility of a respectful melding of cultures, in harmony with nature. That possibility does not come to pass."[121] Malick's use of the *Rheingold* prelude is a form of "environmental Wagnerism," which, according to Ross, emerged in "the late twentieth century, in the shadow of the environmental crisis" as "a story of humanity's suicidal attempt to master nature."[122] In *The New World*, this message, a hallmark of Malick's mature style, could not be clearer. Perhaps it is only fitting, then, that Malick, a classical music aficionado who once upon a time dreamed of scoring his own films, would choose such a mythical piece to introduce his own foray into the realm of myth.[123] Like *Das Rheingold*, like *Life Amongst the Modocs*, *The New World* is, after all, a tale of paradise found and paradise lost. It is "both a celebration and an elegy of the America that was," as the studio's advertising campaign put it, "and the America that was yet to come."[124]

Malick is by no means the first filmmaker to present precolonial life in the Americas as something of a lost Eden, disturbed and ultimately destroyed by greedy colonists. Disney's *Pocahontas*—to take just one well-known example—also has scenes of helmeted Englishmen hacking down virgin forests and digging up pristine soils in a maniacal pursuit of gold: "Mine, mine,

mine," they sing as they toil away. But even if *The New World* echoes the over-all message of its animated predecessor, its style comes from elsewhere.

The way Emmanuel Lubezki shoots the colonists in *The New World*—up close, usually from below, always with inquisitive, handheld cameras—brings to mind the imagery of a very different account of colonial megalomania, one that would have been on Malick's mind when he began working on his original Pocahontas scripts—namely, Werner Herzog's *Aguirre, the Wrath of God* (1972).[125] A depiction of the final days of Spanish conquistador Lope de Aguirre (Klaus Kinski), who perished in pursuit of a fabled El Dorado, Herzog's film does not look kindly upon the first Europeans to explore the Americas. It portrays them as ruthless exploiters overseeing a brutal, violent program of resource extraction, as madmen interested only in their own personal glory.

They may not be as crazy as Herzog's conquistadors, but the colonists in *The New World* are menacing just the same. The scenes filmed in and around the Jamestown fort have a claustrophobic feel. In these, the colonists' meanness of spirit predominates. It is especially apparent in the haughty yet terrified way they look upon their Indigenous neighbors, whom they describe as "the naturals" or, less kindly, "naked devils." When, later in the film, their foodstuffs begin to fail and the colony descends into a mutinous anarchy under Smith's watch (here Malick is drawing upon accounts of the deadly winter of 1609–10, which became known as "the Starving Time"), the malevolence comes out into the open.[126] In one particularly memorable scene, a colonist named Eddie (Eddie Marsan) rants and raves about the need for or-

Figure 21. A colonial Alberich (Eddie Marsan as Eddie in *The New World*).

der while we hear the sounds of Smith being flogged, off-screen, by colonists who have risen up against him. Spitting with rage directly into the eye of the viewer, Eddie could very well be a devil himself, an English Aguirre, a real-life Alberich.

One of the longest-standing, most self-serving fictions of English colonialism in the New World was that it was somehow more benign than that of the Spanish or the Portuguese, mainly because it did not force religious conversion upon the natives. Not only was this so-called Black Legend not true (as scholars from Julián Juderías to Jorge Cañizares-Esguerra have shown), but it also perpetuated myths about the Indigenous peoples of the Americas that have persisted to this day.[127]

The legend originated in the writings of the sixteenth-century Dominican friar Bartolomé de Las Casas. It was he who first suggested—over three hundred years before Joaquin Miller—that the Europeans in the New World who fancied themselves civilizers and evangelists should be viewed as the exact opposite: as devils, that is, not saints. In his *An Account, Much Abbreviated, of the Destruction of the Indies,* Las Casas cataloged, often in horrifying, unrelenting detail, the many crimes committed by the Spanish in the New World. Interested only in gold and power, the conquistadors massacred, raped, and pillaged their way through the Americas, leaving only carnage and desolation in their wake. Las Casas's descriptions of Spanish cruelty were unflinching: "They [the Spanish] would enter into the villages and spare not the children, or the old people, or pregnant women, or women with suckling babes, but would open the woman's belly and hack the babe to pieces, as though they were butchering lambs shut up in the pen."[128]

The *Account* was an impassioned work, motivated by both moral outrage and juridical righteousness. Its author did everything he could to convince his readers that the Spanish colonial project needed reform and fast. Las Casas appealed to the law, to faith, to the prerogatives of royal power, to reason, to sentiment, to anything that might convince or sway his readers. But in his effort to throw the misdeeds of the conquistadors into the highest relief possible, he also ended up romanticizing the Indigenous peoples of the Americas whom he sought to defend, turning them into martyrs for a faith they did not profess. It was Las Casas who introduced the idea that the Indians were more Christian—or at least more Christlike—than the Europeans who claimed to be acting on behalf of the church. Throughout the *Account,* Las Casas portrayed Indigenous people as wide-eyed innocents, as "gentle lambs" or "gentle sheep" led anywhere and everywhere to the slaughter by

conquistadors who were "like fierce wolves and tigers and lions."[129] He denounced these "demons incarnate": perhaps it would have been better "to
condemn the Indians to the devils and the fires of Hell," he suggested with
bitter sarcasm, than hand them over "to these Christians of the Indies."[130]

This was effective rhetoric—so effective that it got colonial laws changed
and earned Las Casas the title "Protector of the Indians."[131] Many today view
Las Casas as a human rights advocate *avant la lettre*. But his work remains
famous not just for its descriptions of tortures and atrocities. The passages
in which Las Casas waxes poetic about an idyllic Indigenous life, unspoiled
by colonial aggression, have also had a long and influential afterlife, one
stretching all the way up to the making of *The New World*.

Like many others before him, Malick was drawn to the romanticized,
Christianizing portrayal of Indigenous communities in Las Casas's *Account*.
His script describes the Powhatan as creatures not yet fallen: "They overflow
with mercy and loving kindness."[132] His production notes contain a lengthy
quotation from the *Account*, saying precisely this: "God made all the peoples
of this area . . . as open and innocent as can be imagined. The simplest people
in the world—unassuming, long-suffering, unassertive and submissive—they
are without malice or guile, and are utterly faithful and obedient."[133] Many
defenders of Indigenous peoples and traditions (including, most famously,
some of the staunchest supporters of liberation theology) have echoed this
sentiment, viewing native peoples as living embodiments of the maxim stat-
ing the meek shall inherit the earth.[134] But in overemphasizing the innocence
and purity of the native inhabitants of the Americas, was Las Casas really
offering his European readers an honest account of their world, or was he
merely helping, once again, to cover it over, simply replacing one European
fantasy about Indigenous life with another?

Efforts to reframe our understanding of the colonial period—even and
especially *The New World*—run the risk of obscuring the very people who
populated the Americas in the sixteenth and seventeenth centuries. Once they
are transformed into symbols, they can no longer be seen as persons. "To cage
a whole people in a state of timeless, static, perpetual goodness," a reviewer in
the *Journal of American History* lamented, "is to rob them of something essential to everyone's lived humanity: their history."[135] Some contemporary
scholars have attempted to place the blame for this tendency squarely at the
feet of Las Casas. After all, he did not question the colonial enterprise itself, he
just frowned upon the violence it engendered. For a time, at least, he even defended the encomienda system that, via the means of mass conversion and

forced labor, did so much to transform the Americas into an enormous plantation economy. That he argued for a more humane system—for some scholars, anyway—is beside the point. He represents but "another face of empire," not its eradication.[136] For a time, he even argued that more enslaved Africans should be brought to the Americas, since they were supposedly better suited to labor under the yoke of the colonial enterprise than the natives.[137]

Tragically, enslaved Africans were brought to the European colonies established throughout the Americas in droves. Jamestown was no exception. Soon after the events depicted in *The New World* took place, enslaved labor, the lifeblood of settler colonialism, came to remake the American landscape. The wealth colonists found in colonial Virginia was not the fabled gold of El Dorado, of course, but rather, as Thomas Hariot and Captain Smith had predicted, the riches stemming from the production of labor-intensive commodities. Chief among these was tobacco, the plantation crop Pocahontas's future husband John Rolfe cultivated with such success in Virginia, introducing non-native species of it that became highly prized back in Europe. Hariot noted how the Algonquins, who called it *uppówoc*, revered the plant, offering it up in sacrifice to their gods.[138] Rolfe revered it, too, but he offered it up to an entirely different kind of god, that of the market—the same market that made slavery profitable.

Worlding

Was *The New World* made with profits in mind? One would think not, or not exclusively, at least. Although it had plenty of marketable components— famous actors, a noted director with a devoted following—*The New World* refused easy commodification from the start. It was "commercial enough," as David Sterritt put it, but just barely. Viewers of the film realized rather quickly that it was not made with "big ticket-sales in mind."[139] After all, *The New World*'s portrayal of Pocahontas did not come predigested, as in the Disney version. No catchy tunes signposted the picture's message with obvious lyrics. Instead, viewers had to actively interpret the film, which meant working to understand how its fragmented images, sounds, and narrations related to each other. Viewers had to make the film meaningful.

They could do this by attending to both the world *in* the film and the world *of* the film. Daniel Yacavone has helpfully differentiated between what he has labeled "world-in" and "world-of" accounts of cinematic works. The former, he argues, describe film worlds as they appear on screen, whereas the latter emphasize connections to contexts beyond or outside the frame—the "world" of a genre, say, or the "world" in which viewers are situated, that is, a certain space and time, a certain existential horizon of meaning.[140] Cinema is an associative art and viewers bring these worlds with them into the movie theater. No film is an island. Watching *The New World*, audiences may think of Disney's *Pocahontas*, but they may also think of *Aguirre, the Wrath of God* or *Black Robe*. They could also think of *The Mission* (dir. Roland Joffé, 1986) or even *Dances with Wolves* (dir. Kevin Costner, 1990). Still, some movies ask their audiences to do more than just situate the cinematic experience in a pre-established genre; they go so far as to probe the limits of the concept of the world itself. *The New World* is one of those films. On one level, it is a motion picture about historical Jamestown. On another, however, it is about the contemporary world—our world, yours and mine. It is also about how nature is both revealed and concealed by these worlds.

As any casual viewer of *The New World* notices rather quickly, nature takes center stage. Grasses, rivers, trees, clouds, birds, and skies receive as much attention from Lubezki's camera as any of the principal actors. Malick uses these images to bridge the gap between the pastness of the events depicted on screen and the immediacy of the audience's contemporary reality, between, we might say, the world-in and the world-of. Far from serving as a metaphor, or as a cinematic interlude between more traditional segments of dialogue-driven narrative, the sounds and images of nature sutured throughout the picture serve as a horizon of meaning, suggesting, as Heidegger once put it, that the world emerges out of the earth.[141]

Lubezki's camera notices the smallest details of *The New World*'s natural settings, and since Malick refuses to relegate these to background material, viewers take note of them, too. After watching the film, viewers come to see their surroundings differently: the earth stands forth in an altogether different manner. The screen is no longer a barrier but a bridge, or what we might call—borrowing from the philosopher Ross Gibson—"an energy field connecting the viewer to the cosmos."[142] What holds it in place is audience attention. With a comportment of care and wonder not unlike that exhibited by Pocahontas on screen, viewers can come to see the trees and hear the birds more clearly. They, too, can see "another world," but it is the same one they already know, just remade by cinema.

The many sequences depicting the subtle ebbs and flows of nature—drifting clouds, rippling waterways, swooping birds—were not things that could be premeditated or staged; they had to be captured on the fly by a crew that was flexible and curious enough to spot them. Almost all of *The New World* was shot outside, using nothing but natural light. Working "like a documentary crew," the members of Malick's team responded to conditions as nature delivered them: nothing was recorded according to "how the script suggested"; filming depended on what the environment allowed. Everything was shot "according to Nature."[143]

Malick told his crew that "the relationship between human beings and nature" should take precedence over everything else.[144] The result is what philosopher Ilan Safit has described as an "eco-film-phenomenology."[145] Even in the most human moments of the film, such as when Pocahontas and Smith begin to fall in love, nature is never far away. Malick filmed many of these scenes himself, apparently, and it shows, for nature is portrayed not merely as a beautiful backdrop for a cinematic love story, but rather as something like a horizon of all human possibility.[146] In Malick's screenplay, Smith teaches Pocahontas astronomy, illustrating the movements of the planets, but it is Pocahontas who teaches Smith to view nature as being imbued with spirit.[147]

The New World shows how worlds come into being, and then, in time, fall away. It was a theme Heidegger explored in *The Essence of Reasons*. As he saw it, the world should not be viewed as a container that held objects: it was not, as was commonly thought, the sum of all things. The world was a phenomenon. It was best understood existentially, in relation to human freedom, temporality, and transcendence. Like *Dasein*, the world was transient. "World never 'is,'" Heidegger wrote (in Malick's translation), "it 'worlds.'"[148] The phrase, in German and English alike, is a strange one, so much so that Malick felt compelled to add a note explaining it. He suggested that Heidegger's notion of *world* was so utterly unique "it can only be expressed tautologically."[149] But hidden in that tautology was the secret of Being itself, a secret that could only be revealed by human existence.[150] Without *Dasein*—"the being for which Being is an issue," as Heidegger famously put it in *Being and Time*—the world would not world. Being had no meaning.[151]

Although it is made of little more than light and sound, cinema is a preeminently worldly art form. Material beings bring it into existence. "Whatever the effort made to intellectualize it," the French philosopher Jacques Rancière has written, "cinema is bound to the visibility of speaking bodies and the things they speak of."[152] There is no escaping the fact that the movie camera is a recording device. However abstract and ethereal they might appear on the surface—and Malick's films have been accused of being both—movies must always return, in the end, to human embodiment, to human worlds. Nowhere is this more apparent than in *The New World*, which juxtaposes not just very different worlds—the so-called old and the new—but also radically different understandings of what it means to be a part of a world: one that sees the earth as little more than "standing reserve" to be consumed and exploited, another that sees it as imbued with spirit. Neither of these ideas appear on screen in the abstract: they are both bodied forth, made possible by *Dasein*.

Writing about the films of the Hungarian director Béla Tarr, Rancière has gone so far as to speak of the "'cosmological' pressure" the process of film-making imposes on every mise-en-scène. In cinema, he argues, the world reveals itself only according to a time "felt by bodies."[153] Following Rancière, we might say that cinema reveals the essential role *Dasein* plays in making the world possible. "To exist means, among other things, to cast-forth a world," Heidegger once claimed.[154] But *The New World* does not rest content dramatizing this insight, for it also points to the ways in which both the world and *Dasein* relate to Being. From his earliest studies in phenomenology and Heideggerian ontology, Malick was aware of the connection. If anything defined Heidegger's work, he wrote in his Harvard thesis, it was this "intimate connection of *Sein* and *Welt*"—"only if we understand what he [Heidegger] means by 'world' can we understand what he means by 'Being.'"[155]

While the visual beauty of *The New World* remains perhaps its most lasting legacy, the patient, improvisational methods Malick and his crew used to capture it were not to everybody's liking on set. Indeed, some of the actors thought Malick spent entirely too much time on scenes of natural splendor. For those who were used to doing things the tried-and-true Hollywood way, the making of *The New World* was too much about Being and too little about coverage, continuity, and directorial control. Many years after its release, word got out that Christopher Plummer had harangued Malick for not sticking to the shooting script. In his opinion, far too much of the production had been left up to chance. He told Malick as much: "You've got to get yourself a writer," he fumed. Because Malick was willing to drop everything at the drop of a hat to try something new or unexpected, Plummer told an interviewer, *The New World*'s actors had no idea what they were doing most of the time. He and Colin Farrell even joked that, in Malick's eyes, they were nothing more than "a couple fucking ospreys."[156]

If the filming of *The New World* resulted in bruised egos, so too did its postproduction. Well-known composer James Horner, who had scored such blockbusters as *Braveheart* (1995) and *Titanic* (1997), had been hired to work on *The New World*, but he quickly realized that it would be an unusual gig. Malick had worked with famous composers before—Ennio Morricone and Hans Zimmer, most notably—but he had never allowed them to dominate his films' soundtracks. Horner quickly realized he would not be an exception. As *The New World* was being edited, his score was cut up, rearranged, and generally relegated to the cinematic equivalent of background music. Bristling at Malick's decision to incorporate popular pieces by Wagner and Mozart into *The New World*'s soundtrack, effectively drowning out his own original orchestrations, Horner threw up his hands in disgust. He claimed to have "never felt so letdown by a filmmaker in my entire life." Even years later, he would maintain that Malick "didn't have a clue how to use music."[157] It was further proof that the director of *The New World* was charting a new course, one that would take him even farther away from Hollywood.

* * *

In his 2013 Jefferson Lecture in the Humanities, delivered at the Kennedy Center in Washington, D.C., Martin Scorsese said, "We need to take pride in our cinema, our great American art form."[158] Revisiting arguments made fifty years earlier by those seeking to establish a national film center such as the American Film Institute, Scorsese said the time had come "to preserve everything."[159] Americans were not solely responsible for the transformation of moviemaking into a veritable art form, he conceded, but American films were part of an international legacy that was too important to lose in the occasional warehouse fire or—just as likely these days—to the underfunding of libraries and archives. Likening the desire to catch life in moving pictures to a "mystical urge," Scorsese held up cinema as "an attempt to capture the mystery of who and what we are." Movies "contemplate that mystery," he said, and if we fail to keep track of them, we will lose an important part of not just our national heritage but also our common humanity.[160]

In the same way that Scorsese attempted to hold up cinema as both a uniquely American art form and an expression of universal values, *The New World* attempts to tell a singular, historical tale about the founding mythology of the United States—"Here, on this strip of marshy land, America is born"—in a way that might make it applicable to other people, from other cultures, all around the globe.[161] It sings a song of worlds lost and worlds yet to come. From Heidegger and Husserl, Wittgenstein and Kierkegaard, Malick had learned that the world is never singular, and that worlds never stay the same.[162] Worlds are made possible by human freedom and transcendence, which means they are always subject to change. In *The Thin Red Line*, Malick gave us Witt, whose defining feature was that he had "seen another world." In *The New World* we are introduced to Pocahontas, who, stranded between worlds, finds her way to another one.

In a late lecture titled "The Good of Film," Stanley Cavell praised cinema's ability to depict what he called "the quest for transcendence." He admired the ability of some films to offer us "access to another world."[163] If anything defines *The New World* it is this quest for transcendence, a quest undertaken not just by seafaring adventurers like Captain Smith or seemingly pious Christians like John Rolfe, but also—and more importantly—by the curious, inquisitive, open-hearted Pocahontas.

From the very beginning of *The New World*, Pocahontas is on a journey. Her opening soliloquy paints her was as a wayfarer, a pilgrim in search of the divine: "Dear Mother, you fill the land with your beauty," she says, "You reach to the end of the world. How shall I seek you?" Throughout the rest of the picture, which could very well have been a catalog of catastrophe—loss, abandonment, banishment, world collapse—she retains hope, a "radical hope," as Jonathan Lear might put it.[164] It is her hope, her quest, that anchors the film. Malick presents Pocahontas as a spiritual seeker until the last moments of her life. "It is the intensity of Pocahontas' search for meaning and the curiosity and courage with which she pursues it," wrote Amy Taubin in an early, laudatory review, "that make *The New World* so moving."[165]

But *The New World* is also, as Taubin recognized, "ultimately tragic."[166] Pocahontas's search for meaning is cut short by her death, and audiences know all too well what was in store for her people: they would endure tremendous hardship in the following years and decades, as settler colonialism upended their lives. The real Pocahontas's last words—"All must die," she reportedly told Rolfe, "Tis enough that the child liveth"—make her out to be something of a stoic, somehow resigned to her fate.[167] But in the final passages of *The New World*, which make use of this famous, oft-quoted line (though transforming it into a voice-over narration from Rolfe), Malick pushes back against this interpretation. He presents his protagonist in a more joyful fashion. His Pocahontas does not merely recognize her mortality, she embraces and even exults in it. "We do not die," she says in Malick's screenplay, "but go on, and on. No one is lost."[168]

Having witnessed the loss of one world, Pocahontas foresees the arrival of another. In the transition between the two she spies the inner workings of the divine: "Mother," she says in her final voice-over soliloquy, "I know where you live." The accompanying images are ecstatic intimations of a happy afterlife. To the sound of Wagner, we see Pocahontas running through gardens, twirling and doing cartwheels; we see her baptizing herself with pond water. She is nothing but smiles, for at long last she has been reunited with her mother, the spirit who still spoke to her through the clouds and stars, as well as the whispering trees.[169] A stirring sequence following these scenes stresses the point. After watching Rolfe's ship heading out to sea, majestically but somberly, we see shots of the natural world: sunrises and sunsets, water rushing over polished rocks, and, finally, tall pine trees, shot from below, swaying gently in the breeze. The Wagner has given way to the sounds of rivers, frogs, and birdsong, which carry on as the screen fades to black.

In something of a happy coincidence, Stanley Cavell published "The Good of Film," a lecture he had given at Princeton University five years before, in 2005, the same year the first cut of *The New World* was released to theaters. We might think of these works as two cheers for cinema. Both Cavell and Malick suggest the movies are uniquely positioned to capture and portray the quest for transcendence that is an inescapable part of being-in-the-world, of being human. Ironically, it is film's very materiality that allows it to aid in this quest. By returning our attention to nature, allowing us to see it as a condition of human possibility, cinema helps us contemplate our own existential thrownness, the origin of our inescapable freedom.

Founded in wonder, shaped by curiosity, filmmaking is the ultimate worldmaking art form. In finding his way back to Pocahontas, sifting through layers of myth and history in the process, Malick stumbled upon a whole new way of worldmaking himself, one that would inform the films he made in rapid succession after *The New World*, during the most daring and productive period of his cinematic career. In these pictures, he continued marveling at the transient "worldhood of the world," but he resorted less often to myth, choosing instead to examine his own existential experience. His focus was now trained squarely on his own being-in-the-world. The result was an ever more personal kind of filmmaking, a new phase in his ongoing search for meaning. The 2011 premiere of *The Tree of Life* at the Cannes Film Festival marked its beginning.

CHAPTER 5

Cosmic Confessions, Part I

The Tree of Life and the Problem of Suffering

A cosmic energy shimmers in all stone and steel as well
as flesh.

—Peter Matthiessen

In *God Save Texas: A Journey into the Soul of the Lone Star State*, journalist
Lawrence Wright suggests there are three levels of Texas culture.[1] Level One
Texas is what one might call originary Texas; it represents the stereotypes
with which we are all familiar: pickup trucks and cowboy boots, steak houses
and honky-tonks. It is the Texas of *Red River* and "Remember the Alamo."
Level Two Texas tries to escape all this, or dolly it up, usually using the proceeds of the oil industry to do so. It represents sophisticated Texas. Level Two
Texas is star architecture and Old World art collections: the Louis Kahn–
designed Kimbell Art Museum, with its vast array of old masters, in Fort
Worth; the Renzo Piano–designed museum for the Menil Collection of antiq-
uities and European surrealism in Houston.[2]

　　If Level Two is the antithesis to the thesis that is Level One, then Level
Three Texas constitutes a Hegelian *Aufhebung*—to use a decidedly Level Two
term—a synthesis or sublation. Level Three mixes authenticity with sophis-
tication. The culture that emerges from it is, in Wright's opinion, nothing
short of transcendent. He finds stirring examples of it in Beyoncé's *Lemon-
ade*, in Alvin Ailey's *Revelations*, and in Robert Rauschenberg's *Gluts*, those
messy, captivating assemblages that reimagine not simply the Lone Star State
but the entire United States. "Telling new stories about who we really are,"
Level Three art and culture is a kind of homecoming: "it returns us to the

familiar."[3] It evokes "the songs we heard as children, the sounds of our labor, the primal smells of the kitchen, the legends of our ancestors, the phrases and intonations we cling to in our language, the colors of our land, the cloud shapes in our sky." Level Three "feels like home. And isn't that point of culture, to come home again with a clear and educated eye?"[4]

If we can get beyond all the awkward talk of levels, it is easy to see Wright's point. It is one that resonates with the arc of Terrence Malick's career, his recent films most especially. What other Texan has spent so much time capturing these things as the director of *The Tree of Life* (2011), a film about growing up, getting lost, and eventually finding one's way back home? The only thing missing from Wright's list to make it fully applicable to Malick's work is the late-summer light filtering through the branches of a grand old Texas oak tree.

For a time, Lawrence Wright and Terrence Malick were neighbors. In the 1980s, they lived two doors apart in the leafy Travis Heights neighborhood of Austin.[5] Both Wright and Malick had returned to Texas after spending a good deal of time away. In Europe, Malick had grown nostalgic for life in the Lone Star State: returning to it "felt like a homecoming."[6] If *God Save Texas* documents Wright's journey home, then *The Tree of Life* depicts Malick's. A 2017 profile of him in *Texas Monthly* supports a Level Three reading of his late-career work, emphasizing his return to his roots. It describes him living a stone's throw from St. Stephen's Episcopal, the boarding school west of Austin he attended as a student in the late 1950s. It was there that his lifelong interest in drama, literature, and philosophy germinated and grew. It was also there that, at the age of fourteen, he met Alexandra "Ecky" Wyatt-Brown, who would become, decades later, his third wife.[7] As David Lynch has put it: "Ecky likes to comment that she and Terry are like a couple of homing pigeons."[8]

I note these biographical details not to expose the private life of a famously reclusive artist, but to highlight the way it informs his recent filmmaking. Many of Malick's late-career pictures depict a cinematic voyage of return, and to fully understand them it is worth exploring just what it is they are returning to. Somewhat paradoxically, these films tell a very private story—a personal story of homecoming and redemption—but in the most public way possible, on the silver screen. Taken together, *The Tree of Life, To the Wonder* (2013), and *Knight of Cups* (2016) represent a unique kind of autobiographical cinema. They are the work of a specific individual—an Oklahoman become Texan; an American; a straight, white, Christian male—seeking to create something truly universal. Attempting to show how one solitary life might be thought of as being connected to *all* existence, they outline an origin story that is applicable to each and every one of us, and perhaps even to the cosmos itself. They are instances of what Heidegger once called, after Kant, "cosmic philosophy."[9]

At the heart of Malick's late-career work is the suggestion that each of us plays some small role in the unfolding drama of the universe. It is an idea animating not just his memoir films, but also *Voyage of Time* (2016), an IMAX documentary (as well as, in a slightly longer version, a theatrical film) that serves as a kind of coda to the trilogy preceding it. Taken together, these four films constitute a unique record of self-examination. They connect the smallest, most intimate experiences of life—the joys and sorrows that populate our private memories, the ambitions and passions that lead us ahead, and sometimes astray—to the grandest story line of all, which is that of the cosmos. Confession, these pictures imply, is the first, necessary step toward communion.

*   *   *

After winning the Golden Palm at Cannes in 2011 for *The Tree of Life*, Malick embarked upon the most prolific period of his career. In a few short years he nearly doubled his cinematic output, creating films that have garnered widespread critical attention—not all of it positive—along the way. Assessing these films, this chapter and the one following it show how Malick broke away, stylistically, from the trail he had blazed in *Badlands, Days of Heaven, The Thin Red Line*, and *The New World*. Eschewing scripted dramas for a more experimental, improvisational approach to filmmaking, he fashioned a distinct "late style."[10] But the notable shift in cinematic technique masked deeper thematic continuities running throughout Malick's career, not the least of which being his interest in the examined life, the search for one's place in the grand scheme of things.

The Tree of Life, To the Wonder, Knight of Cups, and *Voyage of Time* were shot, edited, and completed in rapid succession. Released within a five-year span, these works addressed concerns that had been bubbling beneath the surface of Malick's oeuvre for decades. The look was new, but the questions were not. These films revisited topics that preoccupied Malick in all the various stages of his life: when he was a budding filmmaker in Hollywood, when he studied philosophy at Oxford and Harvard, when he was a boarding-school student at St. Stephen's Episcopal, but also when he was just a curious kid in suburban Oklahoma.

Malick's late-style films depict pilgrimages. They are cinematic celebrations of searching and homecoming rooted in philosophical contemplation and theological consolation. They emphasize not just alienation or exile but also return.[11] Like the protagonists in Malick's earlier films, their central characters at first appear to be existentially aloof or spiritually lost, but they end up taking steps—sometimes rather small ones, sometimes much bigger—to find their way.

Malick has been on this existential journey for decades. The central protagonists of *The Tree of Life*, *To the Wonder*, and *Knight of Cups* are versions of him at different stages in his life—his cinematic avatars. A young Jack (Hunter McCracken) gives us a glimpse of Malick's childhood, which is recalled by adult Jack (Sean Penn) in *The Tree of Life*. *To the Wonder*'s Neil (Ben Affleck) is Malick at midlife, enduring the thrills and trials of marriage, separation, divorce, and, eventually, new marriage. Between the two is Rick (Christian Bale) in *Knight of Cups*, the young artist Malick was in the 1970s, finding fame as a Hollywood scriptwriter and director. Only *The Tree of Life* takes place in a historical period—the 1950s—corresponding to Malick's life history, but all the films are set in and around places where he has lived and worked: the Midwest and the Southwest; Los Angeles, Paris, and Austin.[12] Just one period is missing: those years Malick spent as a philosopher's apprentice at Harvard and Oxford, not to mention the time he spent studying moviemaking at the American Film Institute. But the lessons of those years were ones that stuck, for it was upon their foundation that Malick constructed his trilogy of confessional films. Harvard, Oxford, and AFI helped make it all possible.

When they are viewed together, *The Tree of Life*, *To the Wonder*, *Knight of Cups*, and the coda-like *Voyage of Time* start to look like one continuous project, a singular work of existential self-reflection and spiritual confession that is unique in cinematic history. Malick's confessional films are a reckoning with mortality. As existential philosophers have taught us for as long as they have been around, our finitude—our "being-towards-death," to use Heidegger's terminology—is the only thing that truly individualizes us.[13] And yet, mortality is not entirely singular. It is something we have in common with others—with anyone, or anything, alive. In this regard, at least, death is both personal and universal: it connects each of us to all other forms of life in the cosmos. Everything will die, not just you and me, but also planets, stars, even galaxies.[14]

But what comfort is this knowledge, if, indeed, it is any comfort at all? How should *I* understand *my* mortality in light of the eventual demise of everything? Here is where religious faith often steps in to reassure us, telling us that each ending is in fact a new beginning, that no death is ever truly final. The religiously inclined can view death not as some final exile but as a transition to another stage of life, or even, as a return to something eternal. Our life becomes part of another story, a miraculous rebirth, a homecoming. Ideas of transcendence and providence help take the sting out of finitude. In times of loss and pain we tell ourselves, "God has a plan," or "Everything happens for a reason."

Malick is not the first thinker to search for existential meaning in providential schemes. His confessional cinema sits atop a mountain of previous writing on the subject dating all the way back to Augustine, who found in his own life evidence of transcendent providence.[15] In the words of Garry Wills, Augustine's *Confessions* are best read as a "testimony" bearing witness not just to the particulars of his singular experience, but also, and more importantly, to the greater glory of God.[16] Augustine showed how self-reflection hooked into cosmic contemplation. As Henry Chadwick, one of Augustine's more recent translators and commentators, has put it: "Augustine's personal quest and pilgrimage are the individual's experience in microcosm of what is true, on the grand scale, of the whole creation."[17]

In documenting his own journey from doubt to faith—and in wedding that faith to Neoplatonic ideas, such as those of Plotinus, about the unity of the cosmos—Augustine provided a template for centuries of spiritual seekers to utilize as they narrated their own pursuits of meaning in a seemingly meaningless universe.[18] Augustine shows his readers how to write about spiritual conversions, emphasizing the straying away that leads, in time, to a glorious homecoming. It is the story of every sinner, every convert. It is also the story "of the entire created order."[19] Augustine wants us to see that our wandering is the universe's wandering; that our return is creation's return. He wants us to see that *God has a plan.*

Almost all confessional writing of note can be traced back to the *Confessions.* Augustine's heirs include—but are by no means limited to—Rousseau, Kierkegaard, Dostoevsky, Tolstoy, and Nietzsche. An American branch of the family tree might claim Benjamin Franklin, Ralph Waldo Emerson, Henry David Thoreau, Frederick Douglass, and, in a more experimental vein, Gertrude Stein's *The Autobiography of Alice B. Toklas.* But let us not forget Henry

Adams. In the autobiographical work for which he remains most famous, *The Education of Henry Adams*, he attempted "to complete Augustine's 'Confessions,'" a work he valued as much for its style, it seems, as for its content.[20] To his good friend William James, Adams said that "Augustine alone has an idea of literary form."[21] It may not have been what Augustine was going for exactly, but the remark reveals just how long a shadow his work has cast—all the way into the modern world, the world of the "dynamo," as Adams called it, the world of science, industry, and technology that today seems so very far away from the *Confessions'* talk of salvation.

Other writers have experimented with the "literary form" of confessional writing. Two of them shaped Malick's cinema in particularly noticeable ways, perhaps because they offered him a glimpse of how philosophy could remain a way of life in the modern world. On the surface, Walker Percy and Stanley Cavell had little, if anything, in common: one was a devout convert to Catholicism famous for his popular novels, the other a secular Jew who wrote about ordinary language philosophy. But Percy's and Cavell's careers paralleled each other in interesting ways. Both of them were dropouts: Percy abandoned a career in medicine before he began writing fiction, and Cavell ditched music classes at Juilliard before pursuing graduate studies in philosophy. Neither Walker Percy nor Stanley Cavell viewed philosophy as just another academic discipline. They saw it as an extended exercise in self-analysis. To do philosophy was to figure out just who you were and where and how you belonged. It was confessional. As Cavell remarked in one of his later works: "there is an internal connection between philosophy and autobiography."[22]

Percy and Cavell also loved the movies. Each of them wrote insightfully about cinema throughout their careers. Sometimes this was in award-winning novels, such as Percy's *The Moviegoer*, other times in path-breaking academic monographs, such as Cavell's *The World Viewed: Reflections on the Ontology of Film* and *Pursuits of Happiness: The Hollywood Comedy of Remarriage*.[23] In different ways, Percy and Cavell showed Malick how film, philosophy, and self-reflection could inform each other. In Hollywood, Malick took all he had learned from them and combined it with ideas he picked up from other authors drawn to autobiography and searching, such as the travel writer and spiritual pilgrim Peter Matthiessen. Also important were the films he studied as a fellow at the American Film Institute, especially American New Wave films and the European art-house pictures that had influenced them. Malick was educated by Cavell, influenced by Percy, moved by Matthiessen, but he was truly inspired by the likes of Arthur Penn, Federico Fellini, and, as we shall see, Jean Renoir.

The Varieties of Cosmic Consciousness

I have experienced *The Tree of Life* in a variety of settings. I have seen it on small screens and big ones, in intimate environments and less-than-intimate ones. I have watched it alone in my tiny New York City apartment, but also with a packed, opening-night audience in Hollywood. I have viewed it with family and friends, but also total strangers. I have shown *The Tree of Life* to students, in places as far apart from each other as Lower Manhattan and San Marcos, Texas, near the small town of Smithville, where much of the picture was filmed. I have listened to *The Tree of Life*'s magnificent soundtrack through hand-me-down earbuds plugged into my laptop, while sitting, cramped and claustrophobic, in an uncomfortable seat on a cross-country flight; but I have also heard it played by a live orchestra in a hipster-packed concert hall in downtown Brooklyn. In each of these contexts, Malick's magnum opus has transformed itself, revealing new layers of depth and meaning. *The Tree of Life* is like Heraclitus's river: a different picture every time.

It is reassuring, I suppose, that Malick shares this opinion. Seven years after its premiere, he authorized a significantly longer version of *The Tree of Life* to be released, like all of his previous films, by the Criterion Collection. As the press notices went out of their way to point out, this was not a "director's cut," merely an "extended cut."[24] Malick seemed to be stepping back from the notion of authorizing a definitive version altogether. In fact, he toyed with the idea of producing something that might have undone the whole idea of one. According to numerous sources, he was interested in using new digital technology to produce an infinitely variable movie, with each presentation—in its digital formats, at least—spinning off into different narrative variants. Since the technology for this cinematic shuffle experience was not yet available, Malick settled for a new, longer cut of the existing film instead.

A restless, searching work, *The Tree of Life* is open to many possible interpretations. It is grand yet intimate, awe-inspiring yet also consoling. Different viewers have been drawn to different aspects of it. They have had plenty to choose from, since *The Tree of Life* attempts to capture nothing less than the story of all creation, from the Big Bang and the slow progression of microbial evolution all the way up to the fast-paced present of what scholars are now calling the Anthropocene. But most of the movie focuses on the experiences of just one contemporary character, a disaffected middle-aged architect named Jack O'Brien, whose memories—including a painful one involving the untimely death of one of his brothers—flood back into his thoughts for reasons we come to know only over the course of the film.

It is no revelation to say that *The Tree of Life* addresses themes more often found in Sunday sermons than in summer blockbusters. In this regard, the chief miracle of the picture is that it exists at all. Hollywood's "hedgehog mentality"—to use the words of *Los Angeles Times* film critic Kenneth Turan—has created a cinematic landscape dominated by "sequels and superhero movies and sequels to superhero movies."[25] In it, there would seem to be little room for the kinds of questions—philosophical, psychological, even downright theological—raised by *The Tree of Life*. Malick asks them anyway. His film opens with a quote from the Book of Job—"Where were you when I laid the foundations of the earth," it asks, "when the morning stars sang together, and all the sons of God shouted for joy?"[26] The message is clear: this will not be a story of caped crusaders and evil villains, but rather an exploration of pain, suffering, and loss. It will be, as the initials of the film's protagonist—J. O. B.—suggest, a theodicy.

Jack O'Brien has a wife, a fancy house, and an office job in a downtown skyscraper. We can tell he is unhappy, troubled, at a loss. He is preoccupied with memories that have flashed into his mind, memories of his childhood. These come to life on screen: we see the young Jack and his two brothers, R. L. (Laramie Eppler) and Steve (Tye Sheridan), along with their parents, Mr. and Mrs. O'Brien (Brad Pitt and Jessica Chastain). It is an average, middle-American family at midcentury, one that is well-off enough to have a house, a yard, and an automobile. But this cozy suburban life comes crashing down when news arrives—at a later point in time, judging by the changed setting and fashions—that one of the brothers has died tragically. At this point, *The Tree of Life* becomes inquisitive: What happens to us when suffering strikes? How does one cope with loss? What consolation, if any, might be found in the world? Having glimpsed some of Jack's memories, we now realize that he is in a state of despair, one stretching all the way back to his brother's untimely passing, from which he has never truly recovered. He needs to find meaning in his brother's death.

The German philosopher Gottfried Wilhelm Leibniz usually gets the credit for coining the term *theodicy*. But his 1710 work *Theodicy: Essays on the Goodness of God, the Freedom of Man, and the Origin of Evil* drew upon centuries of preceding philosophical and theological debate.[27] The problem of evil, and of human suffering, featured prominently in Neoplatonism, Augustinian confession, and a wide swath of medieval thought. Already by the sixth century, when the imprisoned Boethius was consoled by the personification of Philosophy—which came to him in the image of a woman, a fact worth remembering when we turn to *The Tree of Life*'s portrayal of gender roles—thinkers in the Western tradition had found a way to explain, or explain away, the pain of suffering. They often did so by juxtaposing our necessarily limited and fallible knowledge of things with God's, which was not only limitless but also, as a result, infallible. "If you could see the plan of Providence," Boethius's consoler assured him, "you would not think there was evil anywhere."[28]

This may have been comforting to Boethius in his prison cell in Pavia, but it did not prevent the bludgeoning that killed him just a short time later. Philosophers and theologians have been arguing about evil ever since. The debate usually centers on matters of perspective and scale. Theodicies like Boethius's and Leibniz's ask us to consider the larger picture, to exchange the "creaturely" perspective for what intellectual historian Mara van der Lugt has called a "cosmic" one.[29] In his *Meditations on First Philosophy*—written over a millennium after *The Consolation of Philosophy* and almost seventy years before *Theodicy*—Descartes suggested that "whenever we are inquiring whether the works of God are perfect, we ought to look at the whole universe, not just at one created thing on its own. For what would perhaps rightly appear very imperfect if it existed on its own is quite perfect when its function as part of the universe is considered."[30] As Descartes saw it, our curtailed, mortal perspective hinders our ability to know God's sometimes mysterious ways, which is why the notion of providence was so important: it allowed one to see their place, as Descartes put it, "in the universal scheme of things."[31]

After Descartes, philosophers often steered clear of theodicy—Kant famously denounced the "miscarriage" of philosophical theodicies.[32] But there were some important exceptions, most notably a certain Danish author who has inspired much of Malick's recent cinema. Nobody wrote more eloquently or extensively about the perplexing nature of Job and the meaning of suffering than Søren Kierkegaard, a thinker who ushered in the existentialism Malick studied as a philosophy student.[33]

Kierkegaard discussed the Book of Job often in his writings, but as Edward Mooney has pointed out, he broke "up his portrait of Job, distributing its fragments over several works," leaving us with the difficult "task of assembling the pieces."[34] Thankfully, there is a recurring theme: Kierkegaard's meditations on Job seek to rescue Christian faith from the twin dangers of modern, secular doubt, on the one side, and self-satisfied, existentially empty orthodoxy on the other, both of which misunderstood—and tried to explain away—the experience of suffering.

In *Repetition*, one of the many pseudonymous works he wrote in a fever, at the height of his powers, in 1843, Kierkegaard describes a Job who has been "kept secret," a Job obscured by traditional church teachings about the "perfection of life."[35] This is not the submissive Job, who is put in his place, but rather the questioning Job, the sarcastic Job. This is the Job who talks back, the Job "who knows how to complain so loudly that he is heard up in heaven."[36] The fictional young man whose letters compose the bulk of *Repetition* urges this Job to "repeat everything" because he thinks there is a fundamental difference between simply recalling one's struggles and being willing to endure them all over again: "It takes youthfulness to hope, youthfulness to recollect, but it takes courage to will repetition."[37] Repetition does not dwell in the past: it reenacts it so as to transcend it.

Viewed from this perspective, Job's "ordeal," as Kierkegaard's alter ego calls it, "is not esthetic, ethical, or dogmatic—it is altogether transcendent," "it places a person in a purely personal relationship of opposition to God, in a relationship such that he cannot allow himself to be satisfied with any explanation at second hand."[38] Job's "ordeal" reveals a pathway to God. It justifies the young man's "carrying on at a scale as macrocosmic as possible in all my microcosmicness."[39] Job shows us that we have every right to question providence, to ask God, "Who am I? How did I get into the world?"[40]

The version of Job that appears in *Repetition*—stubborn, defiant, anything but meek—has had a long afterlife in both Christian theology and existentialist philosophy. But for our purposes here, it is worth noting echoes of it in a book written and published around the time Malick began conceptualizing the film that would later become *The Tree of Life*, a book he read with interest that may have been partly responsible for his two-decade disappearance from the director's chair.

In his 1978 spiritual travelogue *The Snow Leopard*, parts of which first appeared in the *New Yorker*, the travel writer Peter Matthiessen invoked the Book of Job both explicitly and implicitly, putting it in dialogue not only with Christian catechisms and existentialist treatises, but also with the ancient religious and philosophical traditions of the Far East. Matthiessen also connected Job to the latest developments in physics and astronomy, which offered yet another perspective on micro- and macrocosms. Like Kierkeg-aard before him, Matthiessen read the Book of Job as more than just a testa-ment to God's greatness. As he saw it, Job personified a profound curiosity about the cosmos. His Job was open to wonder, the very same wonder that propelled Matthiessen on his travels to exotic locations around the world.

In *The Snow Leopard* Matthiessen praises a "mystical perception" that sees everything as being "in flux," a perception that knows "a cosmic energy shim-mers in all stone and steel as well as flesh."[41] To the question God hurls at Job in the Bible—"Where wast thou when I laid the foundations of the earth?"—Matthiessen provides a novel response: "'I was *there!*'—surely that is the an-swer to God's question," he writes. "For no matter how the universe came into being, most of the atoms in these fleeting assemblies that we think of as our bodies have been in existence since the beginning."[42] This is the Big Bang described in the language of Zen Buddhism, or maybe Emersonian transcen-dentalism leavened with Hopi temporality. It could also be high-altitude eu-phoria, too, induced by the author's wanderings across Tibetan mountains in search of Buddhist enlightenment. Whatever it was, the flash of inspiration allowed Matthiessen to interpret the Book of Job not as a stern warning to wayward mortals from an all-powerful God, nor even as an existential lamen-tation and a call to personal faith (as Kierkegaard's *Repetition* had it), but as a "primordial memory of Creation."[43] If we are all stardust, Matthiessen main-tained, then surely, we *were* there "when the morning stars sang together."

As Matthiessen saw it, we are the cosmos. In coming to know ourselves, we come to know the universe. But the reverse is also true: in seeking to know the universe, we discover ourselves. The spiritual journey inward is but a mir-ror of the scientific quest outward. To underscore the point, Matthiessen quotes Carl Sagan, doing his best impression of Hegel: "Man is the matter of the cosmos, contemplating itself."[44] Needless to say, Kierkegaard, no admirer of Hegel, would not have put it this way. Still, Matthiessen's answer to the Voice in the Whirlwind—as God is described in the Book of Job—achieves something that is nevertheless in keeping with Kierkegaard: it replaces the yearning for justice with a mood of wonderment.

In Kierkegaard's writings, the usual concerns of theodicy are, as Mooney explains, "set aside."[45] In their stead one finds a renewed sense of mystery and reverence, a fascination with the majesty of the world and the cosmos. The marvelous takes precedence over the pious. Kierkegaard had this epiphany walking the streets of Copenhagen. Matthiessen stumbled upon it high up in the Himalayas. But the lesson was the same for both of them: transcendence was out there, and it could be found in the marvels of the cosmos.

In another text devoted to the Book of Job (this one written without recourse to pseudonyms and fictional characters), Kierkegaard made this point explicitly. The fundamental message of the Book of Job was not one of "silent subjection," he argued, but "thankfulness."[46] Despite all his sufferings, Job still "traced everything back to God," not because he was put in his place, but because he came to see the universe as a gift.[47] In Kierkegaard's account, the story of Job's humbling "makes space," Edward Mooney writes, "for the reception of a cosmos wondrously stocked with richly crystallized particulars," including "the great height of starry skies, the wildness of sea-beasts, the wonder of sleet and dew and sunrise, the raw might of a bull, the gentle curve of *this* hawk in flight."[48]

Though the images may differ, a similar sense of awe for such "crystallized particulars" can be found throughout *The Tree of Life*, a picture that moves from grief to gratitude. Its plot hinges on death and loss, but its cinematography revels in the glories of the natural world: water rushing over polished river rocks; the chance landing of a luminous butterfly on an outstretched hand; sunlight illuminating the knotted branches of majestic oak trees. Almost every shot of the film, it seems, is a marvel.

Matthiessen and Kierkegaard wrestled a sublime vision of the natural world from the Book of Job and made memorable confessional literature out

Figure 22. An oak tree outside the O'Brien house in *The Tree of Life*.

of it, but in *The Tree of Life* Malick found a way to transform it into the language of cinema.[49] *The Tree of Life* displays—as John Caruana has put it in an insightful essay on Kierkegaard's presence in the film—"the giftedness of the world": it offers "a sense of the thread that links the human being to the divine source of the gift of the created order."[50] That divine source is represented by images, which bookend the film, of Thomas Wilfred's artistic installation *Opus 161* (1965–66), an ever-changing dance of light and color.[51]

It is not difficult to see why a young philosophy student, eager to find his place in the order of the cosmos, would be drawn—like Kierkegaard, like Matthiessen—to the Book of Job, for Job's story is one of existential turmoil and cosmological homecoming. He is the ultimate searcher, a seeker of meaning. We may never know what Malick intended to show in his proposed Oxford dissertation on the concept of world in Heidegger, Kierkegaard, and Wittgenstein—and we may never know just how much of it may have been conceived with the Book of Job in mind—but already in his Harvard thesis Malick had displayed a familiarity with Leibniz's *Theodicy*, so interpreting *The Tree of Life* as his own attempt at expounding a theodicy-like statement of faith, one rooted in his own search for meaning, helps us appreciate how a film about death can spend so much time marveling at the wonders of nature.[52]

The Bible tells us that God eventually presented Job, whom Satan had tested and tormented, with a world renewed, a world to be viewed with eyes afresh as something marvelous. *The Tree of Life* recreates this world, offering not just the earth, but also the stars and planets of our solar system, as wonders to behold. It is a stunning vision—an instance of what one scholar has called the "postsecular sublime."[53] Moviegoers who wandered into the film expecting only another Brad Pitt vehicle were no doubt confounded. (Theater owners resorted to posting signs outside cinema doors, apparently, warning audiences of what was in store.) But audiences looking for something other than a Marvel movie were mesmerized.

As an exercise in cosmological inquiry, *The Tree of Life* taps into not just the Bible but also some very old philosophical traditions. The modern word *cosmology* comes to us from the ancient Greek: it is a combination of *kosmos*, which in Homer's day described order and adornment (as in "cosmetics") and *logos*, the word, literally, for word, though it usually meant something like reasoned account (as in "logic"). In the words of the classicist M. R. Wright, "*Kosmos* was the name given to the well-arranged, all-containing whole, and *logos* the rational analysis and account for it."[54]

But *kosmos* and *logos* were not so easily combined, at least not at first. Aristophanes, in the *Lysistrata*, went so far as to make their incompatibility the butt of one of his many gender-based jokes: "There's nothing cosmic about cosmetics," one of his characters quips.[55] In time, though, the raunchy jokes gave way to sober inquiry and the science of cosmology was born.[56] *Kosmos* shed its connotations with cosmetics and came to have an abstract, even scientific connotation.[57] Aristotle's *On the Heavens* pushed cosmology from the realm of pure speculation into something resembling empirical observation.[58]

Aristotle showed *how* the cosmos could be studied, but he did not solve the riddle of *why* it should be. Because their scope and scale often exceeded that of the individual human life, ancient cosmologies could make individual human lives seem insignificant. It was Democritus who conceived of a way to combine cosmology's wide-angle perspective with something like a more personal close-up. He showed how the macrocosm and the microcosm reflected each other, how individual creatures embodied, in miniature, the structure of all living things.[59] In the life of one person, in other words, one could trace the outlines of the entire universe. The personal and the universal, the creaturely and the cosmic, went hand in hand—at least until the doctrines of Democritus fell out of favor in the Middle Ages, as Christian theology displaced ancient cosmology.[60]

Leibniz and his follower Christian Wolff brought cosmology back into philosophical fashion in the early eighteenth century. Wolff viewed it as nothing less than the true starting point of all philosophical inquiry. In his 1728 *Preliminary Discourse on Philosophy in General*, Wolff went so far as to suggest that "general cosmology," properly conceived, was the basis of all knowledge. He made the argument that "psychology, natural theology, and physics derive principles from it."[61] But Wolff's intricate theories about micro- and macrocosms were rendered superfluous by the progress of empirical science. By the twentieth century, philosophers agreed that it was probably "better"—one scholar wrote—"to leave the microcosmic theories to lie like fossils scattered throughout the upheaved and faulting strata of the history of philosophy."[62]

The scientific revolution's "destruction of the Cosmos," as the twentieth-century philosopher of science Alexandre Koyré memorably put it, had many consequences, not the least of which was the banishment of God from the universe. Conceptions of a closed, divinely created world gave way to images of a void of "infinite, uncreated nothingness."[63] What Koyré called the "the infinitization of the universe" traded the hierarchical, value-laden conceptions of a bounded cosmos for endless expanses of space and time.

The new science offered no comfort to those seeking order and meaning.[64] It killed off cosmology.

When they are viewed against this intellectual-historical backdrop, Malick's recent films seem like experiments in cosmological reenchantment, the latest installment in "a millennia-old project"—as one commentator has put it—"of visually reconciling the macrocosmos with the microcosmos, finding our local lives situated within the grand scheme of things."[65] They represent post-secular attempts to put some divine warmth back into the void. *The Tree of Life*—like *Voyage of Time* after it—puts the sciences of quantum mechanics and astronomy in conversation with Christian teaching. Malick's grafting of the latest scientific research about an expanding and accelerating universe onto religious discussions of faith and gratitude may be too secular for the theists and not secular enough for the scientists, but it reflects his decades-long personal pursuit of not just knowledge but also meaning.

Some major philosophers in the first half of the twentieth century sought out a similar middle ground between science and faith, among them Arthur O. Lovejoy, Ernst Cassirer, Alfred North Whitehead, and R. G. Collingwood. But these were idiosyncratic thinkers, whose cosmological musings were easily marginalized by a profession becoming more empiricist by the day.[66] Big-picture cosmology was out; pointillist positivism was in. Yet lingering doubts persisted. As the positivist philosopher of science Hans Reichenbach put it in 1942: "We do not want to go blindly through the world." "We desire more than a mere existence," he wrote, and "cosmic perspectives" give us "a feeling for our place in the world."[67] Not only that: Reichenbach also thought the contemplation of the cosmos required "wonder" as well as "sober research and calculation."[68]

More often than not, though, this wonder was relegated to religion. In *The Varieties of Religious Experience*, William James had suggested that the fundamental question around which almost every religion revolves is, fundamentally, cosmological. Whether orthodox or heterodox, Eastern or Western, ancient or modern, all faiths in one way or another ask, "What is the character of this universe in which we dwell?"[69] *The Tree of Life* asks a similar question, but it personalizes it: What is the character of this universe in which *I* dwell?

In both its opening and concluding sections, *The Tree of Life* depicts nothing less than the origin and evolution of all life—from the spectacular emergence of the stars to the smallest sparks of cellular division and microbial flourishing. But these images surround a confessional family drama at the center of the film. To understand the microcosm, Malick seems to be saying, one must understand the macrocosm. To put it in Heideggerian lingo, an understanding of *Dasein* requires a knowledge of Being. But an understanding of Being cannot be attained without first asking about the enigma of human existence, and the only way to get at that is through self-examination. Kierkegaard's *Repetition* offers an example of it: "Where am I?" the narrator asks, "What does it mean to say: the world? What is the meaning of that word?"[70]

In his 1960 book *Theory of Film*, Siegfried Kracauer suggested that movies allow us to take a second look—in some cases, even a third look—at material reality. Cinema trains our attention on all of the sensorial richness of embodied life, and in doing so it offers nothing less than "the redemption of physical reality." In an age of alienating abstraction, Kracauer writes, our "urge for concretion" wants "to touch reality not only with the fingertips, but to seize it and shake hands with it." Movies reacquaint "us with the world we live in," and in doing so they "make the world our home."[71] This is precisely what *The Tree of Life* sets out to accomplish.

Rivers, Trees, and Renoir

The Tree of Life suggests that nature is an elementary component of our world. Malick's films have always taken the great outdoors as their primary backdrop. Earth, sky, fire, and water are their cinematic coordinates; beaches, forests, mountains, and prairies, their primary locations. Almost every one of Malick's pictures has a shot of a majestic tree, backlit by a late afternoon sun. These images provide a kind of meditative break, pulling the viewer's attention away from the unfolding story, redirecting it outward and upward, from the terrestrial to the transcendent.

Malick's attention to nature evokes a tradition of filmmaking preoccupied with finding spiritual meaning in everyday affairs. "In cinema's unique ability to reproduce the immanent," Paul Schrader wrote in *Transcendental Style*, "also lies its unique ability to evoke the Transcendent."[72] Malick's nature montages are moments of wonder. Wherever they are placed in his films, they link the microcosm to the macrocosm, announcing the interconnectedness of all things. They are illustrations of what the famed environmentalist John Muir, channeling the wisdom of Emerson, once said: "When we try to pick out anything by itself, we find it hitched to everything else in the universe."[73]

Muir also famously claimed that "the clearest way into the Universe is through a forest wilderness," which might explain why there are so many

shots of trees in *The Tree of Life*.[74] It is tempting to trace this arboreal aesthetic back to various religious sources—the idea of something like a tree of
life can be found not just in the Judeo-Christian tradition but also in Buddhism, Hinduism, and Islam, as well as in other belief systems stretching
from Mesoamerica to Mesopotamia—but a clear precedent can be found in
cinematic history. *The Tree of Life* is rooted not just in ancient cosmologies,
the Book of Job, and the writings of Kierkegaard and Peter Matthiessen, it
turns out, but also in old movies.

It was a little-known film by the famed French director Jean Renoir, *Picnic on the Grass* (1959), that taught Malick to love trees. On March 20, 1970,
the inaugural cohort of students at the Center for Advanced Film Studies
gathered to discuss the film, which had come and gone from theaters without much fanfare only a decade or so earlier. Its screening at Greystone would
have been a rare opportunity to revel in a rarely shown movie. Though the
Cahiers du Cinéma crowd adored it, Renoir's picture received mostly lukewarm praise outside of Paris. According to Renoir's biographer Pascal
Merigeau, it was a film "fit only to delight Renoirians."[75] Richard Brody claims
it was "screened fairly frequently in New York repertory houses in the mid-
seventies," but one would be hard pressed to find any lasting evidence of this.[76]
Today, *Picnic on the Grass* is dismissed as a minor work in the canon of a major filmmaker; it has never been released on DVD in the United States and
remains rather difficult to track down in its European editions.

Part of the reason may be the film's flimsy plot. Borrowing its title from the
famous impressionist painting by his father's friend Édouard Manet, Renoir's
Picnic on the Grass might be described as a romantic comedy crossed with a
sci-fi farce. It is set in the South of France, in an alternate near future. A famous
biologist, Étienne Alexis (Paul Meurisse), has pioneered a method of artificial
insemination that will make human reproduction more of a science than an
art, producing a supposedly healthier, genetically superior world population,
but one that will be unfamiliar with love, spontaneity, and, well, fun. Dr. Alexis's announced marriage to an aristocratic German cousin of his, Marie-
Charlotte (Ingrid Nordine), an imposing, uniform-wearing scout leader, is an
obvious preview of romantic relations to come: everything will be orderly and
preordained, nothing left to chance. The international nuptials also represent
the destined unification of Europe, of which Dr. Alexis hopes to become the
first president, under the banners of science, industry, and progress.

Things come undone, though, when an alfresco celebration of Étienne
and Marie-Charlotte's engagement is interrupted by a Pan-like peasant,

whose pipe-playing atop the ruins of an old Roman temple to Diana, the goddess of fertility, unleashes the winds of desire, stirring the stuffy, bourgeois picnickers into an orgiastic state. High jinks ensue. All but winking at his audience, Renoir slips in slapstick, sight gags, and silly music to move things along. In the midst of it all, Dr. Alexis falls for Nénette (Catherine Rouvel), a simple farm girl who helps him appreciate all that the largely premodern, Provençal way of life has to offer, including not just naked bathing in rivers, but also meals paired with bottles of the local vintage and midday siestas under shady olive trees (some of the very same trees Renoir's father had immortalized in his paintings).[77] "Perhaps happiness is submission to the natural order," a converted Dr. Alexis muses to his paramour as they recline contentedly under the trees.

After his fling with Nénette, which leaves him marveling at the "inexplicable" glory of nature, Dr. Alexis is promptly shanghaied back into scientific and political service by his scandalized, well-to-do family members, who worry that his newfound love of the peasant way of life will derail their profitable plans for a unified, rationalized, orderly Europe. The marriage is back on. But then, in a denouement straight out of the romantic comedy playbook—the genre Stanley Cavell came to call the "Hollywood comedy of remarriage"—Dr. Alexis accidentally reunites with a now very pregnant Nénette, chooses to wed her instead of his scout-mistress cousin, and declares he will run for president on a platform devoted not to science but rather to science *and* nature.[78]

Picnic on the Grass is never discussed as an influence on Malick's filmmaking, but it should be. Its seemingly Heideggerian critique of modern science—dramatized by a dialogue between Dr. Alexis, representing a technocratic worldview, and a weathered old curate (André Brunot), representing a religious one—seems to prove as much. The country priest laughs down the idea of a destined "dictatorship of scientists," arguing that science has only given the world a landscape of unsightly factories, whereas religion has given it noble cathedrals. The exchange brings to mind the controversy unleashed by C. P. Snow's infamous Rede Lecture—delivered across the Channel at Cambridge the very same year Renoir's film debuted in theaters—about the comparative merits of what he called the "two cultures" of the natural sciences and the humanities.[79]

Such dichotomies can be found throughout Malick's cinema. But the opposition between nature and grace in *The Tree of Life*—personified by a domineering engineer father on the one side and a saintly, ethereal mother on the other—is the one that evokes Renoir most noticeably, especially in the way that it leans into *Picnic on the Grass*'s gendered messaging. Renoir's film suggests that masculinity is synonymous with calculative rationality, whereas femininity somehow manages to temper, if not resist, its relentless drive toward domination. The trope appears in many of Malick's films, including *Badlands*, *Days of Heaven*, and *The New World*, but in *The Tree of Life*, which makes women out to be the sole guardians of God-given grace, it becomes a focal point.

Gender dynamics were not what captured Malick's attention when he first saw *Picnic on the Grass*, though. As a budding filmmaker he was much more interested in Renoir's cinematic style. Tasked with introducing an AFI seminar on *Picnic on the Grass* in 1970, Malick zeroed in on matters of framing and composition, focusing, in particular, on Renoir's use of insert shots depicting the natural world. Interspersed throughout the film, breaking up its narrative, were, Malick noted, images of rivers, grasses, and trees—insects, too. These shots were a "very curious device," he suggested, "because they don't have any immediate relationship to the action." "They aren't meant to contribute to the ambience." "They aren't scenic elements" or "scenic details."[80] Because the "extreme close-ups" of a locust on a piece of bark or "a beetle standing on a dandelion blossom" did not correspond to the progression of the plot, they opened up many different layers of potential experience and interpretation. They drew audience attention to things outside the film's narrative. The inserts revealed a whole other world.

Malick thought Renoir's nature montages were purposefully ambiguous. Unlike the one-to-one equivalences suggested by Eisenstein's editing, they conveyed no predetermined meaning. They were neither a metaphor nor a symbol. They were, rather, a gesture toward "the world in which the characters live." Renoir's nature montages suggested "a world of proliferating mystery that surrounds the characters, that runs parallel with them."

Here is where Malick's singular style, which comes to fruition in *The Tree of Life*, first began to take shape. Just about everything he said in the AFI seminar about Renoir's nature montages—about how they conveyed "a world of proliferating mystery," especially—could be used to describe the most memorable sequences in his own films, including, most of all, the extended cosmos sequences in *The Tree of Life*. Malick's films revolve around shots of the natural world in full, awe-inspiring splendor: the swollen river and whispering trees of *Badlands*; the shining wheat fields of *Days of Heaven*; the long, green grasses of *The Thin Red Line*; the forests, fields, and waterways of *The*

New World. All of these come together in *The Tree of Life*, the purest distillation of his cinematic aesthetic.

Once one is alerted to it, Renoir's influence on Malick's filmmaking is impossible to ignore. Malick was, it seems, a Renoirian from the start. But he was far from alone in rediscovering the power of Renoir's filmmaking. Indeed, something of a Renoir renaissance was well underway when Malick entered AFI. On February 7, 1969, the Los Angeles County Museum of Art opened a comprehensive retrospective of Renoir's work, which led to a resurgence of interest in his films. Writing in the *Los Angeles Free Press* a month after the exhibit opened, Paul Schrader heralded the rediscovery of *Boudu Saved from Drowning* (1932), which until then had not enjoyed a proper West Coast premiere. *Boudu* was a revelation, Schrader wrote, a message in a bottle received at just the right time: it was "as great, or greater, than it was in 1932." He urged his readers to catch its limited-engagement showing at the Los Feliz Theater just as soon as they possibly could.[81]

Malick did not move to Los Angeles until late September, 1969, long after *Boudu* had come and gone from local theaters, but he would have heard about it, and about the Renoir retrospective at LACMA, and maybe not just from Schrader, either. Alexander Sesonske, a philosopher and film studies professor at the nearby University of California, Santa Barbara, was in the process of befriending Renoir at the time. He had invited the French filmmaker up the coast to speak to students enrolled in a seminar devoted to his work. Sesonske would later publish a definitive study of Renoir's early films in the Harvard Film Studies series, which was fitting because Sesonske was one of Stanley Cavell's oldest friends in the philosophical profession. The two of them studied philosophy together at UCLA in the late forties and early fifties.[82] Each had taken a circuitous route to get there: Cavell switching from music, which he had been studying previously at Juilliard; and Sesonske making the most out of the opportunities afforded him by the GI Bill after serving as an artilleryman in the Second World War.[83] Sesonske and Cavell kept in touch over the years, staying abreast of each other's writing on cinema especially. It was Sesonske who introduced Cavell to Renoir in the early 1970s, escorting him to the filmmaker's home in Beverly Hills.[84] Perhaps Malick tagged along.

However he came to discover them, Malick's early appreciation for Renoir's films was boundless. Their unique style left a deep imprint, significantly shaping his development as a filmmaker. He tried to convey their unique power to his classmates at AFI. Aside from a memorable sequence in Charles Laughton's *The Night of the Hunter* (1955), in which a series of shots foreground elements of the natural world—a glimmering spider's web, a frog, cattail grasses illuminated by moonlight—the only other movies Malick could think of that utilized the cinematic technique of the nature montage so effectively were directed by none other than Renoir: *Boudu Saved from Drowning* and *A Day in the Country* (1936).

In *Boudu*, the freedom to be found in parks and rivers stands in stark contrast to the stuffiness of bourgeois society, from which the film's Dionysian protagonist—his full name is Priapus Boudu, an allusion to the always-erect Greek god of fertility—repeatedly attempts to escape. Here, the nature shots hint at freedom, liberation. But the images of the natural world that interrupt the narrative of *A Day in the Country*, a largely light-hearted adaptation of a story by Guy de Maupassant, are different. They place the film's characters—and by extension, the film's audiences—in a particularly reflective state of mind. As Malick told his AFI classmates, Renoir's protagonists are struck by something "outside of their reach." "They are," he said "brought to a stop." Malick resorted to Heideggerian terminology to explain what he meant. Gazing out at a riverbank, a character in *A Day in the Country* is pulled out of "his world of everyday concern." The subsequent shots of the same river leave audiences with a comparable "sense of mystery." The barrier between the world *in* the picture and the world *of* the picture breaks down: characters and viewers alike become aware of the wonder of the world.

Films such as *A Day in the Country* and *Picnic on the Grass* exalt in—as the MIT philosopher Irving Singer once put it—"the sheer wonderment of nature."[85] It was something Malick was particularly predisposed to noticing. In their early English translation and summary of the first fifty-three sections of Martin Heidegger's *Sein und Zeit*, John Wild and his Harvard graduate students—including Hubert Dreyfus, who went on to teach alongside Singer at MIT—described *Dasein*'s ability "to lose himself in what is encountered in the world and to be stupefied by it." This was part and parcel of what Heidegger called the "phenomenon <u>and problem</u> of worldliness"—a topic Malick tried to tackle in his abandoned dissertation project at Oxford just a few years prior to matriculating at the American Film Institute.[86]

Translating such abstruse philosophical ideas into the language of film criticism was not easy. Listening to the tape of the AFI seminar, one can hear Malick's enthusiasm for Renoir's interest in nature but also his frustration trying to explain it. He just about talks himself in circles. Malick admitted that, without the "shots of the river," *A Day in the Country* "would just be a

Figure 23. Proliferating mystery in Jean Renoir's *A Day in the Country*.

plain, saccharine, small human drama, with really nothing to recommend it."[87] But with the river flowing through it from beginning to end—the film opens and closes with haunting shots of water—*A Day in the Country* becomes something else entirely.[88] The question was, why? Why were its fleeting images of nature—passing clouds, falling raindrops, a bird perched in a tree—so compelling?

When pressed by the other seminar members to explain how these insert shots elevated *A Day in the Country* and *Picnic in the Grass* into noteworthy works of art, Malick all but threw up his hands. "I don't know," he said, "You get the sense of banal characters stuck in the middle of some world of mystery. It's very difficult to talk about." He may not have been able to put into words just what Renoir had achieved, but Malick knew exactly how watching his films made him feel, which was bowled over: "that's the effect that's constantly overwhelming me," he said, "just wiping me out when I see it." The images of trees and rivers, insects and birds, suggested that nature was just carrying on, undaunted, "that it has all happened a hundred times before."

The other fellows remained skeptical. Malick urged them to read Penelope Gilliatt's praise-filled profile of Renoir in the *New Yorker*, but the suggestion probably fell on deaf ears.[89] Largely dismissive of *Picnic on the Grass*, his classmates argued that Renoir's use of nature montages was neither as unique nor as profound as Malick had claimed. Paul Schrader likened it to the ways in which Japanese films—about which he had just led a seminar—worked.[90] He also accused Malick of turning Renoir into more of a pantheist than he really was. A vigorous debate ensued, replete with the kind of "intel-lectual rough housing" Malick thought the AFI curriculum could do with-out in those early days of the program.[91]

In the AFI seminar, Schrader insisted that nature montages could be found "all over," in just about every movie. But Malick still thought Renoir's nature montages were unprecedented in cinema, because they were used to "undercut all of the human drama." The images gave audiences glimpses of the "continuity of life." Renoir invited viewers to see a wider world of "pro-liferating mystery."

Seen from this perspective, light-hearted *Picnic in the Grass* was anything but a simple little farce. It was not another tale of nature versus science, which for Malick was a "dead issue" anyhow. Nor was it just some playful exercise in *plein air* pastoralism. Malick thought Renoir was more interested in "how mysterious nature is" than in how beautiful it looked. It was a sense of mys-tery, a sense of awe or even dread instilled by these montages, that set the film apart. Renoir's nature montages were "the most powerful moments in movies, generally," Malick insisted. "These characters just are arrested and see something beyond them that's just completely alien to them, and for a brief moment, the necessity of their lives comes into question. I'm sorry I have to be so vague about that," he said, but it was a mood he was describing, not a theoretical position. "It's an overpowering feeling," he explained, "these people are wandering just as blindly as that locust is."

Comparing shots of the natural world in films such as *Boudu Saved from Drowning*, *A Day in the Country*, and *Picnic on the Grass* with images Ma-lick would go on to insert into his own films years and even decades later, one sees the lingering effect of that "overpowering feeling." Allusions to Renoir's nature montages abound in Malick's pictures: a beetle atop a cactus paddle in *Badlands*; a locust on a stalk of wheat in *Days of Heaven*; a bril-liantly colored bird sitting in a tree in *The Thin Red Line*. Renoirian rivers show up in each of his films, too, from the first one right down to the most recent. Significant portions of *Badlands*, *Days of Heaven*, *The Thin Red Line*, and *The New World* take place in a forest near a river's edge. As they were for Renoir, waterways, for Malick, are places where characters stop and think; they are sites of change and transformation.[92]

Rivers abound in *The Tree of Life*, a film meant to evoke, as one of its pro-ducers put it, the "feeling of a river."[93] But there are plenty of animals, clouds, grasses, insects, skies, and sunsets too. And trees, a whole lot of them. Reno-irian nature imagery suggesting a world of "proliferating mystery" is scattered

Figure 24. River grasses à la Jean Renoir in *The Tree of Life*.

throughout the picture, which helps explain why so many of *The Tree of Life*'s shots feel like an homage to *Boudu*, *A Day in the Country*, and *Picnic on the Grass*. "Renoir's style," Alexander Sesonske wrote in his 1980 study of the film-maker, "proves ideal for the exploration and revelation of nature."[94] Malick celebrates it in *The Tree of Life*. The picture's many luminous images of majestic trees—such as the grand oak tree in front of the O'Briens' family home, which serves as visual centerpiece in the film—recall the quiet, roving shot of trees that follows the opening credits of *Picnic on the Grass*.[95] In addition to this, a particularly haunting shot of water grasses dancing in a river current, which recurs throughout the picture, all but copies similar images in Renoir's film. It is an homage to a filmmaker to whose example Malick has been returning to again and again throughout his career.

From Renoir, Malick learned to focus on the here and now of his surroundings: the world as it is, at precisely this moment, in this exact place. He saw how paying attention to the particular could become a gateway to the universal. As Sesonske, paraphrasing Aristotle but thinking of *Boudu*'s extended closing shot of a river, put it: "it is only through such specificity that true universality can be achieved."[96]

The inaugural cohort of AFI fellows spent a great deal of time studying the films of Jean Renoir in the late winter and early spring of 1970 because he was an influential filmmaker who had been making movies for decades. But they also analyzed his work because their instructors told them to. Renoir was one of the earliest guests of the Center for Advanced Film Studies.

He visited Greystone during what was only the second semester of instruction, just a few weeks after Malick and the fellows had discussed *Picnic on
the Grass*. A pioneer in making films outside the studio system, Renoir was
considered an ideal role model for AFI's aspiring filmmakers, who were being encouraged to work adjacent to the industrial system of Hollywood, if
not outright against it. Renoir proved this was possible. His fame and success demonstrated that one could make unique, personal films and still have
a viable career. As George Stevens Jr. later recalled, the hope was that Renoir
"would bring a distinctive and nourishing sensibility to our process."[97]

This the veteran of "the war of the film-maker against the industry"—to
use the words with which Renoir described himself in his memoir, *My Life
and My Films*, just four years later—most certainly did.[98] He began his remarks at Greystone by reiterating one of his central mantras as a filmmaker,
the very idea that made him such an important role model for the *Cahiers
du Cinéma* crowd: one always can, and should, make "a personal picture,"
he said, a picture that "will be the expression of your personality."[99] Renoir
encouraged the aspiring filmmakers in the audience to think of their films
as being "like literature," more akin to "a state of mind" or an "inner belief"
than the product of an assembly line.[100]

For young filmmakers full of ideas, eager to make something other than
studio filler, this must have been invigorating, liberating advice. Renoir urged
each of them to build up a distinctive cinematic "grammar," to develop their
own "method."[101] Each picture should be thought of as its own "little world"
and directors needed to work from the strength of their "convictions" to realize it.[102] He told the fellows to look within: "After all," he said, "the purpose
of art and moviemaking is to find yourself."[103]

Rockets and Requiems

The Tree of Life is certainly about finding yourself. It marks a significant turn
in Malick's career, inaugurating a trilogy of largely autobiographical films
that dig down into his own personal experience to construct a cinematic
"grammar" uniquely his own. In this regard, Malick took from Renoir and
the directors associated with the *nouvelle vague* who followed in his footsteps
not just a few cinematic techniques but also an enthusiasm for personal
filmmaking.

Malick borrowed liberally from the example of French New Wave directors like Truffaut and Godard (just as the they had borrowed from Golden Era Hollywood directors such as Howard Hawks, Alfred Hitchcock, and Nicholas Ray; just as Renoir, before them, had borrowed from Chaplin, Griffith, and Stroheim).[104] When Renoir visited AFI, Malick asked him for his thoughts about the "French New Wave directors" (this was before Renoir dedicated *My Life and My Films* to them, saying they shared his "preoccupations").[105] Renoir said he was happy to be associated with their work: he liked "belonging to a little group," which far from threatening his "individuality" actually helped him "to find it."[106] Maybe the renegade filmmakers holed up in a Beverly Hills mansion were starting to think of themselves in the same way, as a band of outsiders seeking to find themselves.

Other early illustrious visitors to the Center for Advanced Film Studies offered similar advice. They, too, viewed filmmaking as an intensely personal pursuit. Like Renoir, they told the fellows to look within, to their own lives, for inspiration. "I think it is absolutely impossible not to be autobiographical," Fellini told a rapt audience at Greystone on January 12, 1970.[107] Riding a wave of publicity generated by NBC's unexpected decision to broadcast *Fellini: A Director's Notebook* on network television, Italy's most famous filmmaker was in town to promote his latest film, *Satyricon* (1969), but he was also there to tout the importance of personal filmmaking.[108]

No director is more representative of a personal approach to filmmaking than Fellini. His name is synonymous with subjective, stream-of-consciousness cinema. In fact, in a film that appeared not long after Renoir's *Picnic on the Grass*—namely, *La Dolce Vita* (1960)—Fellini began to trade stories set in identifiably realistic or naturalistic worlds for ones set almost entirely in personal dream spaces of memory, fantasy, and imagination. The result of this turn in Fellini's career, which up until that point had traveled along tracks laid down by the Italian neorealism of the postwar period, was a new kind of moviemaking, a highly personal "metacinema" that drew upon the director's life experiences, often inserting them directly into his films. The most famous example of this is, of course, *8½*, a movie about a director's inability to get a sci-fi movie—like the rocket that is its visual centerpiece—off the ground. Distracted by his own doubts and desires, overcome by memories and reveries that come upon him unexpectedly, Guido (Marcello Mastroianni) is Fellini's avatar. His fruitless struggle to realize a perhaps unrealizable film gives Fellini all the material he needs to complete his own: *8½* is about the struggle to make a movie, but also, and more importantly, about the struggle to find purpose and meaning in one's life.

Situated between *Picnic on the Grass*'s reverence for the wonders of nature and *8½*'s autobiographical mediation on the elusive workings of memory is *The Tree of Life*, a confessional film that is both grandly transcendental and intensely personal. The picture mixes scientific curiosity with searching spirituality, existential phenomenology with cinematic experimentation. It also links cosmic contemplation to personal confession. Using a slightly fictionalized version of his own life story as a starting point, Malick opens a window onto the unfolding processes of all planetary—even galactic—life. In this regard, the film is reminiscent of Heidegger's attempt in *Being and Time* to use the analysis of *Dasein*, or human existence, as a way of gaining access to the larger phenomenon of all existence, or Being itself.

The Tree of Life is not about *Dasein*, though; it is about Malick. In the film, his avatar is Jack O'Brien, the disaffected, middle-aged urbanite who lives in a coolly antiseptic modern house and works in the gravity-defying glass skyscrapers of downtown Houston. The entire film is a kind of reverie rooted in Jack's existence. Like *8½*, it explores memories of childhood—all of its joys, sorrows, and lessons, but also its smells, sounds, feelings, dreams, and visions. These had found their way into many of Malick's previous films, going all the way back to his first, *Badlands*, but never before had they been presented in such an obviously self-referential fashion.

What Dwight Macdonald once wrote of *8½* applies just as well, it seems to me, to *The Tree of Life*: "Everything flows in this protean movie, constantly

Figure 25. Young Jack (Hunter McCracken) in *The Tree of Life*.

shifting between reality, memory, and fantasy."[109] Like Fellini before him, Malick shows us how the work of recollection thrusts us into a hazy realm between extremely private experiences, on the one side, and seemingly universal archetypes on the other. An overbearing father, a saintly mother, a lost brother—these are the tropes of many coming-of-age films, but in *The Tree of Life* they are anything but the building blocks for a generic plot. Instead, these dreams or memories or historical traces of Jack's childhood are woven together into a kind of visual poem or fugue that heralds an emotional, spiritual homecoming. *The Tree of Life* represents nothing less than Malick's attempt at making sense of his own life.

Bookending Jack's coming-of-age story is what I take to be the truly daring part of the film, the one that takes Renoir's nature montages and enlarges them, almost beyond recognition. In both its opening and concluding sections, *The Tree of Life* goes beyond glimpses of rivers and skies to give us the cosmos itself, everything from the spectacular birth of the stars to the smallest sparks of cellular division. They are scenes of "proliferating mystery," captured in the widest, grandest frame. Jack's story is juxtaposed with nothing less than the story of the entire universe.

Jack wanders blindly in despair at the outset of *The Tree of Life*, but by the time the credits roll he has been transformed. We see as much in the smile that comes across his face. What accounts for the shift, for what we might call—to use the words of Hubert Dreyfus—this Kierkegaardian "movement from despair to bliss"?[110] The noticeable change in the adult Jack's mood and demeanor at the conclusion of the film surely does not result from any protracted effort on his part. All he seems to do throughout the scenes in which he appears is stumble through daily chores, obviously preoccupied, lost in his own thoughts. (The extended cut of *The Tree of Life* does try to portray adult Jack as more of a seeker, inserting scenes of him visiting galleries and museums, where he contemplates dioramas of dinosaurs and the paintings of Hieronymus Bosch.) What the adult Jack does do, though, is pray. At one point, we even see him lighting a votive candle. Befitting a film that Roger Ebert famously described as a form of prayer, *The Tree of Life*'s first spoken words are addressed to God.[111] But they also acknowledge the people who made such a prayer possible. "Mother. Brother," Jack's voice-over narration begins: "It was they who led me to Your door."

Remembering his deceased loved ones, adult Jack relives memories of loss and pain. These set him adrift. ("Every human loss"—as one theologian, responding to *The Tree of Life* has suggested—"puts a question mark over the cosmos.")[112] But "to be able to despair," as one of Kierkegaard's famous works, *The Sickness unto Death*, declared, "is an infinite merit," for it has the ability to set one on the path toward faith.[113] Indeed, Jack turns to God not out of joy but out of sadness and confusion. Because everything in his world seems amiss, a somber tone pervades his scenes. They are a far cry from anything in Renoir, but not so far from Fellini. Fellini loved comedy just as much as Renoir did, but he was also preoccupied with the meaning of suffering and the question of faith. Taken together, *La Strada* (1954), *Il Bidone* (1955), and *Notti di Cabiria* (1957), some of his most famous films, form a veritable "trilogy of grace and salvation."[114] They introduce themes—such as the trials of loss and the meaning of faith—that animate *8½*. They are the some of the same themes Malick addresses in *The Tree of Life*.[115]

Fellini's films were among the first pictures shown at Greystone in the fall of 1969.[116] As the aspiring filmmakers at the Center for Advanced Film Studies would have noticed, those pictures became ever more personal as his career progressed. Malick's films are not usually compared to Fellini's, but it seems to me that on this point his confessional trilogy is greatly indebted to them.[117] Especially when it is examined alongside the films that followed on its heels—namely, *To the Wonder* and *Knight of Cups*—*The Tree of Life* starts to look like Malick's version of *8½*. I find it especially significant that the scenes of heavenly reunion near the end of *The Tree of Life* so vividly recall similar shots near the end of *8½*, in which the many persons who have passed through Guido's life over the years reunite on a sandy beach. The same thing happens in *The Tree of Life*. Furthermore, Jack, like Guido, wears a suit of almost funereal cut throughout these sequences. Both films suggest we will be reunited someday with the people who populate our memories; that the lives of our loved ones will be redeemed somehow.

The extended version of *The Tree of Life* shows in greater detail just how entwined Jack's life has been with the lives of others—his mother, father, and brothers most of all. Jack may be the film's protagonist but the story depicted on screen cannot possibly consist of his own memories alone, since so much of the imagery stretches beyond his vantage point. Jack is but the conduit, we realize, for the stories of others—for those who are no longer alive, his brother and mother most especially.

In an insightful video essay included in the Criterion edition of *The Tree of Life*, *New Yorker* classical music critic Alex Ross examines the hauntingly effective way Malick incorporates classical music into his films. A number of the pieces chosen for the soundtrack of *The Tree of Life*, he points out, are memorial works. They range widely in terms of style and mood, from John Tavener's *Funeral Canticle* (1999) to a requiem by Berlioz and, most dramatically, the "Lacrimosa" movements of Zbigniew Preisner's *Requiem for My Friend* (1998). There are works by Bach and Brahms, Górecki and Smetana, too. In short, there is a lot of classical music in *The Tree of Life*, but it is the memorial music that predominates, giving the film an elegiac feel and—as Malick's fellow Harvard philosophy classmate John E. McNees has pointed out—a specifically Christian message.[118]

The use of these requiem pieces in *The Tree of Life* is profound; but the pairing of Preisner's piece with the film's grandiose cosmological sequences is especially so, for the work is a tribute to Preisner's frequent collaborator, the renowned Polish director Krzysztof Kieślowski. Kieślowski was a filmmaker who did not shy away from theological themes, as his unrivaled adaptation of the Ten Commandments—*Dekalog* (1988), for which Preisner wrote the score—amply demonstrates. After the fall of the Berlin Wall, Kieślowski became a sought-after director beyond Poland. His *Three Colors Trilogy* (1993–94) garnered widespread praise, but, tragically, his career was cut short: Kieślowski suffered a fatal heart attack in March 1996 as he and Preisner were collaborating on a "concert that would tell a life story," an event scheduled to debut at the Acropolis in Athens.[119] In the wake of Kieślowski's death, Preisner transformed the music he had already composed for the concert into a memorial honoring the irreplaceable life story of his friend and colleague.

Requiem for My Friend's prominent place in *The Tree of Life* invites us to consider the picture as its own kind of requiem. Malick uses images and music, memoir and scripture, to honor the lives of the mother and brother who, in a roundabout way, made his film possible. When it is viewed from this perspective, the plot of *The Tree of Life* pivots less around Jack's despair and more around the event that brings it about: the death of his brother R. L., a version of Malick's own brother who died at nineteen, while studying music performance in Spain. The painful memory of R. L.'s death, which comes to dominate adult Jack's thoughts and feelings in the early sequences of *The Tree of Life*, is the catalyst that gets the movie's plot, such as it is, underway. It pulls Jack out of the everyday world of office gossip and high-power meetings—what Heidegger called, in *Being and Time*, "idle chatter"—and thrusts him into a meditative mood of reminiscing and reflection.[120] His memories provide the material dramatized in the middle sections of the film. On the outside Jack may appear to be losing his bearings—again, a theme explored at greater length in the extended cut—but inside, he has just started finding his way. Memory points him in the right direction.

Perhaps it is odd that a film titled *The Tree of Life* is so fixated on death, but life and death, it suggests, cannot be separated; they must be thought of together. It is an obvious enough lesson when considered in the abstract, but it is a more difficult one to learn when it becomes a concrete reality in our lives. Jack's ongoing struggle to come to terms with R. L.'s passing so many years later suggests that no amount of philosophy can shield us from the sting of loss. Death retains the power to destabilize everything, which is why we so often find ourselves reeling in the face of it. We go searching for some piece of solid ground on which to stand, some secure corner of the universe where things seem permanent rather than transient. "Grief makes reckless cosmologists of us all," the journalist Kathryn Schulz has written.[121] Maybe it is no accident, then, that the most grief-stricken of Malick's films is also his most cosmological.

Heidegger was not the first philosopher to notice that our mortality, our "being-towards-death," was a central component of human existence.[122] From its inception, philosophy has reckoned with the inescapable fact of death. To repeat a phrase connecting Cicero and Montaigne to the global-warming present, we might say that "to study philosophy is to learn to die."[123] In this regard, Heidegger's reflections on death are part of a long and illustrious tradition. But by stressing how human mortality revealed an essential, often overlooked feature not just of individual existence but also, more generally, of Being, he added a unique twist to the usual narrative. One of the central arguments of *Being and Time* was that Being—like us—could not be understood apart from the question of time. Just as any human being who hopes to find meaning in existence must reckon with death, any inquiry hoping to do justice to the phenomenon of Being must reckon with temporality. As Heidegger saw it, everything passes, which is precisely why the earliest, samizdat English paraphrasing of *Sein und Zeit* produced by John Wild and Hubert Dreyfus translated *Dasein* as "transience."[124]

The Tree of Life interrogates transience from every possible angle. But the picture is not some kind of philosophical exegesis. It is a work of consolation rather than explication. It attempts to alleviate the sense of suffering we associate with impermanence, loss, and death by juxtaposing these with a story of cosmic unfolding, a story of continuing life writ large. While admitting that "suffering must lie at the heart of life, not at its periphery," Malick's screenplay nevertheless suggests a way to endure it: "love," it says, "is the answer to evil and sorrow." Loving "every leaf and every stone, every ray of light," is "the way to the lost kingdom," the pathway to "the eternal."[125] The words are borrowed from a famous passage in Dostoevsky's *The Karamazov Brothers* devoted to the religious teachings of Starets Zosima, Alyosha Karamazov's spiritual mentor: "Love all of God's creation," Zosima says, "love the whole, and love each grain of sand. Love every leaf, every ray of God's light. Love animals, love plants, love every kind of thing. If you love every kind of thing, then everywhere God's mystery will reveal itself to you."[126]

Few novelists were as concerned with theodicy as was Dostoevsky, and *The Karamazov Brothers* represented the culmination of his attempts to make sense of the idea that divinity was everywhere, in all things, even suffering.[127] It is a book Malick knows well, having once recommended it to Martin Sheen when his former *Badlands* star was in the midst of a spiritual crisis in the 1980s. Sheen attributed his subsequent return to the Catholic faith of his youth to the experience: "Terrence was key to my awakening," he said, the person who got him started on his "journey home."[128] We would do well to interpret *The Tree of Life* along these lines, as a document of Malick's return. The picture is a theodicy, urging us to love all things.

This makes *The Tree of Life* sound preachy, but it is hardly a church-sanctioned restatement of religious doctrine. The idiosyncratic theodicy of *The Tree of Life* hinges not on established catechisms but rather on personal experience. It deals with R. L.'s loss in a way that cannot be subsumed under empty, formulaic condolences derived from the Bible: "If the Lord gives, then the Lord takes away; that's just the way He is," says Grandmother (Fiona Shaw) to her distraught daughter, Mrs. O'Brien, R. L.'s grieving mother, whose face betrays disappointment, if not outright disgust, at the hollowness of the sentiment. These lines culled from the Book of Job ring false. They are offensive, insulting, the emotional equivalent of pouring salt on open wounds. True consolation requires something more than clichés. So important was this fleeting scene that Malick reportedly sent his editors back to the cutting room some fifty times before they finally got it right.[129]

The Job invoked by *The Tree of Life* is not the stoic, silently suffering Job of official church teaching. He is, rather, Kierkegaard's Job, the existential Job who dared to shout out his pain to God. This is the Job who "did not disappoint men when everything went to pieces," as *Repetition* puts it. He is the Job who "became the voice of the suffering, the cry of the grief-stricken, the shriek of the terrified, and a relief to all who bore their torment in silence, a faithful witness to all the affliction and laceration there can be in a heart, an

Figure 26. Mrs. O'Brien (Jessica Chastain) confronts the pain of loss in *The Tree of Life*.

unfailing spokesman who dared to lament 'in bitterness of soul.'"[130] That last phrase, pulled directly from the Bible, is what made Job truly "unforgetta-ble," Kierkegaard thought.[131] God may speak louder and more forcefully, but at least Job, in challenging the Lord, prompts "a response"—"a reply from God himself, which even if it crushes a man, is more glorious than the gossip and the rumors about the righteousness of Governance that are invented by human wisdom and spread by old women and fractional men."[132] In *The Tree of Life*, Mrs. O'Brien dares to challenge God, while all her mother—an old woman—can do is repeat empty phrases.

Formulaic talk of providence is, *The Tree of Life* suggests, no consolation at all. It is the equivalent of so much idle chatter. But an intimation of divin-ity achieved through a world-destroying, firsthand experience of loss and suf-fering, the very thing Kierkegaard's Job endured, the very thing Jack and his mother seem to endure? Well, that is something else entirely. As Kierkegaard put it in one of his many commentaries on Job: "When you scan your whole life and think of it as finished, you certainly would not wish to have to make this confession: I was a fortunate one who was not like other people, who never suffered anything in the world, and who let every day take care of it-self or, rather, let it bring me new joys. You would never wish to make such a confession, even if it were true."[133] Untested by hardship or suffering, faith is empty, false, formulaic. It is, in a word, inauthentic.

In contrast to this, the cosmological vision that emerges out of Jack's grief and suffering is authentic—and generative. It leads not just to consolation, but also to reconciliation: reconciliation with others, with the universe, and perhaps even with God. We might also think of it as reconciling Jack with his former selves, for in recalling the loss of his brother, Jack also remembers the various people he has been—the curious child, the excitable adolescent, the brooding and difficult young adult. He comes to terms with them, accepts them.

The Tree of Life's cosmology suggests that our personal life stories are an essential part of the cosmos. What Matthiessen called the "primordial memory of creation" can only be accessed through individual experience. By remembering and recollecting our own lives, we begin to recall the life of the universe itself, we see that "the same power which burns in the stars and nebulae"—Malick's script says—"burns equally in us. Our being is a miracle, equal with the creation of the universe."[134] This is a stunning reworking of Kierkegaard's notion of repetition—a willingness to go through everything again, even the painful stuff, so as to be nearer to transcendence—presented in the widest cinematic frame. It captures both the most personal of memories and the most universal of stories.[135] It recognizes the "cosmic energy," as Matthiessen called it, shimmering in all "stone and steel as well as flesh."

Confessional narratives are works of memory that seek to explain—if not change—the present by way of the past. But such works of self-examination face many obstacles. For one thing, the past is often opaque—"I do not know where I came from," Augustine wrote, because "I do not remember"—and, on top of this, the present never stays still long enough for us to grasp it fully.[136] Since our existence is transient, one might think we are condemned to search in vain for something permanent, something transcendent, in the stories of our lives.

But in the *Confessions* Augustine suggests the opposite. His Christian mother, Monica, taught him to seek permanence not in his own life but in God. In a particularly memorable passage, one that sheds light on Jack's relationship to his mother in *The Tree of Life*, Augustine recounts how he and Monica came to see the divine source of all life. "Step by step we climbed beyond all corporeal objects and the heaven itself, where sun, moon, and stars shed light on the earth." There they saw "a region of inexhaustible abundance," where "all creatures come into being, both things which were and which will be." In this realm, there was "no past and future, but only being, since it is eternal."[137] The vision became the foundation of Augustine's faith. "My humble tongue makes confession to your transcendent majesty," he writes, praising God as the "maker of heaven and earth—this heaven which I see, the earth which I tread underfoot and is the source of the earthly body which I carry."[138]

The very same desire to know both the heavens above and the earth below has animated Malick's lifelong searching. It can be found in his student writings, in his first forays into filmmaking, and in his most mature works as a world-renowned director. The fact that Malick began working on some variant of *The Tree of Life* as early as the 1970s—when the project was called "Q," perhaps short for Qasida, a form of classical Arabic panegyric—is further proof of the coherence and consistency of his filmmaking. *The Tree of Life* is a life project in the most literal sense. It shows us how Malick found and followed a pathway—cut by the likes of Augustine and Kierkegaard before him—from the existential condition of transience to the religious experience of transcendence. It shows us how its director came to understand "his place in the order of the cosmos."[139]

The Tree of Life is also what Kierkegaard would have called "a work of love": it memorializes R. L. and in doing so demonstrates how Jack/Malick came to embrace—and love—the world around him. "The work of love in recollecting one who is dead is," as Kierkegaard put it, "a work of the most unselfish, the freest, the most faithful love. Therefore go out and practice it; recollect the one who is dead and just in this way learn to love the living unselfishly, freely, faithfully."[140] In remembering the dead, we begin to appreciate life itself.

Malick learned this lesson from Augustine and Kierkegaard, but also from Dostoevsky. The coda to *The Karamazov Brothers* has a scene depicting the burial of a young child. In it, Alyosha focuses not on sorrow but rather on love and joy. "Remember that nothing is nobler, stronger, more vital, or more useful in future life than some happy memory," he tells the children lamenting their friend's loss, "especially one from your very childhood, from your family home." Such memories are the key to redemption: "If a man carries many such memories with him," Alyosha says, "they will keep him safe throughout his life. And even if only one such memory stays in our hearts, it may prove to be our salvation one day."[141] When Jack O'Brien finally smiles at the end of *Tree of Life*, it is because he has found just such a memory to hold dear.

It is in this regard, finally, that *Tree of Life* should be viewed as a work of confessional cosmology as theodicy. It seeks to reconcile us, as viewers, with the living world around us, but it does so by recalling the memories of the deceased—and of the world we shared with them. *The Tree of Life* depicts existence as something that is both transient and transcendental, full of meaning, ready for salvation. "We have reviewed the whole of time," Malick writes near the end of his initial screenplay, "in order that we might see what is without beginning or end—without growth, without decay—eternity revealing itself in the phenomena of time—as active in undoing as in doing."[142] It is one part *Being and Time* and two parts heartfelt prayer.

✳   ✳   ✳

From the very beginning, Malick knew just what he wanted *The Tree of Life* to achieve: he wanted to show how his life—his experiences and his memories—fit into the ongoing story of creation. He had found his place in the cosmos and he wanted to help viewers go about finding theirs. To do so, he needed to translate his own private experience into a more universal form. This was the task of what his teacher Stanley Cavell once called "arrogation," "a certain universalizing of the voice" that allowed one to speak not just for oneself but also for others.[143] The arrogation to be found in *The Tree of Life* and the films following it is executed with subtlety. Like Kierkegaard, Malick gave his protagonists names different from his own; like Henry Adams, he made them into manikins or models more than characters. After all, the confessional story should not be his or hers, or yours or theirs, but fundamentally *mine*. Adams stressed this in his preface to *The Education*: "The object of the study is the garment, not the figure."[144]

A brief preface preceding Malick's script for *The Tree of Life* makes his (de)personalizing, arrogating aim explicit: "The 'I' who speaks in this story is not the author," it says. "Rather, he hopes that you might see yourself in this 'I' and understand this story as your own."[145] The wording is borrowed from Johann Gottlieb Fichte's *The Vocation of Man* (1800), a book that transformed technical philosophy into something like a personal testament. Fichte's providential optimism provided Malick with yet another example of philosophy as theodicy. It also gave him an arrogating example to follow: "I still need to remind a few readers that the 'I' who speaks in the book is by no means the author," Fichte had written. "Rather, the author wishes that the reader may come to see himself in this 'I'"; and, in so doing, transform what "is presented to him in this book merely as a picture" into a "philosophical disposition" of his own.[146]

Like *The Vocation of Man*, *The Tree of Life* situates singular, personal experience in a grandly universal story line—the grandest story line of all, in
fact, that of universe. But if Malick's most important film is fundamentally
Fichtean in this regard, it is so by way of Cavell, which means that it presents
skepticism and doubt—Fichte's chief nemeses—not as obstacles easily overcome but more like conditions to be steadily endured. And we learn to endure them by attending to the stories of others, which shed light on our own.
In *A Pitch of Philosophy* Cavell wrote about how "we live lives simultaneously
of absolute separateness and endless commonness." For him, this was precisely why "each life is exemplary of all."[147] The "I" is mine, in other words, but
also yours and theirs.

Like the classic works of the confessional canon, *The Tree of Life* approaches what J. M. Coetzee once called, with reference to the Christian
works of Tolstoy and Dostoevsky, the "limits" of personal introspection, that
fuzzy zone between the existentially singular and the universally shared. *The
Tree of Life* shows—to use Coetzee's words—"analysis not of *one's* self, but of
the self, the soul."[148] (The script for *The Tree of Life* speaks of "the slow, dark
birth of the soul—grander, more mysterious than the birth of worlds.")[149]
Some of the most famous confessions in literary history, such as Rousseau's,
have sought to document their author's radical individuality—"I venture to
believe that I was not made like any that exist," he proclaimed—but Malick's
manikin-like memoir films strive to show, in a more Cavellian vein, com-
monality.[150] For him, confession entails not just, or not only, the disclosure
of private transgressions, but also, and much more importantly, the testify-
ing of faith. Confession marks the spot where self-knowledge, which is always subject to the whims of deceit and self-interest—"learn from Job to
become honest with yourself," Kierkegaard wrote, "so that you do not deceive
yourself with imagined power"—becomes something like an intimation of
transcendence.[151] It is the point at where cynicism—to borrow once again
from Coetzee—gives way to grace.[152]

The Tree of Life puts the isolated individual back into the community of
all living things, the community, believers would say, of divine creation. It is
a fundamentally religious film. Each of Malick's films has tackled religious
themes in one way or another, but *The Tree of Life*, as many theologians noticed, "most clearly exhibits a desire to engage theological issues."[153] And the
engagement is by no means limited to the Book of Job and Kierkegaard. The
film's earliest voice-over narrations—spoken by Mrs. O'Brien, a character
exhibiting all of the hallmarks of the Marian tradition in Christianity—

prepare us for the religious ruminations to come: they reference nothing less than Thomas Aquinas's commentaries on the divergent paths of nature and grace.[154]

For these reasons and many more, *The Tree of Life* received a warm reception among the Christian faithful. Prayer groups and pastors were delighted to see a "film so drenched in prayer" receiving gushing accolades and glowing reviews in the popular press.[155] Even the academics joined their cause: essays, articles, and books addressing *The Tree of Life*'s debts and contributions to theology were rushed into print.[156] But not everyone was convinced. Reviewing *The Tree of Life* for *Film Quarterly*, David Sterritt suggested that the film hooked "into a kind of American religiosity that specializes in affirming static traditions and shoring up reactionary mindsets."[157] Despite admitting that *The Tree of Life* was "a stunning achievement," a true *Gesamtkunstwerk* that was all the more remarkable for how it dared to tackle themes Hollywood normally avoids like some kind of box-office plague, Sterritt looked askance at its effort to replace the "boundless contingency of the human spirit" with a simple tale of Christian providence.[158] It was a too-easy salve for the troubling chaos of human life, he thought, a cinematic failure of nerve.

Sterritt may have had a point. But to make it he overstated the orthodoxy of *The Tree of Life*'s theology. Also, Malick's foray into the realm of what the pioneering Canadian psychiatrist Richard Maurice Bucke over a century ago labeled "cosmic consciousness" may be more emblematic of "the human spirit" than Sterritt allows.[159] Every human culture has produced some variant of "cosmic consciousness." Neither modern philosophy nor positivist science has been able to displace our perennial yearning for it. Religion has tried to contain it; natural science has tried to explain it; philosophy has even tried to interpret it; but none of these efforts has been successful in helping human beings to overcome or abandon it. We still seek a cosmic consciousness that will make us feel whole, or, as Wittgenstein once put it, "absolutely safe."[160]

In the lectures that became *The Varieties of Religious Experience*, William James praised Bucke for putting aside the rationalist assumptions of his medical training to discuss—and perhaps confess?—his own, intensely personal mystical experiences.[161] Peter Matthiessen would do the same some seventy-five years later, in *The Snow Leopard*, a book advertised to readers as "a true pilgrimage, a journey of the heart."[162] One of those readers was Malick, who was starting work on a project that would eventually become, decades later, *The Tree of Life*. Maybe he took the appearance of an advertisement for *The*

Snow Leopard next to Penelope Gilliatt's glowing review of *Days of Heaven* in the *New Yorker* issue of September 18, 1978, as a sign that he was on the right track.[163]

Cosmic consciousness was a key characteristic of what James called "religious life." "Hindus, Buddhists, Mohammedans, and Christians all have cultivated it methodically," he argued in *The Varieties of Religious Experience*. Throughout history, yogis, Sufis, and saints, not to mention Buddhist seekers of Nirvana, have explored the "experimental union of the individual with the divine." But James knew their traditions were, "to the medical mind," incomprehensible.[164] What to make of these ecstasies of cosmic consciousness, then? "To pass a spiritual judgment upon these states," James suggested, "we must not content ourselves with superficial medical talk, but inquire into their fruits for life."[165] When viewed from this perspective—a pragmatist perspective—cosmic consciousness was very powerful indeed. "The mystic is," as James saw it, "*invulnerable*, and must be left, whether we relish it or not, in undisturbed enjoyment of his creed."[166] Is *The Tree of Life* Malick's unshakable statement of faith? Perhaps. But as Malick's next films would show, the search for meaning is an ongoing quest; one can never be sure where it will take one next.

CHAPTER 6

Cosmic Confessions, Part II

The Search for Meaning in *To the Wonder*, *Knight of Cups*, and *Voyage of Time*

The mystery of each thing is the mystery of all things.

—Henry Bugbee

The success of *The Tree of Life* proved Malick's waiting game had paid off. After building a reputation as one of the most talented filmmakers of his generation with *Badlands* and *Days of Heaven*, he ducked out of Hollywood right when independent cinema was about to be swallowed up by summer blockbusters eager to replicate the success of Steven Spielberg's *Jaws* (1975).[1] Although he continued to write, Malick would not sit in the director's chair again for some twenty years. During this time, the name he had made for himself in the 1970s became ever more valuable, as if it were accruing cinematic interest.

A good reputation can do more than open doors in Hollywood—it can *keep* them open. Few other American directors, aside from Stanley Kubrick, have enjoyed this luxury. Maybe Malick knew everything would pay off in the end. Maybe he did not. Either way, the waiting game worked. "It is always difficult to make a film that may not appear to be commercial to investors," Jack Fisk has noted, "but Terry has stayed on course and made films his way."[2] Producers and actors eagerly anticipated his return to filmmaking and their enthusiasm guaranteed Malick would have all the backing he needed to make whatever he wanted. Sean Penn and Brad Pitt would be there to foot the bill.[3] Some of this explains why Malick felt so free to continue exploring the vein of personal filmmaking he had mined in *The Tree of Life*—and to do so without worrying about box-office viability.

To the Wonder and *Knight of Cups*, his next films, failed to replicate *The Tree of Life*'s success. Was it because they were stories of adult disappointment rather than childhood curiosity? Or was it because they were more experimental? Examining the pictures Malick released in rapid succession after *The Tree of Life*, this chapter suggests that *To the Wonder* and *Knight of Cups* are best viewed as extensions of the confessional project inaugurated by *The Tree of Life*. The same applies to the documentary film *Voyage of Time*, which serves as a coda to the trilogy. In all four films we can find evidence of Malick's restless search for "his place in the order of the cosmos."[4] *To the Wonder* and *Knight of Cups* offer updates on Malick's cinematic avatar, Jack O'Brien, but *Voyage of Time* extends *The Tree of Life*'s cosmological ruminations, illuminating not just the deepest recesses of cosmic space and time but also "the slow, dark birth of the soul," which was, as Malick had written in his *Tree of Life* screenplay, "more mysterious than the birth of worlds."[5] Malick's guides during this time were confessional authors who, like Peter Matthiessen, wrote extensively about wayfaring and pilgrimage. Henry Adams and Walker Percy, two other authors who eschewed academia, proved particularly important.

The autobiographical, confessional mode of American writing enjoyed something of a rebirth in the 1960s and 1970s, when Malick first came into contact with the ideas that would define so much of his work as a filmmaker. Authenticity was a watchword of the times, and works that sought to demonstrate it—everything from the Port Huron Statement of the Students for a Democratic Society to *The Autobiography of Malcolm X*—were widely discussed, often because they seemed to make a point that was at once political, philosophical, *and* spiritual.[6] A book published in 1958, just before the wave started to crest, could have defined the genre, but fate intervened, insisting that it be known only as an "underground classic." *The Inward Morning: A Philosophical Exploration in Journal Form* has never managed to shake this double-edged honorific.[7] Penned by the American philosopher Henry Bugbee, it mixed personal meditation with philosophical speculation. *The Inward Morning* addressed self and world, being and becoming, and how everything related, in the end, to nature. Bugbee was denied tenure at Harvard not long before the book was published. He was a victim of the increasingly technical turn academic philosophy was taking at the time, the turn that turned Terrence Malick away from academic philosophy and toward filmmaking.[8]

*   *   *

The Tree of Life tackled the "fractured quality of modern life."[9] But the films that followed in its wake turned the idea into something of a cliché: "A Malick sequence has now become a collection of semi-disconnected shots," David Denby complained in his *New Yorker* review of *To the Wonder*, "individually ravishing but bound together by what feels like the trivial narcissism of Caribbean-travel ads on TV."[10] The *New York Times* film critic A. O. Scott similarly suggested that its imagery looked "more commercial than cosmic, as if plucked from advertisements for perfume, high-thread-count sheets or other luxury goods." Malick's sixth feature film "gestures toward the same kind of transcendence" as *The Tree of Life*, he opined, "but falls short."[11] That Malick went on to direct a perfume advertisement starring Angelina Jolie—with a soundtrack culled from music first used in *To the Wonder*, no less—only seemed to underscore the point.[12]

It is difficult to disagree with such criticisms, but they distract us from what *To the Wonder* seeks to achieve not only as a movie but also as a confessional endeavor. *To the Wonder* extends Malick's autobiographical experiment and the fact that such an experiment even came to fruition is remarkable, for it represents a creative about-face of startling proportions: one of Hollywood's most reclusive directors had suddenly become one of its most unabashed oversharers. Malick once wanted his "personal life to be completely separate from the movies," but here he was, turning it into cinema.[13]

A good deal of Malick's own personal experience finds its way into *To the Wonder* and *Knight of Cups*. If *The Tree of Life* tells the story of Malick's youth, then its follow-up obviously draws from Malick's adulthood, spanning the length of time between his second marriage and the start of his third. *Knight of Cups*, the last installment in the confessional trilogy, fills in the gap between these films, covering Malick's early career in Hollywood, as well as his brief first marriage. The chronology may be out of sequence, but the content is clearly cut from the very same cloth: the fabric of Malick's own life.

Mont-Saint-Michel and Bartlesville: *To the Wonder*

To the Wonder is a work of memory. Its fragmented plot reflects a fundamental truth about our powers of recollection. Rarely, if ever, do we recall our pasts as expertly plotted, fully formed narratives. Instead, we recall an

isolated image here, or a passing mood, a fleeting feeling, there. Mental life is
messy: films attempting to capture it will not display the virtue of tidiness.

In truth, Malick has never been a filmmaker of narrative neatness.
Throughout his career, he has tried to capture what Gilberto Perez once called
the "play of consciousness."[14] His films work not from the outside in but rather
from the inside out. Hence all the voice-overs, all the silent scenes of people
gazing at skies or taking in sunsets. But there is far more to capturing the
mysteries of memory than this. A good deal of formal experimentation and
cinematic innovation is required as well. Malick's recent films utilize jump-
cut editing and constant camera movement to "imitate," as Perez puts it, "the
mind's eye looking back in time." They reflect the fragmentary nature of
memory: "We remember places, the context but not so much the story; we
remember faces, the expression but not so much the event. We remember
parts more than wholes, and try as we might to fit the parts together, discon-
tinuities remain."[15]

Continuing a collaboration that began with his work on *The New World*,
Emmanuel Lubezki once again joined Malick for *To the Wonder*, reuniting
with other longtime crew members, such as artistic director Jack Fisk and
costume designer Jacqueline West. Together, they honed the unique working
methods that had been established on the set of *The New World* and radicalized during the making of *The Tree of Life*. As Lubezki described it in a 2013
interview with *American Cinematographer*: "When we did *The New World*,
we were still shooting like most movies are shot, with scheduled scenes and
coverage in a film that had a fair amount of plot. In *Tree of Life*, we tried to do
less of that and open ourselves to trying new things; we failed all the time, but
in the moments when we got lucky and shot good stuff, that stuff was far more
powerful than anything we had done together before. In *To the Wonder* we
wanted to take that approach to a greater extreme."[16] Over the course of their
collaboration, Lubezki and Malick—along with expert assistants and camera
operators, such as Joerg Widmer—devised a working method they came to
call, in something of a joke, "the dogma." In another interview, Lubezki outlined some of its central tenets: shooting only in "available natural light," using "deep focus," avoiding both "primary colors" and "filters," and remaining
always on the move by shooting only with "steady handheld or Steadicam 'in
the eye of the hurricane.'" Perhaps the most important guideline of the
dogma, though, was its final article: "Accept the exception to the dogma."[17]

As Lubezki was the first to admit, the dogma was "full of contradictions."[18]
But insofar as it oriented the cast and crew toward improvisation, it proved

exceedingly useful. It kept crew members on their toes. It kept actors fresh and spontaneous. Most of all, it kept scenes from becoming too studied or staged. From Jean Renoir, Robert Bresson, and the French New Wave, Malick had inherited a suspicion of artificiality. "Prefer what intuition whispers in your ear," Bresson once wrote, "to what you have done and redone ten times in your head."[19]

This could very well have been Malick's motto for *To the Wonder*.[20] Theatricality was the enemy, so much so that Lubezki even came to think of *To the Wonder* as "a fictional movie shot like a documentary." Describing his work with Malick on the film, he said:

> We want to show things that happen and then capture them before they disappear. Again, this is a form of filmmaking that directly connects to the content of the story. The movie has very little plot; it's more of a contemplation, and we're always looking for the moments that editors normally throw out. In many cases they're the moments before and after the dramatic scenes that make up most movies. I don't want to say that those moments feel more real, but they affect me and I relate to them as an audience member. By leaving out the conventional scenes that explain things, the film invites the audience to create some of the story themselves, and I like that.[21]

These remarks help us appreciate not only what Malick was attempting to accomplish in *To the Wonder*, but also why his film may have confounded critics and audiences expecting more traditional fare.

The later films of Terrence Malick are a fascinating case study in the dialectic between artistic calculation and spur-of-the-moment inspiration. Having made his name in Hollywood as a precise, intensely literary scriptwriter—as somebody who traded in finely crafted sentences and scenes—Malick has more recently proven himself to be adventurously open-minded about how a film can or should be made. In his latest works especially, he has experimented with the usual rules of filming, editing, and producing a movie. Utilizing "the dogma," he has done away with many of the trappings of traditional filmmaking, including even the very thing by which he initially made his name in Hollywood—namely, scripts. Malick's willingness to toss his own expertly crafted dialogue and stage directions aside in favor of a daily search for serendipity on set—the right lighting over here, the flight of a beautiful bird over there—says a great deal about his preference for spontaneity over calculation. As one of his recent editors has put it, "Terry works by intuition."[22]

To the Wonder is often described as Malick's first scriptless film, but this is not entirely correct. There was a script, it just was not shown to actors or much of the crew. Emmanuel Lubezki read a draft of it only because he was "stubborn" and "used to doing things a certain way."[23] But the script did not contain the true story of the film. Malick was adamant that this could only be found during filming, or perhaps even later, during editing. Rather than follow some sort of cinematic blueprint, the cast and crew of *To the Wonder* were told to search for moments of lived experience that might capture the essence of a memory, mood, or feeling. How these might fit together was left open. The subtitle of a recent oral history about Malick's career conveys the paradoxical intent of the method: "rehearsing the unexpected."[24]

As if to signal its allegiance to this improvisational, guerrilla-filmmaking style, *To the Wonder* opens with grainy, camcorder-like footage depicting an American abroad. Neil (Ben Affleck) is in France, and, as usually happens in France, he is in the process of falling in love. The object of his affection is a local named Marina (Olga Kurylenko). Together, they, along with Marina's daughter, Tatiana (Tatiana Chiline), traipse around Paris. Before long, the new couple, in the throes of romantic infatuation, take a road trip out to Normandy, where they visit one of the most famous pieces of architecture in the world, the fortified island known as Mont-Saint-Michel. At this point, the home-movie footage gives way to majestically photographed scenes of Neil and Marina ascending the weathered stone steps leading up to the architectural and spiritual centerpiece of Mont-Saint-Michel: the Gothic abbey known simply as the Merveille ("The Wonder").

For many today, Mont-Saint-Michel may be, like so many other examples of Gothic architecture, nothing more than a tourist destination, but for centuries it was a site of pious pilgrimage. One of the most famous Americans to visit it, well over a century ago, was Henry Adams, who was a pilgrim of sorts masquerading as a tourist. Adams was uniquely qualified to explain the many marvels of the Merveille. In addition to being, among other things, a statesman, journalist, and novelist, he was also once a professor of medieval history at Harvard.

Adams originally wrote and self-published *Mont Saint Michel and Chartres* for his family in 1904. The book was a kind of private travel guide, highlighting for Adams's well-heeled family and friends the remarkable achievements of twelfth-century Norman culture, which they might care to visit on holiday. The book recommended which cathedrals to see, which poems to read, and which theological debates and disputes of the historical past to recall while doing so. For Adams, traveling into the distant past was a refuge from the chaos of modern life: the glories of the Gothic world stood in stark contrast to the dizzying indignities of the fast-paced present.

It was only in 1912, when medievalists began pleading for copies of his work, that Adams agreed to expand the text of *Mont Saint Michel and Chartres* and have it published for a wider audience. An unlikely organization made the project possible: the American Institute of Architects.[25] Its members were drawn to Adams's detailed discussions of noble cathedrals. But *Mont Saint Michel and Chartres* was made up of much more than this. Equal parts architectural guidebook, personal essay, literary survey, philosophical overview, and theological treatise, *Mont Saint Michel and Chartres* is a good example of what we would call interdisciplinary scholarship today. But it opens and closes with discussions of a theme that gets short shrift in the contemporary academy—namely, wonder.

Throughout *Mont Saint Michel and Chartres*, Adams stresses the importance of returning to a childlike state of curiosity so as to appreciate fully the glories of the past. "The man who wanders into the twelfth century is lost," he writes, "unless he can grow prematurely young."[26] Just a few pages later he suggests that "the art of Mont Saint Michel and Chartres" can only be felt by those who are willing "to become pilgrims again."[27] Indeed, Adams repeatedly likens his tour of famous French churches and poems of the past to a "pilgrimage."[28] The term seems especially apt when applied to his detailed descriptions of the architectural and spiritual accomplishments of the Merveille.

For Adams, the most famous piece of architecture atop Mont-Saint-Michel was a pinnacle of medieval culture. It was the rightful centerpiece of a series of structures that "expressed the unity of Church and State, God and Man, Peace and War, Life and Death, Good and Bad; it solved the whole problem of the universe."[29] It was the perfect microcosm, reflecting the harmonic macrocosm of all creation. The Merveille was the visual manifestation of the belief that "God reconciles all." Its message was clear: "The world is an evident, obvious, sacred harmony." Mont-Saint-Michel, with the Merveille ascending from its northern edge, was "a symbol of unity; an assertion of God and man in a bolder, stronger, closer union than ever was expressed by another art."[30]

Unity, for Henry Adams, was everything. But the law of entropy, which he thought applied to human history as well as thermodynamics, meant that dispersal and division were inevitable.[31] Everything—every art, every culture,

Figure 27. Architectural harmony (Mont-Saint-Michel) in *To the Wonder*.

every civilization—loses its vital energy over time. Adams thought his world particularly diminished, for it lacked the harmonious unity that could be found in Gothic cathedrals. Dreaming of the Middle Ages but stuck in the twentieth century, Adams ended *Mont Saint Michel and Chartres* on a note of mopey resignation. Unity and order such as was known in the past may never be seen again, he lamented. Yet, the distant certainties of history could still be glimpsed, so long as people took the time to search for them: "what men took for truth," he writes, "stares one everywhere in the eye and begs for sympathy."[32]

This is a sympathy *To the Wonder* explores in great detail. But it takes a circuitous path to get there. One minute Malick has us contemplating cosmic unity atop a medieval cathedral; the next he sticks us in a tract home in suburban Oklahoma, where Neil and Marina move in together. To go from the Merveille to Bartlesville might seem like a letdown, but this is the entropic narrative arc of *To the Wonder*. A more appropriate title for the film might have been "Away from the Wonder," for in the beginning of the film everything is whole and harmonious as Neil and Marina fall deeply in love; but this feeling soon wanes, and the fragmentation begins.

In whisking us from the heights of the Merveille to the outskirts of Bartlesville, *To the Wonder* finds a way to dramatize entropy at both the personal and communal levels. Neil and Marina's relationship fractures, sending them their separate ways. Neil retreats into a brooding silence, while

Marina searches in vain for solace, which neither the church nor an affair can provide. But it is the residents of Bartlesville who are truly emblematic of modern disunity and discord. They are isolated, suffering, and in pain. Bartlesville becomes a symbol of terrestrial despair. It is entropy incarnate.

The people of Bartlesville fare far worse than Neil and Marina: their prisons are overflowing, their homes are in disrepair, and their groundwater has been poisoned by seepage from oil pumps. Drugs and alcohol, temporary respites from a grinding poverty, are everywhere (in this, Malick's film anticipates the devastating effects of the opioid crisis). So is social decay. We come to know all this through the character of Father Quintana (Javier Bardem), who ministers to the residents of Bartlesville while struggling with doubts and uncertainties about his vocation and his faith. Like so many other troubled confessors in cinematic history—such as the Priest of Ambricourt (Claude Laydu) in Bresson's *Diary of a Country Priest* (1951) and Pastor Tomas Ericsson (Gunnar Björnstrand) in Ingmar Bergman's *Winter Light* (1963)—Father Quintana strains to see the presence of God in such a fallen world. "When did You turn Your back?" he says in a voice-over in the middle of the film. "All I see is destruction, failure, ruin."

During the filming of *To the Wonder*, Bardem shadowed local priests and ministers, speaking to many of the Bartlesville residents they served. These on-camera conversations provided the content for some of the scenes in which Father Quintana appears. Although the people of Bartlesville knew he was merely an actor playing the part of a clergyman, they often ended up speaking to Bardem from the heart. Father Quintana became their real-life confessor. The honesty and sincerity of these fleeting scenes is astonishing, a stark contrast to the perfume-ad aura of the rest of the film. They are scenes of real emotion. They are also a testament to the fact that people want to be acknowledged and recognized—to be, as Bardem put it, "listened to."[33] Eugene Richards, the documentary photographer who helped locate the Bartlesville residents featured in these sequences, worked with Bardem for years to get more of this confessional footage off the cutting-room floor and into theaters. His short film *Thy Kingdom Come* was finally released in 2018. It is a powerful work, one that deserves a far wider release than it has received.[34]

When viewed from this more documentary-like angle, *To the Wonder* hinges less on the trials and tribulations of Neil's and Marina's love life and more on the role of faith in increasingly anxious times. What use is faith in a fallen world? it seems to ask. Is belief just escapism? Can it encourage something other than asceticism or renunciation? As the improvisational interludes featuring Father Quintana suggest, *To the Wonder* is less an exercise in abstract, dogmatic theology and more an exploration of faith as a lived, embodied experience. But just whose lived experience of faith does *To the Wonder* document? It is not just Father Quintana and his scattered flock. Nor is it Neil, Malick's avatar (at one point we even see him reading the Joan Stambaugh translation of Heidegger's *Being and Time*).[35] *To the Wonder* focuses instead on the women in Neil's life. Marina and Jane (Rachel McAdams), an old Oklahoma friend, wrestle with pain and loss long before their love triangle with Neil entangles them in additional sorrows. It is their voice-over monologues that dominate the film's audio track. Marina's voice, especially, is front and center. As many critics and commentators have noted, she, not Neil, should be considered *To the Wonder*'s true protagonist.[36]

Marina's monologues are full of self-reflection and contemplation. We hear her optimistic thoughts about the power of romantic love ("Love makes us one"); her Catholic-tinged gratitude for creation ("What is this love that loves us, that comes from nowhere, from all around?"); as well as her flirtations with temptation ("My God, what a cruel war. I find two women inside me: one full of love for You; the other pulls me down towards the earth"). Many of these ruminations accompany Renoiresque shots of the natural world, radiant in its aura of "proliferating mystery."

Marina's words are the first and last ones heard in *To the Wonder*. Her confession, not Neil's, takes precedence. In preparation for her role, Malick urged Kurylenko to read Tolstoy's *Anna Karenina*, as well as Dostoevsky's *The Karamazov Brothers* and *The Idiot*.[37] How much of this material stuck with her as she portrayed Marina's troubled romance with Neil is difficult to discern in any one particular scene, but it helps explain her character's gradual transformation over the course of the film from whimsical, twirling Parisian into seemingly devout, humble Christian. *To the Wonder* ends with Marina and Neil parting ways in what should be a painful, final farewell, yet her voice-over conveys nothing but gratitude: "The love that loves us, thank you." The scene, staged in an anonymous, antiseptic airport terminal, marks a stunning reversal in the relationship that has occupied our attention for close to two hours. What began as a journey of passionate, romantic love in Paris has been transformed into a divinely inspired prayer of gratitude. The evolution is foreshadowed by one of Father Quintana's sermons earlier in the picture: "You fear your love has died," he says. "It perhaps is waiting to be transformed into something higher."

Ever since Augustine dramatized his Platonic ascent from worldly temptations to transcendent faith, confessional authors have sought out ways to direct our individual passions toward communion with others, with the world, and, ultimately, with the divine. In keeping with this tradition, many of the voice-overs in *To the Wonder* are addressed to God. In some cases, they are overt prayers—at one point Father Quintana recites the prayer of Saint Patrick—but more often than not they resemble fleeting thoughts, rushing in and out of a character's mind like the famously fast tides around Mont-Saint-Michel.

Without a structured narrative to keep it in place, *To the Wonder* never stays still for long. Scenes drift in and out of each other randomly, without purpose. Seemingly important plot points flash past unexpectedly, without narrative explanation. Characters come in and out of focus for no particular reason. Everything is fractured, shard-like, glimpsed only obliquely. Lubezki's camera is always coming, going, or swirling about. Malick instructed him to keep everything in motion so as to emphasize a feeling of transience, a "radiant zigzag becoming" as the approach was called on set.[38] He wanted his actors to remain in motion, too, so much so that Kurylenko likened her performance in the film to "a choreography" or even a version of ballet—precisely what Jessica Chastain had said about her experience working on *The Tree of Life*.[39] All this movement underscores the idea of pilgrimage at the heart of the film's message. The fact that it opens and closes with images of the Merveille suggests that *To the Wonder* depicts a zigzagging journey of return, a homecoming. But *To the Wonder* returns its viewers not simply to some well-known tourist site. It calls them back to their first and most lasting home—namely, the earth.

A feeling of cosmic gratitude permeates *To the Wonder*. In one scene, the normally mute Neil tries to connect with Marina's daughter, Tatiana, by calling her attention to a beautiful sunset. He points out the earth's shadow hanging just above the horizon. She seems uninterested in the impromptu science lesson (one recalling similar astronomy-related set pieces in the scripts for *Days of Heaven* and *The New World*), but Lubezki's camera frames the scene in such a way that we cannot help but be amazed by it. It is a shot reminiscent of Renoir, and it captures a fascination with nature—a true sense of wonderment—that pulses throughout Malick's confessional films. *To the Wonder* presents this wonder as a pathway to God.

Henry Adams also came to see nature and divinity as entwined. But it was not in contemplating the Norman cathedrals or poetry he so admired that he came to this realization. Adams found a way to reconcile God and nature in the life and writings of a mystic by the name of Francis. Francis of Assisi preached a message of cosmic unity requiring no cathedrals or scholastic dialectics to prop it up. Indeed, for him, as Adams pointed out, "the science of the schools led to perdition because it was puffed up with emptiness and pride. Humility, simplicity, poverty were alone true science."[40] Francis taught that love was greater than logic and that nature, not syllogisms, was the true pathway to God. As Adams paraphrased Francis's teachings in *Mont Saint Michel and Chartres*, "All nature was God's creature. The sun and fire, air and water, were neither more nor less brothers and sisters than sparrows, wolves and bandits."[41] Francis's "Canticle of the Sun" captured the spirit. Glossing it, Adams gave his readers a full dose of cosmic fellow feeling: "We are all varying forms of the same ultimate energy," he wrote, "shifting symbols of the same absolute unity."[42] It is the same sentiment William James dared not dissect in *The Varieties of Religious Experience*. *To the Wonder*'s luminous imagery—brilliant sunsets, billowing prairie grasses, flower fields in full bloom—seems rooted in it. All you need is nature, these scenes imply, and love.

The Franciscan idea of cosmic unity rooted in love did not convince the theologians and the philosophers, though. There is a reason Adams concludes *Mont Saint Michel and Chartres* not with Francis but with the greatest scholastic architect of them all, Aquinas. Impressionistic and imprecise, the notion of wonder so central to Francis's faith received at best a lukewarm reception in academic settings. Already in the Middle Ages, proponents of what was then called "natural philosophy" began to disparage it: we marvel at the things of the world we cannot, or will not, explain, it was thought. According to Lorraine Daston and Katherine Park, medieval academicians "marginalized" and disparaged "the passion of wonder."[43] A "distaste for wonder" eventually became the philosophical and theological norm and two currents that had been coursing through the Christian tradition in tandem began to flow away from each other: an Augustinian one, running through Francis and some of the mystics; and a Thomistic one.[44] It was here that our metaphysical homelessness began, for in losing the capacity to wonder we lost sight of our connection to the cosmos.

Cosmic homelessness is an underlying theme in *To the Wonder*, but the film uses suburban sprawl rather than Gothic splendor to contemplate it. A few moments of calm in the middle of the movie bring the point home. Unlike many of the film's other images, they are captured with a stationary camera. They are shots of ordinary, Middle America structures—a couple of homes, an empty service station—in the early evening. The sky above each structure is striated in dark bands of black and blue. In these compositions, a few outdoor lights illuminate driveways and attract insects, but there are no other signs of life. The shots are beautiful to behold but also a little disconcerting, their stillness evoking the paintings of Edward Hopper. A sense of dread builds as the images linger. The buildings of Bartlesville, like those of Mont-Saint-Michel, are expressions of the culture that produced them: they embody the people who have dwelled within them—all those who have lived, loved, and lost in this one particular place on the planet—but they are lonely locales.

The tortured journeys of Marina, Jane, and Father Quintana are intimate portraits of contemporary isolation and loneliness. Their inner monologues are peppered with pained expressions of dislocation, disorientation, and doubt. The scenes in which these characters appear are full of portentous symbolism. A striking sequence that recalls young Jack's betrayal of his brother R. L. in *The Tree of Life*, has Jane, with her hands bound by a rope, telling Neil she trusts him. This cuts to a scene in which Marina undertakes, with some trepidation, a trust fall with him. The meaning is all too obvious: the two women in Neil's life offer themselves to him, only to be hurt and abandoned in return. Bartlesville's disadvantaged residents, who struggle with poverty, addiction, and (actual, not metaphysical) homelessness, have been abandoned, too—not just by a lover but by society. Their presence in the film is a reminder of the real-world entropy all around us. The people of Bartlesville show just how out of joint the world is, polluted not only environmentally or economically, but also emotionally, even spiritually.

Still, there is hope. *To the Wonder* suggests it can be found in nature. Wandering around Bartlesville lost and in pain after her breakup, Marina starts noticing beauty all around her. Just as the forest had pulled Pocahontas back from the brink of despair in *The New World*, the radiance of nature gives Marina something to live for. Toward the end of the film, in scenes that allude not just to *The New World* but also the conclusion of *The Tree of Life*, we see Marina walking through a misty landscape. She appears to be in a state of rapture. Illuminated by an ethereal light, she becomes one with the earth; her alienation and isolation have been overcome. A journey that has taken her from the Merveille to the desolate suburbs of Oklahoma has transformed her, in the end, into a kind of mystic or saint, a pilgrim who, had she been born in another age, could very well have been a follower of Francis.

The suburban ennui Marina ultimately escapes has had a long and storied career in American arts and letters. Indeed, it was a particularly popular literary and cinematic trope in the 1950s and 1960s, precisely when Malick's generation was being raised in suburban environs such as Bartlesville.[45] It practically constituted its own genre, spanning everything from movies and novels, such as Nicholas Ray's *Rebel Without a Cause* (1955) and Richard Yates's *Revolutionary Road* (1961), to pioneering works of nonfiction like Paul Goodman's *Growing Up Absurd* (1960) and Betty Friedan's *The Feminine Mystique* (1963).

Bubbling beneath it all was a midcentury fascination with that literary-philosophical experiment known as existentialism. In the popular imagination, at least, existentialism was often associated with Parisian intellectuals gabbing away in crowded, Left Bank cafés, drinking apricot cocktails.[46] For proof, take a quick glance at Audrey Hepburn's dance scenes in *Funny Face* (1957).[47] But a homegrown variant of the existential search for meaning was already taking root in other, less stylized locales across the United States. By the time Stanley Donen's musical was released, existentialism had even made inroads in southern states, including Texas and Louisiana, where it was often coupled with Christian teaching.[48] We can see evidence of this in a work that displayed a similar concern for the state of the suburban American soul—namely, Walker Percy's *The Moviegoer* (1961), which beat out *Revolutionary Road* for the National Book Award. It was a novel that would have a lasting effect on Malick for decades to come, perhaps because its doubting, searching, pilgrim-like protagonist—a native of New Orleans, not Paris—vowed to live "in wonder, wondering day and night, never a moment without wonder."[49] It may have been this text, more than any other, that led Malick away from academic philosophy and toward the wonder.

The Pilgrim's Progress: *Knight of Cups*

Walker Percy's debut novel appeared as Terrence Malick headed off to Harvard, where he would study with professors who had an abiding interest in existentialism: Cavell, Dreyfus, and Tillich most notably. They played a significant role in shaping Malick's intellectual pursuits, but it was Percy, the largely self-taught philosopher and popular writer, who seems to have had an outsized influence on his later development as a filmmaker. Although Malick abandoned his budding academic career, his subsequent work in Hollywood, much of it inspired by Percy's writings, suggests he did not abandon philosophy—he just went about doing it a little differently.

Walker Percy did philosophy a little differently, too, perhaps because he came to it in a roundabout way.[50] After receiving a medical degree from Columbia University in 1941, Percy contracted tuberculosis interning at Bellevue Hospital. At that time, the only treatment for it was a lengthy stay in a sanatorium. There was a silver lining, though: Percy had plenty of time to read. It was while convalescing at Saranac Lake in upstate New York that he first encountered Kierkegaard and started to think that the mystery of existence might be a topic too important to be left to the doctors, preachers, or professional philosophers.[51] The meaning of life was something one had to explore on one's own, he felt, so with some existential philosophy under his belt, he set out on what he came to call his "search."

The first step was identifying and subsequently studying the writings of like-minded predecessors, the seekers and wayfarers who had come before him. In addition to Kierkegaard and Dostoevsky, he began reading Charles Sanders Peirce on semiotics, Martin Heidegger on authenticity, and anybody else who could help him make sense of the modern predicament of being a "stranger" or a "castaway"—as he put it in a 1959 essay, "The Message in the Bottle"—on planet Earth.[52]

Percy's familiarity with academic debates—some of his earliest published essays were responses to the writings of the pioneering, Harvard-educated philosopher of art Susanne K. Langer—profoundly shaped his development as a novelist.[53] In a publicity interview for *Library Journal* that appeared just a couple months before *The Moviegoer* hit bookstore shelves, he suggested it was "precisely this interest in philosophy which led directly to the writing of a novel." (Percy may have felt it necessary to explain why his book opens with an epigraph from Kierkegaard's *The Sickness unto Death*.)[54] "Although philosophy is usually regarded in this country as a dry and abstract subject," he explained, European philosophers were writing about "concrete life-situations rather than abstractions." The best kind of philosophy was the kind that investigated "the *predicament* of modern man, afflicted as he is with feelings of uprootedness, estrangement, anxiety and the like." This was why the existentialists wrote "plays and novels" in addition to philosophical prose; doing so allowed them to examine life as it was lived, not just as it was theorized. Also, "people would rather read a novel than an article."[55]

Like the physician-turned-philosopher-turned-novelist who invented him, *The Moviegoer*'s protagonist, Binx Bolling, is a spiritual seeker. On the outside, he is a successful New Orleans bachelor, living a life of ease. Behind this facade, though, he is something else entirely. Binx Bolling is a "castaway," a solitary figure alienated from the rituals of contemporary Southern life, including even Mardi Gras, which serves as a backdrop for the novel's plot. His "solitude," as Paul Elie has described it, "isn't that of a rebel or an independent, but that of a man who is alone in a crowd—in a movie theater or on a sidewalk in the French Quarter."[56] In other words, Binx Bolling is somebody who seems to fit in but actually does not. His estrangement from the world is productive, though, because it pushes him to become a pilgrim, a person who pursues higher things.[57] "The search is what anyone would undertake," he says, "if he were not sunk in the everydayness of his own life."[58] Far better to be "solitary and in wonder" than to be immersed in the routine: "not for five minutes will I be distracted from the wonder," he declares.[59]

Percy's novel was a primary influence on not just *To the Wonder* but also *The Tree of Life*, *Knight of Cups*, and *Voyage of Time*. For many years—including those twenty years he spent away from the director's chair—Malick was rumored to be working on a full-fledged adaptation of it.[60] That film never materialized, but Malick's confessional trilogy, which depicts a very Percyan pursuit of meaning, did. The films composing it can be interpreted as an extended, multipart version of *The Moviegoer*, starring protagonists who might be thought of as amalgams of Binx Bolling and Terrence Malick, with a dash of whatever the actors playing them—from Sean Penn and Hunter McCracken in *The Tree of Life* to Ben Affleck and Christian Bale, respectively, in *To the Wonder* and *Knight of Cups*—added to the mix. The confessional feel is reinforced by the fact that the films are set in some of the places where Malick has lived and worked: Texas, Oklahoma, and Southern California. Binx Bolling strolls the streets of Percy's New Orleans, while Malick's avatars wander Texas towns, Oklahoma suburbs, and Hollywood backlots, but all of them are on a similar journey. They are existential searchers.

In an unpublished essay from the 1950s, "Which Way Existentialism," Percy said: "The modern world, not merely the slums of Paris but the pleasant American suburb, is implicated in a special sort of tragedy. This tragedy is not the catastrophic wars of the 20th century—though God knows these are tragic enough. These particular events are only symptoms of the tragedy; indeed they might even be said to be desperate attempts to escape it. The tragedy has rather to do with the fundamental banality, the loss of meaning, of modern life—what Heidegger calls the 'every-day-ness' and the homelessness of life in the modern world."[61] European philosophers may have been the first to call attention to this tragedy, but Americans experienced it, too. No amount of wealth or security could insulate them from existential dislocation—in fact, these things might even make it worse.

Percy's sense of privileged despair buzzes in the background of *Knight of Cups* like a fluorescent light bulb on the fritz. But Malick's film does more than just depict alienation; it also tries to remedy it. In the same way that Percy transformed his personal search for meaning and religious communion into fiction, Malick dramatizes his own quest for philosophical and spiritual fulfillment in *Knight of Cups*.[62] Its debt to Percy, and to *The Moviegoer*, is profound. Although there are a number of allusions to other works scattered throughout the picture, each one of them is mobilized to emphasize a fundamentally Percyan point, which is that the only path out of despair is pilgrimage.

Knight of Cups is a film about a castaway. Its protagonist is Rick (Christian Bale), a successful but disaffected Hollywood screenwriter. He is lost. The first time we see him he is wandering, quite literally, in the desert. Death Valley, to be exact. Why is he there? Where is he going? The answers to these questions can be found in the film's title sequence. As the opening credits appear against a still-black screen, the regal voice of renowned English actor Sir John Gielgud speaks to us from beyond the grave, giving us pointers. He recites the lengthy, extended title of John Bunyan's 1678 Christian allegory *The Pilgrim's Progress from This World, to That Which Is to Come: Delivered Under the Similitude of a Dream Wherein Is Discovered, the Manner of His Setting Out, His Dangerous Journey; and Safe Arrival at the Desired Countrey*.[63] From the film's first moments, then, we are primed for a tale of spiritual seeking, one leading "from the wilderness of this world," with all of its "Lusts, Pleasures, and Profits," to the "Cœlestial City" of heaven above.[64]

Interpreting *Knight of Cups* as a cinematic allegory of conversion and salvation—with Rick standing in for Bunyan's pilgrim, the aptly named Christian—does not take a great deal of effort. Replace the temptations of "Vanity-Fair" with those of Las Vegas, or the ominous threat of that wicked giant "Despair" with clinical depression, and you have the framework for a very contemporary story of religious redemption.[65] We must walk through the valley of the shadow of death, the film implies, so as to find the light of true belief on the other side. (What else is philosophy, or psychoanalysis, Stanley Cavell once wrote, but a process of "leading the soul to light?")[66] But whereas Bunyan dramatizes passages from scripture to point us in the right direction, explicitly showing us the theological scaffolding upon which his allegory rests, Malick takes a more indirect approach. He exchanges Bible references for an assortment of other sources he had amassed over the years, such as *The Moviegoer*, but also Larry McMurtry's *The Desert Rose*, a novel about an aging Sin City showgirl he had adapted into a screenplay in the 1980s.[67]

Not long after invoking the theology of *Pilgrim's Progress*, *Knight of Cups* quickly veers in a different direction, offering us a philosophical account of the nature of the soul, culled not from the Bible but rather from Plato's *Phaedrus*. A different piece of voice-over narration—drawn from the audio archive of another deceased acting great, Charles Laughton—hints that Rick, whom we have now seen wandering aimlessly not just through desert landscapes but also Hollywood nightclubs and parties (hallmarks of a spiritual desert, surely), is searching for transcendence amid a fallen, carnal world. Rick is still a pilgrim, but now we view him through a more Platonic lens: as somebody seeking perfect, transcendental forms.[68]

All this is just the beginning of the quest—and the film. More riffs on pilgrimage are still to come, not all of them so high-minded. Striking a less serious tone, the Hollywood shock novelist Bruce Wagner, playing himself, offers Rick an alternative path to transcendence at a suitably debauched party—the scenes resemble the excesses of Fellini's *Satyricon*—at a gaudy mansion up in the hills.[69] He invites Rick to try Ketamine: "ever been down the K-hole before?" The pilgrim demurs. Sadly, this is one of the few instances in *Knight of Cups* in which Malick successfully channels Walker Percy's sometimes-mordant sense of humor, not to mention his Kierkegaardian wit. Although a number of Hollywood comedy writers and actors appear in the film, including Nick Kroll, Joe Lo Truglio, Thomas Lennon, Nick Offerman, and Dan Harmon, the picture is largely humorless. Wealthy, moody, and aloof, Rick is an unlikable Bruce Wayne–type. It does not help, of course, that Bale, between the making of *The New World* and *Knight of Cups*, played precisely this role in Christopher Nolan's *Dark Knight* trilogy.

Rick's downbeat demeanor is in keeping with the rest of the film, though. *Knight of Cups* is darker and more menacing than Malick's other films. Its tone is reminiscent of Ingmar Bergman's *Persona* (1966) or John Frankenheimer's *Seconds* (1966), fractured tales of identity crisis both. *Knight of Cups'* editing, which recalls *Persona's* experimentalism, seems deliberately designed to keep its audience off balance and at a distance; its frenetic camerawork echoes *Seconds'* existential disorientation.

Knight of Cups places viewers directly into the shoes of its lost, isolated, spiritually conflicted protagonist. Directionless, Rick is buffeted by events, an existential rag doll, which might explain why he remains more or less silent throughout the picture, never making his thoughts or feelings known to those around him. This means much of the heavy lifting required for the progression of *Knight of Cups*' plot falls upon an assortment of characters who pass in and out of his life. Utilizing a technique that he and his collaborators came to call "torpedoing" during the filming of *The Tree of Life*, Malick often sent actors into scenes with Bale unannounced, hoping to elicit responses from him that were spontaneous and natural.[70] As a result, though, Rick's posture is largely reactionary—he is acted upon more than he acts. But his passivity serves as a kind of indirect speech, allowing Malick to universalize Rick's predicament without really having to embed it in the life of a real person. Like Christian in *Pilgrim's Progress* (and like Neil and Jack in *To the Wonder* and *The Tree of Life*), Rick becomes a manikin, a stand-in for anyone, anywhere, at any time.

When Rick's story is overlaid upon the facts of Malick's own journey, though, *Knight of Cups* seems more personal than allegorical. Just as Binx Bolling's wanderings in *The Moviegoer* mirrored Walker Percy's own experiences, there are a number of clues scattered throughout *Knight of Cups* hinting at the film's origins in Malick's own life. Take, for instance, a cameo appearance in the film by Peter Matthiessen, author of *The Snow Leopard*, the book that inspired Malick's own departure from Hollywood after the release of *Days of Heaven*. Portions of Matthiessen's spiritual travelogue had appeared in the *New Yorker*. In an interesting twist of fate, an advertisement for *The Snow Leopard* even ended up accompanying Penelope Gilliatt's glittering review of *Days of Heaven*—"one of the best films about America in a long time"—in the magazine, touting the book as "a true pilgrimage, a journey of the heart."[71]

The Snow Leopard chronicles Matthiessen's arduous but exhilarating journey alongside the wildlife biologist George Schaller through the Inner Dolpo region of the Tibetan Plateau. The mountain trek was but the pretext for another kind of expedition, one not so far removed from John Bunyan or Plato, however much the aspiring student of Zen may have tried to deny it at the time: "To say I was making a pilgrimage seemed fatuous and vague," Matthiessen later admitted, "though in some sense that was true."[72] While Schaller spent his days searching for reclusive blue sheep across snow-covered mountaintops, Matthiessen pursued spiritual peace in remote village shrines. He had journeyed all the way to Nepal to figure out where he belonged. He sought nothing less than his place in the order of the cosmos.

On at least a handful of occasions, Matthiessen came close to finding it: "I have the universe all to myself. The universe has me all to itself."[73] Passages like this are scattered throughout *The Snow Leopard*, forming a figurative trail of breadcrumbs in a metaphysical quest that mixes Gary Snyderesque Zen poetry, *Dharma Bums*–era Jack Kerouac comedy, and lacerating, Augustinian self-reflection.[74] Matthiessen may have traveled halfway around the world, deep into some of the most forbidding landscapes, but what he was really trying to find was a way back to himself. "The search may begin with a restless feeling," he wrote, "but there is a source for this deep restlessness; and the path that leads there is not a path to a strange place, but the path home."[75]

A reporter for *Rolling Stone* noted Malick's own restlessness around the time *The Snow Leopard* was published. The young director was busy finalizing the soundtrack for *Days of Heaven* at Paramount Studios, but he had already made plans for a swift exit from Hollywood. In retrospect, and especially after viewing *Knight of Cups*, it is hard not to read the article as a portrait of a disenchanted filmmaker who, like Rick, is eager to escape the clutches of the culture industry. Malick "knows how to get away," the *Rolling Stone* article concludes: "In a few days he was taking off for Nepal, because he always wanted to see Annapurna."[76] Perhaps he took a copy of *The Snow Leopard*, which had piqued his interest in the region, along with him.[77]

Knight of Cups suggests that what might have started out as an exotic Tibetan vacation turned into a twenty-year journey away from Hollywood and toward home, wherever—or whatever—that was. For this reason, Matthiessen's appearance in the film feels like an especially significant homage, one made all the more poignant by the fact that he would pass away before *Knight of Cups*' official release, transforming his performance into yet another missive from beyond the grave, rather like the audio narrations from Gielgud and Laughton. The brief scenes in which Matthiessen appears—playing, in a thinly veiled cameo, the character Christopher, whose name alludes to the patron saint of travelers—show him conversing with Rick and his girlfriend Elizabeth (Natalie Portman). Sharing stories of his travels, he comes across as a kind of spiritual guide, a fellow pilgrim on the journey of life. Rick listens to Christopher/Matthiessen with rapt attention. It is a remarkable about-face given his distant, distracted demeanor up until that point. Rick is finally listening, finally beginning to come out of his spiritual slumber.

While wandering the beautifully serene Japanese and Chinese gardens of the Huntington Library in San Marino, California—locations Emmanuel Lubezki's camera lingers over with obvious pleasure—Christopher/Matthiessen offers Rick a series of insights or lessons. The most important of these is the wisdom of resisting distraction. Rick's life, as we have watched it play out before us on screen, has consisted of nothing but diversions: nightclubs, parties, an endless string of flirtations. In opposition to all this, Matthiessen stresses the importance of remaining in the present. "I just teach this moment," he says. "Pay attention to this moment. Everything is there. Perfect. And complete. Just as it is." It is an idea he had outlined in *The Snow Leopard*: "the purpose of meditation practice is not enlightenment; it is to pay attention even at unextraordinary times, to be of the present, nothing-but-the-present, to bear this mindfulness of *now* into each event of ordinary life."[78]

The Pilgrim's Progress and the *Phaedrus* lament the fallenness of this world—and what could be more fallen than yet another Hollywood after-party, yet another mindless meeting with agents and managers?—but *The Snow Leopard*, in accordance with the Zen Buddhism Matthiessen spent his life studying, urges us to accept the world as it is, not as we might wish it to be. "There is no hope anywhere but in this moment," Matthiessen writes, "in the karmic terms laid down by one's own life."[79] Whereas Plato asks us to reject the "ugliness and evil" that causes the wings of the soul "to waste and perish," whereas John Bunyan urges us to turn our backs on the world, rejecting all its carnal, corporeal temptations, Matthiessen suggests only that we remain in the here and now.[80] For him, "dark and light interpenetrate the path." Both are important, unavoidable aspects of "the all-pervading presence of the Present."[81] Matthiessen's thinking is at odds with Christian Platonism. Instead of pointing to a transcendental realm of celestial cities, where darkness gives way to shimmering light, it stresses the importance of immanence. Matthiessen asks us to see the "divine in all mankind," rather than somewhere up above.[82]

Although the theology of *The Snow Leopard* animated much of Malick's work from *The Tree of Life* forward, in *Knight of Cups* it is not granted the final word. Indeed, soon after Matthiessen appears on screen, we are treated to a sermon about suffering, delivered with due solemnity by a priest (Armin Mueller-Stahl), who is filmed from below, from the perspective of a seated, perhaps troubled parishioner who has come to him for advice. The scene serves as a kind of counterpoint to those in which Matthiessen appears. The tone here is firmer, more Job-like. God sends us suffering, the priest says, to rescue us. "To suffer," he suggests, "binds you to something higher."[83]

This marks a return to *The Pilgrim's Progress*, and to the providential theology underpinning it. Before passing through the gates of heaven, Bunyan's Christian must cross a dangerous river, one that drowns everybody but the devout. It is Christian's companion, the aptly named Hopeful, who encourages him: "These troubles and distresses that you go through in these Waters, are no sign that God hath forsaken you, but are sent to try you, whether you will call to mind that which heretofore you have received of his goodness, and live upon him in your distresses."[84] Something higher, indeed, and Rick, after listening to the priest's sermon, seems ready to believe in it. At long last, the castaway becomes a pilgrim. He has been converted. Like one of the most famous converts in literary history, Dostoevsky's Raskolnikov, he has glimpsed another world, one in which his "renewal" and "rebirth" will take place.[85]

Given these many allusions and associations—from Plato and *The Pilgrim's Progress* to the Zen Buddhism of *The Snow Leopard* and the Christian faith of Dostoevsky—as well as the film's tarot-card plot structure and gnostic premise (which derives, in part, from the apocryphal Hymn of the Pearl, a tale about "a prince from the East" who is sent west on a journey only to fall into a deep, forgetful sleep), how can we be sure that *Knight of Cups* remains indebted, most of all, to *The Moviegoer*? Allowing actors the final word in anything is foolish—there is a reason Bresson worked only with "models"— but in this particular case their comments reveal a great deal about how Malick conceived of not just the characters in his confessional films, but also the overall meaning of the larger autobiographical project itself.[86] It is revealing to know, for example, that he encouraged Jessica Chastain to consult Renaissance-era paintings of the Virgin Mary and to study the vocal delivery of Lauren Bacall before working on *The Tree of Life*; and that he told Olga Kurylenko to read *Anna Karenina*, *The Karamazov Brothers*, and *The Idiot* before taking on the role of Marina in *To the Wonder*.[87]

Christian Bale's preparation for *Knight of Cups* was no different. At a panel discussion held after the Los Angeles premiere of the film in 2016, he offered some insight into how we might begin to interpret the third installment of Malick's confessional trilogy. Describing the improvisational approach Malick and Lubezki utilized shooting the film, Bale confessed that he never at any point saw an actual script. There were no lines to learn, no backstories to keep in mind, no character arcs to contemplate. To prepare for his role, Malick offered his leading actor just one word of advice: read *The Moviegoer*.[88]

Does this mean *Knight of Cups* should be characterized as an adaptation? It might be better, I think, to call it a reimagining, or even a reappropriation, of *The Moviegoer*. It draws from not just Percy's novel but also his philosophical essays and even his occasional pieces. In fact, a case could be made that *Knight of Cups* resembles another book in Percy's oeuvre more than *The Mov-*

iegoer, a book that synthesizes Percy's fiction, philosophy, and theology and has a title meant for Malick: *Lost in the Cosmos.*[89] If nothing else, it might explain why *Knight of Cups* opens by juxtaposing Rick's wandering in the desert with breathtaking images—shot from the perspective of deep space—of the Aurora Borealis.

One of the recurring themes in Percy's work—emphasized in both *The Moviegoer,* a novel, and *Lost in the Cosmos,* a send-up of self-help books—is the profound importance of pilgrimage. He viewed life as a search for meaning that one had to undertake on one's own. As Percy saw it, the search was a profoundly individual—and individualizing—experience. But it was one available to all of us in common. Literature proved as much. It showed how our singular lives reflect "universal human experience." Great literature demonstrated, Percy wrote in an essay published after his death in 1990, "that it is in one's own unique individuality that one is most human."[90]

This remark illuminates Malick's aims in his confessional films, which attempt to connect his own personal memories—in a Cavellian arrogation—to something like "a universal human experience." We can see as much in their content, but also in how they were made. By running *The Moviegoer* through the story of his own life (and by encouraging his actors to work from their own moods and experiences, something made possible by the improvisational approach articulated in "the dogma"), Malick was treating *The Moviegoer* like a template: others could use it in different ways in the contemplation of their own personal journeys. Rick is Malick, but Rick could also be Christian Bale, or me, or even you.

That said, *Knight of Cups* seems more personally revealing than *The Tree of Life* and *To the Wonder.* Even though it hides its autobiographical elements behind an archetypical tarot-card motif, there can be no doubt that in *Knight of Cups* Malick uses *The Moviegoer* to confront his own personal journey in ways that are far more probing than before. Among other things, it allows him to contemplate the collapse of his first marriage to Jill Jakes, who becomes Nancy (Cate Blanchett) in the film, as well as other failed romances that followed, including a rumored one with Michie Gleason, who was his assistant on *Days of Heaven.*[91] It also allows him to once again grapple with the lasting influence his father (Brian Dennehy, playing the character of Joseph) and brothers (Wes Bentley, playing Barry) have had on his life. Most of all, though, the film gives him a chance to revisit the delirious decade he spent in Los Angeles becoming a world-famous director but also losing his bearings in the process.

Like the protagonist of Frankenheimer's existential thriller *Seconds*, Malick's avatar Rick has been given everything he could have wanted in California, but still he is unhappy. Lubezki's swirling, up-close cinematography, which echoes James Wong Howe's pioneering work in *Seconds*, conveys a sense of existential claustrophobia.[92] Moments of reprieve come from Renoiresque nature montages, but the beauty surrounding Rick in Southern California seems lost on him. At times, the way Los Angeles is depicted in *Knight of Cups*—stunning, but also glassy, soulless, and surface deep—comes close to cliché, but surely it is consistent with how Malick must have felt at that time in his life, longing as he was to escape the Southland and head off to Annapurna.[93]

Whether or not viewers can identify with Rick the way generations of readers have identified with Christian in *The Pilgrim's Progress* or Binx Bolling in *The Moviegoer*—or even Peter Matthiessen in *The Snow Leopard*—depends on how much sympathy they can muster for a privileged white male, wardrobed in nothing but Armani, who enjoys all the glamour Hollywood has to offer, yet nevertheless pouts and mopes. As much as it preaches reconciliation with the world, asking us to pause and contemplate the pulsating energy of the present moment, whether that be a Malibu sunset or a skid row street, *Knight of Cups* can seem disappointingly navel-gazing in this regard.

It is a common critique of Malick's later work, but it is not one that should be dismissed out of hand, for in channeling Kierkegaard and Heidegger (among others) via Percy, Malick flirts with certain reactionary tendencies we would do well to question, such as the isolationist desire to avoid interpersonal interactions altogether, as Peter Matthiessen did on his pilgrimage to the roof of the world.[94] The aloof loner is a long-standing caricature of existentialism, but even cartoons have a basis in reality. A desire to stand out can become an excuse for merely standing alone. "Existential angst"—as George Cotkin reminds us—"powers Percy's Kierkegaardian universe," but too often "it degenerates into a force of passivism and conservatism, as a courage to exist passively, apart from the battles of society." Indeed, the pilgrim's search can represent what Cotkin rightly labels a "philosophical retreat from politics," an avoidance of the world, rather than a true engagement with it.[95]

Only those with a certain level of privilege will have the luxury to confront their existential angst in this way, anyhow. It goes without saying that Rick's enchanted, entitled world is insulated from the material realities of race, class, and gender. Labor, too. *Knight of Cups* is largely devoid of it, showing us only the work of the culture industry, the work of well-paid agents

Figure 28. Existential angst then (Rock Hudson as Tony in John Frankenheimer's *Seconds*).

Figure 29. Existential angst now (Christian Bale as Rick in *Knight of Cups*).

and managers, producers and photographers. Although *Knight of Cups* captures some of the distressing socioeconomic inequality that is now synonymous with sprawling megacities like Los Angeles, it does so only surreptitiously, passingly, usually from afar. Furthermore, these images are merely points of contrast. Skid row poverty is the predictable counterpoint to neon-lit skyscrapers; a cramped and overcrowded garment factory (with Spanish-speaking seamstresses) the antithesis to the spartan bachelor-pad loft

Figure 30. Watching workers, but from a distance, in *Knight of Cups*.

where Rick's troubled brother Barry resides. Only a few brief, blink-and-you-will-miss-them scenes depict the actual work—and the actual workers—required to maintain the immaculate houses and well-manicured gardens where all the parties take place.

These shots of landscapers and gardeners trimming trees or blowing leaves down driveways bring to mind the inventive paintings of Jay Lynn (formerly Ramiro) Gomez, who inserts domestic workers into reimaginings of well-known portraits of Southern California wealth and ease, such as those of David Hockney. But whereas Gomez seeks to make "visible the 'invisible' labor forces that keep the pools, homes, and gardens of Los Angeles in such pristine condition," Malick turns our gaze away from them and toward the region's midcentury modern architecture, its desert cacti, and its sunny skies.[96] The slight may not be intentional, but it is noticeable. As was the case with *To the Wonder*, *Knight of Cups* gestures toward pressing, real-world problems, only to brush them aside. The spiritual search takes precedence over seemingly more mundane terrestrial struggles; material reality is obscured by what Theodor Adorno once called "the jargon of authenticity."[97]

Viewing *Knight of Cups* today, not so long after it was made, throws this problem into high relief. One more example will suffice, though any number of other instances in the film—such as those brief, documentary-like depictions of the down-and-out in downtown Los Angeles, which mimic the scenes of the Bartlesville poor in *To the Wonder*—could be mentioned. Our heightened awareness of gender discrimination and sexual harassment not just in

Hollywood but also throughout contemporary society calls attention to the increasingly one-dimensional, stereotypical portrayals of women in Malick's recent films, which reaches something of a nadir in *Knight of Cups*. M. Gail Hamner is not the only one to find the picture "particularly masculinist and heterosexist."[98]

In Rick's life women appear either as sex objects or spirit guides. The line dividing the two is hazy at best. It is all too easy to lay the blame for such lazy characterizations on Christian theology. In the first part of *The Pilgrim's Progress*, for example, women can either play the role of Wanton, a temptress "all carnal and fleshly," or they can personify Discretion, Piety, Charity, or Prudence.[99] In the second part, the best Christian's wife, Christiana, can do is walk in the footsteps of her husband, whose example she submissively follows. It would be heartening, perhaps, to think of such rhetoric as the hallmark of an earlier, less equitable epoch. But similar tropes surface in many of the other texts marshaled by Malick in *Knight of Cups*. Kierkegaard's troubled romance with Regine Olsen, the impetus for so much of his work, is one example.[100] In many ways, *Knight of Cups* takes up Kierkegaard's notion—first outlined in the many pseudonymous texts composing works such as *Either/Or, Repetition,* and *Stages on Life's Way*—that a personal progression from the aesthetic stage of life through an ethical one might lead, finally, to the most exalted state of existence, the religious stage.[101] It is why we see Rick evolve from a Don Juan seducer, who is interested not so much in finding love as he is in fashioning a "love experience," to a tortured ex-husband, brother, and son, finally becoming a spiritual pilgrim only at the very end of the film.

The arc of Rick's life, with all its romantic dalliances, is also reminiscent of another famous spiritual pilgrim: Augustine. In the *Confessions* the bishop of Hippo also admitted to once being more infatuated with the idea of romance than the experience of true—that is, divine—love: "I was in love with love," he wrote, "but my soul was in rotten health."[102] In faith he found healing and a new beginning. *Knight of Cups* is a film about this kind of starting over. Rick's last whispered word in the movie—the final narration we hear—is "Begin." Women helped get Rick to this point, but they are barred from journeying alongside him to the next stage. The carnal pleasures they represent must be left behind. "Women or ideas are what beckon men out into existence," Kierkegaard once confided in his journals, but "for the thousands who run after a skirt there is not always one who is moved by ideas."[103] As Constantin Constantius (Kierkegaard had a knack for inventing silly names) puts it in *Repetition*: "it is as if God used this girl to capture him." She "is like the lace-winged fly with which a hook is baited."[104]

The women of *Knight of Cups* are Kierkegaardian lures: they are lovers and companions, but mostly they are just bodies. They do not stick around long enough to be portrayed as fully rounded people. Even when their internal monologues can be heard on the film's soundtrack, they speak solely to Rick. As Kristi McKim notes, women appear only as "accessories and muses, caretakers and healers, sexual partners and visual objects, bereft of subjectivity."[105] The women of *Knight of Cups* have none of the personality displayed by Holly in *Badlands* or Linda in *Days of Heaven*. Even Mrs. O'Brien in *The Tree of Life*, who serves mostly as a quiet personification of "the way of grace," gets a chance to develop a character trait or two (the longer cut of the film even gives her something of a story arc, mentioning her hopes for further education, which she puts on hold to raise her brood of boys). The same cannot be said for Della (Imogen Poots), Helen (Frieda Pinto), Karen (Teresa Palmer), or the almost entirely silent Isabel (Isabel Lucas), who flits in and out of *Knight of Cups* from beginning to end without ever receiving any kind of proper introduction. She very well could be a ghost or a sprite, nothing more than a figment of Rick's imagination.

Kierkegaard may be the primary source for such stereotypes, but at least his persistent use of pseudonymous authorship inserts some ironic distance between his personal experience and the often-problematic interpersonal relations described in his texts. I think the blame for such hackneyed portrayals of gender roles in films like *To the Wonder* and *Knight of Cups* is better placed at the feet of Walker Percy. His depiction of women—not to mention "homosexuals," but that is another issue—in *The Moviegoer* and subsequent works is grating at best, offensive and demeaning at worst. This line from *Lost in the Cosmos* is fairly representative: "for every Mother Teresa there seems to be 1,800 nutty American nuns, female Clint Eastwoods who have it in for men and are out to get the Pope."[106] It is a joke, of course, but not a funny one, and it reveals a truth we cannot overlook, which is that Percy's Catholicism is thoroughly conservative, if not outright reactionary, especially when it comes to matters of sex and gender. Too often his spiritual seeker is a lot like him: white, male, and self-assuredly straight.

What if we could imagine women—as well as all other people, regardless of gender expression or sexual orientation—not merely as peripheral characters, not merely as adjuncts to the search, but as searchers themselves? Here it might be worth recalling the prescient warning of Binx Bolling: "The movies are onto the search, but they screw it up."[107] Perhaps the film you need most is the one you have to go out and make yourself. Maybe that is where the journey truly begins, when the story finally becomes your own.

Across the Universe: *Voyage of Time*

How many of us will ever have the resources or the clout to make the movie version of our life's journey? One of the remarkable things about Malick's recent films is the simple fact that they exist; that he and his producers found a way to finance what is essentially an extended autobiographical trilogy. It was made possible by Malick's singular career. Because he emerged as a sought-after director when the reign of the auteur was at its peak, then disappeared when it waned, only to return at a decidedly volatile, uncertain time for the movie industry, when the advent of digital streaming was making endless content the norm rather than a wild fantasy, Malick enjoyed the kind of artistic freedom that is nearly impossible to find in filmmaking today.[108]

Malick put that freedom to remarkably good use, but it was a freedom to fail as much as succeed. The films he made on the heels of *The Tree of Life* did not always live up to the expectations set by its success. *To the Wonder* and *Knight of Cups* share *The Tree of Life*'s overarching plotline, as well as its majestic cinematic ambition, but the latter two films are less-vibrant clones of their predecessor: watching them, one cannot help but feel they are missing something. That something might be the cosmological framing device that makes *The Tree of Life* so astonishing. *To the Wonder* and *Knight of Cups* gesture to the mysteries of the natural world, but they avoid venturing very far across space and time, the way *The Tree of Life* does to such great effect. *Voyage of Time*, however, gives us the stars and more. It is chock full of natural scientific wonder *and* cosmic mystery. An educational guide prepared for is release describes it as "a one-of-a-kind celebration of life and the grand history of the cosmos."[109]

Voyage of Time is a reminder that "astronomy and physics"—as science writer and artist Michael Benson has put it—"were profoundly linked to theology and astrology for much of history."[110] Exchanging the sometimes navel-gazing perspective of the confessional films preceding it for outright stargazing, it veers away from narrative storytelling and becomes something truly unexpected—even for Malick. This time around there is no dramatic plot to serve as a guide rail for viewer interpretations. Not only that, but

Voyage of Time arrived in two rather different versions: a longer theatrical cut narrated by Cate Blanchett—subtitled *Life's Journey*—and a shorter, IMAX experience narrated by Brad Pitt.

Even with name recognition on his side, Malick had a hard time getting *Voyage of Time* made. IMAX projects are expensive. So is years of globe-trotting nature photography in remote locations, undertaken by an ever-changing array of associates and contractors. *Voyage of Time* was a pricey investment. For a time, at least, it looked as if Malick would not be allowed to finish the film: he was sued by investors who were unhappy with the slow pace of his work.[111]

Slow is right. Dating back to the 1970s—when Malick first entertained the idea of making a film about the evolution of the universe, complete with dinosaurs—*Voyage of Time* had an unusually long gestation period.[112] From the beginning, it was going to be Malick's signature work, the film encapsulating his views on everything. Sadly, by the time his passion project finally appeared decades later, it reached only limited audiences. *Voyage of Time: Life's Journey* played in just a handful of festivals around the world. The IMAX version of the film avoided this fate, but just barely, appearing in a few IMAX-specific venues for a limited run.

The IMAX version of *Voyage of Time* gets philosophical fast: "When I was kid, I used to wonder," its narration asks, "why was there something rather than nothing?" Remarkably, the forty-minute film tries to answer this question. Over majestic images of the natural world, *Voyage of Time*'s narrator (a distracting Brad Pitt) asks questions about how and why the universe came about; about what the evolution of life on planet Earth means for us today in the twenty-first century. The film even contemplates the death of our solar system: will that be the end of everything, or just the beginning of something new? In these moments, *Voyage of Time*'s narration resembles mystic poetry: "Out of nothing, a beginning." But in other sections it skews academic: "Mind, consciousness, was it always there?" (Malick told one of his sound designers that he wanted certain scenes "to sound like consciousness.")[113] Sometimes it even resembles prayer, as if the film were a tribute to what many religious traditions call creation.

Voyage of Time does not pit faith against science. Instead of shunning the insights of the astronomers and the physicists, it embraces them. The film is interrogative, inquisitive, searching—more Franciscan, we might say, than Thomist. The world of proliferating mystery it describes is equally available to the theoretical physicist, the wildlife biologist, and the Sunday-schooler.

Divinity is in nature, *Voyage of Time*'s narrations suggest, and wonder helps us see it. "What binds us together, makes us one? Love. Is love, too, not a work of nature?" All this while immense whales swim across the screen. "What is it? This miracle, this gift."

Voyage of Time pulls us out of the churning, spinning now and places us in the immediacy of a present moment ready-made for contemplation. It makes us wonder about our place in the cosmos and returns us to the world with a sense of gratitude. *Voyage of Time* distills Malick's cinematic vision down to its constituent elements: the Renoirian nature montage, the Heideggerian sense of dwelling and being-in-the-world, the Christian appreciation of the gift of grace. All of these can be found in its theatrical release as well, which exhibits a degree of gratitude without equal in contemporary cinema, one that outdoes even its IMAX sibling.[114] But it starts out darker. Recalling the soundtrack of *The New World*, its voice-over narration addresses a "Mother" who deserves thanks. Whether this "Mother" is Mother Nature, the Mother of God, or some other feminine spiritual force that gives life to all things is not entirely clear. Perhaps "Mother" is God Herself. But She is an unseen God, an absent God, a neglected God. The opening scenes of the film depict women suffering and in pain: aged women; unhoused women; ill women wandering downtown streets in obvious distress. If these are the many faces of "Mother," they reveal not a revered and hallowed figure who receives our gratitude, but rather a suffering "Mother" on whom we have turned our backs.

Malick's interest in suffering predates his turn toward confessional cinema. When he was still a fellow at the American Film Institute, he worked on a documentary short devoted to the topic of senility, which surely must have informed the opening scenes of *Voyage of Time: Life's Journey*.[115] Because aging and suffering are reminders of our mortality, they are anxiety-inducing. Suffering leads to searching. But *Voyage of Time* suggests that searching can lead to wonder, and wonder can lead, in time, to gratitude. Over jaw-dropping nature imagery and anthropological footage gathered from around the globe—religious ceremonies in India and Southeast Asia, in particular— Malick's voice-overs search for "Mother": "Who are you? Life-giver, light-bringer." "Speak with me," Cate Blanchett implores. "What am I? Who brought me here?" "Oh Mother," she continues. "All behold you. Blazing. Shining through all time. I tremble, quake, in wonder." Between these spare, infrequent lines of narration, long silences take hold, only to be broken by the riotous soundscape of the earth itself: volcanoes erupting, fumaroles hissing, waves crashing. These sounds and images recall the nature montages of

Malick's earlier films, but the voice-overs add a new layer of meaning to the technique, transforming it into an active questioning: "Nature, who am I to you? You devour yourself, only to give birth to yourself again." In such moments, everything remains an open question, a mystery—our fleeting, temporal existence on this planet the biggest one of all.

The *Voyage of Time* films are not the first artistic works to contemplate the awesomeness of nature, nor will they be the last. (Among the many artistic inspirations behind the *Voyage of Time* films were the magnificent western landscapes of Albert Bierstadt, especially his 1864 masterwork *Valley of the Yosemite*.)[116] But the way in which they achieve their effect is noteworthy, because it shows how expressly *cinematic* Malick's philosophical pursuits have become. His interest in the concept of world was transformed by the power of movies. What he once explored via texts and treatises he now surveys with moving images, sound, and music. His philosophizing has become, quite literally, a work of cinematic art. A close look at some of the special effects utilized in *Voyage of Time* shows how Malick learned to walk the fine line between scientific observation and artistic imagination while searching for philosophical wisdom. Like the outer-space drawings and illustrations of nineteenth-century French American artist and astronomer Étienne Léopold Trouvelot—who worked, for a time, at the Harvard College Observatory—*Voyage of Time*'s images are as beautiful as they are instructional.[117] But they owe their greatest debt not to scientific illustrations but to other movies.

Voyage of Time—as well as *The Tree of Life*'s cosmology sequence—displays the unmistakable influence not only of Stanley Kubrick's *2001: A Space Odyssey* (1968) but also of the 1960 Canadian documentary *Universe* (dir. Roman Kroitor and Colin Low, 1960), which inspired it. Despite being made at very different times, and with very different resources, these works are alike in that they are decidedly pre-digital—painterly rather than programmed. They remain more "natural" than most of the imagery generated by Hollywood today. Indeed, *The Tree of Life* and *Voyage of Time* are holdovers from an aged, analog aesthetic, which debuted with Georges Méliès's *A Trip to the Moon* (1902) and took on something like a definitive shape six decades later in *Universe*. Stanley Kubrick admired the Canadian documentary so much that he shanghaied the person responsible for many of its effects, Wally Gentleman, into working on the project he was in the midst of developing with famed science fiction author Arthur C. Clarke.[118] While Clarke toiled away on story ideas at the Chelsea Hotel, Kubrick experimented with filming techniques, borrowed from *Universe*, that might allow him to depict outer space better than the usual sci-fi B movie. In an abandoned brassiere factory on the west side of Manhattan, he mixed liquids of varying viscosities in large drums, which he then shot close-up and fast. The images he captured mimicked the subtle flows of gases and nebulae, the elemental components of the galaxy. It was the experimental—and slightly toxic—beginning of what would become *2001*.

Unlike the computer-generated images of today, the creation of *2001*'s look was an entirely analog affair, requiring a lot of hands-on innovation. An eager young graphic artist from Southern California named Douglas Trumbull talked his way into a job on the project. His timing was fortuitous, because Kubrick was in the midst of assembling a new team of artists, manufacturers, and technicians to help him realize the increasingly complex designs of his film, including, most notably, its famous Stargate sequence. Trumbull designed much of this material and it launched his career. His work on *2001* earned him a reputation in Hollywood as a special-effects guru. Trumbull went on to shape the look of high-profile sci-fi films, such as Robert Wise's *The Andromeda Strain* (1971). He even got the chance to direct his own picture, the postapocalyptic, environmentalist parable *Silent Running* (1972), which might best be described as an ecological *Canticle for Leibowitz* set in outer space. Trumbull's directorial debut starred a tree-loving protagonist (Bruce Dern) and featured a theme song, Joan Baez's "Rejoice in the Sun," which echoed Saint Francis's "Canticle of the Sun."

It was while developing *Silent Running* that Trumbull met a young screenwriter from the American Film Institute who had worked on adapting *Canticle for Leibowitz* for the big screen.[119] They shared an enthusiasm for spiritually inflected science fiction and amateur astronomy, so they hung out together down in Marina del Rey and Venice Beach for a while (Malick reportedly lived in an apartment in nearby Santa Monica at the time), before eventually taking different paths in and through Hollywood in the years to come.[120] Trumbull and Malick reconnected some twenty years later.[121] In short order, Malick asked his old acquaintance to serve as an adviser on the project to which he was now finally returning, decades later. What began as Q in the 1970s was now in the process of becoming *The Tree of Life* and *Voyage of Time*.[122]

Trumbull suggested setting up a laboratory, in which a special effects crew, led by visual effects veteran Dan Glass, could experiment with analog techniques that might produce the kind of cosmic imagery Malick was after. With a nod to a secret research program in advanced aviation housed at

Lockheed Martin during the Second World War, they dubbed the program "the Skunkworks."[123] The experiments carried out by the team explored, as Trumbull later put it, how best "to use natural phenomena under high-speed photography and use things like liquids and chemicals, water and paint and milk and some of the things that went back all the way to *2001: A Space Odyssey*."[124]

Very little of *The Tree of Life* and *Voyage of Time* was generated by computers. In the place of keystrokes, the elemental stuff of nature took center stage: light, liquid, air, and matter. Thanks to Trumbull, *The Tree of Life* even got a Stargate sequence of its own. But it was science, not fantasy, that mattered most. Joining the Skunkworks team were a number of consultants scattered around the world with expertise in a vast array of fields: astrophysicists from the nearby University of Texas at Austin, for example, as well as scholars of cosmological image-making throughout human history, such as the science writer and artist Michael Benson.[125] But achieving documentary verisimilitude was never the point. Malick emphasized not just scientific accuracy but also "experimentation and discovery," which might lead to something "unexpected," "mysterious, unexplained."[126] Malick was committed, first and foremost, to being curious. In Trumbull's words: "Terry is consumed by wonder and awe for life and everything around it."[127]

Although the *Voyage of Time* films are not properly part of what I have been calling Malick's confessional trilogy, they cannot be separated from the works preceding them. They constitute an epilogue to his autobiographical project, framing the life story presented in *The Tree of Life*, *To the Wonder*, and *Knight of Cups*. If the trilogy inaugurated by *The Tree of Life* examines the uniqueness of one individual life—Malick's life—the *Voyage of Time* films look more expansively at what we might call, in Heideggerian lingo, Being itself. They attend to the natural world, paying close attention to the phenomena of presencing and falling away. In this temporal flux they find evidence of a transcendent continuity, a power surging through all forms of life. A voice-over near the conclusion of *Voyage of Time: Life's Journey* gives it a name: "Joined with you, leaf to branch, branch to tree. Love binds us together."

There is a precedent for this kind of sentiment in American philosophy, one we might locate in thinkers such as Emerson and Thoreau. Thoreau's writings are particularly relevant to the *Voyage of Time* films. Malick was probably pointed in their direction by Cavell, one of Thoreau's more recent champions. In *The Senses of Walden*—a book published the same year Trumbull's *Silent Running* hit theaters, a year before *Badlands* was released—Cavell praised Thoreau's remarkable ability to listen to the natural world. It was a skill that made the author of *Walden* unique, he said. Thoreau understood "that nature is at every instant openly confiding in us, in its largest arrangements and in its smallest sounds."[128] This idea appears in the *Voyage of Time* films, which listen intently to nature. Their soundtracks contain tones from outer space captured by NASA's *Voyager* missions as well as the laughter of little children playing on suburban front lawns. In between, the symphony of the earth takes center stage.

The analytic philosopher Thomas Nagel—who received his PhD at Harvard, studying under Rawls while Malick was an undergraduate there—has described the world as "an astonishing place." "That it has produced you, and me, and the rest of us," he writes, "is the most astonishing thing about it."[129] This might be proof that academic philosophers have finally come back around to viewing the world and the cosmos—not to mention our place in them—as a topic worthy of further exploration. It might also be taken as proof that Malick's cinematic explorations have been running out ahead of the academic consensus, that the analytic mindset responsible for turning Malick away from academic philosophy may be ready, at last, to welcome him back.

Malick's confessional films, stretching from *The Tree of Life* to *Voyage of Time*, are works of wonder that remind us—to borrow Nagel's words—"how little we really understand about the world."[130] They search for a meaningful connection with the cosmos. That connection, a bridge both figurative and real, from our solitary selves to the universe at large, is what Malick failed to find in academic philosophy. The closing shot of *The Tree of Life* is of New York City's majestic, vast Verrazano-Narrows Bridge. It suggests Malick finally found the connection he was seeking—not in philosophy, but in cinema.[131]

*   *   *

As both an undergraduate student at Harvard and a Rhodes scholar at Oxford, Terrence Malick's primary aim was to "understand himself and his place in the order of the cosmos."[132] His confessional films are best understood as a continuation of this quest. They are proof that what Malick could not locate in academia he has sought out in filmmaking. If today philosophers seem willing to entertain such cosmological inquiry, fifty or sixty years ago it was another story. By way of a conclusion to this chapter (and the one preceding it), I would like to speculate, in something of a counterfactual fashion, about how things might have worked out differently.

Not long before Malick made his way to Cambridge, Massachusetts, a philosopher sharing precisely his interests, not to mention his fondness for the grandeur and mystery of the natural world, was denied tenure by the Harvard philosophy department. His name was Henry Bugbee. He, too, thought philosophy should revolve around self-examination and cosmic reflection. He, too, was drawn to Heidegger. And he, too, had a thing for rivers. More inclined to live his philosophy than write it up, though, Bugbee was dismissed from Harvard in 1954.

The perils of publish-or-perish academic life are often bemoaned these days, but in Bugbee's case there may have been other things at play in the decision to deny him tenure. As well as being slow to publish, he did not fit the new mold of what an academic philosopher should be: his work was neither narrowly technical nor highly specialized. An analytical philosopher Bugbee was not, but analytic was what Harvard philosophy was rapidly becoming—by 1960 the department chairperson worried his schedule of classes contained "too much logic," a concern easily dismissed by his colleagues, it seems, since no changes to the course rotation were made.[133]

With interests ranging from Meister Eckhart, Spinoza, and Zen Buddhism to existentialism, Shakespeare, and fly-fishing—and not necessarily in that order, either—Bugbee was an eclectic, ecumenical thinker.[134] His career represents a philosophical path not taken by the Harvard philosophy department, or by the American philosophical profession more broadly, in the 1950s and 1960s. It is a path that bears an eerie similarity to the journey Malick has been on since matriculating at the American Film Institute in 1969.

We get a glimpse of Bugbee's uniqueness in his writings. A few years after his time at Harvard came to end, he published the book for which he is best remembered today, *The Inward Morning: A Philosophical Exploration in Journal Form*.[135] The title was borrowed from Thoreau, but the treatise contained much more than a warmed-over version of nineteenth-century transcendentalism. It was, as its subtitle indicates, an attempt to write a whole new kind of philosophy. For Bugbee, this meant becoming a new kind of philosopher. "I have found myself thinking quite differently from the majority of men who are setting the style and the standard of philosophy worth doing," he wrote in one of the book's many passages of honest self-reflection.[136]

Unlike so many of his colleagues, who were busy paring down the scope of philosophical inquiry, Bugbee sought instead to build it up. Nothing was off-limits. He read Heidegger, *Hamlet*, and the Bhagavad Gita; he listened to Beethoven and made his way through Proust. He developed a fondness for existentialism and a disdain for narrowly conceived variants of empiricism— logical empiricism most especially. Bugbee felt philosophical reflection should be grounded in experience, not expertise. The point of doing philosophy was not to analyze or dissect life, but to live it—and live it meaningfully: "I do not think we can be, or would want to be, professionals—experts—in the conduct of our lives," he wrote.[137] This was not what Hans Reichenbach called—in a 1951 monograph that in many ways set the tone for American philosophy in the decades to come—"scientific philosophy."[138] It was more like "personal philosophy."[139]

Some of Bugbee's antipathy toward overly abstract philosophical systems stemmed from his experiences in the Second World War. His graduate studies in philosophy at Berkeley were interrupted by four years of military service aboard a U.S. Navy minesweeper in the South Pacific, during which he survived both typhoons and kamikaze attacks in coastal waters off the Philippines. These brushes with death left an indelible mark on his philosophical outlook. Years later, friends would tell Bugbee that he wrote philosophy "as a man might write only near the end of his life." Bugbee embraced the description. For him, nearness to death was the best kind of philosophical catalyst: it pointed one in the direction of "eternal meaning."[140]

Returning to Berkeley to complete his thesis only after doing a fair share of therapeutic fly-fishing on the streams and rivers of his beloved Northern California, Bugbee proceeded to finish his dissertation, "The Sense and Conception of Being" ("just a minor responsibility," he later joked, poking fun at the portentousness of the title).[141] While leading a peripatetic philosophical life, teaching first at the University of Nevada, Reno, and then Stanford, before getting the call to head back east to Harvard, his interests deepened and widened. In time, Bugbee came to think of himself as addressing nothing less than "human destiny."[142] Anything and everything became fodder for his reflections: philosophy, poetry, religion, drama, literature, art, hiking, meditation, even his contemplation of the morning sunrise.

Long before Terrence Malick began experimenting with narrative form to portray the interconnected nature of self-examination and cosmic exploration, long before he began searching the deeper recesses of his own memories for glimpses of communion with others and the world at large, long before he was reading Kierkegaard and Heidegger and the Book of Job, Henry Bugbee was doing something similar. In the preface to *The Inward Morning*, he said his book was composed under "the guidance of meditation."[143] It reads like a record of the examined life. *The Inward Morning* contains a few footnotes, and a few quotations from famous philosophers, but mostly it just records a person remarking, remembering, recalling, questioning, and, most of all, thinking. The book is frank and sincere. Its prose is lyrical, but also intellectually demanding and very often digressive. *The Inward Morning* is not the kind of book that gets one tenure at high-profile academic institutions—not then, and certainly not now. Bugbee knew this: "For five years I have been writing in an exploratory way," he confesses, "gradually forced to recognize that this was the case and I must accept it, along with its professional consequences."[144]

Composing *The Inward Morning* was "a precarious business." Bugbee was only "able to transcend the uneasiness and defensiveness incurred in diverging from the main trends of thought in current academic philosophy among English-speaking circles" when he was truly "lost" in his work.[145] But lost in that work he often was. Bugbee seems to have done most of his thinking while wandering outdoors. His "philosophy took shape mainly on foot," which resulted in an unusually rich awareness of places, things, and creatures. His unique writing style tried to capture the insights he gleaned while away from his desk: "I weighted everything by the measure of the silent presence of things, clarified in the racing clouds, clarified by the cry of hawks, solidified in the presence of rocks, spelled syllable by syllable by waters of manifold voice, and consolidated in the act of taking steps, each step a meditation in reality."[146]

During the course of his many walks, Bugbee came to view philosophy as an act of testimony, a practice documenting the thoughts that arise from our personal encounters in, with, and through the world. Philosophy was not about claims or counterclaims, propositions or refutations.[147] It was about bearing witness to one's journey. Bugbee knew that academic philosophy had its place, but in *The Inward Morning* he reminded himself of its limitations, too: "It will ever be important to me to give attention to technical philosophy, but I will never be able to take technical philosophy as the ultimate phase of a reflective life."[148]

Written in a confessional style, complete with a journal-entry format, *The Inward Morning* is a remarkably humble work with very grand ambitions. In it, Bugbee sets out to locate, from out of his own private experience, what he calls—with a nod to his onetime Harvard colleague Paul Tillich—"the ground of ultimate human concern."[149] He examines his own existence with an eye toward understanding *all* existence. He reverses this gaze, too: he looks at the abundance of creaturely life around him hoping it might illuminate the contours of his own life. He paraphrases Spinoza: "The true good is the discovery of the union between oneself and all beings."[150] What follows this remark is a series of reflections on such topics as wonder, experience, communion, mystery, grace, gratitude, truth, confession, memory, subjectivity, simplicity, care, recollection, homecoming, and what Bugbee at one point calls "the gift of all existent things," our "coexistence in communion."[151]

Bugbee thought philosophy erred when it stressed "objectivity" more than wonder and gratitude, when it did everything it could to keep religious insight—that perceived threat to secular science—at arm's length.[152] "To perceive something truly is to be alive to it in its sacredness." The sacred connects all things to each other in both their "individuality" and their "universality." In *The Inward Morning* Bugbee stresses the point: "The mystery of each thing is the mystery of all things; and this—not generalization or the broadening of our scope of attention to wider and wider complexes of things, is the foundation of the idea of universe: the omnirelevance of the experience of something as sacred."[153] In Bugbee's opinion, "the latently religious character of philosophical issues"—another idea he borrowed from Tillich—was not something to be avoided, but rather something to be embraced.[154] This notion also pushed him to the margins of the profession. However much he could find support for it in the Christian theology of Tillich or the Zen Buddhism of D. T. Suzuki (whom he also came to know at Harvard), Bugbee had difficulty locating proponents of such thinking in contemporary American philosophy. Only two philosophers, both of them European, seemed to be on the right track: Martin Heidegger (whose work he read in French translation) and the French Catholic existentialist Gabriel Marcel (with whom he hung out while attending Heidegger's lecture course at Château de Cerisy-la-Salle, France, in August 1955).

Somewhat remarkably, Marcel, a much more senior and famous philosopher than Bugbee at the time, wrote a lengthy introduction for the first printing of *The Inward Morning*. In it, he praised Bugbee's "*experiential philosophy*," comparing it directly to Heidegger's thought.[155] Both espoused what Marcel called "a philosophy of the open air."[156] Bugbee and Heidegger were thinkers of the forest path, of rivers and mountains and leaping trout. They were philosophers of "wonder."[157]

Indeed, many of Bugbee's entries in *The Inward Morning* address the importance of wonder. "In wonder reality begins to sink in," he writes. "It sets us to a questioning which can only find conclusive answer in terms of a deepening of our response to things, which is the deepening, and not the allaying, of wonder."[158] Wonder might arise from religious or philosophical inquiry; but it might also come from elsewhere, from the contemplation of the natural world, say, or from a meaningful encounter with music or art. The point was to be open to it, wherever and whenever it appeared. For Bugbee, "the readiness to receive is all," and whether the "glancing, diving, finning fish" of a steelhead run on the Gualala River or "Beethoven's Opus 135" fostered it made no difference in the end.[159]

Bugbee was not a theologian, but he saw divinity everywhere. He was a post-secular thinker before the term came into fashion, which might explain why so many of his ideas resonate with Malick's post-secular, confessional films.[160] What being out in the wilderness taught Bugbee was that we have no unchanging home. The world around us is constantly evolving, growing, transforming. But so are we. This was the mystery. "The more we experience things in depth, the more we participate in a mystery intelligible to us only as such; and the more we understand our world to be an unknown world." "Our true home," Bugbee thought, "is wilderness."[161] In a 1962 essay entitled "Thoughts on Creation" he put it slightly differently, though no less emphatically: "World is, if you will, always in the building, being forged, to be done; it cannot lapse from dawning and formation. It appears as that which dawns and *is* dawning. So world does appear as world-without-end, and creation with respect to world is continuous creation. Hence the feel of creation is one of fluency and constancy, one of opening out and opening up, one of gathering up and growing together of things and events to enter into this ever-forming of world. Thus, to be in and of the world would be to be in and of continuous creation, and to abide in the world would be to abide in no fixed abode."[162]

Only an "examined life," as Bugbee called it, could bear witness to this coevolution of self and world. The two went hand in hand: we come to know the world through the process of reflecting upon our lives; but we also come to know ourselves by receiving and caring for the world. In Bugbee's words, "the coming to pass of a world and our coming to be as selves are essentially related: we participate in this as selves. World, in turn, seems to come to pass only through our participation in it as selves, and this is ultimately a matter of free consent on our part, by coming to pass through us."[163] That "free consent," for Bugbee, was crucial. It encouraged involvement rather than detachment, an attitude of concern rather than calculation.

Bugbee suggested that only a comportment of "care" toward the world allowed us to receive "all things" as "divine gifts."[164] "The story of creation is an ontological one," Bugbee came to believe, "*the* ontological one."[165] In an unpublished essay written around the same time as "Thoughts on Creation," he turned to the Book of Job. Like Malick, he finds in it "the things of heaven-and-earth, dramatized in their emergent majesty, wonder, and inviolable *reserve*. But *seen* in the mode of this, their being. And seen as if for the first time, yet as belonging to a domain, in which dominion (not domination) reigns, forever and ever: the domain of being itself."[166] This is precisely what *The Tree of Life* and *Voyage of Time* seek to capture.

One of the central themes of *The Inward Morning* is the interconnectedness of self and world. The same idea underpins Malick's confessional cinema, which similarly stresses the importance of communion. Only in working through one's own experiences and memories can such communion be achieved. It is in journeying through our pasts that we become attuned to the abundant gifts all around us. Thinking of Proust, Bugbee at one point considers how moments of "involuntary recall" bring us in touch with what is "essential."[167] "The recollective understanding of one's actual experience," he writes, "is intimately connected with the reflective understanding of reality."[168] Taking up our memories thus becomes a path toward true understanding: "I trust in the remembrance of what I have loved and respected; remembrance in which love and respect are clarified. And I trust in such remembrance to guide my reflections in the path of essential truth."[169] This remembering is "our homecoming." It returns us to the world with understanding and gratitude. "Reflective experience" awakens us to "the idea of grace."[170]

The Tree of Life, To the Wonder, Knight of Cups, and *Voyage of Time* are works of memory and grace. They are cosmic confessions that seek to understand the self and the world. They show both as being interrelated and co-constitutive. Malick's autobiographical films may draw upon the exotic travelogues of Peter Matthiessen, the wayfaring novels of Walker Percy, and the first-person philosophizing of Stanley Cavell, but Bugbee's thinking anticipates them all in almost every way.

How different would things have been if Bugbee and Malick had overlapped at Harvard? One cannot help but wonder. Bugbee could have been the mentor Malick wanted, teaching him to appreciate the enduring legacy of Socratic self-examination, as well as the symbolic beauty and serenity of

Figure 31. Thinking of rivers and existence in *The Tree of Life*.

rivers.[171] In rivers, Bugbee found almost everything he needed to know about existence: "There is a constant fluency of meaning in the instant in which we live," he wrote. "One may learn of it from rivers in the constancy of their utterance, if one listens and is still."[172]

As viewers of his films know, Malick reveres rivers, too. But he had to find a way to them on his own. Although rivers have inspired philosophers for centuries—among them Heraclitus, Thoreau, and Heidegger—there was little room in the logic-centered Harvard curriculum of the 1960s for river-related ruminations.[173] At the Center for Advanced Film Studies, however, one could watch movies featuring rivers—such as Renoir's—and call it a curriculum. No doubt Bugbee would have approved.

In Bugbee's day, personal philosophy was decidedly out of fashion. Although Emerson, Thoreau, and James had considered cosmic questions of "ultimate concern" from a first-person vantage point, it would not be until Cavell found prominence much later that other thinkers in the United States would feel emboldened enough to write in a more autobiographical vein and still feel like they had a shot at tenure and promotion. Bugbee and Cavell were separated by an era of positivist ascendancy that only now appears to be subsiding.[174]

Malick could have followed Cavell's path. Instead, like Bugbee, he continued his search for meaning elsewhere. But this is no reason to exclude him from the philosophical canon. After all, as Jennifer Ratner-Rosenhagen has argued, "we might discover more about the dynamism of philosophy in

America by following the intellectual paths of those who felt the need to break free from it."[175] In this regard, Malick's confessional films document what we might think of as a lost moment in American philosophy. Or maybe it is better to think of them as suggesting, like *The Inward Morning*, a new dawn that is yet to come: "Metaphysical thinking must rise with the earliest dawn," Bugbee writes in one of the book's most memorable passages, "the very dawn of things themselves."[176] This is the dawn depicted in *The Tree of Life*, *To the Wonder*, *Knight of Cups*, and *Voyage of Time*, the dawn that still has the power to amaze and astonish, the power to make us wonder.

CHAPTER 7

Lost and Found

The Gift of Mercy in *Song to Song* and *A Hidden Life*

> Hide the ideas, but so that people will find them. The most important will be the most hidden.
>
> —Robert Bresson

Energized by the success of *The Tree of Life*, Malick continued experimenting. In one sense, this represented the continuation of a bold, new project. In another, though, one might say he was returning to his roots. As a film student he was greatly impressed by European directors such as Jean Renoir, Robert Bresson, and the upstarts collectively known as the French New Wave. More so than generally has been acknowledged, Malick's creative vision was shaped by this cinematic tradition, which prized improvisation and personal filmmaking.

From Renoir and Bresson, especially, Malick had learned to train his focus on the intricacies of the natural world and everyday life, which could only be captured by avoiding premeditation. Overly staged scenes were artificial and inauthentic. Bresson was especially adamant about this. "From the beings and things of nature, washed clean of all art and especially of the art of drama," he wrote in his influential *Notes on the Cinematograph*, "you will make art."[1] Improvisation was an indispensable component of the director's toolkit, because it kept artificiality at bay. As Bresson put it in one of the many aphorisms collected in *Notes*: "Prefer what intuition whispers in your ear to what you have done and redone ten times in your head."[2]

Renoir often expressed the same idea, but more loquaciously and metaphorically, as was his way. "I'm a bit like a man who is in love with a woman and who goes to see her with a bouquet of flowers in hand," he once told Jacques Rivette and François Truffaut, who were interviewing him for *Cahiers du Cinéma*: "In the street he goes over the speech he is going to make; he writes a brilliant speech, with many comparisons, talking about her eyes, her voice, her beauty, and he prides himself in all this, of course. And then he arrives at the woman's house, hands her the bouquet of flowers, and says something completely different."[3] Renoir was quick to add a caveat to this little vignette: "Having prepared the speech does help a little," he conceded, but it was the passion and spontaneity that mattered, not the meticulous preparation.[4]

With his autobiographical trilogy complete and his first proper foray into documentary filmmaking finished, Malick had nothing but open cinematic territory stretching out before him. He did not turn away from it. Instead, he chose to continue the experiment in intuitive filmmaking he had initiated with *The Tree of Life*. Like Renoir's madly obsessed lover, he even attempted, in one project, to forgo speechifying—that is, scriptwriting—altogether. *Song to Song*, a film about indie musicians in Austin, Texas, was shot on the fly with a nimble crew, working from plenty of clues and guideposts—and more than a few shouted directives from its director on set, apparently—but nothing resembling an actual screenplay. Shooting digitally, there was no limit as to how much footage Malick could capture and take back to the editing suite. Now able to improvise to his heart's content, he tested the limits of a prominent Renoirian maxim: "You discover the content of a film as you're shooting it."[5] The first cut of *Song to Song* was eight hours long: Malick had enough material to make not a movie but a miniseries.[6]

With so much freedom to wander, Malick may have gotten himself a little lost. Even edited down to a much more manageable two hours, *Song to Song* still turned out to be one of his least successful pictures. The cool reception it received sent him straight back into speechwriting mode. In a rare appearance in Washington, D.C., where the IMAX version of *Voyage of Time* was being shown, Malick told a surprised audience that his next film, *Song to Song*'s follow-up, began as a detailed script. He had "repented" the idea of working without one, he said.[7] Registered with the Writers Guild of America in 2016, that script—for a film that came to be called *A Hidden Life*—would later be nominated for an Academy Award, proof that even a Hollywood ruled by Marvel movies still loves a Terrence Malick screenplay: what had made Malick famous in the 1970s would make him relevant once again almost fifty years later.

Song to Song was dismissed as a foolish errand into the cinematic wilderness, but Malick quickly found his way back to the kind of filmmaking that originally set him apart from his New Hollywood peers. *A Hidden Life* and (the forthcoming) *The Way of the Wind*, religiously inspired films dramatizing the experience of being lost, then found, heralded his return. The first explored the life of an Austrian conscientious objector who dared defy the Nazis; the second the life and times of a man named Jesus. Having prepared a script for each seems to have helped—at least a little.

*   *   *

The only critics who appreciated *Song to Song* were longtime fans, such as Richard Brody at the *New Yorker* and Justin Chang of the *Los Angeles Times*. Chang lauded the film as a "cinematic symphony."[8] Other critics offered more mixed assessments. In the *New York Times* Manohla Dargis said Malick's music industry movie was "a beautiful puzzle," with "much to admire," but also "much to argue with," too. *Song to Song* was a "film to see," though not really "a film to love."[9] Others were far less kind. One self-professed admirer of Malick's previous work admitted he was tempted to join the crowd of people walking out of the opening-weekend screening he caught in New York.[10]

Hardly anyone walked out of Malick's next film, *A Hidden Life*, a biographical portrait of Austrian conscientious objector Franz Jägerstätter, who was martyred by the Nazis on August 9, 1943, for refusing to take an oath of loyalty to the Führer. The picture was greeted with widespread, fulsome praise. Even the harshest critics of *Song to Song* were happy to declare *A Hidden Life* "a masterpiece," by far "the best American film of 2019," as David Thomson put it.[11] Like many commentators who thought Malick had "seemed to get lost" after making *The Tree of Life*, releasing "confoundingly hollow films" such as *To the Wonder*, *Knight of Cups*, and *Song to Song*, Thomson was eager to welcome the old Malick back.[12]

Perhaps it helped that Malick had a clearer story to tell in *A Hidden Life*, a story centered around ethical resolve in the face of great cultural, social, and political oppression. The dramatic stakes were noticeably higher. Malick's Austin-set picture lacked the obvious moral dilemma posed by the story of Jägerstätter's life and death. In *Song to Song* characters worry about whom they should date. In *A Hidden Life* they wonder what they will do when the Nazis come knocking at their door.

But this stage of Malick's career cannot be so neatly compartmentalized into good films and bad. As much as critics may want to put a film like *Song to Song* into cinematic quarantine, keeping it as far away as possible from *A Hidden Life*, the truth is that these works have much in common. The distance from the small-*m* moral questions posed by *Song to Song* (What kind of person should I be? Should I be sincere or should I put on airs to get what I want?) and the seemingly big-*M* ones of *A Hidden Life* and *The Way of the Wind* (Will I resist evil when I see it, no matter the consequences? Am I willing to die for my beliefs?) should not prevent us from seeing the thread that links them together. In these films, Malick tries to show how morality speaks to the texture of a life, not just a handful of isolated dilemmas that can be resolved according to what the philosopher Bernard Williams once derided as "abstract ethical theory" or "administrative ideas about rationality."[13] Malick's radical experiments in cinematic form stress the everydayness of ethical life, showing it to be a messy, mundane affair rather than an operatic, attention-grabbing one, with easy-to-recognize heroes and villains playing preestablished roles. More often than not, ethical life is but a collection of small, quiet moments of anxiety, doubt, and indecisiveness, which occur well outside the world-historical limelight.

Like all directors, Malick has made some curious choices over the years. Some of his cinematic experiments have worked, others have not. But each has been, in its own unique way, necessary. A close analysis of Malick's late-career work reveals a remarkable degree of continuity with his earliest films. The *style* of his filmmaking may have changed over the course of his career, but the *ideas* animating it have not. Returning, in the years after making *Song to Song*, to the filmmakers who first inspired him to capture these ideas with a movie camera—directors such as Renoir and Bresson, Bergman and Tarkovsky—Malick began writing scripts that eventually became some of the most captivating cinema he has ever made.

Only the Lonely: *Song to Song*

Song to Song is a movie about music. It is set in and around contemporary Austin, Texas, the self-proclaimed "Live Music Capital of the World," where time-honored bars and clubs have nurtured artists working in genres ranging from country and blues to rock and roll and punk, with many other sub-genres in between. Among its many musical milestones, Austin gave Janis

Joplin her start, drew Willie Nelson away from Nashville, and established "the longest running music series in television history," the PBS institution *Austin City Limits*.[14]

Befitting this storied sonic legacy, *Song to Song* is chock full of music-world content: it has concerts, it has crowds, it even has cameos from a plethora of famous contemporary musicians, including Patti Smith, Iggy Pop, John Lydon, and the members of the Red Hot Chili Peppers. There are a number of lesser-known musical acts featured in the film as well, mostly younger musicians trying to make it big. *Song to Song* follows the budding careers of two fictional members of their ranks, the doe-eyed Faye (Rooney Mara) and the reserved but ambitious BV (Ryan Gosling). Their paths cross as they search for music-world wealth and fame. Offering them a golden ticket into the entertainment industry is a malevolent music producer, Cook (Michael Fassbender), who is accustomed to getting what he wants: he dresses in fine suits, drives fancy cars (including, in one scene, an ostentatious Ferrari), and parties in ever more fabulous homes that seem prepped and ready for their *Architectural Digest* photo shoots. Cook takes what he wants from life and does not fret over the consequences. This applies to his romantic relationships, too. Whether they are aspiring indie musicians like Faye, or kindhearted, churchgoing waitresses like Rhonda (Natalie Portman), Cook finds a way to use, abuse, and discard the women in his life whenever and however he sees fit.

Seemingly everyone is ensnared in Cook's hedonistic traps. Long before he gets around to ruining Rhonda's life, he seduces Faye, who works for him as a personal assistant, and exploits BV, whom he hires as a songwriter only to cheat him out of proper songwriting credits. Throughout it all, Cook plays the Mephistophelian role of tempter in chief, cajoling and exploiting, bending the rules to his advantage. (Malick reportedly instructed Fassbender to think of Cook as a version of Satan in John Milton's *Paradise Lost*.)[15] Cook encourages those around him to follow his lead, to live the life they want, unencumbered by duty, obligation, or responsibility. "People changed around him," Faye says, "they did things."

Cook is capitalist excess incarnate, the embodiment of the *business* side of the contemporary music business: "It's all for sale," he says in a voice-over narration, "all of it." His industry-world parties—where Faye and BV first meet—feature fine wines and sushi served atop seminude models stretched out on buffet tables. Such shindigs are about as far away as one can get from queso, chips, and longneck Shiner Bocks. This is not the nostalgic Austin of the past, the city of honky-tonks and Roy Orbison appearing on PBS, but rather the supposedly more cosmopolitan, corporate city of today, the flashier, savvier Austin that hosts the South by Southwest music and media festival—SXSW, for those in the know—and, since 2002, the Austin City Limits Festival, the hipper offspring of its public-television forebearer.

Flush with cash from the coasts, the new, twenty-first century Austin attracts people like Cook. It boasts tech-company headquarters and high-rise condominiums. It looks more like the Bay Area, like Los Angeles or New York, than it does Bastrop, San Antonio, or Waco.[16] Immersed as it is in this context, *Song to Song* comes across as an extension of the Hollywood-set *Knight of Cups*—so much so that many commentators have lumped the films together. In their view, *Song to Song* is just more of the same, the cinematic equivalent of lukewarm leftovers.[17] On a stylistic level, these critics have a point: the visual parallels between *Song to Song* and the films Malick made before it are striking, perhaps because Emmanuel Lubezki was once again responsible for the cinematography and the crew continued working according to "the dogma."

Beyond these visual continuities, though, there are other noticeable similarities between *Song to Song* and *The Tree of Life*, *To the Wonder*, and *Knight of Cups*, most notably its interest in religious themes: forgiveness and redemption, sin and salvation. There is a lot of stereotypically bad rock-and-roll behavior in *Song to Song*, with all the requisite drugs, drinking, and violence—in one scene Val Kilmer, channeling his earlier portrayal of Jim Morrison in *The Doors* (dir. Oliver Stone, 1991), takes a chainsaw to an amp on stage—but there is also the yearning to rise above it. "I want to live a good life," Faye tells us in one of her many plaintive voice-overs. A lot of interpersonal wreckage has piled up before this point is reached, though. All-too-human mistakes and misunderstandings lead to betrayals and broken hearts, giving Malick an opportunity to tell another story about searching for—and possibly finding—a mercy that forgives, a faith that sustains, and a nurturing hope that arrives when least expected.

Song to Song also addresses quintessentially Cavellian themes, such as acknowledgment and avoidance, recognition and (the limits of) self-reliance.[18] Like the romantic comedies and weepy melodramas Cavell spent so much time studying, Malick's Austin movie is preoccupied with the question of how to live meaningfully with others. Falling in and out of each other's orbits, Faye, BV, Cook, and Rhonda struggle to navigate their lives. As BV describes it, they are "drifting, waiting." In a line that gives the film its title, Faye puts it more romantically: "I thought we could just roll and tumble, live from song to song, kiss to kiss." Such naïveté does not last long. *Song to Song* suggests we cannot drift forever: a choice of some kind has to be made eventually. Malick's protagonists waver in the face of this decision, vacillating between a life of unbridled experience, on the one hand, or a humbler life of quiet commitment and devotion on the other. Less comfortable with ambiguity and uncertainty than Cavell, Malick allows no other option in between.

Malick's moralizing tendencies are evident in the story arcs of *Song to Song*'s principal characters. At first, Faye fancies herself a rebel. She has a poster of Rimbaud on her wall: "He did everything," she says. "He exhausted every poison. He knew every form of love, suffering, madness. He experimented." A jump cut from this scene to one depicting John Lydon backstage at a concert suggests a Greil Marcus–like genealogy connecting the *poètes maudits* of the nineteenth century to the punks of the twentieth and the indie rockers of the twenty-first.[19] But does Faye really have what it takes to be as wild and reckless as Rimbaud? Does she dare to be as scandalous as a Sex Pistol? For all her leather jackets and dark eyeliner, Faye also seems to be, deep down, a daddy's girl. Even as she pursues her dreams of indie fame—"I wanted to live, sing my song"—she yearns for that most common of prizes: her father's approval. We see telling scenes of her interacting with him, as well as her siblings, whom she has left behind to make it big in Austin. These sequences hint that Faye might have second thoughts about her decision to live dangerously: perhaps the boring suburban life was not so stultifying after all. Tiring of the rock-and-roll life himself, BV comes to a similar conclusion later in the film: "It'd be awful to have these good times," he says, "and not have life itself."

This existential Sturm und Drang is portrayed in fragmentary scenes largely devoid of dialogue. Snippets of voice-over narration such as the ones cited above string some sequences together, but most of the plot exposition in the film comes in the form of fleeting visual cues: the way a certain shot is framed, for example, or the way one character turns toward, or away from, another. When romantic relationships are going well, Malick's characters cannot keep their hands off each other—they caress, touch, and grope one another in highly stylized choreographies of affection. When things are going badly, they are constantly looking the other way, staring out windows or gazing blankly into the middle distance. Viewers must make sense of the curious ways these affectless characters interact: an occasional come-hither glance or an aloof visage framed by nature is all there is to go on.

The way *Song to Song* was edited—for elliptical suggestion rather than linear consistency—does not help matters. In fact, it infuriated critics, who started suggesting that Malick's foray into experimental, improvisational filmmaking had finally run its course. For them, *Song to Song* was the embarrassing nadir of an otherwise amazing career. Some of the criticisms were especially harsh: "If you could photograph the unwanted urine which dribbles from an old man's penis," Malick's old AFI classmate Paul Schrader ranted online, "you would have a film titled *Song to Song*."[20]

Song to Song is not *The Tree of Life*: it does not open with a quote from the Book of Job. Instead of grand cosmic visions, we get voyeuristic—yet noticeably chaste—glimpses of young people climbing in an out of bed with each other. Torrents of self-destructive passion are hinted at in some of the film's narrations—"I went through a period in which sex had to be violent," Faye says at the outset, "I was desperate to feel something real"—but all we see are the pantomimed embraces of fully clothed actors moving in what seems like slow motion. There is no sex in *Song to Song*, merely the suggestion of it. Standing in for the act are self-censoring close-ups of high-heeled shoes, or a bed's tousled sheets, or a hand wandering over a woman's bare midriff (there are so many of these shots, in fact, that they start to seem fetishistic). Such images—expressing a certain fear of sex, perhaps—can be found throughout Malick's cinema. As Robert Koehler once put it in a scathing piece in *Cineaste*: "Women have always been an issue for Malick, because for all his love of the sensual nature of cinema, he has been visibly afraid of women's sexual power."[21] But here it is especially apparent that his Platonic idea of love is threatened by the very suggestion of actual embodiment.

Throughout *Song to Song*, we get the before or the after, but rarely, if ever, the during. The film seems to be composed almost entirely of deleted scenes. Most of what we see is material usually left on the cutting-room floor, the moments before a threesome with sex workers, say, or the awkward silence following a lovers' quarrel. Although it makes the picture difficult to decipher, the editorial choice was deliberate. As with his previous films, Malick was trying to capture moments on screen that would not come across as overly rehearsed or—as he told an intimate audience just after the film's premiere—"presented."[22] Taking his inspiration from Bresson, who wanted to liberate cinema from the shackles of the stage play—in *Notes on the Cinematograph* the French director denounced "the terrible habit of theatre"—Malick was searching for spontaneity.[23] (His actors, one critic noticed, chased "after the spontaneous moment as if it were oxygen, as if it were reason and meaning.")[24] Malick wanted to avoid giving off the impression that the action in *Song to Song* was "premeditated," which would make it feel too much "like theater."

Stage drama was "wonderful in its own right," he said, but nobody wants "the movies to be like theater."[25]

Malick made sure the editing of *Song to Song* mirrored its narrative content. The film's fragmentary form reflects its preoccupation with the perils of living a directionless life in a fractured world. If *The Tree of Life* offered hope of cosmic reconciliation and spiritual redemption, the films following it dived deeper into the existential malaise of contemporary life: *To the Wonder* depicts a polluted, desecrated Midwest; *Knight of Cups* captures the moral wasteland of the Hollywood culture industry; and *Song to Song* portrays contemporary Austin as a fallen city that has succumbed to temptation and despair.

In something of an ironic twist, though, *Song to Song* premiered at SXSW in 2017. As much as Austin has changed, it remains a place where Malick has deep roots, which might explain why the idea of *home* takes on such great significance in *Song to Song*'s narrative.[26] The film juxtaposes rootedness and rootlessness, dwelling and wandering, being and becoming. It depicts characters—like Faye, like BV—venturing out into the world, trying on and discarding personas like so many wardrobe changes, but ultimately returning to the places and families that initially shaped them. This was something Malick had done in his own life. In Cambridge, Massachusetts, he wore the hat of the philosopher; in New York, that of the journalist; and in Hollywood, that of the successful scriptwriter and famous director. But in Austin he could wear a cowboy hat, or a hard hat, or no hat at all. Austin offers Malick a freedom—and an anonymity—he could not find anywhere else.

Something of this existential changeability finds its way into the character of Faye, who is a sullen rock star (in a bright pink wig) one minute and a dutiful daughter (with her hair pulled back demurely) the next. But all her "snatching at life" exhausts her. She cannot shake the lingering doubt that persists through every costume change: "What if I don't become an artist?" Malick depicts existential anxiety not as some extraordinary limit-experience—Heidegger famously likened it to frontline soldiers confronting their own death on the battlefield—but as something like a teenage or twenty-something rite of passage: young people have to find their way in the world and this is how they do it. It is a simplistic approach to ideas he had explored in a far more nuanced fashion earlier in his career (Holly's stereopticon moment in *Badlands* comes to mind as one instance, Linda's many inquisitive narrations in *Days of Heaven* another).

Indeed, a great deal of *Song to Song* seems silly when looked at closely. Its plot gives us stock characters following along well-trodden cinematic tracks: Faye and BV cope with failure, learn lessons, change their ways, and start over. Rhonda and Cook, by contrast, play with fire and are, like Prometheus, punished. With such a clear and obvious line drawn between good and evil, right and wrong, the film has all the elements of a melodrama and of the "melodramatic moralism"—as Robert Pippin might say—that so often comes along with it.[27]

The message of *Song to Song* is clear, maybe too clear: repent and be saved. After many romantic mishaps and misadventures, Faye and BV eventually find their way back to each other. Together, they turn their backs on Cook and the temptations of the music business, choosing to head out west instead. There they set up a home and begin the process of living less dangerously. BV dons a hard hat and finds work on a drilling rig; Faye ditches the leather jackets and says she is ready for "a simple life." The implication is that their love for each other has grown up, matured, but one could just as easily say that Faye and BV have caved, that they have given in to the very bourgeois moralism Rimbaud spent his short but eventful life railing against. Instead of running away from home, Faye and BV race right back to it. They are the antithesis of Holly and Kit in *Badlands*.

But if *Song to Song* has little in common with *Badlands* or *Days of Heaven* it certainly resembles Malick's more recent films—and not just stylistically. Like *The Tree of Life*, *To the Wonder*, and *Knight of Cups*, *Song to Song* has elements of Malick's own life baked into it. Should we view it as another exercise in cinematic confession? Is it an autobiographical work? The available evidence suggests not. Although parts of *Song to Song* were inspired by Malick's career in Hollywood and his secondhand exposure to the music industry—his friendship with Carly Simon landed him a cameo as a cigar-smoking cowboy on the back cover of her 1976 album *Another Passenger*—no one character in the film stands out as a clear Malick avatar, at least not in the way Jack O'Brien does in *Tree of Life*, or the way Neil and Rick do in *To the Wonder* and *Knight of Cups*.

Song to Song represents a departure in Malick's late-career filmmaking in at least one other sense as well. Prior to its release, nobody would have tagged him as a likely candidate to direct a movie about indie musicians. His previous pictures were full of prerecorded music, but almost all of it was classical or symphonic: Arvo Pärt, Camille Saint-Saëns, Carl Orff, Mozart,

Wagner—the list is endless. Indeed, Malick has inserted so much classical music into his films that just cataloging it is, as James Wierzbicki has remarked, "enough to make the head spin."[28] Consequently, one does not associate Malick with popular music, let alone rock and roll. Mickey and Sylvia singing "Love Is Strange" in *Badlands* is about as hip as he gets, sonically speaking. Malick clearly prefers the sounds of strings and pianos to those of electric guitars. Listen closely to *Song to Song* and you notice that for every track of popular music—BV and an old flame (a cameo by the artist Lykke Li) covering Bob Marley's "It Hurts to Be Alone," for example—there is a snippet of Saint-Saëns, Pärt, or Debussy. In fact, classical sounds accompany almost all of the important sequences in the film.

Malick does know a thing or two about popular music, though. In the late 1980s he even spent time working on a script about Jerry Lee Lewis. Based on the book *Great Balls of Fire*, by Myra Lewis and Murray Silver Jr., the screenplay recounted the familiar tale of a wild, Louisiana-born piano prodigy who captured the attention of the nation and the world by synthesizing gospel, blues, country, and boogie-woogie to create a whole new genre of music, not to mention a whole new kind of musical celebrity, one co-opted from pioneering Black musicians like Little Richard and Chuck Berry and repackaged for white audiences.[29] But Malick's approach to the biopic was unique in the way that he focused less on Lewis's music and more on the state of his soul. In this regard, Malick's "Great Balls of Fire" screenplay anticipates not just the subject matter but also the spiritual focus of *Song to Song*.

Jerry Lee Lewis courted controversy wherever he went. He sang songs about dancing and drinking—"Great Balls of Fire" and "Whole Lotta Shakin' Goin' On" being the most famous—that devout churchgoers denounced as the devil's music. The moral outrage followed Lewis offstage, most notably when, at the age of twenty-two, he married Myra Gale Brown, who was not only his cousin (and third wife), but also just thirteen years of age at the time. Some of the moral controversy that swirled around Lewis's marriage(s) and early performances may have been a direct result of his upbringing in a devout Pentecostal household. In a reality-is-stranger-than-fiction twist of fate, one of his relatives, Jimmy Swaggart, went on to become one the country's most recognizable Christian televangelists. These two cousins from the same Southern family came to represent opposing forces: the saintly preacher in one corner and the possessed performer in the other. But the distance between the saint and the sinner was perhaps not so great as many may have wished to believe.

Spirit possession was a mainstay of the Pentecostal faith in which Jimmy and Jerry were raised, and both of them called upon it in their performances. "The Pentecostal church," as George Cotkin has pointed out, "was a perfect spot for Lewis to perfect his own theatrical style."[30] Indeed, possession became a key part of the Killer's act, but it saddled him with an overly keen sense of Christian guilt. Lewis was torn "between the sins of the flesh in the secular world and the necessity of redemption in the spiritual world."[31] Nick Tosches's *Hellfire: The Jerry Lee Lewis Story* dramatizes the struggle: "the more the music took hold of him, the more it became part of him, the more he suffered, until it sometimes got to where he felt the good and the bad, the Holy Spirit and the Demon, so crowding his lungs with their battle that it was hard to breathe."[32]

Malick's "Great Balls of Fire" script portrays its protagonist in a similar light, as a man possessed, a tortured mystic who "has the gaunt, lonely look of a man who has suffered greatly and kept his suffering to himself."[33] Long before he thought up the story of Faye's and BV's mutual disenchantment with the temptations of the music business, Malick used the story of Jerry Lee Lewis to explore the dangers of a life lived beyond everyday conceptions of good and evil. Like Tosches, Malick was drawn to the spiritually tormented Lewis more than the raucous showman. He was little interested in the gimmicky performer who set his piano on fire.

Malick's "Great Balls of Fire" screenplay opens not with music but with scenes juxtaposing sin and salvation: one sequence, reminiscent of Kit's pursuit of Holly in *Badlands*, depicts Lewis's hot-and-heavy romance with his teenage bride; the other shows Reverend Sun Swaggart, Jimmy's father and Jerry's uncle, denouncing his nephew's transgressions. The contrast sets the tone for everything that follows. Lewis is a man pulled in opposite directions, destined for tragedy: "There's something inside me, I need to let it out," he says in Malick's script. "I have to live the way I sing. I might go down, but I'm going down in a flame of glory!"[34]

Malick's screenplay has plenty of drinking and adultery, not to mention the requisite run-ins with the IRS. But "Great Balls of Fire" also has long sections devoted to the state of its protagonist's soul. It tells the tale of a spiritual reckoning, a realization that rock and roll is not, and cannot be, the highest good. The later sections of the screenplay depict Lewis—like Faye and BV in *Song to Song*—desperately yearning for a change. He, too, is exhausted by all the snatching at life. Lewis is estranged from his wife, struggling both financially and mentally. His confidence is at an ebb and his conscience pulls at him. He lashes out at reporters, rattling the cage of celebrity. "You think rock 'n' roll is about as high as you can get," he yells. "There's plenty higher. There better be." The scales have fallen from his eyes and everything now appears phony, empty, nothing but playacting: "Rock 'n' roll is just about getting off and telling everybody else to kiss your ass," he says, but "I can tear this piano to pieces and ten minutes later you'd be bored again." Like Billy the Kid in Arthur Penn's *The Left Handed Gun*, he has become a prisoner of his own fame: "Rock 'n' roll sets you free? Shit!" he exclaims. "Why ain't I free? Answer me that!"[35]

Lewis has had a change of heart. Maybe everything his uncle and his cousin were saying about secular music being a path to perdition was true. Maybe "Whole Lotta Shakin' Goin' On" really was the work of the devil. Malick describes Lewis recoiling from the "wild applause" the song generates at concerts: "You people are clapping," Lewis says, but "I'm <u>dragging you to hell with me!</u>" Or, worse: "I'm killing you people, and you don't know it. This music sets the demons moving in you."[36] At this point, cousin Jimmy reappears to get Lewis off the road and bring him home to Louisiana. A dramatic tension has been pushed to its breaking point, but the expected narrative reversal only happens when Lewis's young son Stevie dies as the result of a tragic swimming-pool drowning. Jerry Lee Lewis interprets the calamity as a sign from God: "Stevie died for my sins, so that I may be saved . . . I killed him."[37] The Killer now seems on the verge of a true spiritual conversion, so Malick places him in church. There he listens once again to his uncle, Sun Swaggart, who preaches a sermon about the themes of loss and forgiveness in—what else?—the Book of Job.

As in *The Tree of Life*, the official sermonizing about Job from the pulpit's perch rings hollow and trite. Pastor Swaggart is only interested in turning Stevie's loss into yet another notch on his pastoral belt. "Jerry," he says, "will you come forward and receive forgiveness and walk again in the ways of life?"[38] Lewis rebuffs him. Convinced that he is beyond saving, he rejects his uncle's appeal and walks out of the service, scandalizing the hometown churchgoing crowd. Malick's screenplay describes him as "a man who has placed himself beyond the pale of humanity, who refuses to repent."[39] If Jerry Lee Lewis knows all too well that he has made a deal with the devil, he also knows that divine redemption cannot be so easily received. Malick turns him into a character straight out of Flannery O'Connor, a self-mortifying Hazel Motes wrestling mightily with his guilt and worrying over the fallen state of his soul. The Killer has grown skeptical of secular fame and success, but he rejects clichéd versions of Christian salvation, too. Stuck between the two, he chooses a self-imposed purgatory: he is both the stage performer going through the motions to satisfy his audiences and the faithful Christian subjecting himself to an endless period of repentance.

This is not the stuff of the commonplace biopic. Malick's version of "Great Balls of Fire" contains no catharsis, no resolution, no feel-good happy ending. The script ends ambiguously, with its protagonist heading back out on the road, but still broken and unredeemed, a pariah. The vast chasm that has emerged between his public persona and his private pain renders him alienated, isolated, at a loss. Lewis is a stranger to his fans, his family, and maybe even to himself: "For them he is the Killer, the wild man who has lived out every fantasy of freedom, followed every impulse and whim, done what they hardly dare imagine," but audiences "do not see, behind his sunglasses, the great weariness, the solitude."[40] Instead of closing out his concerts with "Whole Lotta Shakin' Goin' On," Lewis starts playing the ballad "Crazy Arms," a song about losing one's true love to somebody else, a song about being forever lonely and alone.

Malick's existential take on the Jerry Lee Lewis story was bleak—too bleak for producers. His longtime agent Mike Medavoy, who was one of them, passed on it, calling it "too dark" for the film he had envisioned.[41] The script that was eventually chosen for the project was cowritten by Jack Baran and the film's director, Jim McBride.[42] A much more conventional story, it deemphasizes Lewis's spiritual crisis and offers a far more cartoonish depiction of the Killer. Whereas Malick tried to humanize Lewis by showing him wrestling with his faith, Baran and McBride opt for hokey one-liners and eyeroll-inducing set pieces. The movie they made—starring a particularly rubbery Dennis Quaid as the Killer, a gee-golly Winona Ryder as Myra, and a very sweaty Alec Baldwin as Jimmy—suffers as a result. *Great Balls of Fire!* makes no attempt to peak behind the sunglasses of its possessed protagonist. In fact, he never even wears them.

Song to Song might be viewed as a belated reworking of Malick's Jerry Lee Lewis script. It takes up many of the same themes: devilish temptation (in the form of Cook's excesses), existential isolation (expressed in the rambling interior monologues of the film's primary characters, especially BV and Faye), and a central narrative tension centered around the choice between being famous—or free, or successful, or happy—and being good. But, unlike *Song to Song*, the "Great Balls of Fire" screenplay ends without mercy or redemption. Jerry Lee Lewis's refusal of divine salvation stands in stark contrast to Faye's and BV's open embrace of it. Indeed, in *Song to Song*'s final act, Faye basks in what appears to be an ethereal light, connoting her newfound state of grace.

In this regard, at least, *Song to Song* seems much closer to another unrealized Malick script—namely, his adaptation of Kenji Mizoguchi's *Sansho the Bailiff* (1954) for the stage. Mizoguchi's film is famous for its oft-repeated moral: "without mercy, man is like a beast," which a kindly governor (Masao Shimizu) passes on to his young son, Zushio (Masahiko Tsugawa/Yoshiaki Hanayagi). The lesson is challenged again and again over the course of the picture. *Sansho the Bailiff* recounts the tragic fate of the governor's family after he is banished for refusing to impose the emperor's harsh directives on the peasants under his jurisdiction. The family is torn asunder: the governor's wife (Kinuyo Tanaka) is forced into prostitution, and his children—Zushio and his sister, Anju (Kyoko Kagawa)—are taken to a distant island and sold, for just a couple of silver pieces, into slavery. The children grow up under the rule of the pitiless landlord Sansho (Eitaro Shindo), who embodies everything their father had stood against. He represents greed, power, malice, and callous selfishness.

Malick's early 1990s adaptation of *Sansho the Bailiff*, which was to be directed by famed Polish auteur Andrzej Wajda for the Brooklyn Academy of Music, reads like a mash-up of Japanese folklore, Zen Buddhism, the Book of Job, and *The Pilgrim's Progress*. The stage play anticipates just about everything Malick made upon his return to directing with *The Thin Red Line* in 1998. On the page, one can see Malick experimenting with big, theological themes. Taking liberties with his source material, he tells a Manichaean tale of good and evil, kindness and cruelty. Most of all, though, he offers a lesson in providential theology. His "Sansho the Bailiff" stage play portrays mercy as a countervailing force—an antidote—to the sorrows inflicted by fate. In Mizoguchi's film, mercy is depicted as the goddess Kwannon, whom we see as a devotional figurine carried by Zushio on his journey. In Malick's stage play she is not just a silent talisman, but also an omnipresent maternal figure hovering above the actors and the audience, stretching "her arms toward us like a mother to her lost children."[43]

Malick's version of *Sansho the Bailiff* offers many a disquisition on the meaning of mercy. Reworking a key scene in Mizoguchis's film, Malick has Sansho's son, Taro (Akitake Kono), who has fled his father's house to become a Buddhist monk, tell a runaway Zushio that mercy is "a readiness, a wish to forgive, an eagerness to help. It is the love which is dependable and cannot go away." It is "the very word," he assures Zushio, "for heaven's way toward

Figure 32. Kwannon in Kenji Mizoguchi's *Sansho the Bailiff.*

men!"[44] If fate is a cruel mistress, mercy, for Malick, is just the opposite: she is "bright and glad," Taro says, a beacon of hope and reconciliation. "She makes good what we have ruined. The pieces of our lives, by her blessing, come together, become riches. Where she leads, you never tire."[45] And indeed, in Zushio's quest to navigate a merciless world and find his mother, all the while trying to live up to his father's teachings—"I am a child again," he says after being reacquainted with Kwannon following his torturous life as Sansho's slave—he does not tire, even after learning that his father has died, that his sister has committed suicide, and that his mother is now a blind, hobbled old woman, living in a dilapidated hut by the sea.[46]

In Mizoguchi's film, Zushio's reunion with his mother is both tragic and redemptive: tragic because it is Zushio who must tell his mother that her husband and her daughter are, after all these years, dead; redemptive because mother and son are finally together again. Their reunion is a work of mercy, she says, the direct result of her son's devotion to his father's teachings. The scene is heartbreaking. As a student at AFI, Malick said it was "one of the strongest scenes I've ever seen," which might explain why his stage play adaptation borrows the exact words (and the same staging) from the film: "you followed your father's words," Mother says, "And that is . . . (gathering her strength). That is why . . . (still not able to say). We can be here together now."[47] But Malick does not end the scene here. Going one step beyond Mizoguchi, he gives Zushio a final soliloquy of gratitude. "I bless this life, Mother, that for all the sorrow it has given us," he says, "I've had you and my dear sister, and Father." Growing emotional, he continues: "I will know what love is now, even though it has killed me finding out." Malick's final lines of scripted direction transform Zushio's dawning awareness of love and mercy and forgiveness into a lesson for all to share. Breaking the fourth wall of the stage, they describe a vision of Kwannon raising "her spread arms, blessing Zushio, his mother, and the audience together."[48] The play has gone from being just a story *about* mercy to being a work *of* mercy in and of itself.

In Malick's vision of things, everyone is deserving of mercy, but they must be open to receiving it. Much of the drama in "Sansho the Bailiff" stems from Zushio's struggle to see all that has happened to him and his family in a providential light. In "Great Balls of Fire," Jerry Lee Lewis wrestles with a similar burden, but, unlike Zushio, he cannot bring himself to acknowledge a mercy hidden behind the cruelties of his fate. In *Song to Song*, however, Faye can—and does. After atoning for her wayward behavior in the final act of the film, she describes the forgiveness she receives—from BV, but also, we gather, from God—as "a new paradise." In lines lifted almost verbatim from Malick's "Sansho the Bailiff" stage play, she speaks of mercy "as a word I never thought I needed—or not as much as other people do," and yet this is precisely what she comes to experience.[49] Divine mercy allows her to "go back to a simple life" with BV, who talks about starting over, "like a kid." Through divine forgiveness Faye and BV are reborn. They no longer have a pathway to music-world fame and success, but they do not need it, for they have everything Jerry Lee Lewis lacked at the end of Malick's "Great Balls of Fire" screenplay: love, faith, a contented domestic arrangement. Mercy has rescued and redeemed them, saved them from sin.

Devilish temptation is a recurring theme in Malick's late-career work. An easily derided trope in most Hollywood biopics—first the rise, then the fall, followed by the inevitable redemption—it pushes *Song to Song* toward preachiness. The film's message is so heavy-handed that it often comes across as judgmental, even puritanical. This is especially true of its depiction of sex. *Song to Song* keeps sex at a safe, suitably virtuous distance, suggesting that love should only blossom in the confines of a committed heterosexual relationship. Any deviation from this norm—Faye's brief romance with an elegant Parisian woman (Bérénice Marlohe), for instance, or BV's dalliance with a much older woman (Cate Blanchett)—is depicted as something of a transgression. (It was enough to give *Village Voice* film critic Melissa Anderson a severe case of "heterophobia.")[50] Faye's story line, especially, underscores the point: she experiments, has regrets, then seeks forgiveness. Along the way,

Christian denunciations of sex out of wedlock creep into her voice-overs, which become riddled with catechism clichés: "I took sex, a gift," she whispers remorsefully, "I played with it. I played with the flame of life."

Playful sex is the kind of sex Cook is into, and that, we are supposed to see, is sordid, so sordid that it corrupts churchgoing Rhonda and leads to her demise. Malick makes Rhonda into a scapegoat. After debauching herself with Cook and the sex workers he routinely hires—one flashback sequence even depicts a ménage à trois with Faye—she commits suicide, perhaps out of guilt or shame, or religious remorse. We are meant to see her as a fallen angel, a victim of Cook's brazen seduction. (To emphasize the threat he poses to her, Malick even incorporates the menacing opening scenes of Dimitri Kirsanoff's 1926 silent picture *Ménilmontant*—an unforgettable Parisian film about murder, seduction, sex, betrayal, suicidal ideation, and, in contrast to all this, small moments of mercy—into a montage depicting their mutual descent into drugs and fornication.) If Faye's story line underscores the grace of forgiveness, Rhonda's is a scared-straight warning about what not to do with the "gift" of sex.

Not all of the temptation in *Song to Song* is carnal, though. There is also the siren call of power (something also explored in the "Sansho the Bailiff" stage play), as well as the allure of complete and total freedom. Here, too, the message is didactic. Malick repeatedly portrays the desire to become somebody new whenever the mood strikes as dangerous. In one scene, Zoey, Faye's Parisian lover, shows off a stylized painting she owns of a snake shedding its skin: "I like this idea of losing your skin," she says suggestively, "starting over." But it was the snake who spoiled things in the Garden of Eden, of course, and so the "starting over" Zoey offers Faye is obviously suspect. It stands in stark contrast to what a relationship with BV offers, which is innocence rather than knowingness. Unlike BV, Zoey cannot help Faye to become "like a kid" again. She is too worldly, too successful, too sure of herself for that. She is too much like Cook: she has the stunning house, the runway-ready wardrobe, the ability to pick up and leave Paris—a city people all around the world dream of one day visiting, let alone living in—on a whim. For all these reasons and more we are supposed to be wary of her, just as we are supposed to be wary of Cook, just as we are supposed to be wary of Satan and the snake in the Garden of Eden.

In both his "Great Balls of Fire" screenplay and *Song to Song*, Malick portrays the changeability that comes with wealth and fame as a wayward path, one full of phony pretense. "It's a stage show," Cook tells BV. "It's all just free fall." In Malick's perspective, all the world is not a stage: intentions matter. As does sincerity. "Am I a good person?" Faye worries. "Or just seem like one so people will like me?"[51] This notion that temptation can make us lose sight of who we are and lead us astray has cropped up repeatedly in Malick's recent films, each more explicitly Christian than the last. *Song to Song* has struggling musicians contemplating offers of sex, fame, and riches, but *A Hidden Life* has a conscientious objector tempted with a chance to avoid the hardships associated with taking a stand against tyranny. *The Way of the Wind* will be even more direct: it has Jesus being tempted by the devil in the desert. The protagonists of these films endure doubt, anxiety, and uncertainty. They lose their grip on the world because the world as they know it has become foreign, strange, ultimately unrecognizable—a world governed not by God's plans but by the devil's games. Only faith offers a way out of the predicament, revealing mercy and providence where others see nothing but meaningless contingency or crushing fate.

   Song to Song invites such overtly religious readings. Conservative critics, in particular, welcomed what they took to be its explicitly "Judeo-Christian" message.[52] They noticed that many of its scenes are set in and around religious spaces, everything from a stately colonial-era church in the Yucatán that Cook, Faye, and BV visit while on a *Jules and Jim*–style vacation to an evangelical megachurch Rhonda attends back in Austin.[53] They also noticed that many of *Song to Song*'s voice-over narrations echo devotional literature. Some critics suggested that the film's title was a deliberate invocation of the biblical Song of Songs, a compendium of poetic meditations on the nature of mortal and transcendental love.[54] But during production, *Song to Song* went by a very different—and far less theological—working title. It was called "Weightless," an allusion, Malick's producers eventually explained, to Virginia Woolf's modernist novel *The Waves* (1931), an unlikely source of inspiration for such a seemingly devout movie.[55]

   They share neither a setting nor a religious sensibility, but what *The Waves* and *Song to Song* do have in common is a fascination with the nature of subjective experience. Woolf's novel and Malick's film wonder about what it means to be a person, a self, a distinct entity in the world surrounded by, as well as living with and through, others. *The Waves* is a densely poetic work. It follows a group of wealthy friends from childhood to old age. Flitting in and out of their respective minds in remarkably seamless prose-poetry, Woolf depicts existence as something flowing and ever changing—regular like the tides, yet as unique and individual as each wave crashing ashore. Woolf's

characters, whom we come to know through extended inner monologues—
the novel is composed of nothing but these—are forever attempting to make
sense of their lives, especially after one member of the group, Percival, dies
midway through the book. Percival's death prompts reflections on mortality,
temporality, and existential purpose from his surviving friends. They use a
variety of metaphors to describe the lives they are living: they liken existence
to "a random flicker of light in us that we call brain and feeling," or to a
"stream," or even to "a grain cast into the air and blown hither and thither by
wild gusts."[56] By the end of the novel most of Percival's friends have come to
see life as both contingent and designed, the product of flux and constancy
simultaneously.

Many of these ideas are expressed by Bernard, a poet who serves as a kind
of authorial surrogate. He asks the inescapable questions posed by life and
death and the irreversible progression of time: What does it mean to be a self,
to inhabit a body that is constantly changing, growing older, heading toward
death? What does it mean to be both a stable thing—a being "that grows rings,
like a tree"—and a spirit that aspires to "weightless" transcendence?[57] Are we
forever doomed to our fallible, limited perspectives, The Waves asks, or is it
sometimes possible to live transcendentally? "How can I proceed now," Bernard says near the end of the novel, "without a self, weightless and vision-
less, through a world weightless, without illusion?"[58]

Malick was so taken with this quote that at one point in Song to Song's
production process he considered giving it its own title card.[59] One can see
why: it sounds very much like a Malick voice-over. In what we anachronistically might call Malick fashion, Woolf's novel ends with Bernard yearning
to become one with the flux of temporal change; to enjoy a transcendental
connection with the tumult of existence. He seeks a cosmic connection with
all things. Malick borrows Woolf's stream-of-consciousness style to explore
the struggles of modern subjectivity, especially its ceaseless grasping at "eternal renewal" in the face of change. Like The Waves, Song to Song transports
us directly into the thoughts of characters searching for meaning. Its
soundtrack is a chorale of pure interiority. There is no external, third-person
perspective—aside, of course, from that of the director's camera, which gives
the film its fundamental unity, its God's-eye-like point of view, showing us
that no mortal existence is ever entirely solitary, for all lives are inherently,
inescapably intersubjective.

On screen, this lesson is imparted by Patti Smith, who serves as Faye's
musical guardian angel. We catch glimpses of her tutoring her charge in a

Figure 33. Patti Smith as Faye's spirit guide in *Song to Song*.

couple of important scenes. Despite being an aspiring *poète maudit* herself once upon a time, Smith does not urge Faye to sacrifice everything for her art, as one might expect.[60] Instead, she talks tenderly about her husband, Fred "Sonic" Smith (of the influential Detroit band MC5), to whom she considers herself still married and devoted, even though he died decades ago, in 1994. Smith shows Faye the wedding ring she still wears, a symbol, she says, of how her marriage transcends mortality. Spying BV off in the distance shortly after saying this, Smith urges Faye to follow her heart, advice that sets up *Song to Song*'s domestic denouement. In it, love and forgiveness conquer all: we watch BV reconcile with his estranged father, Faye with her family, and the two of them with each other. They head off together toward the sunset and, in contrast to Rhonda and Cook, set up a happy home.

Escaping the sparkle and flash of the contemporary music business, *Song to Song* takes refuge in the reassuring comforts of domesticity: the church; the family; the steady, blue-collar job. It is startling just how much of the film, which is ostensibly about the raucous, wild, sexy music industry, is shot not at concerts or in clubs but in humdrum domestic spaces—kitchens, living rooms, bedrooms, even suburban backyards. *Song to Song* is preoccupied—*obsessed* might be the better word—with homes and with what it means to dwell in them. A telling sign of Cook's wealth and power is his ability to purchase a house built from scratch for Rhonda's mother. But this structure, which we glimpse only in half-finished form as it is being constructed, is not a home. Like Cook, it has no soul. Many of the other extravagant buildings pictured in the film do not, either. They are all immaculate, pristine, picturesque,

Figure 34. Searching for authenticity (Ryan Gosling as BV in *Song to Song*).

but they are empty vessels, more staged than lived in. No wonder Faye and BV flee them when they finally decide to start a life together out in the country.

Is life in rural West Texas any more authentic than affluent Austin? Viewing the final scenes of *Song to Song*, for which BV dons a dusty hard hat now that he is a workingman instead of an indie musician, one thinks of Bobby Dupea (Jack Nicholson) in Bob Rafelson's New Hollywood classic, *Five Easy Pieces* (1970).[61] The picture garnered a great deal of praise just as Malick was starting to find scriptwriting work in Hollywood. In fact, some of Malick's first gigs were for Rafelson's production company, BBS Productions, an outfit that went on to produce *The King of Marvin Gardens*, from a screenplay written by Jacob Brackman. Rafelson even ended up receiving an acknowledgment in the credits for *Days of Heaven*.

Five Easy Pieces is a classic example of the "cinema of defection," which foregrounded stories of isolated, conflicted, perpetually uncertain characters running away from society.[62] Bobby Dupea fits the bill in every way. When we first encounter him, he is working on an oil rig down near Bakersfield. He seems no different from the other hard hats around him: when he is not sweating for his pay he bowls, drinks, chases skirts. But all of it is an act, for Bobby is actually a gifted pianist, from a wealthy, musically inclined family up in the Pacific Northwest. (Unlike Jerry Lee Lewis and BV, he plays classical music, not rock and roll.) The oil fields of California were a place to escape the burdens of being a musical prodigy from an eccentric family. In Bakersfield, Bobby was rebelling—or pretending to, anyways.

Figure 35. Jack Nicholson as Bobby Dupea in Bob Rafelson's *Five Easy Pieces*.

Working from a script by Carole Eastman (under the pseudonym Adrien Joyce), Rafelson pokes fun at Bobby's feeble attempt at slumming it. Much of the humor comes from his country-western-singing-waitress girlfriend Rayette (Karen Black), who fawns over him. (Tammy Wynette's "Stand by Your Man" accompanies the film's opening credits.) Bobby treats Rayette horribly, even after learning she might be pregnant with his child. Unlike BV, he comes from money. He and BV are ships sailing past each other, as are the films in which they appear. Rafelson's picture suggests there is no home to which we can ever return. *Five Easy Pieces* famously ends with Bobby fleeing his family, ditching Rayette at a roadside diner and hitching a ride on a truck heading north, away from everything. He has no wallet, no coat, nothing to tie him down. But in *Song to Song* BV does the opposite: he goes home, finds himself, and begins anew. *Song to Song* heralds the kind of homecoming *Five Easy Pieces* rejects. BV embraces all of the things Bobby sneers at: hard work, settling down, raising a family. Whereas Bobby repeatedly tries to shed his skin and start over, choosing the life of the wanderer over that of the dutiful son or husband, BV chooses to be the sincere, unwavering family man, the humorless working stiff. He is everything BBS Productions and the New Hollywood lampooned.

With *Song to Song* Malick put some distance between the New Hollywood–era auteur he once was and the *Tree of Life*–era sage he had become. Reconciliation, forgiveness, and mercy were now his primary themes. The cinema of defection had become a cinema of redemption. In a touching scene near the end of *Song to Song*, we see BV reconnecting with, and gently caring for, his bedridden father. Fighting back tears, he wipes crumbs from the old man's shirt. BV's very obvious care and concern—the scene is one of only two or three in the whole film where he shows real emotion—stands in stark contrast to Bobby's interactions with his own stroke-incapacitated father in *Five Easy Pieces*. Like BV, Bobby cries, but he cries for himself: he knows that his father's death will change nothing, that he still will be lost and alone. For BV it is the opposite: his father's frailty represents a chance to show and receive mercy, to reconcile and start all over again, like a kid.

In his autobiographical films, Malick had searched for an organic, theological unity in the universe, one that might shed light on the paths he has walked over the course of his life: first as a headstrong young adolescent, then as a suddenly famous screenwriter, and, finally, as a searching, middle-aged adult. Through a combination of artistic experimentation, philosophical reflection, and Christian devotion, he eventually found it. *Song to Song* may not dramatize Malick's own life the way *The Tree of Life*, *To the Wonder*, and *Knight of Cups* do, but it nevertheless operates in a similar fashion, as what we might call a form of religious testimony. Buried beneath its glossy surface is a humble message telling us that faith and forgiveness are the keys to leading a rich and meaningful life. Telling us that the dangers of solipsism can only be eluded by embracing the virtues of mutuality and vulnerability. Telling us that to forgive and to be forgiven are an essential part of accepting others and the world. Telling us that seeking and showing mercy might be the first steps toward finding one's path.

There Will Be No Mysteries: *A Hidden Life*

A Hidden Life begins where *Song to Song* ends: at home, away from the temptations and cruelties of the outside world. But this time around the story is set not in twenty-first century Texas but amid the Alpine peaks and valleys of 1940s Austria, a far more fitting place for Malick's pastoral ideal to be realized. His camera—overseen now by Emmanuel Lubezki's longtime collaborator Joerg Widmer—takes obvious delight in the locale (with villages in the Italian South Tyrol standing in for their counterparts across the border). The opening images of *A Hidden Life* are, without exception, stunning: rocky peaks rising majestically into the clouds; waterfalls floating gently down into verdant valleys; village houses, illuminated by candlelight, radiating warmth and harmony. Returning to visual cues that can be found in many of his most memorable films—from the golden wheat fields in *Days of Heaven* to the gleaming stocks of maize in *The New World*—Malick once again depicts a blissful, preindustrial life, sustained by the bounty of nature. But the idyll will not last. Discord, greed, pride, selfishness, and wrath—in short, sin—will poison everything. Though it is situated outside the confines of American history—a first in Malick's career—*A Hidden Life* is very much in keeping with the films that came before it.[63] It is yet another tale of paradise lost.

A Hidden Life tells the story of a humble farmer who takes a heroic stand against evil and is expelled from his Edenic home as a consequence. We hear the voice of this farmer, Franz Jägerstätter (August Diehl), before we see him. "I thought that we could build our nest high up in the trees," he says before anything appears on screen, "fly away like the birds, to the mountains." We quickly see how mistaken he was, for the first images of the film are not of birds or mountains but of Hitler's airplane descending from the clouds. He is arriving in Nuremberg for the 1934 Nazi Party Congress, which Leni Riefenstahl infamously transformed into cinematic propaganda a year later. A montage of familiar images from *Triumph of the Will* flashes by: crowds of enthusiastic Germans lining the streets, jackbooted troops marching in unison, the Führer addressing vast crowds hanging on his every shouted word. "The following is based on true events," a title card tells us. Another one gives us the rest of the relevant background information: "During World War II, every Austrian soldier called up for active duty was required to swear an oath of loyalty to Hitler." As the text fades from the screen, we hear the sound of a scythe cutting through tall grass. It is the sound of reaping; a symbol of harvesting and, of course, death.

After "repenting" the experimental approach he had taken in *Song to Song*, Malick returned to scriptwriting to produce *A Hidden Life*, a film that proved he had not lost the knack. It may have helped that he chose to tell a tale based on actual historical events, which provided him with a harrowing life story—complete with an obvious beginning, middle, and tragic end—for his screenplay. In choosing to dramatize Jägerstätter's life, Malick also had available to him many of the other elements Hollywood loves in historical dramas, such as a clear distinction between good and evil, not to mention a legitimate excuse for trotting out all of the newsreel footage and military uniforms that have reminded Americans they were on the right side of history

Figure 36. The time of reaping as portrayed in *A Hidden Life*.

in the Second World War.[64] Whether in *Hangmen Also Die!* (dir. Fritz Lang, 1943) or *Judgment at Nuremberg* (dir. Stanley Kramer, 1961), *Schindler's List* (dir. Steven Spielberg, 1993) or *Inglourious Basterds* (dir. Quentin Tarantino, 2009), Nazis always appear in Hollywood films as immediately recognizable personifications—"instant avatars," Richard Brody calls them—of evil.[65] Anyone who stands up to them is automatically an audience favorite.

For these reasons and more, *A Hidden Life* was a success in a way that *Song to Song* was not. With a collective sigh of relief, many critics heralded it as a return to form. After a period of wandering in the cinematic deserts of improvisation and experimentation, Malick was back. David Thomson spoke for many when he declared *A Hidden Life* "the best American film of 2019," nothing short of a "masterpiece."[66] It was a career-capping achievement, a picture that excused any and all previous misfires in Malick's cinematic career, most notably the post–*Tree of Life* confessional films, in which he had "seemed to get lost."[67] *To the Wonder, Knight of Cups*, and *Song to Song* were "confoundingly hollow films," which "almost left one nostalgic," Thomson wrote, "for a time when Malick worked less."[68] Worst of all, they were box-office flops (a lifelong Hollywood-watcher, Thomson treats box-office receipts with pious reverence, even and especially when trying to disdain them).

A Hidden Life was none of these things, though. It was solemn, but deservedly so, and it displayed an urgency Thomson failed to locate in the confessional films. Malick's Jägerstätter picture was not a huge generator of ticket sales, but it did land a highly remunerative distribution deal with Fox

Searchlight—a point curiously overlooked by Thomson. What he did not overlook was *A Hidden Life*'s moral power, which relies less on the usual fireworks of a heroic military venture against an evil empire (the stuff, more or less, of *Star Wars*) and more on the quiet daily activities of a man—a son, a husband, a father, a member of the local church and the village community—trying to do what he thinks is right. There are no firefights in *A Hidden Life*, no clandestine meetings or daring escapes. "The old Hollywood scheme," Thomson suggested, "leaves Malick unmoved; he would prefer to be a patient onlooker, a diligent chronicler, attentive and touched, but more rapt than ardent, and still consumed by wonder."[69]

I think Thomson is right, but what narratives like his miss is the unwavering cohesiveness of Malick's cinematic career: *A Hidden Life* was made possible by the journey its director had undertaken after *The Tree of Life*. Malick's confessional films—including even the semi-confessional, or confessional-adjacent, *Song to Song*—were experiments in cinematic technique, but they were also forays into existential and spiritual self-reflection. It was only after undertaking a pilgrimage of his own that Malick was prepared to document Jägerstätter's journey, which led from a peaceful life high up in the mountains to an executioner's chamber in the deepest, darkest bowels of the Third Reich.[70] To tell this story of a largely uneducated peasant who was eventually beatified by the Catholic Church as a modern-day martyr for the faith, Malick first had to walk his own path from existential doubt to sustaining faith.

Traces of the path—philosophical, religious, but also, cinematic—leading from *The Tree of Life* to *A Hidden Life* are evident in the script Malick penned for his Jägerstätter biopic. It opens with a telling epigraph from Kierkegaard, the guiding light of so many of his late-career films. "The tyrant dies," the passage reads, "and his rule is over; the martyr dies, and his rule begins."[71] The quote comes from Kierkegaard's journals of 1848. The entries surrounding it explore themes familiar to readers of his more famous religious texts and treatises from this period of his career—books such as *Works of Love* (1847) and *The Sickness unto Death* (1849), which Malick had utilized in other films.

To understand the arc of history as Kierkegaard does is to see it as a perpetual struggle between materialism and spirit, worldly power and divine mercy. "The first form of rulers in the world," he writes in his journals, "were 'the tyrants,' the last will be 'the martyrs.' In the world's evolution this is the movement from worldliness to religiousness."[72] Anybody who has seen a Malick film since at least *The Thin Red Line* will recognize this idea as a focal point of his cinematic vision. It appears in everything he has directed and written, including works that never saw the light of day, such as his adaption of *Sansho the Bailiff* for the stage.

A Hidden Life is a meditation on Kierkegaard's aphorism, with Jägerstätter playing the role of the martyr, and Hitler—whom we see not just in the clips from *Triumph of the Will* but also, later on, in uncanny color footage, relaxing at his Berghof retreat in Obersalzberg, just across the border from the Alpine village Jägerstätter calls home—that of the tyrant. These two protagonists come from disturbingly similar backgrounds, but the forms of life they represent could not be more opposed. Indeed, the contrast gives *A Hidden Life* all the dramatic tension it needs: the film pits saintly humility against demonic grandiosity, the will to believe against the will to power.

Throughout *A Hidden Life*, Jägerstätter's Bartlebyesque refusal to swear an oath of allegiance to Hitler is questioned, even mocked, by all those around him. Spiritual counselors, village neighbors, even his own wife and mother ask what good his quiet resistance will do in the grand scheme of things. He and his family will face severe hardship—social ostracization, financial ruin, even persecution—and for what? A peasant's refusal to swear an oath to Hitler will not make headlines, will not galvanize opposition to an unjust war, will not put a stop to the unceasing slaughter bench of history or the merciless rule of tyrants. "What purpose does it serve?" an interrogator (Matthias Schoenaerts, in Grand Inquisitor style) asks Jägerstätter in prison. To these questions, which recall ones Welsh poses to Witt in *The Thin Red Line* ("What difference do you think you'll make?"), Jägerstätter has no resounding reply. He repeatedly refrains from offering any sweeping justification for his actions. All he has is his conscience, which tells him that swearing an oath of allegiance to the Führer is wrong.

The Kierkegaard epigraph Malick appended to his screenplay for *A Hidden Life* provides an off-screen explanation for Jägerstätter's principled stand, but it is an absent presence for viewers of the film. Far more visible is a quote that *does* appear in the picture—namely, George Eliot's famous conclusion to her 1871–72 novel *Middlemarch*. The passage serves as a postscript, appearing just before the end credits. Lines borrowed from a sprawling, sentimental story about the English landed gentry of the nineteenth century might seem a curious fit for a film about a humble Catholic farmer refusing to submit to the Nazis (just as a Virginia Woolf novel was an unlikely inspiration for a movie about indie musicians in Austin, Texas), but *Middlemarch* is not altogether foreign to the aims and ambitions of *A Hidden Life*, for it, too, expresses an interest in the morality of everyday life, lived by everyday people, far away from the centers of power.

As it does in *Middlemarch*, village life takes precedence over international affairs in *A Hidden Life*. Nothing that could be considered world historical happens, at least not at first glance. Moments of courage and sacrifice come unadorned, without fanfare. More often than not, they involve intimate decisions, not grand public declarations. The final lines of *Middlemarch*—those quoted in *A Hidden Life*—depict morality as a lived experience that takes place largely offstage, behind the scenes: "for the growing good of the world is partly dependent on unhistoric acts," it reads; "and that things are not so ill with you and me as they might have been, is half owing to the number who lived faithfully a hidden life, and rest in unvisited tombs."[73]

For many years, Franz Jägerstätter's was in fact a hidden life, but only by the standards of the outside world. In St. Radegund, the small mountain village just across the Salzach River from Bavaria where he lived, Jägerstätter's martyrdom was well known, if not always exactly celebrated. Many of his relatives reside there to this day, and some of them still recall how the family was shunned both before and even after Jägerstätter was imprisoned, then beheaded, by functionaries of the Third Reich. Throughout production, *A Hidden Life* was even called "Radegund," an allusion to this place-specific memory, but also to the longer religious history of a Catholicism predating the rise of the nation-state of Austria and the Third Reich of Hitler.[74] The village of Sankt Radegund—to use its full and proper name—was christened in homage to the medieval Thuringian princess famous for founding the Abbey of the Holy Cross in Poitiers. In choosing to call his picture "Radegund," Malick was signaling to curious followers of his work both the provincial nature of the story he intended to tell and its saintly resonance. His would be a film about a beatified martyr—a local saint—who came from a small community named after yet another saint. It would be, in other words, a Christian, if not explicitly Catholic, picture.[75]

By the time "Radegund" arrived at Cannes in 2019, it had become *A Hidden Life*. The new title was less explicitly Austrian, and seemingly less religious, too. But only on the surface. The new title derives from the *Middlemarch* quote with which the picture concludes—a quote nowhere to be found in Malick's original screenplay—but it is also a clear reference to the uncelebrated heroism of Jägerstätter's refusal to serve what he considered to be an immoral regime; a moment of extreme self-sacrifice that had been omitted from the annals of world history, one that stands in stark contrast to the actions of more famous individuals, such as, most notably, Martin Heidegger, who invoked the "inner truth and greatness" of National Socialism even after the end of the Second World War.[76]

It was not until the American academic Gordon C. Zahn published a biography of Jägerstätter, *In Solitary Witness*, in 1964, that his story became more widely known beyond Alpine Austria.[77] A Catholic himself, Zahn depicted Jägerstätter's principled stand as a challenge to authoritarianism, but also, and perhaps more importantly, to the Catholic Church, an institution that had not unilaterally opposed National Socialism and refused to acknowledge Jägerstätter's heroism in the years after 1945. As Zahn put it, Jägerstätter's faith stood in stark contrast to "what seems to pass as Christianity in the modern conformist world."[78]

Zahn was familiar with the kind of collaborationist Catholicism Jägerstätter opposed. A pacifist and a conscientious objector during World War II, he was assigned to alternative service from 1942 to 1946. In the 1950s, Zahn won a Fulbright scholarship to study the demise of the Catholic pacifist movement under Nazism. The book that resulted from that research, *German Catholics and Hitler's Wars* (1962), caused an uproar, in part for suggesting that German Catholics had not done enough to oppose an unjust and immoral war.[79] While conducting research for the book, Zahn stumbled upon stories of heroic resistance, which were noteworthy because they were so few and far between. The story of Franz Jägerstätter was one of them, and it became the focus of his next project, *In Solitary Witness*, which was published just months before the United States embarked on an unjust and immoral war of its own in Southeast Asia.

In the Vietnam era, Zahn's book had an outsized impact, not least because Thomas Merton reviewed it for the pacifist periodical *Peace News* in 1965.[80] The most famous Trappist monk turned antiwar activist of the day reprinted the piece in his widely influential 1968 book *Faith and Violence: Christian Teaching and Christian Practice*, which outlined a "theology of *resistance*" to murderous mass violence.[81] *Faith and Violence* appeared in the year of the "heroic guerrilla," amid global revolution and domestic revolt, the days of rage fueled by political assassinations (Robert F. Kennedy, but also Martin Luther King Jr., about whose murder Malick had cowritten a piece for the *New Yorker*), the brutal escalation of the war in Vietnam, and widespread racist repression.[82] In this context, the lesson of Jägerstätter's refusal to submit to Nazi authority was plain to see: it had less to do with the specifics of German or Austrian history and more to do with the ongoing threat of what

Merton called "white-collar violence," the kind of violence committed not just by the Hitlers of the world, but also—as Hannah Arendt had argued—by the Adolf Eichmanns, the kind of violence military strategists in Washington, D.C., were exporting to Southeast Asia and police departments were deploying in inner cities across the United States.[83]

In Solitary Witness anticipated much of Merton's argument in *Faith and Violence*. Amazed and disturbed by the fact that Hitler, Eichmann, and Jägerstätter were "three men with their roots in the same soil," Zahn set out to find reasons for why they turned out to be so different from one another.[84] What separated those who craved power from those who resisted it, those who blindly followed authority from those who dared to question it? Zahn, a sociologist, thought the answer had something to do with social types: he came to see Jägerstätter as an outsider, a rebel, "an extreme social deviant." He was somebody who put the imperatives of saving his soul over and above those of saving his skin.[85] In this regard, he was a throwback to an earlier age of Christianity, one that produced self-sacrificing prophets and martyrs rather than obedient rule followers. He was a man out of time. "The harsh truth," Zahn concluded, "is that Jägerstätter had chosen to take his stand at a time and in a place where the religious community itself had abandoned all pretensions to the traditions of protest and prophecy that had marked its earlier history."[86] Just as Kierkegaard had railed against the self-satisfied Christendom of his day, Jägerstätter ended up denouncing the fellow-traveling Catholicism of "halfway Christians" in his.[87]

Thomas Merton was less interested in documenting social types than in preaching social action. He thought Jägerstätter's example could lead to a revival of protest and prophecy that might resist the structural violence responsible for "the bureaucratic and technological destruction of man."[88] Only a Christian love expressing itself as resistance could stop it.[89] Christianity was founded upon a "theology of love," he said, but in a world turned upside down by authoritarianism and atom bombs, it might "conceivably turn out to be a theology of revolution," too.[90] Making the stories of religious resisters and revolutionaries more widely known—stories such as Jägerstätter's—might help the world navigate a perilous new age in which evil manifested itself not as isolated, interpersonal crimes but as widespread systems of oppression and destruction. "The real problem," Merton suggested, was "not the individual with a revolver but *death and even genocide as big business*."[91]

Death and genocide remain mostly off-screen throughout *A Hidden Life*. As Lidija Haas pointed out in her review of the film for the *New Republic*, the horrors of total war and the Holocaust are "curiously elided," this despite the fact that the real Jägerstätter may have been at least somewhat aware of the systematic persecution of European Jews taking place all around him.[92] All we see of the mass death now forever associated with National Socialism and the Second World War is one scene in which *A Hidden Life*'s protagonist, while completing his first round of compulsory military training, is forced to watch propaganda footage depicting early Wehrmacht victories on the Western Front. The only explicit reference to the Holocaust in the film comes in the form of a disturbing sequence early on, in which the mayor of St. Radegund (Karl Markovics), a fervent Nazi, rants and raves in the village beer garden about "foreigners" who "swarm over our streets." "And now they tell us to spare these other races" he slurs, "degraded, so contemptible they can no longer despise themselves? They sow the earth with salt."

For daring to question such beliefs—the central tenets of what the historian Claudia Koonz has called, paradoxically, "the Nazi conscience"—Franz Jägerstätter became a so-called enemy of the state.[93] But he also became an outlier in his village community. *A Hidden Life* devotes far more time to the ostracization he and his family face than to the horrors of a war waged against peoples Hitler labeled enemies and pests. We see Jägerstätter threatened by his peers, his wife shunned by their village neighbors, and his children, in one brief but significant scene, taunted and pelted with clods of mud by their classmates. Aside from just a few sympathetic friends who limit their conversations with Jägerstätter to conspiratorial whispers, there is nobody in St. Radegund who dares stand by his side.

These scenes of social exclusion heighten, and perhaps even exaggerate, the treatment the historical Jägerstätter and his family received in St. Radegund, but they are nevertheless in keeping with Zahn's general assessment of how the community still looked askance at his actions some two decades after his execution. "The community continues to reject Jägerstätter's stand," he wrote in a chapter of *In Solitary Witness* titled "The Martyr and His Village," viewing it "as a stubborn and pointless display of essentially political imprudence, or even an actual failure to fulfill a legitimate duty." Everywhere he looked while researching Jägerstätter's life and legacy, Zahn saw only continued evidence of "the community's general disapproval of his action."[94]

In Solitary Witness paints a portrait of extraordinary social isolation. Zahn suggested that Jägerstätter's heroism could only be appreciated in the context of St. Radegund's tight-knit community: only against this backdrop of extreme social pressure did his solitary act of courage stand out as particularly noteworthy—not because it generated widespread attention but precisely because it did not. Jägerstätter's was a mundane martyrdom, little understood by even his closest neighbors. In Zahn's eyes, he was a "rebel-peasant who rejected the *Führer* and refused his orders," paying the ultimate price for it.[95] But in St. Radegund there was no consensus as to whether Jägerstätter's heroism resulted from a profound moral clarity or the fanaticism of an unsettled mind—the consequence, some suggested, of perhaps too much Bible reading.[96]

For Zahn, there was no ambiguity. Jägerstätter's stand represented an insightful fusion of "political thought and moral imperatives," one that was all the more remarkable given both his limited education and the seclusion of his rural world.[97] *In Solitary Witness* marvels at the fact that this otherwise unremarkable Austrian peasant could have seen so clearly what so many of his fellow villagers, not to mention his fellow Austrians and fellow Catholics, could not, which is that Hitler was waging an immoral war of aggression. Jägerstätter's refusal to swear an oath to Hitler was not the impulsive action of a fanatic, but a considered moral decision based on clear, theologically sound principles. It was "political opposition rooted in religious commitment."[98]

Zahn portrays Jägerstätter as an existential hero, what Albert Camus called "the rebel." Invoking this social type—which Zahn connects not just to the author of *L'Homme révolté*, but also Henry David Thoreau, C. Wright Mills, and Peter Viereck—*In Solitary Witness* presents Jägerstätter's case as evidence of the ongoing struggle against conformism and authoritarianism. It was a struggle with a special valence for the faithful, who could see in Jägerstätter's life "the repetition of an old story, the ever-recurring confrontation between Christ and Caesar." This story was, Zahn insisted, a "real life version of the Passion Play."[99]

A Hidden Life is very much a Passion Play, the sufferings of its protagonist recalling the Stations of the Cross. But rather than taking us to the top of Golgotha, it funnels us, through a different kind of Via Dolorosa, into the lower levels of hell. The whole film is a descent: from Alpine meadows to subterranean prisons; from familial, village harmony to interpersonal discord; from hope and happiness to anguish and dread. Viewed from this angle, *A Hidden Life* is less about the horrors of Nazism and more about the meaning and purpose of faith in a seemingly faithless world—a world hemmed in by evil, populated by "halfway Christians" who do their best to look the other way. How does one remain a true and faithful Christian, *A Hidden Life* asks, in a world governed by Caesar? How does one even know what it means to be a Christian when self-proclaimed Christians extol duty to Hitler? As scholars have repeatedly shown since the publication of *In Solitary Witness*, the Catholic Church was not some innocent bystander of the atrocities committed by the Third Reich.[100] And it was hardly alone in this: many other Christian churches and organizations failed to speak out, too, often doing all they could to avoid direct confrontation with the Nazi regime. Worse, some actively collaborated with it.[101]

In these circumstances, what prompts somebody to embrace the life of the martyr or the rebel? What allows one to walk the path of the extreme social deviant? Malick had tiptoed around the subject of deviancy in *Song to Song*, but the story of Jägerstätter's life gives him something far more substantial to work with: a story not merely of a wannabe rock-and-roll rebel, but a committed religious one. But, as it turns out, the real-life Jägerstätter was something of a rock-and-roll rebel himself at one time. Before finding his way to the Catholic faith that informed his moral stand against Nazism, he was, in Zahn's account, a "young ruffian."[102] Like other local youths, he drank and he brawled, usually as part of the local gang. It also appears he fathered an illegitimate child, too. (Zahn notes that Jägerstätter himself may have been born out wedlock, a not uncommon occurrence in rural areas where sexual mores were somewhat more relaxed than in cities.) Locals were just as likely to see young Franz riding around on his motorcycle as attending church services. Somewhere around the time he met and married Franziska (Fani) Schwaninger (played by Valerie Pachner in *A Hidden Life*), though, he changed. So much so that the residents of St. Radegund often spoke of there being two Jägerstätters: "an 'early' Franz, and a 'new' man."[103]

Traces of Jägerstätter's early wild years appear in *A Hidden Life*, but they are few and far between: a recurring image of him speeding down country lanes on his motorcycle, for instance, or a passing line or two from the mayor about the old days. "You were a wild one," he reminds Jägerstätter at one point. "You fought with the police." As Zahn discovered during the course of his research, many people in St. Radegund attributed Franz's newfound religiosity to Fani's influence. It is something Malick signals in his film—"Who changed you?" the mayor asks him. "Your wife?"—but only fleetingly. By and large, the Franz Jägerstätter of *A Hidden Life* hardly comes across as a wild one. He is so mild-mannered as to seem impassive. He is a religious model, a moral exemplar, more than a person. Because his wild days and his return to the faith are conspicuously absent from the film, Jägerstätter's religious devotion, which informed every aspect of his opposition to the Hitler regime, comes across as being somewhat nondescript. It is more of a subterranean force than a daily practice. Some critics have even gone so far as to criticize *A Hidden Life* for downplaying Jägerstätter's deep-seated, "sacramental" faith.[104]

Franz Jägerstätter does not undergo any great transformation in *A Hidden Life*, he merely endures, in Christlike fashion, ever greater torments. First it is the verbal abuse of his friends and neighbors. Then it is the incomprehension of his spiritual advisers, from the local priest all the way up to the regional bishop, who tells him, in no uncertain terms, to obey orders. He does not. Imprisonment, interrogations, even violent beatings follow. All of it culminates in a summary conviction and execution. Throughout these trials and tribulations, Jägerstätter remains resolute. Like Witt in *The Thin Red Line*, he comes across as otherworldly. More concerned with the well-being of those around him than with any personal danger to himself, he does what the martyr is supposed to do: he turns the other cheek, shares his meager rations with other prisoners, and refuses to condemn those who persecute him. "I don't judge you," he tells the head of the military tribunal (Bruno Ganz, in the penultimate role of his long and storied career) that has decided his fate. "I'm not saying, 'He is wicked, I am right.' I don't know everything." All he knows is that he must follow his own conscience: "I can't do what I believe is wrong."

As Zahn showed in *In Solitary Witness*, the real-life Jägerstätter attributed his own moral insight to divine mercy: those around him who failed to see the moral error of Nazism simply had "not been given the grace" to see things the way he did.[105] Or, as he put it in his prison notebooks: "The greater the grace, the greater the responsibility."[106] Even with the gift of grace, though, Jägerstätter faced a harrowing ordeal. Moments of his inner turmoil are scattered throughout *A Hidden Life*. Each time a letter carrier holding what might turn out to be a fatal induction notice whizzes by on a bicycle, he and Fani flinch. Each time he is reminded of the pain and suffering his decisions will inflict on his wife, children, and aged mother, his eyes turn toward the ground. And each time he is interrogated by a Nazi official, or left alone in a prison cell, his thoughts turn to the world he knows he will leave behind.

Still, Malick's Jägerstätter seems to meet his trials—not to mention his final fate, which is shot with almost unbearable realism up until the very moment he is strapped to the guillotine—with a kind of serenity. It is as if he had been born for no other purpose. Although this depiction is in keeping

with some of the testimony Zahn uncovered about Jägerstätter's final days—
he was "completely calm and prepared," one chaplain said—it risks flattening
out some of its protagonist's all-too-human contradictions and complexity.[107] Zahn's *In Solitary Witness* did not make a case for its subject's unwavering saintliness. To the contrary, the very fact that a rowdy rural youth with
a limited education could bravely do what so many of his more privileged
fellow Christians could not was, for Zahn, what made his story remarkable.
The fact that Jägerstätter was not always so saintly, that his formerly wayward life could lead, unexpectedly, to such moral clarity, was a sign of its
fundamental mystery and grace.[108]

To be sure, Jägerstätter was by no means the only Christian to take a principled stand against Hitler. Some well-known religious figures worked actively in the German resistance, one of the most famous being the Lutheran
pastor Dietrich Bonhoeffer, who was executed two years after Jägerstätter, in
1945.[109] Around the same time, the Jesuit priest Alfred Delp also was executed.
Like Bonhoeffer, Delp composed spiritual reflections while awaiting both his
trial and the carrying out of his death sentence. Smuggled out of prison, these
meditations eventually found their way into print in 1958, with an English
translation appearing in 1962.[110] Delp's prison writings reveal a preparation
for martyrdom that was remarkably similar to Jägerstätter's, so much so that
they foreshadow Malick's portrayal of Jägerstätter in *A Hidden Life* and his
decision to include the quote from *Middlemarch*.

Facing certain death, Delp sought to prepare himself—and his friends,
family, and fellow Jesuits—for what was to come. "This is seed-time," he
wrote, "not harvest. God sows the seed and some time or other he will do
the reaping. The one thing I must do is to make sure the seed falls on fertile
ground. And I must arm myself against the pain and depression that sometimes almost defeat me. If this is the way God has chosen—and everything
indicates that it is—then I must willingly and without rancor make it my way.
May others at some future time find it possible to have a better and happier
life because we died in this hour of trial."[111] Such imagery of harvest—the imagery with which *A Hidden Life* opens and closes—is a hallmark of Christian sermonizing. It has its origins in the Bible, most notably the Book of
Ecclesiastes. It is an extended metaphor for divine providence, one that can
be found in many of Malick's films, especially the late-career ones exploring
grace, mercy, and redemption. What theodicy, if any, these films ask, can
make sense of pointless suffering? In a world as cruel as this, where are faith
and consolation to be found? What does it even mean to call oneself a

Christian anymore? After seeing Martin Scorsese's 2016 film *Silence*, which depicts, in intensely graphic detail, the persecution of Jesuit missionaries in seventeenth-century Japan, Malick reportedly sent his cinematic colleague a personal letter, asking him, "What does Christ want from us?"[112]

In prison, Delp asked only that "God keep me in his providence and give me strength to meet what is before me." He reassured himself that his sacrifice would not be wasted: "If through a person's life there is a little more love and kindness, a little more light and truth in the world, then he will not have lived in vain."[113] The letters Franz Jägerstätter wrote to his wife from prison, many of which are quoted directly in *A Hidden Life*, express similar sentiments. The last few of them, written in the final days of his life, are preoccupied with the nobility of sacrifice and suffering. It is "a grace of God," he writes on June 6, 1943, "when one can suffer for his faith."[114] On July 8: "It is a joy to be able to suffer for Jesus and our faith."[115] And in his last letter to his wife, dated August 9, the day of his execution, he writes: "I thank our Savior that I could suffer for him and may die for him."[116]

It was a profound faith in divine providence that sustained Jägerstätter in his final days, allowing him to remain "completely calm and prepared." Fully convinced he was in God's hands, doing what God wanted, he knew that redemption and revelation were on the horizon: "Everything will become clear on the Day of Judgment, if not sooner," he wrote from Berlin-Tegel Prison, an explanation for why "so many people are struggling today" will finally arrive.[117]

Malick brought his script for *A Hidden Life* to a close with scenes expressing these sentiments. Each and every page of his screenplay shows how faithful to his source materials he remained, extracting from Jägerstätter's letters and writings the smallest details of his life—right down to the blackbirds singing outside his prison window.[118] But here, at the very end, Malick takes liberties: he gives Franz's ruminations about the meaning of suffering over to Fani. In an image bookending the harvest scenes at the start of the film, she is gleaning barley outside St. Radegund with her sister Resie (Maria Simon). Her husband is dead and gone, but the work continues. How could everything go on as if nothing happened? What was the point of it all? "I thought you just had to be good," she says. "Wasn't he? Franz!" Her sister offers her a consoling hand as Fani goes on to deliver the final lines of the script: "A time will come when we'll know what all this is for—why there's all this suffering. And there'll be no mysteries. We'll know why we live."[119] A final stage direction tells us that the other residents of St. Radegund are nearby, carrying on with their tasks and chores in the fields: "The life of the land goes on."[120]

Most of these lines are delivered via voice-over narration. They accompany scenes of everyday life in St. Radegund resuming. We see church services and farm labor recommencing; we even see Fani and her mother-in-law whitewashing the building they call home, preparing it for a new beginning. These scenes depicting the continuity of village life eventually give way to a broader perspective, one foreshadowed by the opening images of the film. We see trees and skies, waterfalls and wheat fields. We see majestic mountain peaks. But we also notice conspicuous symbols of loss: an empty bench overlooking a vast valley; a garden gate slightly ajar. Over this montage, Fani speaks words that do not appear in Malick's script. They describe a redemption arriving in and through nature, a rebirth like the ones depicted in *The Thin Red Line*, *The New World*, and *The Tree of Life*. "We'll come together," Fani says. 'We'll plant orchards, fields. We'll build the land back up." "Franz," she says, "I'll meet you there. In the mountains." In the background we hear the hum of swelling strings. The musical cue, from the award-winning composer James Newton Howard, is titled "There Will Be No Mysteries." After it fades, there is nothing but birdsong and flowing water—the sounds, in Malick's cinema, of peace and tranquility.

The meaning of suffering will be revealed, *A Hidden Life* suggests, when one puts one's faith in providence and receives the gifts of mercy and grace, which are evident all around us in nature. This message is in keeping with Malick's other films, but it runs against the grain of postwar reconsiderations of philosophical theodicy, which resisted such easy articulations of consolation.[121] Malick's natural theodicy also borrows a little too liberally, some critics have argued, from the Teutonic *Bergfilm* aesthetic Siegfried Kracauer long ago associated with the cinematic proto-fascism partly responsible for Hitler's rise to power.[122] Most troubling of all, though, is the possibility that Malick's ode to providence elides the expressly political valence of Jägerstätter's actions, the very thing that attracted the attention of those who publicized his martyrdom in the first place.

For religious activists like Zahn and Merton, Jägerstätter was not a symbol of consolation. He was a figure of noble rebellion, somebody who stood up to authority, the kind of person who said "Pfui Hitler" while all those around him shouted "Heil."[123] He embodied Merton's "theology of resistance." Like Delp and the French philosopher and activist Simone Weil, Jägerstätter put conscience before obedience: he was a religious rebel and a political hero who resisted the siren call of conformity. These martyrs did not look the other way when—as Merton put it in his introduction to Delp's *Prison Writings*— "inhuman complacency" came to govern human relations. They were the opposite of Adolf Eichmann, who "considered himself," Merton reminded his readers, "an obedient and God-fearing man!"[124]

In authoritarian times, acts of conscience take on great significance. Writing in the mid-1960s, when Malick was still a philosophy student studying the work of Martin Heidegger (about whom Alfred Delp had written an early study of his own), Merton became convinced that the church (and the world) needed to be awakened from its complacent slumber.[125] "The light and truth which are hidden in the suffocating cloud of evil," he wrote in his introduction to Delp's *Prison Writings*, "are not to be found only in a stoical and isolated individual here and there who has surmounted the horror of his fate. They must appear somehow in a renewal of our entire social order."[126] This meant that religious rebels could not avoid confronting Caesar. Even monks and mystics had an "inescapable responsibility to be involved in politics."[127] In dark times, a champion of the faith had to be not just a believer, or even a martyr, but also a "prophet."[128]

There was plenty of room for prophecy in Zahn's account of Franz Jägerstätter's life. *In Solitary Witness* recounts a dream Jägerstätter had soon after the Anschluss in 1938. In it, he saw a "beautiful shining railroad train that circled around a mountain," along with streams of children and adults clamoring to get aboard it.[129] A voice gave the dozing Jägerstätter a distinct word of warning: "this train was going to hell," it said.[130] In a more wakeful state, Jägerstätter realized that the train represented National Socialism. His dream was a vision of dark times to come. In his review of Zahn's book, Merton focused on this prophetic revelation. It was proof that Jägerstätter's "refusal to fight was not only a private matter of conscience" but also, and more importantly, "the fruit of a particular religious interpretation of contemporary political events."[131] Jägerstätter was not a hero because he fled politics, but because he refused to: he knew the train was coming and he placed himself directly on its tracks.

Trains make a number of appearances in *A Hidden Life*, almost always in a menacing manner. Their movements stand in stark contrast to the many shots of flowing water throughout the film, suggesting calm. Early stockfootage clips of trains racing through countryside locales—imagery resembling the daring cinematography of Jean Renoir's *La Bête Humaine* (1938), a film released the same year Hitler annexed Austria—visualize Jägerstätter's prophetic dream of a national descent into hell. Trains also take Jägerstätter away from his wife and family to his imprisonments in Enns and, after that, Berlin-Tegel. As in the dream-sequence montages, these trains symbolize the unstoppable motion of the state, the inhuman force that, in mobilizing troops and transporting prisoners, determines fates, deciding who gets to live and who shall die. Although Malick does not chose to use any train-related footage depicting mass deportations, it is all but impossible to view these images and not think of the vast transportation network—overseen by functionaries like Eichmann—that made the Holocaust possible.

It is often described as a film about religious faith, but *A Hidden Life* can also be interpreted as an indictment of totalitarian rule. In fact, Malick might very well embrace Merton's "theology of resistance." His script for *A Hidden Life* contains a revealing "Pre-Credit Sequence" set in Tiananmen Square, Beijing, 1989: "A man in a white shirt, holding a grocery sack, stands in front of a line of tanks, blocking their progress toward Tiananmen Square."[132] The scene is familiar to anyone of a certain age living outside the People's Republic of China, where coverage of the pro-democracy uprising—as well as its violent suppression—is extensively censored. By placing such imagery directly ahead of the "Newsreel Footage from the 1930s" that opens the picture, Malick suggests a continuing danger, which we might describe, à la Kierkegaard, as an ongoing struggle between the tyrants and the martyrs of the world.

The Tiananmen Square "Pre-Credit Sequence" did not make it into *A Hidden Life*. Like the Kierkegaard epigraph positioned at the top of Malick's script, it serves as a significant but nevertheless absent presence. Still, the imprint is there. Although Malick avoided doing any publicity for his film, his actors did not hesitate to connect the story of Jägerstätter's heroism to current events, often alluding, in press conferences, to the decidedly undemocratic words and actions of a certain media personality turned U.S. president whose rise to power was predicated on an explicit demonizing of outsiders, minorities, and so-called enemies of the people—the usual bogeymen of authoritarian rhetoric.[133]

Organized, bureaucratic violence is most evident in the second and third acts of *A Hidden Life*, in which Jägerstätter descends from the pastoral Eden of St. Radegund into the labyrinth of the Nazi state, with its barracks and prisons, its military tribunals and execution chambers. Everything in the film changes so as to suggest a Dantesque descent into hell. Open skies disappear behind cold stone walls, grassy greens slide into somber grays, and vast, wide-angle shots give way to confined, claustrophobic close-ups. *A Hidden Life* starts to look less like Robert Wise's *The Sound of Music* (1965) and more like Robert Bresson's *A Man Escaped* (1956), a film about a member of the French Resistance breaking out of a Nazi prison.[134]

Bresson's picture is also about faith: the subtitle he chose for it—"the wind blows where it wants"—references a passage in the Gospel of John (3:8), the same passage Malick has chosen as the title for his next film. I mention this minor detail because, in addition to being a biopic and a historical drama, *A Hidden Life* is also an homage to a certain kind of religious filmmaking, one that inspired not just Malick but also many of his peers. For directors who started making movies in the 1970s, the work of auteurs like Bresson—and Ingmar Bergman and Andrei Tarkovsky, to name a couple others—represented a religiously inflected ideal to which they could aspire. "For me," Martin Scorsese wrote in the *New York Times* in 2019, "for the filmmakers I came to love and respect, for my friends who started making movies around the same time that I did, cinema was about revelation—aesthetic, emotional and spiritual revelation."[135]

Theirs was the generation raised on what Paul Schrader called "the transcendental style," a style that took shape in the films of Carl Theodor Dreyer and Yasujiro Ozu but hit something like a highwater mark in the pictures of Bresson. It was a style that stood apart from secular cinema, a style of searching sparseness and emotional ambiguity. Should we be surprised that some of the most famous members of a movie-mad generation have returned to it in recent years, directing films—Scorsese's *Silence* in 2016, Schrader's *First Reformed* in 2017, and *A Hidden Life* in 2019—about faith, suffering, and the search for redemption, especially as these directors begin to contemplate old age? These films compose an interesting subgenre of their own, demonstrating the long-lasting influence of a midcentury art-house style that is still synonymous with spiritual cinema.

The allusions *A Hidden Life* makes to famous films in the history of cinema are too numerous to catalog here. But focusing on just a few of them demonstrates how indebted the picture is to the examples of Bresson, Bergman, and Tarkovsky. One particular sequence even goes so far as to foreground—in a metacinematic sort of way—the film's own allusionism.[136] In it, we watch Jägerstätter wander into a beautiful, rococo-style church, where he encounters a muralist by the name of Ohlendorf (Johan Leysen) who is working on frescoes depicting scenes from the Bible. "I paint the tombs of the prophets," Ohlendorf says. "I help people look up from those pews and

Figure 37. Art and faith in *A Hidden Life* (Johan Leysen as Ohlendorf).

dream. They look up and they imagine that if they lived in Christ's time, they wouldn't have done what the others did." But this is a fantasy: "They would have murdered those whom they now adore," he says somberly.

Shots of the religious iconography inside and outside the church (the images outside appear to be of a different church, captured on a different day) are interspersed with images of Ohlendorf high up on his scaffolding, hard at work. The labor does not seem to come easily to him. He appears troubled. His next lines reveal why. "I paint all this suffering," he tells Franz, "but I don't suffer myself. I make a living of it. What we do is just create sympathy. We create admirers. We don't create followers."

Are these the thoughts of a peripheral figure in Jägerstätter's life, or do they express the doubts and anxieties of *A Hidden Life*'s writer and director? Ohlendorf's extended soliloquy comes across as a startlingly intimate confession. It offers a window into the soul of an artist struggling to make much more than mere art, an artist who wants to create something that will not just console audiences, but also challenge them into believing. "I paint their comfortable Christ," Ohlendorf says, "with a halo over His head. How can I show what I haven't lived? Someday I might have the courage to venture— not yet. Someday I'll paint the true Christ."

Those interested in Malick's career would have already known, even seeing these images for the first time, that he was at work on *The Way of the Wind*, a movie depicting the life of Jesus. What some viewers may not have noticed, though, was the way in which these scenes with Ohlendorf revisit

Figure 38. Faith and art in Ingmar Bergman's *The Seventh Seal*
(Gunnar Olsson as Albertus Pictor).

and reassess imagery from Malick's first feature film (Holly's father, in *Badlands*, is a sign painter). Even more importantly, they quote Bergman's *The
Seventh Seal* (1957) and Tarkovsky's ode to it, *Andrei Rublev* (1966).[137] Like
these expressly theological films, and in stark contrast to the studied cool of
Badlands, *A Hidden Life* explores the meaning of faith in destitute times and
the role of art in sustaining it. Set in equally bleak contexts—the era of the
Crusades and the Black Death in *The Seventh Seal*; that of the Tatar invasions
in *Andrei Rublev*; and that of the Second World War in *A Hidden Life*—each
of these pictures offers an expressly existential understanding of belief in a
time of geopolitical crisis. Each shows the journey of the faithful to be anything but easy or comfortable.

　These films also suggest that art, if it is to remain a source of hope amid
hopelessness, cannot shrink from the telling of hard truths. Religious art
must confront evil, not avoid it: "Christ's life is a demand," Ohlendorf says
to Jägerstätter. "You don't want to be reminded of it. So we don't have to see
what happens to the truth. A darker time is coming. And men will be more
clever: they won't fight the truth, they'll just ignore it." Malick's script for *A
Hidden Life* has these scenes appearing very early in the picture, almost as if
they were meant to serve as a framing device for the biographical tale that
follows. They foreshadow everything to come. One scene, which did not make
it into the final film, has Ohlendorf criticizing the comfortable Christians of
the day: "They'll count themselves lucky that they didn't live in times like
ours," he says, "when your life might be demanded of you."[138]

In the finished film, the sequences with Ohlendorf appear a little later, after Jägerstätter has completed his initial round of mandatory military training, around the time he begins contemplating a course of action that will put him in direct conflict with the Nazi regime. But Jägerstätter's struggles with his conscience are more explicit in the pages of Malick's script than they appear on screen: "Disturbed by the sense that a decision may soon be required of him," Franz at one point contemplates a local crucifix in the fields, which stares down at him impassively.[139] Later, Franz is "assailed with torment, doubt, and fear."[140] Soon after that, "Franz trembles inwardly." "He alone must decide."[141] Yet Jägerstätter does not decide all by himself. Malick's script has him telling Fani that nature gives him guidance: "I went up to the mountains," he says. "They tell me what to do. The river does."[142] These lines did not make it into the film, though, at least not directly. Malick reportedly told James Newton Howard that he wanted the film's score to evoke the sounds of the Salzach River, but we do not actually hear the mountains whisper or the river speak.[143]

Instead, we get the faces of August Diehl and Valerie Pachner. We see how faces once animated by laughter and smiles begin to display worry lines of anxiety and concern. This is particularly true of Diehl's performance, which conveys inner turmoil via the eyes and the tautness of the jaw. The way Malick's camera frames his face, especially as he sits unblinking before prison guards, lawyers, and military officials, recalls—as many commentators have noted—the poignant closeups of another famous martyr in cinematic history, the one depicted in Carl Theodor Dreyer's religious masterpiece *The Passion of Joan of Arc* (1928).[144] In both films, one feels the weight of authority bearing down on the soul of the protagonist. But an array of officials, alternatively resorting to threats, intimidation, and even cajoling, cannot budge the accused from their stance: earthly authority no longer has a claim over Joan of Arc (Maria Falconetti) or Franz Jägerstätter.

While not as theatrical as Falconetti's, Diehl's performance in *A Hidden Life* similarly suggests an otherworldly subjectivity, one that can endure the trials and tribulations of this life with a certain degree of equanimity because he knows that, one day, there will be no more mysteries, that all the suffering will be justified and redeemed. Malick takes this directly from Jägerstätter's life: "When one's gaze is directed to eternal life," he wrote in his prison notebooks, "this world's afflictions lose their terror."[145] Still, *A Hidden Life* is a portrait of sainthood as forbearance more than vindication. It has its roots in the difficult, often challenging films of Bresson—and not necessarily his own 1962

Figure 39. The protagonist of Robert Bresson's *Au Hasard Balthazar*.

take on the trial of Joan of Arc, either. Besides *A Man Escaped*, which offered Malick a template for depicting Jägerstätter's days in prison, *A Hidden Life* draws a great deal from one the most famous cinematic renderings of the life of a saint, namely *Au Hasard Balthazar* (1966). Those who have worked with Malick after *The Tree of Life* have attested to his unceasing admiration for the director of *Balthazar*. Malick is, they say, "quite fond of Bresson." He has even been known to tell members of his crews that all they "needed to know about making a film" could be found in *Notes on the Cinematograph*. If they took the time to read it, "there was no need for film school afterwards."[146]

The protagonist of *Balthazar* is a long-suffering donkey, an animal that endures indifference, ridicule, and outright abuse from everyone he encounters, except for young Marie (Anne Wiazemsky), whose humiliations and sufferings his own seem to echo. Partly inspired by Dostoevsky's attempt to depict the life of a saint in *The Idiot*, *Au Hasard Balthazar* depicts a Christ-like existence that is at odds with the world around it.[147] Whereas Balthazar is humble and meek, his various owners are proud, greedy, and selfish; whereas he is long-suffering, they are impulsive and impudent. It is Marie's mother (Nathalie Joyaut) who recognizes Balthazar as more than a beast of burden: she calls him "a saint." Balthazar is a barometer for the fallenness of the world around him. His tragic, anonymous death at the end of the picture "underlines," as Bresson scholar Tony Pipolo has put it, "the distance between the Christian message and the world's indifference" to it.[148] The film

Figure 40. An intimation of sainthood in *A Hidden Life*.

asks a difficult question: how can one "believe in a God-run universe in face
of the triumphs of ignorance, brutality, and folly" all around us?[149]

A Hidden Life asks a similar question, and it alludes to *Au Hasard Balthazar* many times while doing so. A donkey appears at least six times in the
film, always at a significant juncture. And always looking just like Balthazar.
The donkey is there at the outset, when Franz and Fani work innocently on
their farm, more or less oblivious to the war raging beyond their Alpine valley. But he is also there when a letter carrier from the *Reichspost* appears,
carrying what might turn out to be Jägerstätter's fateful induction notice,
which would bring their agricultural idyll to an abrupt end. The donkey returns later on in the film, too, after Franz has been imprisoned. These later
shots of the animal serve as both a counterpoint to and a commentary on
Jägerstätter's fate, which is now governed—just as Balthazar's was in Bresson's film—by forces far beyond his control.

Like *Au Hasard Balthazar*, *A Hidden Life* ends with the death of its protagonist. Famously, Bresson has Balthazar, who had been accidently shot, lie
down to die amid a flock of sheep. An image of his lifeless body is the final
scene of the film. Analogously, Malick leads his viewers up to the very last
moments of Jägerstätter's life. But he goes one step beyond Bresson in choosing to capture the scenes before Franz's execution with an almost unbearable point-of-view sequence. It is one of the most visceral moments in Malick's
cinematic oeuvre. The screen cuts to black only after the hand-held camera,
which slowly approaches the guillotine, glances toward the soft sunlight

filtering through the windows of the execution chamber. It is a powerful, poignant, utterly Dostoevskian moment, alluding to a famous scene in *The Idiot*, in which a condemned man realizes "that those rays were his new state of being, and that in three minutes he would somehow merge with them."[150]

This is not the conclusion of *A Hidden Life*, though. Another five minutes' worth of footage awaits, depicting all the images of natural theodicy. The soothing visual coda allows Malick to end his film on a much more consoling note than *Au Hasard Balthazar*. Instead of focusing on the lifeless body of the saint, *A Hidden Life* points to the ongoing presence of his life and legacy in the world he has departed. It is a vision of redemption.

*   *   *

Although it is a film about death, *A Hidden Life* is also, in its own unique way, an uplifting testament to divine love. Given Malick's long-standing interest in Kierkegaard, no great interpretive leap is required to suggest that the title of his Jägerstätter biopic may allude not just *Middlemarch* or to the rural seclusion of St. Radegund, but also to an essay written by the Danish thinker titled "Love's Hidden Life and Its Recognizability by Its Fruits." Written in 1847, not long before Kierkegaard was jotting down notes in his journals about tyrants and martyrs, the piece was first published in his book *Works of Love*.

"Love's Hidden Life" presents Christian faith as a uniquely individual phenomenon. "The divine authority of the Gospel does not speak to one person about another," Kierkegaard writes, "does not speak to you, my listener, about me, or to me about you—no, when the Gospel speaks, it speaks to the single individual."[151] But the "single individual" is part of a larger totality, one sustained by divine love. "What is it," Kierkegaard writes, "that connects the temporal and eternity, what else but love, which for that very reason is before everything and remains after everything is gone."[152] Kierkegaard illustrates this idea by turning to nature: "Love's hidden life is in the innermost being, unfathomable, and then in turn is in an unfathomable connectedness with all existence. Just as the quiet lake originates deep down in hidden springs no eye has seen, so also does a person's love originate even more deeply in God's love. If there were no gushing spring at the bottom, if God were not love, then there would be neither the little lake nor a human being's love. Just as the quiet lake originates darkly in the deep spring, so a human being's love originates mysteriously in God's love."[153] But how can we come to know this hidden source, this spring hidden in the depths of the inscrutable lake, especially when the water's surface reflects back to us nothing but our own, self-absorbed image?

To answer this question, Kierkegaard switches metaphors (from the aquatic to the arboreal). He invokes a famous Gospel verse—"the tree is to be known by its fruits," a line in both Matthew and Luke—to suggest the following: while the sustaining source or cause of all things may remain inaccessible and hidden from view, the effects of its presence are all around us. Mercy and munificence shape the world, but "it is always the individual tree that shall bear the fruits."[154] Christian love provides the seeds, but only individual trees—i.e., individual lives—bring forth the bounty.

Picking up on themes he had explored in works such as *Either/Or* and *Fear and Trembling*, Kierkegaard stresses, in "Love's Hidden Life," the radical singularity of every Christian existence. Each and every tree is unique; each "bears its *own* fruit."[155] As a result, each and every reader of the Gospels must work toward becoming a fruit-bearing tree of their own. To tell the story of Christian love is to tell the stories of individual lives. It is these, Kierkegaard says, that display the fruits of "love's hidden life."

When it is viewed from this perspective, *A Hidden Life* seems very much like an extension of the confessional project Malick had inaugurated with *The Tree of Life*. His Jägerstätter biopic is the story of an individual Christian life. But it is also a story of divine love, too, one that might help audiences recognize such love as the hidden source of all things temporal and eternal. In this regard, *A Hidden Life* stands in stark contrast to what passes for epic cinema today, not to mention what passes for Christian belief. Arriving at a time when faith is as comfortable as it was in Kierkegaard's day—"to be concerned for one's own soul and to want to be spirit looks from the world's point of view like a waste of time," his pseudonym Anti-Climacus had written in *The Sickness unto Death*—it remains as much a challenge as a consolation.[156]

In June 2019, not long after *A Hidden Life* debuted at the Cannes Film Festival, reports surfaced that Malick had begun shooting his next feature film outside Rome. It was going to be about the life of Jesus. Was Malick finally attempting to paint "the true Christ"? Only time will tell if it, or *A Hidden Life*, creates followers instead of admirers. "Let each man examine himself," Christ said. Kierkegaard thought these words needed to be "urged again and again, repeated and addressed to each one individually. Wherever they do not resound," he warned, "Christianity is blasphemy."[157] Franz Jägerstätter went one step further: "Words teach," he wrote in a notebook he kept in prison, "but personal example shows their meaning."[158]

CONCLUSION
———

From Film to Philosophy

There is an often-told story, possibly apocryphal, about a Cambridge student cornering Ludwig Wittgenstein after a lecture. A version of it appears in Frederic Raphael's 1960 novel *The Limits of Love*: "Someone once said to Wittgenstein, 'Professor Wittgenstein, I have a problem: I do not feel at home in the Universe.' 'That,' replied Wittgenstein, 'is not a problem, that is a difficulty.'"[1] Around the scholars' dining table at which this anecdote is told, laughter is the only acceptable response. Knowing the difference between a technical problem in philosophy and a personal difficulty was, in the Cambridge milieu, a telltale sign of intellectual maturity. It was the starting point of serious thought. The real-life Wittgenstein, who sought "to say no more than we know," turned it into something of a mantra.[2] As he put in his most famous work, the *Philosophical Investigations*, "Problems are solved (difficulties eliminated)."[3]

If these kinds of stories were meant to cordon off the sober business of academic inquiry from the personal yearnings of students searching for meaning, then it might be worth mentioning that Wittgenstein explored difficulties on occasion, too. His early notebooks were full of religious rumination, much of it stemming from his reading of Tolstoy and Dostoevsky.[4] Academic philosophy even became something of a dead end for him, a distraction from the important things in life. "The real discovery," he also wrote in the *Investigations*, "is the one that enables me to break off philosophizing when I want to."[5]

Wittgenstein broke off philosophizing often. His academic life was full of fits and starts. Though he hailed from one of the wealthiest families in Europe, he spent time after his own student days in Manchester and Cambridge serving in the military, working as a gardener, and, for one disastrous spell, teaching primary school in rural Austria, where he was particularly fond of offering anatomy lessons using the skeletons of local roadkill he would skin, disembowel, and boil down himself, apparently.[6]

When Wittgenstein returned to Cambridge in 1929, he was well aware of academic philosophy's limitations. He told students as much. Though logic was his specialty—the publication of his *Tractatus Logico-Philosophicus* in 1922 had revolutionized the field—a student group, the Heretics, asked Wittgenstein to deliver a lecture on ethics.[7] It was a topic he was "*keen*" to discuss, he said, so he would not waste the invitation preparing some "lecture about, say, logic."[8] Instead, he would try to show how ethical and religious impulses brush up "against the boundaries of language."[9]

Ethics and religion were beyond logic, Wittgenstein told his audience. Technically speaking, they were "nonsense."[10] Far from delegitimizing such concerns in his eyes, though, this fact made them all the more intriguing. "If a man could write a book on ethics which really was a book on ethics," Wittgenstein told the Heretics, "this book would, with an explosion, destroy all the other books in the world."[11] But how could such a book be written? In something of a nod to his earlier writings on logic, Wittgenstein asked his audience if it was possible to describe the world as something other than a totality of facts, as something more than an assemblage of propositions. Could language capture the "miracle" of the world?[12]

In his lecture on ethics, Wittgenstein made a startling, seemingly religiously tinged confession: "*I wonder at the existence of the world*," he said.[13] But he had a hard time articulating just what this wonder entailed, what it *meant*. Wondering about the world was profoundly important, but finding the words to talk about it was, for Wittgenstein at least, practically impossible, especially if one did not want to be accused of talking nonsense.

In and around Cambridge, Wittgenstein came to be known for his browbeating behavior in seminars. On one occasion, he threatened a visiting guest, the Austrian-born philosopher of science Karl Popper, with a fireplace poker.[14] But his lecture to the Heretics was not one of those moments. In fact, he ended his remarks on a remarkable note of humility. "Ethics, so far as it springs from the desire to say something about the ultimate meaning of life," he said, "can be no science." But it documented a vital "tendency in the human mind" that Wittgenstein could not "help respecting deeply." "I would not for my life ridicule it."[15]

It was an astonishing admission. Philosophers have been arguing about what Wittgenstein meant by it ever since. Just what was "the ultimate meaning of life" for him? Was it the business of philosophy to search for it? Or was it, in the end, a matter for theologians? Wittgenstein had spoken of the religious "experience of feeling *absolutely* safe." It was a "state of mind," he said, "in which one is inclined to say 'I am safe, nothing can injure me whatever happens.'"[16] But it was not clear if Wittgenstein ever came to feel safe himself.

*   *   *

When Terrence Malick arrived as a "surprise participant" at the 1980 Summer Institute on Phenomenology and Existentialism, sponsored by the Council for Philosophical Studies with support from the National Endowment for the Humanities (NEH), at the University of California, Berkeley, he had been out of academia for just over a decade.[17] He had made a stab at journalism, gone to film school, and worked as a rather successful screenplay writer and script doctor, all of which was a step up from his previous employments "as an oil field roustabout, air-hammer operator, short order cook, truck driver, and wheat harvester."[18] Malick had also made a couple of well-regarded feature-length films, *Badlands* and *Days of Heaven*.

As a result of his early success, Malick's prospects in Hollywood were as good as they get. The industrialist Charles Bluhdorn, the head of Gulf and Western (the parent company of Paramount Pictures), loved *Days of Heaven* so much he reportedly told Malick, "I don't care if your movies never make a nickel, you'll always make movies for me."[19] Bluhdorn gave him a million dollars, to be paid out in annual installments of $100,000 to $200,000, allowing the young filmmaker to work on whatever he wanted.[20] But the patronage did not last long: Bluhdorn died of a heart attack just a few years later. It would be almost twenty years before Malick's next picture hit the silver screen.

Some of the reasons for Malick's notorious hiatus from directing might be found in his lecture to the philosophers gathered in Berkeley for the Summer Institute.[21] His talk carried the prosaic title "Why Do Philosophy?"[22] Its content was anything but mundane, though. Like Wittgenstein's lecture on ethics, Malick's presentation was personal, maybe even confessional. A summary of it prepared by the philosophers Hubert Dreyfus and John Haugeland documented Malick's "disappointment as a philosophy major when none of his philosophy courses helped him understand himself and his place in the order of the cosmos."[23] It was not obvious, Dreyfus and Haugeland wrote in their account of the ensuing discussion, that any student should feel entitled to such "metaphysical comfort," but philosophy professors neverthe-less had to address the yearning for it, especially if they wanted to keep their subject alive and well on college campuses.[24]

Unsurprisingly, it took academic philosophers in the United States a long time to come up with an adequate response to Malick's disappointment—at least thirty years if we take the 2011 publication of *All Things Shining: Reading the Western Classics to Find Meaning in a Secular Age* as an expression of it. The book, coauthored by Dreyfus and Sean Dorrance Kelly, addresses the question of how to live meaningfully in an age of "existential uncertainty."[25] The fact that its title alludes to the searching voice-over narrations of *The Thin Red Line* suggests the book was a belated rejoinder to the question Malick had posed decades before, back in Berkeley: Why do philosophy?

Edifying Philosophy

Some of the philosophers in attendance at Malick's 1980 talk were asking themselves the same question at the time. One of them was Richard Rorty. In *Philosophy and the Mirror of Nature* (1979), he famously suggested that academic philosophy was at a crossroads: it could either abandon the narrow, problem-solving mentality it had inherited from Descartes, or it could learn to accept the profession's increasing irrelevance to contemporary life.

Instead of pursuing scientific perfectionism, Rorty recommended his fellow philosophers position themselves as proponents of communication and edification. Unlike many of his colleagues, he thought philosophy had more in common with literature or poetry than science.[26] As he saw it, the aim of philosophical practice was not the attaining of mathematical certainty but rather the fostering of dialogue. He wanted to keep what Michael Oakeshott once called the "conversation of mankind" going, which meant that philosophy had to be open to everybody, not just experts and specialists.[27] Rorty warned of the dangers of science envy and praised the power of the arts: "Edifying philosophers," he wrote, should keep philosophy away from the so-called "secure path of a science" by discussing art and literature.[28] And Rorty practiced what he preached: the years after the publication of *Philosophy and the Mirror of Nature* saw him writing more frequently about fiction—about George Orwell, Vladimir Nabokov, and James Baldwin, for example—than about whatever it was his departmental colleagues were doing down the hall.[29] But in these endeavors to rehumanize philosophical practice, Rorty was not entirely alone. In a book published the same year as *Philosophy and the Mirror of Nature*, Stanley Cavell outlined another path forward for academic philosophy, one that ran parallel to Rorty's. It suggested a similar pivot toward edification, literature, and the arts.

The Claim of Reason: Wittgenstein, Skepticism, Morality, and Tragedy was a Frankenstein of a book.[30] The first sections of it derived from Cavell's doctoral dissertation, "The Claim to Rationality," which had been submitted to Harvard's philosophy department in 1961, seemingly dead on arrival. But as Cavell continued reworking it—all the while teaching and publishing on topics ranging from literature and drama to movies and the writings of Henry David Thoreau—he came to revise his manuscripts extensively, hoping to address the pervasive "*malaise*" he found in contemporary philosophy, "especially among the young who are entering the profession and still deciding whether it can support life."[31] What began as a rather traditional work of academic philosophy exploring, among other things, epistemology, morality, and the thought of Wittgenstein, mutated into a genre-bending, interdisciplinary work that jumped with electrifying and unexpected moments of philosophical daring. In the latter sections of the work, Cavell turned just as often to examples drawn from literature (*Frankenstein*) and drama (*Faust*), from parables (boiling pots) and fairy tales (frog princes), as to any of the proper names commonly associated with Western philosophy.

Injected with all this novel material, Cavell's lifeless thesis became a book that was very much alive. It also became, like Frankenstein's monster, rather strange. In the most inventive part of *The Claim of Reason*—part 4, "Skepticism and the Problem of Others"—Cavell expanded on an idea he floated in the preceding sections, the suggestion that moral life hinged not on "moral argument" but rather on "moral relationship."[32] Unlike orderly logical formulas or rule-governed games, human relationships were messy, complex, and ever changing: they were always and everywhere subject to reinterpretation. Because of this, they did not fit into the tidy schema of analysis and argumentation preferred by most professional philosophers. If we wanted to get a handle on them, we were better off reading literature, because the only sure sign we were on the path to acknowledging somebody else was if we could tell their "story."[33]

Like Rorty, Cavell was suggesting that philosophy had more in common with imaginative literature than calculative science: because "the problem of the other" was, he wrote, "largely undiscovered for philosophy," he felt himself "pushed to pieces of literature" to unearth it.[34] The last section of *The*

Claim of Reason read more like a rambling work of prose poetry than an academic monograph. Its final line was both a confession and a provocation all at once: "But can philosophy become literature and still know itself?"[35]

The book you have in your hands has asked a similar question: But can philosophy become film and still know itself? Terrence Malick's career does not give us a definitive answer, of course, but it offers us plenty of material for a long, hopefully edifying, conversation. Just as Rorty's insouciant questions in *Philosophy and the Mirror of Nature* and Cavell's unique prose in *The Claim of Reason* pushed back the boundaries of academic scholarship, Malick's filmmaking has blurred the lines between professional philosophy and Hollywood movies—so much so that the marriage of film and philosophy might owe a thing or two to him directly.

Malick's privileged position in contemporary film-philosophy scholarship returns us to the beginning of our story, in which I suggested that his departure from academia should be viewed as the start of a cinematic search for some of the very same things he sought as a philosophy student but was unable to find—namely, meaning, purpose, and a sense of his place in the world and the cosmos. In a curious twist of fate, Malick ended up exiting academic philosophy right when his mentors began calling for its reformulation, recommending the turn to literature and art, including film, heralded by the likes of Rorty and Cavell. In other words, Malick began making movies precisely when they were starting to become a subject worthy of philosophical study.

Cavell's *The World Viewed* appeared in 1971, as Malick was embarking on his cinematic career. In the foreword to the second edition of the book, Cavell declared his interest in granting "film the status of a subject that invites and rewards philosophical speculation."[36] One of the films that encouraged Cavell to say this was *Days of Heaven*, which was released just as Cavell was prepping the second edition for publication. Malick may have been disappointed as a philosophy student, but now here he was, making movies that invited "philosophical speculation." With Malick's help, film-philosophy came into being: by the late 1990s, when he returned to directing with *The Thin Red Line*, scholars spoke openly of "the tremendous attraction that films now exert on philosophers."[37] If Malick's first films helped lay the foundations for film-philosophy, then his subsequent ones gave it a blueprint for expansion.

Terrence Malick's filmmaking can and should be viewed as an extended response to the question "Why do philosophy?" It is profitable to think of each of his pictures as another possible answer. This brings the remarkable continuity of his filmmaking into clearer focus. Like Jean Renoir, he is a director who has spent his entire career making—as Jack Fisk once put it—"one big film."[38] This film is an exploration of self and world, of meaning and purpose, of, in short, the examined life. It was a project Malick could not have carried out in academic philosophy, at least not in the way he wanted to. But his career offers us an account of a philosophical journey pursued by other means—a pilgrimage, we might even call it. If Malick's teachers would not set him on the right path, he would find his own way, utilizing the very things his teachers and mentors eventually turned to themselves: poetry, literature, drama, and, of course, the movies. Malick's career demonstrates that he has always been, as Fisk claimed, "a philosopher and an artist."[39]

The Philosophical Condition

Books attempting to show just how much academic philosophy has to learn from the films of Terrence Malick appear regularly these days.[40] Each of them is further proof of his central role in making the movies suitable for philosophical thought. In this regard, Malick's career encapsulates everything the founders of the American Film Institute hoped to achieve in setting up the Center for Advanced Film Studies as a place where filmmakers could learn—as George Stevens Jr. put it—from "philosophers and scientists," as well as Hollywood veterans.[41]

One of those veterans, Gregory Peck, an early champion of AFI, suggested that films "retain the power not only to delight us, but to enlighten us as well."[42] Still, it took a while for this lesson to sink in with philosophers. In a 1982 lecture at the Kennedy Center in Washington, D.C.—a lecture sponsored by the American Film Institute, in fact—Stanley Cavell could still wonder if it was "the nature of American academic philosophy (or of its reputation), together with the nature of American movies (or of their notoriety), that makes someone who writes about both, in the same breath, subject to questions, not to say suspicions."[43] As Cavell feared, it would take a long time for the philosophers to join him at the movies.

But the fact that Malick could be viewed, from day one, as both a philosopher and a moviemaker has helped make the idea of film-philosophy a little less dubious. Scholars are now busy dissecting his films, offering detailed accounts of their contributions to aesthetics, phenomenology, and the philosophy of religion. Some philosophers have even gone so far as to suggest that Malick's cinema offers us an "ontological affirmation," an "acknowledgement" of self and world.[44] The suspicions are falling by the wayside.

There is some evidence to suggest Malick might be falling back into academia's gravitational pull. In recent years, he has shown up at campus film screenings, such as one, at Princeton, of Roberto Rossellini's *Voyage to Italy* (1954). He has taught courses in what we might call humanistic cinema studies. At the European Graduate School in Saas-Fee, Switzerland, he oversaw seminars in which he asked students to read the *Phaedrus* and Epictetus, *The Letters of Vincent Van Gogh* and the Gospel of Mark. He also chose to screen a revealing selection of movies: Akira Kurosawa's *Seven Samurai* (1954), Kenji Mizoguchi's *Ugetsu* (1953), Ermanno Olmi's *Il Posto* (1961), and Federico Fellini's *La Strada* (1954). (Malick chose only one of his own pictures, apparently, *The New World*.) The common thread connecting these various texts and films was, as one of the participants in the discussions recalled, the idea of "redemption." It was the topic to which Malick returned "with the most frequency" in his remarks.[45]

Redemption might be a good way to describe Malick's return to the seminar room. His journey away from Harvard and Oxford and toward Hollywood may have been prompted by a certain perceived narrowness in professional philosophy, but his academic homecoming has been made possible by a growing scholarly interest in film, which his own pictures have fostered. At long last, academic philosophy can talk about movies without risking professional embarrassment: Hugo Münsterberg would be proud.

None of this was preordained. Malick launched himself on a number of very different life trajectories before he ended up in filmmaking. Between graduating from Harvard with a degree in philosophy and matriculating in the inaugural class at the Center for Advanced Film Studies, he tried his hand at research, journalism, and teaching. None of these panned out: he undertook postgraduate study at Oxford, only to depart before completing his thesis; he labored on a long piece about Che Guevara and Régis Debray for the *New Yorker*, which never made it into print; and his stint as an instructor did nothing to dissuade him from the belief that he was "not a good teacher," that he "didn't have the sort of edge one should have on the students."[46]

Without the benefit of historical hindsight, life as it is lived is endlessly open-ended. Kierkegaard famously said that one's life could only be "understood backwards," but it had to be "lived forwards."[47] Even after finding recognition as a screenwriter and a director, nothing guaranteed that Malick would stick around Hollywood. What had begun as "a suicidal little adventure" showed no significant signs of coalescing into a stable career, especially after some of his most influential patrons, such as Charles Bluhdorn, exited the scene.[48] To his friends and coworkers in the 1970s, Malick seemed perpetually conflicted about his own success, unsure if it should be taken as a sign to press ahead or to get out while he still could. It was during this time that he drew up plans for grand, elaborate projects, yet also talked about disappearing to Tibet. It was during this time that he played basketball with Fidel Castro in Havana and appeared on a Carly Simon album cover, yet started to shy away from publicity.[49]

One thing remained constant in Malick's life, though: his openness to wonder. "Wondering" is, Socrates reminds us in Plato's *Theaetetus*, "the philosophical condition." "Philosophy has no other source than this."[50] The more common formulation of the idea puts it plainly: "philosophy begins in wonder." The notion finds its way into most books about philosophy aimed at popular audiences (Dreyfus and Kelly use it as an epigraph for one of their chapters in *All Things Shining*).[51] But the commonness of the phrase should not desensitize us to its power, for it suggests not just that wonder is a useful starting point for thought but also, and perhaps more importantly, that a philosopher who does not wonder is in fact no philosopher at all.[52]

Each of Malick's films originates in wonder. Whether they address historical topics or contemporary ones, whether their perspectives are vastly cosmological or intensely autobiographical, Malick's movies depict a searching that is unique in cinematic history. *Badlands* has a protagonist who contemplates how different her life would have been if she had been born elsewhere, at a different time, to different parents. She even wonders why she had been born at all. *Days of Heaven* contemplates the astonishing worldhood of the world, a topic further explored in *The Thin Red Line* and *The New World*. What I have called Malick's confessional films—*The Tree of Life, To the Wonder,* and *Knight of Cups*—revolve around personal pilgrimages. They explore the mysterious workings of fate, mercy, and redemption in our lives. And whether they have been about the universe (*Voyage of Time*) or indie musicians (*Song to Song*), conscientious objectors (*A Hidden Life*) or Jesus Christ (*The Way of the Wind*), Malick's most recent films have contemplated ethics, faith, and what Wittgenstein called, in his lecture to the Heretics, the "miracle" of the world.

Wonder makes all of it possible. After watching a Malick film, one's vision is altered, transformed. You might find yourself looking up at the sky differently, or noticing, as if for the first time, the way sunlight filters through leafy trees. Everything seems like a revelation, a miracle even, but nothing has changed, except your level of attention. It is not *"another* world" Malick shows us, but rather, as the philosopher of religion Mark Johnston might put it, "this world properly received."[53]

Life Examined

In recent years, a number of philosophers working in the United States have penned books meant to be, like Dreyfus and Kelly's *All Things Shining*, accessible. Aimed at a general readership, these works offer something other than arguments or proofs. They show how readers might escape the clutches of nihilism by offering advice on coping with a predictable midlife crisis or an unexpected divorce.[54] They provide counsel on living "the good life."[55] These books often swerve into self-help, a genre Walker Percy lampooned long ago in *Lost in the Cosmos*.[56] But for every facile popularization of difficult concepts there is also a serious work of honest (self-)reflection, which is why we should look closely at Malick's films, even though they, too, have been accused of offering audiences pseudo-profundity on more than one occasion.[57]

Malick's films demonstrate how philosophy might become a popular pursuit once again. If it was wonder that led him to study philosophy and, later on, to abandon academia for filmmaking, then perhaps a similar kind wonder will lead more people to reconsider his work and, by extension, to rediscover philosophy. As a contribution to this reconsideration and rediscovery, I hope this book has shown just how expansive and ecumenical Malick's vision is. There is no one idea, no single intellectual tradition, thinker, or text, responsible for generating films as different from each other as *Badlands* and *The Tree of Life*, *The Thin Red Line* and *Knight of Cups*. Malick has found exemplars of meaning-making everywhere: not just in philosophy, but also in painting, poetry, history, drama, even, on occasion, in children's literature.

Looking for hidden keys does not make for good philosophy anyhow. It shuts down conversations we would be better off opening up. Film-philosophy is best pursued in a spirit openness and curiosity. Malick's movies show us how philosophy can be something other than, something more than, a discipline: it can be a conversation, a journey, a lifelong pursuit. Philosophy can keep asking questions, keep making meaning, not because philosophers expect to solve anything, but because they, like moviegoers, can be amazed—

or frustrated, or offended, or inspired, or enraptured—by everything. Malick's films liberate philosophical reflection from the shackles of the problem-solving mentality.[58] They make us wonder.

What inspires wonder is different for every culture, for every generation, and, indeed, for every person. Much of what defines us—our language and tastes, for example—is inherited rather than chosen.[59] So it makes sense to speak of traditions, if only as conditions of possibility. In this book, I have attempted to keep my distance from debates about what has, can, or should qualify as the tradition of "American cinema," even though so many of Malick's works investigate defining moments of the American experience, from the founding of Jamestown in *The New World* to the emergence of an indus-trialized, (sub)urbanized, globally powerful nation in *Days of Heaven*, *Bad-lands*, and *The Thin Red Line*, not to mention the even more contemporary *The Tree of Life*, *To the Wonder*, *Knight of Cups*, and *Song to Song*.

Whatever "American cinema" is, Malick's films are certainly part and parcel of it.[60] But a proper genealogical analysis of the ideas and influences animating them takes us well beyond the confines of national borders. Con-sulting the archives allows us to see just how intellectually ambitious and wide-ranging Malick's filmmaking has been. To understand it we must ac-knowledge the influence of Orson Welles and Arthur Penn, but also that of Jean Renoir, Kenji Mizoguchi, and Andrei Tarkovsky; the legacy of Emerson and Thoreau, but also that of Heidegger, Kierkegaard, and Wittgenstein; the imprint of Austin and Los Angeles, but also that of Oxford, Paris, and An-napurna.

If nothing else, Malick's cinema shows us how the American intellectual tradition became, in the second half of the twentieth century, not just more diverse but also more globalized.[61] His films depict quintessentially Ameri-can stereotypes—the gun-toting outlaw, the grizzled GI, the native princess, the Hollywood player—but the inspirations behind them come from every-where: from the slapstick silent films of Harold Lloyd, but also the carni-valesque experimentation of Federico Fellini; from the rebellious iconoclasm of Nicholas Ray, but also the religious searching of Robert Bresson; from Walker Percy and Peter Matthiessen, but also Plato, Augustine, and Stanley Cavell.

Behind all of these figures—yes, behind even Harold Lloyd—is Socrates.[62] In Socrates's famous claim that the unexamined life "is not worth living," one finds the origin of the wondering philosopher, for whom intellectual search-ing is a way of life, not merely a job.[63] As Heidegger once explained to his student Karl Löwith, his work was motivated by a "radical concern for self," one that did not always jibe with "university philosophy."[64] But still, no matter how much he played the role of the renegade philosopher, showing up to lectures in his hiking outfits, Heidegger was very much a university philosopher, the kind of philosopher Terrence Malick is not. Malick's films do not pass themselves off—like Heidegger's writings sometimes do—as the final word. They are not existential orations, but rather invitations to an ongoing conversation, one in which director and viewer are equals, wayfarers in pursuit of shared meaning. As a prefatory note to Malick's script for *The Tree of Life* puts it: "The 'I' who speaks in this story is not the author. Rather, he hopes that you might see yourself in this 'I' and understand this story as your own."[65]

The exhortation copies—almost verbatim—the prefatory remarks of a literary-philosophical work every bit as daring as *The Tree of Life* but created over two hundred years before it. Johann Gottlieb Fichte's *The Vocation of Man* (1800) also sought to transform technical philosophy into something approaching a way of life. In the preface to his hybrid work of philosophy, theodicy, and stirring prose, Fichte told his "readers that the 'I' who speaks in the book is by no means the author. Rather, the author wishes that the reader may come to see himself in this 'I'." Fichte's ideal reader would, he hoped, "converse with himself, deliberate back and forth, deduce conclusions, make decisions," and, "through his own work and reflection, purely out of his own resources, develop and build within himself the philosophical disposition that is presented to him in this book merely as a picture."[66] It is not enough to see the picture: you also have to make it your own.

Although we often watch movies in crowds, with friends and family, with lovers or loose acquaintances, neighbors or total strangers, moviegoing is a fundamentally personal experience. "When you go to the movies," David Thomson has suggested, "you take your history with you. The fantasy is about *you*."[67] Few other art forms have the ability to immerse us in such a self-reflective state as does the cinema, with its total demand of our senses, its beguiling amalgamation of darkness and light, fantasy and reality. Moviegoing is, each and every time, *my* experience, which is precisely why arguing about movies is so much fun, because many of us can view the very same film, yet have vastly different experiences of it. It is in talking about movies that we make them meaningful.

This book aims to keep the conversation going. It is a record of *my* journey, which began with a single paragraph in my previous book.[68] When I discovered, quite by accident, that the Terrence Malick who had translated

Heidegger's *The Essence of Reasons* was the same Terrence Malick who directed movies, I started to think differently about *The Thin Red Line*, a film my dad and I had seen years before at the local theater. I also started reevaluating the arc of recent American intellectual history—not just as an academic, but also as a person, as a moviegoer who grew up at the multiplex. I guess you could say that I began to wonder. I wonder still, but it is my hope that this wonder might somehow become yours, too.

* * *

For as long as philosophy was associated with the question of how to live, it began with and returned to personal experience. But when philosophy became a professionalized endeavor, carried out by degree-holding experts, subjective, autobiographical reflections fell out of favor. Calculative rationality, rigorous logic, and semantic precision took prominence. Philosophers who did not play by these rules, thinkers who did not publish books and articles instantly recognizable as approved scholarship, were pushed to the margins of the profession, if they were not run out of it altogether.

William James may have helped lay the foundations of the Harvard philosophy department, but he never obtained a PhD. In fact, he was quite critical of the "abstract rigmarole" that so often defined academic discussions.[69] By the middle of the twentieth century, it was all but impossible for a philosopher like him to teach at Harvard. The philosopher Henry Bugbee learned this the hard way. But the return of Malick's work to the contemporary academy suggests the reign of rigmarole may be coming to an end and film-philosophy, a field that did not even exist when he was a student, is here to stay.

NOTES

Preface

1. Letter to author, July 17, 1985.

2. Terrence Malick, "Badlands," first draft, November 1971, 2. Margaret Herrick Library, Academy of Motion Picture Arts and Sciences.

3. Dennis McLellan, "Gary Franklin, 79; Popular Film Critic on Local TV Created 1-to-10 Rating Scale," *Los Angeles Times*, October 4, 2007.

4. Plato, *Apology*, in *The Last Days of Socrates*, trans. Hugh Tredennick and Harold Tarrant, with an introduction and notes by Harold Tarrant (New York: Penguin Classics, 1993), 63.

5. See, for example, Carlin Romano, "Afterthoughts on *America the Philosophical*," *Transactions of the Charles S. Peirce Society* 52, no. 3 (Summer 2016): 375.

6. See "Symposium on Intellectual History in the Age of Cultural Studies," *Intellectual History Newsletter* 18 (1996): 3–69.

Introduction

1. "American Film Institute Seminar with Terry Malick," April 11, 1974, 53. Transcript at the Louis B. Mayer Library, American Film Institute, Los Angeles.

2. Only with the release of *Song to Song* has Malick participated directly in the promotion or discussion of one of his films, ending a silence that stretches back some forty years. See Chris O'Fait, "Terrence Malick Makes a Rare Appearance at SXSW 2017 and Digs Deep on His Process," *IndieWire*, March 11, 2017, http://www.indiewire.com/2017/03/song-to-song-terrence-malick -richard-linklater-michael-fassbender-sxsw-2017-1201792562/.

3. See, for example, Lloyd Michaels, *Terrence Malick* (Urbana: University of Illinois Press, 2009); James Morrison and Thomas Schur, *The Films of Terrence Malick* (Westport, CT: Praeger, 2003); Paul Maher Jr., *One Big Soul: An Oral History of Terrence Malick* (n.p., 2012); Steven Rybin, *Terrence Malick and the Thought of Film* (Lanham, MD: Lexington Books, 2012); and Robert Sinnerbrink, *Terrence Malick: Filmmaker and Philosopher* (London: Bloomsbury, 2019). Useful collections of essays devoted to Malick include Hannah Patterson, ed., *The Cinema of Terrence Malick: Poetic Visions of America*, 2nd ed. (London: Wallflower Press, 2007); Thomas Deane Tucker and Stuart Kendall, eds., *Terrence Malick: Film and Philosophy* (New York: Bloomsbury, 2013); and Carlo Hintermann and Daniele Villa, eds., *Terrence Malick: Rehearsing the Unexpected* (London: Faber & Faber, 2015).

4. A. O. Scott, "Fugue for History and Memory," *New York Times*, December 30, 2011.

5. Rev. Jim Tucker, quoted in David Handelman, "Absence of Malick," *California*, November 1985, 129. For more on Malick's time at St. Stephen's, see Eric Benson, "The Not-So-Secret Life of Terrence Malick," *Texas Monthly*, April 2017, http://www.texasmonthly.com/the-culture /the-not-so-secret-life-of-terrence-malick/.

6. Hans Reichenbach, *The Rise of Scientific Philosophy* (Berkeley: University of California Press, 1951).

7. James Miller, *Examined Lives: From Socrates to Nietzsche* (New York: Farrar, Straus and Giroux, 2011), 13.

8. This oft-cited remark comes from W. V. Quine, "Mr. Strawson on Logical Theory," *Mind* 62, no. 248 (1953): 446; reprinted in *Ways of Paradox and Other Essays* (New York: Random House, 1966), 151.

9. Jennifer Ratner-Rosenhagen, *The Ideas That Made America: A Brief History* (Oxford: Oxford University Press, 2019), 176.

10. Jennifer Ratner-Rosenhagen, "The Longing for Wisdom in Twentieth-Century US Thought," in *The Worlds of American Intellectual History*, ed. Joel Isaac et al. (Oxford: Oxford University Press, 2017), 191.

11. A letter from Hubert Dreyfus to Richard Rorty, February 22, 1980, describes Malick's participation in the event, saying he "wants to talk on what Heidegger means by Being." Richard Rorty Papers, University of California, Irvine, Special Collections, Box 22, Folder 2.

12. Council for Philosophical Studies, *Phenomenology and Existentialism: Continental and Analytical Perspectives on Intentionality in the Philosophy Curriculum* (San Francisco: San Francisco State University, Council for Philosophical Studies, 1981), 4. I thank Eduardo Mendieta for providing me with his copy of this document.

13. Robert Bresson, *Notes on the Cinematograph*, trans. Jonathan Griffin, introduction by J. M. G. Le Clézio (New York: New York Review Books, 1986), 66.

14. Walker Percy, *The Moviegoer* (1961; New York: Vintage, 1998).

15. Percy, *The Moviegoer*, 13.

16. Percy, *The Moviegoer*, 42.

17. David Thomson, *The Big Screen: The Story of the Movies* (New York: Farrar, Straus and Giroux, 2012), 507.

18. On the idea of philosophy by other means, see Robert B. Pippin, *Philosophy by Other Means: The Arts in Philosophy and Philosophy in the Arts* (Chicago: University of Chicago Press, 2021).

19. Amy Kittelstrom, "Philosophy vs. Philosophers: A Problem in American Intellectual History," in *American Labyrinth: Intellectual History in Complicated Times*, ed. Raymond Haberski Jr. and Andrew Hartman (Ithaca, NY: Cornell University Press, 2018), 61; and Ratner-Rosenhagen, "Longing for Wisdom," 197.

20. On the question of contextualism, see Daniel Wickberg, "The Idea of Historical Context and the Intellectual Historian," in Haberski and Hartman, *American Labyrinth*, 321.

21. John E. O'Connor and Martin A. Jackson, eds., *American History/American Film: Interpreting the Hollywood Image*, foreword by Arthur Schlesinger Jr. (New York: Frederick Ungar, 1979), x.

22. Daniel Yacavone, *Film Worlds: A Philosophical Aesthetics of Cinema* (New York: Columbia University Press, 2015).

23. See Warren I. Susman, "Film and History: Artifact and Experience," *Film & History: An Interdisciplinary Journal of Film and Television Studies* 15, no. 2 (1985): 26–36. For more on Susman, see Paul V. Murphy, "The Last Progressive Historian: Warren Susman and American Cultural History," *Modern Intellectual History* 14, no. 3 (2017): 807–35.

24. Harvard degrees were awarded to Radcliffe graduates for the first time in 1963, though women were not granted access to Harvard's libraries until four years later, in 1967. See Linda Greenhouse, "How Smart Women Got the Chance," *New York Review of Books*, April 6, 2017, 21.

25. Hintermann and Villa, *Terrence Malick*, 1.

26. Stanley Cavell, *Little Did I Know: Excerpts from Memory* (Stanford, CA: Stanford University Press, 2010), 182, 218.

27. Cavell's longtime friend and colleague Alexander Sesonske called *The World Viewed* "profound and insightful, but also dense and difficult." See Sesonske, "*The World Viewed*," *The Georgia Review* 28, no. 4 (Winter 1974): 561–70, quote on 561.

28. Münsterberg's work has been reprinted in *Hugo Münsterberg on Film: "The Photoplay: A Psychological Study" and Other Writings*, ed. Allan Langdale (New York: Routledge, 2002). For more on early film criticism and philosophy during this period, see Laura Marcus, *The Tenth Muse: Writing About Cinema in the Modernist Period* (Oxford: Oxford University Press, 2007).

29. Münsterberg, "Why We Go to the Movies," in *Hugo Münsterberg on Film*, 172.

30. *Hugo Münsterberg on Film*, 178.

31. *Hugo Münsterberg on Film*, 181.

32. Cavell, *Little Did I Know*, 424.

33. See Robert B. Ray, "Cavell, Thoreau, and the Movies," in *Stanley Cavell, Literature, and Film: The Idea of America*, ed. Andrew Taylor and Áine Kelly (New York: Routledge, 2013), 170.

34. See William Rothman, *The "I" of the Camera: Essays in Film Criticism, History, and Aesthetics*, 2nd ed. (Cambridge: Cambridge University Press, 2004); and Robert B. Ray, *A Certain Tendency of the Hollywood Cinema, 1930–1980* (Princeton, NJ: Princeton University Press, 1985).

35. Carly Simon, *Boys in the Trees: A Memoir* (New York: Flatiron Books, 2015), 179–80.

36. Simon, *Boys in the Trees*, 177. Years later, Malick appeared—with western shirt, cowboy hat, and obligatory cigar—on the back cover of Simon's 1976 album *Another Passenger*.

37. On Brackman and Malick, see Hintermann and Villa, *Terrence Malick*, 6.

38. George Stevens Jr., *My Place in the Sun: Life in the Golden Age of Hollywood and Washington* (Lexington: University Press of Kentucky, 2022), 268.

39. Hintermann and Villa, *Terrence Malick*, 6–7. My colleague Andrzej Krakowski, who studied with Malick at AFI, has told me that Malick knew a great deal about Polish cinema and was a fan of the work Andrzej Wajda in particular.

40. Simon, *Boys in the Trees*, 177.

41. Bruce Kuklick, *The Rise of American Philosophy: Cambridge, Massachusetts, 1860–1930* (New Haven, CT: Yale University Press, 1977).

42. Joel Isaac, "W. V. Quine and the Origins of Analytic Philosophy in the United States," *Modern Intellectual History* 2, no. 2 (2005): 205–34. See also Isaac, "The Rise of Analytic Philosophy," in *The Cambridge History of Modern European Thought*, ed. Warren Breckman and Peter Gordon (Cambridge: Cambridge University Press, 2019), 176–99.

43. See W. V. Quine, "Two Dogmas of Empiricism," *Philosophical Review* 60, no. 1 (1951): 20–43. The essay was collected in Quine's *From a Logical Point of View* (Cambridge, MA: Harvard University Press, 1953), 20–46. Accounting for the institutional success of analytic philosophy in the United States is a notoriously difficult task, but most commentators have stressed the context of the Cold War. See Bruce Kuklick, *A History of Philosophy in America, 1720–2000* (Oxford: Clarendon Press, 2001), 247. See also George Reisch, *How the Cold War Transformed Philosophy of Science: To the Icy Slopes of Logic* (Cambridge: Cambridge University Press, 2005); as well as John McCumber, *Time in the Ditch: American Philosophy and the McCarthy Era* (Evanston, IL: Northwestern University Press, 2001); and, more recently, McCumber, *The Philosophy Scare: The Politics of Reason in the Early Cold War* (Chicago: University of Chicago Press, 2016). For a much better account, see Jonathan Strassfeld, *Inventing Philosophy's Other: Phenomenology in America* (Chicago: University of Chicago Press, 2022).

44. Letter from Roderick Firth to Sargent Kennedy, March 1, 1961, Harvard University Archives, UAV 687.15, Box 5.

45. See Bilge Ebiri, "Quail Hunting Down Rabbit Holes: How Terrence Malick Blended Improv, Dance, and History to Create the Expansive *A Hidden Life*," *Vulture*, January 23, 2020, https://www.vulture.com/2020/01/behind-the-scenes-of-terrence-malicks-a-hidden-life.html.

46. On Heidegger and continental philosophy, see Edward Baring, *Converts to the Real: Catholicism and the Making of Continental Philosophy* (Cambridge, MA: Harvard University Press, 2019).

47. Martin Heidegger, *Being and Time*, trans. John Macquarrie and Edward Robinson (New York: Harper & Row, 1962).

48. Cavell, *Little Did I Know*, 426.

49. Terrence Frederick Malick, "The Concept of Horizon in Husserl and Heidegger" (honors thesis, Harvard University, 1966).

50. Dreyfus knew a thing or two about film, too. His lecture notes for a 1977 lecture course on Heidegger's existential phenomenology contain insightful references to the films of Michelangelo Antonioni as examples of Heidegger's notion of anxiety. Copies are in the Richard Rorty Papers, University of California, Irvine, Special Collections, Box 43, Folder 7.

51. See Hubert L. Dreyfus, "Standing Up to Analytic Philosophy and Artificial Intelligence at MIT in the Sixties," *Proceedings and Addresses of the American Philosophical Association* 87 (2013): 89. Malick was one of the people Dreyfus thanked in his most widely known work, *What Computers Still Can't Do: A Critique of Artificial Reason* (1972; Cambridge, MA: MIT Press, 1992), liii.

52. On Malick's time in Oxford, see David Davies, ed., *The Thin Red Line* (New York: Routledge, 2009), xi. See also, in the same volume, Simon Critchley, "Calm—On Terrence Malick's *The Thin Red Line*," 16–17.

53. Martin Heidegger, *The Essence of Reasons*, trans. Terrence Malick (Evanston, IL: Northwestern University Press, 1969); a bilingual edition, incorporating the German text of *Vom Wesen des Grundes*.

54. I am guilty of this myself. See my "What Is Heideggerian Cinema? Film, Philosophy, and Cultural Mobility," *New German Critique* 113, vol. 38, no. 2 (Summer 2011): 129–57. On the growing tendency to interpret Malick's work through an explicitly Heideggerian lens, see John Rhym, "The Paradigmatic Shift in the Critical Reception of Terrence Malick's *Badlands* and the Emergence of a Heideggerian Cinema," *Quarterly Review of Film and Video* 27 (2010): 255–66.

55. For more on Følesdall and phenomenology at Harvard, see Strassfeld, *Inventing Philosophy's Other*.

56. Over thirty years later, I encountered Heidegger in a similar fashion. See my "Fail Slow, Fail Hard," *Los Angeles Review of Books*, August 28, 2015. See also Martin Woessner, *Heidegger in America* (Cambridge: Cambridge University Press, 2011).

57. Harvard University Archives, HUC 8570.3.1, Box 2 (1961–62).

58. See Ludwig Wittgenstein, "A Lecture on Ethics," *Philosophical Review* 74, no. 1 (1965): 3–12. The essay has recently been republished in an expanded edition as *Lecture on Ethics*, ed. Edoardo Zamuner, Ermelinda Valentina Di Lascio, and D. K. Levy (West Sussex: Wiley Blackwell, 2014), quotes on 51, 47.

59. See Hintermann and Villa, *Terrence Malick*, 1. For more on Tillich and the reception of Heidegger on this side of the Atlantic, see Woessner, *Heidegger in America*, 99–112.

60. See Hubert L. Dreyfus, "Christianity Without Onto-Theology: Kierkegaard's Account of the Self's Movement from Despair to Bliss," in *Religion After Metaphysics*, ed. Mark A. Wrathall (Cambridge: Cambridge University Press, 2010), 88–103.

61. Søren Kierkegaard, *The Sickness unto Death*, trans. Alastair Hannay (New York: Penguin, 2004), 130.

62. Rothman, *The "I" of the Camera*, xiii.

63. Council for Philosophical Studies, *Phenomenology and Existentialism*, 4.

64. Beverly Walker, "Malick on *Badlands*," *Sight and Sound* 44, no. 2 (Spring 1975): 82–83; reprinted in Lloyd Michaels, *Terrence Malick*, 102.

65. In defense of fuzziness, see Richard Rorty, "Science as Solidarity," in *Objectivity, Relativism, and Truth: Philosophical Papers, Volume 1* (Cambridge: Cambridge University Press, 1991), 35–45.

66. Henry Bugbee, *The Inward Morning: A Philosophical Exploration in Journal Form*, introduction by Edward F. Mooney (1958; Athens: University of Georgia Press, 1999), 11. For more on Bugbee's career, see David W. Rodick, "Finding One's Own Voice: The Philosophical Development of Henry G. Bugbee, Jr.," *The Pluralist* 6, no. 2 (Summer 2011): 18–34; and Edward F. Mooney, ed., *Wilderness and the Heart: Henry Bugbee's Philosophy of Place, Presence, and Memory*, foreword by Alasdair MacIntyre (Athens: University of Georgia Press, 1999).

67. Robert M. Pirsig, *Zen and the Art of Motorcycle Maintenance* (New York: William Morrow, 1974). See also Jennifer Ratner-Rosenhagen, "Zen and the Art of a Higher Education," *Los Angeles Review of Books*, July 15, 2018.

68. As David Sterritt has put it, Malick's "opting for the movies didn't mean forgetting his scholarly pursuits." See Sterritt, "Film, Philosophy, and Terrence Malick's 'The New World,'" *Chronicle of Higher Education*, January 6, 2006.

69. Henry David Thoreau, *Walden*, introduction by Edward Hoagland (New York: Library of America, 2010), 14.

70. Stanley Cavell, "The Philosopher in American Life (Toward Thoreau and Emerson)," collected in *Emerson's Transcendental Etudes*, ed. David Justin Hodge (Stanford, CA: Stanford University Press, 2003), 40.

71. John Gregory Dunne, *The Studio* (1968; New York: Vintage, 1998), 23.

72. Mark Harris, *Pictures at a Revolution: Five Movies and the Birth of the New Hollywood* (New York: Penguin, 2008).

73. Michael Wood, *America in the Movies; or, "Santa Maria, It Had Slipped My Mind"* (1975; New York: Columbia University Press, 1989), 195.

74. As Lee Grieveson has shown, American cinema had been a beneficiary of state support since at least the 1920s. See Grieveson, *Cinema and the Wealth of Nations: Media, Capital, and the Liberal World System* (Oakland: University of California Press, 2018).

75. Ted Johnson, "AFI Marks a Momentous Milestone—and Gives D.C. a Political Respite," *Variety*, November 3, 2017, http://variety.com/2017/politics/news/afi-50th-anniversary-morgan-freeman-library-of-congress-1202606251/. See also Jean Picker Firstenberg and James Hindman, *Becoming AFI: 50 Years Inside the American Film Institute*, foreword by Dana Gioia, preface by Patty Jenkins, afterword by David Lynch (Solana Beach, CA: Santa Monica Press, 2017), 120–24.

76. Stanford Research Institute, "Organization and Location of the American Film Institute," February 1967, 7, National Endowment for the Arts Records (MS 686), Special Collections and University Archives, University of Massachusetts Amherst Libraries.

77. George Stevens Jr., "Memorandum on the American Film Institute Center for Advanced Film Studies," no date, Louis B. Mayer Library, AFI. As if anticipating the ways in which this remark might be misconstrued (in the ways I am suggesting), a handwritten note beside these lines reads: "This should be cast in <u>positive</u> terms, I think. Will all who read this understand the context of reference to Soviet Institute? Could be mistaken for Cold War implication."

78. *Report of the Commission on the Humanities* (1964), 2–3; cited in Michael Meranze, "Humanities Out of Joint," *American Historical Review* 120, no. 4 (October 2015): 1311–26, quote on 1317. See also Andrew Jewett, *Science, Democracy, and the American University: From the Civil War to the Cold War* (New York: Cambridge University Press, 2012).

79. For more on the origins of AFI, see Deborah Jae Alexander, "A History of the American Film Institute" (PhD diss., University of Southern Mississippi, 2010).

80. Noël Carroll, "The Future of Allusion: Hollywood in the Seventies (and Beyond)," in *Interpreting the Moving Image* (Cambridge: Cambridge University Press, 1998), 258. The essay originally appeared in *October* 2 (Spring 1982): 51–81.

81. Mike Medavoy, with Josh Young, *You're Only as Good as Your Next One: 100 Great Films, 100 Good Films, and 100 for Which I Should Be Shot* (New York: Pocket Books, 2002), 5, 315.

82. Jeff Menne, *Post-Fordist Cinema: Hollywood Auteurs and the Corporate Counterculture* (New York: Columbia University Press, 2019); see esp. chap. 2, "The Cinema of Defection: The Corporate Counterculture and Robert Altman's Lion's Gate," 75–124.

83. George Toles, *A House Made of Light: Essays on the Art of Film* (Detroit: Wayne State University Press, 2001), 17.

84. M. Gail Hamner, *Imagining Religion in Film: The Politics of Nostalgia* (New York: Palgrave Macmillan, 2011), 144.

85. Paul Schrader, *Transcendental Style in Film: Ozu, Bresson, Dreyer*, rev. ed., with new introduction (1972; Oakland: University of California Press, 2018), 42. Recently, Isolde Vanhee has argued that Malick's cinema echoes Ozu's interest in attempting "to redefine the transcendent in secular life." See Vanhee, "Too Slow to Handle? Ozu, Malick, and the Art-House Family Drama," in *Ozu International: Essays on the Global Influences of a Japanese Auteur*, ed. Wayne Stein and Marc DiPaolo (New York: Bloomsbury, 2015), 93–114, quote on 108.

86. Schrader, *Transcendental Style in Film*, 32.

87. Schrader, *Transcendental Style in Film*, 23. On the question of whether transcendental style is inherently spiritual, Schrader says the following in his new introduction: "In theory, no. In practice, more often than not" (22).

88. I thank Andrzej Krakowski for alerting me to the strong European influence on early AFI curriculum and pedagogy.

89. AFI Fellows' Meeting, March 20, 1970, audio recording in the collection of the Louis B. Mayer Library, AFI.

90. On the politics of labor in the Hollywood studio system, see Ronny Regev, *Working in Hollywood: How the Studio System Turned Creativity into Labor* (Chapel Hill: University of North Carolina Press, 2018).

91. Stanford Research Institute, "Organization and Location of the American Film Institute," 23; see also p. 58: film "has not readily been accorded the status of an accepted academic subject nor treated as a recognized art form."

92. Robert Kolker, *A Cinema of Loneliness*, 4th ed. (Oxford: Oxford University Press, 2011).

93. Mark Cousins, "Praising *The New World*," in Patterson, *The Cinema of Terrence Malick*, 196.

94. For more on the philosophical turn toward film in the 1970s, see Thomas Wartenberg, *Thinking on Screen: Film as Philosophy* (New York: Routledge, 2007).

95. The lecture course has been published as Stanley Cavell, *Cities of Words: Pedagogical Letters on a Register of Moral Life* (Cambridge, MA: Belknap Press of Harvard University Press, 2004).

96. Cavell, *Cities of Words*, 3.

97. Walker Percy, "The Movie Magazine: A Low 'Slick,'" in *Signposts in a Strange Land*, ed. Patrick Samway (New York: Farrar, Straus and Giroux, 1991), 240.

98. Raymond J. Haberski Jr., *It's Only a Movie: Films and Critics in American Culture* (Lexington: University Press of Kentucky, 2001), 173. For a fuller account of the evolution of film studies, see Dana Polan, *Scenes of Instruction: The Beginnings of the U.S. Study of Film* (Berkeley: University of California Press, 2007).

99. Quoted in Jonathan Kirshner, *Hollywood's Last Golden Age: Politics, Society, and the Seventies Film in America* (Ithaca, NY: Cornell University Press, 2012), 27.

100. Thomson, *The Big Screen*, 352–53.

101. See David C. Stewart, *Film Study in Higher Education* (Washington, DC: American Council on Education, 1966).

102. Robert Evans, *The Kid Stays in the Picture* (1994; New York: HarperCollins, 2013), 301.

103. "American Film Institute: Preliminary Program Announcement," p. 2, Box 115, Folder 26, Louis B. Mayer Library, AFI.

104. See, for example, *Siegfried Kracauer's American Writings: Essays on Film and Popular Culture*, ed. Johannes von Moltke and Kristy Rawson, with an afterword by Martin Jay (Berkeley: University of California Press, 2012); Kracauer, *Theory of Film: The Redemption of Physical Reality*, with an introduction by Miriam Bratu Hansen (1960; Princeton, NJ: Princeton University Press, 1997); and Kracauer, *From Caligari to Hitler: A Psychological History of the German Film* (Princeton, NJ: Princeton University Press, 1947). For Warshow, see *The Immediate Experience: Movies, Comics, Theatre, and Other Aspects of Popular Culture*, enl. ed., introduction by Lionel Trilling, epilogue by Stanley Cavell (Cambridge, MA: Harvard University Press, 2002). For Agee, see *Film Writing and Selected Journalism*, ed. Michael Sragow (New York: Library of America, 2005).

105. Norman Malcolm, *Ludwig Wittgenstein: A Memoir*, 2nd ed., with a biographical sketch by G. H. von Wright and Wittgenstein's letters to Malcolm (Oxford: Clarendon Press, 2001), 26.

106. Stanley Cavell, "Film in the University," in *Pursuits of Happiness: The Hollywood Comedy of Remarriage* (Cambridge, MA: Harvard University Press, 1981), 266.

107. Paul W. Kahn, *Finding Ourselves at the Movies: Philosophy for a New Generation* (New York: Columbia University Press, 2013).

108. See Cavell, *Pursuits of Happiness*, 275–76.

109. Cavell, *Little Did I Know*, 423.

110. Stanley Cavell, *The World Viewed: Reflections on the Ontology of Film*, enl. ed. (1971; Cambridge, MA: Harvard University Press, 1979), xvi.

111. Conservatory Fellows Handbook, AFI Center for Advanced Film Studies, 1971–72, p. 1, Box 108, Folder 18, Louis B. Mayer Library, AFI.

112. Conservatory Fellows Handbook, AFI Center for Advanced Film Studies, 1971–72, p. 1.

113. A reference with two relevant meanings: the summer palace described in Coleridge's "Kubla Khan" as well as the mansion in Orson Welles's *Citizen Kane*. Compare Stevens's opening remarks for the second year of the Center for Advanced Film Studies, September 25, 1970, audio file at the Louis B. Mayer Library, AFI.

114. Conservatory Fellows Handbook, AFI Center for Advanced Film Studies, 1971–72, p. 1.

115. See Stevens, *My Place in the Sun*, 271.

116. In *Transcendental Style in Film*, Paul Schrader thanks "the American Film Institute for screening films at my request." The SRI report about the creation of the Center for Advanced Film Studies highlighted the importance of providing "a film library system permitting easy access to, and viewing of, films at the discretion of individual trainees or staff members." See Stanford Research Institute, "Organization and Location of the American Film Institute," 18.

117. Scott Huver, "The AFI Conservatory's Now Accomplished Class of 1969 Recalls Its Inaugural Year on the 50th Anniversary," *Hollywood Reporter*, September 20, 2019, https://www.hollywoodreporter.com/news/afi-conservatory-s-now-accomplished-class-1969-recalls-inaugural-year-50th-anniversary-1241595.

118. Conservatory Fellows Handbook, AFI Center for Advanced Film Studies, 1971–72, p. 10.

119. From the Stanford Research Institute report, "Organization and Location of the American Film Institute," 106: "The advanced Study Center, whose functions would involve the skills, facilities, and other resources found in the theatrical motion picture industry should be located in Southern California where that production industry is centered."

120. Quoted in Stevens, *My Place in the Sun*, 269.

121. George Stevens Jr., *Conversations at the American Film Institute with the Great Moviemakers: The Next Generation, from the 1950s to Hollywood Today* (New York: Vintage, 2014), xiv. See also Firstenberg and Hindman, *Becoming AFI*, 34.

122. Firstenberg and Hindman, *Becoming AFI*, 70.

123. "American Film Institute Seminar with Terry Malick," April 11, 1974, 54.

124. "*Taxi Driver's* Paul Schrader, Interviewed by Richard Thompson," *Film Comment*, March–April 1976, 8. As Deborah Jae Alexander points out in "A History of the American Film

Institute," this claim that AFI was too cozy with the "Hollywood commercial film industry" was widespread at the time, finding support among prominent film critics such as Pauline Kael, Schrader's mentor (155). At least in retrospect, the executives at AFI conceded the point. Jean Picker Firstenberg, who oversaw its move from Greystone to its current location, the former campus of Immaculate Heart College six miles east, has pointed out that AFI had its beginnings in "LBJ's Great Society, with its vision of democratizing opportunity and access. A mansion in Beverly Hills didn't really embody that message." Firstenberg and Hindman, *Becoming AFI*, 55.

125. For evidence of Malick's enthusiasm for Fellini, see his reply to the AFI memo of August 26, 1969, Box 108, Folder 1, Louis B. Mayer Library, AFI.

126. *The Center for Advanced Film Studies: Program Announcement, 1970–1971; The American Film Institute* (Beverly Hills, CA: American Film Institute, 1970), 5, Louis B. Mayer Library, AFI.

127. Jacob Brackman has suggested that *Lanton Mills* is a brand of "peckerwood humor." Email correspondence to author, December 4, 2016.

128. It is worth pointing out that Lloyd's *Kid Brother* has a scene depicting the use of a stereopticon, which may have influenced a similar sequence in *Badlands*.

Chapter 1

Note to epigraph: Warren I. Susman, "Film and History: Artifact and Experience," *Film & History: An Interdisciplinary Journal of Film and Television Studies* 15, no. 2 (1985): 33.

1. "Edited out of utopia," write Mike Davis and Jon Wiener, "was the existence of a rapidly growing population of more than 1 million people of African, Asian, and Mexican ancestry." Davis and Wiener, *Set the Night on Fire: L.A. in the Sixties* (New York: Verso, 2020), 1.

2. See Joel Selvin, *Hollywood Eden: Electric Guitars, Fast Cars, and the Myth of the California Paradise* (Toronto: Ansani, 2021).

3. Edward Ruscha, *Every Building on the Sunset Strip* (self-pub., 1966). See also Alexandra Schwartz, *Ed Ruscha's Los Angeles* (Cambridge, MA: MIT Press, 2010).

4. Reyner Banham, *Los Angeles: The Architecture of the Four Ecologies*, introduction by Anthony Vidler (1971; Berkeley: University of California Press, 2001).

5. Banham, *Los Angeles*, 198.

6. "The divisions between avant-garde art and Hollywood filmmaking," writes Alexandra Schwartz in *Ed Ruscha's Los Angeles*, "were far from distinct" (115).

7. See Nicholas Godfrey, *The Limits of Auteurism: Case Studies in the Critically Constructed New Hollywood* (New Brunswick, NJ: Rutgers University Press, 2018).

8. David Thomson, *The Whole Equation: A History of Hollywood* (New York: Knopf, 2005), 328.

9. For a thorough account of how the critical discussion of *Badlands* has evolved over the years, see John Rhym, "The Paradigmatic Shift in the Critical Reception of Terrence Malick's *Badlands* and the Emergence of a Heideggerian Cinema," *Quarterly Review of Film and Video* 27 (2010): 255–266.

10. After catching *Badlands* on television, Bruce Springsteen was inspired to write the title track of his 1982 album *Nebraska*. Bruce Springsteen, *Born to Run* (New York: Simon & Schuster, 2017), 298. Similarly, in her memoir, Kim Gordon claims that Raymond Pettibon's cover art for Sonic Youth's 1990 album *Goo* was inspired by "the couple in Terrence Malick's film *Badlands*." Kim Gordon, *Girl in a Band: A Memoir* (New York: Dey St., 2015), 165.

11. Tarantino wrote the screenplay for *True Romance* (dir. Tony Scott, 1993) and gave Oliver Stone the story for *Natural Born Killers* (1994).

12. Pauline Kael, "The Current Cinema: *Sugarland* and *Badlands*," *New Yorker*, March 18, 1974, 136.

13. On this point, see Rhym, "The Paradigmatic Shift," 256.

14. See Timothy Corrigan, *A Cinema Without Walls: Movies and Culture After Vietnam* (New Brunswick, NJ: Rutgers University Press, 1991), 153.

15. Vincent Canby, "Malick's Impressive 'Badlands' Screened at Festival," *New York Times*, October 15, 1973, 50.

16. In a 1974 interview, Malick said Fugate "should never have been put in prison. She was only a minor at the time. She never participated in any of the killings." Shaun Considine, "Terrence Malick and 'Badlands'—An All-American Triumph," *After Dark*, June 1974, 70; clipping in the collection of the Margaret Herrick Library, Academy of Motion Picture Arts and Sciences (AMPAS).

17. On New Hollywood filmmaking, see Peter Krämer and Yannis Tzioumakis, eds., *The Hollywood Renaissance: Revisiting American Cinema's Most Celebrated Era* (New York: Bloomsbury, 2018).

18. "Producing the Film Series, with Terrence Malick," December 17, 1974, p. 75, Louis B. Mayer Library, AFI.

19. Mike Medavoy, with Josh Young, *You're Only as Good as Your Next One: 100 Great Films, 100 Good Films, and 100 for Which I Should Be Shot* (New York: Pocket Books, 2002), 5.

20. See Terry Malick, John Milius, and H. J. Fink, "Dead Right," November 3, 1970, p. 15, Louis B. Mayer Library, AFI.

21. Malick cowrote a draft of *The Dion Brothers*—then still called "Gravy Train"—with Bill Kerby. A version of it dated September 6, 1973, can be found in the Margaret Herrick Library, AMPAS.

22. This according to Hellman's obituary in the *New York Times*, April 21, 2021, https://www.nytimes.com/2021/04/21/movies/monte-hellman-dead.html.

23. On the existentialist reception of *Waiting for Godot*, see my "Angst Across the Channel: Existentialism in Britain," in *Situating Existentialism: Key Texts in Context*, ed. Jonathan Judaken and Robert Bernasconi (New York: Columbia University Press, 2012), 145–79.

24. Sylvia Townsend, *Bumpy Road: The Making, Flop, and Revival of "Two-Lane Blacktop"* (Jackson: University Press of Mississippi, 2019), 15.

25. Townsend, *Bumpy Road*, 15.

26. Townsend, *Bumpy Road*, 130.

27. Vincent Canby, "Paul Newman and Lee Marvin in 'Pocket Money,'" *New York Times*, April 20, 1972.

28. Back when Malick still spoke to journalists, he said the following about the origins of *Badlands*: "Except for an eighteen-minute short, I had never directed or produced a film before. But I knew I wanted total freedom, total control, so I stayed away from studio involvement. I decided to raise the production on my own. I made some money writing scripts, *Pocket Money*, and three days on *Drive, He Said*, picking up cash here and there." Considine, "Terrence Malick and 'Badlands,'" 69.

29. *The Wild Bunch* was mentioned in the seminar on "The Western," which Malick moderated. Fellows' Meeting, February 13, 1970, audio file at the Louis B. Mayer Library, AFI.

30. Jacob Brackman quoted in Paul Maher Jr., *One Big Soul: An Oral History of Terrence Malick* (n.p., 2012), 13.

31. Samuel Beckett, *En Attendant/Waiting for Godot: A Tragicomedy in Two Acts*, bilingual ed. (1952, 1954; New York: Grove, 2006), 289.

32. "AFI Fellows Discussion, 9/24/1969," audio file, Louis B. Mayer Library, AFI.

33. "Directors of the Ninth Era," *Esquire*, February 1975. Press clipping in the collection of the Margaret Herrick Library, AMPAS.

34. George Stevens Jr., "Remarks on the Opening of AFI CAFS," September 23, 1969, audio file at the Louis B. Mayer Library, AFI.

35. "Center Schedules, Week of September 22–26 [1969]," Louis B. Mayer Library, AFI.

36. Recalling his AFI days, my colleague Andrzej Krakowski remembers Malick being "pretty quiet," but having a "caustic sense of humor."

37. "Malick, Terry," in "Conservatory Fellows, Biographies, 1969–1970," Box 108, Folder 1, Louis B. Mayer Library, AFI.

38. Actually, one of the AFI instructors who saw it said it had a "Kafkaesque sort of quality." AFI seminar, September 24, 1969, audio file at the Louis B. Mayer Library, AFI.

39. See, for instance, Paul Maher Jr., ed., *All Things Shining: An Oral History of the Films of Terrence Malick*, 4th ed. (n.p., 2017), 58–61. Reno Lauro has suggested the film was made while Malick audited an MIT film course offered by Ed Pincus. See Reno Lauro, "The Smile of Life: Recollections on Malick and the Work of Cinema," in *A Critical Companion to Terrence Malick*, ed. Joshua Sikora (Lanham, MD: Lexington Books, 2020), 247.

40. "AFI Fellows Discussion, 9/24/1969."

41. "First Draft of Center Program for Terry Malick," September 2, 1969, "Conservatory Fellows, Biographies, 1969–1970," Box 108, Folder 1, Louis B. Mayer Library, AFI.

42. "AFI Fellows Discussion, 9/24/1969." In fact, Malick would go on to score his student film at AFI, *Lanton Mills*, though he later described the decision to do so as a "mistake" because he did not "know how to stop." See "American Film Institute Seminar with Terry Malick," April 11, 1974, 100. Transcript at Louis B. Mayer Library, AFI.

43. On Malick's Amarillo Dragway T-shirt, see Maher, *All Things Shining*, 59.

44. Terry Malick to Kay Loveland, "Re: AFI Memo of 26 August 1969," September 8, 1969, Box 108, Folder 1, Louis B. Mayer Library, AFI.

45. Malick to Loveland, "Re: AFI Memo."

46. For a recent statement on the philosophical relevance of Hollywood Westerns, see Robert B. Pippin, *Hollywood Westerns and American Myth: The Importance of Howard Hawks and John Ford for Political Philosophy* (New Haven, CT: Yale University Press, 2010).

47. See Robert Warshow, "Movie Chronicle: The Westerner," in *The Immediate Experience: Movies, Comics, Theatre, and Other Aspects of Popular Culture*, rev. ed., introduction by Lionel Trilling, epilogue by Stanley Cavell (Cambridge, MA: Harvard University Press, 2002), 105–24.

48. Stanley Cavell, "Epilogue: After Half a Century," in Warshow, *The Immediate Experience*, 293–94.

49. Cf. Peter Bogdanovich, *John Ford*, rev. ed. (Berkeley: University of California Press, 1978).

50. See René Girard, *Violence and the Sacred*, trans. Patrick Gregory (Baltimore: Johns Hopkins University Press, 1977).

51. Jeff Menne, *Post-Fordist Cinema: Hollywood Auteurs and the Corporate Counterculture* (New York: Columbia University Press, 2019), 37.

52. Edward Abbey, *The Brave Cowboy* (New York: Dodd, Mead, 1956).

53. Kirk Douglas, *The Ragman's Son* (New York: Simon & Schuster, 1988), 309. Quoted in Menne, *Post-Fordist Cinema*, 35.

54. "The Western: Terry Malick," Fellows' Meeting, February 13, 1970, audio file at the Louis B. Mayer Library, AFI.

55. In early drafts of Malick's screenplay for *Lanton Mills* Tilman's name is spelled Tilmon. Gregory Peck Papers, Margaret Herrick Library, AMPAS.

56. The scene brings to mind an early John Ford Western starring Harry Carey, *Bucking Broadway* (1917), which has cowboys racing down the streets of Manhattan on horseback.

57. Terrence Malick, "Lanton Mills: The Cincinnatus Hiner of Texas," 1970, p. 22. Gregory Peck Papers, Margaret Herrick Library, AMPAS.

58. *Lanton Mills*, dir. Terrence Malick, 1970, Louis B. Mayer Library, AFI. I viewed a digital copy of the film long before the current embargo on its screening was put into place. My reconstruction is from memory and what few notes I took at the time. See also Malick, "Lanton Mills," 23.

59. See "Malick, Terry," in "Conservatory Fellows, Biographies, 1969–1970," Box 108, Folder 1, Louis B. Mayer Library, AFI. See also the two versions of the script in the Gregory Peck Papers, Margaret Herrick Library, AMPAS. Elsewhere I have suggested that *Lanton Mills* should be interpreted along the lines of Malick's interest in the philosophical concepts of worldhood and worldmaking. I recommended viewing its central jump cut as a kind of temporal dividing line, separating the worlds of yesterday and today and emphasizing the theme of existential transience. See my "What Is Heideggerian Cinema? Film, Philosophy, and Cultural Mobility," *New German Critique* 113 (Summer 2011): 129–57.

60. Kevin Starr, *California: A History* (New York: Modern Library, 2005), 142–43.

61. Starr, *California*, 143. For more on Miller, see John Walton Caughey, *California*, 2nd ed. (Englewood Cliffs, NJ: Prentice-Hall, 1953), 345; Andrew F. Rolle, *California: A History* (Binghamton, NY: Vail-Ballou Press, 1963), 426; and Warren A. Beck and David A. Williams, *California: A History of the Golden State* (New York: Doubleday, 1972), 473–74. I thank Thomas J. Woessner, a true California historian, for these references.

62. "Producing the Film Series, with Terry Malick," January 21, 1976, 29. Transcript at the Louis B. Mayer Library, AFI.

63. See Michel Ciment's interview with Malick in *Positif* 170 (June 1975): 30–34. It is reprinted in Lloyd Michaels, *Terrence Malick* (Urbana: University of Illinois Press, 2009), 105–13.

64. Kael, "The Current Cinema: *Sugarland* and *Badlands*," 137.

65. Kael, "The Current Cinema: *Sugarland* and *Badlands*," 136.

66. Brian Kellow, *Pauline Kael: A Life in the Dark* (New York: Penguin, 2011), 213.

67. Kellow, *Pauline Kael*, 130. For a different comparison of Malick's and Spielberg's debuts, see Alberto Spadafora, *In cielo, in terra: Terrence Malick e Steven Spielberg* (Milan: Edizioni Bietti, 2012).

68. See François Dosse, *Gilles Deleuze and Félix Guattari: Intersecting Lives*, trans. Deborah Glassman (New York: Columbia, 2011), 432. See also Gilles Deleuze and Félix Guattari, *Anti-Oedipus: Capitalism and Schizophrenia*, trans. Robert Hurley, Mark Seem, and Helen R. Lane, preface by Michel Foucault (Minneapolis: University of Minnesota Press, 1983).

69. Guy Debord, *The Society of the Spectacle*, trans. Donald Nicholson-Smith (New York: Zone Books, 1995).

70. Andreas Killen, *1973 Nervous Breakdown: Watergate, Warhol, and the Birth of Post-Sixties America* (New York: Bloomsbury, 2006), 194. On this point and others, my reading of *Badlands* is indebted to Killen's incisive account of the film.

71. Killen, *1973 Nervous Breakdown*, 188.

72. On Colin Wilson and the reception of existentialism across the English Channel, see my "Angst Across the Channel," 145–79.

73. Womack and Malick bonded over their shared Oklahoma roots. They have stayed friends since Malick's student days in Cambridge. Womack is the grandfather of the rapper Lil Peep, whose surprising fame and untimely death in 2017 was the subject of a documentary film Malick executive produced: *Everybody's Everything* (dir. Sebastian Jones and Ramez Silyan, 2019).

74. Beverly Walker, "Malick on *Badlands*," *Sight and Sound* 44, no. 2 (Spring 1975): 82–83. Reprinted in Michaels, *Terrence Malick*, 102–5; quotation on 104.

75. Terence Malick, "Badlands," first draft, November 1971, 8, Margaret Herrick Library, AMPAS.

76. Killen, *1973 Nervous Breakdown*, 189.

77. Wittgenstein was fond of a similar cliché: "it takes many sorts to make a world." See *The Selected Writings of Maurice O'Connor Drury: On Wittgenstein, Philosophy, Religion, and Psychiatry*, ed. John Hayes (London: Bloomsbury Academic, 2019), 128.

78. Stanley Cavell, *The World Viewed: Reflections on the Ontology of Film*, rev. ed. (Cambridge, MA: Harvard University Press, 1979), 246 n. 62.

79. Cavell, *The World Viewed*, 246 n. 62 and p. 203.

80. Catherine Wheatley, *Stanley Cavell and Film: Skepticism and Self-Reliance at the Cinema* (London: Bloomsbury, 2019), 77.

81. Jacob Brackman, *The Put-On: Modern Fooling and Modern Distrust*, illustrated by Sam Kirson (Chicago: Henry Regnery, 1971). Parts of the book first appeared in the *New Yorker*, June 24, 1967.

82. Brackman, *The Put-On*, 129.

83. Robert B. Pippin, *The Philosophical Hitchcock: "Vertigo" and the Anxieties of Unknowingness* (Chicago: University of Chicago Press, 2017), 10. See also Cavell, *The World Viewed*, 203.

84. "American Film Institute: Preliminary Program Announcement," Box 115, Folder 26, Louis B. Mayer Library, AFI. On 1970s film feminism, see Maya Montañez Smukler, *Liberating Hollywood: Women Directors and the Feminist Reform of 1970s American Cinema* (New Brunswick, NJ: Rutgers University Press, 2019).

85. In this, Kit is rather like Tilman in *Lanton Mills*. See Terrence Malick, "Lanton Mills," 11: "I think we ought to bury some of our things, and right here," he says to Lanton. "No one else in the world will know where we put them. Just you and me. And someday we'll come back maybe and they won't be any different but we will, you know."

86. Martin Heidegger, *Being and Time*, trans. John Macquarrie and Edward Robinson (New York: Harper & Row, 1962), § 35.

87. Louis Menand, *The Free World: Art and Thought in the Cold War* (New York: Farrer, Straus and Giroux, 2021), 685.

88. In an interview accompanying the 2013 Criterion Collection release of *Badlands*, executive producer Edward Pressman claims Malick "spent at least as much time capturing the nature and the environment around the Badlands area" as he did shooting principal photography with his actors.

89. David Laderman, *Driving Visions: Exploring the Road Movie* (Austin: University of Texas Press, 2002), 120.

90. For a chilling retelling of their murder spree, see Roy Scranton, *I Heart Oklahoma!* (New York: Soho, 2019).

91. To an audience at AFI in 1974, Malick explained that his wife's help on the film was indispensable. "She alienated a lot of people because there are a lot of male chauvinists in the movie business and they don't like taking orders from a woman," but the whole setup "worked out great," he said. "American Film Institute Seminar with Terry Malick," April 11, 1974, 84.

92. Arthur Penn, Harold Lloyd Master Seminar (HLMS), reprinted in George Stevens Jr., *Conversations at the American Film Institute with the Great Moviemakers: The Next Generation, from the 1950s to Hollywood Today* (New York: Vintage, 2014), 428. The text included in this volume draws from two seminars Penn took part in at AFI, one on January 30, 1970, the other on October 7, 1970. The corresponding text can be found on pp. 39–40 of the original transcript of the October 7 seminar, held at the Louis B. Mayer Library, AFI.

93. A carbon copy of a letter from George Stevens Jr. to Maurice Sigler, warden of the Nebraska correctional facility, Lincoln, December 11, 1970, proves as much. It can be found in the administrative file labeled "Terry Malick" at the Louis B. Mayer Library, AFI.

94. Michael Lydon, "Charley Starkweather: Wheel on Fire," *US: A Paperback Magazine*, June 1969, 22–35. Lydon's music journalism was collected in *Rock Folk: Portraits from the Rock 'n' Roll Pantheon* (New York: Dial, 1971).

95. The annotated article, mentioned in the note above, is in a file folder labeled "Terry Malick" in the administrative archive of the Louis B. Mayer Library, AFI.

96. Lydon, "Charley Starkweather," 24.

97. Lydon, "Charley Starkweather," 25.

98. Lydon, "Charley Starkweather," 25.

99. Noël Carroll, *Interpreting the Moving Image* (Cambridge: Cambridge University Press, 1998), 242. The essay originally appeared as "The Future of Allusion: Hollywood in the Seventies (and Beyond)," *October* 2 (Spring 1982): 51–81.

100. Carroll, *Interpreting the Moving Image*, 243.

101. Carroll, *Interpreting the Moving Image*, 260. See Malick to Loveland, "Re: AFI Memo."

102. See Tarantino's exhaustive history of the film in "Targets," *New Beverly Cinema*, March 19, 2020, http://thenewbev.com/tarantinos-reviews/targets/. I thank Chris Rock for the reference.

103. Erin Overbey and Joshua Rothman, "Martin Luther King, Jr., in *The New Yorker*," April 3, 2018, https://www.newyorker.com/books/double-take/martin-luther-king-jr-in-the-new-yorker.

104. "Notes and Comment," *New Yorker*, April 13, 1968, 35.

105. "Notes and Comment," 35–36.

106. On Manson, Hollywood, and the counterculture, see Jon Lewis, *Road Trip to Nowhere: Hollywood Encounters the Counterculture* (Oakland: University of California Press, 2022).

107. Terry Malick, John Milius, and H. J. Fink, "Dead Right," November 3, 1970, 19, 61, Louis B. Mayer Library, AFI.

108. On mimetic or triangular desire, see René Girard, *Deceit, Desire, and the Novel: Self and Other in Literary Structure*, trans. Yvonne Freccero (Baltimore: Johns Hopkins University Press, 1965). I thank Joel Isaac for suggesting—somewhere out in Joshua Tree National Park—this idea.

109. David Riesman, with Nathan Glazer and Reuel Denny, *The Lonely Crowd*, foreword by Todd Gitlin (1950; New Haven, CT: Yale University Press, 2001).

110. Walker's 1975 *Sight and Sound* interview with Malick, reprinted in Michaels, *Terrence Malick*, 104.

111. Walker's interview, in Michaels, *Terrence Malick*, 105, 103.

112. For more on Malick's decision to use Orff's work in *Badlands*, see James Wierzbicki, *Terrence Malick: Sonic Style* (New York: Routledge, 2019), 85.

113. Daniel Bishop, *The Presence of the Past: Temporal Experience and the New Hollywood Soundtrack* (New York: Oxford University Press, 2021), 26.

114. Lydon, "Charley Starkweather," 26.

115. Lydon, "Charley Starkweather," 28.

116. Terrence Malick, "Badlands," second draft, April 1972, 33, WGA Library.

117. Lydon, "Charley Starkweather," 28.

118. Lydon, "Charley Starkweather," 34.

119. Malick, "Badlands," first draft, 44.

120. F. Scott Fitzgerald, *This Side of Paradise*, ed. Patrick O'Donnell (1920; New York: Penguin, 1996), 54.

121. Patrick O'Donnell, "Introduction," in Fitzgerald, *This Side of Paradise*, xviii.

122. F. Scott Fitzgerald, *Flappers and Philosophers* (1920; New York: Penguin Classics, 2010).

123. Fitzgerald, *This Side of Paradise*, 260.

124. Malick, "Badlands," first draft, 20.

125. Jon Baskin, "The Perspective of Terrence Malick," *The Point*, April 4, 2010, https://thepointmag.com/criticism/the-perspective-of-terrence-malick/. On Kit's Deanish mannerisms in the scripts, see Malick, "Badlands," first draft, 85, which describes Kit pretending to be Dean in front of the bathroom mirror.

126. A similar dynamic is at work in *Days of Heaven*, *The New World*, and *To the Wonder*.

127. See Warren I. Susman's seminal essay "'Personality' and the Making of Twentieth-Century Culture," in *New Directions in American Intellectual History*, ed. John Higham and Paul K. Conkin (Baltimore: Johns Hopkins University Press, 1979), 212–26. For more on Susman, see Paul V. Murphy, "The Last Progressive Historian: Warren Susman and American Cultural History," *Modern Intellectual History* 14, no. 3 (2017): 807–35.

128. Fitzgerald, *This Side of Paradise*, 95, 96.

129. Martin Heidegger, "*Per mortem ad vitam*: Thoughts on Johannes Jörgensen's *Lies of Life and Truth of Life* (1910)," trans. John Protevi and John van Buren, in *Supplements: From the Earliest Essays to "Being and Time" and Beyond*, ed. John van Buren (Albany: State University of New York Press, 2002), 35.

130. Malick, "Badlands," second draft, 33.

131. Malick, "Badlands," second draft, 33.

132. As George M. Wilson has put it, the teenagers "react with primitive dread and horror." Wilson, *Narration in Light: Studies in Cinematic Point of View* (Baltimore: Johns Hopkins University Press, 1986), 172.

133. Malick, "Badlands," second draft, 33.

134. Malick, "Badlands," second draft, 44–45.

135. See Heidegger, *Being and Time*, 174ff.

136. In her memoir, Sissy Spacek suggests that the incorporation of the stereopticon was somewhat accidental, having been discovered by Jack Fisk while he was hunting for props for the film. See Spacek, *My Extraordinary Ordinary Life*, with Maryanne Vollers (New York: Hyperion, 2012), 138.

137. Malick, "Badlands," second draft, 45.

138. Walker Percy, *The Moviegoer* (1961; New York: Vintage, 1998), 75.

139. On the concept of anxiety in existentialism, see Samuel Moyn, "Anxiety and Secularization: Søren Kierkegaard and the Twentieth-Century Invention of Existentialism," in Judaken and Bernasconi, *Situating Existentialism*, 279–304.

140. "American Film Institute Seminar with Terry Malick," April 11, 1974, 74.

141. Cavell, *The World Viewed*, 159.

142. Malick, "Badlands," first draft, 70.

143. Cavell, *The World Viewed*, 159.

144. "American Film Institute Seminar with Terry Malick," April 11, 1974, 53, 54.

145. "American Film Institute Seminar," April 11, 1974, 60.

146. "American Film Institute Seminar," April 11, 1974, 59. In a later seminar at AFI, Malick said, "it was the girl in the picture that interested me." "Producing the Film Series," January 21, 1976, 54. Malick's interest in making a picture about a young girl might have stemmed from his professed enthusiasm for the films of Robert Bresson, especially *Mouchette* (1967). For evidence of Malick's fondness for it, see Lauro, "The Smile of Life," 255.

147. Quoted in Helen Thorpe, "The Man Who Wasn't There," *Texas Monthly*, December 1998, https://www.texasmonthly.com/articles/the-man-who-wasnt-there-2/.

148. Spacek, *My Extraordinary Ordinary Life*, 134.

149. "American Film Institute Seminar with Terry Malick," April 11, 1974, 80. In her memoir, Carly Simon suggests that Malick first met Spacek at one of Jacob Brackman's Manhattan soirees. See Carly Simon, *Boys in the Trees: A Memoir* (New York: Flatiron, 2015), 178.

150. Paul W. Williams, *Harvard, Hollywood, Hitmen, and Holy Men* (Lexington: University Press of Kentucky, 2023), 159.

151. "American Film Institute Seminar with Terry Malick," 20; "Producing the Film Series, with Terry Malick," January 21, 1976, 2, 4, 24–25, 38, 46; "Producing the Film Series, with Terry Malick," December 17, 1974, 48, Louis B. Mayer Library, AFI.

152. "American Film Institute Seminar with Terry Malick," April 11, 1974, 76.

153. Malick recounts the "humiliating" experience of going to dentists' offices to fundraise in two of the AFI seminars. See the transcripts of the "Producing the Film Series" seminars of December 17, 1974, p. 24, and January 21, 1976, p. 8. Malick also had to hit up George Stevens Jr. for an emergency loan of $15,000 when one of his initial investors backed out just before shoot-

ing began. See George Stevens Jr., *My Place in the Sun: Life in the Golden Age of Hollywood and Washington* (Lexington: University Press of Kentucky, 2022), 281.

154. "Producing the Film Series" seminar, January 21, 1976, 3.

155. "Producing the Film Series" seminar, December 17, 1974, 74; cf. p. 6. A journalist's account of the seminar picked up on this theme as well. See Martha L. Linden, "Directed by Terrence Malick," *White Arrow* (1975), press clipping in the collection of the Margaret Herrick Library, AMPAS.

156. "Producing the Film Series" seminar, December 17, 1974, 9.

157. See Malick's 1975 *Sight and Sound* interview with Beverly Walker: "I was not a good teacher," he says, "so I decided to do something else." Reprinted in Michaels, *Terrence Malick*, 102.

158. "Producing the Film Series" seminar, January 21, 1976, 32.

159. Audio recording of the AFI Fellows' Meeting, March 27, 1970, Louis B. Mayer Library, AFI.

160. Robert Sinnerbrink, *Terrence Malick: Filmmaker and Philosopher* (London: Bloomsbury, 2019), 162.

161. Fisk interview in *Making Badlands*, a feature accompanying the 2013 Criterion Collection release of *Badlands*.

162. "American Film Institute Seminar with Terry Malick," April 11, 1974, 93.

163. Spacek, *My Extraordinary Ordinary Life*, 146.

164. Spacek, *My Extraordinary Ordinary Life*, 147.

165. Canby, "Malick's Impressive 'Badlands' Screened at Festival," 50.

166. "Producing the Film Series" seminar, January 21, 1976, 43. Billy Weber, Malick's editor for *Badlands*, has also noted the influence of Truffaut's use of voice-over in *The Wild Child* (1970). See the interview with Weber in the Criterion Collection edition of *Badlands*.

167. See Alexander Sesonske, "Time and Tense in Cinema," *Journal of Aesthetics and Art Criticism* 38, no. 4 (Summer 1980): 419–26.

168. Michel Chion, *The Voice in Cinema*, ed. and trans. Claudia Gorbman (New York: Columbia University Press, 1999), 56.

169. Jay Beck, *Designing Sound: Audiovisual Aesthetics in 1970s American Cinema* (New Brunswick, NJ: Rutgers University Press, 2016), 2.

170. Beck, *Designing Sound*, 5.

171. For example, Malick first imagined Kit and Holly meeting outside a church revival tent. Another scene has Kit wandering through an empty cathedral.

172. Walter M. Miller Jr., *A Canticle for Leibowitz* (1959; New York: Bantam Books, 1972). Malick's work on the adaptation is listed in a biographical blurb in the AFI archives: "Conservatory Fellows, Biographies, 1969–1970," Box 108, Folder 1, Louis B. Mayer Library, AFI.

173. See, for example, Walker Percy, "Rediscovering *A Canticle for Leibowitz*," in *Signposts in a Strange Land*, ed. Patrick Samway (New York: Farrar, Straus and Giroux, 1991), 227–33. See also Percy, "Notes for a Novel About the End of the World," in *The Message in the Bottle: How Queer Man Is, How Queer Language Is, and What One Has to Do with the Other* (New York: Farrar, Straus and Giroux, 1975), 101–18; and Percy, *Lost in the Cosmos: The Last Self-Help Book* (New York: Noonday Press, 1983), the final sections of which contain a comical reimagining of *Canticle*.

174. Miller, *A Canticle for Leibowitz*, 153.

175. See Robert Sinnerbrink, "Two Ways Through Life: Postsecular Visions in *Melancholia* and *The Tree of Life*," in *Immanent Frames: Postsecular Cinema Between Malick and von Trier*, ed. John Caruana and Mark Cauchi (Albany: State University of New York Press, 2018), 29–46. See also Robert Sinnerbrink, *Cinematic Ethics: Exploring Ethical Experience Through Film* (New York: Routledge, 2016); and Sinnerbrink, *Terrence Malick*.

176. Considine, "Terrence Malick and 'Badlands,'" 69–71.

177. Considine, "Terrence Malick and 'Badlands,'" 71.

178. On the creation of the New York Film Festival, see Raymond J. Haberski Jr., *It's Only a Movie: Films and Critics in American Culture* (Lexington: University Press of Kentucky, 2001), 144–64.

179. Considine, "Terrence Malick and 'Badlands,'" 71.

180. Considine, "Terrence Malick and 'Badlands,'" 71.

181. "Producing the Film Series" seminar, January 21, 1976, 36.

Chapter 2

Note to epigraph: Hamlin Garland, *Boy Life on the Prairie*, the complete text of the first (1899) edition, with an introduction by B. R. McElderry Jr. (Lincoln: University of Nebraska Press, 1961), 292.

1. Garland, *Boy Life on the Prairie*, xix.

2. Garland, *Boy Life on the Prairie*, 427; from the introduction to the 1926 edition of the book.

3. Garland, *Boy Life on the Prairie*, 273, 416.

4. Garland, *Boy Life on the Prairie*, 217.

5. See Garland's books, *Forty Years of Psychic Research: A Plain Narrative of Fact* (New York: Macmillan, 1936) and *The Mystery of the Buried Crosses: A Narrative of Psychic Exploration* (New York: E. P. Dutton, 1939).

6. Garland, *Boy Life on the Prairie*, 292.

7. See LaWanda F. Cox, "The Agricultural Wage Earner, 1865–1900: The Emergence of a Modern Labor Problem," *Agricultural History* 22, no. 2 (April 1948): 95–114.

8. Garland, *Boy Life on the Prairie* 153.

9. Garland, *Boy Life on the Prairie*, 154, 155.

10. Upton Sinclair, *The Jungle* (New York: Doubleday, 1906).

11. Ted Grossardt, "Harvest(ing) Hoboes: The Production of Labor Organization Through the Wheat Harvest," *Agricultural History* 70, no. 2 (Spring 1996): 283–301; quote on 290.

12. In full, the epigraph reads:

Troops of nomads swept over the country at harvest time like a visitation of locusts, reckless young fellows, handsome, profane, licentious, given to drink, powerful but inconstant workmen, quarrelsome and difficult to manage at all times. They came in the season when work was plenty and wages high. They dressed well, in their own peculiar fashion, and made much of their freedom to come and go.

They told of the city, and sinister and poisonous jungles all cities seemed in their stories. They were scarred with battles. They came from the far-away and unknown, and passed on to the north, mysterious as the flight of locusts, leaving the people of Sun Prairie quite as ignorant of their real names and characters as upon the first day of their coming.

—Hamlin Garland, *Boy Life on the Prairie* (1899)

13. Cox, "The Agricultural Wage Earner," 106.

14. Scot Haller, "*Days of Heaven*: Stunning and Provocative, Terrence Malick's New Film Wrangles with Human Failings and Fate," *Horizon*, September 1978, 27; included in the *Days of Heaven* publicity materials, Margaret Herrick Library, AMPAS.

15. Malick drew upon his own memories of working as a field hand. As he put it in a rare interview after the release of *Days of Heaven*: "Workers and farmers were embodying people whose hopes were being destroyed, some more than others, by opulence or poverty. All were full

of desires, dreams, and appetites, which I hope permeates the film." See Paul Maher Jr., *One Big Soul: An Oral History of Terrence Malick* (Lexington, KY: n.p., 2012), 74. The remarks come from an interview with French journalist Yvonne Baby, first published in *Le Monde* in 1979. This translation is by Maher and Hugues Fournier.

16. On Malick's debt to Wyeth and Hopper, see Stuart Kendall, "The Tragic Indiscernibility of *Days of Heaven*," in *Terrence Malick: Film and Philosophy*, ed. Thomas Deane Tucker and Stuart Kendall (2011; New York: Bloomsbury, 2013), 150. On the political valence of these landscapes, see Maurizia Natali, "The Course of Empire: Sublime Landscapes in the American Cinema," in *Landscape and Film*, ed. Martin Lefebvre (New York: Routledge, 2006), 91–123.

17. Dave Kehr, *When Movies Mattered: Reviews from a Transformative Decade* (Chicago: University of Chicago Press, 2011), 27.

18. Chris Holdenfield, "Terrence Malick: *Days of Heaven*'s Image Maker," *Rolling Stone*, November 16, 1978, 22.

19. For more on the biblical references in *Days of Heaven*, see Kendall, "The Tragic Indiscernibility of *Days of Heaven*," 148–64; and Hubert Cohen, "The Genesis of *Days of Heaven*," *Cinema Journal* 42, no. 4 (Summer 2003): 46–62. Malick used to invoke biblical language less than seriously. The script he worked on for Jack Starrett's *The Dion Brothers* (1974) contains this exchange between its protagonists: "CALVIN: I come to lead you out of all this into the land of milk and honey," to which Rut replies, "Do I have time to change?" "Gravy Train," screenplay by Terry Malick and Bill Kerby, September 6, 1973, 10, Margaret Herrick Library, AMPAS.

20. David Denby, "Museum Piece," review of *Days of Heaven*, *New York*, September 25, 1978; in *Days of Heaven* publicity materials, Margaret Herrick Library, AMPAS.

21. Denby, "Museum Piece."

22. Stanley Kauffmann, review of *Days of Heaven*, *New Republic*, September 16, 1978; in *Days of Heaven* publicity materials, Margaret Herrick Library, AMPAS.

23. Andrew Sarris, "A Thing of Beauty and Almost Joy," review, *Village Voice*, September 18, 1978; in *Days of Heaven* publicity materials, Margaret Herrick Library, AMPAS.

24. Penelope Gilliatt, "This Place," *New Yorker*, September 18, 1978, 159.

25. Gilberto Perez, "Film Chronicle: 'Days of Heaven,'" *Hudson Review* 32, no. 1 (Spring 1979): 99.

26. See Robert Burgoyne, *Bertolucci's "1900": A Narrative and Historical Analysis* (Detroit: Wayne State University Press, 1991).

27. Jeff Bond and Lukas Kendall, liner notes to *Days of Heaven: Music from the Motion Picture*, composed, orchestrated, and conducted by Ennio Morricone (1978; FSM Silver Age Classics, 2011).

28. Alessandro De Rosa, ed., *Ennio Morricone: In His Own Words*, trans. Maurizio Corbella (Oxford: Oxford University Press, 2019), 2. It appears Malick also tried to get Morricone to work on *The Thin Red Line* and a "Japanese musical," likely the stage adaptation of Kenji Mizoguchi's *Sansho the Bailiff* for the Brooklyn Academy of Music.

29. For a detailed discussion of Morricone's compositions, see Bernardo Feldman Nebenzahl, "The Narrative Power of Sound: Symbolism, Emotion, and Meaning Conveyed Through the Interplay of Sight and Sound in Terrence Malick's *Days of Heaven*" (PhD diss., UCLA, 2000).

30. See Joan McGettigan, "*Days of Heaven* and the Myth of the West," in *The Cinema of Terrence Malick: Poetic Visions of America*, ed. Hannah Patterson, 2nd ed. (London: Wallflower Press, 2007), 52–62. On the thematic importance of the farmer's house, see A. Van Jordan, "A House Is Not a Home: The Farmer's House Holds Passion in *Days of Heaven*," *New England Review* 39, no. 2 (Summer 2018): 39–42.

31. Malick, "Days of Heaven," revised draft, June 2, 1976, 108, Margaret Herrick Library, AMPAS.

32. As Steven Rybin has noted, the use of Panaglide shots allowed the camera to "wind its way through the space of the wheatfields without jerkiness," thus establishing a kind of "freedom in exploring and perceiving space." See Rybin, *Terrence Malick and the Thought of Film* (Lanham, MD: Lexington Books, 2012), 70.

33. For a reading of the sonic landscape of these scenes, see Richard Power, "Listening to the Aquarium: The Symbolic Use of Music in *Days of Heaven*," in Patterson, *The Cinema of Terrence Malick*, 110. On Malick's innovative use of Dolby Stereo in *Days of Heaven*, see Jay Beck, *Designing Sound: Audiovisual Aesthetics in 1970s American Cinema* (New Brunswick, NJ: Rutgers University Press, 2016), 204. For an extended philosophical reading of Malick's use of sound in *Days of Heaven*, see James Batcho, *Terrence Malick's Unseeing Cinema: Memory, Time and Audibility* (Cham, Switzerland: Palgrave Macmillan, 2018), 91–113.

34. Garland, *Boy Life on the Prairie*, 213.

35. American cinema would not see anything like this for almost thirty years, until the release of Paul Thomas Anderson's *There Will Be Blood*, which hinges on an almost identical sequence (in this case, the inferno of an oil derrick). Jack Fisk worked on both films and Jonny Greenwood's score for *There Will Be Blood* in many ways mirrors Morricone's for *Days of Heaven*. As George Toles has argued, *Days of Heaven* exerted a great deal of influence upon both the look and the feel of Paul Thomas Anderson's later films, especially *There Will Be Blood* and *The Master*. See Toles, *Paul Thomas Anderson* (Urbana: University of Illinois Press, 2016), 114, 117–18, 149.

36. Stanley Cavell, *The World Viewed: Reflections on the Ontology of Film*, rev. ed. (1971; Cambridge, MA: Harvard University Press, 1979), xiv.

37. Cavell, *The World Viewed*, xv.

38. Charles Champlin, *Hollywood's Revolutionary Decade: Charles Champlin Reviews the Movies of the 1970s* (Santa Barbara, CA: John Daniel, 1998).

39. Haller, "*Days of Heaven*: Stunning and Provocative," 23.

40. Cavell, *The World Viewed*, xvi.

41. See my *Heidegger in America* (Cambridge: Cambridge University Press, 2011), 181–95.

42. Rudolf Carnap, "The Elimination of Metaphysics Through Logical Analysis of Language," trans. Arthur Pap, in *Logical Positivism*, ed. A. J. Ayer (Glencoe, IL: Free Press, 1959); Martin Heidegger, "Overcoming Metaphysics," in *The End of Philosophy*, trans. Joan Stambaugh (New York: Harper & Row, 1973), reprinted in *The Heidegger Controversy: A Critical Reader*, ed. Richard Wolin (1991; Cambridge, MA: MIT Press, 1993), 67–90.

43. For more on Carnap's connection to Quine at Harvard, see Joel Isaac, "W. V. Quine and the Origins of Analytic Philosophy in the United States," *Modern Intellectual History* 2, no. 2 (August 2005): 205–34.

44. Quine, "Mr. Strawson on Logical Theory," *Mind* 62, no. 248 (1953): 446; reprinted in *Ways of Paradox and Other Essays* (New York: Random House, 1966), 151. On this point Quine was not alone. According to intellectual historian Andrew Jewett, "many other postwar American philosophers likewise identified their work as subsidiary to the natural sciences." See Jewett's *Science, Democracy, and the American University* (Cambridge: Cambridge University Press, 2012), 339.

45. In his memoir *Little Did I Know: Excerpts from Memory* (Stanford, CA: Stanford University Press, 2010), Stanley Cavell recounts the story of how, in the early 1960s, Harvard graduate students urged him to start teaching Heidegger (see pp. 503–4).

46. Heidegger, "Overcoming Metaphysics," 75.

47. Heidegger, "What Is Metaphysics?," trans. David Farrell Krell, in *Pathmarks*, ed. William McNeill (Cambridge: Cambridge University Press, 1998), 96.

48. Carnap, "The Elimination of Metaphysics," 69.

49. See Heidegger, *Gesamtausgabe*, vols. 94–96, ed. Peter Trawny (Frankfurt am Main: Klostermann, 2014). See also Sidonie Kellerer, "Rewording the Past: The Postwar Publication of a 1938 Lecture by Martin Heidegger," *Modern Intellectual History* 11, no. 3 (November 2014): 575–602.

50. These have been collected in *Pathmarks*. It is also worth pointing out that Heidegger offered a whole lecture course on the topic in 1935, which was later published in 1953 as *An Introduction to Metaphysics*. See Heidegger, *An Introduction to Metaphysics*, trans. Gregory Fried and Richard Polt (New Haven, CT: Yale University Press, 2000).

51. Steven Crowell, *Husserl, Heidegger, and the Space of Meaning: Paths Toward Transcendental Phenomenology* (Evanston, IL: Northwestern University Press, 2001), 242. See also the insightful essay by Peter E. Gordon, "German Existentialism and the Persistence of Metaphysics: Weber, Jaspers, Heidegger," in *Situating Existentialism: Key Texts in Context*, ed. Jonathan Judaken and Robert Bernasconi (New York: Columbia University Press, 2012), 65–88.

52. Heidegger, "What Is Metaphysics?," 95.

53. Heidegger, "Introduction to 'What Is Metaphysics?,'" trans. Walter Kaufmann, in *Pathmarks*, 277.

54. See, for just one instance, Heidegger, "Introduction to 'What Is Metaphysics?,'" 282. Heidegger's notion of *Seinsvergessenheit*, or the forgetting of Being, also stems from this period.

55. Heidegger, "The Age of the World Picture," in *Off the Beaten Track*, ed. and trans. Julian Young and Kenneth Haynes (Cambridge: Cambridge University Press, 2002), 71. This text underwent a significant transformation between being delivered as a lecture in 1938 and being published in the 1950s. See Kellerer, "Rewording the Past."

56. See David Michael Kleinberg-Levin, *Gestures of Ethical Life: Hölderlin's Question of Measure After Heidegger* (Stanford, CA: Stanford University Press, 2005).

57. Martin Heidegger, *The Essence of Reasons*, trans. Terrence Malick (Evanston, IL: Northwestern University Press, 1969). In a note, Malick explains why he chose to translate the singular *des Grundes* with the plural *reasons*: "'Reason,' as in the phrase 'the reason he came,' would be the best translation, except that in philosophical contexts it can too easily be understood in the sense of a faculty or mental process—a sense reserved for the word *Vernunft*" (133 n. 3).

58. Heidegger, *The Essence of Reasons*, 131.

59. Gilliatt, "This Place," 157.

60. Heidegger, *The Essence of Reasons*, xiv.

61. Heidegger, *The Essence of Reasons*, xiv–xv.

62. Heidegger, *The Essence of Reasons*, xv.

63. Heidegger, *The Essence of Reasons*, xv. Some commentators have suggested that Malick's films are lessons in perspective. These remarks seem to suggest otherwise. Malick, following Heidegger, is interested in things that precede or make possible a "point of view" or a "sense of perspective." See Jon Baskin, "The Perspective of Terrence Malick," *The Point*, April 4, 2010, http://thepointmag.com/2010/criticism/the-perspective-of-terrence-malick.

64. Heidegger, *The Essence of Reasons*, 85. Heidegger scholar William McNeill translates this passage somewhat differently, emphasizing selfhood more than world: "To selfhood there belongs world; world is essentially related to Dasein" (*Pathmarks*, 122).

65. Terrence Frederick Malick, "The Concept of Horizon in Husserl and Heidegger" (honors thesis, Harvard University, 1966).

66. Malick, "The Concept of Horizon," 28, 16–17.

67. In a note in his translation of "Vom Wesen des Grundes," Malick addresses this notion of worlding and references the famous talk of "the Nothing nothings" in "What Is Metaphysics?" As Malick explains it: "Heidegger makes a transitive verb of *Welt* ("world") as he did earlier with *Nichts* ("nothing"), evidently to encourage the reader to think of *Welt* and *Nichts* as existing, or functioning, in a way so peculiarly their own that it can only be expressed tautologically" (*The Essence of Reasons*, 142 n. 44). It is worth pointing out that not all reviewers were convinced by Malick's arguments for the primacy of the concept of "world" in "Vom Wesen des Grundes." See the review of Malick's translation in *Review of Metaphysics* 23, no. 4 (June 1970): 742.

68. Heidegger, *The Essence of Reasons*, 131.

69. Rybin, *Terrence Malick and the Thought of Film*, 74.

70. Heidegger, "Overcoming Metaphysics," 68.

71. In an interview with the *Village Voice*, Manz recounted the story: "No script, nothing, I just watched the movie and rambled on . . . I dunno, they took whatever dialogue they liked." Nick Pinkerton, "Calling Linda Manz," *Village Voice*, June 1, 2011.

72. Ryan Gilbey, "Linda Manz Obituary," *The Guardian*, August 17, 2020, https://www.theguardian.com/film/2020/aug/17/linda-manz-obituary.

73. *Days of Heaven* Release Dialogue Script, January 2, 1979, Margaret Herrick Library, AMPAS.

74. Martin Heidegger, *What Is Called Thinking?*, trans. Fred D. Wieck and J. Glenn Gray, with an introduction by J. Glenn Gray (New York: Harper & Row, 1968), 21.

75. Heidegger, *What Is Called Thinking?*, 235; Cavell, *The World Viewed*, xv.

76. Heidegger, *What Is Called Thinking?*, 237; Cavell, *The World Viewed*, xv.

77. According to Nestor Almendros, Malick "became more daring" over the course of the shoot, eventually "taking away more and more lighting aids so as to leave the image bare." See Almendros, *A Man with a Camera*, trans. Rachel Philips Belash (New York: Farrar, Straus and Giroux, 1984), excerpted in the booklet accompanying the Criterion Edition of *Days of Heaven* (2007), 18–19.

78. "Personality in Focus: An Interview with Jacob Brackman," reprinted in Brackman, *The Acid in the Attic: Legacies of the Sixties—Selected Essays, Reporting, Fiction, Film Criticism, Bits o' Scripts, Song Lyrics and Memorabilia, 1961 to 2018* (Hudson, NY: Shadow Hill, n.d.), 463. I thank Clay Matlin for making this source available to be me.

79. On the affinities between *Days of Heaven* and Hollywood silent films, see Almendros, *A Man with a Camera*, 17.

80. Ryan Gilbey, *It Don't Worry Me: The Revolutionary American Films of the Seventies* (New York: Faber & Faber, 2003), 91.

81. See also Shawn Loht, *Phenomenology of Film: A Heideggerian Account of the Film Experience* (Lanham, MD: Lexington Books, 2017), 157.

82. Heidegger, *What Is Called Thinking?*, 237.

83. Malick, "The Concept of Horizon," n. 26.

84. Malick, "The Concept of Horizon," 44.

85. I discuss this in more detail in chapter 3 of *Heidegger in America*. See also Edward Baring, *Converts to the Real: Catholicism and the Making of Continental Philosophy* (Cambridge, MA: Harvard University Press, 2019).

86. See Andrew J. Mitchell, *The Fourfold: Reading the Late Heidegger* (Evanston, IL: Northwestern University Press, 2015).

87. Martin Heidegger, "The Thing," in *Poetry, Language, Thought*, trans. Albert Hofstadter (New York: Harper & Row, 1971), 173.

88. The idea of a cosmological fourfold can be traced at least as far back as the medieval mapmaker Martin Waldseemüller's *Cosmographie Introductio* of 1507, which debuted "America" as the fourth part of the hitherto tripartite—Europe, Africa, Asia—globe.

89. Heidegger, "The Thing," 179–80.

90. Heidegger, "The Thing," 180.

91. Heidegger, "The Thing," 178.

92. Heidegger, "The Thing," 165.

93. Heidegger, "The Thing," 165. Ilan Safit discusses Malick's use of this imagery, as well as Heidegger's thoughts on technology more generally, in his insightful article "Nature Screened: An Eco-Film-Phenomenology." I thank him for making this manuscript available to me.

94. V. F. Perkins, *Film as Film: Understanding and Judging Movies*, new introduction by Foster Hirsch (1972; New York: Da Capo, 1993), 48.

95. Malick, "Days of Heaven," revised draft, June 2, 1976, 87.

96. Malick, "Days of Heaven," revised draft, 90.

97. George Stevens Jr., *Conversations with the Great Moviemakers of Hollywood's Golden Age at the American Film Institute* (New York: Vintage, 2007), 630.

98. See, for example, pp. 22 and 23 of the "Days of Heaven" revised draft.

99. Jacob Brackman may have been responsible for some of them since, in addition to being a producer on the film, he served as its second unit director.

100. Malick, "Days of Heaven," revised draft, 11, 17, 111.

101. Malick, "Days of Heaven," revised draft, 17, 76.

102. Malick, "Days of Heaven," revised draft, 33, 40.

103. "Days of Heaven" production script, 12, Margaret Herrick Library, AMPAS. On the differences between script and finished film with regard to religion, see Cohen, "The Genesis of *Days of Heaven*," 59: "Although [Malick] excised these verbal references from the film, he reintroduced religious themes in Linda's voice-over monologues."

104. "Days of Heaven" production script, 23. Interestingly, one of the only places where this abandoned plotline survives in the final film is an early shot of the migrant workers riding atop the train taking them out to the wheat fields: one of them wears an Astrakhan hat.

105. "Days of Heaven" production script, 65.

106. "Days of Heaven" production script, 112.

107. Frank Rich, "Night of the Locust," review of *Days of Heaven*, *Time*, September 18, 1978; in *Days of Heaven* publicity materials, Margaret Herrick Library, AMPAS.

108. Rich, "Night of the Locust."

109. Denby, "Museum Piece."

110. Malick, "Days of Heaven," revised draft, 70.

111. *Werckmeister Harmonies* (dir. Béla Tarr and Ágnes Hranitzky, 2000). On Tarr's cosmology, see Jacques Rancière's *Béla Tarr, the Time After*, trans. Erik Beranek (Minneapolis: Univocal, 2013). Compare Malick, "The New World: A Story of the Indies," 37, Margaret Herrick Library, AMPAS.

112. Malick, "Days of Heaven," revised draft, 54.

113. Looming just beyond the time frame of *Days of Heaven* is the rise of assembly-line production: it was in 1917 that construction began on the Ford River Rouge Complex in Dearborn, Michigan. See Joshua B. Freeman, *Behemoth: A History of the Factory and the Making of the Modern World* (New York: Norton, 2018).

114. Ludwig Wittgenstein, *Philosophical Investigations*, trans. G. E. M. Anscombe, P. M. S. Hacker, and Joachim Schulte, rev. 4th ed., ed. P. M. S. Hacker and Joachim Schulte (Malden, MA: Wiley Blackwell, 2009).

115. Karl Löwith, *My Life in Germany Before and After 1933*, trans. Elizabeth King (Urbana: University of Illinois Press, 1994), 28, 30.

116. Löwith, *My Life in Germany*, 31.

117. Carlo Hintermann and Daniele Villa, eds., *Terrence Malick: Rehearsing the Unexpected* (London: Faber & Faber, 2016), 1.

118. *Courses of Instruction for Harvard and Radcliffe* (Cambridge, MA: Harvard University, [1962–66]).

119. Council for Philosophical Studies, *Phenomenology and Existentialism: Continental and Analytical Perspectives on Intentionality in the Philosophy Curriculum* (San Francisco: San Francisco State University, Council for Philosophical Studies, 1981), 4.

120. Walker Percy, *The Moviegoer* (1961; New York: Vintage, 1998), 42.

121. Jack Kroll, review in *Newsweek*, September 18, 1978; in *Days of Heaven* publicity materials, Margaret Herrick Library, AMPAS.

122. On the imagery of the four elements in Malick's work, see Andrea Fornasiero, *Terrence Malick: Cinema tra classicità e modernità* (Genoa: Le Mani, 2007).

123. Garland, *Boy Life on the Prairie*, 120.
124. Patricia Curd, ed., *A Presocratics Reader: Selected Fragments and Testimonia*, 2nd ed., trans. Richard D. McKirahan and Patricia Curd (Indianapolis: Hackett, 2011), 46.

Chapter 3

Note to epigraph: J. Glenn Gray, *The Warriors: Reflections on Men in Battle*, introduction by Hannah Arendt, with a new foreword by the author (1959; Lincoln: University of Nebraska Press, 1998), xx.
1. Thomas Pogge, *John Rawls: His Life and Theory of Justice*, trans. Michelle Kosch (Oxford: Oxford University Press, 2007), 11–12.
2. John Rawls, *A Brief Inquiry into the Meaning of Sin and Faith, with "On My Religion,"* ed. Thomas Nagel, with commentaries by Joshua Cohen and Thomas Nagel and by Robert Merrihew Adams (Cambridge, MA: Harvard University Press, 2009), 262.
3. Ibid.
4. Ibid., 263.
5. Pogge, *John Rawls*, 14.
6. For more on Rawls's relation to religious thought, see the 1998 *Commonweal* interview reprinted in Rawls's *Collected Papers*, ed. Samuel Freeman (Cambridge, MA: Harvard University Press, 1999), 616–22. See also Tom Bailey and Valentina Gentile, eds., *Rawls and Religion* (New York: Columbia University Press, 2015). See also the symposium on his career in the *Journal of the History of Ideas* 78, no. 2 (April 2017): 255–308, with contributions from Mark Bevir, David A. Reidy, P. Mackenzie Bok, Daniele Botti, and Andrius Gališanka. A more recent symposium, "The Historical Rawls," ed. Sophie Smith, Teresa M. Bejan, and Annette Zimmermann, can be found in *Modern Intellectual History* 18, no. 4 (2021): 899–1080. On the rejection of providence and theodicy in American thought at this time, see my "Reconsidering the Slaughter Bench of History: Genocide, Theodicy, and the Philosophy of History," *Journal of Genocide Research* 13, nos. 1–2 (March–June 2011): 83–102.
7. E. B. Sledge, *With the Old Breed at Peleliu and Okinawa*, with a new introduction by Paul Fussell (Oxford: Oxford University Press, 1990); Robert Leckie, *Helmet for My Pillow: From Parris Island to the Pacific* (New York: Bantam, 1957).
8. Recent editions are Richard Tregaskis, *Guadalcanal Diary*, introduction by Mark Bowden, afterword by Moana Tregaskis (1943; New York: Modern Library, 2000); and the slightly retitled John Hersey, *Into the Valley: Marines at Guadalcanal*, illustrated by Col. Donald L. Dickson, USMCR (1942; Lincoln: University of Nebraska Press, 2002). Definitive histories of the period include Samuel Eliot Morison's *The Struggle for Guadalcanal, August 1942–February 1943*, History of United States Naval Operations in World War II, vol. 5 (1948; Boston: Little, Brown, 1984); and James D. Hornfischer's *Neptune's Inferno: The U.S. Navy at Guadalcanal* (New York: Bantam, 2011).
9. Sharon Tosi Lacey, *Pacific Blitzkrieg: World War II in the Central Pacific* (Denton: University of North Texas Press, 2013).
10. See Paul Maher Jr., *One Big Soul: An Oral History of the Films of Terrence Malick* (n.p.: 2012), 101, 117. Malick also was approached to adapt D. M. Thomas's 1981 novel *The White Hotel*. See Thomas, *Bleak Hotel: The Hollywood Saga of "The White Hotel"* (London: Quartet, 2008), 30.
11. Quoted in Carlo Hintermann and Daniele Villa, eds., *Terrence Malick: Rehearsing the Unexpected* (London: Faber & Faber, 2015), 165.
12. James Jones, *The Thin Red Line* (New York: Charles Scribner's Sons, 1962), 263.
13. Jones, *The Thin Red Line*, 277.

14. See Sigmund Freud, *Beyond the Pleasure Principle*, trans. and ed. James Strachey, introduction by Gregory Zilboorg, with a biographical introduction by Peter Gay (New York: Norton, 1990); Freud, *Civilization and Its Discontents*, trans. and ed. James Strachey, introduction by Peter Gay (New York: Norton, 1989); Jones, *The Thin Red Line*, 309.

15. Jones, *The Thin Red Line*, 164.

16. Jones, *The Thin Red Line*, 165–66.

17. Jones, *The Thin Red Line*, 166.

18. Jones, *The Thin Red Line*, 168.

19. On Jones's wartime experience, see Frank MacShane, *Into Eternity: The Life of James Jones, American Writer* (Boston: Houghton Mifflin Harcourt, 1985).

20. Jones, *The Thin Red Line*, 117.

21. Jones, *The Thin Red Line*, 117.

22. Robert Gottlieb, "How Good Was James Jones?," *New York Review of Books*, November 8, 2012, 32.

23. Chris Hedges, *War Is a Force That Gives Us Meaning* (New York: Public Affairs, 2002).

24. Jones, *The Thin Red Line*, vii.

25. Ernst Jünger, "Total Mobilization," in *The Heidegger Controversy: A Critical Reader*, ed. Richard Wolin (1991; Cambridge, MA: MIT Press, 1993), 119–39. On the problematic discourse of heroism in the American literature of World War II, see Roy Scranton's trenchant *Total Mobilization: World War II and American Literature* (Chicago: University of Chicago Press, 2019); and Elizabeth D. Samet's *Looking for the Good War: American Amnesia and the Violent Pursuit of Happiness* (New York: Farrar, Straus and Giroux, 2021).

26. Jones, *The Thin Red Line*, 215.

27. Jones, *The Thin Red Line*, 252.

28. Jones, *The Thin Red Line*, 230.

29. Jones, *The Thin Red Line*, 230.

30. Jones, *The Thin Red Line*, 267.

31. On American representations of Nazi and Japanese enemies, see Robert B. Westbrook's insightful "In the Mirror of the Enemy: Japanese Political Culture and the Peculiarities of American Patriotism," in *Why We Fought: Forging American Obligations in World War II* (Washington, DC: Smithsonian Books, 2004), 13–38. See also Clayton R. Koppes and Gregory D. Black, *Hollywood Goes to War: How Politics, Profits, and Propaganda Shaped World War II Movies* (New York: Free Press, 1987).

32. Michael S. Shull and David Edward Wilt, *Hollywood War Films, 1937–1945: An Exhaustive Filmography of American Feature-Length Motion Pictures Relating to World War II* (Jefferson, NC: McFarland, 1996), 143.

33. *Guadalcanal Diary* (1943; dir. Lewis Seiler). The screenplay was adapted from Tregaskis's book by Lamar Trotti. In fact, the film's depiction of Japanese soldiers is even more problematic than this, since in two disturbing scenes it included documentary footage of actual Japanese prisoners of war.

34. Tregaskis, *Guadalcanal Diary*, 56. For more on Tregaskis's life as a war correspondent, see Ray E. Boomhower, *Richard Tregaskis: Reporting Under Fire from Guadalcanal to Vietnam* (Albuquerque: High Road Books, University of New Mexico Press, 2021).

35. Tregaskis, *Guadalcanal Diary*, 14, 81.

36. Tregaskis, *Guadalcanal Diary*, 71; for Tregaskis's discussion of an "outstanding hero," see, for example, pp. 79 and 110.

37. Tregaskis, *Guadalcanal Diary*, 48.

38. Tregaskis, *Guadalcanal Diary*, 48–49.

39. Tregaskis, *Guadalcanal Diary*, 95, 107, 125.

40. James Jones, "Phony War Films," *Saturday Evening Post*, March 30, 1963, reprinted in the Criterion edition of *The Thin Red Line*, 19, 25.

41. For an excellent meditation on how one war film portrayed death and redemption through the lens of heroism, see Bruce Kuklick, *The Fighting Sullivans: How Hollywood and the Military Make Heroes* (Lawrence: University Press of Kansas, 2016). As Kuklick puts it: "Movies might represent death and trauma at home *if* Hollywood demonstrated the death as redemptive—*if* the film gave positive meaning to the loss" (127).

42. Jones, "Phony War Films," 22.

43. Jones, "Phony War Films," 27.

44. It was a letter to the *Los Angeles Times* from Juliet Green, John Dee Smith's manager, which pointed out the mistake. See "More Thin Red Strands," *Los Angeles Times*, January 16, 1999.

45. An August 28, 1997 memo from George Stevens Jr. suggests Malick thought John Dee Smith's voice-overs would echo those of Sissy Spacek in *Badlands* and Linda Manz in *Days of Heaven*. George Stevens Jr. Papers, AMPAS.

46. In Ford's film, Tom Joad says: "Well, maybe it's like Casy says, a fella ain't got a soul of his own, just a little piece of a big soul, the one big soul that belongs to everybody." It is a slightly expanded version of Steinbeck's original dialogue in the novel: "Well, maybe like Casy says, a fella ain't got a soul of his own, but on'y a piece of a big one." Steinbeck, *The Grapes of Wrath*, introduction and notes by Robert Demott (1939; New York: Penguin Classics, 2006), 419.

47. On the film's use of myth in this "search for meaning," see Steven Rybin, *Terrence Malick and the Thought of Film* (Lanham, MD: Lexington Books, 2012), 108.

48. Editor Billy Weber has spoken of the "very spiritual quality" of Malick's work. See Hintermann and Villa, *Terrence Malick*, 151.

49. Medavoy quoted in Hintermann and Villa, *Terrence Malick*, 183.

50. Stacey Peebles, "The Other World of War: Terrence Malick's Adaptation of *The Thin Red Line*," in *The Cinema of Terrence Malick: Poetic Visions of America*, ed. Hannah Patterson, 2nd ed. (London: Wallflower Press, 2007), 153.

51. Hollywood has a long tradition of turning warriors into monks. Caviezel's portrayal of Witt as a kind of soldier-saint is anticipated by Montgomery Clift's similar depiction of the character of Prewitt in another James Jones adaptation, Fred Zinnemann's *From Here to Eternity* (1953). And Caviezel solidified his saintly on-screen image by later appearing in the title role of Mel Gibson's *The Passion of the Christ* (2004), a film that Gibson more or less remade as a hackneyed World War II film twelve years later, *Hacksaw Ridge*, starring Andrew Garfield.

52. Terrence Malick, "The Thin Red Line," second draft screenplay, 101, Margaret Herrick Library, AMPAS.

53. William Manchester, *Goodbye, Darkness: A Memoir of the Pacific War* (Boston: Little, Brown, 1980), 391. Cited as an epigraph in both the second and third drafts of Terrence Malick's "The Thin Red Line" screenplay, Margaret Herrick Library, AMPAS. Ian-Malcolm Rijsdik is one of the few commentators to note the influence of Manchester on Malick's screenplay. See his "Terrence Malick's *The Thin Red Line*: Some Historical Considerations," *Film & History* 41, no. 1 (Spring 2011): 26–47.

54. Manchester, *Goodbye, Darkness*, 160.

55. Manchester, *Goodbye, Darkness*, 207.

56. Manchester, *Goodbye, Darkness*, 212.

57. James Jones, *WWII: A Chronicle of Soldiering* (Chicago: University of Chicago Press, 2014), 34–35. Jones's text was first published in 1975.

58. David Thomson, *The Big Screen: The Story of the Movies* (New York: Farrar, Straus and Giroux, 2012), 208.

59. Tom Shone, "Lights, Camera, Abstraction," *Sunday Times* (London), February 28, 1999, 7.

60. Stuart Klawans, "Saving Private Malick," *The Nation*, January 4, 1999; Tom Whalen, "'Maybe All Men Got One Big Soul': The Hoax Within the Metaphysics of Terrence Malick's *The Thin Red Line*," *Literature/Film Quarterly* 27, no. 3 (July 1999): 163.

61. As Trevor McCrisken and Andrew Pepper argue, *The Thin Red Line* "poses significant challenges to the quite rigid set of narrative conventions that war films usually follow and audiences expect," including, most importantly, the "discourse of masculine, individualist heroism." See their "Saving the Good War: Hollywood and World War II in the post-Cold War World," *American History and Contemporary Hollywood Film* (New Brunswick, NJ: Rutgers University Press, 2005), 89–130, quotes on pp. 101, 112.

62. Kenneth T. Jackson, "*The Thin Red Line*: Not Enough History," *AHA Perspectives on History*, April 1, 1999, https://www.historians.org/publications-and-directories/perspectives-on -history/april-1999/the-thin-red-line-not-enough-history.

63. One of the few cinematic precedents for Malick's environmental take on the war in the Pacific is the 1968 John Boorman film *Hell in the Pacific*, memorably starring Lee Marvin and Toshiro Mifune.

64. *The Thin Red Line* promotional booklet, p. 1, Margaret Herrick Library, AMPAS.

65. An April 26, 1997 script memo to Malick from producer George Stevens Jr. says "I know this is not a film about taking a hill from the enemy." George Stevens Jr. Papers, Margaret Herrick Library, AMPAS.

66. Terrence Malick, "The Thin Red Line," third draft screenplay, p. 1, Margaret Herrick Library, AMPAS.

67. Malick, "The Thin Red Line," third draft screenplay, 21.

68. *The Thin Red Line* promotional booklet, 5.

69. Promotional booklet, 5.

70. Toll as quoted in Hintermann and Villa, *Terrence Malick*, 159.

71. Malick, "The Thin Red Line," third draft screenplay, 27.

72. A "2nd Unit Preliminary Shot List as of 5 June 1997" lists a number of exotic plants and creatures Malick hoped to include in *The Thin Red Line*, everything from an "Eclectus Parrot" and a "Sacred Kingfisher" to "orchids, frangipani, coral and poinciana trees in flower, coconut and areca palms, cluster figs, papaya and casava fruits, Malay apples, canarium almonds," and "the buttressed roots of various trees," not to mention "red torch gingers for scene toward the end of the picture." George Stevens Jr. Papers, Margaret Herrick Library, AMPAS.

73. Malick, "The Thin Red Line," third draft screenplay, 42A.

74. A strong case for interpreting *The Thin Red Line* through a specifically Emersonian lens is made by Bill Fech, "The Soul Announces Itself: Terrence Malick's Emersonian Cinema" (master's thesis, Oregon State University, 2013).

75. Martin Heidegger, *Being and Time*, trans. John Macquarrie and Edward Robinson (New York: Harper & Row, 1962), §§ 51–53.

76. Robert Pippin, "Vernacular Metaphysics: On Terrence Malick's *The Thin Red Line*," *Critical Inquiry* 39, no. 2 (Winter 2013): 252. Steven Rybin also focuses on the loneliness and alienation that permeate *The Thin Red Line*; see Rybin, *Terrence Malick and the Thought of Film*, 113, 117.

77. 20th Century Fox Fall/Winter Preview, 1999, p. 3, Margaret Herrick Library, AMPAS.

78. Ralph Waldo Emerson, "Heroism," in *Essays: First and Second Series*, with an introduction by Douglas Crase (New York: Library of America, 2010), 144.

79. As Jonathan Levin has put it, "The prophet of self-reliance, then, is also at least in one of his many famously shifting moods, skeptical of the individuated self." See Levin's *The Poetics of Transition: Emerson, Pragmatism, and American Literary Modernism* (Durham, NC: Duke University Press, 1999), 23.

80. In taking up the question of the hero, Emerson was responding to Thomas Carlyle's lectures on the topic. See Carlyle's *On Heroes, Hero-Worship, and the Hero in History* (Berkeley: University of California Press, 1993). For a helpful guide to the literature on heroism as it relates to representations of the Second World War (though one that omits Emerson), see Kuklick, *The Fighting Sullivans*, 183 n.10.

81. Ralph Waldo Emerson, "The Over-Soul," in *Essays: First and Second Series*, with an introduction by Douglas Crase (New York: Library of America, 2010), 156.

82. Emerson, "The Over-Soul," 156.

83. Emerson, "The Over-Soul," 157.

84. Emerson, "The Over-Soul," 158.

85. Emerson, "The Over-Soul," 160.

86. Emerson, "The Over-Soul," 169.

87. Emerson, "The Over-Soul," 170.

88. For a different, more biblically oriented reading of *The Thin Red Line* as a work of theodicy, see Mark S. M. Scott, "Light in the Darkness: The Problem of Evil in *The Thin Red Line*," in *Theology and the Films of Terrence Malick*, ed. Christopher B. Barnett and Clark J. Ellison (New York: Routledge, 2017), 173–86.

89. As Cavell's former student William Rothman has put it: "During the period he was writing *The World Viewed*, it had not yet fully dawned on Cavell the extent to which the unique combination of popularity and artistic seriousness of American movies, especially of the 1930s and 1940s, was a function of their inheritance of the concerns of American transcendentalism. Not coincidentally, during the period he was writing *The World Viewed*, the extent to which Cavell's own way of thinking inherited Emerson's understanding and practice of philosophy also had not yet fully dawned on him." See William Rothman, ed., *Cavell on Film* (Albany: State University of New York Press, 2005), xxii. The most concise statement of Cavell's idea of "perfectionism" can be found in Stanley Cavell, *Cities of Words: Pedagogical Letters on a Register of Moral Life* (Cambridge, MA: Belknap Press of Harvard University Press, 2004), the first chapter of which is devoted to Emerson.

90. Stanley Cavell, "Thinking of Emerson," collected in *Emerson's Transcendental Etudes*, ed. David Justin Hodge (Stanford, CA: Stanford University Press, 2003), 13.

91. Cavell, "Thinking of Emerson," 13. The lines Cavell quotes are from Emerson, "Circles," in *Essays*, 173–84.

92. Cavell, "Thinking of Emerson," 15.

93. Cavell, "Thinking of Emerson," 15–16.

94. Martin Heidegger, "Building Dwelling Thinking" and "'. . . Poetically Man Dwells . . . ,'" in *Poetry, Language, Thought*, trans. Albert Hofstadter (New York: Harper & Row, 1971); Heidegger, *What Is Called Thinking?*, trans. J. Glenn Gray (New York: Harper & Row, 1968).

95. Heidegger, *What Is Called Thinking?*, 141.

96. On Heidegger, Hitler, and Heraclitus (as well as Carl Schmitt), see Domenico Losurdo, *Heidegger and the Ideology of War: Community, Death, and the West*, trans. Marella Morris and Jon Morris (Amherst, NY: Humanity Books, 2001); Emmanuel Faye, *Heidegger: The Introduction of Nazism into Philosophy*, trans. Michael B. Smith, foreword by Tom Rockmore (New Haven, CT: Yale University Press, 2009); and, most thoroughly, Gregory Fried, *Heidegger's Polemos: From Being to Politics* (New Haven, CT: Yale University Press, 2000).

97. Heidegger, *What Is Called Thinking?*, 143.

98. For more on Gray, see my *Heidegger in America* (Cambridge: Cambridge University Press, 2011), 132–59.

99. J. Glenn Gray, "Poets and Thinkers: Their Kindred Roles in the Philosophy of Martin Heidegger," in *On Understanding Violence Philosophically and Other Essays* (New York: Harper Torchbooks, 1970), 88.

100. Hannah Arendt, "What Is Existenz Philosophy?," *Partisan Review* 13, no. 1 (Winter 1946): 46.

101. See Robert Sinnerbrink, "Song of the Earth: Cinematic Romanticism in Malick's *The New World*," in *Terrence Malick: Film and Philosophy*, ed. Thomas Deane Tucker and Stuart Kendall (London: Bloomsbury, 2011), 179–96.

102. For a recent, largely critical, take on Romanticism's and Wordsworth's presence in *The Thin Red Line*, see Elizabeth Bradfield, "Beauty's Failed Seduction: *The Thin Red Line*," *New England Review* 39, no. 2 (Summer 2018): 46–48.

103. As quoted in Paul Maher Jr., *All Things Shining: An Oral History of the Films of Terrence Malick*, 4th ed. (n.p., 2017), 111. The quote comes from Peter Biskind's 1998 article for *Vanity Fair*, "The Runaway Genius," which is reprinted in *Gods and Monsters: Thirty Years of Writing on Film and Culture from One of America's Most Incisive Writers* (New York: Nation Books, 2004), 263.

104. J. Glenn Gray, *The Promise of Wisdom: An Introduction to Philosophy of Education* (Philadelphia: Lippincott, 1968), 37. Gray's interest in environmental themes also appears in the foreword to the 1970 edition of *The Warriors*. For a reading of *The Thin Red Line* as "Heideggerian," see Robert Clewis, "Heideggerian Wonder in Terrence Malick's *The Thin Red Line*," *Film and Philosophy* 7 (2003): 22–36.

105. Jones, *The Thin Red Line*, 60.

106. The sounds accompanying the crocodile's descent are from the opening piece in Zimmer's score, "The Coral Atoll."

107. Actually, the images capture a sunset over Catalina Island, off the coast of Southern California. Carl Plantinga, "Affective Incongruity and *The Thin Red Line*," *Projections* 2, no. 2 (Winter 2010): 86–103; quote on 93.

108. Emerson, "Nature," in *Essays*, 316.

109. Emerson, "Nature," 324.

110. Emerson, "Nature," 325

111. Malick, "The Thin Red Line," third draft screenplay, 181.

112. Malick, "The Thin Red Line," third draft screenplay, 187.

113. Malick, "The Thin Red Line," third draft screenplay, 187. Compare Jones, *The Thin Red Line*, 494.

114. As Emerson's biographer Robert D. Richardson Jr. claims, Emerson "saw process everywhere." See Richardson, *Emerson: The Mind on Fire* (Berkeley: University of California Press, 1995), 341.

115. Emerson, "Circles," 182.

116. On Emerson and Thoreau, see Jeffrey S. Cramer, *Solid Seasons: The Friendship of Henry David Thoreau and Ralph Waldo Emerson* (Berkeley, CA: Counterpoint, 2019).

117. Emerson, "Experience," in *Essays*, 251.

118. Thoreau's *Journal*, January 9, 1853 (see *The Writings of Henry David Thoreau: Journal*, ed. Bradford Torrey [Boston: Houghton Mifflin, 1906], 4:458–59). I thank Dan Wuebben for bringing this passage to my attention. Malick instructed his 2nd unit crew to capture images that "could suggest nature at war with itself." See "2nd Unit Preliminary Shot List as of 5 June 1997."

119. See Mara van der Lugt, *Dark Matters: Pessimism and the Problem of Suffering* (Princeton, NJ: Princeton University Press, 2021).

120. On Emerson's debts to Asian thought, see Frederic Ives Carpenter, *Emerson and Asia* (Cambridge, MA: Harvard University Press, 1930); and Russell B. Goodman, "East-West Philosophy in Nineteenth-Century America: Emerson and Hinduism," *Journal of the History of Ideas* 51, no. 4 (1990): 625–45.

121. Anthony Lane, "Doing Battle," *New Yorker*, December 28, 1998, and January 4, 1999.

122. R. Barton Palmer, "Filming James Jones's *The Thin Red Line*," in *Twentieth-Century American Fiction on Screen*, ed. R. Barton Palmer (Cambridge: Cambridge University Press, 2007), 233. For another detailed account of Malick's fidelity to Jones's vision, see Jimmie E. Cain Jr., "'Writing in His Musical Key': Terrence Malick's Vision of James Jones's *The Thin Red Line*," *Film Criticism* 25, no. 1 (Fall 2000): 2–24.

123. Todd McCarthy, "Malick Looks Poised to Return to Public Eye," *Variety*, October 9, 1992, 25. Malick also impressed James Jones scholars as well: in October 2003, the James Jones Literary Society awarded him a "Lifetime Achievement Award" for "more than thirty years of innovative, profoundly philosophical and literary contributions to the world of film." See the press release "James Jones Literary Society to Study Author's Material at University of Texas or Austin Symposium," October 5, 2003, at http://www.hrc.utexas.edu/press/releases/2003/james-jones.html.

124. The epigraph is drawn from Emerson's essay "History."

125. Steven R. Carter, *James Jones: An American Literary Orientalist Master* (Urbana: University of Illinois Press, 1998), x.

126. Carter, *James Jones*, 35.

127. Carter, *James Jones*, 110.

128. Zack Sharf, "Terrence Malick Told John C. Reilly His *Thin Red Line* Role Was Being Edited Down in the Most Malick Way Possible," *IndieWire*, September 21, 2018, https://www.indiewire.com/2018/09/terrence-malick-john-c-reilly-thin-red-line-role-cut-1202005776/.

129. "The Editing of *The Thin Red Line*: Shaping a Terrence Malick Film," Criterion edition of *The Thin Red Line*. This short compiles interviews with the film's three editors, Billy Weber, Leslie Jones, and Saar Klein. The first cut of *The Thin Red Line* was five hours long, apparently.

130. For an interesting comparison of *The Thin Red Line* and *Saving Private Ryan*, see John Streamas, "The Greatest Generation Steps Over *The Thin Red Line*," in Patterson, *The Cinema of Terrence Malick*, 125–40.

131. Peter Rainer, "War Is Hellish," *New York*, January 4, 1999, 52. Martin Flanagan's "'Everything a Lie': The Critical and Commercial Reception of Terrence Malick's *The Thin Red Line*," in Patterson, *The Cinema of Terrence Malick*, 125–40, usefully surveys some of these reviews.

132. Richard Alleva, "God's Sarcasm: *The Thin Red Line*," *Commonweal*, March 12, 1999, 15.

133. F. X. Feeney, "Human, All Too Human: In Defense of *The Thin Red Line*," *L.A. Weekly*, January 15, 1999, 40.

134. An undated—and unpaginated—"Revised First Draft Screenplay" of "The English Speaker" contains lines such as these: "What is the way beyond sorrow? Beyond suffering and death?"; "It frightens me that I don't understand life"; and "Let me see Providence where I see Fortune." On the incorporation of Malick's adaptation of *Sansho the Bailiff* into *The Thin Red Line*, see Phillip Lopate, "Above the Battle, Musing on the Profundities," *New York Times*, January 17, 1999. See also Maher, *One Big Soul*, 112ff.

135. Cavell's remarks about *The Thin Red Line* come from a 1999 colloquium in Paris celebrating the translation of *The World Viewed* into French. See "Concluding Remarks Presented at Paris Colloquium on *La Projection du monde*," in Rothman, *Cavell on Film*, 282–83.

136. On Homer's presence in the film (Tall quotes the *Iliad* during a significant scene), see Jon Hesk, "Terrence Malick's *The Thin Red Line* and Homeric Epic: Spectacle, Simile, Scene, and Situation," in *War as Spectacle: Ancient and Modern Perspectives on the Display of Armed Conflict*, ed. Anastasia Bakogianni and Valerie M. Hope (London: Bloomsbury, 2016), 313–33.

137. Marc Furstenau and Leslie MacAvoy, "Terrence Malick's Heideggerian Cinema: War and the Question of Being in *The Thin Red Line*," in Patterson, *The Cinema of Terrence Malick*, 179–91. See also Robert Sinnerbrink, "A Heideggerian Cinema? On Terrence Malick's *The Thin Red Line*," *Film-Philosophy* 10 (December 2006): 26–37.

138. Leo Bersani and Ulysse Dutoit, *Forms of Being: Cinema, Aesthetics, Subjectivity* (London: British Film Institute, 2004), 153.

139. Kaja Silverman, "All Things Shining," in *Loss: The Politics of Mourning*, ed. David L. Eng and David Kazanjian (Berkeley: University of California Press, 2003), 324.

140. Simon Critchley, "Calm—On Terrence Malick's *The Thin Red Line*," in *The Thin Red Line*, ed. David Davies (New York: Routledge, 2009), 11–28. For a slightly different, more Freudian reading of the film, see Elisabeth Bronfen, "War and Its Fictional Recovery On-Screen: Narrative Management of Death in *The Big Red One* and *The Thin Red Line*," in *The Philosophy of War Films*, ed. David LaRocca (Lexington: University Press of Kentucky, 2014), 413–36.

141. Hubert Dreyfus and Camilo Salazar Prince, "*The Thin Red Line*: Dying Without Demise, Demise Without Dying," in Davies, *The Thin Red Line*, 29–44.

142. David Davies, "Vision, Touch, and Embodiment in *The Thin Red Line*," in Davies, *The Thin Red Line*, 61.

143. Pippin, "Vernacular Metaphysics," 272.

144. Emerson, "The Over-Soul," 170.

145. Malick chose *Paths of Glory* as one of the "Fellows Choice" films screened during the sixth week of seminars, December 8–13, 1969. See "AFI, Center for Advanced Film Studies, Instruction Material," Louis B. Mayer Library, AFI.

146. "Private Benjamin," an interview with Tom Charity, *Time Out* (London), February 24, 1999, 21.

147. A July 11, 1997 production memo to Malick from George Stevens Jr. refers to the "silent film approach" and the "'silent film' thinking" that guided Malick's vision for *The Thin Red Line*. George Stevens Jr. Papers, Margaret Herrick Library, AMPAS.

148. As quoted in Maher, *One Big Soul*, 157. Many great directors of the silent era maintained that words were extraneous. See F. W. Murnau, "The Ideal Picture Needs No Titles," *Theatre Magazine* 47, no. 322 (January 1928): 41, 72.

149. "Editing of *The Thin Red Line*."

150. "Editing of *The Thin Red Line*."

151. George Stevens Jr., *My Place in the Sun: Life in the Golden Age of Hollywood and Washington* (Lexington: University Press of Kentucky, 2022), 403. In fact, Stevens repeatedly urged Malick not to lose sight of the "big Hollywood war movie" he was making down in Australia. His letters and memos to Malick during this time are full of encouragement, but also suggestions for streamlining, focusing, and clarifying a film that seemed to be growing more unwieldy by the day. Stevens's son Michael, who also worked on the picture, told his father he needed "to go back to a mentor-protégé situation" with Malick, "as it was at AFI, or for *Badlands*." Michael Stevens to George Stevens Jr., July 11, 1997, George Stevens Jr. Papers, Margaret Herrick Library, AMPAS.

152. Of the voice-over recording process, John Dee Smith said Malick "had these index cards, stacks of them that he had typed shortly before, and sometimes he used them, other times it was off the top of his head." Quoted in Maher, *One Big Soul*, 164.

153. On Ives's connection to Emerson, see Michael Broyles and Denise von Glahn, "Later Manifestations of Concord: Charles Ives and the Transcendentalist Tradition," in *Transient and Permanent: The Transcendentalist Movement and Its Contexts*, ed. Charles Capper and Conrad Edick Wright (Boston: Massachusetts Historical Society, 1999), 574–602. For more on Malick's use of Ives's piece in *The Thin Red Line*, see David Sterritt's essay for the Criterion release of the film, "*The Thin Red Line*: This Side of Paradise," 13. For more on Ives and Emerson, see Kyle Gann, *Charles Ives's "Concord": Essays After a Sonata* (Urbana: University of Illinois Press, 2017). Last, this is the testimony of Hans Zimmer: "I think the ultimate piece of music for Terry has to be Charles Ives' 'Unanswered Question.' Because I think that's Terry's life, you know,

that's his mission in life—the unanswered question" (Tim Greiving, "Seeing Terrence Malick Films Through His Use of Music: His Composers Share What They Know," *Los Angeles Times*, January 7, 2020).

154. Sean Penn quoted in Hintermann and Villa, *Terrence Malick*, 229.

Chapter 4

Note to epigraph: Thomas Hariot, *A Briefe and True Report of the New Found Land of Virginia*, in John Smith, *Writings: With Other Narratives of Roanoke, Jamestown, and the First English Settlement of America*, ed. James Horn (New York: Library of America, 2007), 897.

1. See Adam Serwer, "The Fight Over the 1619 Project Is Not About the Facts," *The Atlantic*, December 23, 2019, https://www.theatlantic.com/ideas/archive/2019/12/historians-clash-1619 -project/604093/.

2. Smith, *The True Travels*, in *Writings*, 767.

3. Smith, *The Generall Historie*, in *Writings*, 321.

4. For more on Smith's life and writings, see Peter Firstbrook, *A Man Most Driven: Captain John Smith, Pocahontas and the Founding of America* (London: Oneworld, 2014).

5. J. H. Elliott, *The Old World and the New, 1492–1650* (Cambridge: Cambridge University Press, 1970), 53, 104. See also Edmundo O'Gorman, *The Invention of America: An Inquiry into the Historical Nature of the New World and the Meaning of Its History* (1961; repr., Westport, CT: Greenwood Press, 1972).

6. Smith, *A True Relation*, in *Writings*, 8–9.

7. Richard Ashcraft, "Political Theory and Political Reform: John Locke's Essay on Virginia," *Western Political Quarterly* 22, no. 4 (December 1969): 750.

8. *The 350th Anniversary of Jamestown, 1607–1957: Final Report to the President and the Congress of the Jamestown-Williamsburg-Yorktown Celebration Commission* (Washington, DC: U.S. Government Printing Office, 1958), 4.

9. Daniel Immerwahr, *How to Hide an Empire: A History of the Greater United States* (New York: Farrar, Straus and Giroux, 2019), 75.

10. Nathan Cardon, *A Dream of the Future: Race, Empire, and Modernity at the Atlanta and Nashville World's Fairs* (Oxford: Oxford University Press, 2018), 117–18.

11. *The 350th Anniversary of Jamestown*, 169.

12. *The 350th Anniversary of Jamestown*, 189.

13. Ben C. McCary, *Indians in Seventeenth-Century Virginia* (Williamsburg: Virginia 350th Anniversary Celebration Corporation, 1957), 85.

14. The official website was available previously at http://www.jamestown2007.org/.

15. Jack Fisk, quoted in Carlo Hintermann and Daniele Villa, eds., *Terrence Malick: Rehearsing the Unexpected* (London: Faber & Faber, 2015), 256.

16. John d'Entremont, review of *The New World*, *Journal of American History* 94, no. 3 (December 2007): 1023.

17. *America's 400th Anniversary: The Final Report of the Jamestown 400th Commemoration Commission* (Washington, DC: U.S. Government Printing Office, 2009), 12.

18. Lloyd Michaels, *Terrence Malick* (Urbana: University of Illinois Press, 2009), 79.

19. As editor Saar Klein put it, "I feel that some of the techniques we toyed with on *The Thin Red Line*, we pushed to a greater extent on *The New World*." Quoted in Hintermann and Villa, *Terrence Malick*, 292.

20. Malick had pursued Lubezki for the Che Guevara project. See Paul Maher Jr., *All Things Shining: An Oral History of the Films of Terrence Malick*, 4th ed. (n.p., 2017), 154–55.

21. John Patterson, "The New World: A Misunderstood Masterpiece?," *The Guardian*, December 10, 2009, https://www.theguardian.com/film/2009/dec/10/the-new-world-terrence-malick.

22. "Under the Influence: Chloé Zhao on *The New World*," August 1, 2018, https://www.youtube.com/watch?v=7Ces4ZqX75o.

23. Amy Taubin, "Birth of a Nation," *Sight & Sound* 16, no. 3 (February 2006): 45; Manohla Dargis, "When Virginia Was Eden, and Other Tales of History," *New York Times*, December 23, 2005.

24. Michaels, *Terrence Malick*, 84.

25. On postcolonial theory and film studies, see Peter Limbrick, *Making Settler Cinemas: Film and Colonial Encounters in the United States, Australia, and New Zealand* (New York: Palgrave Macmillan, 2010).

26. Henry Adams, "Captain John Smith," *North American Review* 104, no. 214 (January 1867): 1–30.

27. Monika Siebert, "Historical Realism and Imperialist Nostalgia in Terrence Malick's *The New World*," *Mississippi Quarterly* 65, no. 1 (Winter 2012): 153.

28. "New World: Production Notes, 7/29/03," included with the Criterion edition of *The New World* (2008), 28, 31.

29. Terrence Malick, "The New World: A Story of the Indies," 9, Margaret Herrick Library, AMPAS. The script mistakenly describes Barlowe as James.

30. See Skip Horack, "On Parakeets, in *The New World*," *New England Review* 39, no. 2 (Summer 2018): 49–51. See also the press materials from New Line Cinema, p. 31, Margaret Herrick Library, AMPAS.

31. Robert Sinnerbrink, *Terrence Malick: Filmmaker and Philosopher* (London: Bloomsbury, 2019), 57. Previously published as "Song of the Earth: Cinematic Romanticism in Malick's *The New World*," in *Terrence Malick: Film and Philosophy*, ed. Thomas Deane Tucker and Stuart Kendall (London: Bloomsbury, 2011), 179–96.

32. "New World: Production Notes," 36.

33. See Malick, "The New World: A Story of the Indies," 74, 95, 116.

34. Elizabeth Walden, "Whereof One Cannot Speak: Terrence Malick's *The New World*," in Tucker and Kendall, *Terrence Malick*, 197.

35. Dargis, "When Virginia Was Eden."

36. Press materials from New Line Cinema, Margaret Herrick Library, AMPAS.

37. The work that inaugurated the "myth and symbol" school of American studies was Henry Nash Smith's *Virgin Land: The American West as Symbol and Myth* (Cambridge, MA: Harvard University Press, 1950).

38. Malick, "The New World: A Story of the Indies," 1.

39. "New World: Production Notes," 36. The quotations are from David A Price's popular history *Love and Hate in Jamestown: John Smith, Pocahontas, and the Start of a New Nation* (2003; New York: Vintage, 2005), 233.

40. D'Entremont, review of *The New World*, 1025.

41. Joerg Widmer in Hintermann and Villa, *Terrence Malick*, 279.

42. Dargis, "When Virginia Was Eden."

43. Ludwig Wittgenstein, *Tractatus Logico-Philosophicus*, trans. C. K. Ogden, introduction by Bertrand Russell (London: Kegan Paul, 1922), 31.

44. Ernst Cassirer, *Language and Myth*, trans. Susanne Langer (1946; New York: Dover, 1953), 11.

45. Nelson Goodman, *Ways of Worldmaking* (Indianapolis: Hackett, 1978), 1.

46. On the Davos debate, see Peter Gordon, *Continental Divide: Heidegger, Cassirer, Davos* (Cambridge, MA: Harvard University Press, 2010); and, more recently, Wolfram Eilenberger, *Time*

of the Magicians: Wittgenstein, Benjamin, Cassirer, Heidegger, and the Decade That Reinvented Philosophy, trans. Shaun Whiteside (New York: Penguin, 2020).

47. Cassirer, *Language and Myth*, 11.

48. Heidegger, *Being and Time*, trans. John Macquarrie and Edward Robinson (New York: Harper & Row, 1962), § 38.

49. Martin Heidegger, *The Basic Problems of Phenomenology*, trans. Albert Hofstadter, rev. ed. (Bloomington: Indiana University Press, 1988), 166.

50. Martin Heidegger, *The Essence of Reasons*, trans. Terrence Malick (Evanston, IL: Northwestern University Press, 1969).

51. Terrence Frederick Malick, "The Concept of Horizon in Husserl and Heidegger" (honors thesis, Harvard University, 1966), 39.

52. Malick, "The Concept of Horizon," 39.

53. In his thesis, Malick argued that an understanding of Heidegger's concept of world was essential to understanding his notion of Being: Only by understanding what Heidegger meant "by 'world,'" he wrote, "can we understand what he means by Being'" ("The Concept of Horizon," n.p., "Heidegger (Part II)," n. 11).

54. Hubert Dreyfus, "Being-in-the-World I," Philosophy 185: Heidegger, University of California, Berkeley, Fall 2007. The lecture used to be available as a free download through iTunesUniversity. I thank Joel Isaac for bringing this lecture course to my attention.

55. As producer Sarah Green recalled, Chief Adkins of the Chickahominy tribe in Virginia "wanted to know why we called it *The New World*" since "they had been there for thousands of years." Quoted in Hintermann and Villa, *Terrence Malick*, 258.

56. See Robert Berkhofer, *White Man's Indian: Images of the American Indian from Columbus to the Present* (New York: Knopf, 1978); and Hayden White, "The Noble Savage Theme as Fetish," in *Tropics of Discourse: Essays in Cultural Criticism* (Baltimore: Johns Hopkins University Press, 1978), 183–96.

57. See Edward Buscombe, "What's New in *The New World*?," *Film Quarterly* 62, no. 3 (Spring 2009): 35–40. For more on Pocahontas myths, see Kristina Downs, "Mirrored Archetypes: The Contrasting Cultural Roles of La Malinche and Pocahontas," *Western Folklore* 67, no. 4 (Fall 2008): 397–414; and Camilla Townsend, *Pocahontas and the Powhatan Dilemma: An American Portrait* (New York: Hill and Wang, 2004).

58. In his famous 1891 essay "Our America," José Martí famously indicted "these men born in America who are ashamed of the mother that raised them because she wears an Indian apron." Martí, *Selected Writings*, ed. and trans. Esther Allen, introduction by Roberto González Echeverría (New York: Penguin, 2002), 289.

59. Malick's voice-overs can be divided into two different categories: narrations and soliloquies, neither reducible to the other. See James Wierzbicki, *Terrence Malick: Sonic Style* (New York: Routledge, 2019), 35ff.

60. Malick, "The New World: A Story of the Indies," 34.

61. See Buscombe, "What's New in *The New World*?," 37.

62. The novelist William Vollmann explores this narrative in *Argall: The True Story of Pocahontas and Captain John Smith*, the third installment of his epic *Seven Dreams: A Book of North American Landscapes* (New York: Viking, 2001).

63. On women's roles in Jamestown, see Jennifer Potter, *The Jamestown Brides: The Untold Story of England's "Maids for Virginia"* (New York: Oxford University Press, 2019).

64. Hintermann and Villa, *Terrence Malick*, 275.

65. This according to Jack Fisk, quoted in Hintermann and Villa, *Terrence Malick*, 286.

66. The poem is reproduced, without its full title, in "New World: Production Notes."

67. Vachel Lindsay, "For America at War: Our Mother, Pocahontas," *Poetry: A Magazine of Verse* 10, no. 4 (July 1917): 169–72. Lindsay also was an early champion of the cinema. See Lind-

say, *The Art of the Moving Picture*, with an introduction by Stanley Kauffmann (1915; New York: Liveright, 1970).

68. Lindsay, "For America at War." A typo in the production notes included with the Criterion release of the film exchanges "Nurse" for "Norse." The trope of "new races" being born in the New World is an old one. Compare Mexican philosopher José Vasconcelos's 1925 work *La raza cósmica* (Vasconcelos, *The Cosmic Race: A Bilingual Edition*, trans. Didier T. Jaén, with an afterword by Joseba Gabilondo [Baltimore: Johns Hopkins University Press, 1997]).

69. Rosemary Benét and Stephen Vincent Benét, *A Book of Americans*, illustrated by Charles Child (1933; New York: Holt, Rinehart and Winston, 1961).

70. Benét and Benét, *Book of Americans*, 11. Quoted also in "New World: Production Notes," 33.

71. Benét and Benét, *Book of Americans*, 79.

72. Recent works challenging the long afterlife of the "vanishing Indian" trope include David Treuer, *The Heartbeat of Wounded Knee: Native America from 1890 to the Present* (New York: Riverhead, 2019); and Roxanne Dunbar-Ortiz and Dina Gilio-Whitaker, *"All the Real Indians Died Off": And Twenty Other Myths About Native Americans* (Boston: Beacon Press, 2016).

73. Smith, *The Generall Historie*, in *Writings*, 439.

74. Smith, *The Generall Historie*, in *Writings*, 441.

75. Malick, "The New World: A Story of the Indies," 26, 98.

76. Malick, "The New World: A Story of the Indies," 33.

77. Malick, "The New World: A Story of the Indies," 101.

78. Benét and Benét, *Book of Americans*, 10.

79. Hintermann and Villa, *Terrence Malick*, 276.

80. Malick, "The New World: A Story of the Indies," 35.

81. Hintermann and Villa, *Terrence Malick*, 276.

82. Hintermann and Villa, *Terrence Malick*, 277.

83. Smith, *A True Relation*, in *Writings*, 29.

84. Michael Gaudio, *Engraving the Savage: The New World and Techniques of Civilization* (Minneapolis: University of Minnesota Press, 2008), 62.

85. Some parts of *The New World* were filmed in sixty-five millimeter and others in thirty-five millimeter, with anamorphic lenses. See Hintermann and Villa, *Terrence Malick*, 281–82.

86. Thomas Harriot [Hariot], *A Briefe and True Report of the New Found Land of Virginia: The Complete 1590 Theodor de Bry Edition*, with a new introduction by Paul Hulton (New York: Dover, 1972), 5. I have modernized the type but retained the spellings of the original here and in the following quotations. As this edition shows, Hariot's name was subject to variable spellings, with Hariot or Harriot being the most common. I have chosen to stick with Hariot, unless quoting other sources. Subsequent citations to Hariot's *Briefe and True Report* are to the Dover edition unless otherwise specified. For more background on his life and work, see Robyn Arianhod, *Thomas Harriot: A Life in Science* (Oxford: Oxford University Press, 2019).

87. Hariot, *A Briefe and True Report*, 7–12.

88. Malick, "The New World: A Story of the Indies," 1.

89. Hariot, *A Briefe and True Report*, 24.

90. Hariot, *A Briefe and True Report*, 25.

91. Hariot, *A Briefe and True Report*, 25.

92. Hariot, *A Briefe and True Report*, 29.

93. Hariot, *A Briefe and True Report*, 29.

94. Stephen Greenblatt, "Invisible Bullets," in *Shakespearean Negotiations: The Circulation of Social Energy in Renaissance England* (Berkeley: University of California Press, 1988), 21–65; quotation on p. 31.

95. See Clifford Geertz, "Anti Anti-Relativism," *American Anthropologist* 86, no. 2 (June 1984): 263–78.

96. Malick, "The New World: A Story of the Indies," 63.

97. Stephen Greenblatt, *Marvelous Possessions: The Wonder of the New World* (Chicago: University of Chicago Press, 1991), 8.

98. Nicolás Wey Gómez, *The Tropics of Empire: Why Columbus Sailed South to the Indies* (Cambridge, MA: MIT Press, 2008), 53.

99. See Lewis Hanke, *Aristotle and the American Indians: A Study in Race Prejudice in the Modern World* (London: Hollis & Carter, 1959); and Hanke, *All Mankind Is One: A Study of the Disputation Between Bartolomé de Las Casas and Juan Ginés de Sepúlveda in 1550 on the Religious and Intellectual Capacity of the American Indians* (Dekalb: Northern Illinois University Press, 1974).

100. Surekha Davies, *Renaissance Ethnography and the Invention of the Human: New Worlds, Maps and Monsters* (Cambridge: Cambridge University Press, 2016), 276.

101. Davies, *Renaissance Ethnography*, 276–77; Greenblatt, *Marvelous Possessions*, 20.

102. Price, *Love and Hate in Jamestown*, 183.

103. Malick, "The New World: A Story of the Indies," 1.

104. Rolfe's letter to Dale was reproduced in Ralph Hamor's 1615 *A True Discourse of the Present Estate of Virginia*. Parts of it have been reprinted in Smith's *Writings*; quotation on p. 1164.

105. Smith, *Writings*, 1166.

106. Dargis, "When Virginia Was Eden."

107. Lidija Haas, "The Heavy-Handed Moralism of Terrence Malick's New Film," *New Republic*, December 13, 2019.

108. Leo Marx, *The Machine in the Garden: Technology and the Pastoral Idea in America* (Oxford: Oxford University Press, 1964).

109. Joaquin Miller, *Life Amongst the Modocs: Unwritten History*, introduction by Malcolm Margolin, afterword by Alan Rosenus (1873; Berkeley, CA: Heyday Books/Urion Press, 1996), 387.

110. Miller, *Life Amongst the Modocs*, 205,

111. Miller, *Life Amongst the Modocs*, 90–91.

112. Miller, *Life Amongst the Modocs*, 268–69.

113. Alan Rosenus, "Afterword: The History Behind *Unwritten History*," in Miller, *Life Amongst the Modocs*, 406.

114. Miller, *Life Amongst the Modocs*, 228.

115. In California history, scholars use the term *genocide* to describe the full-scale slaughter of Indigenous populations. See Benjamin Madley, *An American Genocide: The United States and the California Indian Catastrophe, 1846–1873* (New Haven, CT: Yale University Press, 2016).

116. Miller, *Life Amongst the Modocs*, 36.

117. The phrase belongs to the performance artist Guillermo Gómez-Peña. It is cited in María Josefina Saldaña-Portillo, *The Revolutionary Imagination in the Americas and the Age of Development* (Durham, NC: Duke University Press, 2003), 280.

118. Malick, "The New World: A Story of the Indies," 31.

119. Some of the actors who appeared in *Black Robe* also found roles in *The New World*, such as August Schellenberg and Raoul Trujillo.

120. Wierzbicki, *Terrence Malick: Sonic Style*, 92; and Alex Ross, *Wagnerism: Art and Politics in the Shadow of Music* (New York: Farrar Straus and Giroux, 2020), 649.

121. Ross, *Wagnerism*, 649–50.

122. Ross, *Wagnerism*, 650.

123. "AFI Fellows Discussion, 9/24/1969," audio file at the Louis B. Mayer Library, AFI.

124. "Synopsis," *The New World* Press Kit, New Line Cinema, Margaret Herrick Library, AMPAS.

125. Others have made this comparison, though for slightly different reasons. See Michaels, *Terrence Malick*, 85.

126. Price, *Love and Hate in Jamestown*, 127.

127. Jorge Cañizares-Esguerra, *Puritan Conquistadors: Iberianizing the Atlantic, 1550–1700* (Stanford, CA: Stanford University Press, 2006). The idea of the Black Legend was first introduced by Julián Juderías in his 1914 book *La Leyanda Negra y la verdad histórica* (Madrid: Tip. de la Revista de Archivos, 1914).

128. Bartolomé de Las Casas, *An Account, Much Abbreviated, of the Destruction of the Indies*, ed. Franklin W. Knight, trans. Andrew Hurley (Indianapolis: Hackett, 2003), 9.

129. Las Casas, *An Account*, 84, 6; similar imagery appears elsewhere (cf. 82).

130. Las Casas, *An Account*, 29, 75, 65, 85.

131. Las Casas, *An Account*, introduction, xi.

132. Malick, "The New World: A Story of the Indies," 31.

133. Malick, "New World: Production Notes," 31. In Hurley's translation of the *Account*, this passage is on p. 5.

134. See, for example, Enrique Dussel, "Was America Discovered or Invaded?," in *Beyond Philosophy: Ethics, History, Marxism, and Liberation Theology*, ed. Eduardo Mendieta (Lanham, MD: Rowman & Littlefield, 2003), 219–26.

135. D'Entremont, review of *The New World*, 1025.

136. Daniel Castro, *Another Face of Empire: Bartolomé de Las Casas, Indigenous Rights, and Ecclesiastical Imperialism* (Durham, NC: Duke University Press, 2006).

137. See Las Casas, *An Account*, xxx.

138. See Hariot, *A Briefe and True Report*, in Smith, *Writings*, 886.

139. David Sterritt, "Film, Philosophy, and Terrence Malick's 'The New World,'" *Chronicle of Higher Education*, January 6, 2006.

140. Daniel Yacavone, *Film Worlds: A Philosophical Aesthetics of Cinema* (New York: Columbia University Press, 2014).

141. See Martin Heidegger, "The Origin of the Work of Art," in *Off the Beaten Track*, ed. and trans. Julian Young and Kenneth Haynes (Cambridge: Cambridge University Press, 2002), 1–56. On the evolution of Heidegger's essay, see Jacques Taminiaux, "The Origin of 'The Origin of the Work of Art,'" in *Poetics, Speculation, and Judgment: The Shadow of the Work of Art from Kant to Phenomenology*, ed. and trans. Michael Gendre (Albany: State University of New York Press, 1993), 153–70.

142. Ross Gibson, "Searching for a Place in the World: The Landscape of Ford's *The Searchers*," in *The Place of Landscape: Concepts, Contexts, Studies*, ed. Jeff Malpas (Cambridge, MA: MIT Press, 2011), 247.

143. Joerg Widmer quoted in Hintermann and Villa, *Terrence Malick*, 285, 284, 286.

144. Hintermann and Villa, *Terrence Malick*, 286.

145. Ilan Safit, "Nature Screened: An Eco-Film-Phenomenology," *Environmental Philosophy* 11, no. 2 (Fall 2014): 211–35.

146. Hintermann and Villa, *Terrence Malick*, 287–88.

147. Malick, "The New World: A Story of the Indies," 37.

148. Heidegger, *The Essence of Reasons*, 103.

149. Heidegger, *The Essence of Reasons*, 142 n. 44.

150. Heidegger, *The Essence of Reasons*, 47, 49. For a different account of the Heideggerian elements of *The New World*, see Martin Donougho, "'Melt Earth to Sea': *The New World* of Terrence Malick," *Journal of Speculative Philosophy* 25, no. 4 (2011): 359–74.

151. After his so-called *Kehre*, Heidegger abandoned this existential approach to ontology, pursuing a "thinking of Being" that did not privilege *Dasein*.

152. Jacques Rancière, *The Intervals of Cinema*, trans. John Howe (New York: Verso, 2014), 108.

153. Jacques Rancière, *Béla Tarr, the Time After*, trans. Erik Beranek (Minneapolis: Univocal, 2013), 34, 35.

154. Heidegger, *The Basic Problems of Phenomenology*, 168.

155. Malick, "The Concept of Horizon," n.p., "Heidegger (Part II)" n. 11. See also Heidegger, *The Basic Problems of Phenomenology*, 175.

156. Ryan Lattanzio, "Christopher Plummer Penned Letter to Terrence Malick After 'New World': 'Get Yourself a Writer,'" *IndieWire*, February 6, 2021, https://www.indiewire.com/2021/02/christopher-plummer-terrence-malick-get-yourself-a-writer-1234615348/.

157. "Terrence Malick Made an Enemy out of James Horner and 7 More Things We Learned About 'The New World,'" *IndieWire*, July 6, 2011, https://www.indiewire.com/2011/07/terrence-malick-made-an-enemy-out-of-james-horner-7-more-things-we-learned-about-the-new-world-117662/. See also Wierzbicki, *Terrence Malick: Sonic Style*, 83.

158. Martin Scorsese, "The Persisting Vision: Reading the Language of Cinema," *New York Review of Books*, August 15, 2013, 25–27, quote on 27.

159. Scorsese, "The Persisting Vision, 27.

160. Scorsese, "The Persisting Vision, 25.

161. Malick, "The New World: A Story of the Indies," 4.

162. Cf. Heidegger, *The Basic Problems of Phenomenology*, 22: "Because the Dasein is historical in its own existence, possibilities of access and modes of interpretation of beings are themselves diverse, varying in different historical circumstances."

163. Stanley Cavell, "The Good of Film," in *Cavell on Film*, ed. William Rothman (Albany: State University of New York Press, 2005), 344.

164. Jonathan Lear, *Radical Hope: Ethics in the Face of Cultural Devastation* (Cambridge: MA: Harvard University Press, 2006).

165. Taubin, "Birth of a Nation," 44.

166. Taubin, "Birth of a Nation," 44.

167. Quoted in Price, *Love and Hate in Jamestown*, 182.

168. Malick, "The New World: A Story of the Indies," 34.

169. Malick, "The New World: A Story of the Indies," 33–34.

Chapter 5

Note to epigraph: Peter Matthiessen, *The Snow Leopard* (New York: Viking, 1978), 65.

1. Lawrence Wright, *God Save Texas: A Journey into the Soul of the Lone Star State* (New York: Knopf, 2018), 89–111.

2. On the Menil Collection, see William Middleton, *Double Vision: The Unerring Eye of Art World Avatars Dominique and John de Menil* (New York: Knopf, 2018).

3. Wright, *God Save Texas*, 110.

4. Wright, *God Save Texas*, 110–11.

5. Wright, *God Save Texas*, 243.

6. Helen Thorpe, "The Man Who Wasn't There," *Texas Monthly*, December 1998, https://www.texasmonthly.com/articles/the-man-who-wasnt-there-2/.

7. Matthew Odam and Charles Ealy, "Actors, Producers Know Different Sides of Terrence Malick," *Austin360*, June 3, 2001, https://www.austin360.com/entertainment/movies/actors-producers-know-different-sides-terrence-malick/xQCgf6UEFrNZpqXg0f9MHN/.

8. Quoted in Eric Benson, "The Not-So-Secret Life of Terrence Malick," *Texas Monthly*, April 2017, http://www.texasmonthly.com/the-culture/the-not-so-secret-life-of-terrence-malick/.

9. Martin Heidegger, *The Basic Problems of Phenomenology*, trans. Albert Hofstadter, rev. ed. (Bloomington: Indiana University Press, 1988), 8.

10. Theodor W. Adorno, "Late Style in Beethoven," in *Essays on Music*, ed. Richard Leppert, trans. Susan H. Gillespie (Berkeley: University of California Press, 2002), 564–68; and Edward W.

Said, *On Late Style: Music and Literature Against the Grain*, foreword by Mariam C. Said, introduction by Michael Wood (New York: Vintage, 2007).

11. Said, *On Late Style*, 7–8.

12. According to Jack Fisk, *The Tree of Life* is a very personal film, one that Malick began imagining soon after *Badlands*. See Dominik Kamalzadeh and Michael Pekler, *Terrence Malick* (Marburg: Schüren Verlag, 2013), 152.

13. Martin Heidegger, *Being and Time*, trans. John Macquarrie and Edward Robinson (New York: Harper & Row, 1962), § 53.

14. "Only one thing is certain: the universe will end." Priyamvada Natarajan, "All Things Great and Small," *New York Review of Books*, July 1, 2021, 58.

15. On the Augustinian dimensions of Malick's late-career films, see Joshua Sikora, "The Journey Home: A Unity of Memory and Cosmology in Cinema," in *A Critical Companion to Terrence Malick*, ed. Joshua Sikora (Lanham, MD: Lexington Books, 2020), 155–74.

16. Garry Wills, *Saint Augustine* (New York: Viking, 1999), xv.

17. Henry Chadwick, "Introduction," in Augustine, *Confessions*, trans. Henry Chadwick (1991; Oxford: Oxford University Press, 2008), xxiv.

18. On Malick and Plotinus, see Sikora, "The Journey Home," 155–74.

19. Chadwick, "Introduction," xxiv.

20. "Editor's Preface" to Henry Adams, *The Education of Henry Adams*, in *Novels, Mont Saint Michel, The Education*, ed. Ernest Samuels and Jayne N. Samuels (New York: Library of America, 1983), 719.

21. Cited in Robert F. Sayre, *The Examined Self: Benjamin Franklin, Henry Adams, Henry James* (Princeton, NJ: Princeton University Press, 1964), 8.

22. Stanley Cavell, *A Pitch of Philosophy: Autobiographical Exercises* (Cambridge, MA: Harvard University Press, 1994), vii.

23. Walker Percy, *The Moviegoer* (New York: Knopf, 1961); Stanley Cavell, *The World Viewed: Reflections on the Ontology of Film*, rev. ed. (1971; Cambridge, MA: Harvard University Press, 1979); Cavell, *Pursuits of Happiness: The Hollywood Comedy of Remarriage* (Cambridge, MA: Harvard University Press, 1981).

24. See, for example, Chris O'Falt, "Criterion's 'The Tree of Life' Is Not a Director's Cut, but a New Movie from Terrence Malick," *IndieWire*, August 31, 2018, https://www.indiewire.com/2018/08/criterion-tree-of-life-terrence-malick-new-movie-1201999468/.

25. Kenneth Turan, "Hollywood's Lethal Hedgehog Mentality," *Los Angeles Times*, September 21, 2014.

26. Job 38:4, 7.

27. G. W. Leibniz, *Theodicy: Essays on the Goodness of God, the Freedom of Man, and the Origin of Evil*, ed. Austin Farrer, trans. E. M. Huggard (Chicago: Open Court, 1985).

28. Boethius, *The Consolation of Philosophy*, trans. V. E. Watts (New York: Penguin, 1969), 141.

29. Mara van der Lugt: *Dark Matters: Pessimism and the Problem of Suffering* (Princeton, NJ: Princeton University Press, 2021), 95.

30. René Descartes, *Meditations on First Philosophy: With Selections from the Objections and Replies*, trans. and ed. John Cottingham, with an introductory essay by Bernard Williams, rev. ed. (Cambridge: Cambridge University Press, 1996), 39.

31. Descartes, *Meditations*, 39. For a useful comparison of *The Tree of Life* and the Book of Job, see Carol A. Newsom, "The Book of Job and Terrence Malick's *The Tree of Life*," in *Rhetoric and Hermeneutics: Approaches to Text, Tradition and Social Construction in Biblical and Second Temple Literature* (Tübingen: Mohr Siebeck, 2019), 273–88.

32. Immanuel Kant, "On the Miscarriage of All Philosophical Trials in Theodicy," in *Religion and Rational Theology*, trans. and ed. Allen W. Wood and George di Giovanni (Cambridge: Cambridge University Press, 1996), 24–37. On this text in Kierkegaard's thinking, see Ronald M Green,

Kierkegaard and Kant: The Hidden Debt (Albany: State University of New York Press, 1992), 22–24.

33. On Kierkegaard's reception in the United States, see George Cotkin, *Existential America* (Baltimore: Johns Hopkins University Press, 2003), 35–90. On Kierkegaard's influence in the development of existentialism, see Samuel Moyn, "Anxiety and Secularization: Søren Kierkegaard and the Twentieth-Century Invention of Existentialism," in *Situating Existentialism: Key Texts in Context*, ed. Jonathan Judaken and Robert Bernasconi (New York: Columbia University Press, 2012), 279–304; and Habib C. Malik, *Receiving Søren Kierkegaard: The Early Impact and Transmission of His Thought* (Washington, DC: Catholic University Press, 1997).

34. Edward F. Mooney, "Kierkegaard's Job Discourse: Getting Back the World," *International Journal for the Philosophy of Religion* 34, no. 3 (December 1993): 151–69, quote on 151.

35. Søren Kierkegaard, *Repetition*, in *Fear and Trembling/Repetition*, Kierkegaard's Writings 6, ed. and trans. Howard V. Hong and Edna H. Hong (Princeton, NJ: Princeton University Press, 1983), 197.

36. Kierkegaard, *Repetition*, 198.

37. Kierkegaard, *Repetition*, 132.

38. Kierkegaard, *Repetition*, 210.

39. Kierkegaard, *Repetition*, 203.

40. Kierkegaard, *Repetition*, 200.

41. Matthiessen, *The Snow Leopard*, 64, 65.

42. Matthiessen, *The Snow Leopard*, 65–66.

43. Matthiessen, *The Snow Leopard*, 66.

44. Matthiessen, *The Snow Leopard*, 66. The quotation comes from I. S. Shklovskii and Carl Sagan, *Intelligent Life in the Universe* (San Francisco: Holden-Day, 1966).

45. Mooney, "Kierkegaard's Job Discourse," 161.

46. Søren Kierkegaard, "The Lord Gave, and the Lord Took Away; Blessed Be the Name of the Lord," in *Eighteen Upbuilding Discourses*, Kierkegaard's Writings 5, ed. and trans. Edward V. Hong and Edna H. Hong, (Princeton, NJ: Princeton University Press, 1990), 115.

47. Kierkegaard, "The Lord Gave, and the Lord Took Away," 121.

48. Mooney, "Kierkegaard's Job Discourse," 164–65.

49. At the time of his death in 2014, Matthiessen was working on an autobiographical project. See Jeff Wheelwright, "Force of Nature: The Racing Tides Beneath Peter Matthiessen's Literary Achievement," *American Scholar*, June 4, 2018, https://theamericanscholar.org/force-of-nature/.

50. John Caruana, "Repetition and Belief: A Kierkegaardian Reading of Malick's *The Tree of Life*," in *Immanent Frames: Postsecular Cinema Between Malick and von Trier*, ed. John Caruana and Mark Cauchi (Albany: State University of New York Press, 2018), 71. A more expressly theological reading of Kierkegaard's presence in *The Tree of Life* can be found in Nicholas Olson's "They Who See God's Hand: *The Tree of Life* as an 'Upbuilding Discourse," *Other Journal*, May 11, 2012, https://theotherjournal.com/2012/05/11/they-who-see-gods-hand-the-tree-of-life-as-an-upbuilding-discourse/.

51. Gregory Zinman, "Lumia," *New Yorker*, June 20, 2011, https://www.newyorker.com/magazine/2011/06/27/lumia.

52. In the notes to his translation of Heidegger's *The Essence of Reasons*, Malick references *Theodicée* (1710). See Martin Heidegger, *The Essence of Reasons*, trans. Terrence Malick (Evanston, IL: Northwestern University Press, 1969), 143 n. 54.

53. Lambert Zuidervaart, "Hegel, Malick, and the Postsecular Sublime," in Caruana and Cauchi, *Immanent Frames*, 47–67.

54. See M. R. Wright, *Cosmology in Antiquity* (New York: Routledge, 1995), 3.

55. Aristophanes, *Lysistrata*, trans. Douglass Parker, afterword by Judith Fletcher (New York: Signet Classics, 2009), 25.

56. Wright, *Cosmology in Antiquity*, 6.

57. Wright, *Cosmology in Antiquity*, 6. See also Carmen Blacker and Michael Loewe, eds., *Ancient Cosmologies* (London: George Allen & Unwin, 1975).

58. See Aristotle, *On the Heavens I & II*, trans. Stuart Leggatt (Liverpool: Liverpool University Press, 1995).

59. Wright, *Cosmology and Antiquity* 56.

60. George Perrigo Conger, *Theories of Macrocosms and Microcosms in the History of Philosophy* (New York: Columbia University Press, 1922), 134.

61. Christian Wolff, *Preliminary Discourse on Philosophy in General*, trans. Richard J. Blackwell (Indianapolis: Bobbs-Merrill, 1963), 41.

62. Conger, *Theories of Macrocosms and Microcosms*, 138.

63. Alexandre Koyré, *From the Closed World to the Infinite Universe* (Baltimore: Johns Hopkins University Press, 1957), 275.

64. Koyré, *From the Closed World*, 2.

65. S. Brent Plate, "Visualizing the Cosmos: Terrence Malick's *Tree of Life* and Other Visions of Life in the Universe," *Journal of the American Academy of Religion* 80, no. 2 (June 2012): 528.

66. See John Tresch, "Cosmologies Materialized: History of Science and History of Ideas," in *Rethinking Modern European Intellectual History*, ed. Darrin McMahon and Samuel Moyn (New York: Oxford University Press, 2014), 153–72.

67. Hans Reichenbach, *From Copernicus to Einstein* (New York: Philosophical Library, 1942), 12, 11.

68. Reichenbach, *From Copernicus to Einstein*, 12.

69. William James, *The Varieties of Religious Experience*, in *William James: Writings 1902–1910*, ed. Bruce Kuklick (New York: Library of America, 1987), 39.

70. Kierkegaard, *Repetition*, 200.

71. Siegfried Kracauer, *Theory of Film: The Redemption of Physical Reality*, with an introduction by Miriam Bratu Hansen (1960; Princeton, NJ: Princeton University Press, 1997), 297, 300, 304.

72. Paul Schrader, *Transcendental Style in Film: Ozu, Bresson, Dreyer* (1972; Berkeley: University of California Press, 2018), 183.

73. John Muir, *My First Summer in the Sierra* (1911), collected in *Nature Writings*, ed. William Cronon (New York: Library of America, 1997), 245.

74. John Muir, *John of the Mountains: The Unpublished Journals of John Muir*, ed. Linnie Marsh Wolfe (1938; Madison: University of Wisconsin Press, 1979), 313.

75. Pascal Merigeau, *Jean Renoir: A Biography*, trans. Bruce Benderson, foreword by Martin Scorsese (Burbank, CA: RatPac Press, 2017), 701.

76. Richard Brody, "Watching Sandy with Jean Renoir," *New Yorker*, October 29, 2012, https://www.newyorker.com/culture/richard-brody/watching-sandy-with-jean-renoir.

77. Jean Renoir, *My Life and My Films*, trans. Norman Denny (New York: Da Capo, 1974), 277.

78. Cavell, *Pursuits of Happiness*.

79. See Guy Ortolano, *The Two Cultures Controversy: Science, Literature and Cultural Politics in Postwar Britain* (Cambridge: Cambridge University Press, 2009).

80. "Fellows' Meeting 3/20/70," audio recording at the Louis B. Mayer Library, AFI. Subsequent quotations are from this recording.

81. Paul Schrader, "Boudo [sic] Saved From Drowning," *Los Angeles Free Press*, March 21–27, 1969, 26; available at https://paulschrader.org/articles/pdf/1969-BoudoSavedFromDrowning.pdf.

82. See Alexander Sesonske, *Jean Renoir: The French Films, 1924–1939* (Cambridge, MA: Harvard University Press, 1980).

83. For more on Cavell and Sesonske's friendship, see Stanley Cavell, *Little Did I Know: Excerpts from Memory* (Stanford, CA: Stanford University Press, 2010), 251–52, 254, 259, 262; as well

as Stanley Cavell, "Alexander Sesonske Remembered," American Society for Aesthetics, https://aesthetics-online.org/page/AlexanderSesonskeSC?. See also Stanley Cavell and Alexander Sesonske, "Logical Empiricism and Pragmatism in Ethics," *Journal of Philosophy* 48, no. 1 (January 1951): 5–17; and Cavell and Sesonske, "Moral Theory, Ethical Judgments, and Empiricism," *Mind* 61, no. 244 (October 1952): 543–63. I thank Joel Isaac for bringing these sources to my attention.

84. See Cavell, "Alexander Sesonske Remembered." Cavell also acknowledged his "indebtedness" to Sesonske in the enlarged edition of *The World Viewed*, 161.

85. Irving Singer, *Three Philosophical Filmmakers: Hitchcock, Welles, Renoir* (Cambridge, MA: MIT Press, 2004), 154.

86. "*Sein und Zeit*, by Martin Heidegger: An Informal English Paraphrase of Sections 1–53 with Certain Omissions as Noted, by Robert J. Trayhern, John Wild, Bert Dreyfus, C. de Deugd," 45. I thank Bruce Kuklick for generously making his mimeographed copy of this document available to me.

87. "Fellows' Meeting 3/20/70"; subsequent quotations are also from this recording.

88. So fond of rivers was Renoir that he eventually made an entire film dedicated to one: his first color film, shot in India, *The River* (1951).

89. Penelope Gilliatt's "Le Meneur de Jeu," written in Paris, 1968, originally appeared in the *New Yorker* in 1969 and was reprinted in Gilliatt's *Jean Renoir: Essays, Conversations, Reviews* (New York: McGraw-Hill, 1975).

90. Schrader led the AFI Fellows' Seminar on February 20, 1970, focusing primarily on the works of Ozu. Audio recording at the Louis B. Mayer Library, AFI.

91. These remarks come from an administrative document titled "Terry Malick: Status as of March 10, 1970," Louis B. Mayer Library, AFI.

92. Cf. Sesonske, *Jean Renoir*, 255: "throughout Renoir's films the water imagery usually occurs as a context of change, most often a change that involves a loss of innocence."

93. Nick Gonda, quoted in *Terrence Malick: Rehearsing the Unexpected*, ed. Carlo Hintermann and Daniele Villa (London: Faber & Faber, 2016), 340.

94. Sesonske, *Jean Renoir*, 133.

95. The massive, 65,000-pound oak tree was moved from another location for this explicit purpose. See Terry Hagerty, "Oak in 'Tree of Life' Moved to Downtown Smithville," *Bastrop Advertiser*, February 9, 2008, pp. 1A, 2A.

96. Sesonske, *Jean Renoir*, 132.

97. George Stevens Jr., *Conversations with the Great Moviemakers of Hollywood's Golden Age at the American Film Institute* (New York: Vintage, 2007), 608.

98. Renoir, *My Life and My Films*, 11.

99. Stevens, *Conversations with the Great Moviemakers*, 609.

100. Stevens, *Conversations with the Great Moviemakers*, 610.

101. Stevens, *Conversations with the Great Moviemakers*, 612.

102. Stevens, *Conversations with the Great Moviemakers*, 614, 616.

103. Stevens, *Conversations with the Great Moviemakers*, 621. On the rise of "personal" filmmaking in the American cinematic underground, see Robert Sklar, *Movie-Made America: A Cultural History of American Movies*, rev. ed. (New York: Vintage, 1994), 305–20.

104. See *Renoir on Renoir: Interviews, Essays, and Remarks*, trans. Carol Volk (Cambridge: Cambridge University Press, 1989), 169.

105. Stevens, *Conversations with the Great Moviemakers*, 621. Although Malick is not identified in the published version of this seminar, the transcript available at the Louis B. Mayer Library, AFI, lists him by name on p. 34.

106. Stevens, *Conversations with the Great Moviemakers*, 621–22.

107. Stevens, *Conversations with the Great Moviemakers*, 635.

108. See Peter Bondanella, *The Cinema of Federico Fellini*, with a foreword by Federico Fellini (Princeton, NJ: Princeton University Press, 1992), 180.

109. Dwight Macdonald, "8½," in *American Movie Critics: An Anthology from the Silents Until Now*, ed. Phillip Lopate (New York: Library of America, 2006), 373.

110. Hubert L. Dreyfus, "Christianity Without Onto-Theology: Kierkegaard's Account of the Self's Movement from Despair to Bliss," in *Religion After Metaphysics*, ed. Mark A. Wrathall (Cambridge: Cambridge University Press, 2003), 88–103.

111. Roger Ebert, "The Blink of a Life, Enclosed by Time and Space," RogerEbert.com, June 11, 2011, https://www.rogerebert.com/reviews/the-tree-of-life-2011.

112. Peter J. Leithart, *Shining Glory: Theological Reflections on Terrence Malick's "The Tree of Life"* (Eugene, OR: Cascade Books, 2013), 82.

113. Søren Kierkegaard, *The Sickness unto Death: A Christian Psychological Exposition for Edification and Awakening by Anti-Climacus*, trans. Alastair Hannay (New York: Penguin, 1989), 45.

114. Bondanella, *The Cinema of Federico Fellini*, 122.

115. On "anima" in 8½, see Alexander Sesonske, "8½: A Film with Itself as Its Subject," Criterion edition of 8½ (2001). On the imagery of spirit in *The Tree of Life*, see Christopher B. Barnett, "Spirit(uality) in the Films of Terrence Malick," *Journal of Religion & Film* 17, no. 1 (April 2013), art. 33.

116. Though part of Fellini's seminar, January 12, 1970, at AFI has been collected in *The Great Moviemakers of Hollywood's Golden Age at the American Film Institute*, this information, which comes from the opening remarks of George Stevens Jr., is not included. Because so many of his films were among the first screened for fellows when they arrived at AFI, Fellini was, "through his films, the first professor at this Center," Stevens said. Federico Fellini, January 12, 1970, Harold Lloyd Master Seminar Transcript, 2, Louis B. Mayer Library, AFI.

117. Robert Sinnerbrink makes a passing reference to the similarities between 8½ and *Knight of Cups* but does not explore the possibility that a similar claim could be made about *The Tree of Life* as well. See Sinnerbrink, *Terrence Malick: Filmmaker and Philosopher* (London: Bloomsbury, 2019), 186.

118. McNees's remark came in the form of an online comment on a review of *The Tree of Life* published by the conservative Catholic journal *First Things*. See Kevin Collins, "Tree of Life Yields Little Fruit," *First Things*, June 13, 2011. At Harvard, McNees ended up studying with Cavell, though he later went on to become not a philosopher but an academic librarian at Columbia University. For more on McNees's time in Cambridge, Massachusetts, see Cavell, *Little Did I Know*, 422; as well as Abbott Gleason, *A Liberal Education* (Cambridge, MA: Tidepool Press, 2010), 120–23. Malick thanks McNees in his Harvard thesis.

119. See Preisner's website, http://www.preisner.com/.

120. Heidegger, *Being and Time*, § 35.

121. Kathryn Schulz, "Losing Streak: Reflections on Two Seasons of Loss," *New Yorker*, February 13 and 20, 2017, 74.

122. See Heidegger, *Being and Time*, §§ 50–53.

123. For the latest riff on this ancient theme, see Roy Scranton, *Learning to Die in the Anthropocene: Reflections on the End of a Civilization* (San Francisco: City Lights, 2015).

124. See Trayhern et al., "*Sein und Zeit*, by Martin Heidegger: An Informal English Paraphrase of Sections 1–53."

125. Terrence Malick, "The Tree of Life: A Screenplay," first draft, June 25, 2007, https://indiegroundfilms.files.wordpress.com/2014/01/tree-of-life-the-jun-25-07-1st.pdf, pp. 61, 115.

126. Fyodor Dostoevsky, *The Karamazov Brothers*, trans. Ignat Avsey (Oxford: Oxford University Press, 1994), 399–400.

127. Joseph Frank, *Lectures on Dostoevsky*, ed. Marina Brodskaya and Marguerite Frank, foreword by Robin Feuer Miller (Princeton, NJ: Princeton University Press, 2020), 27.

128. Paul Maher Jr. *One Big Soul: An Oral History of Terrence Malick* (Lexington, KY: n.p., 2012), 107.

129. This information comes from editor Keith Fraase. He was interviewed by Eric Hynes at the Museum of the Moving Image on December 7, 2019, as part of the retrospective "Moments of Grace: The Collected Terrence Malick."

130. Kierkegaard, *Repetition*, 197.

131. Kierkegaard, *Repetition*, 197.

132. Kierkegaard, *Repetition*, 198.

133. Kierkegaard, "The Lord Gave, and the Lord Took Away," 124.

134. Malick, "The Tree of Life: A Screenplay," 120.

135. On Malick's use of audio tracks to convey this experience of repetition, see James Batcho, *Terrence Malick's Unseeing Cinema: Memory, Time and Audibility* (Cham, Switzerland: Palgrave Macmillan, 2018), 115–51.

136. Augustine, *Confessions*, 6.

137. Augustine, *Confessions*, 171.

138. Augustine, *Confessions*, 246. For a different account of the Augustinian elements of *The Tree of Life*, see Paul Camacho, "'What Was It You Showed Me?' Perplexity and Forgiveness: *The Tree of Life* as Augustinian Confession," in *The Way of Nature and the Way of Grace: Philosophical Footholds on Terrence Malick's "The Tree of Life,"* ed. Jonathan Beever and Vernon W. Cisney (Evanston, IL: Northwestern University Press, 2016), 139–53.

139. Council for Philosophical Studies, *Phenomenology and Existentialism: Continental and Analytical Perspectives on Intentionality in the Philosophy Curriculum* (San Francisco: San Francisco State University, Council for Philosophical Studies, 1981), 4.

140. Søren Kierkegaard, *Works of Love*, Kierkegaard's Writings 16, ed. and trans. Howard V. Hong and Edna H. Hong (Princeton, NJ: Princeton University Press, 1995), 358.

141. Dostoevsky, *The Karamazov Brothers*, 972.

142. Malick, "The Tree of Life: A Screenplay," 120.

143. Cavell, *A Pitch of Philosophy*, vii. In his commentary "The Lord Gave Away, the Lord Took Away," Kierkegaard suggested we properly call Job "a teacher of humankind and not of individuals" (112).

144. Adams, *The Education of Henry Adams*, 722. As Howard V. Hong and Edna H. Hong put it, "Kierkegaard's view" was "that an author's private experience can legitimately be used in his writing only in transmuted form, that is, as the universally human, not as personal disclosure." The reason Kierkegaard so often utilized pseudonyms in his works, they argue, was "to take himself as author out of the picture and to leave the reader alone with his ideas." See the "Historical Introduction" in Kierkegaard, *Fear and Trembling/Repetition*, x.

145. Malick, "The Tree of Life: A Screenplay," n.p.

146. Johann Gottlieb Fichte, *The Vocation of Man*, trans. Peter Preuss (Indianapolis: Hackett, 1987), 2.

147. Cavell, *A Pitch of Philosophy*, vii, 11.

148. J. M. Coetzee, "Confession and Double Thoughts: Tolstoy, Rousseau, Dostoevsky," in *Doubling the Point: Essays and Interviews*, ed. David Attwell (Cambridge, MA: Harvard University Press, 1992), 251–93, quote on 244.

149. Malick, "The Tree of Life: A Screenplay," 20. Further evidence of Malick's interest in the history of the concept of soul comes from Nicolas Gonda, who got his start working as Malick's driver and assistant during the production of *The Tree of Life*. At that time, Gonda was still completing his undergraduate degree at New York University's Gallatin School of Individualized Study. In a phone conversation in 2014, Gonda told me that Malick gave him a suggested reading list for the undergraduate thesis he still needed to complete, which, after working on *The Tree of Life*, became a thesis on "the history of the soul."

150. Jean-Jacques Rousseau, *Confessions*, trans. Angela Scholar, ed. Patrick Coleman (Oxford: Oxford University Press, 2000), 5.

151. Kierkegaard, "The Lord Gave, and the Lord Took Away," 123.

152. Coetzee, *Doubling the Point*, 392.

153. Barnett, "Spirit(uality) in the Films of Terrence Malick," 1.

154. See Hintermann and Villa, *Terrence Malick*, 341, 351.

155. Leithart, *Shining Glory*, 28.

156. Two of the more useful collections are Beever and Cisney, *The Way of Nature and the Way of Grace*; and Christopher B. Barnett and Clark J. Elliston, eds., *Theology and the Films of Terrence Malick* (New York: Routledge, 2017).

157. David Sterritt, "Days of Heaven and Waco: Terrence Malick's *Tree of Life*," *Film Quarterly* 65, no. 1 (Fall 2011): 52.

158. Sterritt, "Days of Heaven and Waco," 56, 57.

159. Richard Maurice Bucke, ed., *Cosmic Consciousness: A Study in the Evolution of the Human Mind* (Boston: E. P. Dutton, 1901).

160. Ludwig Wittgenstein, *Lecture on Ethics*, ed. Edoardo Zamuner, Ermelinda Valentina Di Lascio, and D. K. Levy (West Sussex: Wiley Blackwell, 2014), 47.

161. James, *The Varieties of Religious Experience*, 359–60.

162. Matthiessen cites Bucke in *The Snow Leopard*, 328 n. 6.

163. Penelope Gilliatt, "This Place," *New Yorker*, September 18, 1978, 159.

164. James, *The Varieties of Religious Experience*, 361.

165. James, *The Varieties of Religious Experience*, 373.

166. James, *The Varieties of Religious Experience*, 382.

Chapter 6

Note to epigraph: Henry Bugbee, *The Inward Morning: A Philosophical Exploration in Journal Form*, with a new introduction by Edward F. Mooney (1958; Athens: University of Georgia Press, 1999), 209.

1. On the structural transformation of Hollywood in the 1970s, see J. D. Connor, *The Studios After the Studios: Neoclassical Hollywood (1970–2010)* (Stanford, CA: Stanford University Press, 2015). A comparison of Malick's career with those of his New Hollywood peers can be found in Dean Yamada, "Auteurs and Movie Brats: Placing Malick's Extraordinary Career in Context," in *A Critical Companion to Terrence Malick*, ed. Joshua Sikora (Lanham, MD: Lexington Books, 2020), 121–35.

2. Jack Fisk, in *Terrence Malick: Rehearsing the Unexpected*, ed. Carlo Hintermann and Daniele Villa (London: Faber & Faber, 2015), 297.

3. On Brad Pitt's "star persona" in the production of other films, see J. D. Connor, *Hollywood Math and Aftermath: The Economic Image and the Digital Recession* (New York: Bloomsbury, 2018), 26–31.

4. Council for Philosophical Studies, *Phenomenology and Existentialism: Continental and Analytical Perspectives on Intentionality in the Philosophy Curriculum* (San Francisco: San Francisco State University, Council for Philosophical Studies, 1981), 4.

5. Terrence Malick, "The Tree of Life: A Screenplay," first draft, June 25, 2007, https://indiegroundfilms.files.wordpress.com/2014/01/tree-of-life-the-jun-25-07-1st.pdf, 20.

6. See Doug Rossinow, *The Politics of Authenticity: Liberalism, Christianity, and the New Left in America* (New York: Columbia University Press, 1998).

7. See David W. Rodick's introduction to Henry Bugbee, *Wilderness in America: Philosophical Writings*, ed. David W. Rodick (New York: Fordham University Press, 2017), 5.

8. On Bugbee's career, see David W. Rodick, "Finding One's Own Voice: The Philosophical Development of Henry G. Bugbee, Jr.," *The Pluralist* 6, no. 2 (Summer 2011), 18–34; and Edward F. Mooney, ed., *Wilderness and the Heart: Henry Bugbee's Philosophy of Place, Presence, and Memory*, foreword by Alastair MacIntyre (Athens: University of Georgia Press, 1999).

9. Malick, "The Tree of Life: A Screenplay," 9.

10. David Denby, "Commitments," *New Yorker* April 15, 2013, 84.

11. A. O. Scott, "Twirling in Oklahoma, a Dervish for Love," *New York Times*, April 12, 2013, C8.

12. See Michael Nordine, "Terrence Malick Directed a Perfume Ad Starring Angelina Jolie, Because of Course He Did," *IndieWire*, February 26, 2017, https://www.indiewire.com/2017/02/terrence-malick-perfume-commercial-angelina-jolie-guerlain-1201787344/.

13. The quote was attributed to Malick's second wife, Michèle, by Peter Biskind in his 1998 *Vanity Fair* article about the making of *The Thin Red Line*, "The Runaway Genius," reprinted in Biskind, *Gods and Monsters: Thirty Years of Writing on Film and Culture from One of America's Most Incisive Writers* (New York: Nation Books, 2004), 255–75, quote on 260.

14. Gilberto Perez, "How We Remember," *London Review of Books*, September 12, 2013, 27.

15. Perez, "How We Remember," 27,

16. Jim Hemphill, "Lyrical Images: Emmanuel Lubezki, ASC, AMC, Continues His Collaboration with Director Terrence Malick on the Abstract, Poetic Love Story *To the Wonder*," *American Cinematographer*, April 2013, https://theasc.com/ac_magazine/April2013/TotheWonder/page1.html.

17. Benjamin B, "Cosmic Questions: Emmanuel Lubezki, ASC, AMC, Creates Emotionally Resonant Images for Terrence Malick's *The Tree of Life*," *American Cinematographer*, August 2011, https://theasc.com/ac_magazine/August2011/TheTreeofLife/page1.html.

18. Benjamin B, "Cosmic Questions."

19. Robert Bresson, *Notes on the Cinematograph*, trans. Jonathan Griffin, introduction by J. M. G. Le Clézio (New York: New York Review Books, 2016), 82.

20. One of the many people who worked on *The Tree of Life* and *Voyage of Time* has suggested that Malick frequently referenced Bresson's work. See Reno Lauro, "The Smile of Life: Recollections on Malick and the Work of Cinema," in Sikora, *A Critical Companion to Terrence Malick*, 255.

21. Hemphill, "Lyrical Images."

22. Keith Fraase, interviewed by Eric Hynes at the Museum of the Moving Image as part of the "Moments of Grace: The Collected Terrence Malick" retrospective, December 7, 2019.

23. Hemphill, "Lyrical Images."

24. Hintermann and Villa, *Terrence Malick: Rehearsing the Unexpected*.

25. Henry Adams, *Mont Saint Michel and Chartres*, in *Novels, Mont Saint Michel, The Education*, ed. Ernest Samuels and Jayne N. Samuels (New York: Library of America, 1983), 337–714; on the publication history of *Mont Saint Michel and Chartres*, see the notes by Ernest Samuels and Jayne N. Samuels, 1217–19.

26. Adams, *Mont Saint Michel and Chartres*, 343.

27. Adams, *Mont Saint Michel and Chartres*, 356–57.

28. Adams, *Mont Saint Michel and Chartres*, 372.

29. Adams, *Mont Saint Michel and Chartres*, 382.

30. Adams, *Mont Saint Michel and Chartres*, 382, 383.

31. For Adams's entropic theory of history, see his *A Letter to American Teachers of History* (Washington, DC, 1910).

32. Adams, *Mont Saint Michel and Chartres*, 694.

33. Lauren Huff, "Javier Bardem Explains Why Filming 'Thy Kingdom Come' Was One of His 'Hardest Experiences,'" *Hollywood Reporter*, March 29, 2018, https://www.hollywoodreporter

.com/news/javier-bardem-explains-why-filming-thy-kingdom-come-was-one-his-hardest -experiences-1097796.

34. I saw *Thy Kingdom Come* alongside *To the Wonder* at the Museum of the Moving Image's Malick retrospective "Moments of Grace," December 7, 2019. See also Matthew Aughtry, "A Universal Priesthood: The Vocation of Being Human in *Days of Heaven* and *To the Wonder*," in Sikora, *A Critical Companion to Terrence Malick*, 231.

35. A Magnolia Pictures press release for *To the Wonder* suggested Ben Affleck prepared for his role by reading, in addition to Heidegger, "Tolstoy, Dostoevsky, and F. Scott Fitzgerald." Margaret Herrick Library, AMPAS.

36. See Paul Maher Jr. and Caitlin Stuart, *Love That Loves Us: Reflections on the Films of Terrence Malick* (n.p., 2015), 109.

37. Kurylenko interviewed in "The Making of *To the Wonder*," *To the Wonder* DVD extra (Magnolia Home Entertainment, 2013).

38. The phrase comes from Margaret A. Doody's introduction to the Penguin Classics edition of Samuel Richardson's 1740 epistolary novel *Pamela*, yet another clue that the film should be interpreted as Marina's story. See Bilge Ebiri, "Radiant Zigzag Becoming: How Terrence Malick and His Team Constructed *To the Wonder*," *Vulture*, April 18, 2013, https://www.vulture .com/2013/04/how-terrence-malick-wrote-filmed-edited-to-the-wonder.html.

39. Eric Hynes, "Muses in Motion, Captured on Camera," *New York Times*, April 14, 2013.

40. Adams, *Mont Saint Michel and Chartres*, 653.

41. Adams, *Mont Saint Michel and Chartres*, 657.

42. Adams, *Mont Saint Michel and Chartres*, 661.

43. Lorraine Daston and Katharine Park, *Wonders and the Order of Nature, 1150–1750* (New York: Zone Books, 1998), 110.

44. Daston and Park, *Wonders*, 113.

45. On the rise of the suburbs in the postwar period, see Kenneth T. Jackson, *Crabgrass Frontier: The Suburbanization of the United States* (Oxford: Oxford University Press, 1985). In a biographical blurb written for the American Film Institute, Malick described himself as being from Bartlesville. "Conservatory Fellows, Biographies, 1969–1970," Box 108, Folder 1, Louis B. Mayer Library, AFI.

46. See Sarah Bakewell, *At the Existentialist Café: Freedom, Being, and Apricot Cocktails* (New York: Other Press, 2016).

47. On existentialism and *Funny Face*, see George Cotkin, *Existential America* (Baltimore: Johns Hopkins University Press, 2003), 103–4.

48. See Doug Rossinow, "Breakthrough: The Relevance of Christian Existentialism," in *The Politics of Authenticity*, 53–84.

49. Walker Percy, *The Moviegoer*, (1961; New York: Vintage, 1998), 42.

50. On Walker Percy's philosophy and fiction, see Jan Nordby Gretlund and Karl-Heinz Westarp, eds., *Walker Percy: Novelist and Philosopher* (Jackson: University Press of Mississippi, 1991).

51. On Percy's turn toward existentialism at Saranac Lake, see Patrick Samway, *Walker Percy: A Life* (New York: Farrar, Straus and Giroux, 1997), 126.

52. Walker Percy, "The Message in the Bottle," in *The Message in the Bottle: How Queer Man Is, How Queer Language Is, and What One Has to Do with the Other* (New York: Farrar, Straus and Giroux, 1975), 144. The essay originally appeared in *Thought* 34 (Autumn 1959): 405–33.

53. Susanne K. Langer was the author of such noted works as *Philosophy in a New Key: A Study in the Symbolism of Reason, Rite, and Art* (Cambridge, MA: Harvard University Press, 1942) and *Feeling and Form: A Theory of Art* (New York: Scribner's, 1953). Percy's first philosophical essays included: "Symbol as Need," *Thought* 29 (Autumn 1954): 381–90; and "Symbol as Hermeneutic in Existentialism: A Possible Bridge from Empiricism," *Philosophy and Phenomenological*

Research 16 (June 1956): 522–30. Both essays were later reprinted in *The Message in the Bottle*. For a recent appraisal of Percy's philosophical contributions, see Leslie Marsh, ed., *Walker Percy, Philosopher* (Cham, Switzerland: Palgrave Macmillan, 2018).

54. "The specific character of despair is precisely this: it is unaware of being despair." Compare Kierkegaard, *The Sickness Unto Death: A Christian Psychological Exposition for Upbuilding and Awakening*, ed. and trans. Howard V. Hong and Edna H. Hong (Princeton, NJ: Princeton University Press, 1980), 23: "not being in despair, not being conscious of being in despair, is precisely a form of despair." For more on Percy and Kierkegaard, see Martin Luschei, *The Sovereign Wayfarer: Walker Percy's Diagnosis of the Malaise* (Baton Rouge: Louisiana State University Press, 1972).

55. Judith Serebnick, "First Novelists—Spring 1961," *Library Journal*, February 1, 1961, 597. Reprinted in Lewis A. Lawson and Victor A. Kramer, eds., *Conversations with Walker Percy* (Jackson: University Press of Mississippi, 1985), 3.

56. Paul Elie, *The Life You Save May Be Your Own: An American Pilgrimage* (New York: Farrar, Straus and Giroux, 2003), 302.

57. In his acceptance speech for the National Book Award, Percy claimed *The Moviegoer* "attempts a modest restatement of the Judeo-Christian notion that man is more than an organism in an environment.... He is a wayfarer and a pilgrim." Walker Percy, "Accepting the National Book Award for *The Moviegoer*," in *Signposts in a Strange Land*, ed. Patrick Samway (New York: Farrar, Straus and Giroux, 1991), 246. Some of Binx Bolling's alienation can and should be traced back to the person who raised Percy, his uncle, the writer William Alexander Percy, author of the Southern memoir *Lanterns on the Levee: Reflections of a Planter's Son* (1941). For more on Percy's biography, see Richard H. King, *A Southern Renaissance: The Cultural Awakening of the American South, 1930–1955* (New York: Oxford University Press, 1980), 85–98.

58. Percy, *The Moviegoer*, 13.

59. Percy, *The Moviegoer*, 42. Percy's notion of "everydayness" is drawn from Martin Heidegger's notions of *Alltäglichkeit* and *das Man* in *Being and Time*, trans. John Macquarrie and Edward Robinson (San Francisco: Harper & Row, 1962), § 27. See Walker Percy, "Another Message in the Bottle," in *Signposts in a Strange Land*, 353. See also Brian Jobe, "The Everyday Lightness of Binx: Being and Time in *The Moviegoer*," in *Walker Percy's "The Moviegoer" at Fifty: New Takes on an Iconic American Novel*, ed. Jennifer Levasseur and Mary A. McCay, foreword by Jay Tolson (Baton Rouge: Louisiana State University Press, 2016), 61–78.

60. See, for example, Lloyd Michaels, *Terrence Malick* (Urbana: University of Illinois Press, 2009), 57; Hannah Patterson, ed., *The Cinema of Terrence Malick: Poetic Visions of America*, 2nd ed. (London: Wallflower Press, 2007), 1; and Biskind, *Gods and Monsters*, 261.

61. This passage is cited in H. Collin Messer, "The Unique Heart: St. Augustine's Influence on Walker Percy," in Levasseur and McCay, *Walker Percy's "The Moviegoer" at Fifty*, 13.

62. On Percy and religious communion, see John F. Desmond, *Walker Percy's Search for Community* (Athens: University of Georgia Press, 2004).

63. John Bunyan, *The Pilgrim's Progress*, ed. W. R. Owens (New York: Oxford University Press, 2003).

64. Bunyan, *The Pilgrim's Progress*, 10, 35, 85.

65. Bunyan, *The Pilgrim's Progress*, 85, 110. On the afterlives of *Pilgrim's Progress*, see Isabel Hoffmeyr, *The Portable Bunyan: A Transnational History of "The Pilgrim's Progress"* (Princeton, NJ: Princeton University Press, 2004).

66. Stanley Cavell, *Little Did I Know: Excerpts from Memory* (Stanford, CA: Stanford University Press, 2010), 234.

67. Interestingly enough, *The Desert Rose* began as a screenplay. See Larry McMurtry, *The Desert Rose*, with a new preface (New York: Simon & Shuster, 1985), 6. On Malick's adaptation, see Joe Gillis, "Waiting for Godot," *Los Angeles Magazine*, December 1995, 62.

68. The narration is a loose version of passages such as this one from the *Phaedrus*: "a man, reminded by the sight of beauty on earth of the true beauty, grows his wings and endeavours to fly upward, but in vain, exposing himself to the reproach of insanity because like a bird he fixes his gaze on the heights to the neglect of things below." Plato, *Phaedrus and the Seventh and Eight Letters*, trans. Walter Hamilton (New York: Penguin, 1973), 56.

69. See, for example, Bruce Wagner, *Force Majeure* (New York: Random House, 1991), and Wagner, *I'm Losing You* (New York: Villard, 1996).

70. Lubezki describes the technique of "sending in a torpedo" in Benjamin B, "Cosmic Questions."

71. Penelope Gilliatt, "This Place," *New Yorker*, September 18, 1978, 159.

72. Peter Matthiessen, *The Snow Leopard* (New York: Viking, 1978), 125.

73. Matthiessen, *The Snow Leopard*, 283.

74. Jack Kerouac, *The Dharma Bums* (New York: Viking, 1958). Kerouac based the character of Japhy Ryder on Snyder.

75. Matthiessen, *The Snow Leopard*, 44.

76. Chris Hodenfield, "Terrence Malick: *Days of Heaven*'s Image Maker," *Rolling Stone*, November 16, 1978, 22.

77. In his November 1985 article for *California Magazine*, "Absence of Malick," David Handelman suggests Malick's interest in this region of the world "was piqued by *The Snow Leopard*," so he set "off for the caves and shrines of Nepal with Bert Schneider, Schneider's wife and Schneider's secretary, aspiring director Michie Gleason." See "Absence of Malick," 129.

78. Matthiessen, *The Snow Leopard*, 249.

79. Matthiessen, *The Snow Leopard*, 300.

80. Plato, *Phaedrus*, 51.

81. Matthiessen, *The Snow Leopard*, 223.

82. Matthiessen, *The Snow Leopard*, 301.

83. The priest's words appear—almost verbatim—in Malick's screenplays for the unproduced "The English Speaker," which has many long soliloquies about the nature and meaning of suffering.

84. Bunyan, *The Pilgrim's Progress*, 148–49.

85. Fyodor Dostoevsky, *Crime and Punishment*, trans. Michael R. Katz (New York: Liveright, 2019), 604.

86. Robert Sinnerbrink also calls attention to Malick's use of this Bressonian technique. See Sinnerbrink, *Terrence Malick: Filmmaker and Philosopher* (London: Bloomsbury, 2019), 165.

87. See Hynes, "Muses in Motion."

88. March 1, 2016, United Artists Theater at the Ace Hotel, Los Angeles. See also Ebiri, "Radiant Zigzag Becoming."

89. Walker Percy, *Lost in the Cosmos: The Last Self-Help Book* (New York: Noonday Press, 1983). For more on Malick's interest in the cosmic perspective, see Marc Furstenau, "Technologies of Observation: Terrence Malick's *The Tree of Life* and the Philosophy of Science Fiction," in *The Way of Nature and the Way of Grace: Philosophical Footholds on Terrence Malick's "The Tree of Life*," ed. Jonathan Beever and Vernon W. Cisney (Evanston, IL: Northwestern University Press, 2016), 59–88.

90. Percy, "Another Message in the Bottle," in *Signposts in a Strange Land*, 359.

91. On Michie Gleason, see Paul Maher Jr., *All Things Shining: An Oral History of the Films of Terrence Malick*, 4th ed. (n.p., 2017), 111. See also Biskind, "The Runaway Genius," in *Gods and Monsters*, 255–77.

92. Malick was certainly familiar with James Wong Howe's extensive body of work—he told his AFI instructors that he found the cinematographer "fascinating." Based partly on Malick's

suggestion, Howe eventually participated in seminars at AFI in 1973. See George Stevens Jr., *Conversations with the Great Moviemakers of Hollywood's Golden Age at the American Film Institute* (New York: Vintage, 2007), 130–43. On Malick's enthusiasm for Howe, see Lauro, "The Smile of Life," 250.

93. Lubezki makes even parking structures, such as the one I parked in when I saw the film a second time in Santa Monica, look like works of art.

94. "The great imaginative failure" of books like *The Snow Leopard*, Kathryn Schulz has argued, "is that they valorize the challenges that arise when we confront ourselves and the wilderness but not the challenges that arise when we confront one another." Schulz, "Cat Tales: What Are We Hoping to Find When We Seek Out the Snow Leopard?," *New Yorker*, July 12 and 19, 2021, 80.

95. Cotkin, *Existential America*, 87.

96. Jay Lynn (formerly Ramiro) Gomez, "Bio/Statement," https://www.cjamesgallery.com /artist-detail/ramiro-gomez.

97. Theodor W. Adorno, *The Jargon of Authenticity*, trans. Knut Tarnowski and Frederic Will (Evanston, IL: Northwestern University Press, 1973).

98. M. Gail Hamner, "'Remember Who You Are': Imagining Life's Purpose in *Knight of Cups*," in *Theology and the Films of Terrence Malick*, ed. Christopher B. Barnett and Clark J. Elliston (New York: Routledge, 2017), 268. A similar critique can be found in Kristi McKim, "Moving Away and Circling Back: On *Knight of Cups*," *New England Review* 39, no. 2 (Summer 2018): 61–72. McKim laments the fact that Rick's journey denies the women in the film "their own longing for enlightenment" (67).

99. See Bunyan, *The Pilgrim's Progress*, 69, 55.

100. See Joakim Garff, *Kierkegaard's Muse: The Mystery of Regine Olsen*, trans. Alastair Hannay (Princeton, NJ: Princeton University Press, 2017).

101. See Søren Kierkegaard, *Either/Or*, parts 1 and 2, ed. and trans. Howard V. Hong and Edna H. Hong (Princeton, NJ: Princeton University Press, 1987); Kierkegaard, *Fear and Trembling/Repetition*, ed. and trans. Hong and Hong (Princeton, NJ: Princeton University Press, 1983); and Kierkegaard, *Stages on Life's Way: Studies in Various Persons*, ed. and trans. Hong and Hong (Princeton, NJ: Princeton University Press, 1988).

102. Augustine, *Confessions*, trans. Henry Chadwick (1991; Oxford: Oxford University Press, 2008), 35.

103. Journal entry, 1854. Quoted in Hong and Hong's "Historical Introduction" to Kierkegaard, *Fear and Trembling/Repetition*, xvii.

104. Kierkegaard, *Fear and Trembling/Repetition*, 185.

105. McKim, "Moving Away and Circling Back," 67.

106. Percy, *Lost in the Cosmos*, 187.

107. Percy, *The Moviegoer*, 13.

108. Malick's time working on *Days of Heaven* under the umbrella of Paramount Pictures is significant in this regard, for it was Paramount that "internalized the auteurist resistance to studio control." See Connor, *The Studios After the Studios*, 72.

109. "Educators' Guide," *Voyage of Time: The IMAX Experience*, p. 3, available at http:// voyageoftime.imax.com/.

110. Michael Benson, *Cosmigraphics: Picturing Space Through Time* (New York: Abrams, 2014), 10.

111. See Mark Olsen, "'Voyage of Time': Digging into the Terrence Malick Lawsuit," *Los Angeles Times*, July 23, 2013.

112. According to the special effects designer Richard Taylor II, who worked on early stages of it: "Terry wanted to recreate the origin of the universe, the earth and life." Paul Maher Jr., ed., *One Big Soul: An Oral History of Terrence Malick* (Lexington, KY: n.p., 2012), 102.

113. Keith Fraase, interviewed by Eric Hynes at the Museum of the Moving Image, December 7, 2019.

114. I saw a screening accompanied by a live performance of the film's soundtrack by the Wordless Music Orchestra at the Brooklyn Academy of Music, November 16, 2018.

115. In the archives of the Louis B. Mayer Library, a file folder labeled "Terry Malick" has a memo titled "Terry Malick: Status as of March 10, 1970," which states that "Malick is almost finished with his documentary, SENILITY."

116. See Lauro, "The Smile of Life," 259.

117. On Trouvelot, see Benson, *Cosmigraphics*, 13. See also the materials associated with the Huntington Library exhibition "Radiant Beauty: E. L. Trouvelot's Astronomical Drawings," April 28–July 30, 2018.

118. Michael Benson, *Space Odyssey: Stanley Kubrick, Arthur C. Clarke, and the Making of a Masterpiece* (New York: Simon & Schuster, 2018), 81.

119. Trumbull and Malick most likely met when the former took part in a special seminar at Greystone on March 12, 1970. "Center Schedule March 9–14, 1970," Louis B. Mayer Library, AFI. See also Lauro, "The Smile of Life," 249.

120. On Malick's time in Santa Monica, see Jeffrey Wells, "Re-Enter the Reluctant Dragon, Terrence Malick," *Los Angeles Times*, March 21, 1993. The original printing of the article—according to a later correction—misstates its author as Mary Williams Walsh.

121. Trumbull quoted in Hintermann and Villa, *Terrence Malick*, 321.

122. Hintermann and Villa, *Terrence Malick*, 309.

123. Hintermann and Villa, *Terrence Malick*, 310.

124. Hintermann and Villa, *Terrence Malick*, 310.

125. Among Benson's works are *Otherworlds: Visions of Our Solar System* (New York: Abrams, 2017); and *Cosmigraphics*. On Benson and Trumbull on *The Tree of Life*, see Benson, *A Space Odyssey*, 447.

126. These quotes come from Trumbull in Hintermann and Villa, *Terrence Malick*, 321, 323, 322.

127. Dan Glass interview, Criterion edition of *The Tree of Life*.

128. Stanley Cavell, *The Senses of Walden*, rev. ed. (Chicago: University of Chicago Press, 1992), 26.

129. Thomas Nagel, *Mind and Cosmos: Why the Materialist, Neo-Darwinian Conception of Nature Is Almost Certainly False* (Oxford: Oxford University Press, 2012), 7.

130. Nagel, *Mind and Cosmos*, 127.

131. Other commentators have addressed the significance of this closing shot, but they interpret it differently. Compare Steven Rybin's "Toward and Away from the World: Subjectivity After Loss in *The Tree of Life*," in *Immanent Frames: Postsecular Cinema Between Malick and von Trier*, ed. John Caruana and Mark Cauchi (Albany: State University of New York Press, 2018), 103. See also Sinnerbrink, *Terrence Malick: Filmmaker and Philosopher*, 150 (though he mistakenly identifies the bridge as the Golden Gate Bridge in San Francisco).

132. Council for Philosophical Studies, *Phenomenology and Existentialism*, 4.

133. A note by Donald Cary Williams on a draft of proposed courses for the 1960–61 academic year. Department of Philosophy Administrative and other records, 1900–1979, Harvard University Archives, UAV 687.15 Box 5.

134. For more on Bugbee's curious position between the analytic and continental factions of the Harvard philosophy department, see Jonathan Strassfeld, "Phenomenology and American Philosophy" (PhD diss., University of Rochester, 2019), 355, 365, 368.

135. In recent years, Bugbee's work has been enjoying something of a revival, especially among philosophers interested in environmental issues. See, for example, Bugbee, *Wilderness in America*.

136. Bugbee, *The Inward Morning*, 79.

137. Bugbee, *The Inward Morning*, 41.

138. Hans Reichenbach, *The Rise of Scientific Philosophy* (Berkeley: University of California Press, 1951).

139. See Edward F. Mooney, *Lost Intimacy in American Thought: Recovering Personal Philosophy from Thoreau to Cavell* (New York: Continuum, 2009).

140. Bugbee, *The Inward Morning*, 11.

141. See "Experience, Memory, Reflection: An Interview with Henry Bugbee," in *Wilderness in America*, 160. Selections from Bugbee's doctoral dissertation can be found in the same volume, 38–59.

142. Bugbee, *The Inward Morning*, 11. The phrase is repeated throughout the work.

143. Bugbee, *The Inward Morning*, 10.

144. Bugbee, *The Inward Morning*, 79.

145. Bugbee, *The Inward Morning*, 79.

146. Bugbee, *The Inward Morning*, 139.

147. Bugbee, *The Inward Morning*, 96.

148. Bugbee, *The Inward Morning*, 139.

149. Bugbee, *The Inward Morning*, 10.

150. Bugbee, *The Inward Morning*, 11.

151. Bugbee, *The Inward Morning*, 209.

152. Bugbee, *The Inward Morning*, 160–61.

153. Bugbee, *The Inward Morning*, 209.

154. Bugbee, *The Inward Morning*, 217.

155. Bugbee, *The Inward Morning*, 21.

156. Bugbee, *The Inward Morning*, 26.

157. Bugbee, *The Inward Morning*, 23–24.

158. Bugbee, *The Inward Morning*, 162.

159. Bugbee, *The Inward Morning*, 86, 112.

160. On the idea of the post-secular in relation to Malick's cinema, see John Caruana and Mark Cauchi, "What Is Postsecular Cinema? An Introduction," in their edited volume *Immanent Frames*, 1–26.

161. Bugbee, *The Inward Morning*, 76. On the ideas of wilderness and philosophical homecoming in Bugbee's work, see Douglas R. Anderson, "Wilderness as Philosophical Home," chapter three of *Philosophy Americana: Making Philosophy at Home in American Culture* (New York: Fordham University Press, 2006).

162. Bugbee, "Thoughts on Creation," in *Wilderness in America*, 75.

163. Bugbee, "Thoughts on Creation," 79.

164. Bugbee, "Thoughts on Creation," 79, 80.

165. Bugbee, "Thoughts on Creation," 81.

166. Bugbee, "A Way of Reading the Book of Job" (1963), in *Wilderness in America*, 125. Harvard philosophers have a long tradition of taking up the Book of Job. See, for example, Josiah Royce, "The Problem of Job," *New World: A Quarterly Review of Religion, Ethics and Theology* 6 (1897): 261–81.

167. Bugbee, *The Inward Morning*, 56.

168. Bugbee, *The Inward Morning*, 105.

169. Bugbee, *The Inward Morning*, 106.

170. Bugbee, *The Inward Morning*, 132.

171. Bugbee, *The Inward Morning*, 61, 63, 83.

172. Bugbee, *The Inward Morning*, 83.

173. Late in his career Stanley Cavell did contemplate rivers, though. See his "Thoreau Thinks of Ponds, Heidegger of Rivers," in *Philosophy the Day After Tomorrow* (Cambridge, MA: Harvard University Press, 2005), 213–35.

174. For a comparison of Bugbee and Cavell, see Edward F. Mooney, "Two Testimonies in American Philosophy: Stanley Cavell and Henry Bugbee," *Journal of Speculative Philosophy* 17, no. 2 (2003): 108–21.

175. Jennifer Ratner-Rosenhagen, "The Longing for Wisdom in Twentieth-Century US Thought," in *The Worlds of American Intellectual History*, ed. Joel Isaac et al. (Oxford: Oxford University Press, 2017), 191.

176. Bugbee, *The Inward Morning*, 52.

Chapter 7

Note to epigraph: Robert Bresson, *Notes on the Cinematograph*, trans. Jonathan Griffin, introduction by J. M. G. Le Clézio (1986; New York: New York Review Books, 2016), 25.

1. Bresson, *Notes on the Cinematograph*, 44.

2. Bresson, *Notes on the Cinematograph*, 82.

3. Jean Renoir, *Renoir on Renoir: Interviews, Essays, and Remarks*, trans. Carol Volk (Cambridge: Cambridge University Press, 1989), 5. The interview originally appeared in 1954.

4. *Renoir on Renoir*, 5.

5. *Renoir on Renoir*, 39–40.

6. Chris O'Falt, "Terrence Malick Makes a Rare Appearance at SXSW 2017 and Digs Deep on His Process," *IndieWire*, March 11, 2017, https://www.indiewire.com/2017/03/song-to-song-terrence-malick-richard-linklater-michael-fassbender-sxsw-2017-1201792562/.

7. See Zack Sharf, "Terrence Malick Vows to Return to More Structured Filmmaking: 'I'm Backing Away From That Style Now,'" *IndieWire*, April 6, 2017, https://www.indiewire.com/2017/04/terrence-malick-radegund-screenplay-style-1201802506/. See also Bilge Ebiri, "Quail Hunting Down Rabbit Holes: How Terrence Malick Blended Improv, Dance, and History to Create the Expansive *A Hidden Life*," *Vulture*, January 23, 2020, https://www.vulture.com/2020/01/behind-the-scenes-of-terrence-malicks-a-hidden-life.html.

8. Justin Chang, "Terrence Malick's 'Song to Song' Finds Beauty, Frustration and Hope in the Austin Music Scene," *Los Angeles Times*, March 16, 2017.

9. Manohla Dargis, "'Song to Song': Terrence Malick's Latest Beautiful Puzzle," *New York Times*, March 16, 2017, https://www.nytimes.com/2017/03/16/movies/song-to-song-review-terrence-malick.html.

10. Matthew Sitman, "Song Without a Story," *Commonweal*, March 29, 2017, https://www.commonwealmagazine.org/song-without-story.

11. David Thomson, "The Wonder of Terrence Malick," *Liberties: Culture and Politics* 1, no. 1 (Fall 2020): 330–47; quotes on 331.

12. Thomson, "The Wonder," 342.

13. Bernard Williams, *Ethics and the Limits of Philosophy* (Cambridge: Cambridge University Press, 1985), 198, 197.

14. This according to the *Austin City Limits* website, https://austincitylimits.com/.

15. Ramin Setoodeh, "Terrence Malick Explains His Unconventional Process in Rare SXSW Conversation," *Variety*, March 11, 2017, https://variety.com/2017/film/news/sxsw-terrence-malick-song-to-song-1202006961/.

16. See Lawrence Wright, "No City Limits: My Town, Austin, Known for Laid-back Weirdness, Is Transforming into a Turbocharged Tech Capital," *New Yorker*, February 13 and 20, 2023, 34–49.

17. See, for example, Robert Sinnerbrink, *Terrence Malick: Filmmaker and Philosopher* (London: Bloomsbury), 161–206.

18. On these themes in Cavell's cinematic thinking, see Catherine Wheatley, *Stanley Cavell and Film: Skepticism and Self-Reliance at the Cinema* (London: Bloomsbury, 2019). On Cavell's appreciation for Malick's movies, see David LaRocca, "Thinking of Film: What Is Cavellian about Malick's Movies?," in *A Critical Companion to Terrence Malick*, ed. Joshua Sikora (Lanham, MD: Lexington Books, 2020), 3–19.

19. See Greil Marcus, *Lipstick Traces: A Secret History of the Twentieth Century* (Cambridge, MA: Harvard University Press, 1989).

20. Michael Nordine, "Paul Schrader Writes an Anatomical Review of Terrence Malick's *Song to Song* and It Doesn't Involve Thumbs," *IndieWire*, May 27, 2017, https://www.indiewire.com/2017/05/paul-schrader-reviews-terrence-malick-song-to-song-1201833222/.

21. Robert Koehler, "What the Hell Happened with Terrence Malick?," *Cineaste* 38, no. 4 (Fall 2013): 4–9, quote on p. 8.

22. Setoodeh, "Terrence Malick Explains His Unconventional Process."

23. Bresson, *Notes on the Cinematograph*, 6.

24. Eric Hynes, "Run Away: The Radical Movements of *Song to Song*," *Film Comment*, March 22, 2017, https://www.filmcomment.com/blog/run-away-radical-movements-song-song/.

25. Setoodeh, "Terrence Malick Explains His Unconventional Process."

26. On Malick's connection to Austin, see Eric Benson, "The Not-So-Secret Life of Terrence Malick," *Texas Monthly*, April 2017, http://www.texasmonthly.com/the-culture/the-not-so-secret-life-of-terrence-malick/.

27. See Robert B. Pippin, *Douglas Sirk: Filmmaker and Philosopher* (London: Bloomsbury, 2021), 76.

28. James Wierzbicki, *Terrence Malick: Sonic Style* (New York: Routledge, 2019), 93.

29. Myra Lewis and Murray Silver Jr., *Great Balls of Fire: The Uncensored Story of Jerry Lee Lewis* (New York: William Morrow, 1982).

30. George Cotkin, *Feast of Excess: A Cultural History of the New Sensibility* (New York: Oxford, 2016), 95.

31. Cotkin, *Feast of Excess*, 95.

32. Nick Tosches, *Hellfire: The Jerry Lee Lewis Story* (New York: Delacorte, 1982), 66.

33. Terry Malick, "Great Balls of Fire," January 6, 1988, 6, Louis B. Mayer Library, AFI.

34. Malick, "Great Balls of Fire," 9.

35. Malick, "Great Balls of Fire," 98.

36. Malick, "Great Balls of Fire," 98 and 99.

37. Malick, "Great Balls of Fire," 114.

38. Malick, "Great Balls of Fire," 114, 116.

39. Malick, "Great Balls of Fire," 116.

40. Malick, "Great Balls of Fire," 124.

41. Mike Medavoy, with Josh Young, *You're Only as Good as Your Next One: 100 Great Films, 100 Good Films, and 100 for Which I Should Be Shot* (New York: Pocket Books, 2002), 193.

42. See Jack Baran and Jim McBride, "Great Balls of Fire," second draft, August 31, 1988, Louis B. Mayer Library, AFI.

43. Terrence Malick, "Sansho the Bailiff: Written for the Stage," second draft (December 1993), 154.

44. Malick, "Sansho the Bailiff," 67.

45. Malick, "Sansho the Bailiff," 67, 68.

46. Malick, "Sansho the Bailiff," 70.

47. AFI Fellows' Meeting, February 20, 1970, audio recording at the Louis B. Mayer Library, AFI. Also, Malick, "Sansho the Bailiff," 162.

48. Malick, "Sansho the Bailiff," 163.

49. Compare Malick, "Sansho the Bailiff," 112: "I believed in mercy, but only for others, not for myself!" The lines are spoken by an old hermit Zushio comes across on his journey.

50. Melissa Anderson, "*Song to Song* Is Chastely Childish," *Village Voice*, March 14, 2017.

51. This voice-over narration echoes a 1996 *Village Voice* review of the first four volumes of Joseph Frank's monumental biography of Dostoevsky by David Foster Wallace, which contains interstitial asides such as: "Am I a good person? Deep down, do I even really want to be a good person, or do I only want to *seem* like a good person so that people (including myself) will approve of me?" Reprinted in Joseph Frank, *Lectures on Dostoevsky*, ed. Marina Brodskaya and Marguerite Frank, foreword by Robin Feuer Miller (Princeton, NJ: Princeton University Press, 2020), 189.

52. Tim Markatos, "Schism in the House of Malick," *American Conservative*, March 29, 2017, https://www.theamericanconservative.com/articles/schism-in-the-house-of-malick/.

53. As Reno Lauro has suggested, *Jules et Jim* is "a film known to be very close to [Malick's] heart for those who know him." See Lauro, "The Smile of Life: Recollections on Malick and the Work of Cinema," in Sikora, *A Critical Companion to Terrence Malick*, 253.

54. For an explicitly religious interpretation of the film, see Elisa Zocchi, "Terrence Malick Beyond Nature and Grace: *Song to Song* and the Experience of Forgiveness," *Journal of Religion and Film* 22, no. 2 (2018), art. 3, available at https://digitalcommons.unomaha.edu/jrf/vol22/iss2/3.

55. See the *Song to Song* press release, specifically "Into the Heart of Austin with Terrence Malick," p. 3, Margaret Herrick Library, AMPAS.

56. Virginia Woolf, *The Waves* (1931; London: Vintage, 2004), 151, 171, 175.

57. Woolf, *The Waves*, 190; see also p. 175.

58. Woolf, *The Waves*, 191.

59. O'Falt, "Terrence Malick Makes a Rare Appearance."

60. Patti Smith has written a couple of highly regarded memoirs about her life in music, poetry, and the arts; see *Just Kids* (New York: Ecco, 2010) and *M Train* (New York: Knopf, 2015). Press materials prepared for the release of *Song to Song* state that Malick and Smith knew each other in the 1970s. Margaret Herrick Library, AMPAS.

61. I thank Nick Norton for suggesting this comparison.

62. Jeff Menne, *Post-Fordist Cinema: Hollywood Auteurs and the Corporate Counterculture* (New York: Columbia University Press, 2019), 75–124.

63. For more on the relation of Malick's cinema to U.S. history, see my "What Is Heideggerian Cinema? Film, Philosophy, and Cultural Mobility," *New German Critique* 113 (Summer 2011): 129–57. The only other film Malick tried to get made that did not have a connection to American history was a story he worked on in the 1990s and early 2000s, "The English Speaker," which explored the origins of psychoanalysis in fin de siècle Vienna.

64. On the American myth of the Second World War as the "good war," see Roy Scranton, *Total Mobilization: World War II and American Literature* (Chicago: University of Chicago Press, 2019); and Elizabeth D. Samet, *Looking for the Good War: American Amnesia and the Violent Pursuit of Happiness* (New York: Farrar, Straus and Giroux, 2021).

65. Richard Brody, "When Bad Nazis Happen to Good Directors: Terrence Malick's 'A Hidden Life,'" *New Yorker*, December 16, 2010, https://www.newyorker.com/culture/the-front-row/when-bad-nazis-happen-to-good-directors-terrence-malicks-a-hidden-life.

66. Thomson, "The Wonder of Terrence Malick," 331. Not everybody agreed with this assessment. The *New Yorker*'s Richard Brody found *A Hidden Life* to be "vague, impersonal, and complacent," especially when compared to his "comprehensively challenging" autobiographical films. See Brody, "When Bad Nazis Happen to Good Directors." Similarly, a *New York Times* report from Cannes suggested that some pundits found the film to be "a whole lot of metaphysical woo-woo." Kyle Buchanan, "Which Cannes Films Will Factor into the Oscars Race?," *New York Times*, May 27, 2019, https://www.nytimes.com/2019/05/27/movies/cannes-oscars.html.

67. Thomson, "The Wonder of Terrence Malick," 331.

68. Thomson, "The Wonder of Terrence Malick," 331.

69. Thomson, "The Wonder of Terrence Malick," 346.

70. Evidence of Malick's journey can be found in works he chose to produce during this time, such as the historical drama *Amazing Grace* (dir. Michael Apted, 2006), about William Wilberforce's campaign to end the British slave trade, and the religiously inflected docudrama *Endurance* (dir. Leslie Woodhead and Bud Greenspan, 1999), about the Ethiopian long-distance runner Haile Gebrselassie.

71. Terrence Malick, "A Hidden Life," July 6, 2016, iii.

72. Søren Kierkegaard, *Papers and Journals: A Selection*, trans. Alastair Hannay (New York: Penguin, 1996), 352.

73. George Eliot, *Middlemarch: A Study in Provincial Life*, ed. David Carroll, with an introduction by David Russell (New York: Oxford University Press, 2019), 785.

74. Scott Roxborough, "Terrence Malick to Tackle WWII Biopic 'Radegund,'" *Hollywood Reporter*, June 22, 2016.

75. *A Hidden Life* premiered at Cannes, but it also received a special screening at the Vatican, with Malick himself in attendance. Sister Bernadette Mary Reis, FSP, "A Hidden Life: Screening in the Vatican," *Vatican News*, December 5, 2019, https://www.vaticannews.va/en/world /news/2019-12/hidden-life-malick-jagerstatter-film.html.

76. Martin Heidegger, *An Introduction to Metaphysics*, trans. Ralph Manheim (New Haven, CT: Yale University Press, 1959), 166.

77. Gordon C. Zahn, *In Solitary Witness: The Life and Death of Franz Jägerstätter* (1964; Springfield, IL: Templegate, 1986).

78. Zahn, *In Solitary Witness*, 177.

79. Gordon C. Zahn, *German Catholics and Hitler's Wars: A Study in Social Control* (1962; Notre Dame, IN: University of Notre Dame Press, 1989).

80. Thomas Merton, "An Enemy of the State," *Peace News*, January 29, 1965, 1.

81. Thomas Merton, *Faith and Violence: Christian Teaching and Christian Practice* (Notre Dame, IN: University of Notre Dame Press, 1968), 9. On Merton, see Paul Elie, *The Life You Save May Be Your Own: An American Pilgrimage* (New York: Farrar, Straus and Giroux, 2003).

82. See Robert Vincent Daniels, *The Year of the Heroic Guerrilla: World Revolution and Counterrevolution in 1968* (1989: Cambridge, MA: Harvard University Press, 1996); and Todd Gitlin, *The Sixties: Years of Hope, Days of Rage* (New York: Bantam, 1987).

83. Merton, *Faith and Violence*, 6; Hannah Arendt, *Eichmann in Jerusalem: A Report on the Banality of Evil* (New York: Viking, 1963). For an attempt to link *A Hidden Life* to Arendt's idea of "thoughtless" evil, see Sam Buckland, "Terrence Malick's 'A Hidden Life' and the Banality of Good," *Los Angeles Review of Books*, December 4, 2019. On the connections between U.S.-led counterinsurgency efforts and domestic policing, see Stuart Schrader, *Badges Without Borders: How Global Counterinsurgency Transformed American Policing* (Berkeley: University of California Press, 2019).

84. Zahn, *In Solitary Witness*, 15.

85. Zahn, *In Solitary Witness*, 6, 203.

86. Zahn, *In Solitary Witness*, 173.

87. Quoted in Zahn, *In Solitary Witness*, 102.

88. Merton, *Faith and Violence*, 6.

89. Merton, *Faith and Violence*, 8.

90. Merton, *Faith and Violence*, 9. On "the religious dimension of American radicalism" during this time, see Jackson Lears, "Aquarius Rising," *New York Review of Books*, September 27, 2018, 8–14.

91. Merton, *Faith and Violence*, 6.

92. Lidija Haas, "The Heavy-Handed Moralism of Terrence Malick's New Film," *New Republic*, December 13, 2019, https://newrepublic.com/article/155960/terrence-malick-film-hidden-life-review-heavy-handed-moralism. Zahn suggests that the residents of St. Radegund may have known about mass deportations to concentration camps because one of them, Mauthausen, was located nearby. See Zahn, *In Solitary Witness*, 113.

93. Claudia Koonz, *The Nazi Conscience* (Cambridge, MA: Harvard University Press, 2003).

94. Zahn, *In Solitary Witness*, 146.

95. Zahn, *In Solitary Witness*, 15–16.

96. For the suggestion that Jägerstätter was "touched in the head," see Zahn, *In Solitary Witness*, 141. The character who seems to represent this idea of the "holy fool" in *A Hidden Life* is not Jägerstätter but Waldland (Franz Rogowski), a simple soul Jägerstätter encounters first during his military training and once again during his imprisonment. It appears that Malick always intended for Rogowski to play the role, since the character is named "Rogowski" in his script.

97. Zahn, *In Solitary Witness*, 116.

98. Zahn, *In Solitary Witness*, 129.

99. Zahn, *In Solitary Witness*, 14, 15.

100. See, in particular, Zahn's chapter titled "The Martyr and His Church," in *In Solitary Witness*, 160–79.

101. See, for example, Doris L. Bergen, *Twisted Cross: The German Christian Movement in the Third Reich* (Chapel Hill: University of North Carolina Press, 1996).

102. "Young Ruffian" is the title of the second chapter of *In Solitary Witness*.

103. Zahn, *In Solitary Witness*, 19.

104. See Nick Scrimenti, "Ways of Heaven: Franz Jägerstätter's Quiet Catholicism," *Commonweal*, January 11, 2020, https://www.commonwealmagazine.org/ways-heaven. Compare this to a much more positive notice in Rand Richards Cooper, "Terrence Malick Deepens the Riddle," *Commonweal*, January 24, 2020, https://www.commonwealmagazine.org/deepening-riddle.

105. Zahn, *In Solitary Witness*, 86.

106. Franz Jägerstätter, *Letters and Writings from Prison*, ed. Erna Putz, trans. Robert A. Krieg (Maryknoll, NY: Orbis Books, 2009), 216.

107. Zahn, *In Solitary Witness*, 106.

108. Zahn, *In Solitary Witness*, 32.

109. See *A Testament to Freedom: The Essential Writings of Dietrich Bonhoeffer*, ed. Geffrey B. Kelly and F. Burton Nelson (San Francisco: HarperSanFrancisco, 1990).

110. Alfred Delp, *Prison Writings*, with an introduction by Thomas Merton (1962; Maryknoll, NY: Orbis Books, 2004).

111. Delp, *Prison Writings*, 160.

112. Alex Stedman, "Martin Scorsese, Robert De Niro on How 'Raging Bull' Avoided Being Shut Down," *Variety*, April 28, 2019, https://variety.com/2019/film/news/martin-scorsese-robert-de-niro-tribeca-film-festival-1203199832/.

113. Delp, *Prison Writings*, 161.

114. Franz Jägerstätter, *Letters and Writings from Prison*, 117.

115. Jägerstätter, *Letters and Writings from Prison*, 124.

116. Jägerstätter, *Letters and Writings from Prison*, 129.

117. Jägerstätter, *Letters and Writings from Prison*, 128.

118. On the sound of blackbirds, compare Malick's "A Hidden Life," 66, with Jägerstätter's *Letters and Writings from Prison*, 106: "One can hear blackbirds loudly singing outside our windows. Even the birds have, it seems, more peace and joy—although they are not rational animals—than we human beings who have the gift of understanding."

119. Malick, "A Hidden Life," 103.

120. Malick, "A Hidden Life," 103.

121. For more on the turn away from theodicy in the philosophy of history, see my "Reconsidering the Slaughter Bench of History: Genocide, Theodicy, and the Philosophy of History," *Journal of Genocide Research* 13, nos. 1–2 (March–June 2011): 83–102.

122. See, for instance, Haas, "The Heavy-Handed Moralism"; and Adam Mars-Jones, "Hammer, Anvil and Scythe," *Times Literary Supplement*, January 24, 2020, 18–19. See also Siegfried Kracauer, *From Caligari to Hitler: A Psychological History of the German Film* (Princeton, NJ: Princeton University Press, 1947).

123. This detail can be found in Zahn, *In Solitary Witness*, 46. Malick dramatizes it in a fleeting scene, but it is one of the few times that his opposition to the regime is expressed publicly or overtly: it is the exception that proves the rule.

124. Merton, "Introduction," in Delp, *Prison Writings*, xxxv. Merton's introduction is reprinted in *Faith and Violence*, 47–68.

125. See Alfred Delp, *Tragische Existenz: Zur Philosophie Martin Heideggers* (Freiburg: Herder, 1935). For more on the context of Delp's philosophical work, see Edward Baring, "A Secular Kierkegaard: Confessional Readings of Heidegger Before 1945," *New German Critique* 124 (February 2015): 67–97.

126. Merton, "Introduction," in Delp, *Prison Writings*, xxxvii.

127. Merton, "Introduction," in Delp, *Prison Writings*, xli.

128. Merton, "Introduction," in Delp, *Prison Writings*, xli.

129. Zahn, *In Solitary Witness*, 111.

130. Zahn, *In Solitary Witness*, 112.

131. Merton, "An Enemy of the State," in *Faith and Violence*, 71.

132. Malick, "A Hidden Life," 1.

133. See Anthony D'Alessandro, "The Epic Three-Year Journey of Terrence Malick's 'A Hidden Life,'" *Deadline*, May 23, 2019, https://deadline.com/2019/05/cannes-film-festival-terrence -malick-hidden-life-box-office-behind-the-scenes-1202618684/.

134. At first glance, it might seem that *A Man Escaped* and *A Hidden Life* offer vastly different story lines. In one film, the protagonist escapes; in the other, he does not. But this overlooks the fact that Jägerstätter's martyrdom is represented as a kind of escape. When he is presented with opportunities to save himself from execution by lawyers and judges, he responds that he is "already free."

135. Martin Scorsese, "I Said Marvel Movies Aren't Cinema. Let Me Explain," *New York Times*, November 4, 2019, https://www.nytimes.com/2019/11/04/opinion/martin-scorsese-marvel .html?smid=nytcore-ios-share.

136. On the genre of metacinema, see David LaRocca, ed., *Metacinema: The Form and Content of Filmic Reference and Reflexivity* (New York: Oxford University Press, 2021).

137. On the connections between *A Hidden Life* and *Andrei Rublev*, see David Michael, "Terrence Malick and the Question of Martyrdom," *Comment*, June 25, 2020, https://comment.org /terrence-malick-and-the-question-of-martyrdom/. For another perspective, see Anthony Parisi, "The Search for Time: Terrence Malick and Andrei Tarkovsky in Dialogue," in Sikora, *A Critical Companion to Terrence Malick*, 137–53.

138. Malick, "A Hidden Life," 14. The script spells the painter's name with two *f*'s instead of one.

139. Malick, "A Hidden Life," 13.

140. Malick, "A Hidden Life," 21.

141. Malick, "A Hidden Life," 25.

142. Malick, "A Hidden Life," 21.

143. See Tim Greiving, "Malick's Stories Told in Music," *Los Angeles Times*, January 5, 2020, E10. See also Bilge Ebiri, "A Long Talk with James Newton Howard, One of Hollywood's Most Accomplished Composers," *Vulture*, January 23, 2020, https://www.vulture.com/2020/01/a-long -talk-with-hollywood-composer-james-howard-newton.html.

144. See, for example, Lidija Haas's review ("Heavy-Handed Moralism") in the *New Republic*.

145. Jägerstätter, *Letters and Writings from Prison*, 224.

146. Lauro, "The Smile of Life," 255.

147. See Dostoevsky, *The Idiot*, trans. Alan Myers, introduction by William Leatherbarrow (Oxford: Oxford University Press, 1992), 59, in which Prince Myshkin describes donkeys as "the most useful of creatures, hard-working, strong, patient, cheap, and long-suffering."

148. Tony Pipolo, *Robert Bresson: A Passion for Film* (New York: Oxford University Press, 2010), 206.

149. Pipolo, *Robert Bresson*, 190.

150. Dostoevsky, *The Idiot*, 64.

151. Søren Kierkegaard, "Love's Hidden Life and Its Recognizability by Its Fruits," in *Works of Love*, ed. and trans. Howard V. Hong and Edna H. Hong (Princeton, NJ: Princeton University Press, 1995), 14.

152. Kierkegaard, "Love's Hidden Life," 6.

153. Kierkegaard, "Love's Hidden Life," 9–10.

154. Kierkegaard, "Love's Hidden Life," 15. For comparable imagery in Jägerstätter's writings, see *Letters and Writings from Prison*, 231: "The seed of God is the sprout of divine life."

155. Kierkegaard, "Love's Hidden Life," 15.

156. Søren Kierkegaard, *The Sickness unto Death: A Christian Psychological Exposition for Edification and Awakening by Anti-Climacus*, trans. Alastair Hannay (New York: Penguin), 88.

157. Kierkegaard, *The Sickness unto Death*, 162. Here Kierkegaard is referring to a passage in 1 Corinthians.

158. Jägerstätter, *Letters and Writings from Prison*, 211.

Conclusion

1. Frederic Raphael, *The Limits of Love* (1960; Glasgow: Fontana/Collins, 1989), 363.

2. Ludwig Wittgenstein, *The Blue and Brown Books* (1958; New York: Harper Torchbooks, 1965), 45

3. Ludwig Wittgenstein, *Philosophical Investigations*, trans. G. E. M. Anscombe, P. M. S. Hacker, and Joachim Schulte, rev. 4th ed., ed. P. M. S. Hacker and Joachim Schulte (Malden, MA: Wiley Blackwell, 2009), § 133.

4. Ludwig Wittgenstein, *Private Notebooks, 1914–1916*, ed. and trans. Marjorie Perloff (New York: Liveright, 2022).

5. Wittgenstein, *Philosophical Investigations*, § 133.

6. Wolfram Eilenberger, *Time of the Magicians: Wittgenstein, Benjamin, Cassirer, Heidegger, and the Decade That Reinvented Philosophy*, trans. Shaun Whiteside (New York: Penguin, 2020), 256. For more on Wittgenstein's days as an Austrian schoolteacher, see Ray Monk, *Ludwig Wittgenstein: The Duty of Genius* (New York: Penguin, 1990).

7. Ludwig Wittgenstein, *Tractatus Logico-Philosophicus*, trans. C. K. Ogden, introduction by Bertrand Russell (London: Kegan Paul, 1922).

8. Ludwig Wittgenstein, *Lecture on Ethics*, ed. Edoardo Zamuner, Ermelinda Valentina Di Lascio, and D. K. Levy (West Sussex: Wiley Blackwell, 2014), 42.

9. Wittgenstein, *Lecture on Ethics*, 51.

10. Wittgenstein, *Lecture on Ethics*, 47.

11. Wittgenstein, *Lecture on Ethics*, 46.

12. Wittgenstein, *Lecture on Ethics*, 49, 50.

13. Wittgenstein, *Lecture on Ethics*, 47.

14. See David Edmonds and John Eidinow, *Wittgenstein's Poker: The Story of a Ten-Minute Argument Between Two Great Philosophers* (New York: Ecco, 2001).

15. Wittgenstein, *Lecture on Ethics*, 51.

16. Wittgenstein, *Lecture on Ethics*, 47.

17. A letter from Hubert Dreyfus to Richard Rorty, February 22, 1980, describes Malick's participation in the event. Richard Rorty Papers, University of California, Irvine, Special Collections, Box 22, Folder 2.

18. On Malick's employment history, see "Conservatory Fellows, Biographies, 1969–1970," Louis B. Mayer Library, AFI.

19. This according to *Days of Heaven*'s editor Billy Weber on the audio commentary of the Criterion edition of the film.

20. Joe Gillis, "Waiting for Godot," *Los Angeles Magazine*, December 1995, p. 61.

21. For an account of Malick's years away from directing, see Michael Nordine, "Hollywood Bigfoot: Terrence Malick and the Twenty-Year Hiatus That Wasn't," *Los Angeles Review of Books*, May 12, 2013.

22. Council for Philosophical Studies, *Phenomenology and Existentialism: Continental and Analytical Perspectives on Intentionality in the Philosophy Curriculum* (San Francisco: San Francisco State University, Council for Philosophical Studies, 1981), 14.

23. Council for Philosophical Studies, *Phenomenology and Existentialism*, 4.

24. Council for Philosophical Studies, *Phenomenology and Existentialism*, 4.

25. Hubert Dreyfus and Sean Dorrance Kelly, *All Things Shining: Reading the Western Classics to Find Meaning in a Secular Age* (New York: Free Press, 2011), 16. Commentators found some of Dreyfus and Kelly's recommendations—such as the suggestion that morning coffee rituals were an adequate substitute for religious practice (cf. p. 217)—wanting. See Garry Wills, "Superficial & Sublime?," *New York Review of Books*, April 7, 2011, 16–18.

26. Rorty's 2004 Page-Barbour Lectures summed up the idea: *Philosophy as Poetry*, introduction by Michael Bérubé, afterword by Mary V. Rorty (Charlottesville: University of Virginia Press, 2016).

27. Richard Rorty, *Philosophy and the Mirror of Nature* (Princeton, NJ: Princeton University Press, 1979), 389. See also Oakeshott, "The Voice of Poetry in the Conversation of Mankind," in *Rationalism in Politics and Other Essays*, rev. ed. (1962; Indianapolis: Liberty Fund, 1991), 488–541.

28. Rorty, *Philosophy and the Mirror of Nature*, 372.

29. See Richard Rorty, *Contingency, Irony, and Solidarity* (Cambridge: Cambridge University Press, 1989); Rorty, *Achieving Our Country: Leftist Thought in Twentieth-Century America* (Cambridge, MA: Harvard University Press, 1998).

30. Stanley Cavell, *The Claim of Reason: Wittgenstein, Skepticism, Morality, and Tragedy* (New York: Oxford University Press, 1979).

31. See Stanley Cavell, *Must We Mean What We Say?*, rev. ed. (1969; Cambridge: Cambridge University Press, 2002), xxv. See also Cavell, *The World Viewed: Reflections on the Ontology of Film*, rev. ed. (1971; Cambridge, MA: Harvard University Press, 1979); and Cavell, *The Senses of Walden*, rev. ed. (1972; Chicago: University of Chicago Press, 1992). Cavell recounts the slow evolution of *The Claim of Reason* in the foreword to the book, xv–xxvi.

32. Cavell, *The Claim of Reason*, 326.

33. Cavell, *The Claim of Reason*, 363.

34. Cavell, *The Claim of Reason*, 476.

35. Cavell, *The Claim of Reason*, 496.

36. Cavell, *The World Viewed*, xvi.

37. Thomas E. Wartenberg, "Beyond *Mere* Illustration: How Films Can Be Philosophy," in *Thinking Through Cinema: Film as Philosophy*, ed. Murray Smith and Thomas E. Wartenberg (Malden, MA: Blackwell, 2006), 19. See also Robert Sinnerbrink, *New Philosophies of Film: Thinking Images* (London: Continuum, 2011).

38. Fisk quoted in Carlo Hintermann and Daniele Villa, eds., *Terrence Malick: Rehearsing the Unexpected* (London: Faber & Faber, 2015), 291. See also, *Renoir on Renoir: Interviews, Essays, and Remarks*, trans. Carol Volk (Cambridge: Cambridge University Press, 1989), 250.

39. Hintermann and Villa, *Terrence Malick*, 291.

40. A partial list includes Steven DeLay, ed., *Life Above the Clouds: Philosophy in the Films of Terrence Malick* (Albany: State University of New York Press, 2023); Joshua Sikora, ed., *A Critical Companion to Terrence Malick* (Lanham, MD: Lexington Books, 2020); Robert Sinnerbrink, *Terrence Malick: Filmmaker and Philosopher* (London: Bloomsbury, 2019); James Batcho, *Terrence Malick's Unseeing Cinema: Memory, Time and Audibility* (Cham, Switzerland: Palgrave Macmillan, 2018); John Caruana and Mark Cauchi, eds., *Immanent Frames: Postsecular Cinema Between Malick and von Trier* (Albany: State University of New York Press, 2018); Christopher B. Barnett and Clark J. Elliston, ed., *Theology and the Films of Terrence Malick* (New York: Routledge, 2017); and Jonathan Beever and Vernon W. Cisney, eds., *The Way of Nature and the Way of Grace: Philosophical Footholds on Terrence Malick's "The Tree of Life"* (Evanston, IL: Northwestern University Press, 2016). These works build on earlier studies, such as Hannah Patterson, ed., *The Cinema of Terrence Malick: Poetic Visions of America*, 2nd ed. (London: Wallflower Press, 2007); Lloyd Michaels, *Terrence Malick* (Urbana: University of Illinois Press, 2009); Steven Rybin, *Terrence Malick and the Thought of Film* (Lanham, MD: Lexington Books, 2012); and Thomas Deane Tucker and Stuart Kendall, eds., *Terrence Malick: Film and Philosophy* (2011; New York: Bloomsbury, 2013).

41. George Stevens Jr., "Remarks on the Opening of AFI CAFS," September 23, 1969, audio file at the Louis B. Mayer Library, AFI.

42. Gregory Peck, foreword to Tom Shales et al., *The American Film Heritage: Impressions from the American Film Institute Archives* (Washington, D.C.: Acropolis Books, 1972), 5.

43. Stanley Cavell, "The Thought of Movies," in *Themes Out of School: Effects and Causes* (Chicago: University of Chicago Press, 1984), 3.

44. Josef Früchtl, *Trust in the World: A Philosophy of Film*, trans. Sarah L. Kirkby (New York: Routledge, 2018), 4, 9.

45. Batcho, *Terrence Malick's Unseeing Cinema*, ix.

46. On Malick's teaching and journalism, see the interviews—with Beverly Walker and Michel Ciment—collected in Lloyd Michaels, *Terrence Malick* (Urbana: University of Illinois Press, 2009), esp. pp. 105 and 102.

47. Søren Kierkegaard, *Papers and Journals: A Selection*, trans. Alastair Hannay (New York: Penguin, 1996), 161.

48. "American Film Institute Seminar with Terry Malick," April 11, 1974, 53. Transcript at the Louis B. Mayer Library, AFI.

49. Carly Simon, *Another Passenger* (1976). The story of Malick's pickup basketball game with Castro is told in Paul W. Williams's memoir *Harvard, Hollywood, Hitmen, and Holy Men* (Lexington: University Press of Kentucky, 2023), 183–86.

50. Timothy Chappell, *Reading Plato's "Theaetetus"* (Indianapolis: Hackett, 2005), 72; this is a translation of line 155d1.

51. Dreyfus and Kelly, *All Things Shining*, 22.

52. See Mary-Jane Rubenstein, *Strange Wonder: The Closure of Metaphysics and the Opening of Awe* (New York: Columbia University Press, 2008).

53. Mark Johnston, *Saving God: Religion After Idolatry* (Princeton, NJ: Princeton University Press, 2009), 187.

54. See, for example, Kieran Setiya, *Midlife: A Philosophical Guide* (Princeton, NJ: Princeton University Press, 2018); John Kaag, *American Philosophy: A Love Story* (New York: Farrar, Straus and Giroux, 2016); John Kaag, *Hiking with Nietzsche: On Becoming Who You Are* (New York: Farrar, Straus and Giroux, 2018); or Massimo Pigliucci, *How to Be a Stoic: Using Ancient Philosophy to Live a Modern Life* (New York: Basic Books, 2017).

55. Meghan Sullivan and Paul Blaschko, *The Good Life Method: Reasoning Through the Big Questions of Happiness, Faith, and Meaning* (New York: Penguin, 2022).

56. Walker Percy, *Lost in the Cosmos: The Last Self-Help Book* (New York: Noonday Press, 1983).

57. See, for example, the parody "Reclusive 'Terrence Malick of the Beltway,' to Release First New Law in 20 Years," *The Onion*, February 9, 2013, https://www.theonion.com/reclusive-terrence -malick-of-the-beltway-to-release-fir-1819595410.

58. See Robert B. Pippin, *Filmed Thought: Cinema as Reflective Form* (Chicago: University of Chicago Press, 2020), 5.

59. See Martin Heidegger, *Being and Time*, trans. John Macquarrie and Edward Robinson (San Francisco: Harper & Row, 1962), § 29.

60. See Andrew Sarris, *The American Cinema: Directors and Directions, 1929–1968* (New York: Dutton, 1968).

61. See James Kloppenberg's "Opening American Thought," in *The Worlds of American Intellectual History*, ed. Joel Isaac et al. (Oxford: Oxford University Press, 2017), 1–15.

62. A *Hollywood Reporter* covering the opening festivities of the American Film Institute, which included a screening of Lloyd's films and a seminar with their bespectacled star, said the following: "It is as old as Socrates, of course, the method that [George] Stevens and the institute have chosen to preserve and regenerate the most American of arts. The institute calls it a 'tutorial' system." Quoted in George Stevens Jr., *Conversations at the American Film Institute with the Great Moviemakers: The Next Generation, from the 1950s to Hollywood Today* (New York: Vintage, 2014), xiv.

63. Plato, *The Last Days of Socrates: Euthyphro, Apology, Crito, Phaedo*, trans. Hugh Tredennick and Harold Tarrant, introduction and notes by Harold Tarrant (New York: Penguin Classics, 1993), 63.

64. Heidegger letter to Löwith, August 19, 1921, in Karl Löwith, *Martin Heidegger and European Nihilism*, ed. Richard Wolin, trans. Gary Steiner (New York: Columbia University Press, 1995), 236.

65. Terrence Malick, "The Tree of Life: A Screenplay," first draft, June 25, 2007, https:// indiegroundfilms.files.wordpress.com/2014/01/tree-of-life-the-jun-25-07-1st.pdf.

66. Johann Gottlieb Fichte, *The Vocation of Man*, trans. Peter Preuss (Indianapolis: Hackett, 1987), 2.

67. David Thomson, *Sleeping with Strangers: How the Movies Shaped Desire* (New York: Knopf, 2019), 17.

68. Martin Woessner, *Heidegger in America* (Cambridge: Cambridge University Press, 2011), 206.

69. William James quoted in George Cotkin, *William James: Public Philosopher* (1990; Urbana: University of Illinois Press, 1994), 15.

INDEX

ACKNOWLEDGMENTS

And now, the credits. I thank the extensive cast and crew—the colleagues, friends, family members, and, on occasion, perfect strangers—who made this book possible. One of those strangers was Terrence Malick. When I began studying his films, he had made just four of them. He has made many more since. Each new release meant more work, but the research never became a burden. I now think of Malick's movies as gifts, and I remain profoundly grateful for them.

I am also grateful for the support that allowed me to tarry with this ever-expanding project. Without the aid of some generous institutions and some kind individuals, this book never would have made it past the pitch stage. I benefited from a Scholar Incentive Award, a PSC-CUNY Research Award, and a much-needed sabbatical leave. Additional support came from the City College of New York's Center for Worker Education, a program committed to the kind of interdisciplinary inquiry I hope this book exemplifies. I thank Dean Juan Carlos Mercado, my faculty and staff colleagues, and my students. Special thanks to Seamus Scanlon, librarian supreme, for tracking down as many obscure references as I could throw his way. Students brave enough to enroll in my course on philosophy and film deserve special recognition, not just for watching and reading as much material as I could cram onto a syllabus, but also, and more importantly, for sharing their honest and insightful reactions to films as different from each other as *The Tree of Life* and *Get Out*. A number of arguments in the preceding pages were shaped in discussions with these budding film-philosophers, many of whom work full-time, care for extended families, and yet still have enough energy and passion to argue with me about *Blade Runner*. I consider myself very fortunate to share a classroom—or a Zoom screen—with them. I also benefited from conversations with CCNY colleagues who know a great deal about Malick, philosophy, and film. My thanks to Andreas Killen and Nickolas Pappas for their encouragement, and to Andrzej Krakowski for taking the time to share his memories of the early days of AFI.

Significant contributions came from audiences at various conferences, colloquiums, and lectures. An invitation from Daniel T. Rodgers to participate in the "Ideas in Motion" workshop at the Shelby Cullom Davis Center for Historical Studies at Princeton University in 2009 offered me a chance to test out some early ideas, which found their way into print thanks to Anson Rabinbach and the editorial staff of *New German Critique*. In 2014, Arne De Boever graciously invited me to think through new material in front of the savvy students at the California Institute of the Arts, this after having tirelessly edited my essays—only some of them Malick-related—for the *Los Angeles Review of Books*. A few years later, Santiago Zabala brought me to beautiful Barcelona to speak at both Universitat Pompeu Fabra and—under the auspices of the European School for the Humanities—the imposing Palau Macaya de La Caixa. I thank him for the opportunity and the hospitality. I also thank Esther Lopera for helping me navigate all the publicity. Last but certainly not least, Ron Haas and the Honors College at Texas State University in San Marcos gave me a chance to talk about Malick on his home turf. Not only that, but Ron (and Tiffany) drove me out to Smithville to see the O'Briens' house(s) for myself—a happy day of cinematic sightseeing.

In between these workshops and lectures, my most sustained feedback came from presentations at annual meetings of the Society for United States Intellectual History. (One presentation at a meeting of the Organization of American Historians also proved beneficial.) To the many co-panelists and audience members who listened to me ramble on about *Days of Heaven*, *The Thin Red Line*, or *Knight of Cups*, I say thank you, for both your many helpful suggestions and your astute criticisms. The same goes for the participants at the Midwestern Intellectual History Group meeting at the University of Notre Dame in 2022.

Research recommendations and tips came from the librarians at the Margaret Herrick Library of the Academy of Motion Pictures Arts and Sciences, the Shavelson-Webb Library of the Writers Guild Foundation, and the Harvard University Archives. Especially generous with their time were the custodians of the many treasures at the American Film Institute's Louis B. Mayer Library in Los Feliz. I am indebted to Mike Pepin, Robert Vaughn, and especially Emily Wittenberg for tracking down so many vital source materials dating back to the dawn of the Center for Advanced Film Studies. Thanks also to Colton Williamson, Terrence Malick's assistant, who provided vital help at a late stage in the research. All AFI archival materials cited in the manuscript, as well as the image of Terrence Malick on the set of *Lanton Mills*, are courtesy of the American Film Institute.

Some passages in this book appeared previously in different form. Portions of the introduction as well as Chapters 5 and 6 showed up in "Cosmic Cinema: On the Philosophical Films of Terrence Malick," in *Philosophy Today* 61, no. 2 (Spring 2017): 389–98. Passages in the introduction and conclusion derive from "What Is Heideggerian Cinema: Film, Philosophy, and Cultural Mobility," published in *New German Critique* 113 (Summer 2011): 129–57.

At the University of Pennsylvania Press, I am indebted to a stellar staff. I thank Bob Lockhart, in particular, for his good humor, steady encouragement, and keen editorial eye—and for lining up peer reviewers whose careful, incisive readings of an earlier draft of the manuscript provided invaluable guidance when I needed it most. It goes without saying that any lingering mistakes are the result of my own stubbornness or inattention. Thanks also to the many folks who saw some promise in my earliest, roughest drafts. Here I shine a spotlight on Casey Blake, Jennifer Ratner-Rosenhagen, and Joel Isaac. I thank Joel, most of all, for keeping the conversation going from Cambridge to Santa Monica, with many points in between. His input over the years has been truly indispensable. I could not have written this book without it.

In the interest of brevity, I will list the names of the rest of this book's supporting cast and crew here, hoping each of them will know just how important their contributions—both big and small—were to the evolution of *Terrence Malick and the Examined Life*: Sarah Bakewell, Jason Chappell, Matt Cotter, Brian Fox, Nick Gonda, M. Gail Hamner, Robert Hernandez, Gregory Jones-Katz, Raffi Khatchadourian, the late (and missed) Richard H. King, Bruce Kuklick, Alan Martinez, Clay Matlin, Kevin McCabe, Dirk Moses, Elliot Neaman, Nicholas Norton, Tom Ort, Álvaro Eduardo de Prat, Dena Richardson, Chris Rock, Daniel Schmidt, Margarete Schwall and the late (and missed) Bertold Schwall, Rachel Toles, Bob Valgenti, Marisa Varallo, Dan Wuebben, and Ben Wurgaft. It was Eduardo Mendieta who first introduced me to the examined life (and who gave me, among many other things, the archival source that got this project going). It was George Cotkin and Roy Scranton who convinced me that one could write about ideas with wit and creativity. All three of them deserve executive-producing credit.

To the crew that is my extended family, a million thanks for knowing when to ask about Malick, and, more importantly, when not to. A very heartfelt thanks to the Woessners in Fayetteville (Beth, Joe, Tyler, Beverly, Trent, and Brooke) and Redding (Gretchen, Jon, Dylan, and Zach), as well as to Meg Hayes in Santa Ynez. Love and support came, as always, from Nanci Brewer and Morris Ignacio in Santa Rosa. And for much of the time that I toiled on this project it also came from Marie Ignacio in San Jose, whose memory still shines very brightly in my life, as I know it always will. To Serene Hayes I owe very much (as she knows), but I will say thanks here for her patience— and for her willingness to put up with all the Kierkegaard.

It was Dad who took me to see my first Malick movie, *The Thin Red Line*. But it was both Mom and Dad, Geraldine and Thomas Woessner, who taught me to seek out, and to appreciate, the important things in life. Most of what I know about grace and love and mercy comes from their example, which is why this book is for them.

www.ingramcontent.com/pod-product-compliance
Lightning Source LLC
Jackson TN
JSHW080713221224
75739JS00021B/93/J